REVIEWER COMMENTS

mav.er.ick (mav'er-ik), *n* 1. an unbranded steer. Hence [colloq.] 2. a person not labeled as belonging to any one faction, group, etc., who acts independently. 3. one who moves in a different direction than the rest of the herd— often a nonconformist. 4. a person using individual judgment, even when it runs against majority opinion.

Maverick Guides by Robert W. Bone
The Maverick Guide to Hawaii
The Maverick Guide to Australia
The Maverick Guide to New Zealand

The MAVERICK Guide to

HAWAII

Robert W. Bone

1984 EDITION

PELICAN PUBLISHING COMPANY
Gretna 1984

ISBN: 0-88289-434-X
ISSN: 0278-6613

Manufactured in the United States of America
Published by Pelican Publishing Company, Inc.
1101 Monroe Street, Gretna, Louisiana 70053

For my parents,
ROBERT O. BONE, JUANITA C. BONE.
Also dedicated with special appreciation to
TEMPLE H. FIELDING

Contents

List of Maps

Preface

Everything in this book represents our own experiences and opinions. If you're looking for mistakes, well, we're sure you'll find a few authentic Boners (as well as a couple of bad puns). This is the eighth edition of the first book in a series of guides to Pacific parts of the world. (Two others are now available—*The Maverick Guide to New Zealand* and *The Maverick Guide to Australia*.) For this reason, we would like your help. If you see an error or note a change in any entry since we investigated it, we'd appreciate it tremendously if you would send the information to us in care of the publisher. You may thereby become one of our most critical editors for subsequent editions. (Use either the special letter-envelope on the back page, or write us reams in your own envelope.)

Let it not be said here that you cannot visit Hawaii without a guidebook. Lots of people do. There are plenty of guided tours that begin by strapping you in on the Mainland and that don't let you off the leash again until you're back home. And there are other visitors who say they do not intend to leave the beach (ouch!) for the entire length of their sun-drenched vacation.

There are also many hotel desk clerks and tour guides to direct you to places in which they or their companies have financial interests. You can get along with these recommendations—in the same way that an automobile which is designed to run more smoothly on low-cost regular gasoline gets along only a *little* jerkily when it is fed expensive, high-test fuel instead.

But we want to keep you rolling smoothly *and* economically, while at the same time gently guiding you along adventuresome beaches and byways. There you can find your own individual fun, as we have done, here in the Hawaiian islands.

Aloha,

BOB AND SARA BONE

Honolulu

p.s. And tell 'em we sent you!

Mahalo a nui loa!

These are the people who helped us the most—not because it was in their interest to do so, or because it was part of their job, but just because they wanted to do so:

Anita Abramson, John Anderson, Laura Baumann, Bruce Benson, Buck Buchwach, George Chaplin, Hugh Clark, Jeanne Creamer, Ron DeLacy, Dave Donnelly, Kani Evans, Jane Evinger, Betty Fay, Victor Givan, Hal Glatzer, Ann Gottlieb, Betty Green, Wayne Harada, Tom Horton, Pat Hunter, Sandra Matsukawa Hu, Stephen Hu, Carolyn Imamura, Ben Kalb, Tom Kaser, Ken Kay, Mike Keller, Ed Kennedy, Arnold Kishi, Bob Krauss, Gerry Lopez, Leonard Lueras, Jeanne McKinley, Ken Metzler, Alan Miley, Barbara Morgan, Dan Myers, Gale Myers, David Pager, Sylvia Pager, Donna Raphael, Rick Raphael, Eunice Riedel, Ross Roberts, Rock Rothrock, Wade Shirkey, David Smollar, Ellen Spielvogel, Lester Spielvogel, Scott Stone, Ed Tanji, Harolyn Tanji, Jan TenBruggencate, Noelani Teves, David Tong, Thurston Twigg-Smith, Janice Wolf, David Yamada, Ron Youngblood, Joan Cameron, Marlene Freedman, Harry Lyons, Frances Reed, Stephen Reed, Spencer Tinker, Carol Johnson, Sally Edwards, Anne Harpham, Sanford Zalburg, Ferd Borsch, Jay Hartwell, Madge Walls, Alberta de Jetley, Peter Wolf, Wendy Long, and especially Frumie Selchen.

Sara and I also appreciate and thank the scores of others, including many business representatives and public relations personnel, who responded so well to our requests for assistance and information.

THE MAVERICK GUIDE TO HAWAII

1

Why and How
to Use This Book

One evening not long ago, we were at Honolulu Airport waiting for friends who were coming in on a late flight from the Mainland. We held flower *leis*—the traditional welcoming gift of the Islands—to place over our friends' heads once they stepped off the Wiki-Wiki bus carrying them from the plane to the terminal.

Nearby, an elderly oriental-Hawaiian woman also waited. She told us she was there to meet her cousin who was returning from a vacation in California. She, too, carried a lei, and she wore a bright *muumuu*, that long Hawaiian dress which, for more than a century, has enhanced the beauty of every woman who has ever put it on.

Not too far away stood two pretty *hapa-haole* girls dressed in ti leaf skirts. Employed by a professional greeting service, they held perhaps two dozen leis in their arms. They had contracted to meet a particular tour group.

After some delay, the first of the buses from the jumbo jet arrived. The tour group soon appeared, and the two hula girls went into their act. The leis were dutifully draped over the shoulders of each who was wearing a certain color gummed label.

Less than a minute later, the label wearers and the hula maidens had finished with each other, and they all moved off—the visiting group toward the baggage area and the young women toward a place to change out of their costumes. Other non-affiliated passengers continued to disembark from the bus.

One Mainlander alighted happily, but immediately let his face fall into an expression of deep disappointment as he watched the two greeter girls disappear into the night.

"Where's mine?" he asked, at first of no one in particular. Then he spotted our friend, the oriental-Hawaiian: "Don't I get some flowers, too?"

The woman hesitated for only a second. Then she stepped forward and placed the lei—the one she had bought for her cousin—around the visitor's neck. She was considerably shorter than the newcomer, so he had to stoop.

"*Aloha!*" she greeted him. The man gave her a smiling kiss on the cheek, straightened up wearing his new lei, and then joined the crowd on a search for suitcases, blissfully unaware that anything out of the ordinary had happened to him.

"What else could I do?" the woman looked at us helplessly. "He seemed so unhappy!"

The vignette at the airport was an illustration of today's Hawaiian contrasts. The once all-pervading Aloha Spirit may have disappeared from the Islands, to be replaced by commercial imitations of its content. Yet the genuine article continues to survive, too, in wonderful and surprising smaller doses.

Our Modus Operandi. *The Maverick Guide to Hawaii* has been carefully constructed mainly for two types of readers: 1. the visitor to Hawaii, 2. the new resident of the state.

There is a Hawaiian word covering both groups—*malihini* ("molly-*he*-knee"). It means "newcomer" or "stranger," and you'll hear it a lot, usually used in an affectionate way.

To continue the language lesson for a moment, this book is specifically for *akamai* ("ak-kah-*my*") *malihinis*. An *akamai malihini* is a newcomer with a certain amount of savvy. He's a visitor who is not cheap, but who certainly is not interested in throwing money around unnecessarily.

Hawaii no longer just happens to welcome visitors who may casually stop off on its shores. The state reaches out for them. It actively seeks *malihinis*, advertising for them, with all the resulting zealousness that a Madison Avenue campaign implies.

Sure it's got a good product, and a visit to Hawaii should be a lot of fun. But although you will seldom be bothered by rain, the good times can still be dampened. It's the purpose of this guide, however, to make sure they aren't.

The tourism business is, by far, the largest industry in the state, its monetary returns having long ago passed the revenues from the traditional sugar and pineapple businesses. And it's likely to remain No. 1 for some time.

But like sugar and pineapple, the growth of the visitor industry in Hawaii has sweet and sour implications.

This book was not written to satisfy, assuage, or coddle those whose profits and livelihood depend on the two-billion-dollar-a-year Hawaiian tourist business. No owners, managers, skippers, drivers, lecturers, maitres d'hotel, or any kind of operator—fast buck or soft sell—have put out money, friendship, or favors to insert anything into (or keep anything out of) this guide.

Our close friends are not in the tourist industry, and we try to keep things that way. We don't play golf with hotel managers. We don't play poker with restaurateurs. And we don't "play ball" with anyone. Except for a few orientation tours, special inaugurals, and the like, which are sometimes extended to legitimate travel writers and press groups, we have paid our own bills for this annual volume. We still don't let restaurants, hotels, rental car outfits, etc., "pick up the bill" for us. And we think this book is perhaps the cleanest travel guide of its type in the world.

We live full time in Hawaii, and we have learned that there is no substitute for walking the ground over and over again in order to keep an accurate picture of today's vacation conditions.

It is, therefore, our earnest belief that the price of this book will save you many times over that investment. And when you meet the poor fellow and his wife who have signed up for two $9 seats on the boat cruise to Pearl Harbor without knowing that the U.S. Navy runs a better one— a *free* one—then we feel sure you'll believe it, too.

The two of us did not grow up in the Hawaiian Islands. But between us, we have lived over much of the world—in the South Pacific, in England and Europe, in North and South America, and in the Caribbean. We also have two teen-age children—David, who was born in Spain, and Christina, a native New Yorker—who are about the most sophisticated travelers for their ages since Bobby Shafto and Dick Whittington.

We think our experiences on the move, plus our living the Island life for more than a decade, have given us special opportunities to realistically assess and appreciate all that we have found in Hawaii.

In addition, Sara, who was born in New Zealand, and the kids all have a smidgen of Polynesian blood wandering through their veins. So again, we are tied to Pacific life, the New Zealand Maoris and the native Hawaiians being at least genealogical first cousins.

But probably most important, the male half of this team is a battle-scarred veteran of the guidebooks to Europe produced by the late Temple Fielding, whom *Time* dubbed "the archon of U.S. guidebook writers." Under Fielding's intense tutelage, I explored hundreds of European hotels, restaurants, nightclubs, guided tours, and other tourist facilities, as well as toiled at home on Mallorca where we pounded the manuscripts into the perfect form that Fielding demanded. My friend and mentor, who died last year, is sadly missed here at the other end of the world.

The Organization. One of the most difficult tasks for any guidebook author is to arrange his book in an easy-to-use pattern. After experimenting with several systems for this volume, we have come up with one which we believe is super-efficient.

After three chapters on such general subjects as nature and people, we devote the subsequent six chapters individually to the six inhabited islands you may visit in Hawaii. Each "island-chapter" is divided into twelve numbered sections, and each section is devoted to a separate subject about that island. The sections and their numbers remain the same for all of the six island chapters:

1. **Around the Island**
2. **The Airport**
3. **Transportation**
4. **The Hotel Scene**
5. **Restaurants and Dining**
6. **Sightseeing**
7. **Guided Tours and Cruises**
8. **Water Sports**
9. **Other Sports**
10. **Shopping**
11. **Nights on the Town**
12. **The Address List**

Once you have become familiar with one of our six island-chapters, you will also be acquainted with the order-of-march through the rest of them, too. With the numbers, you'll learn to find something to eat under "5," the boat trips under "7," the stores under "10," and so forth.

We hope you will read this book before you even leave home. Make some plans on the basis of your homework. Decide which islands you will visit and what you probably will want to do on each. Pick out hotels. If you are considering coming with a group, see how well the itinerary and descriptions given you stack up against what we have reported on in the following pages. Make lists of things you will take with you and of things you may buy in the Islands.

Pick up lots of maps and free travel folders from airline offices and travel agencies. Jot down any changes in prices you have found in this literature.

Finally, long after you have begun to dog-ear this guide during the planning phase, be sure to bring it to Hawaii. As important as it can be in advance preparations, it is as a reference on the scene where the volume will really prove itself.

You will use this book for decisions on the spur of the moment—stores to shop in, for instance, or night clubs to visit. There are those unexpected changes of plans, like suddenly having to rent a car on the tiny island of Molokai on Sunday night. Whom can you call after the sidewalks are rolled up? How exorbitant will be the rates?

You may notice a plethora of telephone numbers in this guide. They're usually in parentheses following the name of a facility of some sort, and they may at first seem impediments to the smooth reading of the text. However, your eye will soon learn to skip over the little (Tel. 555-1212) *until* the times come when you need it. *Use* the telephone; everyone in Hawaii speaks English; and it still costs (keep your fingers crossed) only 15 cents per call from a pay phone. Private telephones are allowed an unlimited number of local calls. (However you may be charged as much as 50 cents per call from your hotel room.)

Anywhere on any one island, all phone calls are local. Only interisland calls are long distance or toll calls. (Look out; it sometimes costs more to call interisland than it does to dial California!) But for local calls, at any rate, you can use the phone for reservations, to find out late changes in operating hours or prices, or just to ask for specific directions and distances on how to get to someplace.

We feel that, although the telephone service is not as dependable as in many areas of the Mainland, it is nonetheless one of the cheapest, most valuable, and yet underutilized tourist aids throughout Hawaii.

And from your own home on the Mainland, you can make good use of the "800" series for toll-free calls direct to some Hawaii numbers. Check the appendix for toll-free numbers of Hawaiian hotels and rental car companies, and don't miss our remarks on these in the Oahu Transportation and Hotels sections (Chapter 5, Sections 3 and 4).

2

Before You Go Holo-Holo

When you consider that only a little over 200 years ago there was no way to get to Hawaii at all, it's little less than amazing how accessible the place is today. Now almost anyone who wants to can go *holo-holo* (make the rounds) in all the Islands.

There are four ways to travel, and two of these—private yacht or military transportation—we'll skip. As a practical matter, you have one choice to make: whether to sail or to fly.

By Ship to Honolulu

If you (1) are a sentimentalist, (2) are pretty well-heeled, and (3) have time on your hands, by all means take a luxury liner to Hawaii. It is the most beautiful and traditional way to go.

Sadly, most of us fulfill qualification number one above, but have trouble with either or both of the other two prerequisites. As a matter of bald fact, so few vacationers travel by ship to Hawaii, and so few passenger-carrying vessels call there anymore, that some may think it's a waste of time to discuss them.

One possibility for luxury-lining to Hawaii is supposed to be coming in the 1952-model S.S. *United States*. It was bought a few years ago by Seattle businessman Richard H. Hadley, who set up **United States Cruises, Inc.** in Honolulu and other cities. The 990-foot, 1,200-passenger vessel, being marketed as a seagoing condominium as well as for regular, fare-paying passengers, is to be home-ported in Honolulu. Still to be completed, however, is a $30-million face-lift, and it again seems that the relaunching of the *SSUS* will be some time in the not-too-near future.

A better chance this year is with the San Francisco–based **American Hawaii Cruises**, which has been making a few trans-Pacific crossings to connect with its week-long sailing around the Islands in the 30,000-ton twins *Independence* and *Constitution*. One or the other of the ships occasionally calls at Seattle, San Francisco, and Los Angeles before sailing to Honolulu. No 1984 rates have been published at this writing, but we'll guess you could count on a minimum fare of around $800 one way for the trans-Pac portion alone. (See Chapter 5, Section 7 for more details about American Hawaii.)

One problem for ship lovers is that it is generally not possible to travel from one American port to another American port on a foreign ship. This "cabotage" procedure is forbidden by an anachronistic law called the Jones Act, which hasn't changed since the day it was passed in 1896.

However, you may visit Hawaii as part of a cruise to many other ports. And if you board any ship at a foreign port like Sydney or Auckland, you are certainly permitted to sail to and even disembark at Hawaii. With these possibilities in mind, there are a few cruise lines to consider.

The **P&O Lines** sometimes sends its 1,500-passenger *Oriana* to Honolulu on its way to and from the South Pacific on two annual cruises that begin in Europe. Also, the P&O's 45,000-ton flagship *Canberra* stops in Honolulu and Lahaina on one of its world cruises, usually in October or November.

The P&O-owned **Princess Cruises** generally operates its *Pacific Princess* on one round-trip cruise from Los Angeles to New Zealand and Australia via Hawaii. The "Love Boat" has been calling at Lahaina and Honolulu in late September on the way Down Under, and then returning on the northbound trip from Sydney and Auckland to drop in on Honolulu on the way home in early November.

Freighter Travel. Another possibility is to climb aboard a passenger-carrying freighter. Also expensive compared to flying, it is otherwise probably the best oceangoing value for the dollars spent, giving you almost luxury accommodations for the price you'd pay for a cubicle below the waterline on a ship like the *Oriana*.

One of these is the cargo/passenger steamer M.V. *Enna G*, operated by the **Nauru Pacific Line**. Leaving San Francisco every six weeks or so, the 100-passenger vessel heads first to Honolulu and then on to the Micronesian islands of Majuro, Ponape, Truk, and Saipan, and eventually returns to San Francisco. Fares run from about $3,000 to $5,000 for the entire 40-day round trip. Shorter segments may be available, but remember, not simply for one-way passage between San Francisco and Honolulu, due to provisions in the aforementioned Jones Act. Unlike most freighters, this one comes equipped with such linerlike luxuries as a swimming pool, a dance floor, and a doctor. Get the details from North American Maritime Agencies, 100 California St., San Francisco, CA 94111.

About the only other freighters to Honolulu are those run by the California-headquartered **Lykes Line**. At the moment, you can only hit Honolulu on the *return* voyage from Japan to Seattle about twice a month. These 12-passenger vessels can be used by persons who want to sail from Hawaii to the Mainland on container ships like the *Colorado*. At about $500 per person for luxury facilities, it's hard to beat this with anything afloat—assuming that all that entertainment whoop-de-doo on a liner doesn't mean much to you.

Long Cruises. A few European-based cruise ships call at Honolulu from time to time. Liners like the *Rotterdam* and the *Sagafjord*, which leave New York or Florida in January, usually make it through the Caribbean, the Panama Canal, and up to Honolulu by about March.

Royal Viking Line ships stop in Hawaii four or five times a year. The *Royal Viking Star* and the *Royal Viking Sea* may call in Honolulu on their return voyage from the South Pacific early in the year on their way to California. Then the *Royal Viking Sky* usually chooses Honolulu as one port on its annual winter/spring cruise.

Also, the Cunard Line's *Queen Elizabeth 2* generally calls at both Honolulu and Kailua-Kona on its annual circumnavigation of the globe.

And now, most of us will return to the real world.

The Air Ways to Hawaii

Many vacationers who go to Hawaii not only spend too much money while there, but actually lay out more than is necessary to travel to the Islands in the first place.

Some jet there First Class, and we would have to agree that it is a comfortable and pampered way to fly—when you have the dough. There are extra-wide, supersoft seats, plenty of leg and arm space, multicourse gourmet meals with elaborate service, all you can eat and drink . . . It's living a luxurious Life of Riley at 30,000 feet. But today more travelers are questioning whether flying First Class is really worth the more than 30 percent price difference.

Coach Class. You'll probably save more than $100 off the one-way First Class (F) West Coast–to–Hawaii fare by moving to the narrower seats in the back three-fourths of the airplane. That means flying Coach, also called "Y Class."

For Coach Class fares, you have to give up a few luxuries. The movie on board will cost you $3 (for the earphones) if you want it. There will be no free drinks (you pay a buck or two for those you want), and your meal will be more limited, with little or no choice of food.

Still not enough savings? Okay, you might cut back your flight expense much more by giving up the free hot meal. That would bring the ticket down another $50 or so each way. This is the old traditional K class, and some airlines are still offering it. And don't worry about missing that meal. The airlines with K class seats usually sell a pretty good box lunch or equivalent, if you want it. And if you do buy it, you'll still save money.

Beyond that, there are special excursion fares (covering a limited period of time); advance purchase fares (APEX), which may also be set up for a limited time only; and some other temporary discount fares designed to better the airline's competitive position.

Also, you just may find a rock-bottom "standby fare," used to fill up those last few empty seats with passengers willing to go out to the airport with their bags full of clothes and hearts full of hope.

All this is a result of airlines becoming less and less regulated as the C.A.B.—the federal Civil Aeronautics Board—heads toward the day when it is scheduled to vote itself out of existence. Airlines now have more freedom to compete, and you have probably read about their controversial decisions to drop unpopular, money-losing routes or to charge passengers more per mile for those high-cost, low-load flights.

Happily, the West Coast–to–Hawaii routes (like the New York–to–California ones) are among the most popular and heavily traveled flights in the country. The airlines seem to keep tripping over each other to offer the most attractive deals they possibly can on the Hawaii runs.

If you aim to get the cheapest possible fare—rather than to choose a particular airline or even a specific date of departure—it is important to find a good travel agent who can instantly come up with the least expensive way for you to make a trip to Hawaii. (More on travel agents later.)

Fare Predictions. All right. For those who insist that we make an attempt to estimate economy airline fares, we'll put on our turban, peer into the crystal jet stream, and make the following, intentionally vague, prognostications:

Early in 1984, some brand-name airlines advertising Hawaii trips on the West Coast will do their utmost to extend some frill-less fares at less than $250 each way to Honolulu. (Add $40 for the new and popular direct Maui flights.) Texans might estimate a barrel-bottom tab of about $375 each way. From Chicago or Cleveland, the full economy fare will probably run around $500. New Yorkers might logically figure a fare of $550 or so. (However, cutthroat competition on the coast-to-coast runs may act together with the competitive California–Hawaii routes to trim those East Coast fares considerably.)

Some of the "bargain" airlines—World, Pacific East, the Hawaii Express, etc.—will probably knock 20 to 30 percent off these figures, although we think we've finally seen the last of the hundred-dollar Honolulu hop from the West Coast.

One way to be sure of getting the best fare possible, especially if you're going to Hawaii later in the year, is to buy your ticket as early as you can and take it home with you. While air fares continue to go up, you will have your ticket stored at home or in a safety-deposit box. Federal "fare guarantee laws" generally keep airlines from forcing price hikes on passengers who already have their tickets (although you will probably have to use them within one year).

The Major Carriers

At this writing, there are about a dozen regularly scheduled trunk airlines on the Mainland–to–Hawaii route. Some can be taken from other countries, along with a few foreign airlines. Pick your airline based on how well it serves your own needs. And always choose a nonstop flight if you can. You may lengthen your trip by an hour each time the plane lands en route.

As to type of equipment (airplanes are called "equipment" in industry jargon), we vastly prefer the jumbo jets—particularly the Boeing 747. (And as always, tell 'em we sent you.)

United Airlines. United is by far the dominant carrier on the route with about 100 flights weekly, most of them on Boeing 747s nonstop to Honolulu from Chicago, San Francisco, Seattle, Los Angeles, and San Diego. Some flights originate in Toronto, New York, and Denver. One DC-10 flight from Chicago via L.A. lands daily at Kailua-Kona on the Big Island. The return flight stops at Hilo on the same island and then continues nonstop to Los Angeles. Also two stretched DC-8 flights from San Francisco and Los Angeles travel nonstop daily to Kahului on Maui.

Western Airlines. Second in the market, Western has about 50 DC-10 flights a week to the Islands. There are nonstops from Anchorage, Salt Lake City, Las Vegas, San Francisco, Los Angeles, and San Diego. Other flights originate in Minneapolis and Washington, D.C.

World Airways. Flamboyant Ed Daly's World pioneered in bargain flights to Honolulu a few years ago. Today, World flies DC-10s between Honolulu and both Los Angeles and Oakland, California, at middle-altitude fares. Some of these are continuations of flights that begin in such faraway places as London, Frankfurt, Newark, Baltimore, and Kansas City.

Northwest Orient. Northwest runs daily Boeing 747 flights between Honolulu and Los Angeles, San Francisco, and Seattle via Portland.

Pan American. PAA sends Boeing 747s nonstop to Honolulu from San Francisco and Los Angeles, one daily from each, in flights originating as far away as Florida, and less frequently from exotic ports to the south and west. (Nonstops arrive from Auckland, Sydney, Guam, and Tokyo.)

Continental Airlines. This Texas-based airline offers two nonstop daily flights between Los Angeles and Honolulu, some flights originating in Houston. (From Down Under, Continental flights to Honolulu also originate in Auckland and Sydney, some flying via Fiji.) All are on DC-10s.

American Airlines. There are daily DC-10 flights nonstop from Los Angeles (originating in Dallas/Ft. Worth) and from San Francisco (originating in Chicago). American also has picked up some Braniff business with newer nonstop flights from Dallas/Ft. Worth.

CP Air. The Canadian international airline has now switched from smaller planes to DC-10s and offers nonstop service between Honolulu and Vancouver, Edmonton, and even (once a week) Toronto. (Coming up above from Down Under, you can fly CP Air to Honolulu on non-stops from Sydney and Fiji.)

The Hawaii Express. This is one of two new airlines that seemed to swoop in out of nowhere recently with one used Boeing 747. Now the Honolulu-based "Big Pineapple" has added two DC-10s and flies two daily flights from Los Angeles and one from San Francisco, offering some low fares to passengers who are happy with a cold-lunch, no-frills trip.

Pacific East Air. Pacific East began flying around the same time as the Hawaii Express, also at bargain rates but in stretched DC-8s. It makes frequent flights from San Francisco, San Jose, and Los Angeles to Honolulu and from Los Angeles to Maui, although the single-aisle craft seems almost an anachronism today. The Civil Aeronautics Board reported recently that PEA had the nation's highest complaint rate. (And one family wrote the Honolulu *Star-Bulletin* in 1983 to say that when they changed their plans they felt trapped by restrictive ticket policies.)

South Pacific Island Airways. Currently this line, equipped with three Boeing 707s (remember those?), is flying between Honolulu and Anchorage, Alaska, and between Honolulu and Samoa and Guam.

Hawaiian Airlines. The longtime interisland carrier may begin 1984 with nonstop flights twice weekly between Honolulu and Seattle, Portland, and San Jose, and possibly even Minneapolis, Boston, Philadelphia, and Pittsburgh. Hawaiian wants to use stretched DC-8s on these runs and on a San Francisco–to–Maui flight. It has also begun talking about starting DC-10 jumbo-jet service between Honolulu and Los Angeles and San Francisco later in the year. Hawaiian has been having financial troubles on its interisland runs, and this is the impetus for some of its blue-sky planning. So recheck all this after our ink is dry. (HAL's 800 number is in the appendix.)

Competition from the newer airlines has been credited with forcing drastic reductions in ticket prices among the big boys, at least those flying from California. It will be interesting to see if the all-out fare wars will continue throughout 1984.

An exception to every rule is a bizarre carrier that is taking off on the Los Angeles–Honolulu run. That is **Regent Air** (formerly First Air), a snob-value executive and celebrity airline that says it will carry gilt-edged passengers between the two cities for $1,500 (one way) amid oriental rugs and expensive artworks, and with a flight crew that includes a manicurist, a hairdresser, etc. Frankly, we think this anachronistic flying carpet is doomed to financial failure. (But we've been wrong before!)

Foreign Airlines. Hawaii is also served by several foreign air carriers. But if you are going from one U.S. destination to another—including Hawaii—the 1896 Jones Act prohibits you from flying between two American cities in a foreign airliner. (It originally covered only ships.) This means most Yankee travelers will have to skip such exotic companies as Japan Airlines, Air New Zealand, or Qantas.

Coming from Australia, however, anyone may fly to Honolulu via Qantas, CP Air, Pan American, or Continental. From New Zealand, your choice is generally Air New Zealand, Pan American, or Continental. These airlines generally have attractive excursion plans for residents of the two countries, worth asking Down Under travel agents about. Some of those routes include free stopovers in such places as Samoa, Tahiti, and Fiji. Also residents of Australia and New Zealand may see Hawaii on the way to the U.S. Mainland, and then return home by a different route. (See *The Maverick Guide to Australia* and *The Maverick Guide to New Zealand* for more information on these routes.)

Baggage Allowance. Currently you're allowed two large suitcases and one small (under-seat) bag free of charge. You'll pay $10 or so per extra piece. CAB regulations require that you affix your name to the outside of each piece of luggage. Surfboards or bicycles will cost you perhaps $20 to take along on the plane with you to Hawaii. But check that out with the specific airline you are considering. Different carriers have different thoughts on these items.

Jet Lag and Time Zones

The first time we flew direct from New York to Honolulu, we couldn't believe what was happening to our bodies. We were dead tired at 7 P.M.—maybe propped our eyes open until 8:00. Then the next day we were awake and up at dawn's early light, waiting impatiently for a breakfast restaurant to open. Everything was mixed up—mealtimes, digestion time, bedtime. We just could hardly cope.

The problem was not the actual distance we flew, or the physical strain of the trip, but merely that we whizzed directly across six time zones— actually seven when the Mainland has Daylight Saving Time (Hawaii never does). In Standard Time, remember that when it's 7 o'clock in Honolulu, it's 8:00 in the Yukon and 9:00 in California. It's also 10 o'clock in the Rocky Mountain states, 11 o'clock in Chicago and the Midwest, and noon or midnight on the Eastern Seaboard. Add one hour to all those times for Mainland areas where Daylight Saving Time is in effect, usually between late April and late October.

Doctors and psychiatrists believe it takes several days to recover fully from jet lag, depending on how many time zones you crossed in a single day and on your own particular constitution. (A lucky few claim they are never bothered.)

We suggest a half-dozen steps to relieve (not prevent) jet lag: (1) Sleep or nap as much as you can aboard your flight. (2) Set your watch to Hawaii time when you get on the plane. (3) Take no sleeping pills and little alcohol during the flight. (4) Rest again when you arrive at your hotel (pulling the shades, if necessary). (5) Schedule no business appointments and make few decisions of any kind your first day in the Islands. (6) Keep to familiar foods and eat lightly your first day on vacation.

Interisland Transportation

For speed and comfort, most visitors to Hawaii opt for the jet trips between the islands offered by the two mainstays: **Hawaiian Airlines**, sometimes called Hawaiian Air or HAL, which flies its 170-passenger, twin-jet stretched DC-9s between Honolulu and seven Neighbor Island airports, and **Aloha Airlines**, which uses 118-seat, tri-jet Boeing 737s to these same destinations. Aloha flies to Kauai and Maui, and to Hilo and Kona on the Big Island. (It has just dropped its Molokai run.) Hawaiian Air adds to that list infrequent schedules to Waimea on the Big Island and to Lanai and Molokai, but uses its De Havilland DASH-7 turboprop planes for those three destinations. Holding 50 passengers, they are also used for some lower-price flights to Maui and Kauai. (No alcohol is served on the DASHes, incidentally.)

Although the two lines have attempted mergers in the past, they now compete fiercely, with each other and against the smaller airlines, and each has its loyal devotees. We usually find it difficult to choose between them. Hawaiian does seem more efficient during heavy-traffic periods in the terminals, but Aloha has a better on-time record. Both are having considerable financial troubles and are trying desperately to capture greater segments of the market.

Hawaiian's regular Douglas fanjets are somewhat quieter than the Boeings in the forward areas. They also have a 3–2 seat configuration, which may give that line a slight edge if you draw one of its newer planes. Aloha's plumper 737s have six across (3–3) seating, but the company claims they can unload baggage faster. Hawaiian has been in the business about fifty years, and Aloha has chalked up more than thirty years of service. Both have virtually perfect safety records, with no passenger fatalities.

Jet flights between the islands are so short—under twenty minutes from Honolulu to either Kauai or Maui, for example—that you are no more up than you start down again. On either of these lines, do check in at the counter no less than 30 minutes—preferably 45 minutes—before flight departure time. Both Aloha and Hawaiian have received slaps on the wings by *Money* magazine for "bumping" passengers more than all other U.S. airlines. That may be unfair because delays are usually short. However, they do not hold reserved space for long, and during busy periods there are many hopeful travelers waiting to slip into any "no show" seats. If you hold reservations and are still caught in a line at the counter 30 minutes before flight time, better speak up just to make sure everything's hunky-dory.

Recently another airline was introduced to the interisland skies. **Mid Pacific Airlines**, the new *jet-prop* outfit, is flying Japanese-made YS-11, twin-motor, 60-passenger aircraft between Oahu (Honolulu), Maui, Kauai, and Kona and Hilo on the Big Island. Flights are normally made at an altitude of only about 7,000 feet, which allows for better sightseeing and picture-taking than the higher-flying pure jet lines. Mid Pacific prides itself on offering flights at somewhat lower fares than those of Hawaiian and Aloha. Long-haul flights between Honolulu and Kona or Hilo, which take about an hour, include free champagne, beer, and even a light meal, unusual on interisland flights. (For some reason, Mid Pac doesn't accept Diners Club cards, we discovered recently.)

In previous editions we went into considerable detail on special discount fares offered by Aloha, Hawaiian, and Mid Pacific airlines, including slashes of up to 50 percent for joining their special travel clubs, taking the first flight in the morning, etc. Throughout 1984 there will be similar bargains, but the picture is changing too rapidly to cover them all in an annual guidebook. Do ask about joining an airline's air-travel club (you might save enough on even one round trip to make it worthwhile). The three lines may be expected to continue their aerial price wars in their attempts to lure tourists and locals alike, and the exact situation in the months after this edition comes off the press is impossible to predict.

Even your travel agent might not be able to keep up to the minute on this, and we suggest that if you want to get the best bargains in interisland flights it would be better to ask all the airlines about their special deals after arriving in the Islands, or to phone their toll-free numbers in the appendix shortly before leaving home. (Check the standby fares, too. If you can stand the uncertainty, they are usually the best deals of all, especially during the week and in off-season periods like May and September.)

Besides the three big boys, there is also a trio of small outfits known collectively as "commuter airlines." They run propeller-driven airplanes, on regular interisland schedules. Our own favorite is **Royal Hawaiian Air Service**, which carries nine passengers (one in the co-pilot's seat, which is best for color photography) on flights in twin-engine Cessna 402s. The newer models of these planes feature wonderfully wide, panoramic windows.

RHAS serves five islands and twelve airports, including such smaller fields as Kalaupapa on Molokai, Kaanapali and Hana on Maui, and sometimes Upolu on Hawaii. Besides those airports, Royal Hawaiian also has scheduled flights to everywhere the jets go, except to Kauai.

We enjoy the low-level prop flights since they allow us to see much more than we can from a high-altitude window. The pilot is right there in the cabin, too, and he'll usually point out the sights and even change the route on occasion to give the best view of the island scenery below the wings.

Like the jets, RHAS has never lost a passenger in nearly twenty years of flying. Fares average about the same as the regular rates on Aloha or Hawaiian airlines or a few dollars more than the travel club or other discount prices on the jets. We continue to receive letters praising the *esprit* of the RHAS pilots, and we fly with them ourselves at every opportunity year after year.

The newest small-craft airline, which has recently been reorganized, is **Princeville Airways**, flying Cessna 404s and De Havilland Twin Otters. It began with hops from Honolulu to the short strip at Princeville on Kauai, which is not served by other airlines. Later it added service to Molokai Airport and to Kahului on Maui. The airline is guided by Bob Fraker, a veteran local pilot, and a big plus is Fraker's two-pilot cockpit policy.

Another interesting company is **Air Molokai**, which caters to frequent local Honolulu–Molokai traffic. They sometimes have the cheapest trip over that route.

Surface Travel? Sadly, SeaFlite, which operated for three years between the islands, has folded its hydrofoils and slipped away to Hong Kong. There are vague plans to bring it back for limited Honolulu–Maui service, but don't hold your breath. Meanwhile, there are a few "fun" boat trips from island to island. These are covered in Section 7 of the island-chapters further along in this book.

Travel Agents

To set up a good trip to Hawaii, we heartily recommend an aggressive, enthusiastic travel agency. Avoid "assembly-line" operations (and these can be the tiny "mom and pop" agencies or the great international giants)—those who seem anxious only to book you on a prewrapped package or just to jet you off into space on any old flight. A travel agency should be able and willing to take the time to tailor the ideal itinerary for you and your family. If the agent can maintain his smile while you exercise your own individuality, chances are he's the one for you.

The only reliable way to choose a travel agent is to take one other travelers you are acquainted with have used successfully. Even if you've never consulted a travel agent before and never expect to see one again, choose him as you would a dentist. Don't pick one blindly from the Yellow Pages. He should be a member of ASTA (the American Society of Travel Agents), and he should be licensed by the ATC (the Air Traffic Conference). Agents who belong to ARTA—the Association of Retail Travel Agents—are also generally reliable. The most respected agents these days have the initials "CTC" after their names. That stands for Certified Travel Counselor, and it signifies an experienced agent who has completed a special two-year, graduate-level travel management program run by the Institute of Certified Travel Agents.

Some Hawaii Experience? Well, it *might* help if your travel agent has been to Hawaii, but don't make that a requirement. Many agents have made whirlwind tours as guests of various commercial enterprises, and their recommendations may be unconsciously colored by these limited experiences. Believe me, we've gotten farther around the state and poked into more out-of-the-way corners than 100 percent of the Mainland travel agents.

Any good travel agent will try to give you what you want, so you can count on the *Maverick Guide* to help you choose your facilities and activities and then seek a good travel agent to put your plans into operation and hone the finer points of your arrangements. Take this book into the travel agency, if you want; you won't be the first to do that with excellent results.

Try to be specific and definite about what you want your travel agent to do for you. Make him have a darned good reason before talking you out of arrangements you have in mind based on your study of this guide. Also, be sure that he obtains letters or certificates of confirmation from hotels and rental car outfits, giving you copies of these, including the rates agreed upon, to take with you.

Remember that travel agents seldom cost you money. Mostly they make theirs from commissions. (Airlines pay them from 7 to 11 percent; hotels and other enterprises usually give them 10 percent.) Sometimes it is proper for a travel agent to charge you a fee, but if he or she wants to do this, ask questions. If you don't like the answers, go see another agent. If the travel agent does book you on a package tour, feel free to ask him *exactly* what you are paying for. Any responsible agent will be only too happy to spell it all out.

For Lone Wolves. Many vacationers like the satisfaction of nailing down all their arrangements themselves, regardless of the availability of travel agents. That's fine, but when writing to or phoning hotels, rental cars, bus tours, etc., remember again to be absolutely specific about the type and price of what you're looking for, the days you will be arriving and leaving, etc., and then save all your confirmation letters and deposit receipts. On the phone, get the name of the person you are talking to and write it down. You probably won't need all this, but it's sound vacation practice to have the evidence of what you agreed on right along with you when you arrive. And as always, it would also be a good idea to tell 'em we sent you.

The Package Tour

Some people are particularly suited to taking a group tour to Hawaii. If you're lonely or gregarious, and feel for one reason or another that you can't or just don't want to make a multitude of arrangements, this is an ideal alternative to more individualized travel.

Others feel that packages seal them against the experience of personal discovery, and if they do choose such a tour it will be mainly a money-saving one that wraps up essentials like the plane, the hotel, etc., and leaves out luaus, nightclubs, and other frills.

If you are considering a group tour, carefully compare the price of the deal with individual arrangements. Sometimes the savings will be significant and sometimes not. By the way, if you're a lone traveler you may pay a special "single supplement" added to the advertised price of the tour, unless you are willing to share a room with someone else.

Extras and Add-Ons. No matter how much you get as part of your package, someone will probably try to sell you more in your "orientation" meeting. Some particular sightseeing tours are good and fun, but others are just not worth it. (See Section 7 in island-chapters 5 through

10.) Be aware that bus tours often list in their literature several destinations that are free and/or easily accessible anyway, and sometimes they list sights that are only pointed out briefly as you zip by in your insulated, air-conditioned coach. (And despite the "tips included" promises, you will be expected to drop some extra change here and there.)

On multi-island package tours, you and your luggage will sometimes seem to be on different itineraries. You'll have to have it battened down early so it can leave each hotel from a half-hour to two hours before you, and it may arrive in each room before or after you. Depending on the necessities (like medicine or film) packed in your Gladstones, that could be a significant inconvenience. On the other hand, you probably will never need to carry them yourself.

On a package tour, you're also expected to join in all the fun and develop a camaraderie with your fellow tour members, taking part in games, community sings, and other activities. Your tour conductor or escort will probably be a lively, fun-loving, and hardworking big brother (or den mother) to you all. More power to him, but he is a professional, after all. You may think you're a gregarious and tolerant person, too— until you sit on bus after bus with that gum-chewing and gabby Mama from Minnehaha and good ole back-slapping Jack who sells widgets and flanges and likes to pinch bottoms.

You may hit some restaurants that give more kickbacks than good food and service, and it's not you that collects the gravy, either. And let's face it; an air-chilled bus with soundproof, tinted windows is just not the way to get out to mingle and experience the Islands.

Hawaii is certainly exotic and different, but it is *not* a foreign country. Everyone speaks your language, your money is just as good as it is at home, all the food and water are safe, and automobile driving is pretty much the same as it is back home. No one will deliberately mislead you if you choose to see the Islands at your own pace and according to your own interests. On the contrary, you'll probably find the local population the most considerate, helpful, and polite people that you will meet anywhere.

So it may not be the fault of any individual tour company, and we admit we are probably wrong in some cases. But for most people, we doubt that the savings are worth joining the big on-the-bus, off-the-bus march of the packaged herds. (We have never managed to sign on incognito to a full-scale, whoop-it-up package tour of Hawaii ourselves. Consequently, we particularly like to have letters from readers who have liked or disliked their own package tour. One couple who wrote recently were absolutely thrilled with their Cartan Tour. We've also had good reports on Island Holidays, Trade Winds Tours, and Maupintour.)

Packing and Wearing

If you've been with us all through the chapter, you now know that a "trunk carrier" is a major airline and *not* someone who will help you with your luggage. And this brings us to something you've heard a thousand times before, but for Hawaii we really mean it: Travel light!

There are two good reasons for this: (1) Hawaii honestly is warm, and life is very informal from a sartorial standpoint. Shirttails are worn outside, shoes are kicked off at the slightest excuse (it is generally impolite to wear shoes inside a private home in Hawaii), and ties and stockings are seldom wanted or needed. (2) Almost no one vacations in Hawaii without buying some clothes on the spot. Men will want to get an aloha shirt or two and perhaps a couple of those eccentric Hawaiian T-shirts. Women can't resist a *muumuu*—long or short. You'll like the informal footwear, too. If you didn't bring sandals with you, you'll probably pick up a pair of leather ones as well as a practical pair of zoris (rubber slippers) at least for the beach.

Men's Wear. Male suit addicts should make it one lightweight model, mainly to wear on the plane to and from the Islands. (Then if you do feel the dress-up urge you'll have that outfit along with you.) Frequent habitués of Hawaii often fly to the Islands in a blazer or sport jacket, if not simply an open-necked shirt.

If you have a couple pairs of easy-care slacks, fine. If you're young and/or plan to explore the boonies, rugged jeans would be useful. Also, white trousers for evening wear are popular in Hawaii, and they are often worn with white loafers (or with sandals for simpler occasions).

You may want to have one or two sport shirts with you (at least one to cover you while you sneak out to buy your aloha shirt). Tuck in lightweight underwear, pajamas, robe, etc. Laundromats are plentiful, and several of the big hotels also have their own self-service machines. Bring comfortable, soft walking shoes for general tramping around, or heavier boots for serious hiking.

If you own Bermuda shorts, by all means feel free to take them along. They're acceptable almost everywhere, any time. Island men usually prefer walking shorts or other models cut differently and shorter than Bermudas. Incidentally, local fashion is not to wear dark shoes, or shoes and socks, with shorts; instead, sandals, zoris, tennis shoes, running shoes, canvas shoes, or even bare feet are considered proper accessories for bare knees. If you're going up in the highest mountains, it may be too chilly for shorts. Take a light sweater up with you, too, or maybe even a parka if you'll hit the Kilauea Volcano area or Haleakala Crater in winter.

Female Fashion. Women should bring the same resort clothes they would use in southern Florida, the Caribbean, or Minneapolis in July, all preferably in loose, easy-to-care-for fabrics. As we said, keep in mind that Hawaii's vast, colorful garment industry awaits any vacancies in your wardrobe. Island fashions are different, but by shopping carefully you can take back aloha wear that can be used for at-home or hostess gowns or for informal/chic occasions. (See Chapter 5, Section 10, "Oahu Shopping.")

Women may want to wear trousers for sightseeing, too, and Sara says a three-piece pants suit is great; the jacket goes on and off as you go in and out of air-conditioned buses, restaurants, etc. Shorts are acceptable nearly everywhere.

If you're not loading up on *muumuus*, etc., you may want to bring something for casual evening wear, as well as regular sun or street dresses. Wear comfortable shoes; you'll be walking a lot. Sandals and zoris will be handy, whether you bring them or buy them here. You'll need heavy-soled shoes for any hiking. And since you may be in and out of the water a lot, bring a hair dryer along, too.

Men and Women. Members of both sexes will want to bring or buy a bathing suit or two. Hotels will provide the towels. Islanders used to short showers turn up their noses at raincoats and seldom use umbrellas, but visitors usually feel happier with either one or both, of the fold-up variety.

Women might like a head scarf to wear in the wind. Men won't need a regular Mainland felt-style hat, but they may want to buy a coconut frond or *lauhala* plantation hat. Sunbathers of either sex should be sure to have some kind of hat to wear during the day.

Toilet articles, makeup, first-aid supplies, etc., may be replenished in Hawaii, just as at home, so don't take lots of extras. All film is available, and you can even get overnight color processing and see how your pictures are coming out before you leave for home.

Besides cameras, some visitors like to bring a small battery radio (hotel rooms are short on radios even if long on TVs), plus a pair of binoculars for looking up at mountains, down into valleys, or across at bikinis. A small cassette tape recorder can be fun for capturing tour guide lectures and Hawaiian music.

Don't forget sunglasses. We like the ones with polarizing lenses (Polaroid and Foster Grant are two brands that make them). Suntan lotion is important; get a kind containing PABA, a four-letter word standing for some multisyllabic monster. One of the best is PreSun, a product tested and proved in the Islands. However, it will sometimes stain light-colored clothing, so apply it carefully. Other good brands are Eclipse and Sundown, both of which seem to stay on well in the water.

Sara personally recommends plenty of plastic bags of all sorts, sizes, and shapes—great for temporarily transporting wet bathing suits, wash-cloths, dirty clothes, old shoes, or whatever must be kept in isolation. You might even come with a roll of Baggies.

You won't need that succession of things you lug around in some foreign country, though. You can get all the familiar soaps, toothpastes, and toilet paper you want. Phrase books and money converters and the like are also superfluous. Just bring the little volume you hold in your hand right now.

When to Go to Hawaii

It might be easier to talk about when *not* to go, and we can think of two possible months. February falls into that category; not only is Honolulu packed with tourists, but it is probably the least dependable month for weather. (We seldom get several days in a row of rain, but if we do, it might be in February.) Then August, the "convention month," is difficult as far as crowds, hotel bookings, etc., are concerned, especially in Honolulu. Also, if we have any month that's hot (85 degrees F. and above), it will surely be August.

Our personal favorite months are in the fall—September to Christmas. And early January (after New Year's Day) is practical, too.

Since Hawaii's weather is much the same as a temperate zone spring the year around, the *real* spring months of April through mid-July are less in demand; too bad, because they're absolutely gorgeous. All the flowers are out, and the trade winds are never so clean and pure as on a day in May or June. And although we would never recommend suddenly zipping off to Hawaii without a hotel and car reservation, well, you might get away with it in the spring or the fall.

If you must come to Hawaii in the peak or near-peak months, that's all the more reason to visit one or more Neighbor Islands, and perhaps skip the Oahu crush entirely. If Waikiki is jammed, you'll find your tropical solitude in, perhaps, Waimea Canyon on Kauai, or the Haleakala crater on Maui, or the Waipio Valley on the Big Island. And even in mid-August or mid-February, we'll bet you can search out that "beach without a footprint" on Kauai, Molokai, Lanai—and maybe even in some isolated areas of Maui. It's worth a try!

3

Where and What Is Hawaii?

An Archipelago Punched Up from the Sea

Despite many intriguing theories, the original and exact meaning of the word "Hawaii" lies, like the bones of its great warrior king, forever hidden in a deep and mysterious past.

It is pronounced pretty much like "Ha-*why*-ee," with a catch of the breath between the last two of those three syllables. Some people sound the "w" like a "v," but that's a recent affectation. Remember, though, that the word does not in the least resemble the interrogation "How are ya?"

Today Hawaii is the official name of our fiftieth state, admitted to the Union in 1959. That's a while back, now, so a visitor will only embarrass himself if he announces in Honolulu that his own home is "back in the states."

In fact, the recipe for instant popularity with your Hawaiian hosts is to recognize their own statehood and U.S. citizenship at once by referring to the rest of the country always as "the Mainland."

Correctly enough, some still call the archipelago "the Hawaiian Islands." And on a few British charts of the Pacific, you may still see printed, with Anglican persistence, "the Sandwich Isles." The latter label was given the Islands by English naval captain James Cook when he came across them in 1778, thus honoring his boss, the Earl of Sandwich and First Lord of the Admiralty. (He was the same card-playing earl who first placed his gambling snack between two pieces of bread, thereby winning himself a much more prominent bite in the history of the world.)

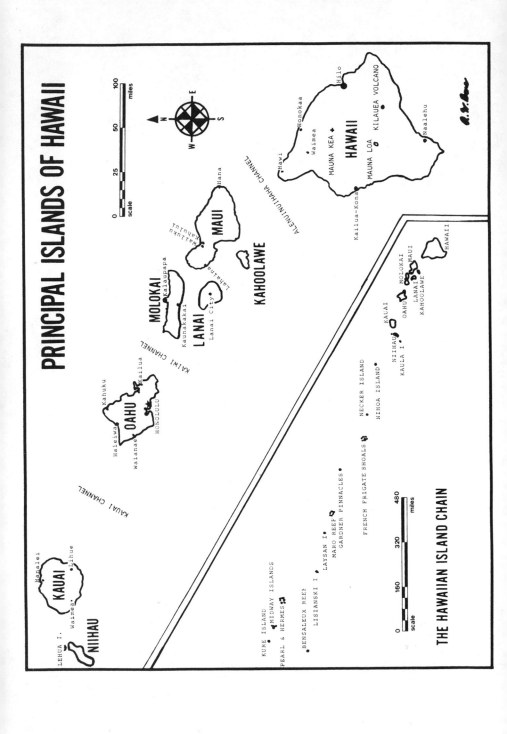

PRINCIPAL ISLANDS OF HAWAII

scale
0   25   50   100
miles

KAUAI CHANNEL

KAUAI
Hanalei
Waimea • • Lihue

LEHUA I.
NIIHAU

Kahuku
Haleiwa
OAHU
Waianae • Kailua
HONOLULU

KAIWI CHANNEL

MOLOKAI
Kaunakakai • • Kalaupapa

LANAI
Lanai City •

MOLOKAI

Wailuku
Kahului
MAUI
Lahaina • Hana

KAHOOLAWE

ALENUIHAHA CHANNEL

HAWAII
Hawi
Honokaa
Waimea •
MAUNA KEA ✦
MAUNA LOA
Kailua-Kona •
KILAUEA VOLCANO
Hilo
Naalehu •

THE HAWAIIAN ISLAND CHAIN

KURE ISLAND
MIDWAY ISLANDS
PEARL & HERMES

BENSALEUX REEF
LISIANSKI I.
LAYSAN I.
MARO REEF
GARDNER PINNACLES

FRENCH FRIGATE SHOALS

NECKER ISLAND
NIHOA ISLAND

KAUAI
NIIHAU
KAULA I.
OAHU
MOLOKAI
LANAI
KAHOOLAWE
MAUI
HAWAII

scale
0   160   320   480
miles

Two hundred years ago, "Hawaii" stood for only one island, the largest and southernmost in the group, and this is not where Honolulu stands. What we now call the "Big Island" still bears the formal title "The Island of Hawaii." But today Hawaii also refers collectively to all the 132 islands, islets, reefs, sandbars, and rock dots that poke up above the surface over a 1,600-mile route running from the northwest to the southeast.

As though it weren't boggling enough that Hawaii is both the name of an entire state and of one single island in that state, there are several other elusive geographic facts on which to spin your compass.

For instance, the Islands are about 2,500 miles southwest of Los Angeles, almost on the same latitude as Mexico City. Incurable romantics might refer to their location in the "South Seas," but they are not in the South Pacific. This is the North Pacific Ocean—more than a thousand miles above the equator, but nonetheless in one of the truly tropic zones of the world.

Discounting the tinier specks, there are eight major islands in the Hawaiian chain:

• Seven of these eight main islands—all except Kahoolawe—are inhabited.

• Six of the seven inhabited islands may be easily visited. Tiny Niihau is taboo.

• Four of those six are much more popular—and populated—than the other two. Thus we set aside little Lanai and Molokai for the moment.

• Two of these four have jetports to which you are likely to fly from the Mainland. You usually have to land on one of the gateway islands—Oahu or the Big Island (Hawaii)—before you can get to Maui or Kauai.

• And one rather medium-size island—Oahu—crowds in four-fifths of the state's entire population.

From the smallest to the largest, the eight principal islands are Kahoolawe, Niihau, Lanai, Molokai, Kauai, Oahu, Maui, and Hawaii. Now let's take them one at a time.

No one other than an occasional very hardy wild goat lives on **Kahoolawe,** the smallest of the eight, although it would be large enough to set up housekeeping on, if you dared. Its 45 square miles have been entirely absorbed by the U.S. Navy since 1941 and adapted primarily for use as one gigantic target range. In the past few years, the bombing of Kahoolawe has become extremely controversial. Hawaiian activist groups have been protesting the practice, using the issue as a rallying point to highlight their demands for social reform. The island is pronounced "kah-ho-oh-*lah-vay*," which is not so different from the sound of the exploding ordnance as it echoes off the pockmarked ridges and valleys.

Not quite so diminutive, but also *kapu* (taboo) to most of us, is the 73-square-mile island of **Niihau** (*"knee-ee-how"*). Niihau supports about 200 people, nearly all of whom are pure Hawaiian plantation workers and their families. One of the few places where the Hawaiian language is still in daily use, the island is private property, owned by a single family. The only island "invaded" on Dec. 7, 1941, this Isle of Mystery has a fascinating story to tell.

The smallest island you may easily visit is the modest and unassuming dollop called **Lanai** ("lahn-*eye*"). Its 140 square miles are virtually all owned by the Dole Pineapple people, and a large portion of it is devoted to a single giant plantation. In a few years it will be developed into a tourist resort. Meanwhile, only you, we, and its 2,000 permanent residents will know of its attractions.

The other sometimes forgotten isle is the friendly neighbor called **Molokai** (*"mole*-oak-eye"). About 6,000 are now at home on the cleared acres of its often rugged and mountainous 261 square miles. Like Lanai, one of Molokai's major selling points is its paucity of tourists; until recently, at least, visitors were about as rare as the Hawaiian *nene* bird. On an isolated peninsula, Molokai once embraced one of the world's most compelling stories of human bondage and personal heroism. You might not be able to resist going over to personally experience its locale.

At 553 square miles, the Island of **Kauai** is more than twice as large, and the 40,000 residents there pronounce their home "cow-*why*" or "*cow*-eye." (There's often debate about that.) It boasts the wettest spot on earth as well as a vast, dry desert canyon, and enough flowers to fill the Houston Astrodome. Its principal town, Lihue, is the seat of Kauai County, which includes the islands of Kauai and Niihau.

The next island up the size scale is 608-square-mile **Oahu** ("oh-*wah*-who"), and it is another source of demographic and geographic obfuscation. The state capital, Honolulu, is located on Oahu. And in a sense the capital *is* Oahu, because the "City and County" of Honolulu encompasses the entire island. (Actually, even more than that; for administrative purposes, nearly all the 100 or so islands in the Leeward chain—skipping over Kauai and Niihau—are part of the city and county.)

Oahu—or Honolulu—is populated by more than 775,000 people, or over 75 percent of the number of residents in the entire state. City and state politicians sometimes compete strenuously, and ridiculously, with each other for the affections of this electorate, due to the high proportion of voters concentrated on the one island. Oahu is also the governmental, commercial, and cultural center of Hawaii. For this reason, islands other than Oahu are known as the "Neighbor Islands" or some-times the "Outer Islands."

At 729 square miles, **Maui** (rhymes with "Howie") is significantly larger in land area than Oahu, and it is a relatively cosmopolitan Neighbor Island of 70,000. It was here that Hawaii's capital was once located, and the island still wears the rusty raiments of past adventure and glory.

Maui is dominated by the vast sleeping volcano of Haleakala, today the center of the 20,000-acre Haleakala National Park. The rustic seaport of Lahaina was once capital of the entire kingdom, but sleepy Wailuku is now the seat of Maui County, which includes the nearby islands of Lanai, Molokai, and Kahoolawe.

Last, there is the king-sized **Island of Hawaii,** referred to by most who live in the state as "The Big Island." With its 4,038-plus square miles, it is more than twice the land area of all the rest of the Hawaiian chain wrapped up together. But for all its bulk, there are only about 95,000 people sprinkled over the vast landscape.

Honolulu folks who vacation on the Big Island are sometimes amazed to find they can drive for long periods there without seeing the sea— only the lofty and majestic mountain masses which are capped by vast snowfields in winter.

It is on Hawaii that the live volcanos of Kilauea and Mauna Loa occasionally put on a show of temper, and the lava from deep within the earth may emerge and then flow to the sea, adding still more land area to Hawaii. From here, too, Kamehameha the Great launched his eighteenth-century war to conquer the archipelago.

The small city of Hilo (*"heel*-oh") is the county seat, and it spreads out a jet airport just a coconut's toss from the city limits. You can fly there direct from the West Coast without passing through Honolulu, and as a bucolic gateway to the Islands, Hilo is highly recommended.

Calculated against the age of the earth's major natural features, the Hawaiian Islands are relative whippersnappers. It all began 25 million years ago when a rift opened up in the floor of the Pacific Ocean. A jet of red-hot volcanic liquid rock from deep within the core of the earth began pushing through the opening, hardening as it hit the cold sea water seven miles below the surface. Gradually the material began spreading out to make the base of what are now Kure and Midway islands at the extreme northwest of the chain.

As each island raised itself up to a point where its own mass congealed and sealed off its birth canal, the pressure moved a little way southeastward and opened up more cracks. These built up new undersea volcanos, some of which eventually reached the surface of the water, thereby earning the name "island."

Geologists now believe that the pressure didn't move along the crack, but that the surface of the globe itself moved—like some Brobdingnagian conveyor belt—over the jet of hot lava. Thus the islands were punched out, more or less, one by one in assembly-line fashion. And according to the same scientific theory, the islands are still drifting toward the northwest at the breakneck speed of four inches a year.

Many of the tiny little islets and underwater extinct volcanos to the northwest once stood high above the sea as respectable-sized portions of real estate. But gradually, due to the islands' own weight and the rising level of the ocean at the end of the last ice age, they began sinking again.

Coral growth sometimes delays their death, but erosion of wind and water combine to eventually wear away the oldest of the volcanic islands. Few of the northwest Leeward Islands are inhabited today, and those that are occupied have become just lonely outposts for military personnel. The rest is a 1,000-mile-long national wildlife refuge.

The eight principal islands of Hawaii also have been significantly eroded since their birth. The island of Kauai is the oldest, so it has been smoothed out the most. Kauai has therefore developed a system of streams and rivers the like of which is unknown on the younger islands.

Oahu, Molokai, and Lanai are more rugged. The volcanic period which created these islands was also so long ago that virtually no trace is found of their original vast calderas. However, several smaller craters were blasted out in a later volcanic period, building such familiar landmarks as Oahu's Diamond Head, which blew up only about 150,000 years ago.

On Maui, the volcano of Haleakala is classified as dormant (not quite extinct), since it last erupted in 1790—just the day before yesterday in geologic time. The only volcanic activity in Hawaii today is on the Big Island, where lava flows and fountains from time to time around Mauna Loa and Kilauea volcanos, the twin nuclei of the Hawaii Volcanos National Park. Kilauea and its satellite pits and vents are always bubbling and steaming, and if you should happen to catch either volcano in eruption, you'll experience one of the grandest and most awe-inspiring shows on earth.

Scenery—Unreal, but Usually True

Driving into Honolulu from the airport, you wonder at first what the difference is. Like many other American airport-to-city routes, Nimitz Highway boasts a healthy collection of car lots, hamburger stands, and gas stations. Yet, there is something different, something mellowing, something that makes these commercial establishments less offensive.

Suddenly you realize it isn't what you did see, but what you didn't see. There wasn't a billboard on that entire route, was there? In fact, there are no billboards anywhere in the state of Hawaii. There haven't been any for over fifty years, after a courageous band of women called the Outdoor Circle finally won a fourteen-year-long battle to grind the oversized advertisements into the dirt. The women, many of whom were wives of Honolulu business and civic leaders, felt that the unusual and special beauty of Hawaii was being sacrificed to the two-dimensional monsters which ate up the views of mountains and valleys.

Followed by larger and larger groups of people, the ladies first boycotted and then shamed most of the outdoor advertising operations into oblivion. Finally, in 1927, there was one holdout, a small billboard firm with a few Mainland accounts. The Outdoor Circle bought the company and closed it down. Only then did the territorial legislature pass a law killing billboards completely throughout the Islands. The law has withstood tests up to the present.

Cynics correctly note that many of the Honolulu views once blocked by billboards have since been obstructed by a succession of Babylonian highrises. But the fact remains that many movers and shakers of Hawaii have not only cared about, but have managed to do something toward, keeping the Islands' reputation for eye-soothing tropical panoramas.

James Michener, the author of *Hawaii*, recently revisited the scene of his epic novel and pronounced himself "astounded" by the development since his days in residence only twenty years ago. Nevertheless, he told Honolulu *Advertiser* writer Leonard Lueras that, taking all the islands together, "It is still the most attractive single state in the country."

Magnificent cliffs, waterfalls, and sunsets have no doubt been Hawaii's heritage almost since the days its creative fires first began to cool, hundreds of thousands of years ago. But it was man's appearance on the landscape which brought to Hawaii and preserved for it the final touches to the "natural" scenery we have today.

This human concern dates back to the ancient Polynesian voyagers who discovered a naked Hawaii, almost completely devoid of trees, with only scrub brush holding tenuously to the desert-like lava fields. On subsequent return trips, these early colonizers brought with them the familiar foliage of their homes in Tahiti and the Marquesas Islands, including coconut palms, breadfruit trees, bananas, and even a few flowers.

But a thousand years later, when the missionaries landed in Hawaii, there was still much gardening to be done. The New England evangelists found natural beauty in a few settlements like Lahaina, but they judged Honolulu one of the least attractive sites in the Islands, noting it was barren, dusty, and provided neither trees nor grass.

Honolulu in the 1800s was distinguished only in the mind of man by its natural deep-water harbor. In fact, the word "Honolulu" is usually translated as "fair haven" or "protected bay." The commercial desirability of this anchorage, of course, led directly to the beautification of the formerly arid real estate immediately surrounding it. Travelers and immigrants brought in species after species of exotic plants, trees, and flowers, most of them with little regard to their effects on the lives of animals and other plants.

Today many of the plants considered Hawaiian can trace their family trees back to the exact date and place of germination which introduced their seed to the Islands. Some truly "native" species, brought here by winds or birds, have long ago been crowded out by the newcomers.

Three miles from arid Honolulu, Waikiki was often a dirty beach 150 years ago, backed by a humid, stagnant swamp which became a breeding ground for mosquitos (admittedly an insect which was inadvertently imported by man in 1827). That marsh was not drained until the 1920s when the Ala Wai Canal was built.

If the Islands of Hawaii were created by volcanos, they were sculpted into esthetic form by the actions of wind, rain, and sea—and then later by a second period of volcanic activity which further dramatized the landscape. This new round of blasting produced such prominent features as Diamond Head on Oahu and provided such new viewing platforms as the Makanalua (Kalaupapa) Peninsula on Molokai, from which the majesty of that island's north shore can be fully revered.

Despite the many sweeping acres of green pineapple, sugar cane, and even colorful flower fields, most of Hawaii's scenic glory is formed by its mountains. The eroded remnants of the ancient volcanos which were the progenitors of the islands are often twisted into rugged shapes which make them seem much taller and more forbidding than the statistics bear out.

Over the centuries, the *palis* (cliffs) have been carved by wind and falling water into a series of giant buttresses, creating a pattern found nowhere else on the globe. You'll see some of the most dramatic examples of this slow-motion erosion as you travel the windward (northeastern) coast of Oahu and gaze toward the 35-mile-long Koolau range. Following a sudden rain, you can often observe these forces still at work as scores of narrow waterfalls drop for hundreds of feet along the grooved buttes.

You'll find the valleys fascinating, too. In Hawaii, valleys often slope *up* for their entire length in a gentle, narrowing incline between two rough-hewn ridges. Like the famous Nuuanu Valley, they may gain gradual altitude on the leeward side of the mountains until reaching the divide, where they climax in a *pali* that plunges straight down for perhaps a thousand feet.

The mountains, cliffs, and valleys of Hawaii are not only rugged, they are green and rugged, in effect that may seem an incongruous combination to the outlander. There is a mountain called Olomana about a mile from our own front door, for instance. From some angles, it's a dead ringer for Switzerland's famous Matterhorn, except that it has been carpeted from base to tip with foliage. And again, it is much shorter than it seems. At less than 2,000 feet, it does not nearly qualify for the official term "Mount."

In a mountainous state, probably the only *true* mountains are the immense 14,000-foot volcanos of Mauna Kea and Mauna Loa on the Big Island and the 10,000-foot dormant volcano Haleakala on Maui. Despite the tropic latitude, in the winter these three peaks are often cloaked with a hood of snow above the tree line.

If you are familiar with the Pacific Northwest on the Mainland, you may notice one feature lacking in the Hawaiian environment—there are almost no natural lakes in which all the green mountains' majesty might be reflected in shimmering symmetry. Generally speaking, the porous lava base of the Islands simply won't hold much water on the surface for very long, and this also accounts for the rarity of rivers and the infrequency of streams over the islandscape.

Strangely enough, just about the highest lake in the United States is here—little Lake Waiau, 13,000 feet up near the summit of Mauna Kea. Hawaii's only large lakes, an intermittent one of 841 acres and a permanent one of 182 acres, are on forbidden ground on the privately owned island of Niihau.

On Oahu, the only natural body of inland water, Salt Lake, was recently filled in by a land developer after a bitter controversy. A tiny portion of the lake serves as a callous reminder of the lost cause—it has been left as a water trap for a golf course. Today Salt Lake is only the name of another Honolulu suburb. As one might suspect, development on the populous island of Oahu has run to the point where the island's natural beauty is in danger of knuckling under to the bulldozer and the jackhammer.

Some of the beauty of the Islands has been preserved simply because many attractive sites are so hard to get to in the first place. Kauai and Molokai contain several examples of these isolated Edens. But in heavily populated areas, environmentalists and conservationists are proving to be needed and, luckily, influential voices in the community.

Although they failed in the battle of Salt Lake and some others, the good guys have thankfully gathered enough political clout to gain some impressive successes, too. Look, for instance, to the clean, green, and unspoiled hills and peaks that form the backdrop to Honolulu. They testify to the prowess of those who fully understand, like the avant-garde ladies of 1927, that in Hawaii there is not only an extraordinary opportunity but a definite obligation to preserve and defend our scenic heritage.

Weather, Climate, and Other Natural Phenomena

You sometimes hear a lot of fuss over the fact that the Hawaiian language includes no word for "weather." Our own judgment on this is that it indicates either an articulate deficiency in the language or a strong indifference among those who spoke it, and not much about the weather itself.

Despite what you may have heard, weather is sometimes more than a figure of speech in the Islands. And for whatever it's worth, the Hawaiians did have words for "hot," "cold," "rain," "snow," "storm," "wind," and even "fog."

It is often difficult to talk about the weather in Hawaii, not because of any language barrier, but just because weather conditions are different to different people living in different parts of different islands.

From custom alone, Islanders now divide their year into four parts, including "spring" and "fall." Nevertheless, the ancient Hawaiians were right when they identified only two seasons in Hawaii—winter and summer.

Winter, which runs vaguely from mid-October through April, means approximately this:

• Daytime temperatures are in the mid-70s to low 80s.

• Nighttime temperatures run from the 60s to the low 70s. (Honolulu's lowest official temperature ever was 57°.)

• The trade winds—northeasterlies, which generally bring on pleasant weather—are more erratic in winter. These "trades" are vigorous at times, but they sometimes become very weak and die completely. In fact, they can be interrupted for days in this cool season, and it always seems that at least once each winter—usually in the coolest month, February— they will cease for more than two weeks straight. Strangely, the trades usually pick up fairly well for a time in December and early January, which makes this "off-season" period a pleasant bargain for some visitors.

• *Kona* winds—westerlies and southerlies which often bring on widespread cloudiness, rain, mugginess, and even thunderstorms—are more frequent in winter. They usually rush in when the trades or other strong wind patterns die.

• Rains increase in frequency, duration, and intensity in winter, although things still might dry out before the day is through. And you can generally find someplace where it is not raining and where the sun is shining even at this time of year.

● Daylight shortens to about eleven hours in winter—still pretty long by Duluth standards.

On the other hand, the Hawaiian summer, running generally from May through mid-October, brings the following:

● Daytime temperatures are in the 80s. (Honolulu's record high is officially 88, but the temperature one steaming day in 1931 reached 100° at Pahala on the Big Island).

● Nighttime temperatures run from the 70s to the low 80s.

● The trade winds are more persistent and consistent, traveling across thousands of miles of ocean from the arctic to keep summer temperatures tolerable here in the tropic zone. Taken on a year-round basis, the trades blow for about 300 of the 365 days.

● *Kona* winds are more infrequent in the summer. However, when the trades occasionally fail and the *konas* do come in, you really know it. There is nothing worse than a sticky summer *kona* wind. If it comes on a day during August, the Islands' hottest and most crowded month, the thermometer can approach 90°, and the misery factor seems much higher. On an August *kona* day, we search out targets—like the Bishop Museum, perhaps—which are air-conditioned. To hang around downtown Honolulu on such a day, wandering its sweltering sidewalks, is a form of summer madness.

● Rains are more infrequent in the summer, except at high elevations, and they don't last long. Summer showers often last only a matter of minutes, and you will nearly always find some place where it is not raining.

● The days lengthen to about thirteen hours. Due to Hawaii's nearness to the equator, there is little difference in the hours of daylight, winter and summer. Such afternoon outdoor sports enthusiasts as tennis players will also note the lack of, or at least the shortness of, twilight in this latitude.

There is so much daylight in Hawaii that the state has never felt the need to "save" it by fiddling with the clocks, so it always remains on Hawaii Standard Time. That's two hours earlier than the West Coast (Pacific Standard) and five hours earlier than places like New York and Washington, D.C. When most of the rest of the country goes on daylight saving time, roughly from May through October, these figures move up by one hour. (It's three hours later in San Francisco instead of two, etc.)

You may have already gotten the idea that weather is very localized in Hawaii. It's true. Somewhere on any given island the skies are clear while only a mile or two away it is just as likely to be raining at the same hour.

If you're staying in Waikiki, you may think of yourself as lucky, from the precipitation standpoint, anyway. Waikiki is one of the driest areas on Oahu. Still, if it is raining in Waikiki, you might head out Makapuu way (Hanauma Bay, the Blow Hole, Sea Life Park, etc.) where it's even more likely to be dry. *Never cancel a picnic in Hawaii merely because your morning window opens on a "rainy day."* Unlike on much of the Mainland, Hawaiian weather seldom remains in a day-long rut.

Perhaps surprisingly, the driest inhabited area in the state is at the verdant Mauna Kea Beach Hotel on the Big Island. The average rainfall there is less than seven inches a year, which means it's a big job to keep the super-luxurious golf course's thirst thoroughly quenched.

The wettest spot on the entire earth is on Kauai. It rains virtually all the time there at the very top of Mount Waialeale—nearly 500 inches per year. And luckily, there is no golf course up there!

Hawaii's mountains have a lot to do with where it rains and by how much. Moisture-laden winds pushed up the slopes are forced by the laws of physics to dump their load at certain cooling altitudes. When you plan a trip around one of the islands and you see lots of dark clouds on high, you might want to stick to the lower elevations, going *around* the mountains instead of *through* them.

The tropical temperatures we have mentioned so far are operative only near sea level. Remember that the thermometer drops at least three degrees for every thousand feet of elevation. This is why Maui and the Big Island boast much cooler climates on their mountains. It snows at about 10,000 feet during the winter, and anyone planning to go up even as high as 5,000 feet should bring at least a sweater to Hawaii, winter *or* summer.

Hawaii's all-time low, for those who keep track of such things, is an astoundingly frigid 11°F. The same temperature was recorded at two places and at two different times—on January 2, 1961, at the summit of 10,023-foot Haleakala mountain on Maui, and on February 11, 1973, at the top of 13,796-foot Mauna Kea on the Big Island. (No one skis on Haleakala, but there is some serious schussing on the upper slopes of Mauna Kea in winter.)

If you're like most *malihinis,* you'll wonder why we have so much artificial air-conditioning. Stewart L. Udall, the former Secretary of the Interior and now head of an environmental planning firm, called the hotel air conditioners in Waikiki an "absurd" waste of energy.

Much of the air-conditioning in Hawaii is to increase the comfort of island residents, not of visitors. Studies have shown that some of us who live here have lessened our tolerances to the extremes of temperature and humidity, and are extra sensitive to small climatic changes. Personally, we have never felt the need to install air-conditioning in our own home, preferring instead the natural breezes which bring to us the delicious feel and smell of Hawaii.

Some books tell you there is no fog in Hawaii, and that is not strictly correct. Clouds can descend to an altitude of only about 1,000 feet. Island roads go that high and a lot higher, and so Islanders often penetrate that cloud-fog while commuting over the mountains to work.

It's another myth that you will never see smog in Hawaii. You may, but it is fairly rare. First of all, there is the "vog," or volcanic smog which on some isolated occasions is blown as far as Oahu by the *kona* winds when Kilauea volcano is erupting on the Big Island. This "natural" air pollution can temporarily increase the levels of particulate matter and sulfur dioxide in the atmosphere to annoying levels, especially when combined with more pollution from Honolulu traffic. (Thankfully, there is virtually no industrial pollution anywhere.)

In 1978, the U.S. Environmental Protection Agency said Honolulu is the only major city in the nation where the air is clean enough to breathe safely. Other studies have shown that the city has only 41 micrograms of particulate matter per cubic meter of air, although we guess the figure refers to the average for the entire island of Oahu, including urban and rural areas.

Hawaii residents often speak affectionately of "liquid sunshine," the "Manoa mist," or the "Hawaiian blessing." This, of course, is rain, even if euphemized through an indulgent smile. These types of gentle rains, however, are usually so light that their tiny drops are blown around as snowflakes are elsewhere in the world. Since the soft rains usually fall at higher elevations during daylight, they provide grist for the rainbow mills in the upland valleys, like Nuuanu and Manoa, which backdrop Honolulu. Rainbows are endemic to Hawaii, and some of them come in gorgeous double- and triple-decker models.

Violent natural phenomena are rare in the Island State. There have been a few hurricanes in the neighborhood. Two of these did serious damage on Kauai, including Hurricane Iwa in November 1982. Tornados can happen, but they usually become waterspouts and remain out at sea. However, on January 21, 1971, a large waterspout came ashore at Kailua-Kona, destroying several buildings and injuring many persons.

Earthquakes, however, are not unknown in Hawaii and, indeed, they are common on the Big Island in association with the active volcanos there. Most of these volcanic earthquakes, up to several hundred daily, can only be perceived by sensitive scientific instruments.

Conventional earthquakes, caused by faulting, are also felt once in a while, although much less frequently than on the Mainland. We all had a brief start on April 26, 1973, when the entire island chain shuddered, and the second floor of an old two-story building collapsed in Hilo. Two people on the Big Island went to the hospital overnight.

Another earthquake, much stronger, occurred only on the Big Island

November 29, 1975. Measuring 7.2 on the Richter scale, it did millions of dollars of damage to homes and buildings in the southern portion of the island. No one was seriously injured in the quake itself, but in a freak aftereffect two persons were drowned when a portion of a beach they were camping on later sank beneath the water as they slept. (Thirty-four others in their group escaped.) The shake-up was the strongest jolt felt in Hawaii since 1868.

Of greater official concern are tsunamis, or seismic sea waves (and somewhat incorrectly called tidal waves). In the past, earthquakes thousands of miles away in the Aleutian Islands or in South America have generated waves which have inundated Hawaii shoreline areas.

The worst tsunami was generated by an earthquake near Alaska and struck Hawaii on April Fools' Day in 1946. One hundred fifty-nine persons died, 1,300 became homeless, and property damage reached $25 million. Hilo was hardest hit—several commercial buildings along the bayfront were completely destroyed. A similar wave on May 23, 1960, took 61 lives in Hilo.

Today the Islands are better protected with an elaborate warning system, involving sensors over thousands of miles of ocean and a series of sirens which cover the coastal areas of all inhabited islands. You might like to have a look at the Civil Defense Tsunami Inundation Maps and instructions in the green pages in the front of isle telephone books. You'll hear those sirens tested at 11:00 A.M. on the first working day of each month.

Plain old sunshine—dry and not "liquid"—is the biggest natural threat to most visitors or new residents of the Islands. Wear good sunglasses (we recommend the brands with polarizing lenses), cover up between swims, and use suntan or sun-screen lotion to avoid burning, a year-round weather hazard in Hawaii.

Fish, Fowl, Flowers, and Fruit (the Natural Hawaii)

They say that if you toss a broomstick into the soil of Hawaii, it will immediately take root and blossom before you can pull it out again. Of course that is not quite the case. But we do recall once laying aside a branch cut from a plumeria tree and forgetting about it for a few days. Then we discovered new bright leaves on it before we ever got around to sticking it in the ground at all.

Not all parts of Hawaii are so fertile, of course. Some areas are genuine desert or have a surface paved with clay or even with asphalt. On the other hand, many places do live up to the image. As Pete Seeger sings, "God bless the grass that grows through the cracks"; some sites in Hawaii are truly jungle, and it seems if you turn your head away for a moment, new growth might take over to force the works of man to crumble into the underbrush.

Even on the capital island of Oahu, there are wild and rugged green mountains, treacherous to the casual hiker, which may host some exciting species of tree, flower, or bush, and maybe even a bird or two that everyone thought did not exist any more.

It is not generally known, but in the hills behind Honolulu there lives an extended family of wallabies. These kangaroo cousins are all descendants of a male and female pair that escaped from a private zoo in 1916. Heaven knows exactly what they eat as they hop from bush to knoll, but the fact remains that they do consume enough wild vegetation to keep alive and reproduce on the fringes of an expanding urban environment.

Food grown in Hawaii. No one really lives off the land in Hawaii any more because there are too many people to do so. Some folks—rugged individualists such as Euell Gibbons—have done it here by working very hard at the project. Personally, we are just as happy to munch on an occasional guava or passion fruit picked up from along a country road or public park.

Also, people who have mango, orange, grapefruit, banana, avocado, or other fruit trees in their back yards often carry a share of the soil's munificence with them when they visit friends.

Some of the best-known fruits and vegetables of Hawaii include the following:

Pineapple has become an unofficial symbol of the Islands, even though it is native to Latin America. This fruit did not take much to Hawaii until James Dole began planting it near the village of Wahiawa on Oahu in 1901. Dole inundated the Mainland market with Hawaiian pineapple, popularizing it among millions who had never heard of it before.

Although the Hawaii hybrid continues to be probably the tastiest of its species in the world, the pineapple companies are now finding production more profitable in such places as Taiwan and the Philippines where labor and other costs are lower. As an Island industry, pineapple is beginning to fade. You may be surprised to discover, too, that pineapple in Honolulu sometimes sells for more than you would pay for the "air flown" fresh fruit in some cities on the Mainland.

By the way, you can buy spears and chunks of delicious pineapple for immediate consumption at a special pavilion on Kamehameha Highway just north of Wahiawa (see Chapter 5, Section 6—Oahu Sightseeing). Best bargains in pineapple packs to take home, however, are usually in the supermarkets (see Chapter 5, Section 7—Oahu Shopping).

Predating pineapple as the most important Island agricultural product is **sugar.** For years, in fact, "sugar and pine" went hand in hand to form the main economic base of Hawaii. But sugar also has been melting from the scene recently, even though the rich volcanic soil, the ample sunshine, and the fluent water supply have combined to help Hawaii produce more sugar per acre than anywhere else on earth.

Sugar cane takes about two years to mature to its maximum juice content. Then the field is burned with controlled "cane fires" to get rid of the leaves. The sweet stalks which remain are trucked to a mill where huge rollers squash the stems and squeeze out the raw liquid sugar. A small amount is refined in Hawaii, but most is sent to a cooperative refinery in California which is jointly owned by all the Hawaiian sugar companies. The sugar is marketed as the "C&H" brand, which stands for California and Hawaiian.

Kids who grew up in the countryside used to hack off a length of cane to chew on their way to school. But today, many of the *keiki o ka aina* (children of the land) no longer know how to do it.

Hawaii grows delicious **bananas**, but not nearly enough to satisfy the demand in the local markets. Many you will see for sale are the Chiquitas from Costa Rica or somewhere else. The tree-ripened Hawaiian varieties—usually Bluefields or Chinese—can sell for about the same price as the imports, depending on the season.

Of course the best bananas are the ones you receive free. Usually they will be given out by friends who grow more than they can use. Besides the commercial plantations, you will occasionally see fruit on the banana plants growing in the wild. But look before you leap; someone will surely claim the patch is his as soon as the fruit begins turning from green to yellow!

Almost as popular a fruit as the pineapple or the banana is the **papaya**. We often eat it for breakfast, in lieu of a melon, and under a squirt or two of lemon juice. Its bright orange pulp has a delightful mild flavor, and it is low in calories (60 in half a papaya). It contains papain, an enzyme which helps digestion, and it is loaded with vitamins. Papaya is also used in Island recipes as a meat tenderizer.

Like pineapple plants, papaya trees need lots of sunshine, water, and good earth. The trees grow easily and quickly, so many homeowners will plant a row of them in the yard. They come in sexes, and would-be papaya farmers must remember that the males bear no fruit. (This leads to lots of bad jokes from guides about "papayas and mamayas.") You can buy papaya fruit the year around, but prices will vary tremendously depending on the success of the current crop.

Then there are **mangos** which, in a good year, bust out all over in June or July. Often compared with a peach, the oblong fruit with the smooth skins are oranger, juicier, and sweeter. Peel before eating; the skin is bitter and some folks are allergic to it. You'll seldom find mangos in the store; you'll have to pick them yourself, have someone present you with an armload, or buy them from a vendor along the highway. (Caution: Because of the occasional presence of a tiny weevil in the *seed* of a Hawaiian mango, it is forbidden fruit on the Mainland, and its strong smell will lead the agricultural inspector straight to your suitcase even if you try to sneak one or two out of Hawaii.)

Hawaiian **coconuts** may be enjoyed, of course, if you can find a ripe one. Coconuts are often trimmed from the trees while they are still green, merely so they won't fall on anyone's head! Better not try to open a coconut until you have seen how the Samoans do it at the Polynesian Cultural Center near Laie. And diet watchers, please note—coconuts are by far the highest in calorie count of any fruit in Hawaii. One cup of grated coconut adds up to 306, and a half cup of coconut milk is loaded with 346!

Since there are two species of **avocado** grown in Hawaii—the Guatemalan type ripens in winter and spring, and the larger West Indian variety is ready in summer and fall—you'll find it in the best Island salads the year around. (If you're making your own, try it with a local brand of dressing called "Tropics Special.") Also calorie-laden, a quarter of the thick-skinned West Indian avocado can add up to 211. Women who do not want to take avocados internally can make use of an Island beauty secret: mashed avocado makes a wonderful face cream, or so they tell us.

The ubiquitous wild **guava** can be found all year, usually clinging precariously to steep banks along the highways. In fact, guava trees are considered pests in Hawaii, and usually no one will criticize your picking all the thin-skinned, heavily seeded fruit you want, as long as your parked car is not a traffic hazard. About the size and color of lemons, guavas are pressed into nectar and used in a popular canned drink sold on the Mainland, too, called Hawaiian Punch.

Another yellow fruit you might mistake at first for guava is **passion fruit**, more often dubbed *lilikoi* in Hawaii. Overly seedy or too tart for most folks, it is also often squeezed and combined with other flavors—usually orange—for consumption as a fruit drink. For some unknown reason, the women in our family like *lilikoi* in the raw, spooned right out of the skins, crackly seeds and all.

Fast becoming another symbol of Hawaii agriculture is the **macadamia nut** industry. Mostly grown in large orchards on the Big Island, the nuts are expensive but popular. Included in several candy combinations, macadamia nuts are also sold shelled, salted, and canned. If you visit the Big Island, you can stop in at major macadamia nut processing plants at Honokaa and Keaau. Incidentally, in its natural state the macadamia nut is probably the most highly caloric nut in the world—about 25 calories per kernel.

Big Island agriculture also includes **Kona coffee**, which is grown there on the west (Kona) coast. It is the only coffee grown anywhere in the United States. To us, Kona coffee has never quite tasted like *real* coffee although we like its flavor in ice cream and even as a liqueur. By all means try at least one cup. It's a unique experience, and the difficulties of growing and harvesting the coffee may one year combine to close down production forever.

Additional edible plants and fruits of Hawaii include **lychee**, really sweet and yummy; **poha**, also known as Cape gooseberry; **mountain apple**, red and vaguely pear-shaped, an ancient Hawaiian favorite; **soursop**, a hard-to-find prickly fruit; **Surinam cherry**, bright red and it makes an excellent jelly; **Kokee plums**, described in the Kauai chapter; **banana lilikoi**, an elongated passion fruit; **taro**, the nutritious Polynesian vegetable from which **poi** is pounded; **breadfruit**, tasting rather like a sweet potato, but no longer popular in the Hawaiian diet; and **Maui russet potatoes** which make some of the best potato chips in the world.

The Dramatic Flowers of Hawaii. Well over 1,000 different kinds of flowers flourish in Hawaii, nearly all of which were brought to the Islands by man. Some bloom the year around. Some come out only during short seasons. One species blossoms only at night.

Several long books have been written on the flowering plants and trees of Hawaii and other tropical lands of the Pacific. You may pick up either cheap or expensive illustrated glossaries of flowers in Hawaii stores, or consult the books in Island public libraries. Meanwhile, here is a brief alphabetical list of the two dozen blooms everybody talks about most:

African tulip tree. One of two brilliant red flowering trees (the other is poinciana), it blooms the year around.

Allamanda. Large, velvet-like, bright yellow blossoms you might see anywhere. Actually a periwinkle, it's a Brazilian native.

Anthurium. Once you've seen one of these naturally waxy creations, you'll never forget it. The usually red (but sometimes orange, pink, white, or green) heart-shaped collar appears pierced with a long, thin finger.

Bird-of-paradise. In profile, at least, the stalk looks like a bird's long neck leading to a "beak" formed by a pointed sheath. This is crowned with a gold or orange crest formed by about six petals.

Bottlebrush tree. These drooping feathery spikes look like a vermilion version of something Fuller might sell you to scrub out a test tube. (Don't confuse it with *lehua,* below.)

Bougainvillea. Not just the purple vines, but varieties of crimson, orange, pink, and even white are seen in Hawaii. Look closely; actually they are not flowers but little colored leaves.

Gardenias. There are many kinds, including the white Tahitian with single star-shaped or pinwheel-shaped flowers.

Ginger. The heavily scented gingers come in red, yellow, and white varieties, and two or three different shapes. One kind or another always seems to be in season.

Gold tree. One of the most magnificent of the flowering trees, the bright gold or yellow flowers usually bloom only in the spring. It's erratic, however, so you may see one even in mid-winter.

Heliconia. There are several, but the kind we always think of is also called a "lobster claw." It's red, and it looks like several claws stacked up together.

Hibiscus. Hawaii's most "important" flower, since it is the official state blossom. There are singles and doubles, and they come at least in red, yellow, pink, orange, and white. There are no less than 5,000 hybrids, but the simple hibiscus that comes to mind has that little thin stamen growing out of the center. A hibiscus blossom generally lasts just about twelve hours—whether you pick it or not—and then suddenly folds up forever. It is the most popular flower for women to wear in their hair.

Jacaranda. "Oh, what's the blue tree?" you may hear someone exclaim. The bell-shaped lavender flowers appear most often in the spring, but you might catch them at any time of year.

Lehua, or *ohia lehua,* is a tuft of red stamens hanging at the end of a tight knot of greyish-green leaves. The flower can also be pink, yellow, or cream-color, and it is generally found in the cool heights of Kauai or the Big Island.

Night-blooming cereus. Between about June and October, it occasionally opens huge white buds at about 8:00 P.M. and closes soon after sunrise. The original was brought to the Islands from Mexico in the last century and planted on the campus of Punahou School, where it still lives.

Oleander. A tall shrub, this poisonous plant grows clusters of single and double flowers on the tips of the branches. They can come in cream, rose, pink, or red.

Orchids. Almost supplanting the hibiscus as the flower of the Islands, several varieties of orchids are now grown commercially, mainly on the Big Island. There are about 700 species, many of which grow wild. Some orchids make gorgeous *leis,* and they are popular for gifts air-shipped to the Mainland.

Passion flower. The blossom of the aforementioned passion fruit (*lilikoi*), it was named because the yellow and purple flower has oddly shaped stamens and petals which once reminded Spaniards of a style of Christian cross.

Pikake. Actually a fragrant white jasmine, it was the favorite flower of the tragic Princess Kaiulani, who was known as the Princess of the Peacocks. In her honor, the blossom was named *pikake*, the Hawaiian spelling of "peacock."

Plumeria. Perhaps the best known and most popular lei flower, the plumeria, or frangipani, blooms white, yellow, pink, or red at the end of stubby tree branches.

Poinsettia. The "Christmas flower," the red-leafed poinsettia is brilliantly prominent in Hawaii during November and December. There are also yellow and pink varieties.

Protea. In recent years these dramatic and bulbous African and Australian blooms have been grown commercially in up-country Maui.

Royal poinciana. Also known as *flamboyant,* the flower produces fiery red and sometimes brilliant yellow umbrella-like trees in June and July.

Shower trees. Delicate pink, white, coral, and "golden" varieties create feathery blossoms annually beginning in about April and often lasting several months.

Silver sword. A dramatic native silver sunflower which grows and blooms in the dry lava near the top of Haleakala on Maui and Mauna Kea on Hawaii.

Ti plant. Ti, pronounced like "tea," is not really a flower, but one variety can develop very red leaves. It was considered sacred by the early Hawaiians.

Wood rose. In its most well-known form, it appears to be a delicately hand-carved rose. Actually it's the dried seed pod of a type of morning glory. A popular souvenir, wood roses are sold in flower shops. They will last for years.

Other Tropical Trees. Some trees of Hawaii which fall into neither the edible nor the floral groups include these:

The **autograph** tree is known for its thick, ovate leaves on which you can scratch a long-lasting inscription. A forest of tall, straight **bamboo** trees makes a heck of a racket in the wind. The **banyan** tree spreads out and sends down so many new roots, it's sometimes hard to tell which was the original trunk. The **baobab** tree is known in Hawaii as the "dead rat tree" because its fruit appears to be small black animals hanging by their tails.

The fragrant **eucalyptus** (gum tree) has become a new source of timber. The twisted, gnarled **hau** (pronounced "how") tree was originally grown to provide outriggers for ancient canoes. **Ironwoods** look something like tall, fuzzy pine trees and serve as excellent windbreaks along country roads. The **kiawe** tree, also called algaroba or mesquite, with its fernish leaves and twisted trunk, appears everywhere.

Koa trees are Hawaiian natives, and their reddish wood is used for furniture and canoes. The **kukui** or candlenut tree has an oily, burnable fruit which provided light for early Polynesians. The polished nuts now make popular *leis* for women or men. Providing excellent shelter from the rain, Hawaii's **monkeypod** trees also are carved into bowls and trays. (Look carefully on these items for sale to see if they are made in Hawaii or in the Philippines.)

The **Norfolk pine** is a perfectly formed "Christmas tree," imported to Hawaii by New Zealand naturalist George Munro. The **octopus tree** has clusters of glossy leaves spreading out like an umbrella's ribs. The **pandanus**, also called the *hala* tree, features a fruit way up in its long pointed branches that looks something like a pineapple. It also has aerial roots which give it its other name, "the walking tree." *Hala* leaves, or *lauhala*, have been woven into baskets, hats, and even houses. Last, be aware that the fruit hanging from the **sausage tree** is not edible despite its name and appearance.

Animals and Insects of the Islands. A short-term visitor to Hawaii will probably see no more than one wild animal. This would be the popular little **gecko**, a tiny (2 to 4 inches) lizard. The harmless creature may come inside your hotel room to eat flies, mosquitos, and other insects. The Hawaiians considered him good luck, and you can pick him up gently in the palm of your hand. But if he becomes frightened, he may run away and leave you a souvenir—his bodiless, still-wriggling tail!

There are only two mammals completely native to Hawaii. These are the **Hawaiian monk seal** and the **Hawaiian bat**. They are seldom seen by anybody, in fact, because they are the rarest seal and the rarest bat in the world. However, there is one Hawaiian monk seal in captivity. His name is Friday, and you can see him any day but Monday at the Waikiki Aquarium.

Driving along the road, you may catch a fleeting view of an elongated, brown furry thing skittering into the underbrush just ahead of your car. It was no doubt a **mongoose**, originally brought to the Islands in 1883 in an attempt to control the rat population. Nobody thought about the fact that rats like to run around at night whereas mongooses are daylight creatures, so the only time they meet is at the changing of shifts. The mongoose went on to contribute to the decline of the ground-nesting bird population of Hawaii.

Living on all islands except Lanai, Kahoolawe, and Niihau, the mongoose only very recently moved to Kauai. The lack of mongooses is the reason Kauai still has had nesting places for native birds that have long been extinct elsewhere in Hawaii, and this latest development is viewed as a potential ornithological disaster.

Game hunters have special seasons in which they may shoot the following mammals: **wild cattle**, found on the Big Island only; **wild pig**, the descendants of the European boar; **wild goats**, the progeny of Captain Cook's gifts of 1778, which are today real problems in some parts of Maui and the Big Island; **wild sheep**, generations removed from those brought by Captain George Vancouver in 1794; **Mouflon sheep**, which were imported especially for game in the 1950s; **axis deer**, particularly seen on Molokai and Lanai; the **blacktail deer**, released on Kauai in 1961, and the **pronghorn**, a type of antelope brought to Lanai in 1959.

Since **dolphins** (porpoises) and **whales** are mammals, not fish, we should mention them in this section. You might be lucky enough to see a whale en route if you take a boat to Maui, and some dolphins frolic in a special pool at the Kahala Hilton Hotel. Most folks run across both these aquatic mammals, however, at Sea Life Park.

You may notice a couple of lawn animals at one time or another. At night, the **bufo** (pronounced "*boof*-oh"), a type of toad, often likes to hop across the grass on a search for insects. (You might catch a few of these on the Royal Hawaiian Hotel grounds.) Then there is the large **African snail**, a pesky land animal who sometimes grows to a size of five inches. You'll usually see him following a heavy rain.

Are there any dangerous animals in Hawaii? Only one—the **wild dog**. You are unlikely to come across any unless you go in for hiking deep into the woods, and even then they are mainly found only on the Big Island. There are also **wild cats**, somewhat of a misnomer since they originated as escaped house cats. Half the 90,000 cats on Oahu alone are strays. (In the pet category, by the way, cats outnumber dogs in Hawaii by 8 to 5. Nationally it's dogs by 3 to 2.)

Believe it or not, there is one single individual **bear** who may still be romping in the Koolau Mountains on Oahu. He escaped as a baby in 1956, but he was always very shy. If he is still alive, he is considered harmless. **Wild pigs**, of course, can be dangerous if cornered or protecting their young. There is a large benign **earthworm** living in the Islands, but no **snakes**, except two of the same sex penned up at Honolulu Zoo. (Technically there is a 4–6-inch long wriggler called the "blind snake.")

There are thousands of varieties of insects in Hawaii. One of these is a clownish fellow called the **click beetle**. If he falls upside down, he snaps his body with the aid of a little spring hinge, noisily jumping up, over and over again, if necessary, until he lands on his feet.

Our most notorious insects are the voracious **termites**. There are two destructive types; and with no winter to cool their appetite, they devour nearly everything and give business to about 81 pest-control companies. There are also **cockroaches**. They can get to be two inches long, and they **fly**!

Yes, Hawaii has **mosquitoes**, as well as **bees** and other things that sting. Two frightening insects include the **centipede**, which can give a painful bite, and the **scorpion**, also a nasty little stinger. Neither is considered deadly, but persons bitten by these two should call a doctor without delay. Fortunately, there aren't a lot of them around. In our years of living in Hawaii, we have yet to see our first scorpion. And centipedes show up about as frequently as a snake in Peoria.

What about the **cricket**? That "harmless" little fellow so welcome on the hearths or in the yards of temperate zone locales is often considered an unwelcome pest in Hawaii. Reason: He loves nothing more than to eat into the eyes of pineapples.

Our Fragile Bird World. Hawaii has the embarrassing distinction of having been the home of more extinct birds than any other single area in the world. At one time, there were more than 70 species of native birds in the Islands. Today, 22 kinds are extinct and 26 more are on the endangered species list. That's about half the number on the list for the entire United States.

Many of the endemic birds have been crowded out by others imported and released here into the wilderness. Others simply couldn't survive with the changes in the environment made by man over the past 200 years.

On the other hand, sometimes a bird thought to be extinct is discovered alive and well in some remote valley. From time to time, a completely new species is found, too. And there are also programs to wipe out some of the harmful birds, such as the papaya- and banana-eating parrots, which were released here carelessly in recent years.

Of the native birds, the **nene** (pronounced "*nay*-nay"), or Hawaiian goose, is the most significant. This is the official state bird, thought to be descended from a flock of migrating Canada geese blown off course several centuries ago. Its feet have meanwhile evolved from webs into claws, and it lives today high on the mountain slopes and lava flows of Maui and the Big Island. No longer is it so rare as to be "endangered," but you'll be lucky to see one nevertheless.

One of the recently rediscovered birds is the **o'o**, or more specifically, the **o'o a'a** (pronounced "*oh*-oh *ah*-ah"). The ancient Hawaiians thought its cry sounded like "oh-oh." And the word *a'a* means, roughly, "dwarf." So this was apparently one of your smaller *o'os*. The **Hawaiian stilt**, an endangered long-legged water bird, can still be found living in isolated ponds, mainly on Kauai or on the Big Island.

The birds you'll most likely meet in Honolulu and other built-up areas number only three. The first is the common **mynah** bird who arrived from India in 1865, and who marches or struts on land, rather than hops. Don't confuse him with the English-speaking mynah, but the Hawaiian mynahs do love to engage in crowded, noisy conventions and arguments in their own raucous language. Usually these take place just above your head in some large tree or other, especially along about sunset. These birds wear a basic black, but just at take-off time, they flash with white at the end of their wings. Mynahs earn their living and the affection of the human suburban population by feeding on the grass-destroying army worms.

Also, **sparrows** are everywhere, usually noticeable picking up the crumbs in outdoor restaurants. Since there are no big grain crops in Hawaii, sparrows are tolerated and are not considered the pests they are on the Mainland. An 1871 import, the sparrow was dubbed *li'ili'i* by the Hawaiians. It means "the little bird."

The third urban bird is the **barred dove**. It has a rattling coo voice and sometimes seems to be saying "hellovalot, hellovalot." Also called the "small dove," the birds are monogamous. They form couples, roost at each other's side by night, and remain forever faithful.

There are four or five birds you'll see in rural areas or in more protected gardens. The most common is the larger **lace-necked dove** or Chinese dove. It coos more slowly and with a deeper pitch than the barred dove. (Hawaii children are taught that it often calls out, "Come to Scho-o-o-o-l.") Both kinds of doves are fair game for hunters during the season. (See Oahu Sports.)

The **Brazilian cardinal** has a bright red head and is fairly tame and friendly, if you offer it some food. The **North American cardinal** is virtually all red, or at least the daddy of the species is. This one likes to whistle a lot. Then there's the **white eye**, or majiro, a greenish Japanese bird with a conspicuous white ring around the eye. All three of these were imported over less than a two-year period from 1928 to 1929.

One of the most interesting birds is only a winter visitor to Hawaii, the **Pacific golden plover** (that rhymes with "lover"). From May to August, the plovers fly away to mate and raise their young in Alaska and Siberia. On Oahu, you will likely see the plovers between September and April in the Punchbowl area.

Some sea birds which hover over Hawaiian waters include the **tropic birds**, both the white-tailed and red-tailed varieties. They're beautiful flyers, often noticed swooping down into valleys and even volcanic craters, but terrible at take-offs and landings, as are the **Laysan gooney birds**. Both types specialize in crash landings. The gooney (albatross) needs a runway to get airborne again, while the tropic birds beat their wings violently against the ground until they finally heave themselves into the air.

The most dramatic of the sea birds is the **frigate bird**, a genuine pirate. He soars aloft, seeming to hover motionless in the sky until he spies another sea bird carrying a fish. Then he harasses his victim into dropping the fish, whereupon the intruder scoops it up. The Hawaiian name for the frigate bird was *iwa*, meaning "thief."

Besides the aforementioned doves, there are twelve birds imported for hunters to shoot in season (about November to January). These are the ring-necked pheasant, Japanese blue pheasant, California valley quail, Japanese quail, Gambel's quail, chukar partridge, Barbary partridge, mourning dove, black francolin, Erckel's francolin, gray francolin, wild turkey, and bamboo partridge.

You may notice that there are no seagulls in the Islands. Seagulls are scavengers who feed on dead fish and debris which are only present where there is a considerable amount of shallow water. The Hawaiian Islands, being only the tip of massive underwater mountains, have grown up steeply in a very deep blue sea. The few gulls who arrive here every year soon leave to find places where the pickings are better.

Hawaii's Fish Story. An estimated 800 different species of fish, of both the decorative and the delicious varieties, frequent Hawaiian waters. (Selected samples of many of these live in luxury at the Waikiki Aquarium.)

With the rise in popularity of salt-water aquariums in American homes, so many Hawaiian fish are being sought that whole species are in danger of being eliminated. Also, certain fish which would delight aquarists elsewhere are sold as food in Hawaii markets.

Some decorative fishes—also called reef fishes because they live close to shore—are included in the following list. (Scuba divers or snorkle enthusiasts may find these at Hanauma Bay Underwater Park or other special places.)

Butterflyfishes, some 21 kinds all together; **Moorish idols**, or **kihikihi**, an old Hawaiian delicacy; **stripeys**, or convict fish; **angelfishes**, who travel in pairs; **damselfishes**, rather drab in Hawaii; **cardinalfishes**, including one type that really is all red; **aholehole**, which means "sparkling," and known also as the "silver perch"; **surgeonfishes**, or "tangs" (some of which have strange single horns); the **wrasses**, and there are more than 3 dozen colorful kinds; **parrotfishes**, which look like they are equipped with bills; **goatfishes**, probably called that because of their goatees; **squirrelfishes**, who are the only "squirrels" in Hawaii, incidentally; **hawkfishes**, which hunt like hawks; **scorpionfishes**, of which all are poisonous, but luckily very shy; **triggerfishes**, including the famous *humuhumunukunukuapuaa*; **pufferfishes**, who can blow themselves up to three times their normal size; **tubemouthed fishes**, including those long, thin vacuum cleaners called trumpetfish; and **moray eels**, who are thankfully not very aggressive despite their vicious, fang-like teeth.

There are, of course, many game and food fishes in Hawaiian waters, and you may charter boats for deep-sea fishing yourself. (See "Sports" sections in the following island-chapters.) Some of these sport and eating fishes include the following:

Pacific blue marlin is the big boy, the sleek billfish everyone wants to catch. The world record is 1,805 pounds, set by Captain Cornelius Choy right out of Honolulu, but normally they run from about 300 to 400 pounds. The **striped marlin** is also a billfish, but averages about 80 pounds. There's also the **broadbill swordfish**, with a much larger bill, and the **sailfish**, with its large dorsal fin.

A favorite food fish in Hawaii is the **mahimahi**, also known as the dorado or the dolphin (but not to be confused with the mammalian dolphin or porpoise). There is also **aku** (skipjack), **ahi** (yellow fin), and a half dozen other types of tuna, as well as **ulua**, or jack fishes, not large but who are fierce fighters.

There are **mullet**, which the Hawaiians raised in fish ponds, the knife-toothed **barracuda**, which can reach six feet in length, and **flying fish**, seldom eaten today but still appreciated for their antics.

As in all ocean waters of the world, there are various types of sharks, including the **great white shark**, the **tiger shark**, and the weirdly shaped **hammerhead shark**. (The ancient Hawaiians thought sharks were gods in disguise.)

Attacks against man by sharks in Hawaii are, fortunately and quite honestly, very rare. In the past ninety years, there have been only sixteen recorded attacks, and of these only five were fatal. Your chances of being struck by lightning anywhere in the world are greater than those of being attacked by a shark in Hawaii.

There are three interesting ray fish sometimes seen off the Hawaiian Islands. The most intriguing is the spotted and somewhat puppy-faced **eagle ray**. Also, there is the **brown sting ray**, which reaches a maximum length of four feet, and the giant **manta ray**, a docile behemoth who can become as wide as twenty feet from wingtip to wingtip.

Although they are not really fish, we should mention there are **squid** in Hawaiian waters, but when boys talk about "going squidding," they really mean they're heading out to the reef to hunt for **octopuses**. Another mollusk popular for food is the **opihi** (limpets). It is a dangerous occupation to scrape these snail-like delectables off the rocks fronting the ocean. The papers are always carrying stories about a sudden high wave which sweeps an opihi-picker into the sea to drown.

Also, there are **oysters** somehow still living in Pearl Harbor, and bearing a few pearls. The water is polluted, however, which means that neither the oyster nor its pearls has any value.

Among Hawaii's more annoying denizens are different species of jellyfish. One, the **Portuguese man-of-war**, looks something like a miniature ship under full sail. The purplish-blue animal floats into shallow, shoreline waters with the tide, usually driven by strong winds. (It even happens in Waikiki when strong kona (southwest) breezes come up in December or January.) If you encounter it in the water or even after it has washed up on the beach, beware: its long, dangling tentacles can cause bitter, stinging welts.

Perhaps not quite so painful is the **pololia** jellyfish, which looks like Saran Wrap floating in the water. Stings from either are easily treated with meat tenderizer (Adolph's is carried by some local beachgoers). Lifeguards are equipped with similar substances. Well-known and usually effective folk remedies include the juice of the green papaya, or urine— although the latter may not be practical on a crowded beach.

And fresh-water fish? There are a few simple shrimp and crayfish, of course. Also you will find **trout** in streams at the Kokee Public Fishing Area on Kauai, as well as **catfish** and **bass** in the Wahiawa and Nuuanu Reservoirs on Oahu. These may be caught with license and permit in season.

4

Islanders—Kamaainas and Malihinis

Hawaiian History in Brief

The dramatic and often violent history of man in Hawaii has been eloquently told in volume after volume. Among the most thrilling is the semi-fictionalized version in *Hawaii*, by James Michener. An enjoyable account which names the real names is the work by Gavan Daws, *Shoal of Time*. And the definitive and scholarly social history is *Hawaii Pono*, by Lawrence Fuchs. A brief summary obviously can be no substitute for books of that caliber.

Much of Hawaii's thunderous and romantic past will become apparent in gentle doses in the island-chapters which follow, mostly in the "Sightseeing" sections. For a ready reference, however, we have included a few basics in the life story of Hawaii and its people.

Pre-Haole Hawaii—A.D. 800 or so to 1778. Almost everyone now agrees that the Hawaiian Islands were first colonized by Marquesan Polynesians around the year 800, give or take a century or two. They were joined by islanders from Tahiti and vicinity in about 1300.

These seafarers made the journey over thousands of miles in great, double-hulled canoes. The first expedition was led, according to legend, by an intrepid navigator named Hawaii Loa, who then lent his name to the Big Island. Following this initial discovery, vessels traveled back and forth for a time, bringing more family members, dogs, pigs, trees, vegetables, and flowers.

Gradually, over scores of generations, ties to the ancestral islands became less important, and eventually even the talent for making the mammoth canoes completely died out.

For a thousand years, the Hawaiians lived alone, their islands composing the entire world as far as they were concerned. The verbal tales of ancient and faraway lands became indistinguishable from the religious and supernatural fairy stories that attempted to explain their environment.

There is some strong evidence that the Spanish navigator Juan Gaetano called briefly at Hawaii in 1555, and that other ships could have followed him. But the Iberians kept their Pacific secrets well, and no proof of what they may have found has survived—only a few old maps which correctly chart the general position of the Islands.

Captain Cook and the Sailor Saga—1778 to 1820. On January 20, 1778, Captain James Cook of the British Royal Navy stepped ashore on Kauai, becoming the first European known to have reached the archipelago. The Hawaiians received him as a white god, old stuff for Cook after his discoveries in the Society Islands. He paid his respects over a fortnight, reprovisioned his two ships, and then headed for the arctic in an unsuccessful attempt to find a northern passage to the Atlantic Ocean.

Cook returned to the Islands in November, this time visiting Kealakekua Bay on the Big Island, which was one of four separate kingdoms. During this second visit, some misunderstandings culminated in what might have been only a minor skirmish between Cook's men and the Hawaiians. But something went awry, and the great explorer was struck and killed on February 14, 1779. His body was later dismembered and only part of it was finally returned to his ship.

One who had been taking in all the excitement during Cook's second visit was the king's alert nephew, Kamehameha. Perhaps then and there he became impressed by the political potential of gunpowder. When his uncle died a few years later, Kamehameha set out to rule the Big Island. A decisive battle in 1791, in which he used some European cannon, won him his goal.

British Naval Captain George Vancouver struck up a friendship with Kamehameha in visits to Hawaii over the next three years, and the Hawaiian chief then revealed his plans to create one single kingdom from the entire Island chain. Kamehameha went on to award some *haoles* (whites) favored places in his inner circle, and with the use of their technical know-how, he began conquering the islands one by one, in a series of ruthless battles.

By 1795, Kamehameha ruled all the major islands except distant Kauai and Niihau. One invasion fleet was turned back by a storm, so he never succeeded in fighting for those northwestern islands. In 1810, however, he tricked their king into ceding the land to him anyway.

During this time, more and more foreign ships called in Hawaii, bearing such gifts and concepts as syphilis and avarice. Kamehameha and the other blue-blooded *alii* (chiefs) developed a taste for foreign finery, but all the chief had to offer for the froufrou of the fur traders and whalers were willing girls and fresh groceries. Eventually, however, Kamehameha decided to set up some more lucrative commerce.

About 1801, the king began to sacrifice his people's entire way of life to the sandalwood trade. Shippers paid him handsomely for the stuff which the Chinese bought to burn as incense in their temples. For this, Kamehameha began breaking the backs of his subjects as they cut trees deeper and deeper in the forests and higher and higher in the mountains. These formerly hard-working people were beginning to ignore their taro patches and their festivals—even neglecting their ancient gods.

Kamehameha made a few liberal concessions, but by and large he is remembered for bloodying streams and beaches in his military victories and destroying souls wholesale in his industrial conquests. Why this Hawaiian Napoleon is so honored today remains a mystery to us.

The old monarch died in 1819, aged at least in his sixties. His body was hidden in a secret place near Kailua-Kona so that others could not obtain magical power from his bones. During his twenty-four year reign, the population of his people had plunged from an estimated 300,000 to about 135,000. Following his death, his weak eldest son, Liholiho, was named Kamehameha II.

Soon afterwards, under the influence of the dynamic Kaahumanu, his father's favorite wife, Liholiho completely abolished the ancient *kapu* (taboo) system, thereby destroying the generally oppressive gods, but at the same time throwing the population practically into religious oblivion. The immediate result as far as liberationist Kaahumanu was concerned was to allow her and other women several privileges which had been previously reserved for men.

But more changes were to come. Into this topsy-turvy atmosphere sailed, on March 30, 1820, the first company of American Calvinist missionaries.

Missionary Hawaii—1820 to 1854. At first there were only seventeen missionaries, led by two ordained ministers, and bearing instructions from their Massachusetts headquarters to convert the heathen of "Owhyee" and to cover the land with fields, houses, schools, and churches.

The women in the party also took it on themselves immediately to cover the ample naked flesh of the female Hawaiians. The pullover garment they whipped up was the ancestor of today's popular *muumuu*.

After receiving the king's permission to stay, members of the company split into three teams, some remaining at Kona, others going on to Honolulu, and still more setting up a mission on Kauai. Later, another church was started at Lahaina, Maui.

The strong-willed Kaahumanu was fascinated with the new religion and the customs of the *haole* women, and through her, the missionaries won greater favor with the king. Of course many of the king's advisors—including resident foreigners—were opposed to the missionary operations.

During this period, Liholiho franchised the sale of sandalwood to his subordinate chiefs, and they, in turn, drove the people to even greater lengths to cut down and ship out this natural resource. Further epidemics of foreign diseases took their toll, and at the same time, more missionaries arrived. Led by Kaahumanu and the king's mother, members of the Hawaiian royal family began to be converted to the faith, and the missionaries standardized a written form of the Hawaiian language.

In 1823, Liholiho and his queen decided to take in London. After a glorious, fun-filled visit to that city, the royal pair died there, in their hotel room, infected by measles. (Hawaiians of the period had no immunity to the disease.) The ruler's teenage brother then became king and was named Kamehameha III.

Kamehameha III was destined for a twenty-nine year reign, always more or less under the influence of the missionaries. Although irresponsible in his younger years, he matured to become almost a storybook wise king in later life. Senior missionary Hiram Bingham, builder of Kawaiahao Church, led the king along the path of righteousness until that minister left the Islands in 1840.

One of the later missionaries, Gerrit P. Judd, eventually left the calling to become the king's secular right-hand man. It fell to these leaders to transfer the semi-feudal society into a constitutional monarchy. Under their management, so many schools were established that Hawaii became one of the most literate nations in the world. Meanwhile, on the commercial front, whaling replaced the sandalwood trade as the Islands' principal means of support.

Civil liberties were born in 1839, when the king proclaimed the Declaration of Rights and Laws. This was followed the next year by a written constitution which set up a two-house legislature. For the first time, representative elections were held in Hawaii.

Conflicts there were aplenty, however, often between the maritime interests and the holy word as interpreted by the missionaries. Sailors, who declared there was "no God west of the Horn," competed with the straitlaced concepts of Jesus for the affections of the loose and mellow Hawaiians, especially the young women of the country. The missionaries continued to stamp out fornication and the hula to the tune of an occasional riot fomented from the vicinity of the waterfront.

There were also troubles with foreign policy. France, a Catholic country interested in exporting her wines and brandies, had plenty to grumble about with the strong Protestant and teetotal abstinence influence in the Islands, and she threatened to annex the tiny nation several times. But the British actually did it—sort of.

It happened in 1843 when the commander of an English frigate forced the king to submit to British rule, alleging that the property rights of Britons in Hawaii were being violated. The Union Jack flew over the Islands for only six months, however, before British Admiral Richard Thomas arrived to repudiate and apologize for the annexation. The festivities ending the occupation took place at what is now Thomas Square, named by a grateful population for the officer who renewed the Islands' independence.

Following that episode, Kamehameha III moved himself and the capital from Lahaina to Honolulu. The whaling trade reached its peak, with hundreds of ships often parked at Lahaina and Honolulu, and then began a fairly steady decline. Several Honolulu commercial establishments still in operation first opened their doors around the middle of the nineteenth century, a number of them begun by former missionaries or sons of missionaries. And agriculture, beginning with cattle ranching, began to assume a new importance in the island nation.

In 1846, the king set up the Great Mahele, which divided all real estate among the king and his chiefs, and even left a few thousand acres to the common people. Many Hawaiians did not understand what they needed to do, but most *haoles* living in the Islands lost no time in registering their claims. A move to support annexation of Hawaii by the United States failed in 1854.

Despite vigorous opposition, Catholics and Mormons had now established missions in the Islands. When Kamehameha III died in December of 1854, with him went more than three decades of American Protestant missionary influence in Hawaiian politics.

The Last Days of the Monarchy—1854 to 1894. The king's nephew, Alexander Liholiho, was named the new ruler, and he assumed the title Kamehameha IV at the age of 21. Two years later he was married to Emma Rooke in a spectacular ceremony at Kawaiahao Church, and together they founded the Queen's Hospital as an institution dedicated to preventing foreign diseases among the Hawaiians.

One disease arrived in 1860, the same year the hospital cornerstone was laid, which could not then be treated. This was leprosy, called the *Mai Pake* (Chinese malady). The board of health chose the spectacular but isolated Makanalua Peninsula (Kalaupapa) on the island of Molokai as a special refuge for its victims. The story of leprosy in Hawaii is long and sad, full of neglect and tragedy, and yet mitigated by cases of high heroism, as that of Father Damien de Veuster, the Belgian priest who worked with the lepers on Molokai until he died himself after contracting the disease.

Two personal tragedies jolted the reign of Kamehameha IV. First, he shot to death one of his own staff in a misunderstanding. Then his four-year-old son and last direct heir to the throne caught a fever and died shortly after the king had held him under running water in an attempt to cool off a childish tantrum. In a spirit of religious fervor, the king embraced the Church of England (Episcopalian) and founded St. Andrew's Cathedral in 1862.

Kamehameha IV died the following year, however, never regaining his interest in public life following the death of his son. The king was 29.

His older brother, Lot, was named Kamehameha V. By this time, the population of Hawaii had declined to less than 70,000, and a very real problem was the lack of available labor to work the burgeoning sugar plantations. (Whaling had died completely as an Island industry as soon as oil was discovered in the U.S. in 1859.)

This fifth and final Kamehameha was instrumental in setting up a Bureau of Immigration to encourage the importation of contract labor. Thus began Hawaii's multiracial character as Chinese, Japanese, Portuguese, and some Europeans began to arrive committed to work under the tropic sun.

At the end of 1872, Kamehameha V died without leaving an heir or naming a successor to the throne. William C. Lunalilo, descended from the half-brother of Kamehameha the Great, was then elected king by the legislature. King Lunalilo didn't accomplish a great deal; he died himself just over a year later.

A new legislative election brought David Kalakaua to the throne after a bitter contest between him and Queen Emma, the widow of Kamehameha IV. King Kalakaua ruled from 1874 to 1891. Now known rather inelegantly as the Merry Monarch, the king was not only into arts, music, and sciences, he was also as peripatetic a ruler as could be imagined, becoming the first king of any country to visit the United States, or even to make a trip around the world for that matter.

Kalakaua's Washington tour and visit with President Ulysses S. Grant resulted in the Reciprocity Treaty which removed the tariff barrier, a tremendous shot in the arm for the sugar industry. The king also granted Pearl Harbor to the Americans for use as a naval base. Kalakaua built the present Iolani Palace, completed in 1882, and then starred in an elaborate coronation ceremony on the palace grounds a year later.

In the 1870s and 1880s, more immigrants arrived from Japan and from Portuguese islands like Madeira and the Azores to work in the sugar fields. Industrialists, foreigners, and persons under foreign influence eventually forced Kalakaua to give up much of his political power, despite a brief revolt by royalists.

King Kalakaua was a tinkerer, or perhaps a minor inventor. He was also the first in Hawaii to acquire any new gadget of the era, such as the telephone and the electric light. He became a friend of Robert Louis Stevenson, who was also interested in Hawaiian history. The king began to bring back and document the nearly forgotten culture of the ancient Hawaiians, including the formerly outlawed *hula*. Kalakaua, himself, wrote the words to the national anthem of the kingdom, "Hawaii Pono'i," which is still sung today as the official state song.

But political strains took their toll on the king. Kalakaua left for San Francisco for his health late in 1890. There he died January 20, 1891.

Queen Liliuokalani, Kalakaua's sister and the last monarch of Hawaii, came to the throne during an economic depression in which the sugar planters were again having trouble getting into the American market. Business interests once more put on the pressure for annexation to the United States.

When the queen attempted in 1893 to declare a new constitution strengthening the monarchy, it was either too much for an American group called the Annexation Club, or—more likely—the excuse they had been waiting for. They formed a "Committee of Public Safety" which asked the United States minister (ambassador) to land troops from a warship in the harbor.

Only one shot was fired—and that one was almost an accident—and a policeman was wounded. Queen Liliuokalani left her throne quietly to avoid bloodshed, and a provisional government was set up. The revolutionists offered the islands to the United States, but after a thorough investigation, President Grover Cleveland haughtily turned down the deal. In a message to Congress, Cleveland said, "It appears that Hawaii was taken possession of by the United States forces without the consent or wish of the Government of the Islands."

The Brief Life of the Republic—1894 to 1898. Hawaii was a republic in little more than name only. Martial law was declared, loyalty oaths were required, and only men of property could vote. The Royal Hawaiian Band, among others, resigned as a body rather than swear allegiance to the revolutionaries and show disloyalty to their queen.

Nevertheless, the United States government never succeeded in restoring Liliuokalani to her throne. The new Hawaii government set about making itself into a semi-permanent arrangement which would last until the climate changed completely in Washington. Sanford B. Dole, a lawyer, sugar planter, and a relative moderate among the members of the new order, was appointed president.

Shots were fired and one man died during a two-week counterrevolution in 1894. The queen did not take active part, but she was arrested anyway and coerced into signing a document renouncing her claim to the crown and swearing allegiance to the Republic of Hawaii. Later found guilty of treason, she was sentenced to five years' hard labor. Instead, she was held prisoner in a second floor corner of Iolani Palace for a total of nine months. During her imprisonment, the queen wrote and composed music, including the Hawaiian words for the famous song "Aloha Oe." (She borrowed the melody line from an old hymn.) After her release, she moved two blocks away to her home at Washington Place. Though she occasionally traveled in a futile appeal for her cause, Liliuokalani continued to live in the mansion until she died in 1916 as a reluctant American citizen.

The election of McKinley's Republican administration certainly helped, but it was the Spanish-American War which put Hawaii's annexation cause over the top. The strategic importance of a Pacific territory was dramatized to all by Admiral Dewey's victory in the Philippines.

A formal transfer of sovereignty took place at the palace August 12, 1898. In the crowd were Americans, Portuguese, Chinese, Japanese, and Filipinos. But according to some accounts, there was not a single native Hawaiian who approached the festivities closely enough to see the American flag raised.

You Had to Know the Territory—1898 to 1959. Business boomed immediately in American Hawaii. Political details took a couple of years to firm up, but by mid-1900, the Islands were handed an official governmental status. President McKinley then appointed former Hawaii president Sanford Dole as the new governor of the incorporated territory.

Meanwhile, out in the fields of central Oahu, James D. Dole, a distant cousin of the governor, was beginning to raise the first commercial pineapples. Contract agricultural laborers from the Far East continued to pour in and spread out all over the Islands.

The native Hawaiians, becoming spiritual aliens in their own land, found some solace in the election of Prince Jonah Kuhio Kalanianaole as Hawaii's non-voting delegate to Congress. Had the monarchy survived, Prince Kuhio would have been in line for the throne. Instead, he served in Washington from 1903 to 1921, and his crowning achievement was the passage of the Hawaiian Homes Commission Act. That law allows Hawaiians who qualify to lease home lots on former government lands for as little as $1 per year, and to use other, larger areas of property for agricultural production.

Upon annexation, considerable lands which had belonged to the crown or the Hawaiian government were set aside for military use, and Hawaii's growth as an armed camp increased, spurred even further by the activity during World War I. Cables, telephones, and airplanes began to link Hawaii more closely to the continental U.S., and tourism gradually became an important industry in the territory. The Moana Hotel was built in 1901, and the new Royal Hawaiian Hotel was completed in 1927. Both have endured to this day.

Virtually all business activities then were held in the grip of an unofficial and paternal corporate club called the "Big Five." Most of these were begun by *haole kamaaina* (Caucasian long-time resident) families who traced their lineage back to the missionaries. These companies, who still command considerable respect today, are C. Brewer & Co., Theo. H. Davies & Co., Amfac (American Factors), Castle & Cooke, and Alexander & Baldwin. Their directors ruled with an iron fist over land ownership and labor activities in the first half of the twentieth century. They could—and did—decide just who would and who would not participate in business in Hawaii.

Hawaii received its worst national publicity in 1931 and 1932 during the "Massie Case," an incident which created high tension between local people and the military establishment. The wife of navy lieutenant Massie said she was raped by some local youths in the swamp now occupied by the Ala Moana Shopping Center. The evidence was meager against those arrested and they were found not guilty. Most civilians, at least, thought they truly were innocent.

But Massie and his wife's mother later kidnapped and murdered one of the accused. In a charged racial atmosphere, the Navy and faraway U.S. congressmen sought to have Massie released without trial. Nevertheless, he was found guilty of manslaughter. His ten-year prison sentence, however, was reduced by the U.S.-appointed governor to one single hour. The conduct of the case, therefore, left no one satisfied and everyone angry.

The Massie case led to Washington efforts to put Hawaii under a more severe form of government. Although this never came to pass, that threat of tough federal domination led others to begin pushing for the political safety offered by statehood.

Sugar, pineapple, and tourism virtually collapsed during the Great Depression, but they were given a psychological boost toward health again by the two-day visit of President Franklin D. Roosevelt in 1934.

The Islands were never the same after December 7, 1941. Although tensions had been building up between the United States and Japan, the actual attack on the Pearl Harbor naval base came as a genuine shock. Thousands of servicemen and scores of civilians were killed in the raid.

Martial law was declared, and many "suspicious" persons, almost all of Japanese ancestry, were rounded up and jailed.

During the war, barbed wire replaced bathing suits on Waikiki Beach. The Islands became the supply and training headquarters for the entire Pacific war effort, and the population jumped by more than 400,000 active duty military personnel. Among them was James Jones, author of *From Here to Eternity,* one of the novels depicting Hawaii during the war.

Americans of Japanese ancestry who attempted to volunteer for the service were, at first, rejected. Later in the war, they were accepted in a body and were formed into two units. The 442nd Regimental Combat Team and the 100th Battalion fought heroically in Italy and France. They sustained the most casualties and became the most decorated American units in World War II.

Following the war, long overdue unionization burst upon the Island scene, seeking to right inequities in the outmoded labor policies of the large corporations. Strikes in sugar and pineapple were bad enough, but when a crippling six-month dock strike took place in 1949, it was almost too much for the water-bound territory to bear.

The rise of McCarthyism led many to equate the union activity with Communist influence. The charges were particularly applied to the International Longshoremen's and Warehousemen's Union (ILWU) and its leaders, after they organized sugar, pineapple, and dock workers, thus controlling the employees of the three most powerful industries in the territory.

The Korean War took a heavy toll on Hawaii, since the Islands contributed more men and more military casualties per capita to that action than any other state in the Union. During that war, too, a new military build-up began in Hawaii, one which has not diminished to this day. In terms of payroll, government employment now rivaled sugar, pineapple, shipping, and even tourism as the Islands' biggest "industry."

By the early 1950s, labor was entrenched and beginning to influence Island political activity. The Big Five no longer held full control over the economy. Many of the *nisei* who had fought in World War II now had used their G.I. Bills to obtain new professional status. The then largest single ethnic group in Hawaii, these Japanese-Americans became the movers and shakers. Led by 442nd veteran and future senator Daniel K. Inouye, they joined with labor elements, represented by John A. Burns (the future governor) to force a 1954 Democratic sweep of the territorial legislature. Thus, they broke Republican political domination in the Islands for the first time.

Two years later, Burns was elected delegate to Congress where he began a long, hard campaign to win statehood for Hawaii. But not everyone wanted statehood. Many prognosticators of doom pointed out the

"Red" influence in the labor unions and spoke direly of Japanese elements in the population "taking over." Native Hawaiians, who probably still favored a return of the monarchy, had nostalgic reasons for opposing statehood. (Tour bus drivers were known to include their opposition to becoming a state in their patter.) Some members of the U.S. Congress also vigorously opposed statehood for various reasons, including racism and the fact of Hawaii's great physical separation from the Mainland.

Delegate Burns worked with the Alaska delegation to help pass its statehood bill in 1958. After that, Hawaii virtually rode in on the same wave. The measure passed overwhelmingly in March, 1959, and President Eisenhower quickly signed it.

The Aloha State—1959 to now. The first state elections ended in a Republican-Democratic split. Republican William F. Quinn, the last appointed governor, became the first elected governor, winning in a close ballot over John Burns. (Burns captured the office from Quinn three years later.) Republican Hiram Fong won one of the U.S. Senate seats, becoming the first Oriental to join that body. (He has since retired.)

Democrat Oren E. Long, another former governor, was voted in as the other senator. The single House post at that time went to Daniel K. Inouye, the first Japanese-American congressman. Republicans took the wheel of the new state Senate, and the Democrats won a majority in the state House of Representatives.

Statehood and the Boeing 707 landed in Hawaii in the same year. With all the national hoopla over the fiftieth state, and a reduction of the former 9 prop hours to 4½ jet hours' time from the West Coast, tourists began funneling into Hawaii on an increasing wave.

Sadly, Hawaii again suffered disproportionate losses in the Vietnam War. In one disturbing incident, President Johnson activated a Hawaii National Guard and Reservist unit as part of a national emergency power play because of the 1968 "Pueblo Crisis" with North Korea. Then the men were callously kept on active duty and sent to fight in Vietnam instead.

Unlike the Korean War, however, Vietnam did not hurt the tourist business. In fact, it actually increased. Thousands of servicemen were flown to Hawaii for their "R & R" time, often to see their families who traveled from the Mainland to Hawaii to meet them.

In the 1970s, Democratic-Republican rivalries became less important than the opposing factions within Hawaii's Democratic party. Former congressional delegate John Burns was elected governor in 1962, reelected twice, and served through 1974.

Development-oriented, Burns was credited with improving the University of Hawaii and helping increase tourism into a greater industry, as well as with some progressive social legislation in public education, welfare, and labor areas. His critics complained that his growth policies worked to the detriment of pollution standards, traffic problems, the housing shortage, and overcrowding of all types.

Before he died, Burns endorsed his even-tempered lieutenant governor, George R. Ariyoshi. In 1974 and 1978, Ariyoshi won the gubernatorial nomination over Honolulu's feisty and colorful mayor, Frank F. Fasi. (The Republican candidates gave only token opposition.) Fasi then lost his own mayoral post in 1980 to Eileen Anderson, a political newcomer who ran on a strong anticrime platform. Ariyoshi again handily won a third term in 1982. His lieutenant governor is John Waihee, the first native Hawaiian in many years to achieve such a high office.

In the mid-1980s, Hawaii finds itself economically dependent principally on tourism, leaving military spending—as well as traditional Island industries like sugar and pineapple—far behind. Tourists now drop a total of about $4 *billion* into the state's economy each year.

This worries many state residents, including Hawaiians (Polynesians) who see the traditional culture of the Islands being subjugated to crass outside influences. Others defend tourism by saying that visitor spending continues to support cultural activities like Hawaiian music and the húla, besides funding the continued preservation of historical sites and similar facilities.

A Rainbow of Peoples

In the volumes on Hawaii produced as school texts or as part of educational libraries over the past twenty years, there is usually a chapter entitled something like "Americans All!" The opening page would display a happy group photograph of smiling, slant-eyed, flat-nosed, olive-skinned, dark-haired, high-cheeked kids, perhaps even with a token towhead in there somewhere. All together, they are as cute a bundle of oriental, Polynesian, and what-have-you kind of joy as you would ever want to see.

It's all true, or at least it is at that tender age. Island youngsters all learn the pledge to the flag together, and they often don't become very conscious of their different ethnic backgrounds until they near their teens. Then it's sometimes a different story.

Meanwhile, the textbook goes on to explain that, yes, these children all speak English, of course, just like boys and girls on the Mainland. But the truth is something more than that; even if they do speak English, most of them would rather speak "pidgin."

The Language is a Queer Bird. Pidgin is a conglomerate of crude English liberally spiced with several Hawaiian words plus a few from other languages. Pure Hawaiian is seldom spoken in Hawaii today, even though it *is* often sung. A few isolated communities on the Neighbor Islands do use a form of the real tongue in day-to-day life, and an older version is still spoken on the tiny island of Niihau, a privately owned strip of water-locked real estate where visitors are forbidden.

Although Hawaiian is a nearly dead language, you still need to know something about it to pick up pidgin and other flavorful aspects of island living. The full-on Hawaiian language includes more than 25,000 words. There is a lot of vowel and throat action, and the speech is considered musical and poetic, though certainly not precise. There are supposed to be 33 synonyms for "clouds," for instance; on the other hand, it takes 8 words to express the idea "across."

The missionaries standardized an easy-to-learn spelling for Hawaiian by using only 12 letters. There are the 5 vowels, "A, E, I, O, U," given the European pronunciation ("ah, ay, ee, oh, oo"), plus only 7 consonants, "H, K, L, M, N, P, and W." To do that, the missionaries cut corners, declaring that all "T" sounds and "K" sounds henceforth would be pronounced like "K," all "R" and "L" sounds would be "L," "B" and "P" sounds would be "P," and so forth.

Thus we have the reason the Polynesian word *taboo* (forbidden or sacred) is interpreted in Hawaiian as *kapu* ("kah-*poo*"). On at least one occasion, the missionaries were known to have corrected King Kamehameha II when he said his name was "Rihoriho" instead of Liholiho.

Now, in a way, there is also one additional consonant in Hawaiian. This is the "glottal stop" between two vowels, represented in print by the use of the *hamzah*. This Arabic symbol is correctly made like a backwards apostrophe or an opening inside quotation mark, as in the word ʻau ʻau ("ow-ow"—to take a bath). You pronounce the glottal stop by doing to your throat what the expression "oh-oh" does—a momentary stoppage of air in the back of the throat between two vowel sounds.

Some folks use a regular apostrophe for the *hamzah*; that makes things easy, though not correct (except on a typewriter). More often, the mark is left out all together and the letter joined together. It can be safely omitted where two of the same vowels are used together (*akaaka*—"ah-kah-ah-kah"—laughter), in other words, where it's obvious the word could not be pronounced correctly without the glottal stop. (Of course, the word Hawaii—Ha-*why*-ee—which may be written Hawaiʻi is another example.)

In this volume, we follow the modern trend, and generally omit the *hamzah* except where there would be some definite confusion without indicating the glottal stop.

An example is *pau*—"pow"—finished, versus *paʻu*—"pah-oo"—a

long skirt, usually worn riding sidesaddle. Used in a pidgin sentence, a
seamstress getting her costume ready for the Kamehameha Day Parade
conceivably could say, "At last my *pa'u* is *pau!*"

As we said, you will almost never hear pure Hawaiian in Hawaii, but
you will certainly hear some degrees of pidgin. The more non-English
words used, together with the more unique pronunciation, lilt, and sentence structure, the heavier pidgin is being spoken.

Linguists say the speech of Hawaii is not a true pidgin, but a softer
form of communication which strictly should be called a creole. Nevertheless, everyone *does* call it pidgin, and in its spoken form, some un-
prepared Mainlanders have trouble knowing just what is being said.

Every visitor to Hawaii picks up some Hawaiian or pidgin words, and
you'll get a head start, because the text of this guide makes use of the
most common of these, just as if we were writing for a local readership.

Here is a list of several words, including some which are more often
written than spoken, and help with the translation of place names. The
most commonly spoken words in the following list are indicated with an
asterisk. You will enjoy your visit more if you do learn the meaning and
pronunciation of them.

aa	a rough type of lava
*akamai	* smart, wise
akua	god
ala	road, way, route (written; seldom spoken)
alii	chief, nobility
*aloha	* hello, goodbye, love, good will
auwe!	alas, ouch, wow!
blalah	heavy-set, amiable Hawaiian man
brah	friend (corruption of "brother")
bumby	after while ("by and by" in pidgin)
*da kine	* whatchamacallit (adjective or noun)
*ewa	* generally west (toward Ewa Plantation)
hala	pandanus tree
hana	work
hanah-buttah	nasal mucus
hanakokolele!	shame, naughty (child's word, chanted to the tune of "Johnny's got a girl friend!")
hanau	born (not spoken—seen on gravestones)
hale	house
*haole	* Caucasian, white, Mainlander
hapa	half, part
hapa-haole	part white and part Hawaiian
hapai	pregnant
heiau	ancient Hawaiian temple
hele on	"with it," "hip," or "hell raising"

holo-holo	to visit about, make the rounds
holoku	a fitted ankle-length dress, sometimes with train
hoomalimali	nonsense talk, flattery
huhu	angry
*hula	*Polynesian dance
huli-huli	barbecued chicken
humbug	trouble, bother
humuhumunukunukuapuaa	tiny trigger fish famous for its long name
imu	underground oven
imua!	forward, onward, *viva*!
kahili	a feathered scepter
kahuna	priest, medicine man
kai	sea, sea water (seldom spoken, except in Hawaiian)
kala	money
*kamaaina	*long-time Hawaii resident, old established family
kanaka	originally "man," but now a familiar, sometimes derogatory term for a native Hawaiian. Hawaiians use it. The rest of us had better not.
kane	men (as written on restroom doors)
kapa	tapa cloth (made from mulberry bark)
kapakahi	topsy-turvy, crooked
*kapu	*forbidden, sacred, taboo
kaukau	food
keiki	child
kokua	help
kuleana	homesite, now used like "bailiwick"
*lanai	*porch, terrace, veranda
lani	heaven, heavenly, sky (not often spoken)
lauhala	leaf of the pandanus tree (for weaving)
laulau	bundled food in leaves
*lei	*garland of flowers
lilikoi	passion fruit
lomilomi	rub, press, massage, type of raw salmon
lua	toilet (originally "two" or "twin")
*luau	*feast, party (originally a taro leaf)
luna	above, overseer, straw boss, heights
*mahalo	*thank you
mahimahi	dorado or dolphin fish (*not* a porpoise)
mahu	homosexual
*makai	*toward the sea (a direction)
make	dead (seen on gravestones)
*malihini	*newcomer, visitor, stranger

malo	man's loincloth
manini	small, cheap, stingy
*mauka	*toward the mountains, inland (a direction and opposite of *makai*)
mauna	mountain (used in names like "Mount")
*muumuu	*long, loose-fitting dress
nani	beautiful (not spoken; seen in names)
nui	big, large, huge
*okole	*bottom, rear, buttocks
okolehao	liquor distilled from ti root
ono	delicious
ono-ono	very delicious
opu	abdomen, stomach
*pali	*cliff (or cliffs)
paniolo	cowboy (Hawaiian corruption of Español)
*pau	*finished (*pau hana*: through work, retirement)
pa'u	long skirt
pahoehoe	type of lava with smooth or ropy surface (contrasted with *aa*)
pikake	jasmine flower, named after "peacock"
pilikia	trouble
*poi	*pasty food made from taro root
*puka	*hole (a *puka*-board is a peg board)
punee	couch with no back, daybed
pupus	hors d'oeuvres (literally, "shells")
pupule	crazy
shaka!	great, well-done, perfect, okay!
tita	sister, but applied to a no-nonsense, spirited, down-home country girl.
*tutu	*grandmother (strictly speaking, *tutu wahine*)
*ukulele	*ukulele
*wahine	*girl, woman, wife
wai	fresh water (used in names)
wikiwiki	fast, in a hurry, quickly (also the airport shuttle bus, which often does not come *wikiwiki*)

A few pidgin postscripts: True pidgin cannot really be written down. Much of pidgin depends on the pronunciation of more or less common words, combined with some unconventional grammatical construction. But as much or more of the flavor is carried by inflection and rhythm, which perhaps can only be inscribed in musical notations, if at all.

Also, there are as many variations on pidgin as there are people who speak it. You may notice there is one general kind of pidgin used by the old folks, and a younger or more "hip" pidgin popular with the under-thirty crowd. It is combined with terms that may be in vogue with the same age group on the Mainland.

Finally, remember that most of the pidgin you will hear is no longer spoken out of necessity, but in a fun sort of way in order to promote comradeship between the speakers. In other words, pidgin is often a type of private game.

Here is a jocular pidgin note we once rescued from a waste basket. It was written by a young woman to a friend named Al to thank him for inviting her to a party.

Eh Al Brah,
Chee was one really ono luau you folks went make! All da kine kaukau stay so ono inside my opu, bumby I come fat, but ho da worth it! Ho dese kine kanakas (you and Les) good okolehao pourers you eh? You like one job in one ba? Ho, da kaukau, okolehao and da floor show you folks went make—really shaka, man.

You know da boss lady I get? She stay crack da whips on top my bod all day, so was one good time you give me. Tanks, eh? You folks went get one good lua, too. I went try em out—da flush kine.

Mahalo plenty again, and aloha.

BARBARA

Racial Groups in Hawaii. Here in the fiftieth state, everyone is a member of a racial minority group. The largest single minority in the state are the *haoles* (Caucasians), but they still make up only a little more than 26 percent of the population.

Hawaii is the only state in the Union where the whites are outnumbered by other races. Japanese add up to nearly 24 percent, Filipinos number some 11 percent, those calling themselves Hawaiian total at least 19 percent. (Some believe this figure should be higher, but actually no more than 1 percent—10,000 individuals or less—are pure Polynesian Hawaiians.) And about 5 percent of the population is Chinese.

Because of this diversification, there is almost no racial friction of the bitter kind known on the Mainland. Also, love and the miracle of reproduction tend to conquer and dilute antagonistic feelings even more; today nearly half the state's 12,000 annual marriages—the highest marriage rate in the country—are interracial. To be sure, group hostilities do exist in Hawaii today, but they are usually shown in more subtle ways, at least among middle-aged and older adults.

Some teenagers, on the other hand, act out prejudices and identity crises more directly, picking fights with other youngsters along racial lines. Usually these take the form of conflicts between established groups and newcomers.

Many of those exhibiting this racial antipathy are the underprivileged

Approximate Population of Hawaii by Race

260,000	or about	26% Caucasian*
240,000	or about	24% Japanese
180,000	or about	18% Part Hawaiian
110,000	or about	11% Filipino
50,000	or about	5% Chinese
15,000	or about	1½% Korean
15,000	or about	1½% Negro
10,000	or about	1% Samoan
10,000	or about	1% Pure Hawaiian
110,000	or about	11% Mixed and miscellaneous
1,000,000	Total state population**	

*Includes the Portuguese, one of the traditional Hawaii minority groups, as well as Hawaii-born, Mainland-born, and foreign-born haoles.
**Hawaii's official resident population at this writing is still less than one million, although it may reach that figure this year. However, its de facto population—the total number of people actually present within the state at any given moment—has been more than a million for at least two years.

minority among young, native Hawaiians who harbor the belief that others have been taking away their land, their beaches, and most of the good jobs for the past century or two. There is some truth in the charge, and there are Hawaiian organizations seeking some intelligent redress of genuine grievances. Nevertheless, the active animosity of the "have nots" for the "haves" seems to lead to police records and prison rosters that are filled with the names of young men of Polynesian blood.

One newcomer group often challenged are the Filipinos. Usually somewhat slighter in stature than the established teenagers of Hawaii, they can become the victims of racial tension. Another newish group—the Samoans—being large and pretty tough themselves, usually manage to hold their own.

The *haoles*, too, are often thought of as newcomers or outsiders, whether they are or not. Young white military enlistees can, on occasion, find themselves challenged by a squad of "locals," a term which generally covers an amalgam of backgrounds, little, if any, of which is Caucasian.

In some neighborhoods, the last day of school is known as "Kill a Haole Day." (Our own children first heard of the event at a tender age and called it "Killer Holiday.") It usually means no more than a day of general boisterousness and mischief-making.

Like the children at any school in the U.S.A., the offspring of Hawaii will—if they can make it past the ten thousand and two traumas of teenhood—probably come out all right.

The heterogeneous destiny of Hawaii was launched in the mid-nineteenth century, when the native Hawaiian population was at its ebb, and when the sugar planters began scouring the world for the labor needed on the plantations. They recruited peasants in Canton, Mongolia, Korea, Japan, Puerto Rico, the Madeira Islands, the Azores Islands, Portugal, Spain, Italy, Poland, Austria, Germany, Norway, Russia, Siberia, Micronesia, Polynesia, Melanesia, and the Philippines. They deliberately chose illiterates of varied and generally docile populations who could not communicate with each other in order to forestall their taking any concerted action to right the often oppressive nature of their employment.

Between 1852 and 1930, about 400,000 immigrants were transported to Hawaii to work in sugar. A few returned home at the end of their contracts, but most stayed on and began to intermarry—with each other, with the Hawaiians, and even with the *kamaaina haoles* who hired them.

All brought aspects of their culture which have remained in the Islands, and this is why we now have such "Hawaiian" institutions as the ukulele (Portuguese), steak teriyaki (Japanese), *manapua* (Chinese), and cockfights (Filipino).

In the rush to Americanize everyone after the turn of the century, Hawaii children adopted baseball and chewing gum with abandon, but they have not been encouraged to learn their own individual heritages. Ethnic diversity doesn't necessarily promote understanding among different groups, and many young people are now understandably angry that the schools do not require Asian and Pacific studies as much as they do courses that reflect traditional American/European thinking.

Nevertheless, in the wake of the distant examples set by the black, chicano, and Indian groups on the Mainland, a slow but encouraging resurgence of ethnic pride is now developing in the Islands.

Most gratifyingly, much of this self-rediscovery is being made by one of the most interesting minority groups, the one which has had the most difficulty adjusting to the social stresses of today, the native Hawaiians themselves.

Government and Economics

At first glance, Hawaii's institutions are largely those of any other American state.

That beautiful and dramatic capitol building, opened in 1969, houses two legislative bodies—a 25-member Senate and a 51-member House of Representatives—plus associated governmental offices and conference rooms.

There is a popularly elected governor (George R. Ariyoshi, a cheerful, somewhat shy fellow with mobile, bushy eyebrows) and a lieutenant governor (John Waihee). Both of them are Democrats.

Hawaii's four Washington legislators are also Democratic. They include Senator Daniel K. Inouye (pronounced "in-*noy*"), who became a national figure as a member of the Senate Watergate Committee, and Senator Spark M. Matsunaga. Both are former House members. The two current congressmen were both first elected in 1978. One is Daniel K. Akaka, the first native Hawaiian ever sent to Washington as a voting legislator. The other is millionaire Cecil Heftel, until recently an owner of television and radio stations in Hawaii.

There are only four counties in the state, and the largest is the "City and County of Honolulu," an official appellation combining what might have been two bodies into a single governmental unit. It includes the entire island of Oahu, with all its smaller communities, plus, for administrative purposes, almost all of the long chain of tiny, mostly uninhabited islets northwest of Kauai called the Leeward Isles.

The other three counties are Kauai (including Kauai and Niihau islands), Maui (Maui, Molokai, Lanai and Kahoolawe islands), and Hawaii (the Big Island). All four counties are administered under a mayor/ council system.

Hawaii is the only American state with just two levels of local government. There are no separate boards for the various towns and villages scattered over the islands, a highly touted fact which should indicate that there is more streamlined government in Hawaii.

To many residents of Oahu, however, the artificial barrier to efficiency set up because of jealousies between the Honolulu government and the state administration often seems to offset any advantages to denying municipalities their own local government.

Also, the centralizing of some super agencies, such as the State Department of Education which controls all 217 public schools throughout the Islands, has created some monolithic monsters and inefficient bureaucratic fiefdoms.

Volatile Politics. There is a strong preoccupation with politics in Hawaii. One sociologist at the University of Hawaii has declared that the state's politics are the "politics of growth" and, at the same time, the "politics of subtle racism."

The Democratic party is firmly entrenched, and it is run mainly by Japanese-Americans. The Republican party has an all-*haole* image and provides no more than token opposition, leaving the most bitter fights generally to the factional splits within the Democratic party.

Government corruption is not unknown, and political favoritism is very much alive and well, aided by a usually apathetic electorate. If you are in the real estate, construction, or allied businesses, it will help to have friends or relatives in the city or state governments—and hurt if you don't.

Politics also thrive on a strong feeling of "localism," which some translate as racism. It is reflected in policies designed to promote cautious state development while at the same time discouraging "outsiders" from moving into the state.

Where the Money Comes From. Hawaii's main economic base has now been firmly captured by tourism, which today is a three-billion-a-year business. There is some controversy over this, with protests from a few members of the environmental community against the practice of shuttling 4 million vacationers per year—more than the entire United States sends annually to Europe—in and out of the state, most of them funneled through the overdeveloped peninsula of Waikiki.

However, most of Hawaii's people realize that their economic cake is iced with visitors and agree with Hawaii's Senator Dan Inouye who says that it is, with proper control, a "non-polluting industry," and an ideal one because it draws on the traditional Hawaiian "Spirit of Aloha"— something you won't find in Miami Beach.

Until a few years ago, the federal government provided the greatest income source for Hawaii. With Hawaii's position as the single most important Pacific outpost for the United States Armed Forces, the defense establishment is still an important Island "industry."

The largest industrial operation in the state, as a matter of fact, is the Pearl Harbor Naval Shipyard, not to be confused with the Pearl Harbor Naval Base next door. The shipyard repairs and overhauls more than 800 ships annually, and it has the greatest civilian payroll of any organization in Hawaii.

There are well over 120,000 military personnel and dependents in Hawaii at any one moment, almost half of them with the navy. All service branches are represented, however, and you'll find that much of the wild outback of the Islands is still fenced off for military training and maneuvers. On Oahu, more than 25 percent of the acreage is under direct control of the military. The unified command for the entire Pacific American forces, CINCPAC (Commander in Chief, Pacific) is at Camp H. M. Smith, in the hills overlooking Pearl Harbor.

There are more than a dozen other important military commands and installations in Hawaii, nearly all of them on Oahu. This has led to Hawaii's description in some quarters as a "sugar-coated fortress." And sad to say, there is sometimes social antipathy between local groups and members of the military community, misunderstandings and tensions that date back to the "Massie Incident" of the 1930s.

These relationships are not helped by a system which keeps servicemen and their families generally leading separate, insular lives on military posts, buying cheaper groceries, liquor, and other products in the post exchanges, and generally not learning more than a superficial amount of Hawaii culture or taking part in activities of the community at large.

Happily, there are a few heart-warming exceptions, such as the Marines' "Toys for Tots" program, under which the leathernecks repair discarded playthings and present them to needy Island youngsters at Christmas time.

"Sugar and Pine." The traditional agricultural partnership of the Islands has, in the past, kept the state green in more ways than one. But sugar and pineapple have now been reduced to a long third and fourth place, respectively, in economic importance. Both were being steadily cut back until very recently when talk of a worldwide food shortage caused some reprieves in planned plantation closings.

There are still about a dozen and a half sugar companies and several hundred independent growers in the state, employing about 7,000 persons altogether. About 200,000 acres of cane grown on Oahu, Maui, Kauai, and Hawaii compose about three-quarters of Hawaii's cultivated lands.

But compared with tourism's $4 billion, and the federal government's $1½ billion, sugar's annual income of about $400 million seems very modest. Creeping water shortages are also threatening sugar in Hawaii. It takes a ton of water to produce one pound of refined sugar. Still, sugar may yet take on new economic life with the advent of gasohol, a fuel which can be used in cars and other engines. It is a combination of gasoline and alcohol, the latter of which may be made from sugar once fuel prices rise to the point where its manufacture would pay off.

Pineapple, almost the symbol of the Islands for so many years, has reduced its domain to three companies—the main firms are Dole and Del Monte—and six plantations. It is grown on all major islands except Hawaii, employs around 3,000 full-time workers, and garners a total income of around $200 million.

Pakalolo. That's the Hawaiian word for marijuana ("crazy tobacco"), and it's true that the cultivation of these illegal crops of "Maui Wowie" and "Kona Gold" now forms Hawaii's largest agricultural industry. The Hawaii state statistician has said that shipments of *pakalolo* from Hawaii County (the Big Island) alone have been estimated at 250,000 pounds per year, with annual sales from this crop running from $250 million to $750 million. Of course a certain amount of this product is regularly harvested and destroyed by the police.

Other Business. Heavy industry includes two oil refineries on Oahu, plus several factories supporting the large construction business—two cement plants, one small steel mill, an aluminum extrusion plant, a concrete pipe plant, and the like.

On a completely different scale, there are more than 100 garment manufacturers in the state, mainly producing colorful Hawaiian sportswear.

Other light industries are those which produce Kona coffee, tropical fruit drinks, jams and jellies, candies, macadamia nuts, oriental and Hawaiian foods, dairy products, beer, sake, rum, okolehao (a ti-root "whisky"), and all kinds of soft drinks.

Labor. Employees in Hawaii's main industries have been organized at least since the early 1950s. There may be a total membership in all unions of about 150,000 but it's difficult to get honest figures. Industry-wide contracts are negotiated in plantation industries and the stevedoring companies.

Two of the most influential unions are the International Longshoremen's and Warehousemen's Union (ILWU) and the Teamsters, but the largest is probably the Hawaii Government Employees Association (HGEA).

Problems in Paradise

Citizens of Hawaii are fond of calling their state "Paradise," and some members of the chamber of commerce awhile back got a lot of mileage by throwing away a preposition and turning the name of the state into an adverb: "Lucky You Live Hawaii!" the boosters wrote, and everybody oohed and ahhed.

Some realists, however, characterize such catch phrases as only whistling in the sunshine. The traditional beachboy pidgin phrase "Lucky You Come Hawaii" is more accurate. For as delightful a destination as are the Islands for an upbeat vacation, many Hawaii-philes who return year after year still feel that you *can* get too much of a good thing—that there is an enervating surfeit of surf, sun, sand, and somnolence which is fine for a vacation but not conducive to efficient and productive living on a year-round basis.

Some call the disease "Polynesian Paralysis," and others diagnose it as "Rock Fever" or "Islanditis." At any rate, it is a feeling that eventually creeps over many transplanted Mainlanders that there just isn't enough wide open space to move around in in "Paradise," whether physically, economically, or intellectually.

(This malady is not limited to Hawaii, of course. We've come down with it ourselves after long stints in Puerto Rico and on Mallorca. Others have reported its effects in Jamaica, Bermuda, and the Virgin Islands.)

It is true that the Hawaiian Islands promote love and romance where the potential previously exists. But it is equally true that many boys and girls who meet here and later form themselves into life companions do not stay to live, work, and raise their families. They return to the Mainland to make their home chiefly because the prohibitive cost of living in Hawaii, combined with a shortage of professional opportunities, is just too much.

The living costs also make it difficult for the state to compete with the Florida Gulf communities or even those in southern California in attracting the nation's retirees to some sunshine to warm up their remaining years.

There's a popular myth in Hawaii to the effect that Mainlanders are moving to the Islands in droves to escape the harsh winters, race riots, and crime waves that Islanders imagine are always gripping the Mainland. It's just not true. There is a large *turnover*, but the ratio of those who move to Hawaii and those who move out annually is not dramatically different—about 45,000 coming and 40,000 going, and about half of these are military personnel and their families.

The population of Hawaii has been increasing, to be sure. But mostly it's a natural increase (births over deaths amount to more than 12,000 annually), augmented by immigration from foreign lands (perhaps 9,000).

Now despite the higher living prices, Hawaii is generally no more expensive to vacation in than any other American playground—cheaper than many, as a matter of fact, and certainly less costly than such exotic foreign capitals as London, Paris, or Tokyo.

Local cynics harumph that this is because visitor expenses reflect a balance between the high cost of material goods and the lower wage scales paid to those who serve the visitor. (And they say this same low-wage level and high-priced products combine to make life difficult for permanent residents who are "paid in sunshine.")

No one can tell you for sure why things are more expensive in Hawaii. The most accused villain is the cost of shipping, but others say that cargo costs account for only a small percent of the difference. Somehow, though, there seems to be a tradition of extra middle men chipping away at the goods as they travel through the merchandise funnel on the way to retail shelves.

Although these are factors, it is more likely that the cost of living is tied more or less directly to the cost of real estate. Prices paid for land are astronomical, largely because there just isn't much of it available in the state.

There are a little over 4 million acres in the major islands, and much of that is untenable, wild and wooly land, and a large chunk, of course, is agricultural. Be that as it may, 42 percent of all the land is owned by the state, county, and federal governments, and 47 percent is owned by a few major private owners (each one having at least 1,000 acres), who often will lease—not sell—their farm and home sites.

Less than 11 percent of all Hawaii is owned by small landowners—in "freehold" or "fee simple," to use the legal terms.

You may have heard that you can pay several times as much for a house and lot in Hawaii as you would for a comparable home in other parts of the country. That's entirely correct. Hawaii's housing units are the most expensive in the nation. The median value of owner-occupied dwellings is about $120,000, more than double the Mainland median, and most single-family homes available cost much more than that. Many middle-class, white-collar workers have given up on the idea of owning their own homes any time soon. They rent houses or apartments instead, until such time as a relative may die and leave them enough— hopefully—for the required down payment. Even then, many forego the fee simple house to build on a leasehold lot.

After the cost of groceries and housing, most Hawaii residents would certainly name crime as an important problem in the Islands. Crime gets a lot of attention in the media, and it's apparently causing public concern as the statistics begin to approach the crime rate common on the Mainland. Hawaii's rate of violent crimes, however, is still below those for most American states, although its property crime rate (car theft, burglary, etc.) is above average.

Juvenile crime, drug abuse, and vandalism are up, as they are everywhere. But a different type of lawlessness, organized crime, has accounted for a number of murders in the Islands over the past several years. No, there is no branch of the Mafia. Organized crime in Hawaii has a distinctly local flavor, with the perpetrators of the violence usually called "The Syndicate." Competing factions often are warring for power throughout the Island's Lilliputian underworld.

Like its Mainland counterparts, the Syndicate dabbles in gambling, prostitution, extortion, and drugs. Meanwhile, the tumult continues in front of a public which is little concerned, since the victims of the occasional mayhem are virtually always only fellow members of the same criminal subculture. Juvenile and amateur crime, on the other hand, get much more public attention since they are perceived as greater threats to the average citizen.

Recently some violence has been attributed to an "us and them" attitude among low-income, unsophisticated youths who seek a target for their hostility among outsiders. They are most often from families of Hawaiian or mixed blood who are generally forced to live at the bottom of the economic scale. Another factor contributing to their problems is the lack of good education, both at home and in the public schools.

Some critics also blame the rapid development of Hawaii, some of it by large, international corporations that have little or no sense of the social consequences of their intrusion into what was, until a short time ago, a relatively simple society.

The tensions created can erupt in fights between young locals and young military men. And unfortunately, a few members of these criminal or disadvantaged groups have preyed upon visitors to the islands who innocently wander into economically depressed areas. (Sadly, we now advise our friends not to visit the Waianae Coast on the western shore of Oahu, and not to camp overnight anywhere on that island.)

Visitors to Hawaii are invariably surprised to learn that crime is a concern here at all, since it is usually invisible over a short-term stay. But no matter how polite and friendly most island citizens are, remember that just like in any large Mainland city, it's a good idea not to leave valuable things unguarded on the beach or even in the trunk of your rental car, and not to visit dark, lonely places at night.

By the way, everyone should be aware that on Oahu, at least, policemen are *tough* and not to be argued with, even over a simple speeding ticket. Under the law, if you talk back to a Honolulu Police Department officer, you can be handcuffed, arrested, and booked for "harassment." It doesn't happen often, of course, and by and large the cops are friendly, considerate, and polite, especially to visitors. But if you feel any polemics coming on, save them for the courtroom.

Virtually all HPD officers, by the way, chase around the highways in late-model, souped-up, unmarked cars that they purchase and care for themselves. A Honolulu policeman is considered to be always available for duty, whether in uniform or not, and he always carries a gun, whether it is visible or not. (And by the way, television notwithstanding, there is no "Hawaii Five-O," or any other state police force.)

Taxes take a big bite in Hawaii. Per capita, Island residents pay the third highest state and local taxes in the nation. There is a 4 percent excise tax on absolutely everything you buy or rent.

As we mentioned in Chapter 3, environmental problems come in for their share of concern in Hawaii today. Air pollution fortunately is rare, but unfortunately not completely absent in the state. A few consecutive days of stagnant or Kona winds in the winter months can combine with the effect of the thousands of infernal combustion engines and maybe some sugar cane fires on Oahu—and sometimes with some volcanic haze drifting up from the Big Island—to create a daytime smog.

The effect has been known as "stealing the Waianaes" ever since science writer Bruce Benson observed this modern phenomenon, which occasionally eliminates the traditional view of the distant Waianae ("*Why*-an-eye?") mountain range from some parts of Honolulu. There has been talk of limiting the number of motor vehicles on Oahu, but a planned 14-mile mass transit system has stalled in the political tunnel.

Alternate Energy. Hawaii takes the energy crisis more seriously—and is handling it better—than many places on the Mainland. Not long ago, Dr. Edward Teller, the atomic physicist, suggested that a line of windmills might be used to harness the strong, dependable trade winds, an idea that seemed almost laughable at the time.

But there are two serious experimental operations producing energy from the volcanic action under the ground at Pahoa on the Big Island. Even more dramatic was the breakthrough made in 1979 when the state government was the first in the nation to produce electricity through ocean thermal energy conversion. In this OTEC project, Hawaii's warm seawater is used to change ammonia from liquid to vapor within a heat exchanger. The vapor then turns an electrical generator, after which the vapor is condensed by cold water pumped from deeper in the ocean, and the cycle is repeated.

As already mentioned, there is considerable interest in converting sugar cane to alcohol to make gasohol. And there is also a system to burn bagasse, the waste residue from sugar harvesting. Combined with the discarded shells from macadamia nut farms, this "biomass" energy now provides more than 58 percent of the electricity used by the Big Island. One firm also has an "energy tree farm" sprouting nicely.

Solar energy is also big in a state with so many hours of dependable sunshine. Hawaii has about 201,000 families, and there are 20,000 solar water heaters atop residential roofs. The main hospital on Kauai now gets most of its electricity from a field of photovoltaic cells, and for about 200 isolated homes in rural areas of the Big Island similar devices are the only regular source of power.

And what about that wind-power idea? The Hawaiian Electric Company is now receiving power from an experimental wind generator installed near Kahuku, a particularly breezy spot on Oahu. And the U.S. Department of Energy has installed some prototype windmill generators on Molokai and the Big Island. A private corporation has plans for an entire wind farm somewhere in the islands.

To wrap up some of the state's other difficulties, there is vocal opposition to the storage of nuclear weapons on Oahu. One activist group claims there are 3,000 atomic bombs in the West Loch area of Pearl Harbor, but the military remains mum on the subject.

There are some union problems, made particularly difficult by the occasional threat of a dock strike, which would affect Hawaii's shipping lifeline. The state is said to suffer one of the highest alcoholism rates in the country, and it pays out almost as much in welfare checks as New York State.

It seems safe to say that 99 and 44/100ths percent of the visitors who came to Hawaii last year had a darn good time, but the numbers may not be so impressive for those who moved here to begin a new life. The Midwest Research Institute, which uses a computer to rate the "quality of life" in 243 American cities, placed Honolulu a modest 31st in its list of metropolises worth living in.

We don't know what they fed into that computer, but two complaints we almost forgot to mention have to do with the problems of communications in the fiftieth state. Most of Hawaii's TV programs are shipped here on tape by air freight, so they generally get on the stations about a week later than on the Mainland. And a bug in the ears of island residents for years is an erratic and often utterly inefficient telephone service.

Art and Handicraft

The Hawaiians of old were adept at crafts of many types, but most of these skills were laid aside and forgotten in the face of imported talents and technology. **Tapa** is a good example, for the production of this kind of Polynesian cloth probably achieved its highest level with the Hawaiians.

In some long-lost way, they beat the bark of the mulberry tree until a material similar to felt was achieved, but today you will probably see this quality product only in the Bishop Museum. Samoans and Tongans still turn out tapa, and you'll find that sold in Honolulu instead, along with a few samples of locally manufactured material using the methods developed in other Pacific islands. In the past 100 years, no one has been able to duplicate the quality of the traditional Hawaiian tapa—including the Hawaiians themselves.

In ancient Hawaii, the people were perhaps best known for their use of **feathers** in creating clothes and other ornaments. The most dramatic of the objects of feather art were the cloaks, helmets, and *kahilis* (cylinders made from feathers mounted on a pole to indicate high social status).

There were not enough birds sporting the proper colors to clothe everyone, however, so only the *alii* (the nobility) wore the royal colors of red and gold produced by the tailfeathers of the *mamo* and *o'o* birds. Some feather art continues to be turned out today, but only in modest and expensive quantities. You'll occasionally see it in hatbands for the country folk and perhaps in a rare feather *lei*.

Almost the only genuine handicraft that has survived intact from the early days is the production of **leis and necklaces**—not usually made of feathers, but of garlands of flowers, leaves, *kukui* nuts, sea shells, and even seeds. Everyone, man and woman alike, wears something around his neck in Hawaii, at least once in a while.

The art of weaving **lauhala** (the leaf of the pandanus tree) and coconut fronds has not been lost. But now, instead of fences, walls, and floors, the leaves are generally used in smaller products like hats, baskets, slippers, and table mats.

Woodcarving was an old Hawaiian art, and it's still kept alive by some modern operations in Hawaii. The traditional native woods are *koa*, monkeypod, and *ohia*, but many of these materials are now shipped in from the orient, either as finished products or raw for working here in Hawaii.

The wooden bowl or calabash—now largely used for tossed salads—is authentically connected to the past and it is still the traditional company retirement gift in the Islands. But you can get wood carved into any pattern imaginable, from attractive *koa* coffee tables through pregnant hula girls and up to those ridiculous giant-sized spoon and fork sets.

It surprised us to learn that some **ukuleles**—the best and most expensive ones, as a matter of fact—are made in Hawaii, although thousands of cheap (and satisfactory) ones are stamped out in Japan and then shipped to Hawaii.

One of the most fascinating of Hawaiian handicrafts was begun after the missionaries showed the Hawaiians how to make bedspreads. But instead of the simple patchwork of New England, a new form of **Hawaiian quilt** utilizing island designs began to evolve. There are embroidered fruits, flowers, leaves, landmarks, and legends, usually in a single-color pattern over a white or another solid background. Designs are jealously guarded by the few Hawaiian quiltmakers, generally older women, who are around today.

The quilts take perhaps a month to make with the quiltmaker working full time. You will seldom find a Hawaiian quilt for sale, however. Usually they are made for a member of the family and presented to him at a special event. On the rare occasion that a price is put on a Hawaiian quilt, the tag will read about $1,000.

Another ancient art, recently revived, is **scrimshaw**. This carving on whales' bones and teeth was not a Hawaiian form, but a type of primitive etching done by *haole* sailors who spent long boring hours at sea between catches, dreaming of Lahaina or New Haven while patiently scratching away at a leviathan's molar. Original scrimshaw, of course, brings antique prices. But there are several local artists turning out modern versions of the old art on whales' teeth, walrus tusks, and other material.

The authentic folk arts and crafts of Hawaii are on exhibit in the Bernice Pauahi Bishop Museum in Honolulu, the repository of all artifacts of historical significance to Polynesia.

More modern handicraft or factoricraft being performed today encompasses (take a deep breath) jewelry manufacture of all types, including those made from pink, black, and gold coral, olivine and shells; several different types of porcelain, ceramic, and pottery operations; freeze-dried flowers coated with plastic; other flowers petrified in gold; collage boxes made from such Hawaiian souvenir items as macadamia nuts, shells, and ancient post cards; artificial flowers made from shells and what-have-you; various glass-blowing and/or etching processes; zillions of types of scented and unscented candles; little bottles filled with layers of colored sugar; dolls of all kinds; monkeys made from coconuts; and figurines of little hula girls and tiki gods molded from pulverized lava rock or monkeypod sawdust.

Much of the above sounds worse than it is; much of the above is even worse than it sounds. Some of it is even good, and all of it is discussed in detail in our "Shopping" sections (No. 10), farther along in the island-chapters.

Artists in Hawaii. Many artists with sketch pad and canvas have been depicting the flavor of the Islands since they were discovered by Westerners in 1778. Two talented members of Captain Cook's scientific expedition, **John Webber** and **James Clevely**, accurately documented the first visit.

Other ships' artists included **Louis Choris**, who visited in 1816 and whose incisive, sensitive works are heavily acclaimed today. **Jacques Arago**, who drew heroic Hawaiians in 1819, and **Robert Dampier**, who sketched here during an 1825 stopover, are also important.

By the mid-nineteenth century, the missionaries had begun to train a few local artists, and the Hawaiians lost the inclination to continue scratching out petroglyphs during this same period. Petroglyphs, apparently only the casual scribble of a pre-literate people, have their own special charm, however, and several artists of today have incorporated petroglyphic design into their work.

In the late nineteenth and early twentieth centuries, many artists came to live and work in Hawaii. Today it is generally agreed that four were particularly outstanding. **Madge Tennent**, an Englishwoman who arrived from New Zealand and Samoa in 1923, is remembered especially for her bold oils of large Hawaiian women. She is often known as "Hawaii's Gauguin," and many feel her works will attain international recognition. The Tennent Art Foundation Gallery at 203 Prospect St. in Honolulu exhibits her work exclusively.

Huc M. Luquiens became famous for his landscape etchings. **John M. Kelly** was also an etcher, but one who chose the human form instead of scenery for his subject.

Jean Charlot, who came to Hawaii in 1949 already famous for his

Mexican murals, remained to become the unofficial captain of Hawaii's art community until he died, aged in his nineties, in 1979. There are about three dozen other recognized artists doing significant work in Hawaii today.

The most important collection of art in Hawaii is displayed at the Honolulu Academy of Arts at 900 South Beretania St., known not only for its Western exhibits but also for its huge oriental collections. There are several other galleries, however.

In addition to the art sold at private galleries in Hawaii, current works may be purchased at the outdoor "art marts," the most well-known of which is displayed along the fence near Honolulu Zoo on Saturdays and sometimes Sundays. Similar exhibitions are held at Lahaina on Maui and at Kailua-Kona on the Big Island.

Hawaiian Music and That Ol' Hula Moon

Irving Kolodin once told us while he was music critic for the *Saturday Review* that the lure of Hawaiian music alone could account for the large number of visitors who have come here over the past several decades. "The music of the Islands has brought more people than the airplane," Kolodin said.

Certainly no other state in the Union is so musical—or at least can boast styles of music so distinctively influenced by local custom. Who can say he has listened to *Aloha Oe* or *Lovely Hula Hands* and never dreamed of experiencing the Islands in person?

Not everyone is a Hawaiian music fan, of course. Groucho Marx once grumped that all Hawaiian songs sounded the same to him, and he suspected they were all written on the same day. And Kolodin politely said that he seemed to hear the wrong kind all the time on the Mainland.

Most impressions like Groucho's are formed on hearing only a limited sample of popular tunes, usually those churned out for a Hawaiian-hungry appetite among Mainland masses during the 1930s. Hawaiian music produced today is often rich and varied, containing the traditions of the Pacific as well as the modern sounds of American jazz, rock, and country.

In ancient Hawaii, music consisted solely of chants (usually religious), for which rhythm was much more important than the few tonal changes it possessed. There was no scale at all, only relatively random notes, usually limited to two or three.

When the American missionaries arrived in 1820, they made their most immediate and dramatic effect with the hymns they brought with them. Not only was the diatonic scale immediately embraced by the natives, but the whole concept of harmony almost caused a cultural revolution.

Recognizing this valuable commodity, the holy folk lost no time in organizing a singing school and in translating many Calvinist hymns into the Hawaiian language. It was music which brought the Hawaiians to church in droves—not the long, monotonous sermons which now held about as much attraction for the Hawaiians as their discontinued chants.

The Hawaiians soon began adopting the Christian hymns and giving them new, secular lyrics in their own tongue, although they were all called *himeni*—a word still in the language for slow and dignified music. They were sung *a cappella* in four-part harmony and not accompanied by dancing, which for many years was strictly prohibited by missionary influence.

The mid-nineteenth-century *himeni* were often sad, usually reflecting a longing for some place or person far away. The reason was not only because the islands seemed very large and distances between them huge in that day; it resulted from the social legacy of King Kamehameha I who sought to "unite" the island nation by dispersing elements of the population over the entire chain.

The potential political action by the people against the king and his successors became a reduced threat. And a song like *The Thirsty Winds of Kohala* (a district on the Big Island) was probably composed by a sentimental and homesick Hawaiian transplanted from Kohala to Oahu or Kauai.

In the 1870s and 1880s, Hawaiian music underwent several rapid changes. First, there was the increased popularity of the guitar, learned by the *paniolos* (Hawaiian cowboys) on the Big Island from the Spanish-speaking *vaqueros* who had been imported to teach the local boys how to punch cattle. (The word *paniolo* is a Hawaiian corruption of *Español*.)

The *paniolos* probably had been playing the Spanish guitar in the isolated hills of Waimea for the previous twenty years, but it was only the inauguration of regular interisland shipping which brought it to the attention of the entire land. By this date, the Spanish had gone back to Mexico, and the Hawaiians had changed the guitar strings from the original tuning to what is now called "slack key." Basically, it is a method of loosening the strings, creating a more distinctive style of plucking and strumming. (To a large extent, "slack key" guitar continued to lead an obscure life in the back country until very recently.)

Also during this period, the first of thousands of Portuguese immigrants arrived in the Islands. They, too, brought guitars and a livelier style of folk music. Still further, they shipped in several other types of string instruments among which was a relatively tiny, four-stringed affair variously called the *braga*, the *braguinho*, or the *cavalquinho*. The Hawaiians took a look at Portuguese hands strumming quickly across the *braga*'s neck and concluded it could not look more like a dog trying to scratch a persistent flea. They therefore named the new instrument the "jumping flea," or, in Hawaiian, *uku-lele*.

In a very few years, there were few thatched huts in the Islands that did not have at least one guitar or ukulele stashed in the corner, ready for instant inspiration by its Hawaiian owner. And when the instrument was picked up, it was more likely to play a happy ditty than in times past. Missionary influence on the Hawaiians and their rulers decreased in the latter half of the nineteenth century, and Hawaiians began to dance again.

The newer, fast-paced numbers which accompanied the dancers became known as *hula* songs. Rhythm again became important, and the Hawaiians drew upon the old beats used prior to the missionary influence on their music. Some singers also picked up the yodeling methods put forth by the Big Island *vaqueros* and changed it into today's style of falsetto singing.

Another important development occurring at almost the same time was the arrival in the Islands of Henry Berger, the German musician hired by Kamehameha V as music teacher to the royal family and to whom was entrusted the formation of the Royal Hawaiian Band.

The Hawaiians soon found themselves led musically as well as socially by their own monarchs. King David Kalakaua wrote the words (to Berger's music) of Hawaii's national anthem, *Hawaii Ponoi*, which is the state anthem today. Queen Liliuokalani is credited with *Aloha Oe* which she wrote in her own hand in 1878, although nit-pickers note that the tune is much like the old hymn *The Rock Beside the Sea*.

Shortly before the turn of the century, a young student at Kamehameha School for Boys, Joseph Kekuku, accidentally dropped a comb on his guitar and as it skittered across the strings he heard a new sound. One thing led to another, and soon Kekuku had changed the gut strings to wire and was turning out a steel bar in the school machine shop. He used the bar to play the world's first instrument of its type—the one the rest of the world knows now as the "Hawaiian guitar."

In Hawaii, however, it was always called the "steel guitar," and no sooner had Kekuku popularized it in the Islands, he left to perform on the Mainland. There he continued to entertain and teach for twenty-seven years until he died in New Jersey in 1932. Kekuku never returned to Hawaii, and his Hawaiian guitar was adopted by every Country and Western group in America. A few years later, it was electrically amplified, and to some musical ears outside of the Nashville sphere of influence, the steel guitar just plain committed suicide—killed as a serious instrument simply by overuse.

In Hawaii, the steel guitar had firmly captured the melody line from the violin and flute which led earlier Hawaiian orchestras. It generally held the lead clear into the 1960s, although today in the most modern Hawaiian arrangements the steel guitar is a much more subtle instrument or absent altogether. Nevertheless, Hawaiian musicians are nothing if not sentimental, and many are still very attached to the old twang.

In truth it is hard to imagine the likes of *Princess Pupule, Sweet Leilani, Little Brown Gal,* and the *Cockeyed Mayor of Kaunakakai* holding up their treble clefs without a healthy dose of steel guitar. These are *hapa-haole* songs—Hawaiian music written in English or partly in English, and largely influenced by Hollywood and Broadway—which became the successors to the old *hula* songs. There are hundreds of *hapa-haole* songs written over four decades, and a few are still being composed today.

During the 1960s, a terrible thing seemed to be happening to Hawaiian music. It was disappearing altogether. In the bars, clubs, and showrooms of Waikiki, the ukes, the steel guitars, the melodious Hawaiian language, and the familiar themes of surf, rustling palms, and fragrant flowers all had faded from the scene in favor of hard-rock music, much of it imported from Las Vegas.

Only a few stalwarts like the perennially popular entertainer Don Ho continued to sing the traditional favorites—*Tiny Bubbles, Pearly Shells, Beyond the Reef*—all known widely on the Mainland but which were haughtily put down by hip elements of Honolulu. Ho tried to back up his own songs with some modern arrangements and a few new songs (*Suck 'Em Up, Ain't No Big Thing*) with some semi-rock influence. Nevertheless, he still found himself virtually alone, patronized mainly by older generation tourists, while the upcoming musicians of the Islands looked beyond Hawaii's shores for their professional inspiration. Loud outcries by visitors and residents alike ensued, bemoaning the imminent demise of Hawaiian music. Still, nothing they could do seemed to bring the *Hawaiian Wedding Song* or *Blue Hawaii* back onto Kalakaua Avenue.

But Hawaiian music was not really defeated. It had only made a strategic withdrawal until it was re-formed, revitalized, and ready to enter the field again. Beginning in 1970, some new and exciting patterns emerged, many of them traditional songs or themes, but clothed in some brand-new styles.

The new groups eschewed names like the Royal Hawaiian Serenaders or the Waikiki Beachboys, titles which conjured up images of happy-go-lucky brown lackies always ready and willing to evoke whatever images you remember from Bing Crosby movies of old. Calling themselves names of the land—the Sunday Manoa, Hui Ohana, Na Keonimana—the new groups combined close harmony with hard-driving rhythms influenced by jazz, rock, and the best C&W, but above all infused with a sense of the Hawaiians' recently rediscovered cultural identity. Digging into the past, they came up again not only with the slack key guitar, but with a whole group of other instruments—strings like the tiple, the requinta, and even the mandolin, plus percussions like the *ipu* (a gourd drum), *'ili'ili* (stone castanets), *pahu* (a sharkskin drum), and a *'ulili* (triple gourd rattle).

So today, there are many forms of traditional and modern Hawaiian music, the latest still in transition. Those new to the medium may only be able to discern a narrow range of style, in the same way that persons who are not accustomed to seeing faces of another race have trouble at first recognizing personal differences. But to seek out and carefully listen to Hawaiian music is to gain a special appreciation of Hawaii—perhaps the most valid experience of Hawaiian culture today.

Some musical postscripts:
• A list of Hawaiian entertainers and local musical groups, together with a brief description of each, will be found in the Oahu chapter's Section 11—Nights on the Town.
• If you want to hear Hawaiian music at any hour, you may turn your radio to KCCN, the only Oahu radio station playing Hawaiian music exclusively—and indiscriminately. There at 1440 kilocycles (it's on AM only), you'll hear all the best and all the worst, side by side.
• The Royal Hawaiian Band—the same organization set up more than 100 years ago by Henry Berger—is still going strong. It's often on the dock to welcome a cruise ship to the Islands, but it's now better known for its free concerts Friday noons at the Coronation Bandstand on the grounds of Honolulu's Iolani Palace.
• Western classical music is not unknown in Hawaii, and the Honolulu Symphony Orchestra, founded in 1900, is well regarded. The symphony has a regular concert series plus several special appearances and traveling tours. The symphony also sponsors the Hawaii Opera Theatre, which features guest artists and local singers.
Some brief words on the hula: Believe it or not, the first *hula* dancers were men. In pre-discovery Hawaii, the *hula* was a religious ritual, and it was thought too sacred for women to perform.

The missionaries tried to suppress the *hula*, considering its gyrating motions sinful and sexually suggestive no matter who performed it. The *hula* never really died, however, although some versions of it were forgotten and others underwent several changes. By the time it re-emerged into public consciousness in the late nineteenth century, most men had dropped the dance, leaving it to women who gradually adapted it into a more graceful, interpretive performance.

The grass skirt, incidentally, is a relatively recent innovation brought by Gilbert Islanders to Hawaii. *Hula* skirts were all at least knee length 100 years ago. Usually they were longer, and there were no thighs to be seen. The ti leaf skirt, however, is genuinely Hawaiian, although it takes fewer such leaves to make today's *hula* skirt, to be sure.

In recent decades, *hula* hand motions have become almost a musical sign language, but it is not true that you can follow the story by watching these movements. And the swiveling hips—once downplayed in importance—have indeed been increased to a sensual proportion, at least in some *hapa-haole* and comic hulas.

As with Hawaiian music, there are then several different types of *hulas* ranging from the traditional and classical to a graceful grind of good fun, vamps, and rolls. Be aware that you will see *hulas* from many other Pacific Islands performed in Hawaii. One of the favorites is the extremely fast-hipped version danced in Tahiti (remember *Mutiny on the Bounty?*), and often mistaken by newcomers for a genuine Hawaiian *hula*.

A Calendar Full of Activities

With the possible exception of Aloha Week (see "September" below), we wouldn't suggest that you pick your vacation dates on the basis of what's going on. One thing to remember this year is that several Silver Jubilee events (for which dates are not yet set at this writing) will be scheduled up to and including August 21, 1984, to mark the 25th anniversary of statehood for Hawaii.

Meanwhile, here's a hopefully handy guide in capsule form to other yearly activities that you might look for during the period you are visiting Hawaii. As indicated, sometimes specific dates will vary considerably.

JANUARY

January 1: New Year's Day. Sunshine Music Festival (rock music) in Diamond Head Crater.

First Saturday afternoon: Annual Hula Bowl College All-Star Football Classic. Aloha Stadium on Oahu. (Colorful half-time pageantry.)

Some Sunday afternoon: Annual Carole Kai Bed Race, Kapiolani Park.

Mid to late January: Chinese Narcissus festival begins. A selection of events off and on different evenings and weekends over the next five weeks. (Watch newspapers closely or you'll miss them.)

Third Wednesday in January: State legislature opens in colorful ceremony at capitol. (Entrance without ticket could be difficult.)

FEBRUARY

About February 1: The four-day Hawaiian Open International Golf Tournament. Waialae Country Club, Oahu. (Usually shown live on

Mainland TV resulting in immediate visitor crush over the next four or five weeks!)

About mid-February: Hang Ten American Professional Surfing Championships.

During February: Three- or four-day ski meet atop Mauna Kea on the Big Island sponsored by the Ski Association of Hawaii.

Late February, early March: Eleven-week Cherry Blossom Festival sponsored by the Japanese community on Oahu begins. Extends into April with various events, including cooking demonstrations, a fashion show, tea ceremony, etc.

MARCH

One day during the month: Kite-Flying Contest at Kapiolani Park, Waikiki.

March 3: Japanese Girls' Day.

Early March: Polo season opens, Mokuleia, Oahu.

A Friday evening in March: Kamehameha Schools Song Festival, Neal S. Blaisdell Center.

March 17: St. Patrick's Day Parade in Honolulu.

March 26: Prince Kuhio Day. (Celebrated as a festival on Kauai, the prince's birthplace.)

APRIL

Early April: Four- or five-day Merry Monarch Festival, honoring King Kalakaua, Hilo, Hawaii.

During April: Miss Aloha Hawaii Pageant, Hilo, Hawaii.

One Sunday: Bishop Museum Festival, continuous entertainment on museum grounds, Honolulu, Oahu.

One Weekend: Children's Fair, at La Pietra, estate housing Hawaii School for Girls, 2933 Poni Moi Rd., Honolulu.

Sunday close to April 8: Buddha's birthday celebrated, Blaisdell Center Concert Hall, Honolulu.

Easter Sunday: Sunrise service at the National Memorial Cemetery of the Pacific, Punchbowl Crater, Honolulu.

Late April or Early May: Flora Pacifica exhibition, flowers and plants of Hawaii.

MAY

May 1: Lei Day, with flowers, contests, and pageants in afternoon at Kapiolani Park, Honolulu.

May 5: Japanese Boys' Day. Look for paper carp flying outside homes where young boys live.

Mid-May: Honokaa Rodeo, sponsored by the Hawaii Saddle Club at Honokaa on the Big Island.

Mid-May through Mid-June: Fiesta Filipina, a series of Philippine culture events on Oahu.

Last Monday: Memorial Day. School children decorate Punchbowl graves with flower leis.

JUNE

Wednesdays: Zoo programs begin with entertainment each Wednesday through August at 6 P.M., Honolulu Zoo.

Early June: 100-mile Around-the-Island Canoe Race, usually on a Saturday and Sunday starting on beach fronting Moana Hotel.

June 11: Kamehameha Day, honors the conqueror of the Islands. Features a colorful parade in Honolulu. Other events on other islands.

Mid-June: Molokai Rodeo on Molokai.

Late June: Japanese "Bon Dances" at Honpa Hongwanji Buddhist Temple, 1727 Pali Highway.

JULY

July 4: Independence Day. Lots of fireworks may remind you of old-style Fourths of July on the Mainland. In Hilo, look for the special Fourth Fest Day.

Early July: Summer Crater Festival, rock music inside Diamond Head Crater, Honolulu.

Early July: Several rodeos, including the Makawao Rodeo on Maui and the Parker Ranch Rodeo and Naalehu Rodeo on the Big Island.

Weekends in July & August: Japanese Bon Dances begin at various Buddhist temples. Visitors are welcome.

Mid-July: International Festival of the Pacific—one week of parades and pageants in Hilo.

Mid-July: Prince Lot Hula Festival, Moanalua Gardens, Honolulu.

Mid-to-late July: In odd-numbered years, contestants in the Trans-Pacific Yacht Race arrive at the finish line off Diamond Head.

Late July: Following the Trans-Pac (see above), the Around-the-State yacht race takes six or seven days.

Late July: Run to the Sun, a 37.5-mile ultramarathon from Kahului to the summit of Haleakala on Maui.

Late July: The Kapalua Music Festival, a week-long classical and Hawaiian presentation, at the Kapalua Bay Hotel on Maui.

Late July, Early August: Hawaiian Billfish Tournament at Kailua-Kona on the Big Island, not to be confused with the international event that follows it.

AUGUST

Early August: Hawaiian International Billfish Tournament over 10 days at Kailua-Kona. Anglers from all over the world compete for prizes for catches of giant marlin.

A Sunday during August: Ukulele Festival, usually in the afternoon at Kapiolani Park Bandstand, Honolulu.

Another Sunday: Hula Festival, also at Kapiolani Park.

Mid-August: Water Week. Board of Water Supply takes interested people on cable car far underground where water is tapped and pumped.

During August: Fiftieth State Fair usually opens. It has not been distinguished in recent years.

During August: Hawaii State Surfing Championship two-day meet. Also, another weekend, the Honolulu Body Surfing Championship. Beach locations can vary from year to year.

August and September: Several canoe regattas and races on various islands.

SEPTEMBER

September 1: Labor Day. The Waikiki Rough Water Swim over two miles from Sans Souci Beach to Duke Kahanamoku Beach. Labor Day Rodeo on Kauai. Labor Day Fishing Tournament on Maui.

Early September: Seniors Tennis Tournament, Mauna Kea Beach Hotel on the Big Island.

Early September: One-day Garden Fair by Foster Botanic Garden, corner Vineyard Blvd. and Nuuanu Ave., Honolulu. Floral displays and plant sales.

Mid-September: Five-day Na Mele O Maui, a music festival on Maui.

Mid- to late September: Aloha Week celebrations on Maui, the Big Island, and Oahu. Look for outrigger canoe races, luaus, royal balls, athletic events, parades, etc.

OCTOBER

Early October: Aloha Week festivities on Kauai and Molokai.

During October: Kanikapila Hawaiian Music Festival two nights at Andrews Outdoor Amphitheater on University of Hawaii campus. Usually features contemporary Hawaiian music.

During October: Scottish-Hawaiian Games at Waikoloa resort community on the Big Island.

Late October: Molokai-to-Oahu Canoe Race. Finish is about noon at beach by the Moana Hotel in Waikiki.

Late October: Iron Man Triathlon endurance contest at Kailua-Kona.

Late October: Annual orchid show at Honolulu International Center over four days.

Late October: Hawaii County Fair in Hilo.

Late October: Open Pro-Am Golf Tournament, Maui.

NOVEMBER

Mid-November: Bull and Horse Show at Kamuela on the Big Island.

Mid-November: Kona Coffee Festival at Kailua-Kona on the Big Island.

Late November or December: Smirnoff World Pro-Am Surfing Championship, and the Duke Kahanamoku Surfing Classic, North Shore, Oahu.

DECEMBER

December 7: Pearl Harbor Day. Memorial service aboard the USS *Arizona* Memorial.

Early December: Festival of Trees for five days at the Blaisdell Memorial Center.

Early December: Bodhi Day. Day of Enlightenment celebrated by Buddhists on a Sunday in several temples.

Early December: Honolulu Marathon. Thousands run 26 miles beginning before dawn at the Aloha Tower and finishing around noon in Kapiolani Park.

Mid-December: Kamehameha Schools Christmas Concert at the Blaisdell Center Concert Hall, Honolulu.

Christmas Week: Mission Houses Museum Christmas Candlelight Tour. Music, costumes, refreshments, etc. Honolulu.

Late December: Makaha Invitational Surfing Championship, Oahu.

December 31: New Year's Eve. Thousands of firecrackers like you've never heard before!

The Spirit of Aloha

John F. Kennedy once commented that Hawaii is what the rest of America is striving to be.

Like so many other public figures who have experienced Hawaii at first hand, the late president apparently admired the state's racial harmony as shown so clearly in its chop suey population. But this is merely one manifestation of a social resource dubbed in recent years the "Aloha Spirit."

What is this Aloha Spirit, if there really is any such thing? This question has been perplexing many in the Islands today. Some say that even if it once did exist, it is now dead. Others claim that the Aloha Spirit is around, all right, but that it often hides, leaving the pressures of the city to reside farther *mauka*—inland—and on the Neighbor Islands, where country folks more freely exude the natural, relaxed feeling of good will toward their fellow man.

Not long ago, a 35-member State Commission on Environmental Planning met to find, among other things, a way to pin down and examine the supposed Aloha Spirit. At the conclusion of the session, the group solemnly announced that it assumed that "there is such a thing as an aloha spirit, even though it may be hard to define, and that it is identified with empathy, tolerance, graciousness, friendliness, understanding and giving."

The same report, however, went on to issue a warning: "The aloha spirit is fragile and can be shattered by population pressures and a highly competitive society." The commission concluded, too, that the Aloha Spirit partly springs from Hawaii's natural environment as well as from the heritage of traditional Hawaiian lifestyles: "If we cannot prove that our Island geography, a benign climate, and beautiful vistas create this spirit, we nevertheless are sure that the people who live here would act very differently in a different environment."

Sociologist Harry Ball once speculated aloud that the roots of the Aloha Spirit were in the *hanai* or the "extended family" system of ancient Hawaii: "It was a totally open society. People were very open in their feelings, free of themselves, and generous," Ball said. "This openness, which I think the aloha spirit is all about, was really the character of Hawaiian society."

Others have noted that it was strictly *kapu* for the old Hawaiians to *helu*—to count what they did for other people in a "tit for tat" or mutual backscratching sort of way. Favors were just done, that's all, with nothing expected in return. But as more and more members of other groups entered Hawaiian life, this began in greater or lesser degree to break down.

Andrew W. Lind, senior professor emeritus of sociology from the University of Hawaii, recently wrote admiringly, though sadly, of the Aloha Spirit: "It is this universal facility of entering imaginatively and sympathetically into the experience of others, unmindful of differences of skin color, age, sex, or social position—we may call it aloha—which, if anything, 'makes the whole world kin.' Thus, however defined, aloha has a moral and emotional quality and, like love, so frequently equated with it, is fragile in nature and can easily be turned into apathy or even hatred if neglected or mistreated by those to whom it is directed."

In the book *The Frontier States* (the Time-Life Library of America), author Richard Austin Smith poetically follows a similar theme:

> The aloha spirit permeates the 50th state like a benign contagion. It can be heard in the timbre of laughter and felt in the simple friendliness of a business contact. Even a short exposure to such good will has a way of turning up the corners of mouths that hostility had clamped in a thin line. . . .

It would be a mistake to assume that all Hawaiians are responsive to the aloha spirit—they are not, human nature being what it is. Nor do those affected respond in equal measure. But there can be no doubt that what might be called a mainstream of the aloha spirit flows through Hawaiian life continuously, if variably.

The result is a slow but steady tempering of self-interest, aggression, acquisitiveness, ambition. How else can it be explained that the Hawaiians are not at one another's throats like so many groups elsewhere?

Bob Krauss, the perceptive columnist for the Honolulu *Advertiser*, has taken up President Kennedy's theme, declaring aloha to have import far beyond the shores of Hawaii and defining its spirit as a potential gift not only for the nation, but the world. Wrote Krauss: "Aloha, as a weapon of survival, may be the greatest contribution our small, island state has to offer in the future of a tiny, crowded earth island as it whirls alone in space."

5

Oahu,
the Capital Island

1. Around the Island—Gateway to the Fun

To millions upon millions who have coursed through the Pacific over two centuries, the island of Oahu simply *is* Hawaii. Although it was of minor importance in early history, this medium-sized landfall has, for the past 125 years, overwhelmingly dominated politically, economically, and culturally all the other territory in the Hawaiian chain.

Unlike the Outer Islands, Oahu does not deign to call itself also by some identifying name or phrase. Nevertheless it is the "Capital Island" because Honolulu, once the nexus of the Hawaiian nation and now a modern highrise city and seat of the state government, is firmly established here.

The word *oahu* has been translated as "the gathering place," certainly an accurate description in the present day since more than 775,000 people work and play within its 608 square miles. That number, in fact, is over three-quarters of the population of the entire state.

In at least one way, Honolulu and Oahu really are synonymous. The governmental body called the City and County of Honolulu encompasses the entire island, even though several smaller settlements also dot the islandscape.

The metropolitan area itself stretches several miles on the map to the left and right of Honolulu harbor. It is one of the world's long and narrow cities, hemmed in between sea and mountains along a thin line. This two-sided squeeze causes considerable concern among job commuters and land developers.

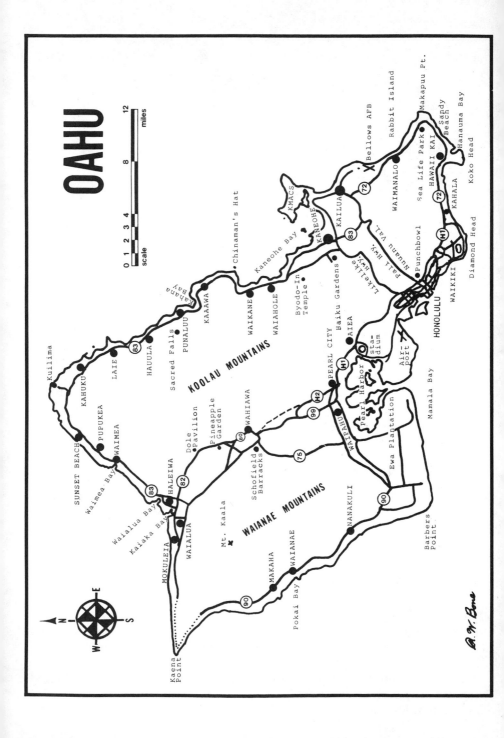

The mountains which channel the physical growth of Honolulu are called the Koolaus (vaguely, "*ko*-oh-louse"), and the range runs for some 30 miles from the southeast to the northwest. They look rugged, but they're pikers by Rockies standards, the tallest peak reaching up only about 3,150 feet.

Honolulu is in the lee of the Koolaus, and there are two superhighways over these heights to take you to the area called the "windward side," dominated by the towns of Kailua and Kaneohe. A third highway has long been planned, but it has become a controversial project in this environment-conscious age, so it remains blocked—for a time or forever.

A second set of mountains, up to 1,000 feet higher but only half the length of the paralleling Koolau range, dominates the western portion of Oahu. Called the Waianaes (vaguely, "*wine*-eyes"), they are largely controlled by military installations. The only paved pass over the Waianae Mountains is not open to the public. The Armed Forces occupy fully 25 percent of the acreage on Oahu, and most of that is perpetually off limits to civilian traffic.

The gently sloping area between the Waianaes and the Koolaus traditionally has served as a wide agricultural belt, mostly composed of sugar and pineapple plantations. These green areas are still there, although there are examples of creeping urbanization now cutting into the fields.

The shape of Oahu is so irregular, and its routes of commerce so winding, that standard compass directions are seldom used. Instead, today's population has maintained the ancient Hawaiian system of direction finding. There is *mauka* for inland or toward the mountains, and *makai* for toward the sea. Otherwise, the directions are indicated by naming known landmarks that lie farther along the same general path. In Honolulu, for instance, you not only travel *mauka* or *makai*, but you can also go *ewa* ("*eh*-vah"—toward Ewa Plantation—generally west or northwest) or "diamondhead" (toward Diamond Head crater—east and/ or south).

Oahu has been the scene of not one but two particularly violent and tragic military conflicts. The Battle of Pearl Harbor, of course, exploded the United States into World War II at 7:55 A.M., Sunday, December 7, 1941. You may visit the site of this attack and stand on the floating memorial over the rusty body of the battleship USS *Arizona*.

But a lesser known engagement which took place here nearly a century and a half earlier also captures the imagination of all who step up to its climactic location for the first time. This was the Battle of Nuuanu, in which King Kamehameha I took on the forces of Oahu and drove them up the sloping and narrowing Nuuanu Valley behind Honolulu until the

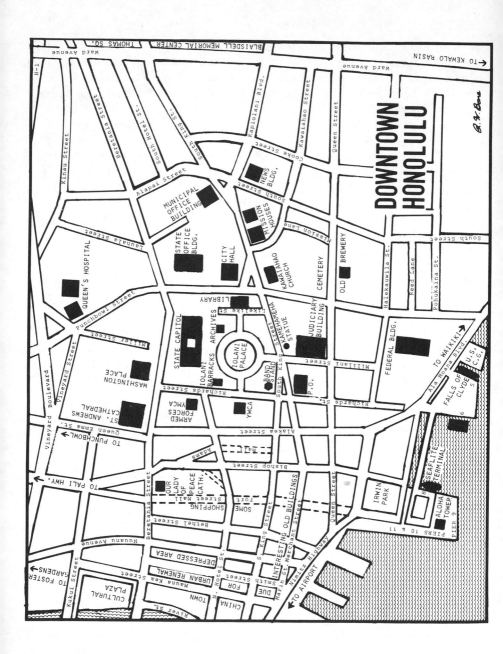

defending army reached the dramatic and gale-swept cliff known as the Nuuanu Pali.

According to surviving accounts of the 1795 battle, hundreds of the Oahu soldiers were driven over the sheer *pali* to plunge nearly 1,000 feet to their deaths. This was the end of the seventh and most decisive battle by which Kamehameha established his dynasty over the island chain. The spot, which provides one of the most beautiful views in the state, is made doubly dramatic by the memory of the bloody event which took place there.

In the minds of most visitors, the city of Honolulu is divided into two distinct areas. First, there is "downtown," a formerly rather seedy but now largely revitalized city center. Downtown also boasts the dramatic and modern state capitol, as well as the Victorian and quaint Iolani Palace, the former royal residence of the last monarchs of Hawaii. The second area is Waikiki, the vacation suburb just 3 miles from downtown. Here, most of the hotels vie for position on or near the gently curving and world-famous beach, backgrounded by the profile of Diamond Head, an extinct volcano.

Today, Waikiki is a seven-tenth square mile peninsula, bounded by the gentle surf on one side and the Ala Wai Canal on two other sides. Between the sand and the artificial waterway is a curious mixture of hotels, shops, open spaces, trees, snack bars, souvenir stands, and bikinis. A hodge-podge of architectural styles has sprung up in Waikiki, and some have justly criticized its lack of central planning.

Don't let anybody tell you, however, that Waikiki is simply "another Miami Beach." It is not, and you have only to walk it from one end to the other to verify our impression.

Begin your sandy stroll at the Hilton Hawaiian Village or Fort DeRussy and head "diamondhead" along the water at about sunset in order to keep the rays from your eyes. For the next mile or two, while the sky changes color and darkens, you will take in the smell of the sea, the sounds of Hawaiian music and laughter from the hotels, and the sight of millions of pinpoints of light which come alive in the hills beyond and the towers above, many of them reflected in the friendly moving waters lapping at your feet.

There's nothing quite like it in this world.

2. Honolulu International Airport

Honolulu International Airport is modern and well marked, but perpetually under construction. It's also strictly elbow-to-elbow during the peak periods of 7 to 11 A.M. and 5 to 9 P.M.

One of the busiest airports in the nation, Honolulu International is almost a small town in itself, with nearly 8,000 persons making a living

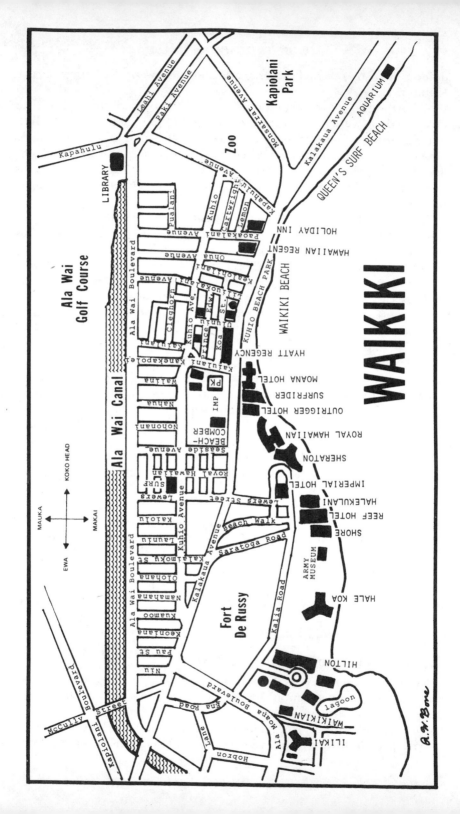

there. Besides the usual airline accouterments, you'll find a bank, post office, restaurants, bar, barber, several kinds of stores, a foreign money exchange, and a duty-free shop for foreign departures.

There is no hotel on the campus (although two are nearby). In the main terminal building there is a unique facility called the Shower Tree, where at nominal fees you can shower, shave, and even nap between flights.

If you have a problem, look for the office of VIVA, the local travelers' aid organization.

And be aware that like many airports on the Mainland, Honolulu International is occasionally chosen as a begging ground by members of the Hare Krishna. They may or may not be in costume.

The principal airport structure, more formally known as the John Rodgers Terminal Building, has two main floors. The ground level is set up for arriving passengers (with baggage claim areas, taxis, rental car booths, etc.). The second level is generally for departing passengers (luggage check-in, ticket counters, and waiting lobbies).

There is also a third, topmost story acting mainly as a right-of-way for the Wiki-Wiki articulated buses that shuttle to and from distant gates carrying those who don't want to walk.

Airlines that fly to and from foreign countries are generally assigned to gates at the western wing, better known as the **Ewa Concourse** (pronounced "*eh*-vah")—Gates 26–31. Other jumbos, on Mainland flights, may dock there, but more likely they will park at the eastern wing, called the **Diamond Head Concourse**—Gates 6–11. If your gate is near the end of this wing, you may choose to ride between the plane and the terminal on a free Wiki-Wiki bus.

The Y-shaped **Central Concourse**—Gates 12–25—also serves some Mainland flights with facilities designed especially for DC-10s. However, some of the interisland carriers, notably **Mid Pacific Airlines** (Tel. 836-3313), are also assigned to these Central Concourse positions. (Mid Pacific is *not* in the "Inter-Island Terminal." More on this in a moment.) If you have some time on your hands, wander outdoors through the yoke of the "Y" to see the three charming little gardens—one Hawaiian, one Chinese, and one Japanese. Flocks of ducks and geese swim between them, oblivious to the scream of nearby jet engines. They must be either the most tolerant or the most hard-of-hearing birds in the Pacific.

If you are being met at the airport from a Mainland flight, your friends may decide not to trudge out to the arrival gate itself but instead to find you in the ground-floor **baggage claim area** whose number is listed on the "Arrivals" TV monitor for your flight. There are three rooms: One for Areas 7–11, another for 12–14, and the third for 15–17.

But if you are landing on an *international* flight, everyone will have to look for you outside the **International Arrivals Center**, the sanctum sanctorum where mysterious Customs and Immigration rites are performed, and where outsiders are not allowed to enter.

Be forewarned that there are *two* doors from International Arrivals. They are about fifty giant steps apart, and on crowded days they are not even quite in sight of one another. When both these doors are in use, your loved ones may be performing mad dashes between them, hoping to catch you at the right exit. (The TV monitors there are confusing and not helpful.) For whatever it's worth, most individual (non-group) passengers emerge through the door on the left (diamond-head) side.

In two parts of a separate structure at the western extreme of the main terminal complex is the traditional **Inter-Island Terminal**. Closest, at Gates 46–51, you'll find most jets operated by **Aloha Airlines** (Tel. 836-1111). And farther along, Gates 52–59 are the assigned parking areas for most jets and turboprops of **Hawaiian Airlines** (Tel. 537-5100). (See Chapter 2 for descriptions of their services and equipment.) Shuttle buses run between the Main Terminal (catch them outside in front of the second level) and the Inter-Island Terminal. The fare is 50 cents.

Traffic is heavy in the Inter-Island terminal in the early morning until 9 A.M. and from 3 to 5 in the afternoon, perhaps largely due to the number of business persons traveling between the islands.

The crush has been getting steadily worse. The airlines are carrying greater loads, but expansion plans for the Inter-Island Terminal may be postponed or cancelled, since both Aloha and Hawaiian have asked to be relocated in the main terminal near their competitor, Mid Pacific. The two have been granted temporary ticket check-in counters there, and this can save a little time and confusion for interline passengers who have already checked their luggage through to a Neighbor Island destination.

Aloha and Hawaiian have inaugurated a new free connecting bus system that carries transferring passengers from Mainland flights directly to the Aloha and Hawaiian departure gates. The route, already inside the airport operations area, thus bypasses further security checks. And besides that, some Aloha and Hawaiian flights are now leaving from the Y Concourse, a new move guaranteed to confuse and delay a lot of passengers who are understandably accustomed to always boarding their interisland flights at the Inter-Island terminal. (Perhaps they will come to their senses by the time you read these words and that half-measure system will be dropped.)

Another building, a temporary structure, has been put up at the eastern end of the complex—about 500 yards from the main terminal—

for the small, commuter airlines. At the moment, these include **Royal Hawaiian Air Service** (Tel. 836-2200), which is older and better known, and **Princeville Airways** (Tel. 836-3505), which is generally less expensive.

A third commuter line is in the low-rent district on the other side of the runways. This is **Air Molokai** (Tel. 536-6611), which offers free parking at its private headquarters at 203 Lagoon Drive.

For a description of all these interisland airlines—exactly who they are and where they go—please see Chapter 2.

Back at the main terminal, on the opposite side from the aircraft, you'll find the large parking lot and parking building. It is accessible to pedestrians from the first or third floor of the terminal only, the latter reached via elevator to the overhead footbridges. (Parking has been holding at a maximum of $4.50 for a 24-hour day—pretty cheap as airports go.)

Near the parking lot outdoors is a line of flower lei stands where you can buy a lei for $4 that would probably cost $5 or $6 at the flower shop inside the terminal (or $3 in Downtown Honolulu).

On the elevated roadway in front of the second level is the **city bus stop**. For a grand sum of 50 cents, it is the most economical way to go to Downtown or Waikiki in one direction, or Hickam A.F.B. in the other. However, the driver is not supposed to let you on board carrying anything larger than a shopping bag—not even a backpack—and this politically inspired rule supported by the island taxi industry forces us nickel-knucklers to ride something more expensive. (If you think that's mean, we suggest you call the City's Office of Information and Complaint at the number in the back of this chapter and let them know your feelings.) The bus route—No. 8—takes about 45 minutes between the airport and the hotel area.

On the other hand, if you're tired it might be a better idea anyway to climb aboard the **Gray Line Airporter** which waits just outside the baggage claim area on the *ground* level. It will drop you at your Waikiki hotel in about half as much time as the bus and cost about $5 per seat. If there are two or more of you, however, it may be as cheap or cheaper to share a cab, which usually runs about $12 to Waikiki.

3. Transportation—Honolulu and All of Oahu

Not counting sightseeing buses, cruise boats, and the like, there are several ways to make your way around the Capital Island. (All those other things we cover under Section 7, "Guided Tours and Cruises," farther along in this chapter.)

Taxicabs. You'll find most cabbies polite and friendly, the cars new and sometimes air-conditioned, and the fares—set by law—fair. Current rates are $1.40 at the drop of the flag, plus 20 cents for each ⅙ mile thereafter. This means you will pay about $12 for the approximately 9-mile trip from Waikiki to the airport, or about $5 to downtown. Drivers are allowed to charge 25 cents per suitcase.

There are zillions of taxi companies, but three large ones stand out with 24-hour service, radio-dispatched cars, and island-wide service. They are **Charley's** (Tel. 531-1333), which operates a gigantic fleet of company-owned cabs, although with drivers of varying experience, **SIDA of Hawaii, Inc.** (Tel. 836-0011), a cooperative of individually owned hacks whose name comes from State Independent Drivers Association, and the **Aloha State Cab, Inc.** (Tel. 847-3566), a third biggie serving the entire island.

Limousine Service. A VIP service, complete with chauffeured Rolls Royces and Bentlys, made its Honolulu debut in 1978. The **Silver Cloud Limousine Service** (Tel. 941-2901) hires out its shiny carriages with liveried drivers for about $50 an hour. Reserve from P.O. Box 15773, Honolulu, Hi. 96815. We have had no personal experience with the firm, but it does sound elegant!

Buses—City and Others. The City and County of Honolulu is justly proud of its bus operation. It is known almost affectionately by the two pushed-together words painted on the sides of the white-yellow-orange-brown striped vehicles, **TheBus** (Tel. 531-1611 up to 10 P.M. for schedule information). Every ride now costs 50 cents, and you can travel for hours and hours at that price, virtually circling the island, if you want, and still qualify for one free transfer to another line, if you ask for one when boarding. Students (grades 1–12) pay only 25 cents, and tykes under 6 travel free. *Exact change is required, in coin only.* Senior citizens (65 or over) may apply for a special pass allowing them to ride free everywhere. But it does take two to three weeks for the pass to come through—an intentional and politically inspired delay.

Unfortunately the new, colorful bus stop signs were apparently designed by people who don't catch buses. They are marked only on the front side—more useful in telling the drivers where to stop than the passengers where to wait. (Thus it is difficult to walk against the traffic flow while searching for a bus stop.)

Bus headquarters, where you apply in person for your senior citizens' pass, is at 530 South King Street near downtown Honolulu (open until 4 P.M. weekdays).

If you are headquartered in Waikiki, your important bus routes will be Numbers 2, 4, 5, and 8. You can always get home on those. Buses run anywhere from five minutes to one hour apart, depending on the route and time of day. Throughout this chapter, we often give bus routes applying to popular Oahu destinations. Unfortunately there is no official route map, although some privately published ones are sold in drug-stores and other places.

You will see other buses (besides tour buses) occasionally making their way around town. Sometimes these are free buses which take you to commercial establishments like garment factories, boat trips, tours, etc. Another valuable bus is the commercial **Arizona Memorial Shuttle Bus** (Tel. 947-5015), which costs $3 per person one way, $5 round trip. It may save a lot of hassle on the Pearl Harbor trip—*if* it shows up. (The last time we called for one, it never arrived!)

Rental Cars. If there is a more aggressive and competitive pursuit in Hawaii than the U-Drive game, we don't know what it is. You will find it hard to believe the number of auto-renting companies which seek your patronage.

During slack periods, rates will drop to amazingly low levels, and you may be stopped in the street by people who want to put you in a car with a special rate "today only." It could cut to half the rates prevailing a week ago. Yet there are times—like in August, late December, or February—when it seems you cannot find a car of any kind. In heavy periods, much of the hoop-la about special deals seems to evaporate. Due to the wildly fluctuating situation, few firms continue to issue any literature describing the types of vehicles they offer at what prices.

The Hawaii State Office of Consumer Protection has received complaints about every rental car agency in town, from the largest to the smallest. Your only real protection is to be as *akamai* as you can about how they operate. Most complaints, incidentally, center on extra charges the customer said were not mentioned or not clear at the time of rental. Here are some things you should consider before you rent a car:

• **Mileage rates and flat rates.** An example of mileage rates is the deal that runs $20 a day and 20 cents a mile. Flat rates, with unlimited mileage, might be $25. In this example, if you average more than 25 miles a day, you'll save money on flat rates ($25 \times \$0.20 = \$5 + \$20 = \$25$). For either, you buy your own gas.

• **Weekend and weekly rates.** These are three-day and seven-day specials which may save you more than 10 percent off the daily flat rates. (Weekend rates, however, are among the first bargains to disappear during peak periods.)

• **Discount specials.** On a "fly-drive" deal, you'll save between 15 percent and 20 percent off some rates if you fly a certain airline, either to the state or between the Islands. These may be limited to the number of discount days according to the number of adult tickets of adult drivers in your party. After that, the rates may jump back up again. Also, the advertised special may be for one "ten-hour day" or something similar. Before going out of your way to make a fly-drive arrangement, you should ask plenty of questions—like what will they do if they are out of the particular type car the deal applies to. Will they give you another at the same price?

● **Mileage minimum.** This may occur in a company that advertises a very cheap daily rate. If, for example, the rent is $1 a day plus 24 cents a mile on a 100-mile-a-day *minimum*, that car is going to cost you at least $25 for any day, even if you only use it for occasional trips to the grocery store. Look these over carefully.

● **Age minimums and maximums.** Several companies won't rent cars to persons under 25 or over 70, and this is certainly a debatable practice. (However, some companies will not rent to military personnel or will do so only with outrageously high deposits, and some will not rent to Hawaii residents! We have attempted to eliminate these latter two types of companies from our list below, because we believe the feelings behind such discriminatory practices also lead to other elements of customer dissatisfaction.)

● **"Insurance."** Auto-renting agencies are not really licensed to sell genuine insurance. They have a sort of self-insurance, and some companies now charge $5 extra a day for what they call "damage waivers." If you are a licensed driver who already owns a car, you are probably already insured to drive a rental car with the same coverage you have on your own car. (You should check this with your insurance man before leaving home to be sure.)

It is a waste of money for you to pay extra for "full damage coverage" *if* your regular policy already covers that. Of course if you don't already have auto insurance—or not enough—you may want to play it extra safe with the additional coverage.

● **Deposits.** Deposits, of course, are meant to discourage folks from running away *with* a car or from running away *from* the car without paying for the rental, so don't be surprised if the company asks $50 or so. The only way to avoid paying a deposit is to carry a major credit card. (However, some rental agencies no longer accept Diners Club.) By the way, if you keep the car longer than you planned, give the company a call or you may find it missing—repossessed by an agency who believes you stole it or skipped town.

● **Drop-off charges.** There are more of these around than you might think, even with the big companies. For instance, if you rent a car in Waikiki but leave it at the airport, even at the agency's own facilities, they may charge you from $5 or more for that convenience.

Other differences in the rate you pay will depend on the type of car you want to rent. In generally descending order, they are the following:

● **American sedan.** This is the top dollar car, and you probably won't get one for a flat rate of less than $35 anywhere. If you do, and you want one, grab it.

• **American compact.** When you can find it, you might save $5 or $6 below the flat rate for the above sedans.

• **Foreign compact.** The real competition is in this class. You could pay $10 below the daily flats for an American sedan, and even a dollar or two less than American compacts.

• **Automatic and standard shift.** Where standard shift is available, it could save you another dollar or so per day off automatic drive. Of course you also get better gas mileage.

As in other parts of the U.S., car rental rates vary widely and wildly in Hawaii, depending on the year, the season, the weather, and perhaps the heartburn of the manager and the phases of the moon. Here is a run-down on a selection of *some* car rental agencies in Honolulu. (Phone numbers listed here are local. You can use them while in Honolulu to reserve a car on Oahu or at Neighbor Island branches. If you're calling from the Mainland, be sure to see the WATS toll-free numbers listed in the back of this book.)

Until recently, the expensive rental companies were the four who had concession booths at the airport. Three of those are still there: **Hertz Rent A Car** (Tel. 836-2511), **Avis Rent A Car** (Tel. 836-5511), and **Budget Rent-A-Car** (Tel. 922-3600). The fourth—and somewhat cheaper—airport agency is **Dollar Rent A Car** (Tel. 922-6415). Dollar also offers "Celebrity Tape Tours," professionally produced recorded narrations with music for a rental fee of $5.95 per tour. (We've tried them; they're a little hokey, but fun.)

Other outfits will come over to pick you up at the terminal when you phone them. Now this includes the other member of the original big four, **National Car Rental Systems** (Tel. 922-6461).

One of our personal favorites has always been **Tropical Rent-A-Car Systems** (Tel. 836-1041). Headquartered near the airport (550 Paiea St.), Tropical can be over to the terminal in a jiffy. We've been recommending Tropical since it was a two-cylinder operation a decade ago, and now it's the largest car-rental operation in the state and has even expanded to the West Coast. There can be discouragingly large crowds standing around the offices, but that annoyance is ameliorated somewhat by the gracious Hawaiian *tutus* (grandmas) there whose only job is to be friendly to the customers. (If for some reason you don't get what you want, ask for Gene Hirst, the president.) In any case, at minimum flat rates of perhaps $22 this year, Tropical is probably worth waiting for.

We also like two other local choices for low prices. **Holiday Rent-A-Car Hawaii** (Tel. 836-1974) is now shepherded by Don Hillis, the first

father of the above-named Tropical. Coincidentally it is parked where
Tropical used to be at 2881 Ualena St., near the airport, and they'll also
pick you up on demand. Holiday has compacts, standards, vans, and
convertibles—plus a VIP lounge and *tutus*, too. On the minus side, it has
been experimenting with a bothersome and rather tacky gas tank policy.
The other bargain (sometimes) is the venerable **Robert's Hawaii Rent-
A-Car System** (Tel. 947-3939), an efficient *kamaaina* company that will
even rent to *married* 18-year-olds.

Other low-priced agencies include **South Seas Rent-A-Car** (Tel. 941-
0570) and **United Car Rental Systems** (Tel. 922-4605), either of which
might put you in a car for $15 or less during the off-peak seasons—*if*
they're still around when you get there (no guarantees by us).

A few last words on car rentals:

A disturbing trend, now, even among the top-dollar outfits, is to provide less service at the various island airports. That is, even though you
check out a car at an airport counter, some companies are beginning to
bus you to a separate location to pick up the car and perhaps to complete
the paper work. Sometimes you may be able to rent a car and pick it up
from the airport, but you must return it to another location, from which
you will be bused back to the terminal—when they're ready to take you,
that is.

Such busing operations traditionally have been the way for the bargain outfits to provide good service to those who choose them, and that's
fair enough. But we join those who protest that it is inconvenient to business people and others who are paying top dollar for their buggies and
need the most convenient arrangements. We will try to clear up this picture in the year ahead. Meanwhile, if this concerns you, it would be a
good idea to check the policy out in advance with any car company
you're considering renting from on any island.

Before driving away in a rented car, always make sure it is in good
condition. Try the brakes and hand brake, the horn, the lights, the turn
signals, the windshield wipers, the trunk and door locks, etc. Look for
any body damage, and point it out to the agency, asking them to write it
down so that you won't be charged for it. Check the tire tread, and make
sure a jack and a spare tire are in the trunk. Try to drive the car for
awhile right after you take it; if you notice anything wrong, return it
immediately.

Remember, too, that if you rent a jeep, a beach buggy, or similar open
car, there is usually no place to lock your things up if you want to take a
hike away from the vehicle. And one of those fringe-topped "Fun Buggies"—usually a VW "Thing"—might be fun in the sun, but a real drag
in a serious downpour. Don't assume these Things and other things
are genuine "off-road" vehicles, either, unless the agency tells you they

are. And you'll probably need a four-wheel-drive vehicle (Jeep, Land Rover, or Land Cruiser) if you're planning on bouncing along the beach track around Kaena Point. Frankly, we'd skip it. Going camping? We wouldn't—not on Oahu, anyway. If you are, though, don't tell your U-drive. They might not let you have the car.

Hawaii on two wheels? We know of just one motorcycle outfit that has been in business for some time. This is **Aloha Motorcycle U-Drive** (Tel. 942-9696), recently merged with Aloha Funway Rentals, at 1984 Kalakaua Ave., across from Fort DeRussy. Rates run from $27 to $52 daily, depending on the displacement of your "hog" or "chopper."

Then there are the little motorized bicycles which may be rented from the above or from other, less permanent outfits. Look, perhaps, for **Sunshine Moped Rentals** (Tel. 923-6083) at 351 Saratoga Rd. Rates may still be $17 for an eight-hour day or else $5 an hour. Top speed on these putter-power jobbies is only about 25 m.p.h.

Frankly, if there is more than one of you, these two-wheeled rentals are very problematical as a bargain, compared with car rental rates. Of course if you're a bike addict, that's something else again, and you might consider flying your own over with you.

Driving on Oahu. If you drive in your home state, you should not hesitate to get behind a wheel while visiting Oahu, or on all the Islands of Hawaii, for that matter. Laws do not vary from Mainland ordinances, any more than they do among most other states back home. Traffic is no worse than a lot of places—perhaps better than most—and other drivers are usually polite. All in all, we think driving your own route and at your own pace is the best way to experience Hawaii.

However, there are a few local quirks of the open road that should be remembered:

• One annoying traffic characteristic results from the very politeness of the drivers, and it concerns an "after you" philosophy toward left turns. An island driver whose car faces yours at an intersection will often wait and wave you across in front of him, if he believes you would have to wait a long time to make your left. He means well, of course, but he, like you, cannot see any other car which might be coming up fast in the right lane beside him. We often refuse to make these dangerous turns.

Another aspect of the same practice is the opposite situation, where an island driver will assume you will do him the same courtesy—giving up your right-of-way to allow him to turn across in front. (He'll also wait until the last second to signal, incidentally.) Try to remember that it's a matter of custom, be careful and patient, and you'll be all right.

• Hawaii residents have had divided highways for much less time than on the Mainland. Therefore, there is not a well-developed tradition to stay in the right lane except when passing.

● Avoid crossing a solid white line, and never cross a double white line. This law is often mercilessly enforced in Hawaii.

● On Oahu, you may generally turn right, from the right lane, on a red light (after a safety stop), unless you see a sign specifically prohibiting it at the intersection. Similarly, you may make a left turn, from the left lane of a one-way street onto another one-way street, also on a red light (after stopping), unless prohibited.

● Horn-honking is a general no-no. It's usually not that it's specifically prohibited. It just isn't done in Hawaii, except in emergencies and the most obvious situations, and some people take considerable offense at the sound of a horn.

● Watch your signs carefully—including arrows on the pavement— for there are a lot of exotic traffic patterns. Kalakaua Avenue in Waikiki, for instance, is one-way *except for buses and bicycles* which are allowed to go in the opposite direction for a few blocks in a special lane!

● Zoris and similar one-thonged Japanese slippers are great and popular footwear in Hawaii. However, don't drive while wearing them; they have a way of catching your control pedals in just the wrong way. We would rather drive barefoot—much safer.

● Try to avoid rush hours (7–9 A.M. and 4–6 P.M.), especially on main arteries like the H-1 Freeway or the Pali Highway.

● About the best overall free highway map of Oahu is the Shell map, but Union 76 has a better street index. For a couple of bucks, though, there's an excellent all-around map called "Travel Map, Island of Oahu" sold at the bookstores in Hawaii. If you want to pick up some maps before leaving for the Islands, check on those sold mail order by the Forsyth Travel Library, P.O. Box 2975, Shawnee Mission, Kansas 66201.

● Speed limits are generally lower than on the Mainland, a factor which cuts down the auto accident rate. If you're leisurely sightseeing, though, pull over now and then to allow other traffic to pass.

● Parking meters on the streets are inoperative Sundays and holidays, but municipal parking lot meters are in effect at all times. They range from 25 to 40 cents an hour.

● Since you'll pay for your own fuel in a rental car, look for the cheapest prices. (Gasoline runs about 10 cents a gallon more than on the Mainland.) For example, you'll find discount gas at **Holiday Mart,** corner of Makaloa and Poni streets, a block off Kalakaua, and at **Lex Brodie's Tire Co.,** 701 Queen St. About the only gasoline credit cards accepted in Hawaii are Union 76, Standard, and Shell. Many stations welcome Visa and MasterCard, though.

● Look out for pedestrians. They have the right of way, especially on the specially marked crosswalks. (Note to pedestrians: Don't count on it!)

Oahu Air Routes and Charter Aircraft. There is only one more-or-less regular air trip within Oahu. This is the golfers' helicopter trip from Ala Wai Helicopter Pad (near the Ilikai Hotel) to the course at the Makaha Inn. (Check with **Makaha Golf Tours** at 696-9488.)

According to the travel agents' magazine *Discover Hawaii*, there are three large air-charter firms on Oahu: **Associated Aviation Activities** (Tel. 836-3106), 218 Lagoon Drive; **Hawaii Air Academy** (Tel. 836-2237), 3031 Aolele St.; **Aviation Centre Hawaii** (Tel. 836-0006), Attn: Bob Wong, 104-D Lagoon Drive—all zipped at Honolulu 96819. We have had no personal experience with any of them.

Pedicab service. Shades of Saigon! Someone who remembered the popularity of two-passenger pedal vehicles in the Orient has organized a pedicab, or rickshaw, service in Waikiki. These companies have changed hands a few times, but the service will probably be in operation under some name or other. Last we looked, the fare was $3 for a point-to-point connection (for one or two people) in Waikiki or about $20 to tour the peninsula for one hour.

Hitchhiking. State law prohibits hitchhiking, unless the counties specifically permit it. On Oahu, the issue of hitchhiking has been fought back and forth for several years. As of *this writing*, and subject to change and re-change by sudden vote of the City Council, hitchhiking is permitted on Oahu from bus stops only. If you are on the roll of the Society of the Upturned Thumb, you'll have to check with your fellow members for the latest on this soon after arrival.

4. The Hotel Scene—Waikiki Havens to Rural Resorts

Unless you come to Hawaii during peak seasons like February or August, the chances are good that you will not have any trouble with hotel rooms. Hotelkeeping is an honored and highly competitive profession here—especially in Honolulu, where most vacationers want to stay. And now, as more and more visitors are on repeat trips, these establishments will usually knock themselves out to be helpful to their guests.

Unless you come in slack months, like May or October, your arrangements should be hammered down and sealed up as far in advance as possible. Many hotels will not confirm a reservation without at least one night's deposit, and this is as good a guarantee for you as it is for them. If your plane is delayed or if something else goes awry, the place should not feel it must give your room to someone else, since it has actually been paid for that night, anyway.

In the past, there have been some highly publicized overbooking scandals in Honolulu, usually in February and sometimes January. Most

of these tearful incidents concerned large tour groups—few if any independent travelers with reservations were affected—and the groups
squawked loudly and with justification when they were shunted to airport hotels and rural rooms far from the ocean and the action in Waikiki. In some cases, they were even sent to the Neighbor Islands.

There are several tiresome technical reasons for this unhappy hap-
penstance, having to do mainly with block booking practices by tour
wholesalers before they even sign up their tourists. But any traveler
should realize that nearly all hotels—at least the large ones—do over-
book, even if they may prefer to call it "compensation for shrinkage."

Hotels will confirm up to 120 percent of their rooms, knowing that
generally 30 percent of their customers just won't show up. Therefore,
they end up most of the time 90 percent full. The rub comes, of course,
when more than a third of the expected no-shows do indeed arrive. The
hotel is then admittedly overbooked, and no more playing with words.
Although that happens to only a tiny part of Hawaii's 4 million annual
visitors, emotions run high and the fuss can reverberate loud and long.

If you *are* one of the fraction of one percent who arrive with a confirmed reservation in hand, and your hotel will not give you your room,
our advice is not to budge. Do not allow the hotel merely to give you
your deposit back. Do not remain satisfied to speak to the desk clerk.
Deal only with the manager or the assistant manager on duty, and demand firmly and politely that he find you a room, either in his hotel or a
comparable one in some other hotel. If he will not, you point out, you
will immediately describe the situation by telephone to (a) the two Honolulu newspapers, (b) the State Office of Consumer Protection, (c) the Visitor Satisfaction Committee of the Hawaii Visitors Bureau, (d) the Better
Business Bureau of Hawaii, (e) the Chamber of Commerce of Hawaii, (f)
the Hawaii Hotel Association, (g) the mayor's office, and (h) the governor's office.

A traveler and his family who stand their ground with a definite idea
of the fairness and justness of their request have a good chance of ending up with a room after all—perhaps even in the presidential suite (at
a lower price), if no other accommodation is genuinely vacant in the
house.

Fully 99 and 44/100ths percent of the visitors to Hawaii this year will
not have booking difficulties with their hotel. Most Hawaii hotels are efficient and are staffed by friendly people who are constantly aware of the
value of the Aloha Spirit.

Choosing a Hotel. Generally, the greatest hotel problem visitors face
is simply picking one out in the first place. If you are equipped with advertisements or tourist brochures for some hotels that's fine, but look

over the literature carefully. Naturally, any business wants to put its best and most attractive foot forward in a slick, full-color production.

Pamphleteers are on to lots of tricks. Like placing their cameras down low on Waikiki Beach so that a hotel that is actually far across the street looks as if it were right on the sand. Snaps of some scenes in the brochure may not have been taken on the hotel grounds at all. Other pictures of "typical rooms" may be made in the two or three luxury suites in the house. Frankly, we think the word pictures we have drawn in the following pages are more accurate than many of these fancy publications.

Not counting the suites, most hotels divide their rooms into three categories, usually called "standard," "superior," and "deluxe." There is no legal definition of these terms, however, and some hotels try to avoid "standard" as a pejorative word. Whichever are the cheapest rooms may be considered standard in the traditional sense, and there may be several different price levels above that.

The three terms may or may not have anything to do with the room facilities. Often you find all the units in the hotel are exactly alike except that suites and deluxes are high up and face the ocean, superiors might look up and down the beach from a middle altitude, and standards are often low down and/or face the mountains (fine)—or even the parking lot (not so fine).

The rates for many Hawaii hotel rooms have remained near their levels last year, with only a few making the customary great leap upward. It does look like there will still be higher winter rates. There is no good, honest reason for seasonal room rates in Hawaii. Hotels face pretty much the same level of expenses all year. It's just a question of greed—of being able to get away with it.

Hawaii hotelmen have for years fought a proposed special state tax, a relatively low 4 percent on hotel rooms. The revenues would be used for public works, which would ultimately improve the attractiveness of Hawaii to the visitor. The hotels, however, have successfully argued that even such a modest add-on would begin to send holidaymakers elsewhere—to Mexico or Europe—for their vacations. But without batting an eye, some of these same managers have arbitrarily tacked on a surcharge of 10 to 15 percent for rooms sold from mid-December through March.

If you don't like seasonal rates, we think you should tell the hotels—and then consider patronizing those who don't lay on such a surcharge. Defenders of Hawaii hotel rates say they are still at least a little lower than those in most large cities and resort areas on the Mainland or in many foreign countries. That may be true—but it doesn't make it right.

Dial Hawaii 800. Hawaii is now partway on the toll-free WATS system, and many hotels in the Aloha State may be telephoned directly from the Mainland U.S. and Canada. These "800" numbers are a boon for individual guests or travel agents who want to make instant, accurate reservations.

Our list of the latest 800 series for some Hawaii hotels appears as an appendix in the back of this edition, just in front of the index. (Other numbers listed in the text of this volume are for regular local telephones.)

By the way, once you do have a satisfactory hotel room, remember to be burglary conscious. Valuables should be kept in the hotel safe. When leaving our room for a day of sightseeing or an evening of merrymaking, we generally leave a light on and the radio or TV playing. If you're counting pennies, incidentally, be aware that local phone calls from hotel rooms are sometimes 50 cents each. On the other hand, a few hotels don't charge anything at all. The pay phone down in the lobby costs 15 cents, and calls from private telephones are unlimited within the monthly tariffs.

Another way to save on hotel expenses without sacrificing quality: If you're traveling with others—two or three couples together, for instance—look into the possibility of renting a suite or an apartment. It could be that you'll have a lot more luxurious and commodious living accommodations—sometimes with kitchens—in a one- or two-bedroom suite which charges the same price for up to four or six persons than you would if you took the per-person tabs and applied them to regular double hotel rooms.

Whatever hotel you choose to call home, you will probably visit some of the others described in this book. The major hotels in Honolulu are almost sightseeing attractions themselves. You'll certainly be visiting their restaurants and night clubs, and, of course, some of these are described more thoroughly in Sections 5 and 6 in this chapter.

We have divided Oahu hotels into six main categories, which we think you can use to efficiently pick your own headquarters. In Hawaii, a hotel is usually not "just a place to sleep." You may remain for several days or weeks, and much of the atmosphere of your vacation and many of your memories will be affected by your hotel and its surroundings.

You want a hotel that answers your requests with quick, friendly service. But you may also want one with good swimming facilities, gardens, restaurants, showrooms, group activities, or whatever, and perhaps a place where you are likely to meet other people with similar interests. Hotel ambience is not something that can be precisely defined, but you'll find it an important ingredient in your Hawaiian vacation.

Because most people who come to Honolulu prefer to bed down in Waikiki—and because that's where most of the beds *are*—we lead off our discussion with those hotels, separated into four groups of eight to ten establishments each, and in each set we generally slide from our first choices to our last within the group. The categories we have set up are as follows:

a. Hotels directly on Waikiki Beach;
b. Waikiki hotels very near the beach;
c. Major Waikiki hotels off the beach;
d. Waikiki budget lodgings;
e. Big hideaway resorts;
f. Other Honolulu hotels outside Waikiki.

As this is a volume of subjective judgment, we regularly get some brickbats on the choice of categories as well as on the entries in each classification. Nevertheless, this is the way we see it as the most helpful to you, the visitor.

And, of course, tell 'em we sent you!

HOTELS DIRECTLY ON WAIKIKI BEACH

"On the beach" means with no argument from anyone. By our definition, a hotel is not a beachside hotel if there is any intervening street or other geographic feature, despite such modern devices as the Ilikai's long footbridge or the lagoon beach behind the Waikikian. In all Waikiki, there are only ten choices from which you'll be able to run right out the back door into the ocean.

Of these beachside hostelries our present favorite is the 20-acre complex of conveniences called the **Hilton Hawaiian Village** (Tel. 949-4321). In this mammoth enterprise, now the largest resort in the state, Uncle Conrad has done his name proud, although the Village actually was the dream of the late industrialist Henry J. Kaiser nearly two decades ago. The still-expanding hotel is a self-contained resort yet within the boundaries of high-density Waikiki. Guests may participate as much as they want or don't want in the life of the community at large.

We've visited this campus dozens of times, and here's the way we see it: no wider, cleaner, prettier, or safer part of Waikiki beach than the sand bordering the Village; the only hotel with its own dock and large catamaran; decorative private lagoon (where we don't swim, though); long list of excellent beach facilities; four fresh-water pools; five living towers including the newest, the Tapa Tower (35 stories; over 1,000 rooms) plus the Rainbow, Ocean, Lower Ocean, and Diamond Head towers; private street off Kalia Road leading to confusing conglomeration and activity in the Main Lobby with its three macaws, and thence to the peaceful and lovely lobby with orchid walls in the Rainbow Tower; beautiful grounds with ponds, putting greens, gardens, etc.; many trees and plants labeled for easy identification; free classes in Hawaiiana; a total of 10 restaurants, led by the Rainbow Rib Lanai; several showrooms including the famous Hilton Dome and swinging Garden Bar; fantastic collection of shops, many in the unusual Rainbow Bazaar, featuring Japanese, Chinese, and South Pacific architecture.

Top-price, top-quality rooms this year still in the Rainbow Tower at an even $115 double (nicest panoramas are on the Ewa side, but avoid the top—31st—floor with its noisy air-conditioning compressors and elevator mechanism); Deluxe rooms at $100 (high up) and Superiors at $90 (lower down) mostly in the new Tapa Tower, in the center of the complex, just across from the convention center; Medium category rooms at $80 and Standards at $70 in the Ocean Tower and Diamond Head Tower, with categories depending more on vistas than amenities. Some Standards also in the Lower Ocean Tower, with views of the grounds instead of the ocean; color TV; some with executive refrigerators; none with kitchen facilities; children free in their parents' rooms.

Do not confuse this establishment with the more prestigious Kahala Hilton Hotel in the suburbs (see later); it's not the Kahala, but the Hilton Hawaiian Village is a fine hotel and the leader among Waikiki beach houses. About the only criticisms we might venture are: (1) we think they should discourage swimming in the almost still-water, if otherwise charming, little lagoon, (2) we wish the *luau* garden were on the beach side instead of the street, and (3) it is quite a hoof for some older folks to all the rest of Waikiki. (Reservations from the hotel at 2005 Kalia Rd., Honolulu, Hi. 96815.) A sure bet for the world-famous shoreline and happily recommended to all.

A beach hotel in the center of the action is the twin-winged, thirty-story **Sheraton-Waikiki Hotel** (Tel. 922-4422), which will continue to undergo massive refurbishment and redecoration into late 1984, the first complete renovation of the rooms since the hotel opened in 1971. It's the flagship of a fleet of five Sheraton-operated hostelries in Waikiki. Breezy entranceway, often cheerfully rattling with thousands of windchime Capiz shells; very large circular lobby with green-leaf and flower patterns in floors and furniture; lobby may be redone by the time of your check-in; commodious public areas; spacious space-capsule-shaped pool, site of the Thursday Polynesian Aquacade; smaller, round pool to one side; gorgeous outdoor garden setting for the evening *luau*; sometimes narrow section of sand; a short walk to a wider stretch at the Royal, however; several restaurants including the viewful Hanohano Room (where we've had good luck), reached by the glass-walled outdoor elevator, the Safari Steak House (not our favorite), the very decorative, second-floor Kon Tiki Room, reached by an elevating "grass shack," and the Ocean Terrace (where our own buffet was okay); Oahu Bar showroom; "Infinity," a far, far out discotheque; Sheraton guest charging privileges also in the nearby Royal, Surfrider, Moana, and "P.K." hotels.

Generally roomy rooms, gradually changing from the original greens, blues, and whites to more earthy tones. All have *lanais*, color TVs, etc. (but you pay extra for the closed-circuit movies), and you'd better make special arrangements if you want your room made up early in the day. We would opt for the oceanfront rooms, $130 for two, preferably on the Diamond Head wing. Oceanfront suites up there run from around $200 up. Some high *mauka*-side rooms are considered "partial ocean view" for $110. There are also "high mountain views" for $95 and "low mountain views" for $79. Charges may be up $10 or so beginning December 21, 1984. A third adult charge is $10, but there are no extra add-ons for children in the same room as their parents. (Reservations through any Sheraton on the Mainland or by mail to Sheraton Hotels, 2255 Kalakaua Ave., Honolulu, Hi. 96815.) The Sheraton-Waikiki is a little too architecturally overwhelming for our personal taste; nevertheless, it's a professional operation in a good position. A solid choice on the sand.

Repeaters gush over the **Royal Hawaiian Hotel** (Tel. 923-7311), also known as the "Pink Palace" or the "Pink Lady." Built in 1927 in a stucco Mediterranean style, the hotel is reminiscent of the days when the well-to-do came to Hawaii by ship and then moved into the Royal with their steamer trunks to stay for weeks. Now it's literally under the wing and in the shadow of the next-door Sheraton; both these places and several others around are owned by Japanese industrialist Kenji Osano, but are still ruled wisely and well by a local regency.

High, wide, long, and handsome corridor/lobby; crystal chandeliers downstairs; shiny, black stone floors; lots of places to sit; acres of tall mirrors, an arcade of tasteful shops; famous red-and-gold Monarch showroom; sun-blessed Surf Room on the edge of the strand; Mai Tai Bar nearby; the beach itself very wide and welcoming at this location.

There are vastly varying rooms. All have color TVs and air conditioning, but not all have been brought entirely into the current decade. Our favorites are not the $135 doubles in the architecturally Philistine tower; those might as well be any ho-hum hotel on the beach. Instead, we like the high-ceilinged, wallpapered, old-style ocean view units in the original structure for about $125, even though none have any *lanais*. There are some nice garden view rooms, too, for perhaps $110, but some very small mother-in-law quarters for about $90. (Reserve at the Sheraton-Waikiki's address—2255 Kalakaua Ave., Honolulu, Hi. 96815.) The Royal Hawaiian valiantly maintains an elegant tradition in Waikiki. Incidentally, Osano, the hotel owner, and Bishop Estate, the land owner, are fighting the efforts to place the hotel on the National and Hawaii Registers of Historic Places. It's becoming "obsolete," and there's talk about tearing it down. If that bothers you as much as it does us, we suggest you complain about it whenever and wherever possible.

Surrounded on all sides by the more-or-less flamboyant Sheraton entries, the **Outrigger Waikiki Hotel** (Tel. 923-0711) is the anchor in the local Kelley chain. It turns out to be a very pleasant, if more conventional, beachside hotel—nicer than we realized before our own intensive Waikiki ramble: lower lobby admittedly a hodge-podge, more like a cheap department store; down there also, Perry's Smorgy, a cafeteria bargain, and the nautical but nice Monterey Bay Canners fish restaurant; very large pool a few steps above a good section of beach; Davy Jones Locker bar for peering under the surface; up the escalator to a very large upper lobby; friendly though busy reception folks on our visit; large showroom where the Krush and the Society of Seven have alternated for years; Malolo Kai dining room in one corner, built of bamboo, mainly; good Chuck Machado Luau outdoors once or twice a week.

We closely inspected three sample rooms: No. 701 was a nice, bright, large standard—officially a "city view," but a little drop of the ocean was detectable, too—for about $60 double. No. 1521, a superior, had an excellent view of the sea for around $75. No. 1525, an oceanfront, was terrific with a large *lanai* for about $95. We also saw a small suite (No. 622) which would suit a team of four very well for $115. Many units are similar to these, and there were cheerful, warm-toned furnishings in all. All, of course, had TVs and air-conditioning, and many held refrigerators, coffee pots, etc., but no stoves. (Reservations from the hotel at 2335 Kalakaua Ave., Honolulu, Hi. 96815. Remember that there are four or five other Outriggers in Waikiki, but this is the only beachside model.) The Outrigger may not have developed a strong buoyant personality, but for the right crew, she'll sail very well in her class.

The ancient, Victorian **Moana Hotel** (Tel. 922-3111), matriarch of Waikiki, seemingly hasn't changed much since opening day, March 12, 1901. Not unlike a big, old-fashioned, white-walled summer boardinghouse of another age, the Moana has only partially succeeded in keeping up with the twentieth century, aided in recent times by the efforts of the Sheraton organization.

Excellent beach location; famous Banyan Court and its century-old Robert Louis Stevenson tree, now unattractive by day, due to the set-up for the nighttime show; elegance of the H-shaped building itself detectable behind the junk; Captain's Galley Restaurant (not one of our favorites) in the newer wing (also personally unloved); wide hallways, high ceilings, and double doors in the original structure, creating a romantic Old World atmosphere.

There are widely varying quality rooms, starting at a low double price of about $50 (and you can be sure most un-air-conditioned models will funnel in the sound from the street or the frenetic nightly Polynesian show). We would try hard for the oceanfront rooms at the ends of the wings in the Main Building (perhaps $70). The anachronistic appendage called the Ocean Lanai building was erected in about 1953 as the old, original Surfrider, but does offer the only terraces and more air conditioners. The rooms are not bad ($75 and $95), but they're not the Moana. (Today's Surfrider has now moved to the Ewa side—see next entry.) Some wayfarers with an archeological bent really dig the Moana, but it helps if they groove on a lot of drums, too.

Joined to the Moana by an interior walkway is today's version of the **Surfrider Hotel** (Tel. 922-3111), and the two are often mentioned together as a single establishment (they share the same phone number, too): double-deck lobby similar to the Outrigger, with which it is often confused; upper one marred by its dual purpose as a parking garage; a noisy escalator nearby; low ceilings; ground floor Beachside Cafe, still doubling as a showroom at night; second-level Ship's Tavern restaurant, not our cup of grog; some very poor standard rooms about $70; so-so superiors with some decent views for $90 or so; ocean view deluxes, the same size and shape as others, approaching and exceeding $95.

But why go on? Frankly, we only liked the suites (now $170 to $200). It's a good beach position, but we felt the spiritless Surfrider hangs on a high-priced board for low-wave returns.

Over next to the Army Museum and Fort DeRussy, the 100-unit **Waikiki Shore Apartments** (Tel. 923-3283) remains etched in our memory mainly as the victim of the next-door Reef Hotel's noisy air conditioners. There is almost no lobby, no restaurant, no pool, and virtually no spirit to these premises, in our opinion. Frankly, we'd skip it.

Lying right alongside, the **Reef Hotel** (Tel. 923-3111), formerly the Cinerama Reef, is cheap for the beach, but sure looks it, too: one of the most jumbled, over-commercial, and constantly crowded lobbies in Hawaii; reception desk often staffed by harassed clerks on our visits; several rooms with apparently severe maintenance and housekeeping deficiencies. Some ascetic, viewless doubles run as low as $32, but we never saw what we'd call a decent unit here below about $70. (Try for the $77 rooms.) On the other hand, there's a nice large pool, the beach is good, and there's some free Sunday fun on the sand. At this writing, the Reef has just begun "a complete renovation program." Good. We can't think of any major hotel that needed it more. If you must have a shoreline, mid-Waikiki hotel at a bargain price, this is it. Otherwise, we might spend the night on the *offshore* reef.

For the fortunate few, there is the fairly new, 416-unit Army hotel, the **Hale Koa** (Tel. 955-0555), meaning "House of the Warrior," on the grounds of Fort DeRussy. It has some of the most inexpensive doubles on the strand, ranging between about $30 and $60. This vacation headquarters and satellite facilities are available only to military personnel and their families, and you've got to be able to prove it or you won't even get an ice-cream cone. If you're service-connected, though, scoop it up.

A longtime favorite whose foundations were laid prior to World War I was the venerable **Halekulani Hotel** (Tel. 923-2311 or 526-3541). Now the former cottage-style hotel has been transmogrified into a new stair-stepped high-rise. In fact, it almost seems as if a small city has been constructed on the site at the foot of Lewers Street, with different levels all capped by a stylized version of Hawaii's famous "Dickey roof." The old main building has been spared for use as a couple of restaurants. Also basically unchanged are the gardens and the "House Without a Key," the bar inspired by the first Charlie Chan novel. A new beachside pool is nearby.

The surrounding wings now enclose 456 modern, wood-and-marble guest rooms, all unusually spacious, filled with fancy furniture and phones, and with ample *lanais*. The announced price scale *begins* at an ambitious $145 daily for Gardenview rooms. Oceanviews go for $185, Oceanfronts for $225, and suites start at $285 and then shoot into the stratosphere. The first C-notes will begin to change hands just after our final deadline for this volume, so our comments must be limited.

The Halekulani has always mistranslated itself as the "House Befitting Heaven." The correct meaning is the "House Befitting Royalty." Never mind. The dowager Halekulani, a gracious lady, will be sorely missed. We'll reserve final judgment until next edition, but if the Regent International organization lives up to its advance planning, the new Halekulani might yet be dubbed the Queen of Waikiki.

WAIKIKI HOTELS VERY NEAR THE BEACH

Generally speaking, this category covers hotels that are just across the street from Waikiki Beach, except for the Ilikai and the Waikikian, which fit in here because they are just far enough away so we don't call them beach hotels but not removed enough to be "off the beach" either. The group does not include places that are "just across the street and through another hotel to the beach." These you will find in our "off the beach" listings.

The 39-story, twin-towered **Hyatt Regency Waikiki** (Tel. 922-9292), generally agreed to be Waikiki's most dramatic hotel, is another link in the glittering chain that spans the country from Atlanta to Albany, from San Juan to San Francisco, and now to Hawaii. The block-long, block-wide, 1,260-room Gulliver is directly across the avenue from one of the best and most popular public sections of Waikiki Beach:

Mammoth Diamond Head side porte cochere with acres of teak and bronze; luggage whisked directly above by special elevator; colossal Great Hall, an open, 10-story landscaped atrium, the hallmark of the Hyatts, featuring three waterfalls and occasional band concerts; popular Harry's Bar fronting the water; Trapper's, an elegant jazz club, also at Basin Street level; grand stairway plus escalators to the second-floor lobby; separate tour-group entrance off the back street; lobby level also with buffet supper club called the Hana Hou Room, and the Colony, A Steak House, with British "Indjah" overtones.

Another moving stair to the third-stage promenade deck for the dinner-only Bagwells 2424 gourmet restaurant in the Ewa Tower and the Terrace Grille, a fancy coffee shop in the Diamond Head Tower; tiny outdoor pool there, too, serving better as a lighted fountain at night; footbridges for crossing the Great Hall and admiring the 4,500-pound, 34-foot-high hanging metal sculpture; lots of dangling plants and other greenery; downstairs again to Furusato's, for Japanese dining, or to Spats, an Italian *ristorante* by day and a disco after dark; about 75 different stores on all three levels; no general public areas above the third floor, designed that way for greater guest security.

Since there are two towers in the Hyatt Regency, there are two presidential suites, each at this writing renting for about $800 a day. Eight penthouse suites are perhaps $550, and 68 smaller suites go for around $250. Units on Hyatt's Regency Club floors sell for $150 and $175, depending on position. Most rooms fall into double prices running from $75 a night for "Mountain View" through $90 for "High Mountain View." The "Ocean Views" go for $105 in '84, except for the "Ocean Fronts," which are $120.

Some sleeping units have unusual shapes due to the octagonal architecture. Models we saw were furnished well but not startlingly. Designs are in muted tones of beige, peach, and blue. All have couches, some of which are convertibles, plus the usual color TVs, terraces, and other luxury amenities. But some penny pinching may surprise you—like having only one reading lamp between two beds. There's 7-to-11 room service and unusual features like setting your own wake-up time on the telephone computer system.

Some readers have complained to us about the tortuous route they must take from the street entrance to the elevators. Nevertheless, the Hyatt is a championship establishment and a firm fixture on the Waikiki funscape. (Reservations from the hotel at 2424 Kalakaua Ave., Honolulu, Hi. 96815.) For elegant Hyatt-rise living overlooking Waikiki, it's highly recommended.

One of Honolulu's great establishments, even if it isn't quite in the center of the action, is the widely recognized **Westin Ilikai Hotel** (Tel. 949-3811), often featured in scenes on TV's "Hawaii Five-0." The Ilikai is within striking distance of the Duke Kahanomoku section of Waikiki Beach via a long, private footbridge, and at the same time, it's only a short walk in the other direction to Ala Moana Center. However, the hotel is now netting a new reputation as the tennis center of Honolulu: viewful position alongside Ala Wai Yacht Harbor; three basic structures, including Marina Tower Building for longer term rentals; no grounds or ground floor; most facilities on a sort of main deck above the street and parking garage; programmed fountain with changing patterns and colors at night; free evening entertainment on the mall; a score of shops; four dining rooms including the up-top Champeaux's, reached by outdoor glass elevator, the Pier 7, a rather expensive coffee shop, and the Maiko Japanese restaurant; several cocktail lounges; Annabelle's Nightclub; two swimming pools; extensive convention facilities; seven—count 'em—seven tennis courts in three locations.

Some low-down viewless standards still about $80 for two in the older, L-shaped Yacht Harbor Building; no ocean views below about $100, best units for $120 or so, with kitchens, in the Y-shaped Tower Building; some of these totaling an unusually large 650 square feet; the $150 suites surprisingly without stoves, but those above (up to $275) with full facilities; reportedly good service throughout the house. The Ilikai, owned by Westin Hotels, a subsidiary of United Air Lines' parent company, is fun when not loaded to the wingtips with conventioneers. (Reservations from the Hotel at 1777 Ala Wai, Honolulu, Hi. 96815.) Consistently a high flyer.

Three blocks farther along Kalakaua from the Hyatt Regency is the well-respected **Hawaiian Regent Hotel** (Tel. 922-6611), also across the traffic from the same beach. The Regent has been locally known not only as a good hotel, but as the home of Honolulu's best restaurant. Now, with its newer 33-story Kuhio Tower, the establishment has 1,346 rooms, making it the third largest hotel around (after the previously described Hilton and Sheraton): Excellent physical plant with intelligent landscaping; large open patio with trees, ferns, flowers, and fountains; outdoor stairway in the original section leading to The Third Floor (the award-winning restaurant), The Library (a cocktail piano lounge), and The Point After (a popular cabaret/disco); the Summery coffee shop and the Garden Court Lounge on the ground floor; pleasant outdoor deck with ample pool three levels up; sunsets often visible from there; newer section boasting another pool and terrace bar; Tiffany Steak House and Cafe Regent rounding out the restaurants; convenient hospitality suites for guests before check-in or after check-out.

Ample rooms with twin double beds, good, colorful furnishings with sizable baths and showers, color televisions, and large lanais; five basic price levels; best rooms the Oceanfront *Corners* ($115) as opposed to regular Ocean Front ($108) and Ocean *View* ($94), which the corner combines. (Reservations from the hotel at 2552 Kalakaua Ave., Honolulu, Hi. 96815.) We call the Regent really comfortable and a real sleeper.

The Regent is often confused locally with another entry a block down the street, the **Holiday Inn-Waikiki Beach** (Tel. 922-2511). At 25 stories and 636 rooms, this is the World's Innkeepers' largest in the U.S. A leap across the street from the sand, it's also only a few bounds away from the Honolulu Zoo. Perhaps in honor of its motel roots, it is one of the few inns in Waikiki to offer free guest parking.

Downstairs side-street entranceway with travel desks and the tiny Waiaha Bar; long escalator ride up and up to the brown and yellow lobby and nearly everything else; swimming pool only a splash away from the reception desk; nautical motif Captain's Table dining room (see Section 5); a doctor and nurse in an office on the premises.

Confusing rate schedules, depending on seasons and perhaps phases of the moon, start at $63 overlooking the pool and run up to $93 for ocean views. Lots of units here offer king-size beds. A child under 12 is free, but add $10 for a third adult. Try for the high floors for less noise and good views. The room amenities are certainly adequate in this efficiency-conscious operation. (Reserve from the hotel at 2570 Kalakaua Ave., Honolulu, Hi. 96815, or from toll-free numbers listed in some Mainland phone books.) Although we don't sense a strong individual personality, the inn certainly is a dependable holiday headquarters.

(There are two more Holiday Inns. One is the well-known old Hale Makai at 2045 Kalakaua Ave., now renamed the Holiday Inn Makai. The other is at Honolulu Airport, designed mostly for transit passengers. Nevertheless, there is a pool, bar, restaurant, etc., all of which are fine. Prices run slightly lower out there, although not quite as low as the Ramada Inn, which offers similar facilities in the same neighborhood.)

In a jump again to the other side of the Waikiki peninsula, the modest, Polynesian-style **Waikikian Hotel** (Tel. 949-5331) huddles between the Ilikai and the Hilton. It has loads of character, although we would never swim in the nearly still-water Duke Kahanamoku Lagoon which forms its "beach." (It doesn't matter, though, because you can squeeze past the end of a fence and stroll over to the sandy shore fronting the Hawaiian Village.)

Entrance off busy Ala Moana into the high-peaked "Ravi Lobby"; free Tuesday Mai Tai party under the banyan tree; acres of palm trees and other tropical foliage; good, fresh-water swimming pool; locally famous Tahitian Lanai Restaurant; fun and camaraderie usually available in the Papeete Bar.

We like the twenty-year-old part of the Waikikian, with rooms strung out in the four long, two-story wooden Tiki Garden buildings. Each unit there either opens onto the greenery on the ground floor, or onto a private lanai overlooking it all from the second deck. The accommodations themselves feature lots of wood, rattan, lauhala mats, overhead fans (not air-conditioning), sliding louvres, and other South Seas accoutrements. Bedrooms in these buildings run between about $64 and $70 in winter, and $55 and $61 in summer. Also, four persons may divide up an excellent bargain in the suite (about $100). In general, we don't like the shelters in the newer air-conditioned Tiki Towers building, many of which overlook the parking lot. And in the buildings we do like, there may be occasional complaints about revelers noisily departing the hotel's bar and restaurant. (Reservations from the hotel at 1811 Ala Moana, Honolulu, Hi. 96815.) The Waikikian is getting a bit rough around the edges, but many still give it an "A" for atmosphere. Let's hope they leave very good alone.

The vastly improved **Pacific Beach Hotel** (Tel. 922-1233) is an ambitious entry that falls into the category since the well-polished façade of its older section sits directly across Kalakaua from the shoreline:

No-nonsense, solid construction in one highrise and one higher rise; gargantuan 280,000-gallon aquarium featured in the newer, 40-story Ocean Tower; two swimming pools; three dining rooms, including the coffee-shoppish Oceanarium Restaurant (no shorts or slippers, please, even on the kids!), more elegant Neptune Restaurant, and the Shogun Restaurant with Japanese fare; Atlantis discotheque. Total of 850 bedchambers, many in blue and white with brown-patterned bedspreads, radio, and TV; a few kitchenettes in the older Beach Tower; double rates now in five categories ranging between $68 for Standards and $102 for Ocean Fronts ($6 less from mid-April to mid-December); suite prices from $195 to $395 (with four bedrooms).

The hotel also offers free shuttle-bus service to Ala Moana Shopping Center and its sister Pagoda Hotel. (Reservations from the hotel at 2490 Kalakaua Ave., Honolulu, Hi. 96815.) Altogether, it's becoming a handsome choice along the avenue, especially in the newer section.

A budget entry overlooking the beach is the nearby, well-named and unmistakable **Waikiki Circle Hotel** (Tel. 923-1571), the only cylindrical hotel in Honolulu. About fifteen stories tall, it provides some views of the beach and mountains which would cost twice as much in other establishments. There are 100 oddly shaped, often hard-used rooms with couches that make up into beds, and ample terraces. The baths and showers we saw were cramped. Rates this year will probably run between $30 and $40 double and $25 and $35 single. (Write the hotel at 2464 Kalakaua Ave., Honolulu, Hi. 96815.) Not bad for the low prices, maybe, and at least you won't get cornered in the rooms.

Next door, the **Waikiki Surfside** (Tel. 923-0266)—not to be confused with the Waikiki Surf—is perhaps for more ascetic voyagers. The ocean-front units at about $35 to $45 double aren't bad, and overlook a banyan tree toward the beach. There are mountain view models for maybe $35 and some claustrophobic inside cells where the only view you'll get is a foggy one on the TV for about $30. Frankly, we think you may do better in some budget choices farther inland.

MAJOR WAIKIKI HOTELS OFF THE BEACH

There are eight or nine well-known Waikiki hotels which are neither planted right on the sand nor just across the street from it, but all are within easy strolling distance of Waikiki Beach. Some, like the "P.K." and the Beachcomber, are just across the street from other hotels which *are* on the beach. Except for the capsule entries at the end, we have taken pains in this group to eliminate discussion of hotels which almost exclusively cater to large tour groups.

The oh-so-trim and still super-neat **Princess Kaiulani Hotel** (Tel. 922-5811) is a favorite of many annual returnees. If you want to sound local, you'll either pronounce it "Kah-ee-oh-*luh*-nee" (glottal stopping the first two syllables) or else call it simply, "the P.K." It's the only hotel under the Sheraton aegis which is not on the beach, and its guests generally pad along Kaiulani Avenue or through the P.K. garden a few yards, cross Kalakaua with the light, and then march through the lobby of the old auntie Moana to get to the shoreline.

Convenient location across from King's Alley; L-shaped main building backed by a newer, thirty-story tower; two spacious and colorful lobbies; portrait of the princess herself (on whose former estate the house sits) opposite the front desk; large oval pool just outdoors; lots of palms and other greenery in the surrounding garden; slurpy "Beyond-the-Reef" Muzak playing incessantly—even outdoors; courtyard skyline dominated by the Moana, Surfrider, and Outrigger hotels; several respectable restaurants including the American-style Cafe Colonnade (where we once had a good meal), the Japanese-cuisine Momoyama and the Mandarin-motif Lotus Moon (both untried by us); friendly Kahili Bar; no showroom; a host of good meeting rooms.

Several different types of accommodations are available at the P.K., starting at an amazingly low $50 double for an inside standard without view or terrace. But even those rooms have full air-conditioning, color TV, and good furnishings. Others include better mountain views (and *lanais*) at $55, charming King's Village vistas at $60, and poolside panoramas at $85. In the tower, mountain and city views have been unified now at $80, but insist on the 14th floor or above at that price. Full-on ocean views (eighth through twenty-ninth floors) sell for $95. Suites at about $130 are excellent bargains for four persons per unit. (Reservations from the Sheraton-Waikiki address.) Heartily suggested for those to whom sleeping near the water's edge is not a must.

The giant Amfac Hotels and Resorts, a subsidiary of Amfac, Inc. and known more for its Neighbor Island hostelries, is nevertheless also responsible for the **Waikiki Beachcomber** (Tel. 922-4646). It's about a block down Kalakaua Avenue, and right above the Liberty House department store, owned by the same corporate parent.

L-o-n-g escalator ride past several carved panels up to a third-floor lobby; attractive reception area with potted *tis*, ferns, and an artificial skylight; lots of facilities nearby including the Surfboard Bar, the Veranda Coffee Shop, the well-known Don the Beachcomber restaurant (we like it), the Bora Bora Room, featuring a Polynesian show (not the best), and the DBC discotheque; three or four rather nice shops nearby; pool and terrace outdoors overlooking the palm-lined avenue at frond level.

There are only a few lower-floor standard rooms at $53. We inspected No. 1503, a well-decorated superior room at $60, although the Princess Kaiulani Hotel blocked a view of Diamond Head, even at that height. Only a room divider separates your washbasin from the rest of your bedroom, perhaps a concern for some modest folks. (There was a door to the shower, tub, and toilet, however.) Deluxe rooms we saw at $67 featured views up and down Kalakaua and, of course, the Pacific Ocean. Watch the suite prices, here. They're quoted for *two persons* ($140 and $160 this year). Rates about $5 lower April through mid-December. Extra bodies will cost $10, now, any time of year. (Reservations from AMFAC Hotels, P.O. Box 8519, Honolulu, Hi. 96815.) Groups will like the place pretty well, but it's not a bad choice for the "free and independent" traveler (FIT), either.

We've nothing against the **Outrigger Prince Kuhio Hotel** (Tel. 922-0811) except its position, which is at the corner of Kuhio and Liliuokalani avenues in the part of Waikiki they used to call "the Jungle." The 620-room, L-shaped plant is well designed and generally attractive, its Protea Restaurant is well regarded, and the hotel features several other welcome touches like room safes, refrigerators, marble bathtubs, and a newspaper delivered daily (except Sunday) to each room. Double rates run from about $58 to $92 for most rooms with special top-floor units in the "Kuhio Club" perhaps in the $120 range this year. (Reservations from the hotel at 2500 Kuhio Ave., Honolulu, Hi. 96815.) It's a little farther than most want to walk from the sands of Waikiki, but an oasis of sorts when you get there.

The **Waikiki Tower of the Reef Hotel** (Tel. 922-6424, same telephone as the Edgewater) is certainly a mouthful of words. Despite the shared name with one hotel and shared phone number with another, the WTOTRH is a self-contained establishment which does not quite qualify as a beach hotel in our book. It sprouted like Jack's beanstalk in the late, lamented garden of a battered brother, the Edgewater, which explains the strange, cutoff look of the swimming pool. But it is not a part of the Edgewater, nor the nearby Reef Towers, nor their aging grandmother on the sand, the Reef. This young sibling is the Cinderella of that otherwise lackluster family.

The rooms are small, and cost-cutting fixtures and furniture have been installed; but all is neat, clean, and comfortable. Even the stamp-sized viewless standards have air conditioning and color TVs for two at $33 and $35 this year. Ocean view doubles at $44 and $52 are also good buys for those tabs. (Reservations from the hotel at 200 Lewers St.) If maintenance continues high and rates continue low, the Waikiki Tower will stand out as a tall bargain in the neighborhood.

A little farther along Kaiulani Avenue than the P.K. is the second of the three or four (depending on how you count them) Kelley-owned Outrigger hotels, the **Outrigger East** (Tel. 922-5353). Unimpressive public facilities; a second-floor lobby that looks like a shopping arcade and sometimes smells of cooking; 25 steep steps up to a prosaic pool; bedchambers, however, much better; nice views above the twelfth floor; several with refrigerators and kitchen sinks; excellent maintenance and housekeeping in rooms and corridors. Standard units at about $40 surprisingly commodious; No. 1722 and similar a great deluxe Diamond Head view for about $52; suites at $60 to $72 with full kitchens excellent buys for four sharing. (Reservations from the hotel at 150 Kaiulani Ave., Honolulu, Hi. 96815.) If you forget about your downstairs—and lots of people do—the Outrigger East holds up very well.

Now begins some confusion, for our next choice is another Outrigger, sometimes called the **Outrigger West** (Tel. 922-5022) and other times referred to as the Outrigger West—Kuhio Wing. (There's also an Outrigger West—Surf Wing—see below.) This one is even farther away from the sand, around the corner on Kuhio Avenue: Tiny hodge-podge of a lobby; up the elevator to a nice pool and pool deck overlooking the street; no trees around, however; bar and snack bar next to the pool; again, some nicely kept rooms, most in this entry with full complete kitchenettes, another potential money-saver, full air cooling, TV (some color), small *lanais*, etc.; double rates ranging from about $36 to $46; two-bedroom penthouse an excellent deal for up to six people at around $75. (Reservations from the hotel at 2330 Kuhio Ave., Honolulu, Hi. 96815.) Good prices for the rewards.

Our last Outrigger now is the **Outrigger Surf** (Tel. 922-5777), sometimes known as the Outrigger West—Surf Wing, even though it is a building or two removed from the Outrigger West—Kuhio Wing along Kuhio Avenue; tiny, but very neat lobby in browns and greens; small pool just outside; Rudy's Italian Restaurant extending up to the brink; generally viewless standards with B&W TVs, convertible punees, and kitchen facilities about $35; better superiors about $39 with the same amenities; very roomy deluxe models, some almost suite-like with a *shoji* screen sliding between the bed and the punee at $43. (Reservations from the hotel at 2280 Kuhio Ave.) In general, the rooms seemed more stale to us than the other Outriggers.

The **White Sands Garden Hotel** (Tel. 923-7336), at 431 Nohonani St., is undergoing a successful metamorphosis, but primarily to attract members of its new time-sharing club. Supposedly it will still take hotel guests in 1984, though, at rates from about $40 to $60. There are no advance reservations. This attractive oasis surrounding a cool pool is justly popular and recommendable—if you can get in.

If you can't, **The Breakers** (Tel. 923-3181) has a similar feeling, but in a more frenetic neighborhood at 250 Beach Walk. Doubles around $50; garden suites much nicer from $67 to $82; all with kitchenettes. Swimmers like the large pool here.

The **Reef Towers** (Tel. 923-3111), farther inland on the same street, is known as the home of the Polynesian Palace, the club built especially for entertainer Don Ho, but there the fame stops. The house isn't quite as haphazard as its beachside brother, the Reef, but we thought lots of repair and cleaning operations were needed when we trudged through the sleeping areas. Double rates run between about $30 and $45. We might take it in a pinch.

Another Reef, known as the **Edgewater Hotel** (Tel. 922-6424, same as for the WTOTRH) is the last member of the Gang of Four. On the plus side, it's the home of an excellent Italian restaurant, and some doubles may be worth the $22 to $38 tab. But the Edgewater, which is not at the edge of the water, still seems a little too soggy for us.

WAIKIKI BUDGET HOTELS

There are still decent hotels in the Waikiki peninsula where you can get a good double room for less than $40 a night—sometimes even under $25. Here are a few we explored for this volume.

Our happiest find was the exceedingly well-scrubbed, well-decorated, and well-managed **Waikiki Surf Hotel** (Tel. 923-7671) at the corner of Lewers and Kuhio: convenient bus stop location in a semi-residential area of Waikiki; pleasant, breezy open lobby in red tones with leather furniture; friendly reception folks; small pool and terrace off to one side; no bar or restaurant; really lovely, clean rooms in blues and greens;

many with nice, full kitchenettes with large refrigerators; bathroom/ dressing rooms with flocked wallpaper.

We inspected four types of rooms and found them all to be excellent bargains. Most rooms probably renting for (depending on height above the ground) $24, $26, and $30 double this year (without cooking facilities), sometimes connect with superiors (via both the internal door and a common lanai) which rent for about $30, $34, and $38 (*with* kitchenette). Deluxe corner units with all food-preparing amenities go for about $44 for two. The best bargain, however, was a four-person, two-room family suite, renting in different positions for a low of about $40 and a high of about $48. All rooms are fully air-conditioned, but TV is an optional extra at additional cost. (Reservations from the hotel at 2200 Kuhio Ave., Honolulu, Hi. 96815.) We didn't explore the East Wing extension nearby, but everything is under the watchful eye of general manager Mildred Courtney, so we feel they can't help but be a comparable bargain. Enthusiastically suggested.

At the narrow end of Kuhio Avenue, not far from Kaiulani Avenue, is the fifteen-story **Kuhiolani Hotel** (Tel. 922-1978), which offers full kitchen facilities throughout: neat, wood-paneled lobby; no other central areas; 98 clean if unspectacular accommodations in four classes renting for $32, $39, $47, and $55, double or single. There's no pool, but for some reason this one is a favorite with circus people when they come to town. (Reservations from the hotel at 2415 Kuhio Ave., Honolulu, Hi. 96815.) Hardly the greatest show on earth, but it's got its act together, nonetheless.

A fairly short hoof from Kalakaua Avenue, the family-operated **Royal Grove Hotel** (Tel. 923-7691) is a riot of pink on its façade, but mercifully it does not continue into the lobby. There's a nice pool out back, and a friendly looking card room with a waiting piano. Bedchambers are in three different constructions. Simple units in the old building are very small, clean, have B&W TVs, and sell for $28.50 to $30.50, double or single. There's more elbow room, air conditioners, color tellies, and kitchen facilities in the newer edifice for perhaps $34 to $40. In the low, cinderblock poolside units out back are L-shaped quarters with pullman kitchens for $40, which we'd choose if we just *had* to have such a cabana. (Reservations from the Leonard Fong family, Royal Grove Hotel, 151 Uluniu Ave., Honolulu, Hi. 96815.) Pretty good for the category.

Over at 250 Lewers Street, the 110-room **Coral Seas Hotel** (Tel. 923-3881) is a possibility: wide lobby; Perry Boys' Smorgy restaurant entrance nearby; no swimming pool; some hard-used rooms; few, if any, views; rooms varying between about $20 and $30 double. So-so.

One street over, a brother hotel to the Coral Seas is the **Reef Lanais** (Tel. 923-3111), which is also no beauty. Try for a high floor on the Honolulu side. If you can pick up a twin billet here for $25 or so, it may or may not be worth it.

Finally, the **Waikiki Terrace** (Tel. 923-3253) may be the cheapest hotel in town at $20 doubles, $16 singles, but we still call it overpriced for the battered and beaten rewards. Not recommended by us.

THE BIG HIDEAWAY RESORTS

There are only three—and some would say one or two—which fall into this category. These facilities generally represent self-contained vacations, which to a greater or lesser degree are enjoyed far away from the madding crowds.

The best hotel in Honolulu—if not in the entire state—isn't on Waikiki Beach at all. Conveniently sited on its own reclaimed beach on the edge of one of the city's most desirable residential sections is the super-prestigious, super-deluxe, very impressive **Kahala Hilton Hotel** (Tel. 734-2211). To erase any immediate misimpression, the Kahala Hilton, operated by the Hilton International Co., is separate and distinct from the Hilton Hawaiian Village, owned by the Hilton Hotels Corp. chain. "The Kahala," as it is often called locally, has been and continues to be the home away from home of more kings, presidents, entertainers, etc., than all other Honolulu inns combined. It will knock itself out to give all the luxury and all the privacy that its guests may desire.

Located in the Kahala district, between the Waialae Golf Course and Waialae Beach; basically two offset, ten-story rectangles faced with an exterior concrete trellis; balconies dripping with bougainvillaea; thousands of other flowering plants and trees on 6½ acres; specially groomed 800 feet of golden beach with two man-made islets; a trio of dolphins and other sea creatures cavorting in a tropical lagoon out back; 35-by-80 foot oval pool for human fresh-water fun; saline waterfall, a favorite wedding backdrop.

Old-style palatial lobby with three giant chandeliers; drinks and tea served there; interior inspired by Hawaiian monarchy period plantation house; Thai teak parquet floors; understated, high-quality, mellowed furnishings and artworks in the public areas; about 10 good shops nearby; excellent, prize-winning Maile Restaurant in the basement; Maile Terrace (Saturday and Sunday brunch) overlooking the lagoon; beachside Hala Terrace restaurant, now also used as a supper club (probably still featuring Danny Kaleikini's show); poolside kiosk for sips and snacks; Plumeria courtyard cafe off the lobby.

There are 370 rooms, including 33 suites. Most are in the main structure, but 84 are in the cottage-style Lagoon Terrace near the dolphin playground. Bedchambers, about half with *lanais*, feature tasteful but muted color schemes. You'll find excellent furnishings including plenty of chairs, lamps, sofas, a desk, color televisions *and* radios, refrigerators, and the unique "his and her" bathrooms (he can mix drinks, shave, shower, etc., while she tubs, makes up, or does nails in the opposite side of the same complex). There are no kitchens in the units, but room service is a proud feature of the Kahala.

Daily rates are the most expensive in town, and depend more on position than facilities. This year the $135, $155, and $175 rooms generally have mountain views. (A very few are without *lanais*.) Ocean or Lagoon views run $225 and $245 and beachfront bedrooms are $310. The junior suites by the lagoon are $330. One-bedroom suites begin at $400. Two-bedroom suites cost $755, except in the Lagoon Terrace, where they are $970. The Presidential or the Governor's Suite is $660 with one bedroom or $970 with two bedrooms. (All suites are the same price for up to four persons.)

The Kahala Hilton bases its reputation mainly on service, and many guests are annual repeats. The house keeps records on any preferences or quirks of its residents so as to be better able to welcome them again next time, and it prides itself on unexpected homey touches like providing pineapples and newspapers. (Reservations from the hotel at 5000 Kahala Ave., Honolulu, Hi. 96816.) If you have to worry about the money, the hotel is at least an interesting tourist attraction. But to those who can well afford the outlay, there simply is no other place on Oahu worth considering.

The 487-room **Hilton Kuilima Resort** (Tel. 293-8811) seems something like a giant Waikiki entry that was lifted bodily and then plunked down on a roughish piece of oceanfront land on a windy peninsula on the North Shore, a full hour's drive from Honolulu and Waikiki. There's a nice piece of beach, and the Kuilima is the only Oahu hotel both right on the sand and with its own golf course, too. Two cool pools, one large and one small; ten lighted tennis courts; three-mile jogging path. Hilton Hotels Corp. has just taken over at this writing, and everything is closed for reconstruction, so our judgment will have to be withheld until next year. Better recheck that phone number, too.

The Kuilima, now planned as the nucleus for a whole new 800-acre resort, improved mightily after it was bought from Del Webb by the Prudential Insurance Company. Prudential first assigned Hyatt to polish this outback piece of the rock. Now, under Hilton management, maybe it will become a gem, and maybe not.

The third establishment in this category, the **Sheraton Makaha Resort** (Tel. 695-9511)—way out in the boonies on the Waianae Coast, 45 miles from Waikiki—is certainly "far out" in that sense. The area is marginal, at best, and many readers have not felt welcomed by their neighbors. Golfers, of course, go for the excellent championship course surrounding the hotel, and readers who said they never left the campus during their entire stay tell us they liked it a lot. To us it still seems an island of luxury surrounded by a sea of geographical and social uncertainty.

OTHER HONOLULU HOTELS OUTSIDE WAIKIKI

Of this final group of six hotels, the first three are often thought of as Waikiki Beach hotels, even though they are far along the shoreline by Diamond Head. Then there are two in the Ala Moana Area (within striking distance of the shopping center), and we wind up with another one in central Honolulu.

The elegant **Colony Surf Hotel** (Tel. 923-5751) and its next-door companion, the **Colony East**, have been favorites with some elements of the "in" crowd for years: main building in an excellent, beachside location way up by the Natatorium; a neighbor to the exclusive Outrigger Canoe Club; sumptuous but small marble and green-walled, mirror-lined lobby; famous and very French Michel's restaurant in the Colony Surf; super-hip and fun dining in Bobby McGee's Conglomeration in the Colony East; no swimming pools, but a nice piece of beach.

The rooms in both buildings are all "one-room suites," with fully equipped kitchens, ample living areas (*very* large in the Colony Surf), two queen-size beds, and color TV. The Surf features 25 feet of windows, but no balconies. The Colony East boasts a small *lanai* with every room. All apartments are well done, mostly in cool blues and whites. Four-stage rates depend on position and view, but we doubt there are really any *bad* views from these two buildings. In the Colony Surf, they range from $100 to $200, and in the Colony East from $80 to $110. One extra person is $15. Say Hi! to general manager Judy Daniel for us. (Reservations from the hotel at 2895 Kalakaua Ave., Honolulu, Hi. 96815.) All together, very, very nice for the type.

Much improved is the former bargain bet, the **Diamond Head Beach Hotel** (Tel. 922-1928), at 2947 Kalakaua Ave. Gradually pyramiding, fifteen-floor, pink façade; sandy yard in back; short walk on the seawall to the genuine beach; friendly reception at a window on the walkway; total of 76 units in five types, most with two double beds, a few with twin single beds, and some with one queen-size bed. All are well decorated with new furnishings and equipped with terraces and TVs. Double rates will run from about $70 to $150. At deadline, we haven't been able to see the face-lift on this establishment. (Reservations from Colony Resorts, Inc., 733 Bishop St., Honolulu, Hi. 96813.)

Between Waikiki and downtown Honolulu, and next door to the shopping center whose name it bears, is the 36-story 1,268-room **Ala Moana Americana Hotel** (Tel. 955-4811), not to be confused with the

Moana in Waikiki. Half owned by the Pick Hotel chain, the place advertises itself as "Nearest the Fun," and if your fun is shopping, that's certainly true. (There's even a special walking ramp between the hotel and
Ala Moana Center.) It's not, however, "at the entrance to Waikiki Beach,"
another piece of Madison Avenue hyperbole, although it is only a stroll
to a city-owned beach park.

Busy location on Atkinson Drive; free shuttle bus to Waikiki; very spacious lobby featuring lots of artwork and several shops of its own; dozens
of meeting rooms on two floors; third-floor pool and deck, lined with
acres of Astroturf; good 24-hour Plantation Coffee House nearby; the
Summit Supper Club way up on the roof. The rooms, most of which run
approximately $55 to $110 for two, were ordinary but certainly adequate. We recall decorations in brown and beige, quilted spreads on twin
beds, radios, color TVs, nice baths, and good views from the higher
floors. (Reservations from the hotel at 410 Atkinson Dr., Honolulu, Hi.
96814.)

Two or three blocks farther *mauka* is the **Pagoda Hotel** (Tel. 941-6611)
in a highrise residential area, and under the same ownership as Waikiki's
Pacific Beach Hotel, with whom it shuttles a bus. Neat lobby of bamboo,
wicker, leather, straw and a striated shag rug; tiny ovoid swimming pool
just outside; waterfall and carp pond just beyond, surrounding the well-
known "floating" restaurant; clean but generally uninspiring bedchambers in the main building, none with balconies, but all with kitchen facilities, running between $42 and $50 double; best bargains across the
street in the Pagoda Terrace, maybe $40 for two or $46 for a one-
bedroom family apartment, holding four, or $52 for the two-bedroom
units holding six. Not bad for the price.

What you might call a very basic, no-frills, but still clean and decent
establishment is the **Nakamura Hotel** (Tel. 537-1951) in a nowheresville
location at 1140 South King St. Nevertheless, it is on a bus route, and the
cinderblock building is neat, and most of the orange and white rooms
are air-conditioned. (No phone, no pool, no pets; don't know 'bout ciga-
rettes!) At last report, all of its 41 units still went for under $23 for two,
but that could be up a dollar or two by now. Certainly a relief for the
painfully pinched traveler.

5. Dining and Restaurants on Oahu

There are few things so personal as a taste in food. Some travelers are
always adventuresome—ready to try every strange new dish, no matter
how exotic, haggis horrid, or squid squishy, whether the morsel is dead
or alive, and regardless of how long it has been in its particular state of
mortality.

Others, of course, approach their vacation fare with the grim determination that whether in Hanapepe or Dar es Salaam, they will root out, if it exists, the only underground ground beef and mashed potatoes joint within a hundred-mile radius.

We fall somewhere between those extremes, but have broadened our dining interests in both liberal and conservative directions to prepare this volume. We want you to know where to look for the raw fish and where you'll find the hot dogs. Whether you regard the information at either end of the culinary spectrum as warning or invitation is up to you.

If we do lean a little toward the unusual, well, that's what this book is all about. Throughout Hawaii, you will enjoy special foreign accents in the food as much as in the modes of dress and in the customs of the people. It's simply another attraction that makes a stay in the Islands more stimulating than another trip up to Moose Lake.

Now, there is no such thing as absolutely genuine Hawaiian cuisine prepared today. This is true whether you are talking about the ancient Polynesian Hawaiians (who ate dog, among other "authentic delights"), or whether you mean simply a particular style of cooking which is strongly preferred today by the general island population.

The comestibles consumed by Hawaii residents of all racial extractions during this decade are largely American, and it's a trend which becomes more true with every generation. Some dishes do survive in ethnic purity. *Poi* is one of these. It does *not* taste like paste, by the way. There are different kinds of *poi*, too—bland, sour, thick, thin, fermented, and all made from well-pounded taro root. *Poi* is an acquired taste, like mashed potatoes, and you are not likely to fall in love with it at first smack.

Nevertheless, most island favorites are not so historically and culturally accurate, representing instead a polyglot of palates. Take *saimin*, for example, and you should try it at least once. A type of noodle soup flavored with chicken, beef, or shrimp, and garnished with meat slices and chopped onions, it was invented in the last century by Orientals living in Hawaii. Islanders often stop briefly at a little hole-in-the-wall *saimin* stand and order a bowl or paper container for about 75 cents. It's usually served with one of those funny-looking porcelain or plastic Chinese spoons and a pair of wooden chopsticks. You're supposed to use that spoon to slurp up the broth, and the chopsticks are for the noodles. Of course there's no law against using the spoon for the noodles.

There are lots of *saimin* stands in Honolulu, but few in Waikiki, although some regular restaurants in Waikiki also have *saimin* on their menus. You can even get it at McDonald's, now, but according to Honolulu writer Mark Matsunaga, who's as *saimin*-savvy as they come, the best local flavor is served up by **Washington Saimin Stand**, at 1117 So. King St., between Pensacola and Piikoi Streets.

A second popular "Japanese" plate (and, unlike *saimin*, the basis of a full meal) is found in restaurants of many types throughout the Islands. It is steak *teriyaki*, or *teriyaki* beef. Sometimes it is known as just plain "teri." This beef is first marinated in a saucy combination of *shoyu* (soy sauce), *sake*, sugar, ginger, and garlic, and then broiled. It's delicious, and an absolute must for visitors. But again, beef *teriyaki* is almost a Hawaiian adaptation; although the *teriyaki* recipe is known and enjoyed in Japan, it is usually applied there to fish, whereas this is virtually never the case in Hawaii. There are even "teriburgers," nowadays, and they are usually darned good, too!

Teriyaki is so ubiquitous and generally well-prepared all over Hawaii that we never order it at a genuine Japanese restaurant. There we would choose a more authentic imported dish instead. As a rule, delicious beef *teriyaki* may be found at any of the good American steak houses on Oahu, listed right in there alongside the prime rib and the New York sirloin.

Another important "steak house" specialty bears a Hawaiian name—*mahimahi* (pronounced "*mah*-he-*mah*-he"), and this one is a fish. A strong local favorite, when broiled or otherwise prepared properly, *mahimahi* certainly deserves its popularity. Don't become confused and saddened if someone tells you the English name for *mahimahi* is "dolphin." This is *not* the charming, personable porpoise you see performing tricks at Sea Life Park. The dolphin you *eat* (that is, *mahimahi*) is a genuine fish, not an aquatic mammal. It's quite devoid of any sympathetic temperament or the smiling visage you find on the other kind of dolphin.

The lust for *mahimahi* among Islanders is so intense that the demand for it long ago outstripped the supply available in local waters. Most *mahimahi* consumed in the state today has been caught off Taiwan, Japan, or perhaps Ecuador, and then quick frozen and shipped to Honolulu. When thawed and broiled, this frozen *mahimahi* is usually still very good. Some expensive restaurants, such as Nick's Fish Market and the Third Floor, do offer the genuine island-fresh variety, and it does have a definite gustatory edge on the imported stock. But then it darn well ought to for a price tag that can run more than twice as high.

To *saimin*, beef *teriyaki*, and *mahimahi*, the three "musts" in the culinary portion of a Hawaii vacation, some would add still a fourth specialty—*kalua* pig.

This Hawaiian fresh-pork preparation is the center of the *luau*, and it is almost the only thing about that traditional Hawaiian feast which is sometimes concocted in the centuries-old manner. The entire animal, eviscerated but loaded with salt, steams for hours or all day in an underground hot-rock oven called an *imu*. It's a very salty dish, and there's where the *poi* comes in handy—to chase the pig with, and contrast favorably with that salty shredded meat.

If you don't agree that *kalua* pig is *ono-ono*, never mind. Most *luaus* serve plenty of other food, too. In a Waikiki hotel *luau*, you may find such familiar fare as baked ham or broiled steak, garnished with pineapple. (The latter, incidentally, is a recently arrived fruit that the old Hawaiians never saw.) For that reason, a hotel *luau* costs over $25 per person as compared with prices about half that for a church-sponsored *luau*, which makes almost no concessions to Mainland taste habits. (More about *luaus*, later.)

Our personal additions to the ethnic food list might be some Portuguese contributions to island preferences. First, there is Portuguese sausage—mild, medium, and hot. You can eat it for breakfast, but it's also used as a base for an excellent bean soup. There is Portuguese sweet bread, which is sometimes still known as *pão dulce*. Then there's a stomach bender called *malasadas*, made of deep-fried dough which is later dunked in sugar. (*Malasadas* are not unlike the *zeppoles* of Italy or the *bunuelos* of Spain.)

Other goodies that, like *saimin*, belong in the Japanese snack category are *sushi* (singular and plural), little vinegared rice clump concoctions that are nearly as popular in Hawaii as they are in Tokyo. The boiled rice is tossed with Japanese vinegar, sugar, and salt, and then rolled up with tiny pieces of vegetables or fish mixed through it. Usually they are first formed into cylinders, held together by seaweed, and then sliced into sections about one inch thick. Eaten with the fingers, they are delicious and a real lunch-time bargain, too.

You may also hear a lot about another tid-bit whose name, at least, is Hawaiian—*manapua*. But this is an adaptation of a Chinese dumpling specialty called *dim sum* by purists. You often find *manapua* at the same shops that sell *saimin*. The original *dim sum* comes in more than a dozen different varieties. You'll find them in their purest forms at certain Chinese restaurants. Two favorites are **Yong Sing** at 1055 Alakea St., downtown, and **China House**, at the top of the ramp at 1349 Kapiolani Blvd., near Sears at Ala Moana Center.

The closest to *manapua* among these Chinese recipes is *char siu bao* (*bao* dumpling stuffed with *char siu*—sweet roast pork). Some other popular *dim sum* include steamed bread dough, coconut *bao*, curry chicken turnover, crabmeat *fun goh*, and chicken or shrimp *siu mai*. Yong Sing and China House both serve other, more familiar, Cantonese Chinese dishes too, so ask for the special *dim sum* menu when you come in.

There's a third *dim sum* restaurant in town, **Fat Siu Lau** at 100 North Beretania St., in a corner of the Cultural Plaza. There they serve *dim sum*

Hong Kong style, which makes choosing easier and faster. No
involved—you pick the ones you want visually from a circulating
They're all delicious!

While in Hawaii, you'll probably hear a lot about "having *pupus*" be
fore dinner or with cocktails. The word literally means "shells," but is
used idiomatically for hors d'oeuvres. In fact, *pupus* can mean snacks of
any kind. Maybe butterfly shrimp, pieces of *char siu*, some Korean meat-
balls, barbecued spare ribs, crisp *won ton*, or even just plain peanuts to go
with your beer.

One innocent-looking little dish you may be given automatically as a
pupu at some bars is *kim chee*. If so, watch out! It looks like nothing more
than a clump of day-old tossed salad, but it's a super-hot Korean concoction which may remove the roofs of unwary mouths. This pickled *won
bok* (Chinese cabbage) takes a lot of getting used to. We rather like it now,
in moderation, but it took years for us to come around. Made with garlic
and red-hot peppers, *kim chee* has a way of hanging around your breath
for hours, and it's become somewhat of a socially controversial product.

Now, what about your raw fish? That's simply a Japanese appetizer
called *sashimi* (not to be confused with the previously discussed *sushi*).
Usually *sashimi* are very thin slices of fresh tuna. Using chopsticks, you
dip them into a mixture of *shoyu* (soy sauce) and hot mustard or in another special sauce. Strangely, *sashimi* has no "fishy" odor or taste. When
made from *ahi* or *aku*, two kinds of local tuna, it feels like and has the
flavor of tender beef.

The specialties discussed so far cross several ethnic lines—Hawaiian,
Chinese, Japanese, Portuguese, and Korean. Of course, such American
snacks as popcorn and hot dogs will also be found in profusion throughout the Islands, and are beloved by everyone. In fact, you'll generally see
more Orientals and Polynesians than anyone else in the neighborhood
McDonald's.

The other popular dishes of Hawaii are taken up in conjunction with
the different restaurants which follow. We have divided our listings into
separate categories. You'll find some of Honolulu's most famous restaurants covered in the Continental/French group, of course, but remember that the capital leads the country in some of its choices of Pacific and
Eastern specialties. It is in these that you will find the extraordinary flavors associated with living in the Islands.

Listed alphabetically, here are the categories in which we have divided
our Oahu dining experiences: American/Cosmopolitan (including steak
houses), Chinese—Cantonese and Mandarin, Continental/French, Filipino, Hawaiian, Indian, Indonesian, Italian, Japanese, Mexican, Seafood Selections, and Thai. Following these, we will wrap up the major
portion of our gastronomic grouping with a discussion of a few well-

known buffets, coffee and snack shops, and some unusual or out-of-the-way spots. And, at the very end of the section, there is a brief description of some rural Oahu restaurants under our "Kitchens in the Country" heading.

A word about prices: We think an expensive restaurant in Honolulu is one which runs $25 or more per person for dinner. We do not imply that such an establishment is *too* expensive. In fact, you'll usually have to pay those prices to experience the city's best culinary offerings. If the same place is also open for lunch, you probably won't get away for under $15 or so for a midday meal.

In general, we consider a moderately priced dinner as something in the $15 neighborhood. (Of course this will vary; $15 or $16 for, say, a Chinese or Mexican meal—which often costs much less—would certainly be thought expensive.) A moderately priced lunch, in our view, is one which runs $6 or $7.

Although it is less than convenient and not as much fun for many travelers, one way to eat well on a budget is to take your big meal of the day at some beautiful and delicious dining room at noon or early afternoon, and then just get by on a snack in the evening hours. Visitors who have rented hotel rooms with kitchen facilities can do even better by preparing something simple upstairs, and then using the resulting savings to help them take in a Hawaiian show later in the evening, or to pay for some cruise or sightseeing tour the next day.

By the way, if you are a credit card addict, it might be helpful to know that in Hawaii there seem to be many more restaurants, etc., which accept the bank-issued plastic cards such as Visa and MasterCard than prestigious membership accounts like American Express and Diners Club. The latter especially seems to be going out of style. Out-of-town checks are sometimes hard to cash in a restaurant, but travelers' checks (in U.S. dollars) are welcome nearly everywhere.

By the way, the dress in Hawaii restaurants—even for dinner—is basically informal. Women may wear their muumuus, if they wish. Coats and ties are okay but virtually never required for men. A nice aloha shirt or other neat open-neck model is fine. And wherever you go, please tell 'em we sent you. (You won't get a better price, but it will mark you as a discriminating traveler who keeps us advised of your successes and failures.)

AMERICAN/COSMOPOLITAN RESTAURANTS

Restaurants in this group cannot really be characterized by cuisine—at least not beyond the obvious specialties turned out by steak houses. Therefore, our preferences in this collection often include what might be called the most "fun" dining in Honolulu. These are places that seem to operate with an overall style and flair, even if the type of cooking falls into no particular or exclusive ethnic pattern. (Unless otherwise noted, always reserve for dinner at the following addresses.)

Of that *genre*, one of our favorites continues to be the rollicking **Horatio's** (Tel. 521-5002). Just across Ala Moana Boulevard from the Kewalo Basin cruise boat docks, the place is upstairs at the Ewa end of the Ward Warehouse shopping complex. Inspired by Admiral Horatio Nelson and his flagship, the decorations are of the most incredible collection of seventeenth- and eighteenth-century nautical memorabilia gathered together this side of the Greenwich Museum. Scores of different seating arrangements—sometimes in old skiffs, other times in a wardroom, fo'c's'le, or crew's quarters; the Admiral's Deck, a favorite bridge overlooking it all; wonderful olde baroque muzake; pleasant waitresses garbed as "serving wenches." On one luncheon voyage, we enjoyed the Yardarm, an open-faced sandwich with chopped beef, mushrooms, tomatoes, zucchini, and topped with Swiss cheese. Another in our party enthused over the shellfish *saute* (scallops, shrimp, and vegetables fried in a butter-wine sauce). A third member of the gang gobbled up every ounce of the Admiral's Topside Broil, a thinly sliced flank steak. Don't think of disembarking without dessert. Our favorite is the Burnt Cream—about a dollar—a caramel custard like we've never had before. (They've got the recipe all printed up if you ask for it.) Most meals at Horatio's have been running in the (cross your fingers) $15 to $16 range, but we believe its continued popularity could force prices up to the crow's nest. At this writing, it has some unusual reservations policies, which may change, so you had better recheck when and where things are booked and when and where things are first-come-first-served. Despite the mob scene often at the gangplank, we still give this admiral his four stars.

Another establishment where the quality of the fare survives pretty well over a far-out decorating scheme is closer to Waikiki—in fact, just up Kalakaua Avenue in the Colony Surf East Hotel. **Bobby McGee's Conglomeration** (Tel. 922-1282) is filled with a $300,000 inventory of hodge-podge you'd associate with a large, overfull antique and cast-off store scattered throughout five dining rooms. A couple of these, like the Indian Room or the Library, are designed in somewhat of a theme, but the others—the Victorian, the East, and the West Rooms—are, well, merely a conglomeration. Excellent service by waiters and waitresses in every costume imaginable, from a wild Wyatt Earp and a sappy Superman to a flip Florence Nightingale and a hip Cleopatra; all-you-can-eat salad fixings from the bathtub; all-you-can-slurp soup of the day from atop the ancient wood stove; free potatoes (baked or French) or rice with everything. Our party of four enjoyed the Prime Ribs (about $15), the

Shrimp Kabob (with bell peppers, pineapple chunks, and mushrooms—
about $14), and the Rainbow Trout (about $14 at this writing). After dinner, they'll set you up at a table in the discotheque portion, if you wish.
There are no windows and nothing to look at, save the nutty things on
display in the joint itself. Although the food is good, it is not *haute cuisine*.
Perhaps it's more enjoyable for a gang than a couple. In any case, we like
it a lot.

One of the loveliest and most expensive restaurants in Waikiki is
Canlis' (Tel. 923-2324), sometimes called Canlis' Broiler, and one of the
few Honolulu restaurants where coat and tie are strongly encouraged.
(They place you in a second-rate room if one man in your group hasn't
placed his neck in a noose.) The Canlis chain was founded in Honolulu a
quarter century ago, and for many of those years it may have been about
the best restaurant on the island. Many faithful old-timers return every
time they are in town, and the nicest room is the one with the chandeliers that looks like a church. The best table is the first banquette upstairs on the left. Although the famous Canlis' salad is still good, as well
as some of its just desserts, the main courses were a disappointment in
some way to each one of our group of four. We judged it at least inconsistent—perhaps too inconsistent for the high tariffs asked.

A very Polynesian theme is carried by the torch-lit old favorite called
the **Tahitian Lanai** (Tel. 946-6541), just off the beach in the Waikikian
Hotel. Try for a table in one of the little separate thatched huts along the
walkway. The place is cosmopolitan with local overtones; the Hawaiian
Dinner (about $10) is pretty good for its type, if you want to give that a
whirl. The Tahitian Style Chicken, served in a coconut, was more our
own speed. There's also a good shrimp dish with garlic sauce. Some call
the Tahitian Lanai a little corny, but what sarong with that?

Similar fare, but with a few more exotic accents thrown in, is served in
an indoor, straw-lined, and South Seas-soned cave called **Don the Beachcomber** (Tel. 922-4646). In the Waikiki Beachcomber Hotel, 2300 Kalakaua Ave., the dining room is known for its rakish rum drinks. The
food, however, is also interesting, and we heartily enjoyed our curry dish
here recently. There were only two small criticisms: The air conditioning
can be c-c-c-cold (we thawed our hands over a candle), and somehow we
found ourselves whispering because the sound seems to carry (others
across the room were creating a racket every time they shook a sugar
packet). A newly installed waterfall might break the silence. It's also
known for good pies. Recommended—for warm and perhaps quiet folk.

Trader Vic's (Tel. 923-1581), in the International Market Place, is
very similar in tone and taste to Don's (above) except that there are fewer
"American" items on the menu and more Americanized Chinese dishes.
The long-gone original Trader Vic's used to be on South King Street, but

they trucked over tons of the same junk and installed it here. Our meals weren't bad in the new Vic's, although we still prefer Don's for the type.

Yet another of these Cosmo/Polynesian places is located in the Sheraton and is called **Kon Tiki** (Tel. 922-4422). Ride up in its "grass shack" elevator to a dramatic "outdoors-indoors" layout. We passed up the Lobster Dean Martin, but the sweet-and-sour victuals we sampled were tasty and inexpensive.

As good or better than the previous three or four entries, but far from the usual tourist haunts, is the open-air, Hawaiian-style, 39-year-old **Willows** (Tel. 946-4808). It's a lovely inland setting under the willow trees by a spring-fed Hawaiian fishpond in an otherwise prosaic neighborhood at 901 Hausten St. Now under the very professional management of Randy Lee, who shepherded the old Halekulani Hotel for most of its final years, this thatched-roof emporium has expanded its menu considerably to include several continental classics. Note the special Hawaiian entertainment and local foods for Tuesday lunches. We like it very much any day or night of the week.

Beyond that, the Willows has also opened up something ultra-special called the "Kamaaina Suite," a separate area designed to be a restaurant within a restaurant. It even has a separate chef, specifically Kusuma Cooray, F.C.F.A. (C.G.). All meals are about $50 at this writing (plus tax and tip), and each table is sold only once per night, so there is never any rush. We haven't been in the new room yet, but reports have been glowing. If they keep Ms. Cooray over the coming years, it could turn out to be one of the city's top dining rooms.

Another choice with a beautiful setting and fair-to-middlin' cuisine is the **Pagoda Floating Restaurant** (Tel. 941-6611), attached to the Pagoda Hotel at 1525 Rycroft St. Order something simple, take your time, and don't forget a stroll through the garden to admire the colorful carp. (This "floating restaurant" doesn't *really* float, by the way. There *is* a genuine floating restaurant in Honolulu, but throughout the world we have avoided such establishments, whose design we believe is intrinsically unsafe in an emergency.)

In the "theme" category (like Bobby McGee's or Horatio's) is a Kapiolani Boulevard entry, **Victoria Station** (Tel. 955-1107), of the successful Mainland train chain. Crammed with railroad accessories and souvenirs of a trip to England, Victoria Station also has portions of actual trains—strangely American, not British—tacked onto the building. Specializing in prime ribs (prices between $14 and $20, depending on the weight) and barbecue ribs (perhaps $13), this wood-burner is generally a smooth express at the right fare. Once you get in, you can keep up full steam in round trips to the salad bar, etc. But then there's the hitch— "once you get in." At this writing, Victoria Station has a *no reservations* *policy*, and that may keep you sidetracked in the cocktail caboose for 45 minutes or more on a busy noon or night, watching your drinking budget go down the line while waiting for space in the dining cars. We sometimes try to climb aboard on a slow night. There's also a branch line (Tel. 946-9545) next to the Ilikai Hotel on Ala Moana.

A quartet of dining places, at least three of which we like a lot, has been installed in the new Ward Centre, a chic shopping block at 1200 Ala Moana Blvd., between Ala Moana Center and the Ward Warehouse. At the top of the heap, literally and figuratively, is the noisy, bright, barnlike, crowded, and hectic **Ryan's Parkplace Bar and Grill** (Tel. 521-4866). Here's a place with no privacy at all, lit with institutional light globes, but with plenty of loud merriment, and somehow it works. It could be the quality of the fare. The menu proudly states that all the recipes were "personally supervised and approved by Sharon Kramis, widely known West Coast food writer, consultant and instructor." There's a lotsa pasta, scadsa salads, and about two dozen kinds of beer in addition to some innovative meat and chicken dishes. A lot of food and a lot of fun.

A modest place called the **Yum Yum Tree** (Tel. 523-9333) is a notch or two above your average coffee shop. Ask for an outdoor umbrella table, for the full tropical flavor. Some of its pies are famous. Also on the pastry file is **RoxSan Patisserie** (Tel. 526-9533), started by a young couple with gourmet tastes and abilities. Go early or late for lunch, or you probably won't get in at all.

Right at the top of the twenty-five-story Ala Moana Building is **La Ronde** (Tel. 941-9138), the very first of the world's now-proliferating revolving restaurants. Despite the name, the cuisine is not French. On our 2½-revolution trip, the service and meals were disastrous, and the prices were as high as the view. The view, however, was terrific, and next time, we're going around for a drink only.

Miso and Mango in the Ala Moana hotel was a disappointment. Here they tore out an excellent Japanese restaurant and replaced it with a glorified coffee shop.

And downtown, on the Pacific Trade Center mall, is a black-and-shiny, pink-lit, mirror-bound place called **Del Centro** (Tel. 521-7714). We thought it terribly overpriced, despite the decorous waitresses.

STEAK HOUSES: Here's a little American/Cosmopolitan subcategory designed to answer the question "Where can we go to get a really good hunk of steak?" Besides the meat served in the places so far mentioned, we do have a few more likes and dislikes. (Don't forget, you'll probably be offered teriyaki and mahimahi along with the T-bones in these broilers.)

A champion in Waikiki has always been the moderately priced **Black**

Angus (Tel. 923-1919), which has moved from its former site to the nearby Coral Reef Hotel. The Black Angus really *is* black, too, but if your eyes ever get used to the firefly-power illumination, you'll see some attractive Spanish appurtenances. Steaks are in the $14 range, and we usually find the waiters efficient and the beef delicious. The **Captain's Galley** in the Moana Hotel was a bummer for us, except for the sunset which can be super. The **Colony, A Steak House**, in the Hyatt Regency Hotel, is not our side of beef. There were too many tables crowded into the room—not enough space for runs to the salad bar—although many lap up the products of its Margarita Machine. **Hy's** (Tel. 922-5555), a sparkling local link in a Canadian chain at 2440 Kuhio, has been attracting a loyal clientele. Stick with steak, and you've got a shot. Also in Waikiki, over on Lewers St., is the below-stairs **Chuck's Cellar**. The meat was no more than okay, and we felt rushed by their *modus operandi*. A *lower priced* entry in the immediate neighborhood which is more or less dependable for the modest tariffs is in a corner of the Edgewater Hotel: **Chuck's Steak House**. A newer branch, up in Manoa Valley, however, is a much more friendly and tasty address.

Out of Waikiki, and back into the top-dollar steak emporia, the **Whaler's Broiler** in the Ala Moana Hotel is generally dependable, as is **Byron II** nearby in the shopping center. The viewful **Chart House** in the Ilikai Marina Apartments always *used* to be good, but we haven't sliced into it since it was charbroiled but good in an expensive fire. The House has risen from the ashes, however. Further along Ala Moana Boulevard, **Stuart Anderson's** (Tel. 523-9692) is a dependable local link in the western beef chain. **Buzz's Original Steak House** (Tel. 944-9781), which opened a new branch at 2535 Coyne St., was okay at that address, although many prefer to drive over the Pali to the *original* "Original" in Kailua. Then out in the Kahala Mall, some folks are faithful to the old Reuben's, now renamed the **Spindrifter** (Tel. 737-7944). We haven't been around since the Reuben's chain was bought by Jolly Roger. But Louis Cofer, the respected restaurant critic for *Aloha, The Magazine of Hawaii*, gives it plaudits as a dependable suburban dining room. If we were in that neighborhood, though, we might head for the **Pottery** (Tel. 737-0633), nearby at 3574 Waialae Ave. in the Kaimuki District. While waiting for a table, you can watch the ceramists at work spinning out the dishes, cups, etc., which you may also buy. The steaks are probably all good, but you might like something different such as the Teriyaki Kabob. Happily remembered and recommended.

CHINESE COOKING IN HONOLULU

Chinese restaurants always seem more enjoyable with a group, because you can order "family style"—choosing several kinds of dishes to pass around and sample among each other. There always seems to be some new things to try that none of the gang has ever heard of before. Probably no other style of cooking, in fact, can come up with such a large number of diverse delectable items as Chinese. Nevertheless, in our listings below, we have also tried to find places where two people can enjoy a good sampling of the bill of fare.

It is far beyond our scope to go into the intricacies of Chinese cooking. But you may want to remember that in Hawaii, at least, there are two general types. **Cantonese cooking** tends to be rather mild and sweet. Most Chinese restaurants throughout the U.S., in fact, are actually Cantonese. The other style is generally called Northern, Szechwan, or **Mandarin cooking** even though, strictly speaking, those three terms are not exactly interchangeable. The dishes tend to be on the hot and spicy side, and it's this kind of Chinese restaurant that you may not find back home. Incidentally, rice is usually *not* included "free" with a Chinese meal. Some readers report misunderstandings on the subject.

Now, a brief word about *chopsticks.* Why be intimidated? If your chopsticks are jumping and sliding over your fingers, for heaven's sake, ask for a fork. This is especially true with Chinese chopsticks, which tend to be long, slippery, and hardest to handle, as opposed to the wooden Japanese models. If the restaurant can provide us with disposable wooden ones—the Chinese often call them "picnic chopsticks"—we use 'em. Otherwise, depending on what we ordered, we might ask for western utensils, too. (Also, see our discussion on chopsticks operation under the Japanese category.)

CANTONESE RESTAURANTS: One convenient old reliable, equally practical for lunch or dinner, is the **House of Hong** (Tel. 923-0202) at 260-A Lewers St. Walk inside, past the Red Chamber Bar, and on upstairs to the Dynasty Dining Room. Attractive black-and-gold decorations; high-glossed tables; low ceilings with patterned bronze characters meaning "longevity"; gold patina, carved teakwood mural to one side; quiet, perhaps taciturn (but attentive) waitresses; low noontime prices; high dinner fares. We enjoyed very much our combination lunch (spare ribs, chicken, shrimp, pork chop suey, rice, etc.) here for under $7. Others praise the $10, $11, and $12 dinners. Evening reservations are advisable. Unlike many Chinese restaurants, this one has kept the same chef for years. Bending at the waist, we happily award it *Won Lo Bao.*

The reincarnated **Lau Yee Chai** (Tel. 923-1112) is setting a high standard of Oriental opulence up in the new Waikiki Shopping Plaza, near its old address at Kalakaua and Seaside. We'll try the cashew chicken or the almond duck again after the gold dust settles. Also in Waikiki is the dinner-only **Golden Dragon** (Tel. 949-4321), which boasts a famous reputation in the Hilton Hawaiian Village. This restaurant has had a continuously successful history for the past ten years. The house specialty is the lemon chicken.

The above should not be confused with the **Golden Duck** on McCully Street, or the **Hon Kung** on Harding Avenue, both of which may be slipping too far. The obscure **Hee Hing Chop Suey** is holding a firm fan club at 477 Kapahulu Ave., a chopstick's throw from the Ala Wai, although the traditional champion of the chop suey sweepstakes is still **McCully Chop Sui** at McCully and King Streets. Despite its traditional hold in Chinatown, the century-old **Wo Fat** (Est. 1882—Tel. 537-6260) sometimes has trouble keeping the quality of its fare up to date. Some Wo Fat fans disagree, however, and it is certainly interesting to dine in a sort of local Cantonese museum.

Also downtown, and in a much more savory environment, is the new-ish **Fat Siu Lau** ("the Happy Man"—Tel. 538-7081) in the Cultural Plaza. Although we know it for its delicious *dim sum* (served only up to 4 P.M.), it is developing a happy reputation for full meals and take-out orders, too. A similar story is the decorous **China House** (Tel. 949-6622), across the parking lot mauka of Sears' second floor.

For cafeteria-style Chinese fun, the traditional favorite in the Ala Moana Shopping Center is **Patti's Chinese Kitchen**. It's always crowded, but the line moves pretty quickly, and to many it's worth the battered elbows to get to the ginger sauce chicken and other high-quality delights. If you want to sit down and be served, pay more for **Patti's Noodle Kitchen** next door. And a newer entry, now relished by Chinese gourmet David Tong, is the **Asian Garden** (Tel. 955-6674) at Young and McCully streets. There's usually an excellent special of the month—also a separate menu for parties of 10 or more. **The Great Wok of China** (Tel. 922-5373) is an attempt to capture some of the panache of the Japanese *teppan* table and put it in a Chinese setting. We found it unoriginal, but enjoyable. Try the Butterfly Dream Beef Steak.

MANDARIN RESTAURANTS: For spicy, Northern Chinese cooking, we have two favorites, neither one of which is in Waikiki. The easiest for a *malihini* to find, perhaps, is the recently redecorated **Mandarin** (Tel. 946-3242), at 942 McCully St., near the corner of Beretania St. Back in the days when we thought we didn't like Chinese restaurants very well, we dined here and gobbled up everything that was brought out. They make their own noodles, which we love with beef chunks in a hot sauce. The eggplant and pork are good, as are the Shanghai style steamed dumplings, and the Mongolian beef (sauteed with green onions and red peppers). We wish the Mandarin *fu-lu-shou*—"wealth, luck, and longevity."

A much better-known establishment is the **King Tsin** (Tel. 946-3273) at 1486 South King St.: very simple but very neat decor; excellent service; tables often attended by owner Sylvio Wang or his family members; the hot and sour soup a must; the Crackling Chicken also a popular choice; the Szechuan beef a personal favorite; most dinners in the $12 range. At present, the King Tsin is "in." Except Tuesday, when they're out. Equally dependable, but perhaps a little harder to find for strangers in the city, is the **Maple Garden** (Tel. 941-6641), at 909 Isenberg St.—a fly ball away from the park that used to be the old Honolulu Stadium. Home-run favorites include the very meaty Szechuan smoked duck and eggplant with hot garlic sauce. Mmm! The new **Szechuan Garden** (Tel. 536-5527), an attractive dining nook on Wilder Avenue, we thought was just okay on our single dining experience. We plan to check it out again, though. The **456 Restaurant** (Tel. 947-6456), across King Street from the King Tsin, has slipped. We might now rank it 4,5,6 on a scale of 8,9,10.

The **Mongolian Bar-B-Que** (Tel. 533-7305) has been the leader of a clutch of Oriental dining dens developing downtown in the Cultural Plaza. Besides the title dish, it also features a *Chinese* shabu-shabu, which we haven't yet dipped into. The **Hong Kong Noodle House** (Tel. 536-5409) nearby at 100 North Beretania sometimes has them standing in line outside—for good reason. Ditto the **Mini Garden** (Tel. 538-1273), at 50 North Hotel. But we'd skip the **Yang-Tze**, thank you. The **Paradise Garden** (Tel. 941-8073), near Waikiki at 1665 Kalakaua Ave., is good. At lunch, try the Spicy Beef with Pancake. (Skip McGoun wrote us from Anchorage, Alaska, to say it was the best food he'd ever had in Hawaii!)

CONTINENTAL AND FRENCH CUISINE

Some may wonder what the subtle difference might be between a "Cosmopolitan" restaurant and a "Continental" one. I don't think we can explain it, and I'm not sure we even understand it. Our personal working definition has been that Cosmopolitan restaurants are "not quite all American," and that Continental restaurants are "not quite all French."

A few things we are sure of: It takes more to make a Continental restaurant than translating an American menu into French. You also cannot merely take an island "two scoops rice" joint, expand the wine cellar, and dim the lights. Hmm. But then, if you replace the mahimahi with a Lobster Newburg . . . , perhaps hire an Italian waiter . . . ? (We're only kidding.)

Anyway, we know one when we see one—or taste one—and in this book there are seven or eight Continental candidates who belong with the three or four French restaurants in Honolulu.

The best restaurant on Oahu for the past several years has been **The Third Floor** (Tel. 922-6611), in the Hawaiian Regent Hotel. Entrance like walking into the Horn of Plenty—cascades of fruit, vegetables, salami, and cheeses; large, yet intimate dining area; high-backed rattan chairs creating almost a private room effect; multi-colored banners on high; small fountain and fish pond in the center; impressive copper chandeliers; elegant parquet tables; strolling minstrels on occasion.

The decor is lovely and dignified, but the cuisine is absolutely superb. First of all, if you wish, take the "Promising Start," an appetizer buffet with such delights as fresh hearts of artichoke, vinaigrette shrimp, marinated herring, goose liver pâté, et cetera, et cetera, et cetera. Our last time, we skipped the Start to save room for the dinner, which includes a relish tray anyway (Greek olives, baby corn, pickled tomato, and more), together with a wonderful house salad and Indian *naan* bread. About ten dinners are listed on the menu, including, typically, scampi, a shellfish special, lobster tails, a veal dish, rack of lamb, prime rib, New York steak, Chateaubriand (for two), saddle of venison, and perhaps a pheasant specialty. All are likely to be excellent. There are always seasonal entrees not listed, and these may include fresh local fish.

We saw and experienced terrific service by a young, intelligent, happy (though very correct) crew of several men and women. This restaurant just might have the largest staff-to-customer ratio in the state. Desserts are extra, and you might not have room, anyway. A dozen different coffees and a dozen different teas are available. All meals are finished off with chilled bon bons, dramatically served in a floating dry-ice mist. The sommelier offers about 100 wines.

We take pride in our objectivity, and we accept no advertising and not so much as a free artichoke from any restaurant, but we can hardly find anything critical to say about this dining palace—except that we wish we could afford it more often. Count on spending at least $30 apiece; some uninhibited diners add in wine, the appetizers, the coffees, dessert, etc., and find they blow a lot more without blinking. Be that as it may, The Third Floor is the standard by which we measure all other restaurants in Hawaii.

Probably a little more expensive is the **Maile Restaurant** (Tel. 734-2211)—pronounced "*My*-Lee"—in the super-deluxe Kahala Hilton Hotel, 15 cab minutes from Waikiki. Spiral staircase leading one floor down from the lobby; orchids blooming on a lava rock wall; trellised ceiling; copper and glass chandeliers; several fountains and "outdoors" touches seeking to bring the room visually up out of the cellar; overall decor in orange, brown, and yellow; pleasant and very efficient waitresses, incongruously clad in kimonos; piped-in guitar music from the nearby lounge; the room sometimes a little noisier than we prefer.

The delicately garlicky Taiwan shrimp makes a good appetizer. Another in our party liked the lightly curried turtle soup. The roast duck, with fruits and a Grand Marnier sauce, was excellent, as was the fresh island fish called *opakapaka*. This is one of the few places in Honolulu where a jacket is *required* for male diners (but they may have a few extras on hand to lend you). It's expensive, but not out of line for the quality usually offered.

Michel's (Tel. 923-6552), in the Colony Surf Hotel, 2895 Kalakaua Ave., is certainly more beautiful, more elegant, more famous, and more expensive than many Oahu choices. The fare is sometimes better, too. Unusual setting, with one entire wall open to the beach, palms, and sea; best sunset views at an early dinner; lunch panoramas also excellent; well-decorated rooms with crystal chandeliers, fine china, velvet chairs, and white table cloths; fast-moving, sometimes smart-talking waiters. Roast loin of veal with cream of cognac sauce is a specialty. Ask for a table by the window. In the evening, men must wear a jacket. Usually excellent, but not everyone agrees.

Now, don't become confused, because the original Michel, after whom the above restaurant was named years ago, owns and runs another excellent French restaurant called **Chez Michel** (Tel. 955-7866). It has recently moved from 2126-B Kalakaua Ave. to Eaton Square, 444 Hobron Lane, near the Ilikai Hotel. *Most unfortunately*, still a third restaurant with the word "Michel" in its name has taken over Chez Michel's old address and even its old phone number. (We haven't been to that one, but that part of Kalakaua Avenue is currently rather unsavory anyway.) Chez Michel's is expensive—most main courses are over $20—but the sweetbreads or the Duck a l'Orange will probably be worth the price. Anyway, it's giving a fresh breath of Gallic life to the neighborhood as well as new meaning to "Eatin' Square."

Another of Honolulu's gourmet restaurants, **Bagwells 2424** (Tel. 922-9292), is firmly installed in the Hyatt Regency Hotel. Tiny lights sparkling from indoor tree branches; booths and tables in warm, orange colors; Franciscan china place settings; a talented guitarist around the corner somewhere. Only one person (never a woman) is handed a menu with prices, an out-of-date pretension. Main courses run around $20, and everything else is extra. Some have praised the almond-glazed duck or the Pacific salmon. Bagwells has snagged what may be the best chef around, Yves Menoret, a Gallic champion who apparently likes living in Hawaii and has even adapted some of the best local foods to international culinary standards. We agreed completely when *Gourmet* magazine wrote recently: "Bagwells is flawed by cumbersome serving-cart service and a young, unseasoned dining room staff, but there is a serious chef in the kitchen who cares." (Order carefully if you want to keep your final tab under $35 per diner.) Bagwells may yet become the ranking restaurant in Waikiki.

Champeaux's (Tel. 949-3811), at the top of the Ilikai Hotel's glass-walled elevator, is making a serious bid for recognition, and on our taste test scored very high indeed. We don't think their low-cholesterol *nouvelle cuisine* dishes are always dependable, but their classic French and Continental dishes are generally successful. We have been happy with our Tournedos de Boeuf Rossini and other dishes with French sauces. Go early for the sunset. There are better tables for four and six than there are for two. Enjoyable.

In the Prince Kuhio Hotel, at 2500 Kuhio Ave., the **Protea** (Tel. 922-0811) seeks to join the ranks of Waikiki's finest dining places. Named for a pink island flower (which you'll see displayed there); abounding in shades of protea pink plus warm oranges and yellows; subdued lighting behind gigantic fans; lots of greenery in outsize pots; a wall of translucent wine bottles on one side; a skylight effect on the other; piano music drifting in from the bar. We had a very good Filet Mignon Henry IV with artichoke heart and sauce béarnaise and veal steak with chanterelle mushrooms (over $20 for either). The service was impeccable with the *sommelier* particularly knowledgeable and entertaining. Altogether, an enjoyable evening.

A smaller but no less serious address is the **Cafe de l'Isle French Restaurant** (Tel. 735-5504) at 799 Kapahulu Ave. We particularly enjoyed the French provincial atmosphere at the Cafe de l'Isle, where some of the day's specials are listed on a blackboard menu. (Sara had a delicious lobster-tail dinner.) We recently enjoyed the pricier **Bistro at Diamond Head** (Tel. 735-4444), not far away at 3058 Monsarrat Ave. This is also a favorite of Jim Nabors and Burt Reynolds, when they are in town.

The Holiday Inn-Waikiki has launched the **Captain's Table** (Tel. 926-1700) in an attempt to recapture the atmosphere of "boat day" in Honolulu. Some call it a little hokey, with its recordings of ship-type sound effects, but most take it as a fun theme in this era of theme restaurants. A galley special is Steak Diane, flamed at table-side. It's not the QE-2 to be sure, but some land-lubbers lub it.

In a very different vein, the **Hanohano Room** (Tel. 922-4422), atop the Sheraton-Waikiki Hotel, is also not bad. Up the transparent lift to the end of the line; best seats by the windows or close to the orchestra/dance floor; wonderful panoramas of night-light Honolulu; usually a good orchestra for dining accompaniment and dancing; unusual terrace construction giving more tables a view over the city; acoustics difficult in some areas. We might stay with the beef here (the pepper steak is spectacular). When you take it as a whole experience (altitude, music, dancing, food), you might like it a lot.

Yacht Harbor Restaurant (Tel. 946-2177) is very dignified and very pleasant—if you can find it. It's perched atop the five-story parking garage attached to the Yacht Harbor Towers apartments at 1600 Ala Moana Blvd., corner of Atkinson Drive. On foot, we had to trudge up the automobile ramp and then ask questions.

FILIPINO FOOD IN HAWAII

There are several Filipino restaurants in Honolulu, and if you have a background in Philippines culture, you might enjoy them all. But we neophytes would consider only one.

The **Mabuhay Cafe** (Tel. 537-2493) is at 186 North Hotel St., and we therefore would suggest it only for lunch in this marginal neighborhood. The atmosphere is nothing more nor less than a very simple, friendly, store-front cafe. Filipinos are pork or chicken eaters, and of the 45 things on the menu, we'd pick the Pork or Chicken Adobo (simmered with garlic, vinegar, salt, black pepper, and bay leaves), perhaps still under $4. Some folks like the equally cheap Kare Kare, an oxtail stew with eggplant and long beans. The main dishes tasted all right, but the Filipinos' highly favored and relatively expensive fruit-cocktail/milkshake dessert called *halo-halo* said goodbye-goodbye to each of our group of six. Other than that, we found the Mabuhay a different and rather interesting experience.

HAWAIIAN FOOD

Sadly, Hawaiian cooking is almost an alien in its own land. It holds onto its precarious status largely out of cultural sentiment plus the fierce devotion of a small group of fanciers who will not let it die.

In addition to *poi* (which can be fresh and bland or a few days old and nicely fermented) and the *kalua* pig, both of which we mentioned previously, look for *laulau* (tender pork and beef, sometimes with butterfish, wrapped in taro and ti leaves). Also there is *lomi* salmon (a mixture of smoked salmon, tomatoes, peppers, onions, and crushed ice); if you like lox, you may like *lomi* salmon. For dessert, look for *haupia*, a coconut pudding or *kulolo*, a pudding made from coconut and brown sugar.

Non-Hawaiian restaurants, such as the Tahitian Lanai, the Whaler's Broiler, or the Columbia Inn, to name three that come immediately to mind, will often offer a Hawaiian plate special of the day, and it is this that we might find ourselves ordering, rather than setting out especially to find an honest-to-*kaukau* Hawaiian restaurant.

They do exist, however, and we have had occasion to lunch at one recently, the **Culinary Studio** (Tel. 537-4528), in the Cultural Plaza at the corner of Kukui Street and the River Street Mall. Owner Flossie Shiroma had been catering successfully for so many years previously that it was logical her new restaurant would prove *ono-ono*. It's very simple, neat, clean, inexpensive, and worth a try.

Other favorites include **Helena's Hawaiian Foods** (Tel. 845-8044) at 1364 North King St. and **Ono Hawaiian Foods** (Tel. 737-2275), good and cheap, at 726 Kapahulu Ave. However, most Hawaiian food is experienced by visitors solely at a *luau*, a more-or-less modern version of an ancient Hawaiian feast. Since *luaus* now are usually more entertainment than an authentic Hawaiian dining experience, we will take them up in Section 11, "Nights on the Town."

INDIAN RESTAURANTS

Honolulu historically has had a difficult time keeping Indian restaurants. One good one that has been around for more than a year, now, is **India House** (Tel. 955-7552), located far from the tourist area at 2632 So. King St., near University Avenue. There's no atmosphere to speak of, but the important thing is that owner/chef Ram Arora supervises everything himself. Some choose the Maharaja's Dinner, a mixture of Tandoori chicken, lamb curry, and fish tikka, at about $11. The curry and kabob dinner (about $10) is also popular. If you like it authentically hot, speak up. Otherwise you'll get the milder western version of everything. (Closed Mondays.)

A second entry, the **Shalimar** (Tel. 923-2693), is more convenient. It serves up both Indian and Pakistani dishes from a niche in the Waikiki Holiday Hotel, 450 Lewers St. Besides the curries, you might try the Tandoori chicken or the shrimp Bhunna. We liked it once for lunch awhile back, but somehow never gave it a thorough dinner workout. Let us know what you think.

INDONESIAN FOOD

Finally, after we have lived in Hawaii for years, not only one but two Indonesian restaurants have opened here. And they have similar names.

We recently enjoyed the **Bali Room** (Tel. 949-4321) at the bottom of the new Tapa Tower in the Hilton Hawaiian Village Hotel. The *Rijstafel* was very good (even if not on a par with the famous Bali Restaurant in Amsterdam). There was plenty of it, too, and well worth the tab of $15 per person (we took home about three doggie bags). The other entry, the **Bali Indonesian Restaurant** (Tel. 922-1669), we haven't yet tried. It's on the fourth floor of the Waikiki Shopping Plaza, 2550 Kalakaua Ave., at Seaside. If it's still in business this year, however, we'll get there, too.

ITALIAN DINING

The dependable **Trattoria** (Tel. 923-8415) is in a corner of the Edgewater Hotel at Kalia Road and Beach Walk. Those experienced in the ways of Roman dining may call the place more a fine *ristorante* than a modest *trattoria* in the original sense. And the real significance of the place is that it offers some of the more subtle *al burro* dishes (cooked in butter instead of olive oil) of central and northern Italy. On our most recent visit, we thought the lasagna very good, the Correletto di Vitelo alla Parmigianna and the Pollo alla Romana even better. We have sometimes found the elbow-to-elbow seating disturbing, and although the guitarist is good, we were once placed so near him that we couldn't hold a conversation among our group. Prices are generally moderate. Watch your seating, and you'll probably enjoy yourself. (Open daily, dinner only.)

At the corner of Kuhio and Seaside avenues, in the relatively obscure Marine Surf-Waikiki Hotel, is **Matteo's** (Tel. 922-5551), a Hollywood-type Italian dining spot, often a haunt of local and visiting entertainers. (One pepper steak is named after Frank Sinatra.) Large and dark with lots of oil paintings and orange lights; relative privacy in well-padded booths; excellent house salad or antipasto; specialties in veal good and perhaps worth the price; a very attentive cadre of professional waiters; a nice selection of Italian wines, plus an expensive (but not bad) house carafe. For the food, you'd better figure on at least $25 per person here. If that seems high for an Italian restaurant, you may be right, but plenty of people are happy to pay. (Open daily for dinner only.)

Downtown, far from the usual tourist haunts, are two more Italian addresses. The most *elegante* is **Matteo's Royal Tavern** (Tel. 524-4870) in a historic building at No. 2 Merchant St. (It is said to have been a bar patronized by King Kalakaua a century ago.) We enjoyed our Chicken Rolletini (perhaps $12 at dinner, $8 at lunch). Other dinner specials of veal and fish. Highly favored by the local *cognoscenti*.

Another spaghetti emporium is a barn of a place, the furnishing of which must have denuded the Tyrol of every antique it ever possessed. It's called **The Old Spaghetti Factory** (Tel. 531-1513, but currently taking no reservations). Amid the stained glass and bedsteads of brass are scores of happy spaghetti slurpers. Some don't like the crowds here, but large families lap up the prices. Dishes begin in the $5 neighborhood (cheaper for kids). Light and dark draft beer or decanted *vino di tavola* is available. Hardly gourmet, but fun nevertheless.

Another high-quality Italian room, which serves lunch too, is **Sneeky La Pasta** (Tel. 922-2702), formerly Comito's East, back in Waikiki in the Ilima Hotel at 445 Nohonani St. A dark rendezvous with leather-like tablecloths and doctored photos of Ital-lionized local celebrities; large menu with most dinners in the $10 range; noontime chicken and bell peppers at around $5 a tasty deal. We haven't been in a while, so keep your fingers crossed.

Another super-decorous salon is **Spats** (Tel. 922-9292) in the Hyatt Regency Waikiki. Furnished à la 1920s speakeasy—but much nicer, come to think of it—this Al Capone-ish cellar was once billed as a "family style" dining room. The menu is longer than that, although the service might be as friendly as at your Uncle Giovanni's. (Some booths are small, though; the tables are a more commodious bet.) Spats' Mamma Mia banks her fires about 10 P.M., and after the family goes to bed, the place turns into a disco for the *bambini*. Fun—and often very good, too.

More modest Italian entries include the well-advertised **Rudy's** (Tel. 923-5949) in the Outrigger Surf Hotel and **Bella Italia**, in Ala Moana Center. They're okay for tomato paste lovers but far from the quality of those preceding. We haven't yet tried **Renown Milano** (Tel. 947-1933) at the Discovery Bay condo, or **Papa's** (Tel. 949-8848), a BYOW place at 1614 S. King St.

JAPANESE FARE IN HONOLULU

The Japanese are always quick to pick up on a new thing, embracing new experiences in food as they do other things of quality, so it is sometimes difficult to tell what is genuine Japanese cooking. Many of the most famous Japanese dishes may have started out as Portuguese, Chinese, Korean—even American.

Such as *teppanyaki*, which has become immensely popular over the past several years. (*Teppan* means a metal plate and *yaki* means broil or fry.) It involves grilling steak, chicken, shrimp, etc., on a heavy steel top which forms the "*teppan* table" around which the diners sit. The chef cuts, slices and sprinkles with a deft click-click, clack-clack, zip-zip, putting on a show of dexterity along with the food preparation, then he serves them out right there, along with bean sprouts and other vegetables.

This kind of Japanese steak house was developed in Tokyo not long ago to appeal to Americans and other foreigners, but the Japanese soon took to it themselves with equal fervor. In Honolulu, some Japanese restaurants also have *teppan* tables, some have them exclusively, and some don't have them at all. It is probably now the most popular style of Japanese cooking for Americans, although some folks don't like sharing a table—lunch counter style—with others.

As a general rule, Japanese food is water based and cooked quickly. Fish, chicken, or beef is either broiled, boiled, fried, simmered, or steamed (never baked). There are several interesting seasonings, including *shoyu* and *sake* (rice wine). Vegetables play an important role, including such different ones as *tofu* (soybean curd), bamboo shoots, and *daikon* (white radish). Everything is served with rice—not the light, fluffy "*haole* rice," but sticky and gooey so it is easy to pick up on chopsticks! Full meals also have soup and green tea.

Other dishes which are always favorites for Mainlanders include *suki-*

yaki (*suki* means "slice thin"), in which thinly sliced meat and vegetables are fried in a flat-bottomed pan. (The Japanese like it served with a raw egg, which can be whipped in at the table, but, well, frankly we always ignore or send back the egg.)

Shabu-shabu is another favorite, and works rather like a Swiss fondue. You pick up a slice of meat, cook it in the boiling broth for a moment, then dip it into some special sauce before eating. It's really very good, but a certain amount of work is involved all through the meal, of course.

Then there's *tempura*, an uncharacteristic cooking method imported to Japan by sixteenth-century Portuguese. Vegetables, fish, and, most popularly, shrimp, are cooked in a batter in very hot oil.

Japanese food is usually cut up into small pieces so it may be easily picked up with chopsticks. If you are not adept at chopsticks, let the waiter or waitress show you how to use them. In Hawaii, they often come as one piece of bamboo or wood, partially slit apart. Break them the rest of the way and rub the small ends against each other to remove any tiny splinters. Chopsticks are held so that the bottom chopstick is stationary and the top one movable. The bottom stick should be in the crotch of the thumb, and the thumb forces the stick tightly against the inside tip of the ring finger. The top chopstick is held by the thumb and the first two fingers, much like a pencil, and is moved up and down by bending the fingers. If you want to try it, find a friend who knows something about chopsticks to show you exactly how, and then practice it by using two fresh, unsharpened pencils.

With the unfortunate closing of the Mon Cher Ton Ton, the best all-around Japanese restaurant is probably the very attractive **Restaurant Suntory** (Tel. 922-5511) on the second floor of Building B in the Royal Hawaiian Center (very near the Sheraton). The Suntory runs the gamut in foods Japanese, although so far we've only tried the offerings in the *teppan* room, which were delicious. Everything was à la carte, and offerings are in a wide price range from $15 to $25. Others have praised the Shabu-Shabu dinners, the Beef Sukiyaki, or the many fish dishes. There is also an elegant version of a Tokyo *sushi* bar on the premises. Things can add up here fast. Service will probably continue to be excellent.

For *teppanyaki* exclusively, no Honolulu restaurant can beat the simple elegance of its own link in the ubiquitous chain **Benihana of Tokyo** (Tel. 955-5955), on the grounds of the Hilton Hawaiian Village. We've never liked its advertising, but we do like its food. Outfitted like a very neat, old-fashioned Japanese farmhouse; a half-dozen *teppan* tables, most holding seven diners; some private rooms around the edge of the large open area; athletic chefs with excellent memories as to who ordered what; lunchtime bargains still about $8 (for chicken) to about $10 for a hibachi steak special; dinner prices from about $14 to $20 for a super spread including soup, hibachi shrimp, salad, special steak, hibachi vegetables, and ice cream. There's an unfortunate local trend to look down on Benihana for its very popularity. It does tend to be more expensive, and some evening diners say that they feel constrained to rush. But otherwise, we can't fault it. Delicious and fun.

The decorous little **Maiko** (Tel. 946-5151), downstairs in the Ilikai Hotel, is a charming choice for several Japanese dishes. We cooked the Genghis Khan Steak at our table, and enjoyed it. The bill for two was about $35. Then at 2057 Kalakaua Ave., next to Fort DeRussy, is **Kyo-Ya** (Tel. 947-3911), which significantly attracts a considerable number of tourists from Japan. If you haven't yet tried *sukiyaki*, this might be the place. The **Kobe Steak House** (Tel. 941-4444), at 1841 Ala Moana, near the Ilikai, offers good *teppanyaki* by entertaining chefs—once you get to the table. Despite our reservation, our large party was kept in the bar for nearly an hour. (It's American beef—not Kobe—by the way.) This restaurant is perhaps slightly cheaper than Benihana, about a block away. We also liked the very simple, very friendly **Regent Marushin** (Tel. 922-6452) in the Hawaiian Regent Hotel for old-style dining.

The traditional Japanese favorite in town is **Furusato** (Tel. 923-8878, for the one at 134 Kapahulu Ave.), although now there are many new spots which seem to have passed it by over the years. It may still be the most beautifully decorated Japanese restaurant, however, and it surely is the only one which announces each guest's arrival on a gong! Make special arrangements if you don't want to sit on the floor, for there are some conventional table and chairs available. A new branch of Furusato's has now opened in the Hyatt Regency Waikiki.

If you are a party of four to six, you'll probably get your very own small *teppan* table at **Chaco's** (Tel. 732-9333). This was the first restaurant to bring *teppanyaki* to Honolulu, several years back. Now it's a little out of the way at 2888 Waialae Ave., but the meals are still good. At the top of the tank in the Pacific Beach Hotel, the little **Shogun** (Tel. 922-1233) offered *teppanyaki* that was all right, but *sushi* and other authentic Japanese finger foods were particularly appealing. We were not too impressed with the **Miyako** (not to be confused with previously named Maiko), at the top of the Kaimana Beach Hotel. We thought the food was no more than okay, and that the portions were small. Some folks like the **Suehiro** (Tel. 949-4584), a simple establishment at 1824 South King St. We would go there again *only* if we can sit with our own group in a *tatami* mat room. Otherwise the ambiance is quite ordinary. It's inexpensive, at any rate. (Closed Tuesday.) One of the most authentic Japanese restaurants around is **Yanagi's Sushi** (Tel. 537-1525) in a modest address at 762 Kapiolani Blvd. downtown. You can watch them make the stuff on the premises. Also good is the Alaska King Crab, they say, but we haven't tried it. And sorry, we still haven't visited **Tanaka of Tokyo** (Tel. 922-4702) on the fifth floor of the Waikiki Shopping Plaza. However, Monty Strauss of Lubbock, Texas, pronounced it "delicious." (Thanks, Monty!)

MEXICAN RESTAURANTS

There are always a half-dozen or so Mexican restaurants in town, but most of them are about as stable as a *sombrero* in a high wind—moving addresses, switching owners, or changing their names at the drop of a *serape*. One of the old favorites, however, is **La Paloma** (Tel. 533-1272), not too conveniently sited at 1216 Kapiolani Blvd. Nice, comfortable ambiance of stucco and dark wood; comfortable red-leather booths and mahogany tables; Mexican music on the stereo; fairly standard, taco-enchilada-based fare; large portions generally; a little mild for the true *aficionado*; hot sauces on the tables, however. Altogether, a dependable, inexpensive family operation.

A newer entry on the Mexican scene is **Popo's** (formerly Pepe's, Tel. 923-7355), sharing a *hacienda* with the South Seas Village at 2112 Kalakaua Ave. It opened in time to capture the *jefe de la cocina* from the defunct La Fonda, which means the menu is not limited to the spicy border foods, but also offers some sophisticated selections from Mexico City. Lots of stucco and wrought iron around; no air conditioning; diners in the loggia watching the passing parade; generous dinner helpings in the $8 range. We were certainly *satisfecho*.

A newer branch called **Popo's Cantina** (Tel. 955-3326) has opened on the ground floor of Canterbury Place, a condominium apartment building at 1910 Ala Moana Blvd., on the corner of Ena Road, and not far from the Hilton Hawaiian Village. Some tables are outside.

An attractive address in the Royal Hawaiian Center is **La Mex** (Tel. 923-2906), and many have spoken well of its offerings. On our night, however, the billed *mariachi* music was recorded, the fare was bland, and the service was almost nonexistent. We'll try it again this year.

For really inexpensive south-of-the-border fare, you might look into **Mama's Mexican Kitchen** (Tel. 537-3200), even more out in the cactus at 378 North School St. The original Mama has long ago folded her apron and moved away, but someone always seems to keep the ovens hot, for better or for worse, and for richer or for poorer. Next, far out at 1134 Koko Head Ave., is **Jose's** (Tel. 732-1833), which has been slipping and sliding in this Kaimuki neighborhood. In the same precincts, some prefer the **Azteca** (Tel. 735-2492) at 3569 Waialae Ave. **La Cocina** at Ala Moana Center is not bad, but it's cheaper at the outdoor window. (The taco you loved for 90 cents on the sidewalk becomes $1.80 if you sit down inside.) Last, but for California-style food fanciers perhaps not least, there are two branches of the ubiquitous **Taco Bell** Mexican-style take-out chain. One is on South King Street, and the other is on Kapahulu Avenue, about five blocks in from Waikiki. You can't miss it.

SEAFOOD SELECTIONS

Many head first for the modestly titled **Nick's Fish Market** (Tel. 955-6333), an underground den in the Waikiki Gateway Hotel. Very dark, stucco-walled grotto; flashlights sometimes needed to decode the menu; super-chummy waiters who just might join in your conversation (described by one local wag as "beach boys in tuxedos"); most fish dishes excellent, especially swordfish, abalone, mahimahi (of course), ualu, opakapaka, and a super-expensive air-flown Maine lobster; accompanying vegetables sometimes bland by comparison; a superb Greek salad available, however; one of the highest priced wine menus in town. Some whose opinions we respect have enjoyed the Crepes Madagascar. Not everyone likes the atmosphere here, and reservation policies are erratic, but if fish is your thing—and you're willing to pay through the gills— Nick's is a good catch.

A second champion of the ocean is far out of Waikiki, but convenient enough with your own wheels and a map. That's the architecturally inspiring **John Dominis Restaurant** (Tel. 523-0955), launched by Republican state senator D.G. "Andy" Anderson, who occasionally and unsuccessfully runs for mayor or governor. His restaurant, however, is a winner— both as an eye-dazzler and a tummy-tempter. Look for it at 43 Ahui Street, which is next to the channel entrance to Kewalo Basin. Island fish are prepared in several different ways. There are also a few very nice meat dishes in the chef's repertoire. All are expensive, to be sure, but we've never met a dissatisfied diner at Dominis.

In the same general neighborhood, and not to be confused with the above, is **Fisherman's Wharf** (Tel. 538-3808), which ties up to the tuna boats and harbor cruise ships at Kewalo Basin. Decor of stuffed denizens, glass balls, flotsam and jetsam; friendly but sometimes overworked waitresses; checkered tablecloths; generally good local specialties; often crowded; open for lunch and dinner. Try the Shrimp Louie Salad in Abalone Shell for lunch. Admittedly more informal and more modest, and certainly less complete and less expensive than Nick's or John Dominis, the Wharf nevertheless holds up pretty well for the shallower investment. Across the street, we don't like the **Chowder House** at the prices asked for the small portions offered.

Still on the waterfront beat, downtown at 923 Nuuanu St., the modestly titled **Jameson's Merchant Square Oyster Bar** (Tel. 523-7906) is much more than that. Open for lunch and dinner (always reserve), it also features shrimp, prawns (raised right on Oahu), scallops, and freshly caught fish, served in indoor and outdoor settings. Some specialties include the clam chowder, the seafood quiche, and artichoke stuffed with seafood. Sourdough bread is flown in from San Francisco. And is there an oyster bar? You bet, and bivalve fans say there's none better this side of the Sydney Rocks. To round out the fish scene, they're making quite a splash at the **Monterey Bay Canners** (Tel. 925-5161), both at the Outrigger Hotel on the beach and over at Ward Centre. Our own experience was not such a buoyant one, however.

THAI DINING

The Thai-style **Mekong** (Tel. 521-2025) has inherited the mantle—and the menu, cook, waiters, and dishwashers—of the late, lamented Khun Mariam's. Nowhereland location at 1295 South Beretania; Thai posters on the walls; eight tables and a bar, evocative of a waterside cafe in Bangkok; spicy meals served in a friendly manner; most dishes in the $8 or $9 range. Try the Thai crispy noodles, the satay beef or pork, the spring rolls, or that staple of Southeast Asia, meatball rice noodle soup. Adventurous diners conjure up the Evil Jungle Priest (sliced chicken or pork sauteed in hot spices on a bed of cabbage). Smooth the way with Ching Mai salad. For dessert, there's a dollar delight of bananas in warm coconut milk. Open daily except no lunch on Sunday. Delicious. Much closer to Waikiki, and owned by the same outfit, is **Keo's** (Tel. 737-8240) at 441 Kapahulu Ave., just about 1½ blocks from the zoo. Also recommended.

The newer **Thai House** (Tel. 521-1606), at 1243 S. King St., offers several sea-soned specialties: Steamed crab in bean sauce, fish cake with cucumber sauce, squid salad, or whole fish deep fried with chili peppers. No atmosphere, but also inexpensive and also good.

Sorry, but we couldn't get to the newest of this Thai quartet for a personal look-see-taste before this volume went to press. However the **Royal Thai** (Tel. 949-0481) at 2671 S. King St. has been packing in fans of this fare, and we know some who have pronounced it better than the other three.

SOME WELL-KNOWN BUFFETS

The spread offered on Sunday only at the **Maile Terrace** (Tel. 734-2211) is rapidly gaining fame. The Maile Terrace—which should not be confused with the basement-sited Maile Restaurant—overlooks the Dolphin Lagoon at the Kahala Hilton Hotel. The price will probably be about $16 per person this year. Same price for children.

The evening buffet at the **Ocean Terrace** (Tel. 922-4422) begins at 6 P.M. daily in the Sheraton-Waikiki Hotel. It's a beautiful ocean setting, and you can stuff yourself while the sun sets for probably around $14. Our only minor criticism was that we were not fond of the precooked rice we found there on our night. Everything else was good, and the atmosphere is unsurpassed.

We thought the **Summery** in the Hawaiian Regent Hotel was vastly overrated in its evening buffet activities on Friday and Saturday. Somehow, though, the Summery remains fine as a daytime coffee shop. But the **Marco Polo** buffet, in the apartments of the same name, represented one of our most unsuccessful voyages despite the low tabs.

COFFEE SHOPS AND EFFICIENCY RESTAURANTS

Here are some diners that do not fall easily into the categories listed previously. Generally speaking, they offer all three meals, and some will be open around the clock.

The best all-around coffee shop in Honolulu is the **Wailana Coffee House** (Tel. 955-1764) in the Wailana Apartment Building at 1860 Ala Moana Blvd., just across from the Hilton Dome. Open 24 hours; validated parking underneath; warm gold and yellow decor; often crowded; best booths at the window; fast, generally efficient service; choice of full dinners or snacks; the broasted chicken a best seller; steaks at under $12; excellent dinners on holidays and special occasions; perhaps the waffliest waffles in town. Here are good, well-served meals in the best American tradition, yet with distinct and flavorful local accents, too. Warmly recommended for the type.

Some prefer the nearby **Tops Canterbury Coffee House** (Tel. 941-5277), 1910 Ala Moana Blvd. Open 24 hours, it features booths in olde oake style, fake faded petit point, lions and unicorns etched in glass, etc. We gave it an "A" for atmosphere and a "C" for bill of fare.

Much better is the place we seem to receive more letters about than any other, **Coconut Willie's** (Tel. 923-0777), at 270 Lewers St. in Amfac's Holiday Isle Hotel. Decor is vaguely British Colonial with koa wood paneling, parquet flooring, oriental area carpets, period chandeliers and fans, etched and stained glass, and waitresses and waiters in campaign jackets. Food, however, is American with a dash of Hawaii—lots of burgers, steaks (including teriyaki), barbecues, omelets, salads, and ice cream specialties. Dinner will run around $11. There are several luncheon specials for around half that.

Downtown near the state and city government buildings, the **Columbia Inn** (Tel. 531-3747) is a 24-hour favorite for many at 645 Kapiolani Blvd. It owes much of its fame to the fact that it has been the standard feeding trough and watering oasis for so many newspaper workers at the next-door Honolulu *Advertiser* and Honolulu *Star-Bulletin*. If you're an

L.A. Dodgers fan, you'll feel at home in the baseball bar. The best batter is the shrimp *tempura*—at least a three-bagger and sometimes a home run.

The **Terrace Grille**, third floor in the Diamond Head tower of the Hyatt Regency, is a classy coffee corner, but despite its early ambitions, it is no longer open around the clock. The **Minute Chef**, operated by the P.K. at the corner of Kalakaua and Kaiulani, has generally well-prepared combinations. And the **Veranda**, in green and white, is a pleasant appendage to the lobby level of the Waikiki Beachcomber. A blue plate gourmet we know named Milt Guss declares its specials to be especially good bargains.

Unpretentious, inexpensive, and down-home food, local style, is served at the **Flamingo**, one wing of which is at 574 Ala Moana, where no restaurant ought to be, and the other at 871 Kapiolani, also a rather strange address. Substantial meals are served for about $10 per diner per evening. It's hard to beat for the low prices, but another contender is the efficient **Likelike Drive In**, which is really a sit-down cafe at 735 Keeaumoku St. (And that's pronounced "leaky-leaky," like the highway of the same name.)

The **Rigger Restaurant** at 2335 Kalakaua Ave., in central Waikiki, is a good table-and-booth bazaar for burgers and the like. Decorated in slick Polynesian, it has lots of localized dishes like a Beach Boy Special, Surf Burgers, etc.

You'll find several addresses for the **Jolly Roger**, but our most recent foray was into one at the corner of Kuhio and Kaiulani avenues in Waikiki. Naugahyde and formica abound, and it was noisy with the clatter of dishes and the recorded music which tried unsuccessfully to drown out the chorus of dancing plates. Nevertheless, our charcoal-broiled burgers and coffee tasted fine, and service was quick and good. Breakfast is fun at 2244 Kalakaua Ave., especially if you draw a table by the sidewalk. We have not been as jolly in some of their other branches, however.

Perry's Smorgy is one of those all-you-can-eat cafeterias. At the moment, you can find one in the Reef, another in the Outrigger, and a third in the Coral Seas hotels. For five or six bucks, you can fill up on spaghetti, chicken, pot roast, and several other things. Not bad for a starved trencherman on a bottom budget, but we wouldn't look for any gourmet bargains.

Another traditional penny-squeezer's pal has been the **Colonial House Cafeteria** in the International Market Place. But we thought the house was pretty battered and beaten recently, both in its dining room and in its kitchen products.

In the Ilikai Hotel, the **Pier 7** is neat and popular, but we've always thought it overpriced. **Coco's**, the conical 24-hour spot at the corner of Kalakaua and Kapiolani, we've never been fond of. It's the kind of place that might charge us an extra 15 cents if we want a slice of onion on our hamburger. And **Tops**, at 298 Beachwalk, was the "bottoms" as far as we were concerned. The pleasant decor was soured for us by bumbling service, soggy french fries, and a virtually inedible sandwich.

The meals at the Waikiki **Woolworth's** aren't bad for the low tabs. There's no longer a kosher-style "deli" on Kalakaua Avenue, but a somewhat similar establishment in the Ala Moana Shopping Center is **Lyn's Delicatessen**. It used to be a madhouse between 12 and 1, but it seems to us like they've reduced the size of their sandwiches lately and the lines aren't quite as hefty, either.

For the past year or two, however, the sandwich queen of Honolulu has been **Heidi's Bread Basket**, with addresses in several nooks and crannies around town. You can get your beerwurst, headcheese, or Danish ham on about a dozen different kinds of bread. In a hard-to-find corner on the ground floor of the Davies Pacific Center (Bishop and Merchant streets), **The Haven** builds some wonderful, healthy sandwiches. Our favorite is Avocado and Bacon Bits on nine-grain bread. M-m-m-m-m! A newer branch at Ala Moana Center is not as good.

For a wide variety of local and Mainland-style snacks, head for a diner with lots of genuine local character, **Zippy's**. There are several sites, including a new one near Waikiki at 601 Kapahulu and its familiar "Saimin Lanai" at 1725 South King St. Take a minute or two to peruse the wall-mounted menu, and you might like to try a *saimin*, a teri beef and rice plate, *sushi*, etc. Of course it has hamburgers, chili, etc., too. Zippy's is not much more than a snack bar, of course, but it's a good one, with a definite Hawaii accent.

Yes, there are **McDonald's** in Hawaii, as there are in Tokyo and Melbourne. They're still usually a bargain as compared with many other places (but the Waikiki one is usually a little higher). Until recently, the only thing different about McDonald's in Hawaii were the wide-open walls and the aloha shirt uniforms worn by the workers. Now they have made a couple of small concessions to popular local tastes in some branches—adding papaya and Portuguese sausage to their breakfast menu and *saimin* at all hours of the day. We're still waiting for them to add a McTeri burger to balance all those Mainland Macs, however. You'll also notice a clutch of **Kentucky Fried Chickens**, although strangely not at the moment in Waikiki. If you like it at home, you'll probably like it in Hawaii, too. Other fast-food chains represented in Honolulu include Jack-in-the-Box, Wendy's, Burger King, Church's, Taco Bell, Pizza Hut, and Shakey's.

SPECIAL AND UNUSUAL EATING PLACES

In an outside corner of the Honolulu Academy of Arts is one of the best and least-known culinary bargains in Hawaii, the **Garden Cafe** (Tel. 531-8865). Open only for lunch—two sittings, at 11:30 A.M. and 1 P.M.— Tuesday through Friday, about September through May; operated by volunteer ladies connected with the academy; each lunch with a different specialty soup, salad, and sandwich; no choice; all at a single price ($6 or so); sometimes dessert as an extra. *Reserve always.* (We would ask for the menu of the day and the exact price by phone.) Very pleasant.

Not far away, and at this writing all the rage, is **T.G.I. Friday** (Tel. 523-5841), at the corner of King Street and Ward Avenue, across from the Blaisdell Center Concert Hall. Outdoor section a little too close to the traffic for comfort and conversation; a cooler, quieter, and cleaner indoors simply loaded with interesting antiques; large menu with unusual and clever specialty items (I loved my "potato skins" filled with various spicy delights); champagne Sunday brunch for around $9; currently on a "no reservations" policy. Friday's is fun any day of the week.

About the farthest thing from Hawaii is **Marrakech** (Tel. 955-5566), a Moroccan-style feast nightly at 1855 Kalakaua, with belly dancers, finger cymbals, navel jewels—the whole bit. If you can take two hours of that kind of music and writhing, the Casbah specialties like couscous, pastilla, chicken, and rabbit are pretty good. Figure about $22 per pasha, here, plus whatever bills you lose playing Pin the Dollars on the Dancers. Some folks love it.

For ribs, try **Tony Roma's** (Tel. 942-2121) at the corner of Kalakaua Avenue and Pau St. The barbecued baby back ribs are a bargain at lunch, more expensive at dinner.

The Salvation Army's lovely, half-century-old **Waioli Tea Room** (Tel. 988-2131) up in Manoa Valley suffers from TMT—too many tourists—in our opinion. They come in by the belching busload—often in several diesel coaches at the same time—and literally swarm through its premises. For a late lunch—after the crowds have left—it's not too bad. Try the *mahimahi*. Skip the Robert Louis Stevenson steak.

Pub dining. The warmth and informality of the English or Irish pub is approximated in several drinking/eating establishments in Honolulu this year. For authentic Victorian atmosphere (they brought in all that mahogany from England) nothing in Hawaii beats **Dickens** (Tel. 531-2727), unfortunately located in a modern building at 1221 Kapiolani Blvd. A recent change of ownership, however, has resulted in a new menu which is less British and less inspiring. It's still fun for a beer, anyway. The **Rose and Crown** in King's Village concentrates on drinking and some eating (meat pies and the like). Atmosphere depends on the crowd. **Jameson's Irish Coffee House** is pretty nice for Irish coffee, quiches, omelets, etc., for late, light dining. There are two addresses— 342 Seaside in Waikiki and 12 Merchant St. in the revitalized downtown area. Also in the same immediate neighborhood is **O'Toole's Irish Pub** (Tel. 536-6360), 902 Nuuanu Ave., which offers a full menu and live piano music. We've yet to try their Shillelagh hamburger.

Vegetarian fare. The most charming, most delicious, most friendly, and most attractive vegetarian address is the tiny **Laulima** (Tel. 947-3844), which is somewhat out-of-the-way at 2239 S. King St. We never thought much of vegetarian food before we sat down at their shiny butcher block tables, but the things they do with avocados, melted cheese, peanut butter, mushrooms, etc., are amazing. It opens at 11:30 A.M. daily, and if you go between 12 and 1, you probably won't squeeze in. You might have to sit on the floor here anyway, but if you're mellow about it, it's worth it. (No smoking.) And not so strictly vegetarian, but of the same general genre, is **Johnny Appleseed** at 932 Ward Ave., across from the Concert Hall. It's deservedly popular.

Pancakes and waffles. A downtown favorite is **Jake's**, at Bishop and Hotel streets. Then, at the little, plain shopping center at 1414 Dillingham Blvd., there's the **Original Pancake House** (Tel. 847-1496) from a Seattle franchise (and seemingly just about as much out of the way).

Pizzas. You won't get two people to agree on this, either. We like the ones baked by the branches of **Shakey's Pizza Parlor** (Tel. 946-2821 for the one at 805 Keeaumoku St.). Others swear by **Mama Mia Pizza & Deli** (Tel. 947-5233) at 1015 University Ave., or **Harpo's** in the Ward Warehouse.

Submarine sandwiches. There's just one champion sub manufacturer, as far as we are concerned, and that's **Mister Sub** (Tel. 945-3511) at 1035 University Ave., next to Mama Mia's in the Puck's Alley shopping complex. M.S. makes at least 40 combinations, of which a personal favorite is the "Opu Buster" with Russian dressing. We can always dive into that one, even if we have trouble floating afterwards. Wow!

Ice cream. Now all the rage are the hot fudge sundaes at **North Shore Fudge** in the Diamond Head end of the Moana Hotel.

Shave ice. This local dessert—compared to, but much more wonderful than, a snow cone—is perhaps best sampled in Honolulu at the **Waiola Store**, a "mom and pop" grocery at 2135 Waiola St., off McCully Street. Shave ice aficionado Tom Brislin, an editor on the Honolulu *Advertiser*, likes his with vanilla and coconut syrups mixed half-and-half over a large shave ice with an ice cream base. Mmmm!

KITCHENS IN THE COUNTRY

Here's a brief round-up of restaurants you may run across by design or by accident on a trip around the Island of Oahu:

PEARL CITY. The **Pearl City Tavern** (Tel. 455-1045), corner of Kam (Kamehameha) Highway and Lehua Ave. A first-rate restaurant specializing in Japanese food, but with several other choices, including excellent lobster. Also famed for its Monkey Bar and its collection of bonsai trees. To sound like a local, just call it the P.C.T.

MAKAHA. The **Sheraton** (Tel. 695-9511) on the Makaha Valley Road is expensive and probably good. More unassuming fare will be found at the nautically decorated **Fogcutter** (Tel. 695-9404).

WAHIAWA. The most famous restaurant in this center-island community is on the shores of little Lake Wilson, across Route 99 from Schofield Barracks; it's called **Kemoo Farm** (Tel. 621-8481). Keep your eyes open or you'll miss it. It's great for a cool lunch on a hot day, overlooking the water and the eucalyptus trees. Reservations advised in the evening.

HALEIWA. Famous for baking its own pies is the **Sea View Inn**. (Try the banana or blueberry cream.) The new **Jameson's By the Sea** may be nice. It's a branch of the Honolulu operation of a similar name. Getting up a lot of steam these days is **Steamer's**. Seafood is the specialty, but steaks and chops are also available. The nearby Mexican entry, **Rosie's Cantina**, does a willing, credible job with standard, south-of-the-border dishes. It shares a front door with a pizza place we haven't tried. The **Tic Toc** offers little more than very cold air conditioning and too many echoes, we thought. Zeke Wigglesworth, the perspicacious travel editor of the San Jose *Mercury-News*, says some of the best hamburgers on the island come from **Kua Aina**, a tiny Haleiwa shop. We might also save Haleiwa as a dessert to a Wahiawa lunch by searching out the **M. Matsumoto Grocery** at 66-087 Kam Highway, and ordering cones of "shave ice" (flavored crushed ice). We prefer the kind with either ice cream or sweet *azuki* beans in the bottom of the paper cone.

WAIMEA. The **Proud Peacock** (Tel. 638-8513), at Waimea Falls Park, is a pleasant room in a beautiful garden setting. Our roast beef was fine.

KAHUKU. Sorry, the Kuilima dining rooms, under the new Hilton banner, are a mystery at deadline.

LAIE. This is the home of the Polynesian Cultural Center, which traditionally offers great displays and entertainment but only fair fare. Readers have complained of long lines and cold food.

HAUULA. Try the **Texas Paniolo,** if you dare. It's the only restaurant in Hawaii to offer rattlesnake meat!

PUNALUU. There's just one restaurant, **Pat's at Punaluu** (Tel. 293-8502), and without it, you might not know where Punaluu is. Although there are several who lament (correctly) that it was much nicer when "Pat" was alive, it's nevertheless still a very pleasant, beachside dining room. It's now the bottom floor in a huge beachside condo.

KAAAWA. Actually, the **Crouching Lion Inn** (Tel. 237-8511) is just on the *outskirts* of Kaaawa(!) nearer Kahana Bay, and about 2 miles from Punaluu. Time was when no one would think of tripping around the island without a stop at the Inn. Now the lunches are so crowded that it's not much fun during the day. If you can get to this charming site for dinner, however, try the Slavonic Steak, carved at your table—about $33 for two.

KANEOHE. For steaks, a salad bar, etc., you can do worse than the galley at **Rosey's Boat House** (Tel. 247-0039), on Kam Highway, for the evening meal. For lunch (or dinner) in a charming green setting, however, search out **Haiku Gardens** (Tel. 247-6671) at 46–336 Haiku Road, about a quarter mile *mauka* of Kahekili Highway. **Mexican Gardens** (Tel. 235-4141) is no Xochimilco, but it is reasonably good. The hard-to-find site is near the Times Supermarket.

KAILUA. There is one very nice little French salon in this bedroom community, open for dinner only. **L'Auberge** (Tel. 262-4835) at 117 Hekili St. is a popular local choice and certainly *très bien*. Then there's **Orson's Bourbon House** (Tel. 262-2306) at 5 Hoolai St., perhaps a little pretentious, but savory, in the New Orleans style. There are two nicely decorated coffee shops, **Rob Roy's** (Tel. 262-6992), open for three decent if unspectacular squares at 26 Hoolai St., and **Bib's Family Restaurant** (Tel. 261-8724), at 315 Uluniu St., which we now like much better. The new **Yum Yum Tree** didn't open before deadline. For pizza, try **Alexander's**, across the parking lot from Emjay's market. For beef, one of our favorite feederies on the island is **Buzz's Original Steak House** (Tel. 261-4661), at 413 Kawailoa Rd., across from Kailua Beach Park. Many consider it worth driving to especially from Waikiki. **Buzz's Original Fish House**, however, is another story. It's not nearly as good a catch.

6. Sightseeing Oahu

Face it—the Capital Island has so many targets for ogling, ooing and ahing that it is impossible to see everything on a single vacation. And, praise be, not everything appeals to everybody. So the lists included below are designed so you can cut in and cut out of them as desired.

Sightwise, we've divided Oahu into five parts. The lead pair are walking tours; they are first, *Waikiki*, and second, *Downtown*.

Next we sweep nearly everything else in the metropolitan area into *Greater Honolulu*. It is arranged generally alphabetically, since no itinerary could efficiently cover them all in a single swing anyway.

Finally, there are two circuits more suitable for a set of wheels. The first is the relatively short *East Oahu Circle*, a good morning's or afternoon's jaunt by car. The second we call the *Big Middle Island Round Trip*. You could almost handle that in a half-day, too, but we think it would be a mistake to do so. In both these motor excursions, like the walking tours, we have tried to cover things in the order you may run across them.

A WAIKIKI WALK—THE PARK TO THE YACHT HARBOR

"Waikiki is *not* Hawaii!" someone will tell you. Unh-hunh, and we tell you, "Nonsense." Of course you could say it is no more Hawaii than, say, Kilauea Volcano *is* Hawaii, or Waimea Canyon *is* Hawaii, or Schofield Barracks *is* (or *are*) Hawaii. The point is that Waikiki is an integral and vital part of today's Hawaii, regardless of anybody's opinion as to whether it should be or not.

Travelers who have visited Waikiki in the past and then returned later almost invariably claim it was much nicer twenty years before (and when they were twenty years younger). They say it in the '80s about the '60s, just as they said it in the '60s about the '40s.

You can almost imagine the first American missionary landing on Oahu at Waikiki, looking around, and announcing to his guide, "A very nice island you have here, brother!"

"Nice?" the other man says incredulously. "Whadaya mean, nice? You should have been here before King Kamehameha and his gang swept in and ruined everything! Twenty years ago—that's when it was really beautiful around here!"

Mark Twain came to Hawaii for a few months in 1866, when he was thirty-one years old, and then wrote and spoke admiringly of the Islands throughout the rest of his life. The Hawaii Visitors Bureau has been quoting and gloating over his words ever since. But Twain suffered from what Honolulu newsman Gerald Lopez always called the "Old Oaken Bucket Delusion," and the HVB can be thankful that the great author never returned to find that his youth was not here waiting for him. Not only would he not have composed some of that glowing prose of his later years, he would surely have angrily turned his pen to eloquently damn nearly everything in sight.

Meanwhile, Waikiki continues to grow up, and not without a few scars inflicted and lessons learned in the school of hard knocks. To outsiders—like us—its beauty spots far outshine the marks of its mistakes. We'll bet you'll enjoy Waikiki today, and we won't be surprised if you come back again in the 1990s and say, "Oh, but you should have seen Waikiki back in the 'Eighties!"

The dominant feature of Waikiki, and almost the symbol of Hawaii, is

Diamond Head, a volcanic crater extinct for 150,000 years. It's only 760 feet tall, and you can clamber around via some rough paths on the slopes, if you're the hardy type (enter the trail at Makalei Place, off Diamond Head Road). Most will be content to merely gaze at the mountain the Hawaiians thought resembled a fish profile. They called it *Leahi* (forehead of the *ahi*—yellowfin tuna). Its English name came from calcite crystals discovered there by some nineteenth-century sailors who apparently thought they were diamonds.

That end—the "diamondhead boundary"—of Waikiki is more or less guarded by **Kapiolani Park**, named for the wife of King Kalakaua. Within its hundred acres are several other attractions including the **Waikiki Aquarium** (Tel. 923-5335), a wonderful, state-owned collection of sealife, with an entrance fee currently at a reasonable fee of $1.50, or free if you're under 16. The aquarium has more than 300 species of Hawaiian and South Pacific marine life, including the giant clam, chambered nautilus, sharks, deep-water crustaceans, sea turtles, salt-water crocodiles, and harbor seals. You can also rent a hand-held receiver to listen to the short-range recorded broadcasts, providing a sort of narrated tour of the aquarium. (Open daily, 9 A.M. to 5 P.M.)

Try not to miss the free **Kodak Hula Show** (follow the crowd at 9:30 A.M. to get good seats for the 10 A.M. show Tuesday, Wednesday, and Thursday—plus Friday in the summer). The one-hour performance takes place at some bleachers just off Monsarrat Avenue near the **Waikiki Shell**, another and more permanent outdoor amphitheatre.

Nearby is the **Honolulu Zoo**, also free admission, and you'll miss an experience if you don't pop in and say hello to at least a few inhabitants. The unusual design allows you to peek at the animals through the foliage, giving them a little more security and creating a natural feeling instead of putting them "on stage." At 7 P.M. Wednesdays, during the summer, there's usually some kind of free show inside the zoo. (Picnic lunches welcome.) And a **Weekend Art Mart**, featuring the works of local artists, is held along the outside of the zoo fence Saturday and Sunday. (See Section 10, "Shopping.")

Somewhat out of the way at the corner of Paki and Monsarrat avenues is the **Kapiolani Rose Garden**, with blooms feeding on such delicacies as giraffe manure from the zoo. There's no fee, but there's no picking, either. The roses are protected by some "magic *kahuna* stones." There are also picnic tables in the park, a driving range, an archery set-up, tennis courts, and a special joggers' track. On the bandstand, the Royal Hawaiian Band often performs weekly, usually at about 2 P.M. Sunday afternoons. It's also free.

Over by the water's edge, there's the **Waikiki War Memorial Natatorium**, a crumbling 1927 structure recently saved for renovation. The sections of beach along the park are known as Sans Souci and Queen's Surf. It was once a bathing area for Hawaiian royalty, but now there are showers and other facilities there for us all.

The principal thoroughfare through Waikiki and the park, by the way, is **Kalakaua Avenue**, named after the last king of Hawaii, King David Kalakaua ("kah-la-*cow*-wah"). Please don't let anybody tell you it is "Main Street." That's condescending, a cop-out, and decidedly unfair to the memory of a good king.

Just out of the park begins **Waikiki Beach**, a 2½-mile-long strand of wide, curving sand. Waikiki Beach is actually made up of several smaller beaches, and the section just at the foot of Kapahulu Avenue is called **Kuhio Beach Park**. It is particularly well protected from the heavy waves and ideal for young children and timid souls—usually. (See Section 8.) The checkerboard tables there are also free, *if* you can find a vacant one.

At the end of the beach park, across Kalakaua from the big twin-towered Hyatt Regency Hotel, is the **Waikiki Beach Center**, where you can rent a surfboard (look for all the racks) and take surfing lessons or maybe a surfing canoe ride. (More details are in Section 8, "Water Sports.") Next to the beach center are four **Kahuna Stones**, repositories of magic healing powers perhaps for several hundred years. (A plaque explains it all.)

One of three "theme-type" Waikiki shopping emporia is **King's Village,** renamed that after being known as King's Alley for several years. It's a collection of nineteenth-century-style buildings which Honolulu *Star-Bulletin* writer Pierre Bowman called "Waikiki's Disneylandic confection in concrete." It's across Kaiulani Avenue from the "P.K." (the Princess Kaiulani Hotel), and there's free entertainment at the main entrance beginning at 6:15 P.M. daily.

The other cutesy shopping arcade in the neighborhood is the twenty-year-old favorite **International Market Place**, 2330 Kalakaua Ave., largely sheltered by a gigantic banyan tree. Formerly a section of an old royal estate, it's now mostly a group of rustic shopping stalls, snack bars, etc., all of very varying quality, plus even a night club or two.

Don't miss a stroll through the old wooden **Moana Hotel**, across from the International Market Place. The Moana was built in 1901, and for a quarter-century it was the only real hotel on the beach. Today you can enjoy the banyan tree and the *makai* view as much as Robert Louis Stevenson did.

Two other landmark hotels in the immediate area include the venerable "pink palace," the **Royal Hawaiian Hotel**, still glowing in 1927 splendor, plus its dramatic if gaudy young cousin, the **Sheraton-Waikiki Hotel**. On the second floor of the Sheraton is a "Waikiki Historical Room" exhibiting old photographs of the neighborhood. If the owners of the Royal have their way, it will soon exist only in old photos. We invite you to join us in protesting the unthinkable idea that the grande dame of Waikiki should be razed.

Kalakaua Avenue below Lewers Street (the 1900, 2000, and 2100 blocks) has become a little sleazy. Turn left on Lewers. At the end of the street is the 1917 **Halekulani Hotel**, site of the first Charlie Chan detective novel, *The House Without a Key*. Just next door is the **Reef Hotel**, which features free beachside entertainment Sunday nights. Stroll along the beach or Kalia road to **Fort DeRussy**, whose grounds are maintained much like a park. The **Army Museum** (Tel. 543-2639) is headquartered in the old coastal artillery battery building. If it looks something like a ruin, that's because they once tried to batter the building down, but it was too tough to raze. Admission is free, but there's an intimidating donation box at the entrance. You can reserve a "free" guided tour (Monday–Friday) by calling 543-2687.

You can't buy anything at the army's **Hale Koa Hotel** without military I.D. Of course you're welcome to swim along here, however. In Hawaii, all beaches are public property by state law.

Farther along the beach is the Hilton Hawaiian Village Hotel and its attractive **Rainbow Bazaar** shopping arcade. The beach ends here, but Waikiki is considered to extend just a little farther to the Ilikai Hotel and the **Ala Wai Yacht Harbor**. It's perhaps best seen by riding the glass-walled elevator which crawls up the spine of the Ilikai.

DOWNTOWN—HAUNTS OF MISSIONARIES AND MERCENARIES

All the tearing down and building up that goes on in Waikiki often seems to be doubled downtown, and the core area appears destined for a high state of flux over the next several years. Nevertheless, Honolulu's downtown is not a Wall Street or some other impersonal blocks of stone mortared into a rectangular maze. There are happy islands of intriguing history and inviting tranquility throughout, bordered by an active waterfront and some spicy activities in part of a decaying urban area, too.

You may follow the stroll we have designed below from the description, although you might like to pick up a map, too.

If you're busing from Waikiki, take the No. 2 and, after it goes along Beretania Street, get off at Lauhala Street. (See map near the beginning of this chapter.) Walk *makai*, past the tall Municipal Office Building, and at a point near City Hall cross King Street to get to the **Mission Houses Museum** (Tel. 531-0481), at 553 S. King St. These are the earliest American buildings on the island. The white, wooden frame house was prefabricated in New England, shipped around "the Horn," and then, in 1821, erected as a dwelling place for the first missionaries to the Sandwich Isles. The adjoining two coral block buildings (in one of which the visit to the museum begins) were added slightly later and also became part of the mission complex. The museum, which includes many mementos of that exciting period in Hawaiian history, is well run by members of the Hawaiian Mission Children's Society—the descendants of the missionaries themselves.

Open daily except Monday from 9 A.M. to 4 P.M., the museum costs $3 for adults and $1 for children. A guided tour is optional but included in the price. Ask for a guide; *don't* just wander through without the talk. A visit to the Mission Houses is essential to anyone who wants to understand some basic history of the Islands. The museum also serves as the headquarters for an excellent two-hour tour conducted by the society over the entire central historic district, including the Mission Houses and several sights listed below. (See Section 7, "Guided Tours," etc.)

The unusual sculpture across King Street is **Sky Gate**, a somewhat controversial art work that is the site for many city-sponsored concerts, etc.

Just across the little street from the Mission Houses is **Kawaiahao Church** (Tel. 538-6267) at King and Punchbowl streets. Sometimes called the Westminster Abbey of Hawaii, the church has served as a royal chapel for the coronations, weddings, and funerals of kings and queens. But it was as a mission church for the Hawaiian people that it was consecrated. Construction began in 1837 on the 14,000-coral-block structure which replaced four previous thatched-roof models on the same site. It was dedicated in 1842. Today the Rev. Abraham Akaka conducts services at 10:30 A.M. on Sundays in English and Hawaiian. Visitors are usually invited to tour the church afterwards.

Graves of missionaries and their families are behind the church. Those of the early congregations are on the *makai* side. In front of the church is **King Lunalilo's Tomb**, which was built in 1876. (Lunalilo did not wish to be buried at the Royal Mausoleum in Nuuanu Valley.)

Across King Street from the Kawaiahao Church you will notice **Honolulu Hale** (City Hall), built in Spanish style in 1929. But we would continue our walk along King for a block to the **Kamehameha I Statue**. This black and gold impression of the conqueror of the Islands was erected in 1883. It was the second such statue cast; the first was aboard a ship which sank on the way to Hawaii from Italy. (See Chapter VIII.) On Kamehameha Day, June 11, it is festooned with scores of long flower leis.

The statue's backdrop is **Aliiolani Hale**, now also known as the Judiciary Building, built in 1874. Originally designed as a royal palace, it was modified for use as the House of Parliament during the monarchy. The lawmakers moved out and the courts moved in when Hawaii was declared a republic in 1893.

Across King Street and set in elaborate grounds is the highly revered Victorian structure named the **Iolani Palace**. Built by King David Kalakaua in 1882, it is now known as the only royal palace in the United States. The architecture has been called American Florentine, along with lots of other things, and it almost surely was inspired by something on King Kalakaua's world tour. One mystery is the little-known fact that it is virtually a duplicate of the famous mansion built in Athens by German archeologist Heinrich Schliemann, the discoverer of Troy.

Over the past decade, the palace has been beautifully restored, and it has now been reopened for 45-minute guided tours *by reservation only, from Wednesday through Saturday*, 9 A.M. to 2:15 P.M. But if you telephone 536-2474 a few days in advance, you should be able to get on a tour. Or you may write in advance to the Friends of Iolani Palace, P.O. Box 2259, Honolulu, Hi. 96804. Admission price is $4 for adults and $1 for children 12 and under.

The palace is not yet furnished, but all the architectural detail, woodwork, lighting fixtures, and other features have been brought back to 1882. Only twelve people are allowed on a tour, and twenty tours are offered per week.

Out on the palace grounds, you will see the **Kalakaua Coronation Bandstand**, only the dome of which remains unchanged from the 1883 ceremony during which King Kalakaua placed a crown on his own head. Today the stand is used sometimes for public events—the governor was inaugurated there—but it primarily serves on Friday noons as the site for the free public concerts by the Royal Hawaiian band.

The fortlike structure a few hundred yards *mauka* of the bandstand is **Iolani Barracks**, originally built in 1871 to quarter the Royal Household Guard. It used to stand near the present state capitol, but it was moved stone by stone to make way for the capitol.

Behind the palace is the multi-trunked **Iolani Banyan**, a still-spreading tree which may be 100 years old. According to some accounts, it was planted by Queen Kapiolani, wife of King Kalakaua. The modern-looking and out-of-place building next to the tree is the **State Archives**, whose tucked-away treasures are not immediately accessible.

Out on the grassy mall, which used to be a segment of Hotel Street, is the new **Queen Liliuokalani Statue**, installed in 1982. She faces the bold and dramatic **Hawaii State Capitol**, an architectural wonder unduplicated anywhere. Completed in 1969 at a cost of $25 million, the capitol takes its inspiration from Hawaii's natural history. The House and Senate chambers externally resemble volcanos rising up from a "sea," or reflecting pool. The columns are evocative of palm trees, and the open central court seems to invite the gentle climate of Hawaii to enter the most important building in the state. (The offices and chambers around the railings, however, are fully air-conditioned.)

If you take an elevator to the top floor, you can appreciate the rotunda from another angle as well as walk to two opposite terraces to enjoy impressive *makai* and *mauka* views over Honolulu. The governor's office is up here, too. Look for a giant koa door which says: "E Komo Mai" (Please Come In). Sometimes there is a free booklet available inside describing the capitol and surrounding area.

Outside the capitol building on the *mauka* side you will find the excellent though controversial bronze statue of **Father Damien**, the hero of the leprosy settlement at Kalaupapa on the island of Molokai. (See Chapter 8.) It was hammered out in modern style by Marisol, the Venezuelan sculptress.

The capitol grounds are bordered on the mountain side by Beretania Street, the closest Hawaiian pronunciation and spelling could come to honoring Britannia, the ancient Latin name for Britain. Directly across this street is the new **Armed Forces Memorial**, a non-objective sculpture with obligatory eternal flame.

A walk toward town on that side of the street will bring you to the gates of **Washington Place**, 320 S. Beretania St., the official mansion of the state governor and the oldest continuously occupied house on the island. Built in 1846, it eventually was inherited by Queen Liliuokalani, who resided there until her death in 1917. Today you can peek at it through the closed iron gate. It is not open to the public.

A few steps farther, at the corner of Queen Emma Street, is **Saint Andrews Cathedral**, the Episcopal (Church of England) headquarters. Construction was begun in 1867, supervised by Queen Emma, the widow of Kamehameha IV, both of whom were anglophiles. The building was designed in Britain, and some of the materials were shipped from there.

On the *makai* side of Beretania Street, and two blocks farther on, is **Our Lady of Peace Cathedral**, the modest nexus of the island's Roman Catholics. It was built between 1840 and 1843, after local opposition to Catholicism finally eased.

The cathedral fronts on the **Fort Street Mall**, which meanders for seven blocks to the waterfront. The former street, now redesigned and relandscaped entirely for shopping and strolling pedestrians, represents a generally successful 1969 attempt to revitalize the former mercantile center of the city.

If you're running short of time, you can follow Fort Street directly to the waterfront, the Aloha Tower, etc. But if you're not, and if it's daytime, we'd take a slight detour to see as much of **Chinatown** as still exists since urban renewal was begun in the neighborhood. Turn right (*ewa*) off the mall and walk four blocks along Hotel Street, past the adult film houses, fortune tellers, and other elements of a honky-tonk neighborhood (popular with servicemen), and then turn left (*makai*) on **Maunakea Street**, and poke around in the little Chinese groceries, herb shops, import stores, etc., on the way to King Street. (The *mauka* end of Maunakea Street is bounded by the Cultural Plaza, which is covered in our Shopping Section, No. 10. You can discover more of Chinatown, by the way, on the Tuesday morning tours sponsored by the Chinese Chamber of Commerce, described in Section 7.)

Turn left at King Street, cross King at Smith, go along Smith for a few yards, and head down tiny Marin Street past an antique gas station and several other buildings to get to **Merchant Street**. Along here several late-nineteenth- and early-twentieth-century buildings have been preserved and are being turned into some smart shops, bars, and restaurants. The 1871 Kamehameha V Post Office recently restored there may become a postal museum. Recently it has been used for several courtrooms. Now return to the Fort Street Mall, this time at its lower end.

Turn seaward on the mall and cross Queen Street to see what was saved from the fort, razed in 1857, which gave the mall/streeet its name—a single, solitary cannon. It was one of forty which once poked through the bastion built in 1817 by Kamehameha I. (A nearby plaque covers the details.)

Use the traffic lights and carefully cross Nimitz Highway, walk straight through **Irwin Park**, take the escalator to the second deck of Pier 9 (where virtually all ship passengers disembark), and follow the signs for the elevator up to the **Aloha Tower**.

Built in 1921, the state-owned Aloha Tower for several decades was the tallest structure in Honolulu. Its purpose then, as now, was to direct the ship movement in Honolulu Harbor. You can ride free to the tenth-floor observation deck for a 360-degree view of the city any time between 8 A.M. and 9 P.M.

Walk down the ramp. You'll pass the Oceana Floating Restaurant at Pier 6. Repeat visitors may remember that at Pier 5, on the other side of the parking lot, the museum ship *Falls of Clyde* was permanently berthed. Unfortunately, the ship was heavily damaged during Hurricane Iwa, and is being repaired elsewhere. Her ultimate fate is unknown at deadline, and she may or may not return to her former resting place during 1984.

If you're not driving, you can return to Waikiki from this area by catching the No. 8 city bus on nearby Nimitz Highway.

GREATER HONOLULU

As we mentioned earlier, no routing could wind through this next group in a logical order. Nor should it, since it is doubtful that any traveler will aim for every target on the list.

So now that we have wandered through Waikiki and downtown, we here cover the rest of Honolulu more or less alphabetically, sometimes indicating which others in the group are in the same or nearby neighborhoods.

If your feet weren't tired from our *Waikiki Walk* (above), you might have stumbled a little farther along Ala Moana Boulevard from the Ilikai Hotel to the **Ala Moana Center**, one of the most gigantic shopping souks in the world. (From and to Waikiki, take Bus No. 8.) There are more than 150 stores and restaurants over three levels with artwork, colorful fish and birds, children's play areas, free shows on the outdoor stage, etc. On Honolulu excursions, Neighbor Islanders often stay at the adjoining Ala Moana Hotel so they can lay in supplies at this merchandising oasis. Note that some of the same articles for sale in Waikiki hotel shops may be found more reasonably priced at Ala Moana or other shopping centers. (See Section 10, "Shopping," for complete details.)

Across the boulevard named Ala Moana (Ocean Way) from Ala Moana Center and Ala Moana Hotel is **Ala Moana Park**, a long strip of trees, grass, and calm-water beach popular with some local folk.

The man-made peninsula which juts from that park into the ocean is called Magic Island, once the site of an ambitious but abortive "Tivoli Gardens" style amusement park project some years ago. Although the fun and games never got under way, the park, which forms one side of the channel to the Ala Wai Yacht Harbor, now provides an excellent view of the Waikiki coastline.

The highly revered **Bishop Museum and Planetarium** (Tel. 847-1443), at 1525 Bernice St., should not be missed—or at least the museum part shouldn't. The museum, founded 1899, is the repository for all things Polynesian, and the center for much of the scholarly archeological work throughout the Pacific. Headquartered in an old stone structure, it appears deceptively small. But winding its stairways and threading its corridors to closely examine all exhibits can easily take a half day.

Here are not only the thrones, crowns, and other relics of the elegant monarchy period of Hawaiian history, but also the feathered cloaks and carved gods of Kamehameha I and the "pre-European" ages of the Island. Next door, the museum has opened a new "living theater" structure, a sort of thatched-roof pavilion called the Atherton Halau. The arts and crafts of Hawaii are demonstrated there on a variable schedule, and classes may also be arranged. And the museum's shop (in the new Ululani Jabulka Pavilion) sells books, recordings, and artifacts you may not find for sale elsewhere.

The next-door Planetarium is also well-run, but of more interest locally, perhaps. Check out the old Oahu Railway train and other outside exhibits, too. Last time we were at the museum, admission was still running a price of $4.75 for adults, $2.50 for children 6 to 17. Open 9 to 5 every day except Sunday, when it remains locked up until noon.

Take City Bus No. 2—"School Street" (not No. 2—"Liliha"), get off at Kam Shopping Center and walk *makai* for a block. With a car, take the Houghtailing Street exit from the Lunalio Freeway, then drive to the grounds via Houghtailing and Bernice streets.

The sports arena, exhibit hall, and concert auditorium recently named the **Neal Blaisdell Center** is still often known locally as the HIC—Honolulu International Center. One goes to the circular arena, at Kapiolani and Ward, for events like the circus, the fights, or basketball games. The nearby concert hall, at Ward and King, hosts the Honolulu Symphony Orchestra or the Hawaii Opera Theatre in season.

Also seasonal are the visits to the **Dole Pineapple Cannery** (Tel. 536-3411) which are conducted on a tour basis only at the plant, 650 Iwilei Road. Generally the $2 rounds are made weekdays from about May through August, but hours and details vary, so phone the above number. (Take Bus No. 8—"Airport/Hickam" from Waikiki.) They give you free pineapple juice, by the way. It sure tastes great—but yes, it *is* canned. Dole explains that there really is no such thing as *fresh* pineapple juice.

All too often, visitors miss the **Foster Botanic Gardens** (Tel. 531-1939), a large and tranquil oasis in the midst of the hustle and bustle, at 180 N. Vineyard Blvd. Open from 9 A.M. to 4 P.M., this unusual city park is a living museum of virtually every type of fern, vine, tree, orchid, and other flower which can exist in the tropics—about 4,000 species.

Admission to the nearly 1½-century-old park is free. (Call 538-7258 to find out about guided tours sometimes available.) Look for the gigantic trees called the earpod, the Queensland Kauri, and the kapok, all planted by the originator of the garden in 1855. Wander, too, through the Prehistoric Glen, a mysterious cul-de-sac of ferns, strange palms, weird grasses, etc., which has received national recognition. Visitors are welcome to pick up anything which has fallen on the ground—seeds, flowers, leaves, etc.—but nothing off the trees or plants, of course.

You can get to the garden by a pleasant one-block walk *mauka* along the river from the Cultural Plaza. There is a parking lot for cars. Or busing from Waikiki, take No. 4 to Nuuanu Avenue and Vineyard Boulevard. Don't forget that early closing time, but don't forget to go, either.

Across Thomas Square from the concert hall is the **Honolulu Academy of Arts** (Tel. 538-3693), and entrance is free to the beautiful building with its six open courtyards and thirty-seven gallery rooms. Best known for a rare collection of Oriental art, the academy also includes European and American masterpieces as well as the best work of Hawaii-based artists. (Somehow, though, the galleries are arranged so that the Eastern art is in the west and the Western works are east!) Open Tuesday, Wednesday, Friday, and Saturday, 10 A.M. to 4:30 P.M.; Thursday, 11 A.M. to 8 P.M.; and Sunday, 2 to 5 P.M.; 45-minute guided tours at 11 A.M. Wednesday and Friday. Closed Mondays.

Besides the galleries, notice the academy shop, which has for sale a large selection of books on art and Polynesian lore, plus some gift items. Also, the Garden Cafe there serves gourmet lunches by ladies of the Academy Volunteers Council from September through May. (Reserve at 531-8865.)

To bus to the main academy building, take No. 2 from Waikiki. Your destination is 900 South Beretania St., between Victoria and Ward; on-street metered parking is usually available in the area. If you ever visit art galleries anywhere, you should add this one to your list.

Kewalo Basin, often (incorrectly) called Fisherman's Wharf after the restaurant there, is at the lower end of Ward Avenue, just across Ala Moana Boulevard. This commercial harbor, the home of most of Oahu's fishing fleet, is the place to charter deep-sea fishing boats. Most of the dinner cruises, Pearl Harbor tours, glass-bottom boats, etc., also leave from here. At the end of one pier is the Bumble Bee tuna cannery, not usually noticeable unless there is an off-shore (Kona) breeze.(!) Across the boulevard from the basin is the Ward Warehouse, a new shopping and restaurant complex. (From Waikiki take the No. 8 "Airport/Hickam" bus.) The area makes a nice walk on a sleepy Sunday—at least if the trades are blowing.

Up in Manoa Valley, **Paradise Park** (Tel. 988-2141) is mainly into exotic birds—teaching them to do tricks on the high wire and the like. The park itself has recently expanded to 15 acres, and includes a rain forest and more than 100 species of tropical plants. It's certainly fun for the kids ($3.75); adults fork over $7.50 now. The parrots, of course, are not native to Hawaii. There's also an electronic "Dancing Waters" fountain show three times a day. The flowers and trees, at least, are authentic, and the whole park is probably a good place to take a lot of nature pictures. The tickets are steep, but visitors who are not getting out into the country or over to the Neighbor Islands may think it worth the price.

From Waikiki you may take Bus No. 5 on a long, roundabout route for 45 minutes to the end of the line. If you make the bus trip but decide not to hit the park, and if your hiking legs are in good shape, take the beautiful, free (but often slippery) trail at the end of Manoa Road behind Paradise Park for one mile (about 30 minutes) to **Manoa Falls**. Fresh-water swimming is permitted, and it's a wonderful place for a picnic.

Known rather simply as **Punchbowl**, the National Memorial Cemetery of the Pacific is really the Arlington of this part of the world, a last resting place for more than 20,000 servicemen on the 112-acre floor of a long-extinct volcano. Punchbowl Crater was called Puowaina (Hill of Sacrifice) by the ancient Hawaiians, and it was indeed the site of human sacrifices in pre-history.

You almost need a car or taxi to visit Punchbowl, and note that there's less traffic after noon. It's at the end of Puowaina Drive, and the city buses don't go on into the cemetery. If you're truly busbound, transfer to No. 15 downtown, explain to the driver, and he'll let you off on Puowaina Drive, where your walk will be a scenic half mile or so into the cemetery.

The gates are open 8 A.M. to 5 P.M. For details on the memorial and other aspects of the cemetery, see if you can pick up the Veterans Administration pamphlet in the Administration Building, near the flagpole.

Queen Emma's Summer Palace (Tel. 595-3167), at 2913 Pali Highway, was once a summer retreat of the wife of Kamehameha IV. (They were the same royal couple responsible for Queen's Hospital and St. Andrew's Cathedral.) Built in 1843, the palace, whose real name is Hanaikalamalama, is now maintained as a museum by the Daughters of Hawaii. Notice the little koa wood cradle for Emma's son, the prince, heir to the Hawaiian throne and godson of Queen Victoria, who nevertheless was to die tragically at the age of four. The museum, open 9 A.M. to 4 P.M. Monday through Friday and to noon Saturday, costs $3, which seems a lot for the rewards. (A better deal if you show up at 2 P.M. Mondays, when you'll receive a guided tour.) Take Bus No. 4.

In the same general part of town, at 2261 Nuuanu Ave., is the 1865 **Royal Mausoleum** (Tel. 536-7602), which holds the remains of most members of the Kamehameha and Kalakaua dynasties. The 3-acre grounds, the chapel, and the crypt are open daily except Sunday from 8 A.M. to 4 P.M., and from 8 until noon Saturdays. Look for a free state parks folder inside, or you might be lucky enough to get a guided tour by Lydia Maioho, the custodian and herself a descendant of the Kamehamehas. (And out of alphabetical order, here, but just around the corner at 42 Kawananakoa Place is the dramatically ornate **Chinese Buddhist Temple of Honolulu**. Turn down the street. You'll know it when you see it!)

Sand Island, the traditional dumping ground across Honolulu Channel from the Aloha Tower, has been developed into a long-overdue park—or at least part of it has—which affords a nice view of downtown Honolulu. The route to it isn't all that salubrious, however. Take Sand Island Access Road off Nimitz Highway, but only if you're in the neighborhood.

If you can dream up an excuse to get on the U.S. Coast Guard Base at Sand Island on the way to the park, have a look at the two unusual sculpted hula girls there. These figures, with hair, bathing suits, and make-up in the styles of forty years ago, are all that remain of a group of six statues. They were crafted there by lonely Italian prisoners of war. For some reason lost to history, the Italians were penned in a compound on the property in 1944.

The **Tantalus-Round Top Drive**, named after the two tall hills it crosses, is a favorite excursion made by Honoluluans with Mainland guests. It sometimes provides appreciation points for Oahu's most spectacular sunsets, especially in the winter. Part of the route goes through a tropical forest reserve, and you'll often be able to pick up guavas or passion fruit along the winding, two-lane road. It's cooler on Tantalus, and the few folks who live along the way often have fireplaces to cozy up to in the wintertime. Don't miss the little *Ualakaa Park*, and particularly its wide-angle, eagle-eye view of Honolulu from Koko Head to the Waianae Mountains. (The park closes at dusk.) City bus No. 15 also makes its way along this 7-mile route.

At 203 Prospect St., on the slopes of Punchbowl, is the **Tennent Art Foundation Gallery** (Tel. 531-1987). It is devoted to displaying the works of the late Madge Tennent, probably the best-known island artist. Open Tuesday through Saturday 10 A.M. to noon, Sunday 2 P.M. to 4 P.M.; closed Mondays. Admission free.

The University of Hawaii and the East-West Center are on a joint 300-acre campus in Manoa Valley. (Bus No. 4.) Architecturally, the institution is a disaster—a real stylistic jumble, but the grounds are botanically interesting if you're into those subjects. Ask for the map and guide at the University Relations Office in Bachman Hall (Dole Street near University Avenue). Student guided tours are offered both of the university and of the East-West Center, the unique institution set up in 1960 to promote cultural exchanges between Asian-Pacific and Western peoples. (See Section 7.)

A traditional watering hole for hundreds of tour buses through Manoa Valley is the **Waioli Tea Room** (Tel. 988-2131) at 3016 Oahu Ave.

Although it is run by the good folks from the Salvation Army, and although they have installed on its grounds an old *pili* grass house which is supposed to be (but we doubt it) the one once used by Robert Louis Stevenson in Waikiki, we feel the place is generally overrated and too often overcrowded. Its bakery, however, often has delicious mango bread and other local goodies. If you stop here, go in the afternoon to avoid the hordes. They're open until 4 except on Sunday.

THE EAST OAHU CIRCLE

This trip, a good morning or afternoon tour, is designed mainly for travelers who have equipped themselves with a rental car. Nevertheless, two buses cover basically the same route, both called No. 57. From Ala Moana Center, you can take this jaunt either clockwise or counterclockwise as we describe it below.

Both this section and the next are circle routes. We have put it down here our way, just because that's the way we like to drive it ourselves.

Pick up a road map, of course, and if you want piped-in local atmosphere along the way, you might turn your car radio to the only Oahu radio station which plays all Hawaiian music. It's KCCN, at 1420 kilocycles, crowded in amidst two dozen island stations who vie for position on the AM dial.

Look for the little Hawaiian Warrior markers along the road, but don't count on them. Some sights are relatively unrecognized, or the Hawaii Visitors Bureau sign may have disappeared.

Diamond Head, the extinct volcano crater which was a starting point to our Waikiki Walk, also serves as a take-off point in the opposite direction for our wheeled excursion. You can drive through a tunnel into the crater, by the way, and then hike to the rim. Get permission from the Hawaii National Guard headquarters behind the two cannons at Fort Ruger. (Take Monsarrat Avenue through the zoo and then up behind the mountain for 1.5 miles.)

Until the crater becomes a park someday, most people prefer to save that excursion, driving instead *makai* of Diamond Head along Diamond Head Road, past the Amelia Earhart Monument and into the lush, green, and palm-shaded **Kahala District**, which holds some of Honolulu's finest homes and gardens.

If you continue on Kahala Avenue (while other traffic turns *mauka* onto Kealaolu Avenue), you'll wind up at the beautiful and prestigious **Kahala Hilton Hotel**, which has hosted the likes of kings and presidents for the past decade and a half. The buildings and grounds are lovely, and you can watch the porpoises and turtles get fed at 10:30 A.M. or 12:30 and 2:30 P.M. (Ask at the front desk for a pamphlet outlining a walking tour of the grounds.)

The next-door golf course is the **Waialae Country Club**, scene of the Hawaiian Open tournament in January.

Now back to the aforementioned Kealaolu Avenue, then drive to the Lunalilo Freeway (H-1) and take it in the *kokohead* direction (vaguely, east). The road becomes the famous Kalanianaole Highway. (When you can pronounce that, then you're supposed to be a *kamaaina*. And take heart, for the Honolulu Police Department usually calls it simply "Kalani" highway.)

Skirting the residential neighborhoods of Aina Haina, Niu, and Kuliouou, the highway emerges alongside a sort of tropical Venice developed by the late industrialist Henry Kaiser. Called **Hawaii Kai**, the area is still growing in, around, through, and over an ancient Hawaiian fishpond. Notice that not only are there two cars in nearly every garage, but that many back doors also boast a boat dock, with Evinrude or Chris Craft tied up there.

Out the starboard side of your windshield, above the ocean, humps the landmark known as **Koko Head**, an extinct crater, not to be confused with its steeper cousin to the left of the road which is called **Koko Crater**. (Years ago, a military aerial tramway used to cut straight up the side and you can still just barely make out its route.)

If you turn into Hawaii Kai on Lunalilo Home Road at the light, the shopping center on your immediate left again is **Koko Marina**. Besides the stores installed in rustic, nautical trappings, there really is a marina, which sometimes offers free, narrated boat rides through the surrounding waterways.

Back on the coastal highway, if you continue up the hill, you can turn right to **Hanauma Bay Beach Park**. Go peer over the edge by the parking lot to view what appears to be a nearly circular bay. (Actually, it's more horseshoe-shaped, but the perspective is deceptive.) This is an extinct volcano crater, breached on one side by the sea. It now boasts a lovely beach, and also an underwater park, where thousands of colorful reef fish swim among the submerged rocks, observed and enjoyed by skin and scuba divers. You can only see the creatures by using a face mask, however, and such snorkeling is one of our own favorite island diversions.

Elvis Presley had a grass shack on Hanauma Bay in the film "Blue Hawaii," and the beach was also used in "From Here to Eternity." The "Beach Bus" goes there from Monsarrat Avenue in Waikiki. No. 57, the circle island route, also heads for Hanauma.

If you continue along Kalanianaole again, you'll see HVB markers pointing out to sea identifying the islands of Molokai and Lanai, about 30 miles away. *Sometimes*—usually during the winter months— you *can* see them, and maybe even Maui as a ghostly shape beyond Molokai when the conditions are perfect.

Just a little past a fishing shrine, a memorial to some men once swept into the sea near here, is the **Halona Blow Hole**. From the lookout, you can often see the waves shoot a spout of water up through an old lava tube. Lock your car or take everything with you, as thefts from "locked" vehicles are common. And watch your step while walking, too.

Sandy Beach Park, just beyond, is popular but dangerous for persons not accustomed to handling its often violent and tricky waves. It is not recommended for visitors. Even locals are regularly injured here, and a number of sharks sometimes patrol about 100 yards out, too. (See our discussion on beaches in Section 8—Water Sports.)

If you are into cacti, desert plants, etc., you can take nearby Kealahou Street *mauka* to the **Koko Crater Botanic Gardens**, just behind the Koko Head stables. The garden is a project of the Succulent Society of Hawaii.

The windswept shoreline beyond Sandy Beach, known as **Queen's Beach**, or Wawamalu Beach, was once planned for a major resort by the Kaiser-Aetna corporation, but the state has now become interested in the area as a future park. Meanwhile, most of it is covered with huge boulders that Kaiser-Aetna dug out of its new residential areas in nearby Kalama Valley.

Just past the **Hawaii Kai Championship Golf Course** the road heads through a dry, low pass, where it almost never rains, to the windward side of the island. Pull over at the lookout for a spectacular view of the windward—or northeast—coastline.

The lighthouse up on the hill marks the land's end in these parts. The most prominent islet in view is Manana, more well-known as **Rabbit Island**. It is supposed to look like a rabbit with flattened ears, but then rabbits once did live there, for that matter. During the abortive 1894 counterrevolution, arms and ammunition to support it were buried on the windward side of Rabbit Island. Today it is a bird sanctuary, as is the smaller **Turtle Island** (Kaohikaipu) next to it. (The silhouette in the far distant view that *looks* like a "turtle island" is actually a peninsula on which is established Kaneohe Marine Corps Air Station.)

Perhaps the only beach more treacherous, yet more fun for body surfers, than the aforementioned Sandy Beach is the little **Makapuu Beach Park** tucked away below the lookout. It's a wonderful place for a picnic, however, but again, lock your car or—preferably—empty it.

Across the road from the beach is the widely hailed **Sea Life Park** (Tel. 259-7933), a highly successful commercial park operation displaying the life and antics of fish, fowl, and water animals. It costs nothing to visit the Galley Restaurant and the shops, but you'll pay $7 or so (or around $5 ages 7–12) to be admitted to the show portion. This includes the 300,000-gallon Hawaiian Reef Tank, where a spiral ramp leads you, in effect, three fathoms under the sea to see hundreds of creatures, sometimes including a special demonstration during which they are hand-fed by a scuba diver.

Other shows in the park include the Ocean Science Theatre, featuring a production on the training of porpoises and penguins, and the Whaler's Cove show, which includes small whales taking part in a sort of water pageant. Their tricks are complicated and good. You may also feed sea lions and sea birds, if you buy the food, and listen to mini-lectures at different points in the park. You'll also find a small but excellent collection in the whaling museum.

If you haven't seen Marineworld or Marineland back in California or Florida, you should definitely go, but some feel that even for dolphin-show veterans, the distinctly Hawaiian flavor at Sea Life Park makes the show worthwhile. (TIP: It doesn't cost anything to enter the restaurant portion of the park. From there, you can see the museum and the sea lion pools for free. Use the lower level entrance past the restrooms, etc.) The park is open from 9:30 A.M., and the last show goes on about 4:30 P.M. The setting is also gorgeous, and if the price is no object, then don't miss it.

(Remember that you can reach Sea Life Park also by public bus. Climb aboard any Route 57, although from its beginning at Ala Moana Center, it may be a little shorter trip if you use the clockwise route—via Kailua, Waimanalo, etc.—rather than the opposite system we've been following here.)

Throughout this whole Makapuu area—especially on a Sunday—you may cast your eyes skyward to see Hawaii's newest sport. The updrafts along the nearby cliffs are particularly suited to **hang glider flying**, and as many as a dozen at a time wheel and turn as they jockey for air space in the neighborhood. Unfortunately, over the past few years there have been some fatalities registered in this popular activity here.

Continuing via the highway, you'll see at the end of a long pier the **Makai Undersea Test Range**, a commercial marine research station (visitors not welcomed).

Waimanalo Beach Park, farther along, is attractive, but we do not consider it safe to camp there overnight. As a matter of fact, it leads the list—along with Makaha and Nanikuli parks—of sites of several crimes and various unpleasantness. If you see a rough crowd here, better let them have the place all to themselves.

Under a long row of ironwood trees behind a white fence *mauka* of the road, you may catch sight of several portable stands selling everything from pickled mangos to puka shell necklaces. These vendors and craftsmen, who used to create a colorful if hazardous collection directly alongside the traffic, have banded together into a *hui* (cooperative) called Pine Grove Village. It's still somewhat unsettled and experimental, and you may have to search out the parking area. But some visitors have been picking up some good handicraft bargains under the trees, especially on weekends.

The entrance to **Bellows Air Force Base**, today only a recreation installation, is along here. Its park and camping areas are open to civilians for camping and general frolicking on weekends and holidays. The beach is lovely, clean, uncrowded, full of beautiful waves, and generally safe for swimming and body surfing.

The village of **Waimanalo** is now somewhat of a poverty pocket. Formerly the nucleus of a large sugar plantation, the rich soil in the area is used today for flower and fruit production. Most of Oahu's banana, papaya, and anthurium supply comes from Waimanalo. It is not, however, considered much of a visitor attraction.

The sharp, double-spiked mountain you can see in the distance past Waimanalo is **Olomana Peak**. Hikers often like to tackle that one, but sometimes they become stranded on its slopes and must be picked off by rescue helicopter.

If you're not running late, take the main junction with Kailua Road (Route 63) to the right (*makai*) to visit **Kailua**, a small bedroom beachside community within easy commuting distance of Honolulu. Ask directions to **Kailua Beach Park**, basically at the corner of Kailua Road and Kalaheo Avenue, for another popular beach.

Returning up Kailua Road again toward Honolulu, a short way out of the village and behind the YMCA is the hard-to-find **Ulu Po Heiau**. To the non-scholar, it looks like a mere pile of rocks on the edge of **Kawainui Swamp**. If you're going to search out the Puu O Mahuka Heiau on the North Shore (in the next few pages), you can certainly skip this one.

Beyond the intersection at which you turned toward Kailua, the Kailua Road becomes for all intents and purposes the four-lane Pali Highway (Route 61). It winds its way up into the Koolau Mountains to dive through the twin Pali Tunnels into the upper reaches of the **Nuuanu Valley**.

Now please don't strain your neck or let your car run off the road, but if weather conditions are right, you may see far up in the right-hand rim of the valley "Waipuhia" or **Upside Down Falls**. Strong winds and heavy rain runoff often combine here to blow the waters *up* once they reach the edge of a small cliff.

A half-mile farther is the turnoff to take you back up the old road through the rain forest to the point above the tunnels called the **Nuuanu Pali Lookout**, by far the most dramatic elevated view on Oahu, and ranking among the two or three best in the state. It is a low point eroded in the Koolau Mountains, and through which the trade winds usually rush with such force that you can virtually lean against them. But watch anything you're carrying. It just might be blown right out of your hands.

This is the dramatic, 1,000-foot cliff over which Kamehameha I drove the forces of the king of Oahu in 1795. Somewhere between 400 and 10,000 warriors (casualty lists were casual) jumped or were pushed over the *pali*, and for a hundred years afterward their bones were taken by souvenir hunters from the ledges below the cliff.

Try to ignore the recently overbuilt concrete observation platform and enjoy the aspect from the little railing below it, but watch your step everywhere. When the old, two-lane highway ran over here, it was at this lower point that you stopped to enjoy the panorama of mountain, sea, and shore which—thankfully—has not appreciably changed over the centuries.

The view is most dependable and the light is considered best in the mid-morning, but in those hours you may have to share it with the occupants of scores of tour buses. We like to hit it between noon and about 4 or 5 P.M. The overlook is also open at night, but it is deserted and unguarded, and we don't think the views of the lights of Kailua and Kaneohe are worth the potential risk. It is fun and safe during daylight, but again, be sure to take your valuables with you when you park the car.

(If you do not follow the route we have been describing here, you may come up the Pali Highway directly from the Honolulu side, turning onto a different, well-marked spur just before the tunnels. After your ooing and ahing, you can either come back to the highway there and continue through the tunnels into Kailua, or you may return to Honolulu via the old road just described. Unfortunately, as of this writing, there is absolutely no way to travel to the Pali Lookout by public bus.)

However you get there, the site is Oahu's crowning glory. You cannot go home without experiencing it firsthand. When the weather's good, we absolutely defy you to shrug your shoulders and walk away!

From the Lookout, return to the Pali Highway which will take you into downtown Honolulu again. We suggest you check the map and use Bishop Street, Ala Moana, and Kalakaua Avenue to return to Waikiki.

PEARL HARBOR AND THE BIG MIDDLE ISLAND ROUND TRIP

Like the East Oahu Circle route, you really need a car for the excursion as we've outlined it here, although several of the targets may also be hit by public bus (most of them with Route No. 52, which goes in a four-hour circle). Allow all day for this trip, and be aware that although we have included Pearl Harbor and the Polynesian Cultural Center here, you may logically prefer to make those trips on separate days.

By car, there are two different ways to reach Pearl Harbor. The low road, or *makai* route, is basically via Kam (Kamehameha) Highway past the airport and Hickam Air Force Base. Then keep watching your signs carefully for "Halawa Gate" or "Arizona Memorial."

However, there is so much construction continuing along this thoroughfare that it may be much easier to take the high road. This *mauka* route means the Lunalilo Freeway through the city in a west or north direction. At about Exit 19, it's called the Moanalua Freeway (Route 78).

If you're picnicking, consider a stop about halfway along at **Moanalua Gardens**, a private, 26-acre park open to all. The monkeypod trees are magnificent, and the cottage on the grounds was built about 110 years ago for bachelor King Kamehameha V and his card-playing cronies.

Back on the highway, keep a lookout for the new $32 million, 50,000-seat **Aloha Stadium**, a history-making construction that moves into baseball or football configurations virtually at the touch of a button. Across from the stadium is the new **Castle Park**, a dizzy-land appealing more to residents than transients. Near the stadium, bear right at the sign to "Aiea" first, and then left to merge into Kam Highway (Route 90) *south* to go to Pearl Harbor. Soon after, you make a right turn through the Halawa Gate to get to the shuttle boat landing for the **USS Arizona Memorial**.

Finally, after years of bureaucratic warfare, the shoreline waiting arrangements for the memorial have been vastly improved. No longer are there long lines to stand in, regardless of the weather. The new $5 million Visitor Center includes new docks and an attractive new building with a museum, a movie theater, a bookstore, and a snack bar.

After arriving at the Center (any time between 8 A.M. and 3 P.M.), you'll be issued a free ticket and a group number by the National Park Service. You can walk around, take pictures, muse through the museum, or browse through the bookstores until your group is called to view the film. It is a 20-minute documentary on the Battle of Pearl Harbor and subsequent events. Then your group files out of the theater and onto a U.S. Navy launch to go to the memorial.

The boat lands you directly *on the memorial*, a 184-foot-long floating bridge of white concrete, which was dedicated in 1962. It spans the width of the sunken U.S.S. *Arizona*, which stands upright on the bottom in 38 feet of water. (The flag is mounted on a part of the ship's superstructure which is still above the surface.)

The memorial is magnificent and a fitting tribute marking the grave of 1,177 men. Their bodies are still aboard the battleship whose hull you can discern in ghostly outline just below. You may notice a slight oil slick coming from the depths, and it is said that after more than four decades, the ship itself is still bleeding.

Be sure to enter the shrine room, at one end of the memorial, where the names of all who were killed on the ship Dec. 7, 1941, have been engraved on a wall of white marble.

The Navy has several rules and regulations, of course, some of which prohibit children under 6 and anyone wearing a bathing suit or not wearing something on their feet. Also the Center is closed and boat trips are suspended on all national holidays *except* Memorial Day, Independence Day, and Veterans Day. The trips may be suspended, too, for any period when it is raining hard or when there are high winds.

The Arizona Memorial is the state's most popular tourist attraction, and more than one million will go through it again this year. As it stands, now, the memorial is *closed on Mondays*. This makes the heaviest day for tourist traffic on Tuesday, gradually reducing to lighter crowds later in the week. The morning is usually your best bet, too. Some Tuesday afternoon waits are over two hours long.

For the latest official information on the hours, tours, etc., take pencil in hand, and then telephone the U.S. Navy's recorded message at 471-3901.

Remember that if you take the $8 to $10 three-hour *commercial* cruises from Kewalo Basin to Pearl Harbor, they're not allowed to let you off on the memorial. On the plus side, you won't have to do any waiting.

There are four different numbered buses you may board from the suburban bus stop on Kona Street on the *mauka* side of Ala Moana Center, including Routes 50, 50-A, 51, and Route 52, the big circle run. (Be sure to take it in the "Wahiawa" direction.) If you start from Waikiki on Bus No. 8, you must change to one of these routes at the bus stop on the *makai* side of Ala Moana Center. Do not become confused and take Route No. 3 unless you're going to the sub base only (see below) and not the *Arizona* Memorial. In any case, better ask the driver before dropping in your two quarters. It's a faster trip on the special shuttle bus (Tel. 947-5015), which costs $2 each way, if they remember to pick you up. (They left us behind once recently.)

Within walking distance of the Visitor Center, on the other side of the Ford Island ferry landing, you may now visit the U.S.S. **Bowfin**, a World War II submarine. It has been installed there through the auspices of the Pacific Fleet Submarine Memorial Association, which has been restoring the old vessel, and you will be asked for a donation to walk through it. The *Bowfin* went on nine Pacific combat patrols and is credited with sinking 38 Japanese ships. (Closed Mondays.)

A little-known but interesting military sight at another part of Pearl Harbor is the **Pacific Submarine Museum** (Open Wednesday through Sunday, 9:30 A.M. to 5 P.M.). To get there, however, you'll have to ask directions to Nimitz Gate (the Main Gate), or take Bus No. 3. Tell the marine at the gate where you want to go, and he'll issue you a special pass and point you in the right direction. Again, it's better to have a car; otherwise it's a 20-minute walk after you get off the bus and pass the marine guard. For military buffs, however, the museum is essential. It includes portions of actual submarines (both American and captured foreign models) and you can twiddle the dials to your heart's content.

To continue the circular trip, head back north (*ewa*) on Kam Highway, continuing either on that or (better) the H-1 Freeway through the towns of Aiea ("I-*A*-ah") and Pearl City.

We do not recommend driving out to Nanakuli, Waianae, or Makaha unless you have a specific reason for doing so. That coastline has become a poverty-stricken, high-crime area where rebellious youths sometimes take out their frustration on strangers in the area.

Check your map and take Kam Highway (when it is numbered 99) or the new H-2, now that it is completed, inland through the sugar cane and pineapple fields to the battered old plantation town of **Wahiawa**, which now borders the home of "Hawaii's Own" 25th Infantry Division, **Schofield Barracks**. (If the barracks look familiar, maybe it's because you remember Burt Lancaster on the roof shooting down attacking airplanes with a BAR in "From Here to Eternity.") Also on the post, the **Tropic Lightning Historical Center** is less interesting since many exhibits have moved to the Army Museum in Waikiki. The material now relates only to the 25th Infantry Division and Schofield Barracks. (Closed Monday and Tuesday.)

Also in Wahiawa, at 1396 California Ave., is the **Wahiawa Botanical Gardens** (open daily, 9 to 4). We might give it a half-hour stroll or so, but only if it's not raining.

Kam Highway out of Wahiawa (Route 80) goes over a bridge and then on the left passes a dirt road which leads about 300 yards to Kukaniloko—the **Hawaiian Birth Stones**. It was to this sacred site that Hawaiian *alii* preferred to come for ceremonial births, and you can sit on the same stones as they did for the royal blessed events. The area has been slated for restoration, and the access road may be moved to the west.

Continuing on Kam Highway, you'll pass Del Monte's **Pineapple Variety Garden** on your left (illustrating the evolution of the pineapple from primitive to modern varieties), and then almost immediately on the right come to the **Dole Pineapple Pavilion** (open 9 to 5). There you may purchase hunks of fresh pineapple for about a dollar and then chomp on it while wandering over to the edge of the fields to see how they grow. (Grab plenty of napkins, first.) We've noticed that when pineapples are plentiful, you can often buy whole pineapples at this pavilion at prices cheaper than in the stores. When pineapples are in short supply, however, the Dole pavilion doesn't seem to raise their prices; they just stop selling whole fruit entirely, offering instead the little packages of spears and chunks, and cups of juice only. The juice, by the way, is canned.

Continuing along the highway, glance to your left to the **Waianae Mountains**. Yes, there is a road over them, but you can't take it because of military restrictions. The army at Schofield Barracks will sometimes let you go up their side, but if you don't have military identification, the navy won't let you go down theirs. (In many ways, the Armed Services still seem to think of Hawaii as a foreign country, and they have placed much of Oahu permanently "off limits" to the taxpayers. The image of the Islands as a "sugar-coated fortress" is thus perpetuated.)

The tallest peak in the Waianaes—the tallest on the island, in fact—is **Mt. Kaala**, at 4,046 feet.

We have directed you away from Kaukonahua Highway which you may notice on the map. It may be scenic, but it's one of the most dangerous roads on the island, due to some deceptive illusions and other effects along its curves.

At the Weed Traffic Circle, you might head west to **Mokuleia** ("Mo-cool-lay-*ee*-yah"), where the polo matches are held at 2:30 Sunday afternoons in the spring and summer, or on a little farther to the **Dillingham Airstrip** where you may watch the gliders any day of the week, or even take a ride in a three-seat sailplane yourself with members of the Hawaii Soaring Club. (See Section 7.) Never having quite made it aloft ourselves, and being a little unsure of our insurance policies, we can't vouch for it one way or another, but it sounds like fine fun for the daring.

Somewhat retracing the route brings you to **Waialua** ("why-a-*loo*-wah"), another old sugar plantation town. There are several ways to wend through it until you cross the stream into **Haleiwa** ("Holly Eva"). At the turn of the century, the village was a fashionable beach resort at the end of a railroad line. Today the tracks are gone and the hotels are closed, but it's sometimes fun for just poking around in, admiring its little boat harbor, etc. At the country stores, you can buy cones of shave ice. (See Section 5, "Restaurants—Kitchens in the Country.")

Continuing east along the north shore Route 83, you will pass several beaches and beach parks, not nearly as populated as any near Honolulu. During the week, they can be completely deserted. Seven miles from Haleiwa, just at a lovely little bay, is the turnoff for **Waimea Falls Park**, a privately owned nature reserve (Tel. 638-8511, open 10 A.M. 'til dark, admission about $6 for ages 13 and over, $4 for youngsters 7–12).

The park is usually a much more pleasant stop for the money than other expensive commercial gardens. You can take the mile-long ride in a free electric tram to the 55-foot falls, and then swim if you want in the pool at the base. (*Careful*—there is no lifeguard, and diving is dangerous unless you know *exactly* where the rocks are.) There are plenty of beautiful trails in the area. You can walk them yourself, occasionally meeting up with helpful young guides, or else take the guided tours at no extra charge.

At one time, the entire Waimea Valley was the home of thousands of Hawaiians, and Captain Cook's ships stopped to take on fresh water in 1779, after his death, on their way home. Today it's a lovely place for a picnic, and you can either bring in your own basket or buy the fixins at the park's "Country Store." Waimea Falls Park also includes an arboretum and a few exotic birds—some caged and some free. Our only caveat is that the park is sometimes just too darn crowded. We now avoid it on weekends, particularly in the afternoon. (Like most of these sites, it's on Bus Route No. 52.)

Back on the main drag, **Waimea Beach Park** is across the road. This coast is a famous winter surfing area where waves often break up to 35 feet high. (See Section 8.) Just around the bend—if the weather is dry—take the Pupukea Road across from the fire station up the hill for about 7/10 mile, then look for an HVB marker and a red dirt road which leads, after 7/10 mile, to the **Puu-o-Mahuka Heiau**. The ruins of this ancient Hawaiian *heiau*, or temple, are now a registered National Historic Landmark. Human sacrifices took place here, including those in 1794 of three of Vancouver's crewmen who ran afoul of the local population. In case you doubt that all the old pagan beliefs are now dead, have a look around you at all the sacred *ti* leaves, recently held down by rocks, given as offerings. The view from the bay side of the *heiau* is beautiful, and not so different than it was when the structure was built several centuries ago.

Just up the road, **Sunset Beach** is the home of the infamous Banzai Pipeline, a curl of fast-breaking waves and a supreme challenge for super surfers. This whole shoreline is often the site of winter surfing championships and the center of a whole youthful subculture in Hawaii.

Somewhere midway up a cliff *mauka* of Sunset Beach you're supposed to see the **George Washington Stone**, a natural formation that tour bus drivers say looks like a bust of the first president. The old Hawaiians noticed it, too, and called him Kahiki-lani—a surfing prince who was turned to stone for being unfaithful. We usually don't think much of this kind of thing, since it usually takes a powerful amount of imagination, plus knowing just exactly where to look. Near the stone, by the way, is the COMSAT (Communications Satellite) station, which is much easier to see. It's the one with the big white dish.

Almost at Oahu's windy and most northerly point is the **Hilton Kuilima Hotel**, representing an attempt to plunk a luxury resort down into the sticks. Certainly an architectural success, it has been less fortunate economically. The developer, Las Vegas' famous Del Webb organization, sold the place and now Hilton is trying to take a firmer hand on the property. If you think you hear cannons in this neighborhood, by the way, you may be right. The U.S. Army has a major field training area in the hills beyond.

A very unusual sugar-sweet museum attraction is the **Kahuku Sugar Mill** (Tel. 538-3841), which reopened in 1976 to considerable fanfare at Kahuku. The mill had closed in 1971, after ninety years of processing sugar cane, when it became an economically unviable operation. Five years later it reopened, its machinery turning again, albeit slowly, in a color-coded demonstration of how such Hawaii mills operated. The ironic thing is that the mill is again. A new owner hopes to open it again one of these days.

The town of **Laie** (pron. "*Lie*-yay") is headquarters for the Mormon Church in Hawaii. (The Church of Jesus Christ of the Latter Day Saints is the formal title.) Here it operates Brigham Young University—Hawaii Campus, and the nearby 1919 **Mormon Temple** is considered a point of interest. (We don't think much of its slide-show production, however.)

The champion presentation at Laie—and worth a separate trip—is the church-run **Polynesian Cultural Center** (Tel. 293-3333, 923-1861). Open daily except Sunday, the center consists of authentic replicas of several different Polynesian villages, where there are intricate demonstrations of art, craft, music, dance, costumes, and other cultural aspects given by real natives of the islands they represent. Nearly all the employees there, in fact, are students at BYU-Hawaii earning their academic tuition. The recently enlarged center almost seems to take you on a trip through the cultures of ancient Hawaii, Samoa, Fiji, Tonga, the Marquesas and New Zealand (The Maori culture).

For a daytime visit, late morning or early afternoon is best. We wouldn't spend the *kala* to enter the center at all unless we got there by at least 3:00 P.M., in time to find a good front seat to see the Pageant of the Long Canoes. (The huts begin emptying out after 4:30 or so, and some readers have complained that although tickets are still sold, few or no staff are around in the late afternoon.)

The 1½-hour nighttime show, "This Is Polynesia," although not totally authentic, is perhaps still the most entertaining Polynesian music-dance-and-costume show in Hawaii. It goes on stage about 7:30 P.M. Every performance is sold out, sometimes long before show time; so if you haven't made advance reservations, be sure to ask if you can be put on the waiting list immediately after your arrival.

Note that village admission and evening show prices are separate. We have seen them both climb drastically over the past few years, although we believe general admission will hold at $14 this year. The evening show will be around $15, and it is excellent. (Children from 5 to 12 are half-price.)

There are package deals that include an evening meal, but we would avoid the dinner at almost any price. (Try the nearby Crouching Lion, or the Kuilima Hotel—see Section 5.) Remember this is Mormon country, and no alcohol, tobacco, coffee, or tea is available, and smoking is prohibited in some areas. If you're traveling by city bus (No. 52, either direction), note that the show ends at 9:15 P.M., and many will be joining you with the hope of crowding on the last bus for Honolulu at 10 o'clock.

Add it all up carefully in advance, for it may cost a family of four over $100 to experience the whole banana. If you can okay the outlay, the PCC earns a high combination entertainment/cultural recommendation. (And again, a reminder—it's open *never on Sunday*.)

Just on the other side of **Hauula** ("how-*oo*-la") are a couple of nice beach parks. A little farther, about 4 miles from Laie, those with a hiking itch might like to keep an eye out for a sign on the right indicating the way to **Sacred Falls**, which is being turned into a new state park. You may hike a sometimes rough trail for about an hour—only one mile—and swim in the clear pool at the base of an 87-foot waterfall.

The falls are lovely when you get there, but definitely avoid the trek in wet weather. The trail is particularly dangerous and treacherous when muddy, and there is also the possibility of flash flood. (Our family enjoyed this excursion, but we might not do it on a first trip to Hawaii. Also, if you're going to Hilo, Hawaii; Wailua, Kauai; or Hana, Maui, you'll see nicer falls with less work involved on the way.)

Just past Kahana Bay Beach Park, you might notice the ruins of **Huilua Fishpond**, one of several such mullet-raising pens created when the ancient Hawaiians built stone walls out into the sea. This one was in use until the 1920s.

Beyond the inn and restaurant by the same name is a mountain ridge profile called the **Crouching Lion**. You've got to get in just the right position to see this leonine illusion, of course, and it took us several trips here to find it. In Hawaiian lore, it goes as usual: Somebody—a demigod, not a lion—was turned to stone for some kind of religious transgression.

You'll pass the ruins of an **Old Sugar Mill** along here. It's just about the first one on the island, dating back to 1863 and operated only until 1871. Out to sea, you'll recognize the little conical island known as **Chinaman's Hat**. Hawaiian name is Mokoli'i, which means "little dragon." It's supposed to be the visible part of the li'l fella's tail, the rest of him apparently stuck somehow underwater. The **Molii Fishpond** you may be able to make out along here is actually still in commercial fish-raising operation. It was originally built before recorded history in the Islands, probably as long ago as 700 years. You can see it better if you enter the nearby **Kualoa Regional Park**.

Farther along the road, the lush areas full of papaya, taro, bananas, etc., and often dotted by very modest Hawaiian dwellings, are known as **Waikane** and **Waiahole**, together currently forming a symbol of modern-day struggles and perhaps tragedy in the Islands as the agricultural leaseholders, most of whom are native Hawaiians, are being forced off the property by landowners who want to develop new housing in the area.

We do not believe the several souvenir shops along here will provide any better bargains than you can find in Honolulu, although some are attractively arranged. Others are tourist traps that survive because of the under-the-bus payments made to tour drivers who choose to stop there. Fruits and vegetables sold along the road, however, can sometimes be genuine bargains.

Just beyond Waiahole, near a local landmark incredibly called the Hygienic Store, you'll have to choose routes at a fork in the road. Route 83 (Kahekili Highway) goes to the right and leads to the charming **Haiku Gardens**, at 46-316 Haiku Rd., a former private estate now crowned by a restaurant. The highway also goes to the **Byodo-In Temple**, a beautiful replica of a famous Japanese building, for which you'll have to go through the Valley of the Temples (a cemetery) and pay $1 a head. (It's lovely, but we liked it more when it was free.)

If you're a clever map reader, and if you want to, you can backtrack later to either or both of those last two targets. You would instead take the left-hand fork at the Hygienic Store (Kamehameha Highway, Route 836) along the shoreline to the **Heeia** area ("hay-ay-*ee*-yah"). At the end of the pier, there is the **Coral Garden Glass Bottom Boat** (Tel. 247-0375). Captain Tom Smith charges $5 or so for an hour tour (maybe $2.50 for children), and points out live coral and tropical fish. Ask about the day's viewing conditions before signing up.

In **Kaneohe** ("Connie-*O*-He") you can turn right on the Likelike ("leaky-leaky") Highway (Route 63) to return to Honolulu via the Wilson Tunnel. Or you may take Kam Highway (Route 83) farther on to the Pali Highway (Route 61) described at the end of our East Oahu Circle Route and return via the Pali Tunnels. Either will bring you to the Lunalilo Freeway which you take diamondhead (eastish) toward Waikiki. Drive carefully!

7. Guided Tours and Cruises

A-lo-o-o-o-*ha!* Hawaii's equivalent of the school cheer is the word *aloha*, but not spoken straight and simple. When the tour guide gives you his *aloha*, he intones it slowly, ending with a special oomph, and then cocks his ear so that his faithful dozens of charges can shoot it back to him again in a resounding echo—ah-lo-o-o-o-o-*HA!*

There is no definite record of who first started giving this *banzai/* Geronimo treatment to such a kind and gentle sentiment as *aloha*. It is certainly not authentically Hawaiian and surely did not exist before the tourist industry developed in Waikiki.

According to humorist H. Allen Smith, the long, drawn-out *aloha* originated with a little man named Freddie who used to operate the elevators at the Moana and the old Surfrider Hotel in the 1940s and '50s. But those elevators are self-service now, and if there really was a Freddie, he has long ago alo-o-ha-ed himself into obscurity, officially unrecognized for his contribution to Hawaiian culture.

The tours in this section are not the umpteen-day, "all-inclusive" type. These "packages" are discussed in Chapter 2. The kind of guided tour we're talking about usually goes in a bus, limousine, or taxi, for anywhere between three hours and all day. It may or may not be part of one of your large package tours. But whether yours was all-inclusive or not, your bus driver's last and most dramatic trick will be his demonstration of the fastest hand in the Islands—palming with a "secret handshake" any tip you may offer him.

He generally hopes for a buck a head. However, we have quite successfully slipped him less and even stiffed him completely on occasion. No driver ever said a word—just smiled in anticipation of shaking the hand of those directly behind us. Therefore, if we were going to give any advice on this, we might say that if you're *not* going to tip, it might be wise not to be the last off the bus!

There is no official standard to which guides must measure up. Since they do have to pass a government test to be bus drivers, chances are they will be better at manhandling a bus than they will be at pointing out the interesting things about their islands.

You might like to know, too, that some of the stops made by a bus driver have more to do with the kickbacks he may receive from nearby commercial interests than from any determination that the point will be of particular interest to you.

Nevertheless, many a driver/guide is fun and smart and genuinely likes pointing out over and over again, day in and day out, the things he is proud of about his island. It is difficult to ask him a question he hasn't heard and answered a hundred times before, usually with just as big a smile and as much patience the hundredth time as the first.

There are three or four things to remember which may help you get a good tour: **(1)** The smaller the vehicle, the more rapport and responsiveness between the driver/guide and passengers, and the better time is

194MAVERICK GUIDE TO HAWAII

had by all. Of course taxis are the most expensive tour vehicles. Limousines, or "stretch-outs" (carrying 11 passengers) are less expensive and a good compromise. The big motor coaches (40 passengers or so) are the least costly, but you have a somewhat higher chance of drawing a dud for a guide, and it will be harder to get to know him, in any case.

(2) Try to find out if your guide is a graduate of the voluntary Hawaiiana class taught by the State Department of Education. If he is, you're probably in good hands. Unfortunately, the tour companies don't send their drivers to this class. They go on their own time, although the best companies do at least reimburse their drivers for the tuition providing they finish the course.

(3) In general, remember that long tours tend to be better than short tours, since there is more chance for passengers and guide to get to know one another. The worst tour, for instance, would be the short trip on a big bus. We are reminded of the "City/Punchbowl" trip we suffered through at the hands of Trade Winds for one morning a while back. Unfortunately, that particular tour—by whatever company—is often the "free" tour, included in the price of a package. The other tours—those you have to pay extra for—are likely to be better.

(4) It is a strange and interesting fact that if you are a member of a group, all of whom know each other from back home, you will probably have a better time on a guided tour. You may end up by voting your driver an honorary member of the club!

Most standard bus and limousine tours cost exactly the same prices among companies. The tariffs for each are approved by the State Public Utilities Commission, and the firms must justify any applications for increases.

There are only a few major tour bus companies (and scores of small ones) on Oahu. Without going into exhaustive detail, here are the larger ones, more or less listed in our personal order of preference. As we mentioned, you might draw a dumb driver in the best of them, or a really snappy, entertaining and informed expert in the worst. (We would be very happy to hear of your experiences with these outfits—good, bad, or indifferent.) All have sedans, stretch-out limos, and full-size buses available.

SOME MAJOR TOUR BUS COMPANIES

Charley's Tour & Transportation, Inc. (Tel. 955-3381), 1682 Kalakaua Ave., Honolulu, Hi. 96815. Charley's caters also to local business, and seems responsive to the potential of repeat trade.

Gray Line Hawaii, Ltd. (Tel. 836-1883), 435 Kalewa St., Honolulu, Hi. 96819. We like its strict "no kickbacks" policy and the fact that it sometimes sends out undercover company personnel posing as passengers to check out the drivers. It's now owned by InterIsland Resorts, a hotel chain.

Robert's Hawaii Tours, Inc. (Tel. 947-3939), 444 Hobron Lane, Honolulu, Hi. 96814, which also prohibits its drivers from accepting commissions from roadside businesses.

Aloha State Tour & Transportation (Tel. 949-2975), P.O. Box 22612, Honolulu, Hi. 96822.

Here are a few sample tours offered by these and some other companies on the island of Oahu. PUC-approved rates below are in effect at press time, but some of these may change before you climb aboard. Use them as a general guide only.

City-Punchbowl (Honolulu Tour). Morning. Three hours. University of Hawaii, Waioli Tea Room (a stop), Manoa Valley, Punchbowl Cemetery (a stop), Downtown Honolulu, Iolani Palace. $11.50 on the bus; $13.50 on a limousine. (And worth the $2 difference on this crowded run.)

Pearl Harbor and Punchbowl. Half day. Includes a *drive past* Pearl Harbor, central Oahu pineapple fields, the Nuuanu Pali Lookout, Punchbowl Cemetery, Downtown Honolulu. $15 on the bus; $17.50 on á limousine.

Little Circle Island. Half day. Diamond Head, Koko Head, suburban Honolulu residential neighborhoods, Hanauma Bay, the Blow Hole, Makapuu Point, and Windward Oahu, returning to Waikiki via the Nuuanu Pali Lookout (a stop). $13 on the bus; $14 on a limousine.

Circle Island. 7 hours. Nuuanu Valley, Pali Lookout (a stop), Kaneohe, (Byodo-In—w/Charley's only,) Mormon Temple (a stop), Sunset Beach, Waimea Bay, Haleiwa, Wahiawa, Pearl Harbor. (Or reverse.) $17.50 on the bus; about $23 in the limousine (definitely preferable). A lunch stop is made—probably at the Kuilima Hotel.

Sea Life Park. Afternoon, 4 hours. Diamond Head, Koko Head, Hawaii Kai, Hanauma Bay (a stop), the Blow Hole (a stop), Sea Life Park (admission not included), Waimanalo, Wilson Tunnel. $15 on the bus and probably about $18 on the limousine.

Polynesian Cultural Center. Afternoon and evening. Includes center admission, buffet dinner, and evening show. About $55 on the bus (children's fare about $35).

Small-group tours, specializing in (but not limited to) waterfall and nature itineraries, are offered by the minibus-equipped **E Noa Tours** (Tel. 941-6608), 1110 University Ave., Honolulu, Hi. 96826. The excursions can vary somewhat depending on the interests of the passengers and the predilection of the driver. Prices vary from around $16 for a four-hour sunset tour, to $30 or $35 for an all-day, 8-hour, round-the-island excursion.

E Noa pioneered in the van tours, but several more are now being cranked up. **Akamai Tours** (Tel. 922-6485) may also be a smart bet. Others include **Polynesian Adventure Tours** (Tel. 922-0888), **Hauoli Tours** (Tel. 836-3656), and **Kiwi Tours** (Tel. 923-2228).

All four have slightly different itineraries but comparable fares. The only danger with these tours is that they may grow large. At groups of a dozen or less with a driver-guide, they form an ideal way to get a good feeling for Hawaii. Another point is that *big* buses tend to be resented by the local population. (They block traffic, create fumes and noise, and interrupt TV reception in rural areas.) A smaller vehicle, and by extension all who sail in her, often receive a better blessing throughout Hawaii.

Still another possibility is to hire a personal driver-guide, a more expensive but sometimes much more satisfying arrangement. You'll find it upwards of $200 a day for such private service in roomy, air-conditioned Cadillacs and taxis. There are several around, but a Beverly Hills attorney has written a favorable brief on the personalized tour given by **Danny's Tour & Limousine Service** (Tel. 941-6381, or you can even phone Danny in his car at 526-6164). We haven't yet met the gentleman ourselves, but we would like to hear from more readers who have used such individual tour services in Hawaii.

Here's a mouthful—the **Diplomat's Passport to Polynesia** (Tel. 847-3511), a tour guided by the prestigious Bishop Museum. It utilizes a big, red, London double-decker bus between Waikiki and the Museum/Planetarium in Kalihi Valley, plus admission to the Mission Houses Museum. The Diplomat's is the guided tour, still running at $10, and far preferable to the $7 Passport to Polynesia, which provides transportation and admission but no narration. We've yet to take this tour. Let us know if it's as good as it sounds. (Leaves daily at 8:30 A.M. from King's Village.)

The preceding two "passports" should not be confused with the similarly named but lesser-known **Passport to Paradise** (Tel. 988-2141), run by Paradise Park. This $15 all-day tour *also* includes the Bishop Museum and environs, but winds up at Paradise Park. (And then, Paradise Park has still another arrangement, a "deluxe tour" that is basically a tour through the park, including transportation to and from Waikiki. It costs $9.50—$2 over the park admission price.)

For exploration on foot, you might try **Hawaii Hiking Trail Tours** (Tel. 836-8648), which offers special excursions through Nuuanu Valley, up Diamond Head, out to Kaena Point, and even to Pearl Harbor. The firm also conducts nature tours through Waimea Valley and backpacking trips on the Neighbor Islands. Say hello for us to Kele Kameha, the Hawaiiana expert who leads most of these personally.

Offering 4- to 16-day camping and hiking tours on the Neighbor Islands, but from an Oahu base, is **Trek Hawaii** (Tel. 235-6614), formerly called Sea Trek. Fares begin at a fair $275. We've not yet had the chance to go with these people, but the itineraries look fascinating. Write Nancy Pendleton at Sea Trek, P.O. Box 1585, Kaneohe, Hi. 96744, and say we suggested asking for the brochure.

History buffs should not miss the **Historic Downtown Walking Tour**, a two-hour stroll offered by the volunteers from the Mission Houses Museum (Tel. 531-0481). For $5 or so, the ladies will meet you about 9:30 A.M. weekdays and lead you through the historic government center, winding up with a tour of the Mission Houses themselves. *Reservations are essential.* We recommend it particularly for a Friday. Then you can finish the morning off with the noontime band concert on the lawn of Iolani Palace.

The **Walking Tour of Chinatown** (Tel. 533-3181) is also pretty good. Sponsored by the Chinese Chamber of Commerce, the tour goes every Tuesday at 9:30 A.M., rain or shine, from the CCC at 42 North King St. Last time we checked, it was still $2.50 for the tour and about $4 for the optional Chinese lunch following the three-hour excursion.

The free **University of Hawaii Tour** and the **East-West Center Tour** take place one right after the other Monday through Friday. Meet at the entrance to Bachman Hall, at the corner of University Avenue and Dole Street, at 1:30 P.M. After about an hour viewing what Honolulu *Star-Bulletin* writer Murry Engle calls "a phantasmagoria of architecture set in an impressive collection of plant life," your student guide will leave you at Jefferson Hall, the headquarters of the East-West Center.

Another guide will pick you up there a few minutes later and explain the purposes of the East-West Center, etc. Interesting for those with a definite academic or botanical bent—a bore for others.

AIR TOURS

We normally do not recommend any one-day flying tours of all the Islands. One such company has an unenviable safety record, and another has an unenviable public relations image. The problem usually comes—as it does with so many activities—during busy periods when somebody gets greedy and wants to pick up all the fares he can. In this kind of business, it's a temptation to scrounge extra planes and extra pilots besides the regular ones when necessary. The substitute personnel and/or equipment just might not be satisfactory.

Many readers have written to disagree with this assessment because their own experience has been good—or lucky. Still, we decided long ago that as long as there was any possible problem, we wouldn't recommend or even list these outfits.

Now, however, the picture seems to have changed for the better with the launching of **Hawaiian Airlines** (Tel. 537-5100) into the air-tour business with its "Islands in the Sky" program. One of the long-established scheduled interisland airlines (with an impeccable safety record), Hawaiian Air flies neither its big jets nor tiny puddle-jumpers, taking off instead in its 50-seat British-made De Havilland DASH-7 turboprops.

The peripatetic trips cover seven islands in eight hours, viewing Oahu, Molokai, Lanai, Kahoolawe, and Niihau from the air, and making stops at Kauai and Maui. Currently the flight does *not* go to the Big Island, which we call a plus since it would cram far too much into the day's schedule (a problem with other operations). The program is thus divided into totals of about four hours' flying time and four hours on the ground. The fare of about $200 per person includes breakfast on board, lunch on the ground, a boat ride to the Fern Grotto on Kauai, and a van tour of the Hana area on Maui.

Some passengers will certainly be exhausted after the long day, but others are sure to love it. At this writing we haven't yet tried this "Islands in the Sky" excursion ourselves. And, since this is a relatively new operation, we will be particularly happy to hear any reaction you may have to it.

HELICOPTER OPERATIONS: You may or may not find some whirly-bird sightseeing trips of Oahu available. Chopper firms have a way of cranking up and shutting down so fast that many in existence today will have flown into a cloud tomorrow.

One outfit that has become fairly well established is **Hawaii Pacific Helicopters** (Tel. 836-1566), headquartered at the Ala Wai Heliport behind the Ilikai Hotel. (Viewers of TV's "Magnum P.I." will recognize the site, but this is decidedly *not* "T.C.'s" operation.) Hawaii Pacific has been offering seven "Cloud 9" tours ranging from a short $15-per-person six-minute skip along Waikiki Beach to a $200 excursion to the end of the Koolau Mountains. Hawaii Pacific launches these in one Hughes 300 two-passenger helicopter and one four-passenger Bell Jet Ranger.

Another company is **Royal Helicopters** (Tel. 836-2868), which usually uses the same Ala Wai pad. Prices are comparable to those of Hawaii Pacific. A third outfit that may still be hovering around is **Moore's Hawaiian Helicopters** (Tel. 623-9862), headquartered at the Hilton Kuilima Hotel on the North Shore. Moore's has a popular 20-minute, $50-tour which includes Waimea Falls and other sites in that outback neighborhood.

We have yet to climb on any of these commercial trips and can offer little advice, except to be sure to confirm how long each trip lasts for the amount you're paying. Better check by phone with any of these, as a matter of fact, just to be sure you'll find them out at the pad. Happy landings!

CRUISES ON OAHU

There are several interesting trips on the briny from the Capital Island, running all price ranges. And, in fact, we think it would be a dogfish shame if any voyager to Hawaii did not manage to get out on the water at least once. The sea is an important part of Hawaii's heritage, and it should be experienced, even if only in the most minor or cornball way.

SUNSET AND TWILIGHT DINNER CRUISES

Affectionately called "boogie boats" by their crews, a half-dozen or more craft swing out at 5:15 or 5:30 P.M. daily, generally from Kewalo Basin ("Fisherman's Wharf") for a two-hour cruise toward Diamond Head and back. Most run pretty smoothly, although we generally prefer the sailboats to the mechanical power operations. There's a lap dinner (usually barbecued chicken), free drinks, live music, an emcee, and dancing. Fares are running around $35 this year.

Companies offering the sunset/twilight cruises include **Aikane Catamarans** (Tel. 538-3680), whose newer boats are the *Aikane*, the *Aikane II*, the *Aikane III*, and the *Aikane VI*, all of which resemble ancient Polynesian canoes. Also its 30-year-old humpbacked cat, *Ale Ale Kai*, made famous by Henry Kaiser in the mid-50s, has been refurbished. All offer tables-and-chairs seating.

Another well-established outfit is **Windjammer Cruises** (Tel. 521-0036). Windjammer has owned several boats, but it's currently most proud of its massive, refurbished *Rella Mae*, a sort-of replica of a clipper ship, which was a New-York-based Hudson River excursion boat. This 284-foot, three-deck, four-masted leviathan almost seems to feature everything an ocean liner does, and it can carry 1,500 passengers. It takes about 20 minutes to hoist the 20 sails. Both Aikane and Windjammer vessels sail from Kewalo Basin.

Another dinner operation is conducted by **Rainbow Cruises** (Tel. 955-3348). The catamaran with the distinctive striped sails leaves from its own dock off the beach at the Hilton Hawaiian Village in Waikiki. Two which cast off from the Aloha Tower area include **Hula Kai Catamarans** (Tel. 524-1800) at Pier 11 (the Ewa side of the tower) and **Hokunani Cruises** (Tel. 531-9981), which parks its 82-foot Polynesian-style craft at Pier 8 (on the Waikiki side of the tower area).

Perhaps also underway this year will be **VIP Cruises** (Tel. 524-7315), which has been piloting a magnificent 160-foot, all-aluminum vessel called the *Royal Prince*. (Formerly the *Avalon*, it used to carry passengers

between San Diego and Ensenada, Mexico.) The launch, which originally cost a reported $3 million, seats 500 persons.

MOONLIGHT AND STARLIGHT TRIPS

This is the same two-hour dinner cruise as above but repeated later in
the evening, usually at 8:15 or 8:30 P.M. Aikane Catamarans, Hula Kai
Catamarans, and Windjammer Cruises (see above) all offer it. Rainbow
Cruises and VIP don't.

PICNIC CRUISES

Picnics are seldom definitely scheduled. It depends more on the demand than anything else. The most dependably offered *pikiniki* this year
will probably be by Hula Kai Catamarans for 2½ hours. Usually there's a
cold lunch, complimentary mai tais or soft drinks, an off-shore swim,
and dancing to live music. It should be priced around $15.

Lunchtime cruises for $5 are sometimes offered by Hokunani Cruises
(Tel. 531-9981).

PEARL HARBOR BOAT RIDES

Most commercial Pearl Harbor cruises—not to be confused with the
free Navy tours—last 2½ to 3 hours and depart Kewalo Basin twice
daily, at 9:30 A.M. and 1:30 P.M. The fare now varies between $8 and $13.
Passengers view, *but do not get off at,* the USS *Arizona* and USS *Utah* me-
morials. The trip will be narrated, and hard and soft drinks and snacks
are for sale on board. Color slides and various souvenir books will also be
hawked, to be sure.

This year, we expect the sailing cruises to the harbor to cost more than
the power operations. Aikane Catamarans (Tel. 538-3680) will probably
get $12 for the trip, and Rainbow Cruises (Tel. 955-3348), leaving from
behind the Hilton, may charge $13.

The power boats include **Hawaiian Cruises** (Tel. 923-2061), with
their 110-foot vessel *Adventure V*, **VIP Cruises** (Tel. 524-7315) in their
majestic 160-footer *Royal Prince*, and **Paradise Cruise** (Tel. 536-3641),
with its 550-seat, 128-foot *Hawaii State*, which also features some glass-
bottom viewing over the reef when weather and other conditions permit. They also run the cruise sometimes in the 110-foot vessel *Hawaii*.

GLASS-BOTTOM BOATS

It seems every year there's a different glass-bottom boat operation in
Honolulu, so don't blame us if this is out of date by the time this perishable research comes off the press. At the moment, however, the only
company is **Glass Bottom Boats Hawaii** (Tel. 537-1958), operating the

74-foot, 149-passenger *Ani Ani* in a one-hour cruise off Waikiki. (The *Ani Ani*, which has glass viewing ports, used to be the old *Captain Cook VI* from the Kona Coast on the Big Island.) We'll make an educated guess that the fare for bottom viewing and skyline viewing will run about $8 this year.

AN OVERNIGHT CRUISE

A fairly new operation is the overnight cruise from Honolulu aboard the 85-foot **Spirit of Adventure** (Tel. 926-4785). The 85-foot motor yacht of that name currently leaves Honolulu Harbor at 5 P.M., returning the following day at 1 P.M. after sailing along the coastline of Oahu and anchoring in some secluded cove during sleeping hours.

The yacht has 14 cabins, some with queen-size beds. Fares at this writing run from about $100 to $250 per person, depending on sleeping arrangements. We have not experienced the trip so can draw no conclusions. Details may be available from the firm at 119 Merchant St., Honolulu, Hi. 96813 (although they didn't answer *our* recent letter). *Bon voyage!*

CRUISING INTERISLAND

An unusual four-day sailing adventure that specializes in sailing from Maui *to* Oahu has been launched by **Trek Hawaii** (Tel. 235-6614), formerly Sea Trek, whose camping tours are mentioned earlier in this section. The trips stop at Lanai or Molokai en route.

For several years this academically oriented organization provided marine life tours for the Waikiki Aquarium. Snorkeling and fishing are featured en route. Per-person fares on the 38-foot sailing yacht currently run about $400. (Add to that your air fare to Maui, of course.) Write for information to the company at P.O. Box 1585, Dept. MG, Kaneohe, Hi. 96744. (Tell 'em we sent you.)

The only regular sailings from Honolulu to the Neighbor Islands are the week-long luxury trips offered by **American Hawaii Cruises** (Tel. 521-0384) aboard two historic 30,000-ton sister ships. Originally built in 1951, they have several stories to tell. Grace Kelly and her wedding party sailed to Monaco on the S.S. *Constitution;* it was also used for filming *An Affair to Remember* with Cary Grant and Deborah Kerr. And President Harry Truman traveled aboard the S.S. *Independence*, when both ships were owned by the old American President Lines. Amazingly they still have much òf their original furniture and decorations, although they have been vastly refurbished, too.

Sometimes both vessels are in operation, but on opposite itineraries. Other times, only one ship may be making the island rounds while the other is used for a Trans-Pacific cruise (between Honolulu and San Francisco or Los Angeles), routine maintenance, or other activities.

The original itinerary is better: In this one, the ship departs the Aloha Tower in Downtown Honolulu on Saturday night; sails around the island of Molokai (enjoy its rugged north shore in the morning), then between Lanai and Kahoolawe and Kahoolawe and Maui during the day on Sunday; calls at Hilo on Monday; Kailua-Kona on Tuesday; Kahului, Maui, on Wednesday; visits Nawiliwili, Kauai, on Thursday and Friday; and returns to Honolulu early Saturday morning.

The alternate itinerary we think is a little more unwieldy: The ship seems to have a difficult time using up 30 hours to cover the 100 miles between Oahu and Kauai, where it stops Monday for the day. Then the sail by Molokai and Kahoolawe, etc., is made during the night. It calls on Tuesday in Hilo, Wednesday in Kailua-Kona, and then spends Thursday night in Kahului. The ship begins its return by cruising along the famous north shore of Molokai Friday afternoon (don't stay below deck!) before returning to Honolulu on Saturday morning.

At this writing, the *Constitution*, the more attractive of the two ships, is taking the original itinerary. If that continues, choosing between them should be easy.

Other differences: The *Independence* has a gymnasium, an art gallery, a video games room, a Teen Room, a larger dining room, and a larger hospital. The *Constitution* carries 800 (50 more than her sister), and sports two separate dining rooms, plus the attractive Starlight piano bar open into the wee hours on the top deck (where the gym is located on the other vessel). Both ships have three other bars and each has two swimming pools, four elevators, a shopping arcade, and a children's playroom. Interiors are in a sort of '50s revival of the '30s *art deco* style.

American Hawaii, headquartered in San Francisco, is fully versed in the traditional cruise activities, keeping you busy almost around the clock or allowing you to laze every day in a deck chair if you'd rather. All nightclub acts, music, movies, games, and other entertainment is included, as, of course, are food, accommodations, and your built-in transportation. (Drinks on board and shore excursions—available at Hilo, Kailua-Kona, Maui, and Kauai—are extra, payable with cash or credit card, but not with personal checks.)

Letters from Maverick readers who have traveled on either ship have been generally favorable. We enjoyed our own inaugural cruise on the *Constitution*, except perhaps for the feeling of isolation from the world at large and even from today's Hawaii. (No newspapers or magazines were sold on board, it was difficult to impossible to get radio news, and there was no TV anywhere for passenger use.) Understandably, many will find all that a big plus. To us, the general feeling is that the operation is somewhat more "mainland" than Hawaiian, apparently reflecting its San Francisco management.

The meals were good to excellent, although within a limited range of cuisine due to central menu planning. (We would like to have seen more Hawaiian and European choices.) But there was plenty of food, especially when you count afternoon tea, the midnight buffet, pizza parties, etc. The generally young crew (more than 300 in number) were almost universally pleasant to everyone. (Count on a minimum of $35 in tips, by the way.) You'll save time on returning to port if you can carry your own luggage off.

Fares for 1984 will run from $995 to $3,295 per person in 11 categories, except on the *Independence*, where there are a few smaller, inside upper and lower bunk C Deck cabins for $895. Children under 16 sail for $350, except that during the summer months two in their parents' cabin are carried free. Choose your accommodations carefully, consulting a deck plan and a good travel agent. (You might save $150 or more apiece if a porthole doesn't mean that much to you—maybe more if you forego the "prestige" of residence on an upper deck. Or you might get more elbow room lower in the ship for the same amount of money.) If you do choose a porthole room, incidentally, we think the port (left) side is preferable. All cabins have private toilets and showers. Many have separate lower berths. Several have double or king-size beds (but watch out for kings in cabins that are really not large enough for them). A few have upper bunks.

For full details, write American Hawaii Cruises, 3 Embarcadero Center, San Francisco, Calif. 94111, or call the toll-free number in the appendix. All in all, we judged it a trip to remember—for all the right reasons.

SPECIAL BARGAIN TIP: American Hawaii also has begun selling shorter cruises of three and four days. At this writing, these "*kamaaina* cruises" are intended to attract local residents. They are being marketed in Hawaii only, and so you would have to chance making arrangements after arriving in the Islands.

For the three-day cruise you join the ship in Maui and travel to Kauai and Honolulu. For the four-day cruise you sail from Honolulu to Hilo, Kona, and Maui. The price of a plane trip between Maui and Honolulu is included in the fares, which currently range upwards from about $450 for the three-day trip and about $500 up for the four-day version.

8. Water Sports on Oahu

Oahu's beaches are generally gorgeous, and of the island's 50 miles of sand, 2 miles of the safest and the most fun line right up against the vacation precincts of Waikiki.

Many of the things you want to do in the water you can do very well at Waikiki Beach. You can swim, you can surf (better for boards than for bellies), you can paddle, you can skin dive (snorkel), and even scuba dive in calm and clear waters, including the famous "100-foot hole" beyond the reef. But with no talent at all, you can also shoot the waves in an outrigger canoe, or even catch wind and wave together on the small-size catamarans that run up onto the sand. Or you can sun yourself (not too much, too soon!), and maybe learn to play the ukulele.

WAIKIKI BEACH

After years of careful grooming, Waikiki Beach today runs uninterrupted for the entire length of the peninsula. It is generally considered to begin at Kapahulu Avenue, and end in front of the Hilton Hawaiian Village. (To the left or "diamondhead" of Kapahulu Avenue is a half-mile narrow strand not strictly part of Waikiki. Called Queen Surf Beach, it runs generally along Kapiolani Park and is a popular place for island families to picnic and play.)

For most, Waikiki Beach begins just past Kapahulu at a small and protected portion of shoreline called "Kuhio Beach." With the long breakwater cutting the rough waves down to kiddie size, it's a good place to take young children. Curiously, Kuhio Beach is also popular for strolling, wading, and sometimes swimming tourists from Japan. If you don't swim, watch out for deep holes here.

Just along from Kuhio Beach is the **Waikiki Beach Center**, repository of several scores of red surfboards and headquarters of the **Star Beachboys, Inc.** (Tel. 841-7884). It is just one of a half-dozen similar concessions along the beach. You may take surfing lessons for about $10 an hour, including board and instructor.

If you're already into surfing, you can rent the boards alone for maybe $4 an hour. And if all seems a little too tricky, you might approximate the thrill very well on an outrigger canoe ride. Usually the beachboys will take you and others out and let the boat catch three waves—which takes about 20 or 30 minutes—for about $4 per person.

Similar beach concession outfits along the shore include the **Aloha Beach Service** (which serves the Sheraton hotels and has extensions on their phones) with desks in front of the Moana/Surfrider, the Royal Hawaiian, and the Sheraton.

The **Outrigger Beach Services** are operated by the Outrigger Hotel, and we like the way this group cleans up the cigarette butts from the sand along here. The **Halekulani Hotel** also has its own beach stand. Two more beach concessions are operated by **Nathan Napoleon** (Tel. 923-6137) at the Reef Hotel and at the Fort DeRussy Beach. Like the

Outrigger and the Halekulani, the **Hilton Hawaiian Village** runs its own beach operations.

Each section of the beach has its own particular characteristics, and the surfing areas in the water in front of them are nearly all named. The aforementioned Kuhio Beach, tame close in, has fast, crowded waves called "Queens" out in front of its seawall.

The wide Moana/Surfrider beach section has a lovely outdoor bar and that's a good place to sit and watch surfers and outriggers taking the "Canoes," a portion of waves which break close enough so you can get good views and photographs of the action. The Outrigger's beach is also wide, but usually jammed anyway. The Royal Hawaiian is less crowded, partly due to the ropes set up above the high water line to give its guests a little more elbow room. The "Malihinis," gentle waves in front of the Royal, are close in and a good beginner's surfing lesson spot.

The beach narrows at the Sheraton, then widens a bit at the Halekulani. The "Populars" offshore are often populated with surfers. The Reef beach might have a festive atmosphere, perhaps with impromptu ukulele music and lessons in the evening (mainly on Sunday). The long Fort DeRussy Beach you'll find primarily used by military men and their families.

Finally, the Hilton Hawaiian Village Beach has an affluent air about it. You'll see lots of Sunday volleyball here on the wide, tree-studded sand.

At several points along Waikiki Beach, there are catamarans pulled up onto the shore. Usually they offer one-hour rides for $6 or $7, and perhaps half that for the *keikis*.

Before leaving Waikiki Beach, a few words about the famous—or notorious—beachboys. James Michener wrote about the fabled Kelly Kanakoa, a bronze Adonis who was no smoother on a surfboard than he was at satisfying the fantasies of hundreds of lonely *haole wahines* who felt far away from home and reality on a pre-jet Waikiki Beach. This extracurricular image may be slipping a little in the 1980s, but the fact is that the beachboys' *official* talents, at least, are not. All beachboys must be licensed by the Hawaii State Department of Transportation. They not only have to know how to teach surfing, but they must be regularly qualified in lifesaving tests. The requirements are even stiffer for surfing canoe captains, and catamaran skippers must also be licensed by the U.S. Coast Guard.

Still, beachboys will be beachboys, and they shouldn't be confused with life guards, of course. The younger instructors still are good at good-natured hustling—lessons and rides by day, and maybe a few free drinks, a meal, and impromptu friendships after dark. They give the appearance—like one of their traditional songs—of "Livin' On Easy." Nevertheless, they know their job.

OTHER BEACHES ON OAHU

If you don't remember anything else about Oahu beaches, note that although most are beautiful, several are downright dangerous. Lifeguarding isn't all that it should be, and some Mainland beachgoers may be shocked to learn that beaches are always open, whether a life guard is on duty or not. So unless you're an Olympic swimmer, it's a good idea at *any* beach to see if there's a guard tower nearby, and more important, see whether or not that tower is occupied.

Safety rules: Here are several precautions specifically for *malihinis* in Hawaiian waters.

• *Never* swim alone. The powerful waves of Hawaii can tire a swimmer almost before he knows it. Have someone around to call to.

• Don't swim where the waves are large, along a rocky coast, or at a steep beach.

• If you're caught in a riptide (undertow), don't fight against the current. Swim parallel or diagonally in relation to the beach toward the white water until out of the current, then turn back toward shore.

• If you're in the water but not surfing, stay clear of surfers. Runaway boards are dangerous.

• Obey warning signs, red flags, etc., at the beaches.

• Avoid all fresh-water swimming unless you know exactly what you're getting into. There are sharp rocks at the bottom of mountain pools. Also some clear natural pools—especially those near residential areas—are nonetheless polluted.

Progressing from Waikiki in order along vaguely the south, east, and north shore of Oahu, here are several beaches or beach parks you may run across. Most parks will also have picnic facilities—barbecue grills, etc. (We do not recommend stopping at any beach along the western shore—the Waianae Coast. First is a large number of burglaries which often occur from rented cars—even from locked trunks—in that area while the drivers and passengers are on the beach or in the water. And sometimes visitors and military men have been victims in more violent incidents with residents of this high-crime area.)

Diamond Head Beach Park, on Diamond Head Beach Road below the lighthouse. Poor and dangerous swimming, but a nice place for a walk and observing life in the tidal pools.

Waialae Beach Park, 4925 Kahala Ave., and others along a five-mile shoreline including **Wailupe**, **Kuliouou**, and **Maunalua Beach Parks**. Poor swimming in all due mainly to shallow underwater coral. Scuba divers know, however, that off Waialae lies the famous Fantasy Reef, but that's accessible only by boat.

Hanauma Bay Beach Park, 7455 Kalanianaole Highway. Yes, there is good swimming in this beautiful, semi-submerged volcanic crater, but its *raison d'etre* is the easy yet dramatic snorkeling and—in the deep water beyond the rocks—gentle but still lovely beginners' scuba diving waters.

The bay is a Hawaii underwater park, so no fishing is allowed. The fish seem to know this, now, and if you look under the surface with mask and snorkel, even in shallow wading areas, you can see hundreds of different kinds and colors of reef fish. Bring a crust of bread into the water, and we'll almost guarantee it! Hanauma Bay is one of our favorite excursions. (If you take snorkel or scuba lessons, the chances are they'll bring you out here. There's no better place of the type on Oahu.)

Farther along the highway is **Sandy Beach** (also known as Koko Head Beach Park). *Do not even think of entering the water here!* This is the most notorious and dangerous body surfing beach in Hawaii. There are hazardous, crunching shorebreaks causing broken necks among many but the most expert body surfers who have grown up with these waters. Strong currents and riptides are common. Regardless of how many people you see here, skip it!

Around on the windward side, now, you'll note below the scenic lookout **Makapuu Beach Park**, a famous body surfing beach. But to all but the expert, it is virtually as dangerous as the previously named Sandy Beach. Swells over 4 feet will bring in hazardous currents on top of everything else.

Waimanalo Beach Park, at 41-741 Kalanianaole Highway, has good swimming, but you occasionally see a rough crowd hanging around. We skip it and go on a couple miles to Bellows.

Bellows Field Beach Park, however, is administered by the U.S. Air Force and is only open to the civilian public from Friday noon to Sunday midnight and on federal holidays. There is excellent swimming and good safe body surfing, plus lots of excellent picnicking facilities.

Follow your map carefully to find **Kailua Beach Park**, 450 Kawailoa Rd., at the edge of the windward bedroom community of Kailua. There is excellent swimming, but the little "Flat Island" you'll see is farther away than it looks! Body surfing is sometimes fun when the "surf's up." Sailing and boating are also excellent.

Kaneohe Beach Park, as well as others like **Laenani** and **Waiahole Beach Parks**, borders polluted Kaneohe Bay. These parks are fine for picnics and sunning, but don't go near the water.

Kaaawa Beach Park, 51-392 Kam Highway, near Kaaawa, has good swimming and snorkeling. But skip **Swanzy Beach Park**, about a mile along, where swimming is difficult due to a coral shelf.

Kahana Bay Beach Park, at 52-222 Kam Highway, is a real sleeper. Here is a beautiful location with good swimming, fishing, and boating. There's a nice beginners' body and board surf close in to the beach, too.

Punaluu Beach Park, 53-309 Kam Highway, also has good swimming, but **Hauula Beach Park**, 3 or 4 miles farther, has poor swimming due to a rocky bottom.

Ehukai Beach Park is the site of the experts-only "Banzai Pipeline" and other high winter surf. In the summer, when the ocean is flat, this is a pretty good swimming and snorkeling area. **Sunset Beach**, nearby, has body and board surfing, but for experts only. Both of these are killers in the winter. They're not even safe for strolling.

Waimea Bay Beach Park, 61-031 Kam Highway, often features dangerous swimming and very strong currents. In the winter, as a matter of fact, there's a danger that beach strollers may be picked right up off the beach by high waves and then washed out to sea. In the fall and winter, avoid the water here as well as at nearby **Pupukea Beach Park** like a pariah. Snorkeling is fun in calm surf during the summer. By the way, in the winter, remember that the entire shoreline between Kahuku and Haleiwa, including the preceding four entries, is often *exceedingly dangerous*. If you can't find a life guard to tell you the latest information, *don't even walk at the water's edge!*

Haleiwa Beach Park, 62-449 Kam Highway. Good swimming and snorkeling in the spring and summer. Surfing for experts only (dangerous reef and current farther out). **Waialua Beach Park**, 66-167 Haleiwa Rd., now just renamed Haleiwa *Alii* Beach Park, also has good swimming in spring and summer. And **Mokuleia Beach Park**, 68-919 Kaena Point Rd., a popular camping spot, has poor swimming.

SCUBA DIVING AND SNORKELING INSTRUCTION

Several "dive shops" offer lessons in how to get along underwater, but we think it would be best and safest to stick to the big ones—and the ones who have been in business for at least five years—especially for scuba which has some dangerous aspects. A half day of classes and diving will run about $45 or so. (Snorkel lessons will total maybe $20.) Prices usually include transportation from and to the hotels and all necessary paraphernalia. (Of course, if you are already a certified scuba diver, you can rent equipment from most of these shops, too. You'll have to have your "C" card to prove it, however.)

Here are four "old reliables" on the scuba scene: **Dan's Dive Shop** (Tel. 941-2284), at 1382 Makaloa St., offers a catamaran scuba tour for around $50, a five-day scuba course for about $225, and a half-day snorkel tour for $25 or so. **South Seas Aquatics** (Tel. 538-3854), in the Ward Warehouse shopping center, has half-day beginning scuba lessons for about $50, two-tank boat dives for around the same price, and half-day snorkel tours for around $20.

American Dive Hawaii (Tel. 732-2877), 3684 Waianae Ave., offers half-day scuba tours for around $50 and snorkel tours for about $20. And the **Aloha Dive Shop** (Tel. 395-5922), a somewhat newer outfit in Koko Marina out at Hawaii Kai, has one-tank dives for about $50, two tanks about $75.

For snorkeling lessons only, the best deal is to latch onto the inexpensive classes given by the City and County of Honolulu Department of Parks and Recreation. They usually take place March through June and cost $5 or $6. For information, call the department at 524-1257. Also, some readers have written in praise of **Dave's Snorkel City Tours** (Tel. 734-0788), three-hour trips that leave Waikiki twice a day for about $10. All equipment and lessons at Hanauma Bay are included.

SAILING LESSONS AND RENTALS

Figure $60 or $70 a day for sailing lessons. One outfit is **Hawaiiana Yacht Charters** (Tel. 521-6305), at McWayne Marine Supply, 1125 Ala Moana (next to Kewalo Basin). It also offers interisland courses as well as sailboat rentals (both crewed and uncrewed).

By the way, if you're already qualified on a Hobie Cat, that 12- to 15-foot beach-based catamaran, you can rent one from the beach services desk at the Hilton Hawaiian Village. Please do not attempt to handle these tricky craft without experience!

DEEP-SEA FISHING

Hawaii has some of the best sport fishing in the world, and on Oahu you may charter boats from 40 feet to a luxurious 63 feet in which to try your luck. Of course marlin and other billfish are the most famous and dramatic catches, but even when they aren't running, you can fish for skipjack tuna (*aku*), *mahimahi*, jack crevalle (*ulua*), wahoo, yellowfin (Allison) tuna (called *ahi* locally), bonefish, or even barracuda.

There are three major charter boat areas on Oahu. Most bookings are made from the **Kewalo Marine Basin** in Honolulu (Ala Moana Boulevard, foot of Ward Avenue, next to Fisherman's Wharf restaurant). But there are also a couple of good boats at **Pokai Bay** on the Waianae Coast, and at **Haleiwa Boat Harbor** on the North Shore. When the big spring and summer tuna and marlin runs are out that way, it's a lot more convenient to drive directly to those harbors than it is to work your way around by boat from Honolulu, taking more than four hours to get to the fishing grounds. (Of course everyone else wants to do this, too!)

If you make your inquiries and your Honolulu bookings through the half-dozen addresses listed below for Kewalo craft, you'll most likely get a good boat and a fine captain and mate. All these boats must maintain high standards and they generally keep the latest equipment aboard. By and large, it's not worth saving a few pennies by trying to find some independent operator, who may have trouble staying . . . well . . . shipshape.

The newer and better sport fishing boats have at least a flying bridge above the deck house so the skipper can get an elevated view of the telltale sea bird action, and even see the distant fish breaking the surface while feeding. The very latest boats might even have a "tuna tower," a tall framework which extends even higher over the flying bridge.

If you're new at the game, say so. Hawaii charter skippers won't take you for a ride you don't want. And if you want to fish for Pacific blue marlin, and the marlin aren't running, they'll probably suggest you'll have more fun after putting out lures for something else, like wahoo or maybe *mahimahi*.

The best season for blue marlin, incidentally, is in the summer. And the tuna run around Oahu begins about the second week in June and continues until the end of September. Winter is fairly quiet, with few big fish, except for periodic battles with a type of young, striped marlin (up to about 130 pounds). These marlin appear shortly after Christmas and may continue running through Hawaiian waters to the end of February.

Charter rates will run from $325 to $450—but mostly hold at about $375—for a full day (about 7 A.M. to 3:30 P.M.) for up to six persons. Half-day trips cost from around $275. Tackle, lures, etc., are included, but not lunches. If there are only one or two of you, call the booking offices anyway. They may be able to fit you in on a boat short of its full complement of anglers. (On a share-boat basis, per-person rates will run between $70 and $75 for full day, $55 to $65 for a half day.)

The largest association of Kewalo Basin skippers is **Sport Fishing Hawaii** (Tel. 536-6577), firmly guided by Captain Bill Shelton. Queen of that fleet is Shelton's 63-foot *Catherine S.*, which is certified for up to 18 persons. (She has several staterooms, too, and is often chartered by the more well-heeled for interisland cruises.) Shelton's association books a total of 19 different boats, all of which can be relied upon.

Nearly as hefty an outfit is **Island Charters** (Tel. 536-1555), which represents some of the same boats as Sport Fishing Hawaii, plus a handsome, twin-diesel-powered sampan fisher called the *Aukai*, a popular boat owned and operated by Captain Freddie Knight.

There are other small groups of boats which are "self-booked." They include the **Coreene-C's** (Tel. 536-7472), which charters out the *Coreene-C II*, and the larger (60-foot) *Coreene-C III*. This operation is conducted by Captain Cornelius Choy, famous as the skipper who caught the world's largest marlin, an 1,805-pound monster that now hangs at the International Market Place. We have been out on the *Coreene-C III*, and were impressed with the efficiency of the Choy operation. However you will not always get Choy himself as your captain.

Recommended individual charter craft from Kewalo Basin which are not represented by any of the above include the **Kono Charters Ltd.** (Tel. 531-0060) with the *Kono*, a popular 61-foot twin diesel, and the island's only gyro-stabilized vessel, captained by Toots Tsutahara.

Although nearly all of Oahu's fishing boats berth at Kewalo Basin, there are two boats over at Pokai Bay particularly convenient for covering the Waianae fishing grounds. The best is the **Kamalii Kai** (Tel. 696-7264), owned by Dr. Lynn B. McKinney.

Over at Haleiwa, the best charter vessel is the **Haole Queen** (Tel. 637-5189), captained by Les Walls. He keeps his boat immaculately clean and in perfect condition.

It's customary to tip following a fishing charter. If everything has gone really swimmingly—the captain and the mate have worked hard, etc., and especially if they've gotten you some fish, someone in your party should hand the skipper at least a $20 bill—maybe a higher minimum if you're going to have the fish mounted rather than give it to him. Normally the captain does expect to keep the fish.

If you do tip the captain, he'll take care of the mate for you. Some folks prefer to tip the mate only, and if he's worked hard—fish or no—it's nice to slip him a ten-spot. Of course if you didn't like your boat or your crew, don't tip at all. (And then please write us and tell us why you were dissatisfied.)

Is sport fishing a thrill? You bet it is, and if you're visiting Hawaii in the summer, at least, it seems a shame to pass it up. If, of course, you can swing the price.

9. Other Sports and Games on Oahu

Blessed with a year-round mild climate, Hawaii seems ideally suited for any sport, except those few that actually call for cold weather. Islanders, in fact, have always been sports crazy, apparently because of their natural heritage as an outdoor people.

The ancient Hawaiians had a wide variety of athletic events, all of which were effectively shut out by the missionaries. Due to this Calvinist upset, the old games are no longer popular, nor indeed are they really remembered, although there are occasional efforts to revive such activities as *ulu maika*, a kind of bowling, and a few other obscure pastimes. The Hawaiians also had a large number of warlike games involving spear throwing, wrestling, boxing, etc.

But today the popular sports in Hawaii are much like those of most areas of the Mainland. High school football is followed avidly. Now a member of the Western Athletic Conference, the University of Hawaii plays against first-rate Mainland competition in football and basketball, and it enjoys popular local support in both. Professional golf and bowling make annual stops, and professional boxing does better here than in most Mainland cities. Amateur and professional baseball also have wide followings.

SPECTATOR SPORTS

One of the earliest American sports in the Islands was **baseball**. This was undoubtedly because the father of modern baseball, Alexander J. Cartwright, moved to Honolulu from New York City not long after designing the baseball diamond and setting up the first clubs and written rules in 1845. He was just as active in promoting his sport here in the Islands as he had been in New York.

Today the state is proud of its professional baseball team, the Islanders of the Pacific Coast League.

The Islanders play in the new 50,000-seat Aloha Stadium near Pearl Harbor. This gigantic contraption can be shaped for football or baseball by sliding its massive grandstands on a thin cushion of air, a trick that received world attention when it was first performed in late 1975.

In the **football** configuration, the stadium accommodates several high school and University of Hawaii football games. It also is the home to three post-season contests that are telecast live to the Mainland, including the traditional Hula Bowl in January, which brings the country's leading college senior players to Honolulu for an all-star game. Then there's the Aloha Bowl, which pits two top collegiate gridiron teams in a Christmas-week game.

Finally, Honolulu now hosts the Pro Bowl, the last football game of the season, usually played the first weekend in February. This is the National Football League's all-star game, putting the American Conference up against the National Conference.

On game nights, there are usually express buses to and from the stadium. They usually leave from the suburban bus stop on Kona Street, next to Ala Moana Center, and sometimes also from Monsarrat Avenue near Kapiolani Park. (Telephone 531-1611 for details on times and fares.)

The island is nuts over **basketball**, too, particularly University of Hawaii basketball. The U.H. Rainbow Warriors play in the 7,852-seat Neal Blaisdell Center arena at the corner of Kapiolani Boulevard and Ward Avenue. The same arena is host to the annual Rainbow Classic Basketball Tournament during Christmas week, which brings some of the nation's leading college teams to town.

You'll find that same arena used for professional **boxing** events from time to time, as well as for Japanese **Sumo wrestling** and various other forms of martial arts.

Out in the countryside next to the obscure village of Mokuleia, a popular spectator sport every Sunday, beginning at 2:30 P.M., is **polo**. The season opens in early March and continues into September. Admission price this year is uncertain, perhaps around $3 for adults.

There is no pari-mutuel horse racing in Oahu, but there are several other kinds of races. **Outrigger canoe races** are sponsored by two different associations on Saturdays and Sundays off several different beach parks around Oahu between June and August. Statewide, there are more than 50 clubs, some of which trace their history back to the nineteenth century. There are numerous regattas all summer long, and there is even a high-school league.

Members of the Hawaii Power Boat Association hold **motor boat races** usually the third Sunday of every month at Keehi Lagoon from around 10:30 A.M. to 2 P.M. Just take the road to Sand Island, turn right, and follow the noise. It can be an exciting free show.

And **automobile races** at Hawaii Raceway Park are often held on Friday and Saturday nights. To get there, take the H-1 Freeway past Makakilo and turn *makai* on Kalaeloa Boulevard. Recommended only for car nuts.

Something quiet, more genteel, perhaps? Head for Kapiolani Park at noon, and somewhere, right about in the middle of that large green space, you might run across a rousing match held between teams formed by the Honolulu **Cricket** Club. You may not be surprised to learn that because of Honolulu's ideal weather—as opposed to that of Merrie England—some authenticity must of necessity be lost: In this climate, there simply is no such thing as a "sticky wicket."

PARTICIPATION SPORTS

Perhaps inspired by the annually televised Hawaiian Open Golf Tournament at the end of January and beginning of February, many newcomers head directly for one of Oahu's twenty-six golf courses, at least fifteen or sixteen of which welcome visiting drive, slice, and putt artists. The eight military clubs are off limits to civilians, and that's too bad because the Navy/Marine club at Leilehua and the Air Force course at Hickam, for instance, are beautiful.

The Waialae Country Club, used for that Hawaiian Open and the prestigious old Oahu Country Club in Nuuanu Valley limit play strictly to members and their personal guests.

The **Ala Wai Golf Course** (Tel. 732-7741), just across the canal from Waikiki, looks tempting and convenient, but you'd better skip it. There's just too long a wait to get a starting time. The 6,855-yard **Hawaii**

Kai Championship Course and the 2,610-yard **Hawaii Kai Executive Course** (Tel. 395-2358 for both) are in a beautiful setting, fanned by trade winds, although way out by Sandy Beach.

The best deal going may be at **Olomana Golf Links** (Tel. 259-7926). It's a lovely location, and a challenging but not sadistic course. The **Pali Golf Course** (Tel. 261-9784), the one you see from the Pali Lookout, is also soothing and stimulating.

Of those less convenient to Honolulu, the big one is the **Sheraton Makaha Country Club** (Tel. 695-9511). The West Course, at 7,252 yards, is the longest in the island. Another important club is the **Kuilima Country Club** (Tel. 293-8811), a 7,061-yard course supposedly laid out with the wind in mind.

Other golf links include the par-three **Bay View Golf Center** (Tel. 247-0451) at Kaneohe; the **Hawaii Country Club** (Tel. 621-5654) on Kunia Road, *makai* of Wahiawa; the **Kahuku Golf Course** (Tel. 293-5842), nine holes at the northern tip of Oahu; the **Mililani Golf Club** (Tel. 623-2254), 6 miles past Pearl City on Kam Highway; the **Moanalua Golf Club** (Tel. 839-2411), a nine-holer near Tripler Hospital; the **Pearl Country Club** (Tel. 487-2460), which overlooks Pearl Harbor; and the **Ted Makalena Golf Course** (Tel. 671-6488), located on Waipio Peninsula.

In recent years, **tennis** has become popular—so popular, in fact, as to nearly overrun the courts available on Oahu. There are free county courts at twenty-six different locations, only four of which are at least remotely in the area of Waikiki.

Visitors who want to get on a court with less waiting should play weekdays, and even then only before 4 P.M. (You are allowed 45 minutes per turn. And foursomes take preference over twosomes.)

There are ten lighted courts at **Ala Moana Park**, 1201 Ala Moana Blvd., but that does *not* mean no waiting. Still, it may be a smash compared with **Diamond Head Tennis Center** (Tel. 923-7927), 3908 Paki Ave., which has seven courts, and for which there can be as much as a two-hour delay (you'll see players reading books to pass the time).

You might do better at **Kapiolani Tennis Courts**, 2748 Kalakaua Ave., which has four courts. They're lighted at night, too. And you'll sometimes find spirited matches going at 4 A.M. The courts just mentioned are closest to Waikiki, but visitors sometimes drive the short distance to the six-court **Koko Head District Park**, 423 Kaumakani St. in Hawaii Kai.

Private courts available for public use include six courts at the **Iolani Tennis School** (Tel. 941-9555), 563 Kamoku St., and the **Punahou Tennis Club** (Tel. 946-2951) on the campus of Punahou School, 1601 Punahou St.

You may reserve a specific time at the **Westin Ilikai Hotel** (Tel. 949-3811). Now known as Oahu's tennis hotel, the Ilikai has seven courts—including two stadiums—scattered around its various rooftops. Open 7 A.M. to 5 P.M. There's also a single court at the **Hawaiian Regent Hotel** (Tel. 922-6611) for the same price. Out of Waikiki, a better bet might be the **King Street Courts** (Tel. 947-2625), 2220 So. King St. Its four lighted courts rent for about $5 per person per hour.

There are lighted tennis facilities at the Kuilima Hyatt Resort on the North Shore and at the Makaha Inn on the Waianae Coast. There is no fee, but they are normally reserved for hotel guests only.

Surprising to many, **hunting** is very big throughout Hawaii. But of all the islands, Oahu is the worst target for that activity. There is a year-round season for feral goats and wild pigs on the island. Bird hunting season on Oahu runs from approximately November through January. Game birds include several types of pheasant, quail, partridge, dove, francolin, and wild turkey.

There are twelve hunting areas on Oahu, but we advise skirting the often muddy and dangerous grounds near Kaena Point. Non-resident hunting licenses run $15. For more information, see the Division of Fish and Game, State of Hawaii Department of Land and Natural Resources (Tel. 548-4002). You'll find it in the new State Office Building on Punchbowl Street across from the capitol (Honolulu, Hi. 96813).

If you want to go **horseback riding**, we know of two outfits that are saddling up trail rides this year. One is **Koko Crater Stables** (Tel. 395-2628), which offers guided rides into Koko Head Crater. And **Kualoa Ranch** (Tel. 237-8202) may still be offering rides in that windward area out near Chinaman's Hat.

Running has been gaining great strides in Hawaii, as it has everywhere, but Honolulu has been called the runningest city in the nation. If you want to join the sessions of the Marathon Clinic, show up at the Kapiolani Park Bandstand at 7:30 A.M. Sundays (March to November). The Honolulu Marathon itself is run by thousands on a Sunday in early December.

If you're into **hiking and backpacking**, we strongly urge you to first contact one of three organizations before trekking out into the wilderness. The most all-encompassing is the Hawaii Geographic Society (Tel. 538-3952), which runs a small bookstore at 217 South King St. The Hawaiian Trail and Mountain Club meets at the *mauka* side of Iolani Palace usually at 8 A.M. Sundays (or sometimes at 1 P.M.) for a weekly hike, and they welcome newcomers. If you want to write them in advance—a good idea—the address is Box 2238, Honolulu, Hi. 96804. If you send a check for $4.50 and mention our name, they'll send you a veritable care package of information. (They might even do it if you don't say you read it here!) The other outfit is the Hawaii Chapter of the Sierra Club (Tel. 946-8494), which has hikes about once a month. Its address is Box 22897, Honolulu, Hi. 96822. (Send a stamped envelope if you want advance information.)

Hikers who just want to poke around on their own may pick up a free trail map from the Division of Forestry, State Department of Land and Natural Resources, on the third floor of the State Office Building on Punchbowl Street. Also the city has a free, safety-conscious booklet on hiking trails. Pick one up at City Hall or at any fire station. Due to unusual geological and climatic conditions, there are special hazards to hiking in Hawaii. Talk to local hikers before going out, and *never* hike in Hawaii alone!

If you're going **camping**—whether by backpack or by wheels—you'll need a free permit from the city and county to bed down in the various public beach parks. Obtain that document between 8 A.M. and 4 P.M. Monday–Friday at the ground floor Parks and Recreation Department Office of the Honolulu Municipal Building. That's the tall, fortress-like structure at the corner of King and Alapai streets. Then see our general remarks on some of these beaches in our "Water Sports" (Section 8). Frankly, however, we don't recommend camping on Oahu. Chances are everything will be okay, but be warned that there are occasional middle-of-the-night incidents between campers and young toughs out on a toot. It is better to camp in groups of four or more—and always only where you can see other campers, too.

Visitors who refuse to have an ordinary land-locked or water-logged vacation, might get their trip really off the ground by **gliding or soaring**. The more "conventional" version of such things is to go out to Dillingham Airfield near Mokuleia and buy a ride in one of the all-aluminum gliders stationed there. (Tel. 623-6711 for information.)

Believe it or not, the ancient Hawaiians reportedly had a similar game to that, too. According to some old accounts, they practiced gliding on air currents near the Nuuanu Pali by the use of a kind of feathered contraption. This, too, apparently became a lost art. But among the more far-out activities in Hawaii over the past two or three years has been something very like it—**hang gliding**.

For this, the more daring set sail on little more than wings of song and dacron off the Makapuu cliffs. Despite several fatal accidents, some say the location off the ridge provides the finest hang-gliding site in the world.

Would-be hang glider pilots should first write the Hawaii Hanggliding Association, Ltd., Box 22232, Honolulu, Hi. 96813.

You might enjoy this sport more by watching it from below the cliffs near Sea Life Park. Actually taking off from those thousand-foot cliffs is not for the fainthearted . . . and that includes *us* chickens!

10. Shopping and Browsing on Oahu

There are at least fourteen definable areas in which to shop in Honolulu, and we will discuss below some that are relatively good and convenient.

But first, what should you buy? The answer to that puzzler largely relates to your own taste as well as the preferences of the folks back home for whom you are buying. Here, with just a little attention paid to our own prejudices, are things for sale that have interested other visitors to Hawaii, together with some particular kinds of shops.

Two points to remember: One is that Hawaii has a refund law which states that stores can refuse to give you your money back if they conspicuously post a notice of their no-refund policy. The second is to avoid buying products that are supposed to be shipped, at least from small stores. The Better Business Bureau is sometimes flooded with complaints about packages that didn't arrive. And *never* have something shipped to friends as a gift. You may never know if they received it or not, and you'll be too embarrassed to ask!

ITEMS SOLD AND TYPES OF STORES

Aloha wear—Bright and light-hearted patterned shirts for men and gaily designed *muumuus* or *holokus* (long, loose-fitting Hawaiian dresses) for women are called aloha wear. The cheaper and gaudier models from the "Garment Factory to You," etc., will probably hold up long enough to use while your vacation lasts, and may look out of place back home anyway. More expensive, tasteful, and better-made aloha styles from prestige stores like Liberty House will last much longer and will probably serve on festive occasions back home, too. (In Hawaii, everyone wears aloha clothes at one time or another, but we might mention that it is not the local fashion for couples to don *matching* aloha outfits.) **Artworks**—Honolulu has about four score commercial galleries, often featuring paintings of people and places in Hawaii. Avoid the so-called "investment art," unless you know *exactly* what you are doing. Art salesmen are often very persuasive. **Artificial flowers**—Some good ones, and some bad ones, are made of shells. The best of the shell group may be those crafted by Sue Lange, and they are sold in several stores.

Bamboo and rattan—Bamboo is made into lots of things, from flutes to furniture. **Books on Hawaii**—You'll find hundreds in bookshops, department stores, and the five and dime, along with special cookbooks with Pacific accents. **Calendars**—Some have nice Hawaiian pictures, but the ones with the months and days in the Hawaiian language may drive you nuts after the novelty wears off. **Candles**—You see different designs in candles all over the place. Some give off the scents of Hawaiian flowers. **Candy**—There are candies shaped like Hawaiian flowers, but macadamian nut candy is perhaps a better bet to take back home. **Caricatures of yourself**—The ones drawn by the artist in the International Market Place are pretty good. **Ceramics**—Lots of pot-throwers come to Hawaii, and you'll see their work everywhere. Consider the Pottery, a restaurant which also makes pots and plates on the side. (See Section 5.) **Chinese preserved seeds**—Sometimes called "crack seed." Islanders love 'em, chew them up like candy; most Mainlanders do not. **Chinese goods**—Lots of stores carry Chinese objects along with other things. You might stop by the China Silk House in Ala Moana Center. For genuine Red Chinese products, however, look up Camelot East in the Rainbow Bazaar at the Hilton Hawaiian Village.

   Clothing stores, men's—Besides the department stores, some of the big names are Ross Sutherland, Andrade's, Reyn's, Kramer's, Palm Beach, and Sato. **Clothing stores, women's**—Well-known shops, not counting department stores, include Carol & Mary, Andrade Store for Women, Alfred Shaheen, Elsie Krassas, Fumi's, Villa Roma, and Ethel's. **Clothing—large sizes**—The traditional place is the Trunk, in Kilohana Square. But there is also one shop which has had at least a couple of name changes near the top of King's Village. **Coconuts**—If you can find, or buy, the kind with a smooth husk, you can paint on an address and paste on the stamps and post them home just like that. **Coconut syrup**—Canned, and not much cheaper than you might find it in any city on the Mainland. **Coffee cups and mugs**—You can get them with your name in Hawaiian baked right on. Most we've seen were overpriced.

   Coral jewelry—There are polished necklaces, rings, pins, and other eyecatchers fashioned out of three types of Hawaiian coral—black, pink, and gold. Some of the best but not necessarily *all* of the best, is produced by Maui Divers, Inc. Coral is sold all over Hawaii. You should see and price it in several locations before choosing, for price tags can vary by more than 50 percent for similar pieces. (Be aware that the very deep red coral, which you'll also see, is Mediterranean, not Hawaiian.) **Craft shops**—There are several, but you may want to drive directly to Lanakila Rehabilitation Center. It's somewhat inconveniently sited at 1809 Bachelot St. in the Nuuanu area, but everything is made on the premises by handicapped workers. **Department stores**—The big ones are Liberty House, Sears, and Penney's, all in Ala Moana Center and other locations. **Discount department stores**—These include Holiday Mart, Gem, Gibson's, and Payless. **Drug stores**—Stewart's and Royal are the main ones in Waikiki. *Discount* drug stores include Long's and Thrifty. **Dolls**—

There are dolls in Hawaiian clothing at several stores, including a Hawaiian Barbie. **Duty free shops**—You may only use them if you've got a ticket out of the country. Designed largely for Japanese tourists, they have few genuine savings for Americans.

Fabrics—Many stores sell colorful printed Hawaiian yardage for persons who want to sew their own. **Flowers**—Orchids or dozens of other Hawaiian flowers you may wear as leis or mail or take to the Mainland. Remember about quarantine restrictions: Most fresh flowers are okay, except those of mauna loa, gardenia, rose, and jade vine. Plants in soil are also forbidden. (If you have any questions, call 841-4342.) **Fruits**—Like flowers, many are prohibited for removal to the Mainland. All pineapples and coconuts are okay. Avocado, banana, litchi, and papaya must be treated first. *All other fresh fruits are banned.* (For information, telephone 841-4342.) **Glassware**—Some of it is made with etchings of Hawaiian flowers. (We liked those turned out by Arts Hawaii.) **Gold-plated items**—Shells, flowers, etc., which have been dipped in gold are sold all over the place. Check it to see if it has retained fine detail. (Lately, gold-plated Hawaiian *cockroaches* have been all the rage in some quarters!) **Grass skirts**—Generally only souvenirs for children. They should, of course, be marked "flame resistant," or something similar.

Hats—Coconut hats, webbed out of palm leaves before your eyes, are the tourist traditional (about $4). Some kind of hat is advisable for the hot Hawaiian sun in any case. Men sometimes like a straw style "planter's hat," a wide-brimmed legacy from plantation days. **The Hawaii Dollar**—One of those Chamber of Commerce gimmicks, and some places it really does cost a dollar. Perhaps not a bad souvenir for that price. **Imported goods**—Everywhere. Stores that specialize include India Imports, Bamboo Barn, Philippine Handicrafts, Badillo's, Bali Ha'i Mekong Company, and many of those places in the Rainbow Bazaar and the Cultural Plaza. **Jade**—Due to the popularity of jade among the Chinese, lots of it is bought and sold in the Islands. You'll generally find a greater variety available and more technical knowledge among the dealers than in many places on the Mainland. **Jams and jellies**—Several are made from tropical fruits like guava, passion fruit, mango, papaya, poha, etc., and are packed for gifts or mailing. These products are more popular with visitors than with residents. **Japanese stores**—Some of the most well-known include Shirokiya (a Japanese department store), Hotei-Ya, Iida, Dai'ei, Hakubundo, and Musashiya. You might like to check these for good deals in kimonos, happi coats, and other Oriental items.

Kona coffee—Make sure you *like* Kona coffee first, for the price is steadily rising with the world coffee shortage. **Kukui nut leis**—A traditional necklace for women and men, these are finely polished nuts from the official state tree. Buy them only from reputable stores, and save your receipt. If they weren't prepared properly, they may burst or rot. Beware of peddlers' bargains in kukui nuts. **Kukui nut oil**—We'd skip it. All of it has been high priced and we can find no useful purpose for it. We would never use it for suntan lotion.

Lauhala products—Lauhala is about the only genuine traditional Hawaiian handicraft left in the Islands. You can get it in floor mats, table mats, hats, slippers, purses, and other things. These are made from the leaf (*lau*) of the pandanus tree (*hala*), and you can often watch the process in person under the banyan tree in the International Market Place. **Lava products**—We don't think much of the artistic merits of most stuff made from lava. The little statuettes—most of which are not historically accurate designs—are not carved lava, but powdered lava mixed with resin and poured into molds. They're solidly made and hold up pretty well, however. If you want this kind of thing, the best is made by Coco Joe. (The outfit also makes some figures out of "Hapa-wood." It's the same process, but using sawdust instead of pulverized lava.) **Lava flower pots**—They're porous, so supposedly they allow the plant roots to "breathe." Of course they also leak. **Lava-lava**—This wrap-around cotton skirt for men is not worn in Hawaii (except sometimes by Samoans), but it is sold here. We call it a non-authentic souvenir. **Leis**—In addition to flower ones, there are those made of kukui nuts, various kinds of seeds, and even—rare—from feathers. **Liquor and liqueurs**—In the old days, Hawaiians drank a kind of ti-root "whiskey" called *okolehao* ("iron bottom"). Virtually nobody partakes of it nowadays, but you can buy it still, along with lots of alcoholic "cordials" made from pineapple, passion fruit, etc. The best of these liqueurs is Kona coffee, which some people (not us) compare with Kahlua. There is also a Hawaii-made *sake* (Japanese rice wine).

Macadamia nuts—Grown on the Big Island, there are two big brands. We like Mauna Loa (formerly called Royal Hawaiian—the blue can) best, but Hawaiian Holiday has a larger choice of types—flavored with hickory smoke, Maui onions, etc. The two are competitively priced, but relatively expensive everywhere. **Music and recordings**—Hawaiian music, of course, is distinctive. The best prices in records are at the department and discount stores (and you *won't* find them when you get back home). For sheet music and books, check the House of Music in Ala Moana Center, although their record prices are usually higher than some other places. **Olivine**—Unless you really go for this green gem, we think you should pass it up in Hawaii. Virtually all olivine for sale is brought into the state, generally from Arizona. It is *not* mined here, and it only occurs in "sand sizes" on the famous Green Sand Beach and a few other shorelines.

Patterns—For making Hawaiian dresses, etc., you can buy patterns (look for the ones called "Patterns Pacifica.") At Alfred Shaheen they come together with the suggested material already precut to the right length. **Perfumes**—There are three local brands. Royal Hawaiian has the big local factory, but there is also Liana and Perfumes Polynesia. Supposedly, they capture the essence of Hawaiian flowers. The better perfume displays have tester bottles, so you can see how it sniffs on a piece of your own skin. (There is even a perfume scent called "Hibiscus," which is a flower without a smell!) **Photographs of old Hawaii**—For something different, pore through the albums at the Archives of Hawaii downtown and order some prints specially made. They usually cost less than $3 each. **Pineapples**—If you're taking them home, get them packed in a carrying box with a handle, etc. The better prices are usually at the supermarkets or perhaps at the Dole Pavilion out near Wahiawa. **Posters**—Several stores sell surfing posters or others with Hawaiian scenery.

Shells—Some of the most beautiful individual shells in the world are gathered from Hawaiian waters. Check what's for sale at Shellworld Hawaii, 2381 Kalakaua Ave. We thought them a little snippy, but their selection is snazzy. (Prices start at two for $1—no, not one for 50 cents!—on up.) Some of the most sought-after shells are the eensy ones from Niihau. **Straw mats**—Islanders lay them out on the sand instead of using beach towels. You see them at variety stores for under $2. **Sugar**—We think some of the most doubtful things for sale are those little jars of colored sugar—the ones poured into layers to create a sort of swirly, rainbow effect. The price is about $3 for five ounces. If you're going to use it at a party soon, so be it. Otherwise, be aware that it might fade out within a few months after you put it on display. **Supermarkets**—There are four big food chains here, listed in our general order of preference: Times, Safeway, Star, and Foodland or Food City. In those you'll save as much as 50 percent over some stores on Kalakaua Avenue. **Surfboards**—More than a dozen shops make and/or sell surfboards. If you get with the surf scene in Hawaii, you'll pick up better and later recommendations than we can give you here.

T-shirts—There are lots with distinctive Hawaiian designs. Some of the best are made by Crazy Shirts, which has several outlets. Count on paying as much as $15 for the best ones. At Woolworth's you'll get them a dollar or two cheaper. **Tapa cloth**—Tapa designs are usually good and the beaten bark material is texturally interesting. It all comes from Samoa, Tonga, or Fiji, however. Tapa-making is a lost art in Hawaii. **Ti logs**—The kind you take home, water, and grow are okay. They come in red or green varieties. **Tiki torches**—These are a popular way to light up a garden party. Just buy the heads and put them on your own poles back home. **Tunafish**—See if you agree that the Coral brand, available only in Hawaii, beats anything else in a can. (Hawaiian tuna are caught by the pole method, too; there's no chance of any porpoises getting pulled in with the nets, as on the Mainland.) **Ukuleles**—Lots of ukes sell for $10 or less (OK, but mostly made in Taiwan or Japan). No really good ones go for under $50 or so. Kamaka is the best local brand, and you might look for a cut-rate price at Holiday Mart and other discount stores.

Wood products—Monkeypod and koa are the two popular—and expensive—woods of Hawaii. Much of what is for sale is cheaper and imported from Taiwan or the Philippines, even though it may be nicely finished off in Hawaii. Salad bowls are often a good buy, but look at lots of samples. Something different is sandalwood jewelry. **Woodroses**—A seed pod that looks like a flower makes a practical gift that will last indefinitely. If you've never seen a woodrose before, it might look like some kind of delicate carving. **Zoris**—Sometimes called go-aheads, they are a type of one-thong Japanese slipper. The cheap varieties may cost $1.99. But there are thick-soled kinds called Kamabokos and a personal favorite made out of mats called goza slippers (or sometimes, jokingly, "Nanakuli suedes"). All zoris are practical for this brand of indoor-outdoor living, particularly since it's polite to slip off your footwear before entering a private home in Hawaii.

ALA MOANA CENTER

The gigantic, well-architected emporium called Ala Moana Center is a 5-minute bus ride (via No. 8) west of Waikiki. (On the map, the 50-acre lot is bounded by Ala Moana Boulevard, Piikoi Street, Kapiolani Boulevard, and Atkinson Boulevard.) It's open seven days a week—until 9 P.M. weekdays, with most stores closing at 5:30 P.M. Saturday and 4 P.M. Sunday.

Your first serious shopping should be done at Ala Moana, in the same stores where much of the permanent population of Honolulu shop. Then, if you want, hit every other place in town.

Guarded on opposite ends by Sears and by Liberty House, the shopping center is lined up along two basic levels and includes more than 150 shops and stores. With notable exceptions, you'll generally find food and restaurants on the street level and more concentrated shopping activity up on the mall level. (Parking is better up there, too.)

With its sunlit wide spaces, trees, and fishponds, the mall level is more casual, open-air, and fun for strolling. The street level seems darker and stuffier.

Sears, Roebuck & Co. (Tel. 947-0247) turns out everything you'd expect in a Mainland Sears, *plus* a wide, wide selection of local goods, including pretty dependable souvenir items and lots of generally good aloha wear. For years it's been the largest single store in the state. Moving down the mall, **Long's Drugs** (Tel. 941-4433) is crowded but inexpensive. **Woolworth's** (Tel. 941-3005), next door, has some of the least expensive (but not lowest quality) Hawaiian knick-knacks and clothing in town.

Across the mall, **Security Diamond** (Tel. 949-6432) is one of the big name jewelers. Their Hawaiian Heirloom rings, bracelets, etc., nice as they are, are *inspired* by the monarchical period, and are not a recreation of particular antiques. **Watumulls**, nearby, is a link in a local chain, and sometimes has a few interesting aloha items. **Sato Clothiers** (Tel. 949-4191) is one of several good men's stores. **Carousel** (Tel. 941-0907) rounds up some good quality children's wear, if a little pricey. Mod clothes for a somewhat older set (teens and twenties) are next door in the **San Francisco Rag Shop** (Tel. 946-2808). **Reyn's** (Tel. 949-5929), nearby, is another with some nice things on the expensive side. **Ethel's** (Tel. 946-5047) has a fairly wide, middle-of-the-road selection of dresses.

Across on the *mauka* side again, we're not fond of the duds at **Hartfield's** or at **Aloha Fashions**. And **McInerny's** is a large, conservative store that Sara likes better than I do.

Again on the *makai* side, the Hawaiian gift shop thereabouts is representative of several small souvenir stores in the neighborhood which generally leave us cold. But **Andrade's Women's Store** (Tel. 949-3951), which appeals to mature clientele, is pleasant and well-stocked.

Across Fashion Square and on the mountain side of the street, **Carol & Mary** (Tel. 946-5075) has chic women's and children's clothing styled for the carriage trade. There are many designer items and European modes. The **Ritz** store we thought crowded and unappealing.

Two large stores take up the remainder of the block on that side. **Penney's** (Tel. 946-8068) is a branch in the Mainland Penney tree, but with a definite Hawaiian bent. You'll find some good aloha fashions there, some Hawaiian-type jewelry, and a souvenir section running the gamut from el schlocko on up. Next door is the intriguing Japanese department store **Shirokiya** (Tel. 941-9111), and it really *is* Japanese. A wonderful place to browse and discover some unusual gadgets. (Also, check the upstairs food section.)

Across from Carol & Mary is **Ross Sutherland** (Tel. 946-2888), appealing to the older and more well-heeled man. The next-door **Center Art Gallery** we think unexciting, but if you know what you like, go to it. **Waltah Clarke's** (Tel. 949-0197) has some nice dresses generally well displayed.

Along here are two men's stores, **Kramer's**, with nice, if limited, selections, and **Andrade's Men's Store** (Tel. 949-3951), which sets out lots of quality wear for older men. An Andrade man might find his daughter next door in **Otaheite** (formerly Cook's Bay, Tel. 941-5470), a sort of far-out Polynesian boutique. The **Pocketbook Man** has a nice selection of luggage and traveling accessories. And right next door, the snazzier, snobbier **Louis Vuitton** displays some super-classy *mallettes* that M. Baedeker may have carried across the Alps.

At the end of the mall is **Liberty House** (Tel. 941-2345), Honolulu's best department store. It's the most up-to-date in island styles and trends in all merchandise, all attractively displayed on three big floors. We've always thought the clerks the politest and most helpful of any department store in Hawaii. (Some California readers have complained to us that their mainland Liberty House cards aren't accepted. We've found, however, that LH cardholders may quickly make arrangements for a "courtesy account" at the store's credit office.)

On the *street level* of Ala Moana Center, some shops at random include **Honolulu Book Shops** (Tel. 941-2274), stacking up the island's widest and most complete selection of reading material. There are two Japanese stores, including **S. M. Iida** (pronounced "E-*E*-dah," (Tel. 946-0888), in two locations, with paper lanterns, simple toys, nice teacups, wooden trays, etc., and **Hotei-Ya**, with somewhat less exciting offerings. **Tahiti Imports** (Tel. 941-4539) hangs up some nice aloha wear. **Hale Kukui Makai** (Tel. 949-6500) has a large variety of candles, some made on the premises. **The Jeans Machine** (Tel. 955-0649) displays young, casual fashions. **Crazy Shirts** (Tel. 949-6900) turns out the widest selection of Hawaiian T-shirts. **India Imports** (Tel. 946-7707) has domestic and foreign clothes and doodads from everywhere and is fun for browsing. **Honsport** (Tel. 949-5591) is the city's premier sporting goods store.

Beside Patti's Noodle Kitchen, the **ABC Store** posts some of the lowest prices for tourist junque in town, and also does pretty well with macadamia nuts, liquor, etc. It's often crowded—with good reason. Next door to that, at **Fromex One-Hour Photo System**, you can watch your color pictures coming right off the production line. (You'll find lower film prices at ABC, Longs, or Sears, however.) Near the bookstore, **Morrow's Nut House** is attractive but expensive. How expensive? Well, you have to go inside to find out. After you're hooked, *then* they'll tell you. Absolutely no prices are posted, and that's one reason we never go in.

There are some lovely imported fabrics at the **China Silk House**, and we like the little gifties we find in the midget-size **Summer's Place**. Nearby, **Paniolo Trading** seems to be an urban tack stall cashing in on the rhinestone cowboy craze. At the **Crack Seed Center**, you can try that gooey stuff that island kids are so in love with, if you want. And, sharing a stall with a doughnut shop near McDonald's, **Mrs. Fields' Chocolate Chippery** sells the most delicious cookies in town (about 50 cents each).

INTERNATIONAL MARKET PLACE AND KUHIO MALL

Back in Waikiki, the second most popular visitor shopping bazaar is the outdoorsy International Market Place at 2330 Kalakaua Ave., across from the Moana Hotel. This quarter-century-old casbah crowds in dozens of stalls and stores, all gathered under, around, and near a gigantic banyan tree. Places worth wandering into include the **Gem Tree**, just at the entrance, for coral and similar goods. (There are even some you can string yourself or have mounted at home.) Some well-designed women's clothes (aloha and other) are at **Fumi's**, way in the back.

To the rear, across Kuhio Avenue, is the new **Kuhio Mall**. It's a three-story Polynesian/Oriental complex designed around a central courtyard with fountains, tropical plants, and the like. Shops and carts sell craftwork from Southeast Asian countries.

KING'S VILLAGE (NEE ALLEY)

After a decade of calling it King's Alley, a pretty good name, by and large, the owners of this cobblestone souk across from the P.K. Hotel have for some reason decided to promote it to a "village." It's a gossamer version of Hawaii's sentimental monarchy period (the 1880s), all gussied up into a winding street of shops. At night it affects an especially festive air. Evenings at about 6:15, a costumed drill team "changes the guard" with a free precision rifle and marching show. You'll probably find many local people still refer to the place as King's Alley.

Mark Christopher, near the guardhouse, lays out the usual blah mementos over most of its floor space. But in one little quality corner of the store you may see some well-displayed coral jewelry. We thought it expensive, but well made, at least.

The best part of the alley/village is the little "Open Market" square right at the top. The storelets there change hands often, of course. You'll also find in the alley small branches of some well-known quality stores like Liberty House and Alfred Shaheen. The Bishop Museum has a good book selection in the shop on the ground floor.

WAIKIKI SHOPPING PLAZA

At Kalakaua and Seaside avenues, the slightly spectacular Waikiki Shopping Plaza is making a big splash. Its principal feature is a 75-foot tall "water sculpture," best enjoyed while traveling the escalators flanking the fountain.

The bottom floor is devoted to fast foods—pizza, sushi, tacos, burgers. Then there are four stories of stores. **Buck's**—sportswear and jewelry—advertises it was established in 1955, but we never saw it before. The **Center Art Gallery** has works by Red Skelton and seems to feature clowns with big red noses; **Waldenbooks**, a link in a well-known chain, has a good selection of best-sellers and Hawaiiana. Some lovely cigar and pipe odors emanate from **Jacques Tabac**, a third-floor smoke shop. The two highest levels in the plaza are devoted to individual restaurants, some of which seem to be having a hard time drawing folks to the top of the fountain.

KALAKAUA AVENUE IN WAIKIKI

Not a shopping center *per se*, but there are nevertheless several interesting stores right on Kalakaua Avenue, Waikiki's "Main Street." If aloha wear at the cheapest possible price is what you want, head for those multi-branched stores at several Waikiki addresses called **Island Fashions—Garment Factory to You**. There's no "factory" in Waikiki, of course. The stuff is stamped out in long-used patterns, but at maybe $9 for aloha shirts and perhaps $19 for muumuus, it's a way to get into Hawaii at less than half the price of some other stores. They have same day or overnight alterations.

However, it might be a good idea first to see what the best and most current Hawaiian fashions look like and add up to. You can do this at **Liberty House**, whose Waikiki store is at 2314 Kalakaua Ave. LH has some of the most tasteful goods in town.

Several interesting shops have been installed in the Hyatt Regency Hotel on Kalakaua—not the ground floor shops, which generally seem to have the same frou-frou as everywhere else, but the quality establishments on the Hyatt's second-floor mezzanine. Among them are **Chapman's**, a good men's shop, and **Alfred Shaheen**, a somewhat conservative but very nice women's wear store.

At the little stands and pushcarts in **Duke's Lane**, an alley beside the Waikiki Beachcomber Hotel, you can sometimes haggle your way into a bargain.

The massive **Royal Hawaiian Center**, a three-block-long emporium walling off the Royal Hawaiian and Sheraton hotels, is now open for business. In all, there are more than 150 shops, anchored by McInerny, a branch of the Ala Moana department store. (Other shops include Waltah Clarke, House of Jade, Butik Copenhagen, and Camelot East.) Also fairly new is the $15.5 million **Rainbow Promenade**, in the triangle formed by Kalakaua and Beachwalk. Mitsukoshi, Ltd., one of Japan's largest department store chains, occupies the first three floors. The other six are devoted to individual shops and restaurants. Most customers are expected to be Japanese tourists, but you might find something unusual there.

THE RAINBOW BAZAAR

Like the International Market Place and King's Alley, the Rainbow Bazaar, at the Hilton Hawaiian Village, is a "theme" shopping center. It is divided into three sections—Imperial Japan, Hong Kong Alley, and South Pacific. The settings are very well done, and it generally features quality merchandise at premium prices. Some of the Oriental furniture at **China Fair**, for example, is as good a rosewood or teak as you'll find anywhere west of the East. For Philippine and Oriental antiques, look into **Badillo's**, which has a large selection. The Rainbow Bazaar should not be confused with the aforementioned Rainbow Promenade.

FORT STREET MALL, AND DOWNTOWN

In downtown Honolulu, the former Fort Street has been almost entirely converted into a walking and sitting street in a noble experiment somewhat more successful here than in some other cities—at least for resident weekday shopping. The best time to visit is around noon Friday when you will see office workers shopping or lunching in attractive aloha clothing. (Use Bus No. 2.)

The big stores downtown are now **Woolworth's**, not quite as interesting as the ones in Waikiki and Ala Moana, and **Liberty House**, the department store which has moved to fancy quarters at King and Bethel Streets. **T & H Leather Wear** (Tel. 538-1214), at 1120 Fort St. Mall, is the only place in town anymore that will custom make leather sandals. They're priced from about $40.

THE CULTURAL PLAZA AND CHINATOWN

An idea perhaps a little ahead of its time is the struggling but still charming Cultural Plaza, on the fringe of Chinatown in the block bounded by Kukui, Maunakea, and Beretania streets and the Nuuanu Stream. It's an easy stroll from Foster Gardens. (Bus No. 2.) When more urban renewal projects are completed in adjacent neighborhoods, this project—designed to exhibit the multi-cultural make-up of Hawaii—might really bloom. Meanwhile, there are several interesting restaurants and stores in this ethnic center, most of which are Chinese.

If you're going to seek out what's left of shopping in Chinatown proper, it's somewhat of a hoof from the Cultural Plaza through a sometimes unattractive area. Most interesting stores are in a one-block area on the east side of Maunakea Street running between Hotel and King streets. There are Chinese jewelry shops, ceramic shops, spice shops, herb shops, grocery stores, and acupuncture supplies. If you want to chew on lotus root candy, you'll almost have to buy it along here. For porcelain, check into the **China Emporium** at 1040-A Maunakea. By the way, there are several lei shops on Maunakea Street, where the flowers are usually much cheaper than anyplace else in town.

Note: Some people understandably consider Chinatown a marginal area, and it's true that at Hotel Street and other areas, perhaps, Chinatown crosses with Porno Town. It's a safe and sane area in the daytime, at least, but depending on your predilections, you may feel better staying away from that part of Hotel Street at night. It is, however, heavily patrolled by police after dark, and it usually features more barkers than biters.

THE WARD WAREHOUSE

Across Ala Moana Boulevard from Kewalo Basin is the Ward Warehouse, 1050 Ala Moana, a contemporary shopping center with a natural wood beam feeling and which mixes retail and light industrial establishments. (Take Bus No. 8.) Some folks wander over after coming off one of the daytime cruises.

Check the beautiful hand-blown art glass at **Rare Discovery** (Tel. 524-4811), the lovely artificial flowers at the **Miyuki Art Flower Studio** (Tel. 536-5020) on the second floor, and the products of local artists at **The Artist Guild** (Tel. 531-2933).

PEARLRIDGE CENTER

The top suburban shopping center now is Pearlridge, inconvenient for most visitors way out at Pearl City, near the intersection of Kamehameha Highway and the Waimano Home Road. (Suburban buses from Ala Moana Shopping Center—Nos. 53, 51, 50, or 50A.) Hawaii's first monorail is here, connecting the two parts of the center which are 1,000 feet apart. There are 90 stores, one of the most interesting of which is **Dai'ei** ("*die*-yay"), a Japanese department store.

KAHALA MALL

In the high-priced residential district of Waialae/Kahala near the H-1 Freeway is Kahala Mall. (Bus No. 14.) It was Hawaii's first fully enclosed, air-conditioned shopping mall. There's a branch of **Joseph Magnin** (Tel. 737-7989), the only Magnin that has a Gucci Boutique. But you might also check into a husband/wife import store called **Fabulous Things** (Tel. 732-7070).

KOKO MARINA

The island's only shopping complex at the water's edge is Koko Marina, sometimes called the Waterfront Village, which borders the lagoon harbor way out at Hawaii Kai. (Bus No. 1.) The attractive, nautically inspired center unfortunately has been having economic troubles, and individual stores may continue to open and close unpredictably. The 16-acre center has now been bought by the Prudential Insurance Co., which seems to be breathing new life into the place. We always liked to stop at Koko Marina for hot pretzels, but what with the corporate twists and turns, we can't guarantee the dough will still be around this year.

11. Nights on the Town

Only one oasis in the United States is a bigger entertainment town than Honolulu. That's Las Vegas, Nevada, which draws crowds to the desert bright lights with the aid of open gambling. In Hawaii, of course, gambling is strictly illegal, but night life goes on, perpetuated by a strong, local tradition of music, song, laughter, and booze, with thanks to the millions of tourists who help finance all this nighttime revelry.

In Waikiki you will find big, professional headliner shows, largely designed to appeal to visitors to these shores. But you may also attend performances by accomplished entertainers who are stars only to those who avidly follow the latest trends in contemporary Hawaiian music and entertainment.

Outlanders are often bemused by this local audience/entertainer rapport, not being blessed with the necessary island background to appreciate it. There might be lots of in-jokes in pidgin, sometimes at the expense of the *haoles*, and which have special meaning to a resident crowd only.

Nevertheless, most accomplished Hawaiian entertainers succeed in spanning the distance between both cultures, sizing up their audiences and gearing their acts to the people responding to them.

SHOWTIME

Many well-advertised, high-priced performances will be offered at both a mid-evening **dinner show** and then later at a **cocktail show**. Usually the sit-down or buffet dinner will begin at 6 or 7 P.M., with showtimes set for 8 or 9.

We usually feel that to pay for the dinner merely because it is connected with a certain show is a waste of money. We'd rather pick a restaurant on its own merits and then go on to attend a show we think will be good entertainment, even if it is under a different roof—maybe even if we have to pick a different show than the one we chose first.

In fact, the only reason for going to a dinner/show combination as far as we can see is to make sure you get a good table to see and hear the performance. This we will do on some occasions, and if we don't like the position we are taken to, we can always leave immediately without owing a thing.

But showroom reservations people who tell you that the *only* way they will sell a certain show is with the dinner included in many cases are being less than truthful. We have often skipped the dinner/show combination (perhaps at $22) and showed up later at showtime to pay only about $10 to catch the act without having absorbed the "required" $12 plate of roast beef. You'll often save by making dinner/show reservations yourself directly with the hotel. As part of a tour operator's "package," it could be 20 percent higher.

COVER CHARGES AND MINIMUMS

If you arrive to see the show *only*, there will likely be a cover charge and/or a two-drink minimum (sometimes both combined in a **show charge**), whether or not you see the early show (maybe 8 or 9 P.M.) or the cocktail show (starting somewhere between 10 and 11 P.M.). At that second show you will almost surely pay *both* cover charge and minimum (or a hefty show charge), especially if it is a Friday or Saturday night.

Standard cover charges vary between about $2 and $5 per person. The drinks might be $2 or $3 each.

THE LATE-LATE SHOW

Some acts have a very late or post-midnight show, perhaps on a Friday or Saturday only. These are almost always presented without a cover charge, although sometimes they keep the drink minimum.

If you can take the hours, they usually are a good deal. You might find other Waikiki entertainers whose shows finish earlier generally walk in to catch the act. Often they are enticed onstage.

USE THE PHONE

All of these factors—starting times, cover charges, drink minimums, etc.—change regularly everywhere, and so we always try to reserve shows by calling ahead, asking all the questions right there on the phone. If any showroom doesn't take the time to spell out everything we want to know, we say bye-bye and look for another production.

LATE INFORMATION

Most entertainment events are listed in the half-dozen or so "throw-away" tourist publications in Waikiki. The free papers with the zappy color pictures on the front are usually the most complete, probably because they are well-established and are bountifully favored by advertisers. We use them both.

The **Hawaii Tourist News** has probably the most complete list of shows in its "What's Happening After Dark" column that winds throughout the paper, and it generally lists more prices, a big plus. The **Waikiki Beach Press** divides everything up more conveniently—keeping the discos out of the luaus, etc.—and seems to include fewer prices but more telephone numbers.

Remember that these and any other free visitor publications generally don't list anything commercial which has not bought advertising space.

ORDERING DRINKS

We always ask for standard drinks by their brand names in the clubs ("Dewars," "Jack Daniels," etc.). By asking for "scotch and soda," or "bourbon and water," you might open yourself up for an injection of Olde Rotgute, which is probably no less expensive than the Chateau Real McCoy, anyway.

However, **"exotic" drinks**—Mai Tais, Blue Hawaiis, Chi Chis, Wipeouts, Catamarans, Zombies, or whatever—may be ordered by those names without fear. Most of them are rum concoctions and are filled up with sugar plus pineapples and other fruits of the tropical loom. They will cost considerably more than call drinks, however.

The two-drink requirement in many clubs usually works for any kind of drink, incidentally—even beer, although you may have to pay $2 for a bottle of Primo. By the way, this former Hawaiian brew is no longer made in the Islands. It is "imported" from California!

If you want to change your poison in mid-show, by the way, you'll have a hard time catching your waitress on the fly. She might be so busy that the next time you see her will be when she swoops in on automatic pilot with the second round of exactly the same stuff that you originally ordered.

THE OFF SEASON

Watch out for the slump season on the club show circuit. Any time between November and late December—after Aloha Week and before the holidays—the big names of Honolulu entertainment may be found on vacation or in Vegas. In some big rooms there are substitutes—some on the way up and some rusting old stars perhaps beginning to dip below the popularity horizon.

WAIKIKI SHOW BIZ—WHO'S WHO AND WHAT'S WHAT

Most Waikiki entertainers and some big productions move around from clubroom to clubroom too frequently for us to pin down their particular shows and admission prices in an annual publication. But here are some of the big names—people and show titles—on the night scene. Only a few will be performing at any one time, and some may only appear in guest spots.

The Aliis—A six-man Hawaiian vocal group which successfully blends music and yuk-it-up humor. Plenty of variety in a big, well-paced show. **Arias, Rodney**—A Hawaiian baritone at home with both local and Mainland songs. **Azama, Ethel**—A newly popular jazz singing stylist. **Beamer, Keola and Kapono**—Two brothers from a famous Hawaiian musical family. They sing, play guitar and cut up with lots of local feeling. **Bumatai, Andy**—Hawaii's most popular stand-up comedian. **Borges, Jimmy**—Popular and informal island singer, even more at home in jazz than on Hawaiian numbers.

Cazimero, Roland and Robert—Now billed as the "Brothers Cazimero," they are ⅔ of the old and lamented "Sunday Manoa," which now only exists on recordings. At their best in a small room with an intimate, mostly local audience. **Chillingsworth, Sonny**—Now the foremost slack-key guitar artist in Hawaii. **Cypriano, Nohelani**—Island singer with a Mainland wallop, popular on the concert circuit, but sometimes busy with local engagements, too.

Davis, Charles K. L.—A Hawaiian operatic tenor, and more versatile than that might indicate. He has a vast repertoire of old Hawaiian songs. **DeLima, Frank**—He mixes music and mirth successfully along with a comic pair called Na Kolohe. Wild, local-style humor. **Denny, Martin**—Pianist/composer/orchestra leader trying to outlive his bird calls and jungle sound fame of bygone years. **Garner, Loyal**—Once the biggest thing to hit Waikiki in years, and she's still pretty big. A radiant personality with voice and piano ability to match. Sometimes schmaltzy, but always fun.

Hannemann, Nephi—Once a popular Samoan/Hawaiian entertainer, he seems to be devoting his time to bit parts in films, now. **Harrington, Al**—Another leading Waikiki professional who formerly played a regular on "Hawaii Five-O." An appealing personality, but not a strong singer. **Here Is Hawaii**—A multi-ethnic music and dance program. Probably not such a good bet for the money.

Ho, Don—Mister "Tiny Bubbles" himself, the king of Hawaiian entertainers, and the handsome prince for the thousands of grandmas he's kissed on stage over the decades.

It is perhaps unfortunate that Ho is almost the only Hawaiian entertainer known on the Mainland, but he's good—at least once, and on your first trip to Hawaii. It's just about the most expensive show in town. As a guess, probably near $35 with drinks and dinner this year, or maybe $20 or so for the cocktail show.

Jensen, Dick—Another powerful, first-line Hawaiian showman, Jensen stands 6-foot-2, and they call him "Giant." Lots of excitement, dancing, etc., in his show, and he's known for a slip, glide, and slide routine as well as a group of humorous sound effects.

Kai, Carole—A bouncy and expressive wide-eyed local girl who can really belt it out in Mainland and Hawaiian numbers. She's also pretty good on the piano. **"Kailua Madrigals"**—A delightful chorus of high school students. **"Kalo's South Seas Revue"**—The Polynesian show probably still thump-thumping it up in the Hawaiian Hut, a nicely designed showroom in the Ala Moana Hotel. We would rank it about third in Waikiki shows of the type.

Kaleikini, Danny—Almost as well known as Don Ho, he has been the star at the Kahala Hilton for more than 15 years. Honolulu *Advertiser* critic Wayne Harada says he offers "Hawaiiana with simple elegance." In a brisk show, he demonstrates several talents including his famous nose flute performance. Kaleikini's good voice can retreat to the back of his throat, and then the orchestra might overpower it. We had one of the bad tables in the Hala Terrace, certainly not the best of showrooms. **Kapono, Henry**—A former member of a duet, now going it alone. He appeals to a young audience.

Keale, Moe—Once a character actor, now making it as a singer and ukulele artist. **Keawe, Genoa**—She's a genuine, old-time Hawaiian entertainer, a great-grandma specializing in falsetto voice.

Kinimaka, Iva—A dependable Hawaiian entertainer, also capable of singing jazz and rock. **Krush, The**—Energetic eight-member modern musical group.

Larrin, Jay—A lounge performer whose own piano and voice compositions are appreciated by locals and visitors alike. **Leed, Melveen**—Hawaii's hottest female down-home style singer at the moment, Melveen Leed is known as the "Tita" (pidgin for "sister") from Molokai. Specializes in "Hawaiian country" music, and was the first Hawaiian singer to appear at the Grand Ole Opry in Nashville. **Lincoln, Bill**—A solid, old-style Hawaiian falsetto singer and guitarist. **Lopaka, Al**—A genial Hawaiian singer-guitarist. He's a musical rogue who would rather play polo, and trades in his instrument for a mallet in season. **Lupenui, Darryl** (and his Men of Waimapuna)—An expansive figure leading a prize-winning hula group, noted for its earthy Hawaiian songs and dances.

McCall, Azure—A jazz trouper with a powerful voice. **Makaha Sons of Niihau**—An excellent down-home Hawaiian group. **Mendes, Sonya**—A 5-foot-2 bundle of energy, she's considered Hawaii's "new rock" music queen. A vocalist who can double on keyboard and guitar. **Meyers, Audrey**—Formerly a luau performer, she has become an energetic headliner. **Mossman, Sterling**—Policeman turned entertainer, with a heavy local beat. **Moon, Peter**—The wayward member of the former Sunday Manoa, a talented guitarist and composer who recently formed the Peter Moon Band, specializing in modern island songs. **"Music Magic"**—A four-member combo specializing in jazz. **Nabors, Jim**—Go-o-o-lly, it's Gomer, all right, in his new home in the Islands. **Namakelua, "Auntie Alice"**—Now in her eighties, she is still among the foremost slack-key guitar players and composers in the Islands. She seldom performs in public, except as a guest.

Nievera, Roberto—A former member of the "Society of Seven," now making it nicely on his own. Once known as the "Johnny Mathis of the Philippines," he has now gone far beyond that. **"A Night in the Philippines"**—A dinner/show combination. We caught the show recently and thought it sometimes graceful, but generally dated and soon boring. I think we would have been unhappy to have paid the price for the whole ball of wax and wan. **Nueva, Vida**—A new jazz and pop group we haven't seen yet.

Ohta, Herb—Known also as "Ohta-san," he's probably the Islands' foremost and most accomplished ukulele artist.

Paulo, Rene—Quick, nimble, and precise, he ranks as the dean of the keyboarders in Hawaii. His wife, Akemi, often sings with him. **"Polynesian Aquacade"**—One of our most un-favorite Waikiki shows. We didn't take the dinner, but showed up poolside to pay $10 for the privilege of jamming up on tight, uncomfortable, rickety bleachers to watch dancers/swimmers perform to canned songs and music, actually mouthing the words. There are one or two nice splashy numbers, but for us that was only a drop in the bucket.

The Reycards—Filipino performers Ricky Castro and Reynaldo Ramirez sing, do impressions, etc. **Reiplinger, Rap**—Like Andy Bumatai, another former member of the defunct island comedy group, "Booga Booga." Now a popular comic on his own. **Rowles, John**—A powerful Maori singer from New Zealand, often attempting to make it on the Mainland, but who keeps returning to Waikiki where he is more appreciated.

Sai, Marlene—Powerful singer with a regal style. Hawaii's only gold-record female vocalist. **Santos, Jerry**—Singer and guitarist who writes and performs folk-pop Hawaiian music popular among Island youth. The **"Society of Seven"**—Also known as S.O.S., they're a long-run favorite at the Outrigger Hotel's Main Showroom, often alternating weeks with the Krush. **"Sons of Hawaii"**—A five-man, no-nonsense, all-Hawaiian string and song group led by ukulele virtuoso Eddie Kamae. **Stevens, Frankie**—Like John Rowles, a part-Maori singer with good audience rapport. **"Surfers"**—Another dependable island musical-comical combo which harmonizes on Hawaiian and some pop. Now stripped down from a former top-heavy seven to lithe, four-part harmony. **Tanaka, Teddy and**

Nanci—Okinawan/*haole* couple specializing in contemporary and Japanese melodies. Locally very popular.

"Tavana's Polynesian Spectacular"—Sometimes called simply "Tavana," the show in the International Market Place has perhaps remained the best Polynesian review in Waikiki, surpassed only by the teetotaling show out at the Polynesian Cultural Center in Laie. Of the same ilk, the **Moana Polynesian Review** in the Banyan Court behind the Moana Hotel is also pretty good. **"Tihati's South Seas Spectacular"**—Another all-Polynesian review, it's also fine, even if we still prefer the outdoor production at the Moana.

Vaughan, Palani—Singer and Hawaiiana scholar, specializing in songs of the King Kalakaua era. **Veary, Emma**—Affectionately dubbed "Ol' Golden Throat," Emma brings a cultured, classical voice to her Hawaiian songs and a special misty-eyed reverence for the monarchy period of island history. Some find her a little cloying, especially during the prayerful patter, but others judge her to be gracious, dignified, and charming. We like her best on Broadway show tunes and light opera. **Woodward, Mike**—A former bongo player turned *haole* comic in Hawaii. **"Zoulou,"** who used to spell his name "Zulu"—Always pointed out as that fat guy who played in the first three or four seasons of "Hawaii Five-0." That's unfortunate, for Zoulou deserves his own good reputation as a first-rate versatile showman—singer, dancer, comedian, and a top-grade performer on the uke, too.

By the way, the **Laff Stop** (Tel. 955-8863) has opened in Honolulu at 301 Cooke St. Similar to the Comedy Store in L.A., it features a revolving roster of comedians, some of whom are nationally known.

THE LUAU SCENE

Stop thinking of a luau as a "feast." It is not, especially as set up in Waikiki at present. It is true that you will sample some Hawaiian food, and that may be a valuable cultural experience. Nevertheless, less than one percent of the visitors to Hawaii like Hawaiian food. As far as we are concerned, luaus are better in direct proportion to the amount of non-authentic comestibles one is offered in addition to the traditional fare.

Most folks are most interested in the entertainment, and there's where a luau can be fun. Depending on the emcee, the other entertainers who take part, and the camaraderie in your own group, the luau should be a whoop-it-up, happy-go-lucky Hawaiian experience.

Remember that a luau should be *outdoors* to capture the full flavor of the event, and we would skip any which are not. Don't expect to sit on the ground in this day and age, however.

Here's a list of best bets in Oahu luaus for 1984. All may run in the neighborhood of $35 for adults, $20 for children. Reserve in advance, either by phone after arrival or (in some cases) using the toll-free numbers in the back of the book:

Germaine's Luau (Tel. 949-6626)—It may be the most expensive by a few dollars, but letters from our readers have been almost universal in their praise of the goings-on several nights a week at a secluded beach near Ewa. (One woman, who took her children, complained of the bus driver's off-color jokes on the way, and said there were too many people when they got there.)

Chuck Machado's Luau (Tel. 836-0249)—A long-established, well-regarded local firm presenting luaus outside the Outrigger Hotel.

Paradise Cove Luau (Tel. 945-3539)—A new one seemingly modeled after Germaine's. Guests are taken to the beachfront estate of the late Kamokila Campbell near Ewa.

Royal Luau (Tel. 923-7311)—The regular Sunday luau presented by the Royal Hawaiian Hotel on their Ocean Terrace.

Sheraton-Waikiki Luau (Tel. 922-4422)—A good show *if* it's held out on the lawn. (We were once packed into an indoor version here, which was not much fun.) Tuesdays.

Those are our top five, but you'll also find other luaus of varying quality, opening and closing frequently. Until we can check out the stability of any others, we suggest you stay with one of the above.

DISCOTHEQUES, CLUBS, AND CABARETS

Nearly all establishments serving liquor must by law close their doors at 2 A.M. The exceptions are those with "cabaret" licenses, generally singles' rock music and dance spots, which the city allows to jump until 4 A.M. They're not truly "discotheques," by the way. One requirement for the cabaret license is that there must be live music—no records.

The most popular such spots featuring the best musical groups are usually easy to find—there's a capacity limit, so they're the ones with the longest lines outside. And it may not be fair, but some of these admit card-carrying "members" before a newcomer to the scene.

The best honest-to-groove discos are restaurants that have banked their fires and heated up the Hi-Fi along about 10 P.M. Beginning generally with the best, those the local discomaniacs dig the most include **Spats** at the Hyatt Regency, **Nick's Fishmarket** in the Waikiki Gateway Hotel, 2070 Kalakaua, **Bobby McGee's Conglomeration** far out at the Colony Surf East Hotel, 2885 Kalakaua Ave., the **Parrot House** in the Hotel Miramar, and the **Tiki Broiler** in the International Market Place.

Annabelle's is under the aegis of the prestigious Juliana's of London on the top floor of the Ilikai Hotel, the **DBC's Dance Menagerie** is in the Waikiki Beachcomber Hotel, **Atlantis** is the entry alongside the giant fish tank at the Pacific Beach Hotel, and the new **3-D Ballroom**, 2260 Kuhio Ave., is big with the punk-rock crowd.

The big rock band clubs, most with a 4 A.M. weekend closing time, are—in approximate order of descending desirability—**Wave Waikiki** at 1877 Kalakaua Ave., the **Point After** on the second floor of the Hawaiian Regent Hotel, **Infinity** in the Waikiki Sheraton, **Da Sting** in the P.K. Hotel, the **Foxy Lady Too** (sometimes a disco) in the Waikiki Beachcomber Hotel, **Rumours** in the Ala Moana Americana Hotel, and the **Hula Hut** at 286 Beach Walk. All six are 110-decibel dating-and-mating grounds for singles. You'll find a cover charge (for men) and a two-drink minimum on live band nights. There are plenty of other hot spots opening and closing their doors and changing their names by the dozens almost monthly. The scene will surely be shifted by the time this perishable research hits the strobe lights.

By the way, the drinks in these clubs will be at least $2—maybe $3— even for a Coke. Big outfits like the Point After and Infinity will levy cover charges, too, but not the places which are restaurants earlier in the evenings.

Mellower music and dancing? One of the big favorites today is the sophisticated lounge called **Trapper's** in the Hyatt Regency. Also, you might try **La Dolce Vita**, underneath the Trattoria Restaurant.

Jazz? Currently some of the best sounds are at **Valentino's** in the Imperial Hotel, 205 Lewers St., and at the **Marcus Restaurant**, far out of Waikiki at 1630 Kapiolani Blvd. (the Pan Am Building).

HONOLULU ON THE SEAMY SIDE

There is no Sin City in Hawaii, but there is plenty of racy action for anybody with the curiosity, the inclination, and, of course, the money. Traditionally much of this has been centered along the porno palaces, kook book shops, and X-Y-Z-rated film houses in and around the low numbers on North and South Hotel streets downtown. Some cheap sleaze has also invaded Waikiki, from the 1900 to the 2100 block of Kalakaua.

Honolulu's long-standing strip-tease and burlesque joint is Downtown—the **Club Hubba-Hubba** (Tel. 536-7698), at 25 N. Hotel. The action is continuous and exhausting from about 4 to 4—that's P.M. to A.M., of course. No cover, and no cover.

You'll also find nude go-go dancing at places like the **Lollipop**, 2131 Kalakaua Ave.

HOSTESS BARS

Probably due to the Oriental influence in Hawaii, the B-girl enjoys just a little more *geisha*-like respect in Honolulu than in Mainland cities, and the places in which she works are a little less likely to be ripoffs. They are known here as "Korean Bars," and the young women who will sit on a customer's lap for as long as he buys the drinks are almost always Korean, often J.O.B's not much more conversant in English than a breathy "yes-s-s." There are usually ten hostesses for ten tables.

Her drinks cost the same as yours—perhaps as much as $3—and of course it's all on your tab. Perhaps that's harmless enough, but look out when she gives you her only other English word—"Champagne." Then your wallet has begun to get serious. Of course if you can afford $50 for a $7 bottle of Barney's Backyard Bubble, great.

The free *pupus* in the better Korean bars are usually delicious, and you *can* turn down the professional companionship if you just want to sit and talk business with your buddy. (A date, however, would feel very uncomfortable in there, of course.)

Among the "respectable" Korean bars is the big-band, 4 A.M.-closing establishment called **The Rendezvous** (Tel. 955-4666) at 1420 Kapiolani Blvd. A simpler place, without band and closing earlier, is **Sir John's** at 1210 Queen St. There are about 50 more, however, usually recognizable by a woman's name following the word "Club" or preceding the word "Lounge," as in "Club Penelope" or "Geraldine's Lounge." (To our knowledge, at least, neither of these examples exists at the moment.)

Most are all right as long as you accept their basic premises. And don't expect the girl to topple over on the stuff *she's* putting away.

There may be a Korean bar around someplace that will try to make you pay for something you didn't order. We'd talk loudly about notifying the Honolulu Liquor Commission—*if* we were sure of our ground, of course.

GAY BARS

The gay scene changes quickly, of course. At this writing, there is no bar or club devoted exclusively to the fraternity. Gays do frequent the aforementioned Club Hubba Hubba, however. In Waikiki, and billing itself as a "megasexual discotheque," is **Hula's Bar and Lei Stand**, 2103 Kuhio Ave., at Kalaimoku Street. Hula's closes at about 1:30 A.M., at which time many mega-patrons move over to Wave Waikiki to ride out the evening.

DRINKING AND CHATTING

There are several nice lounges, but one of our favorites is a quiet piano bar called **The Library**, next to the Third Floor Restaurant in the Hawaiian Regent Hotel. The pubs mentioned near the end of our dining suggestions (Section 5) are also good and popular, as is the aforementioned **Trapper's**.

A place which doesn't seem to fit into any category is **Sherlock's Palm Garden** (Tel. 523-8511), downtown in the back patio of the old Blaisdell Hotel, 1154 Fort Street Mall. Drinking, light dining, and contemporary Hawaiian entertainment are often featured in the ambiance of an earlier-day Honolulu. Call first; depending on the program, this can be a real find out of the usual tourist precincts.

AND AFTER 4 A.M.?

Night owls who get hungry following their evening hoot often float back to earth at the **Wailana Coffee Shop**, 1860 Ala Moana Blvd., or perhaps sit down for awhile with **Eggs 'n Things**, nearby at 436 Ena Rd. Happy Landings!

12. The Oahu Address List

Art supplies—Pacific Gallery and Art Supplies, 1253 S. Beretania St. Tel. 533-1197.

Bakery—Leonard's Bakery, 933 Kapahulu Ave. Tel. 737-5591.

Barber—Percy's, 2255 Kalakaua Ave. (Sheraton-Waikiki). Tel. 922-1591.

Beauty salon—Paul Brown's Cutters, 1347 Kapiolani Blvd. Tel. 947-3971.

Bird information—Hawaii Audubon Society, P.O. Box 22832, Honolulu, Hi. 96822.

Bus information—Tel. 531-1611.

Camper rentals—Beach Boy Campers, 1720 Ala Moana Blvd. Tel. 955-6381.

Camping equipment rental—Hawaiian Rent-All, 1946 S. Beretania St. Tel. 949-3961.

Chamber of Commerce of Hawaii—735 Bishop St. Tel. 531-4111.

City Office of Information and Complaint, 530 S. King St., Room 301. Tel. 523-4381.

Dry cleaners—Al Phillips, International Market Place. Tel. 923-1971.

Fire department—Dial 911 for all emergencies.

Fishing supplies—Amfac Marine, 1125 Ala Moana Blvd. Tel. 945-8711.

Florist—Polynesian Exotics, 410 Nahua St. Tel. 926-3556.

Hawaii Visitors Bureau—2270 Kalakaua Ave., Suite 804. Tel. 923-1811.

Health food store—Aloha Health Foods, Ward Warehouse. Tel. 531-7703.

Hospital—Dial 911 for all emergencies. (Closest hospital to Waikiki is Kaiser Foundation, 1697 Ala Moana Blvd. Tel. 949-5811.)

Laundromat—Outrigger Hotel Arcade, 2335 Kalakaua Ave. Tel. 923-0711.

Pharmacy—Outrigger Pharmacy, 2335 Kalakaua Ave. Tel. 923-2529.

Police—Dial 911 for all emergencies. Headquarters is at 1455 South Beretania St. (near the end of Kalakaua Ave.) Tel. 955-8111.

Post office—Waikiki Branch Post Office, 330 Saratoga Road, Tel. 941-1062.

Public library—Waikiki-Kapahulu Library, 400 Kapahulu Ave., at the Ala Wai. Tel. 732-2777.

Supermarket—Safeway, 1121 South Beretania St. Tel. 538-7315.

6

Kauai,
the Garden Island

1. Around the Island—A Verdant Outpost

Is there really no such thing as a sleepy tropical paradise any more? Are such ingredients as rustling palms, fragrant *mokihana* berries, pure untouched sands, azure seas, wheeling frigate birds, and an unhurried pace of life all mixed together solely in someone's imagination—a scenic recipe only affirmed in the films of Hollywood?

Maybe. But then where do the movie-makers go to capture these images of Elysium?

They go to the Island of Kauai. Perhaps the director must cart along an improbable collection of characters, but there is virtually no need for anyone called a set designer.

Honoluluans often save Kauai for their honeymoons. The distance from the capital—103 miles—serves as a psychological barrier to state residents. They may visit all the other islands in the chain before they finally fall in love and set out for Kauai.

Together with its satellite, Niihau, Kauai is the only major piece of real estate in the archipelago which cannot be seen from any of the other Hawaiian Islands.

Maps produced by airlines and other commercial operations often draw Kauai artificially closer—to the point where it is nearly touching Oahu. This is an usurpation of artistic license, for the island's distance and more northward latitude helps us to understand its bucolic isolation and somewhat cooler mien.

Kauai is not on the way to anyplace else, unless you count the unin-

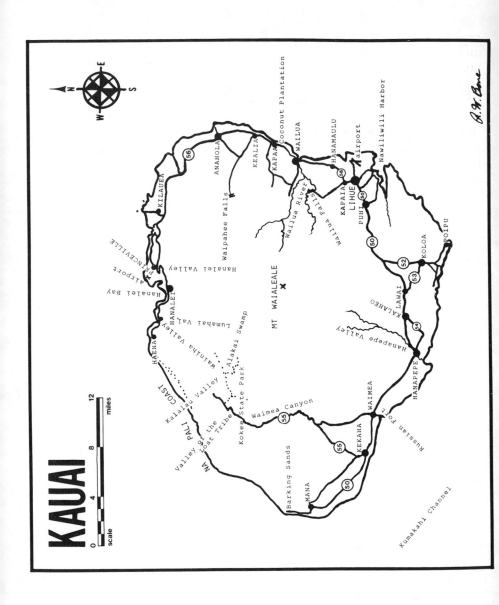

habited atolls, islets, and shoals which form tiny, wave-swept stepping stones dotting the direction to Japan. In the eighteenth and nineteenth centuries, this separation from the islands to the southeast saved Kauai residents considerable bloodshed. Here is one island which was *not* conquered by Kamehameha the Great. It was finally given to him, though a little less than amicably, by Kaumualii, the king of Kauai, in 1810.

To statisticians, the Garden Isle consists of 553 square miles, making it the fourth largest of the islands. It is also the oldest, since it thrust itself above the sea about 8 million years ago. It has had considerably more centuries to be eroded and otherwise moulded by wind, rain, and tide. Perhaps partly for this reason, it could also be called the Island of Rivers, features which are generally missing from the younger islands in the state.

Kauai was built by one massive volcano. Today's tallest peak, Mt. Waialeale ("why-Ollie-Ollie") is all that remains of that volcano's eastern rim. The 5,243-foot mountain, whose name can be translated as "overflowing water," is almost the wettest spot on earth. A geologic fluke has created a funnel which collects masses of moisture-laden trade winds and forces them up to an altitude where they must cool and condense. The rainfall atop the cloud-shrouded *massif* averages more than 460 inches annually, and one pluvial year it measured 624 inches.

The island spent much of 1983 recovering from the physical and psychological effects of Hurricane Iwa, a violent November storm during which winds were recorded at more than 100 miles per hour. Amazingly no one was killed or even seriously injured on Kauai, although Iwa caused more than $200 million worth of damage. Some evidence of the tempest is still visible, particularly in the Poipu area on the southern shore.

Most of Kauai's 40,000 residents live around the rim of the island, leaving the sprawling and often rugged interior to sugar cane, wild goats, and pigs. Two natural features dominate the outback—the deep gash called Waimea Canyon, and the virtually impenetrable sloping valleys and green sea cliffs on the northwest shore called the Na Pali Coast. Because of this rugged obstruction, no road will ever completely circle the island. There are gorges in Na Pali which have not felt a human foot for centuries, and there are others which have never been explored at all.

The first Polynesians came to Kauai in about 800 A.D., but there are tales of mysterious groups of people having preceded them. Hawaiian legends speak particularly of the *Menehunes* ("Many-*Hoon*ies"), a race of "white dwarfs" who were adept at stonemasonry but who were physically subjugated by the more powerful Polynesians.

Did the *Menehunes* really exist? You will see examples of very sophisticated fitted stone on Kauai which are found nowhere else in the Islands. And even the journals of Captain James Cook tell of a servant class on Kauai—men and women he saw who were shorter and light-skinned.

For more than 150 years, the Hawaiians have been telling us that the *Menehunes* simply went away one day. According to legends, they pulled up stakes and disappeared into one of the hidden valleys along the Na Pali Coast. The Hawaiians say they may be living there still.

2. Airports—Lihue and Princeville

Most travelers to Kauai enter through **Lihue Airport** after a seventeen-minute jet trip from Honolulu via either of the two scheduled air carriers, Aloha Airlines or Hawaiian Airlines. A few, however, take the forty-five-minute Cessna flights between Honolulu and Princeville via Princeville Airways. (See Chapter 2.)

There is no chance of getting lost in the tiny terminal, even though there are often large crowds at some hours—when hundreds of people and thousands of flowers seem to be arriving and departing simultaneously. Major new construction will be getting under way at the airport this year, however.

Lihue Airport needs several technical improvements. They are now on the way. Meanwhile, we take the advice of pilot friends and never fly into or out of Lihue in obviously bad weather or at night—preferably not after 6 P.M., when traffic gets heavy.

Facilities at Lihue Airport include a Visitor Information Center, airline counters, the Menehune Restaurant and Cocktail Lounge, Greeters of Hawaii (leis, fruit baskets, etc.), the Driftwood Gift Shop, a newspaper-cigarette stand, tour operators, rental car counters (outdoors, across the roadway), and taxis.

Kauai's smaller landing strip is **Princeville Airport**, alongside the road a couple miles or so east of Princeville. It's one of the most beautiful sites for an airport in the country. The terminal, a squarish, plantation-style gazebo, is set in a garden of greenery and backdropped by the Hanalei Mountains.

3. Transportation on Kauai

To travel from the airport to Lihue or your hotel, your choices are simple: Take a shuttle bus, hire a taxi, rent a car, or—if that's your duffle bag—hike.

Hotel transfers (shuttle service) from the terminals now have standardized prices on all tour bus companies. It will cost you somewhere between $3 and $6, depending on the distance, to be carted off with your luggage to most lodgings via these buses or limousines.

There are two taxi companies stationed at the airport: **Garden Island**

(Tel. 822-4612) and **Tony's Taxi** (Tel. 245-2774), both long-time companies. Approximate taxi rates from Lihue Airport to some destinations
run as follows: Lihue—$6; Poipu Beach hotels—$23; Coco Palms Hotel
(Wailua)—$13; Coconut Plantation Hotels—$15; and Princeville at Hanalei—$35. Drivers are allowed to charge 25 cents extra per large suit-
case.

There are at least seven other taxi ownerships on the island at this
writing, each generally associated with separate communities. Check
with your hotel for specific taxi information.

Most travelers not on conducted tours will prefer to rent a car. In
Kauai, too, this is a highly volatile and very competitive business. As of
yesterday afternoon, there were no less than fifteen competing companies there. Impossible? You bet, and there are bound to be many
changes by the time you're ready to slide into the driver's seat.

The picture is more confused because of the current "fly-drive" deals,
which appear to be—but seldom are—the best deals around. (Please see
our long discussion on rental car agencies in Chapter 5, Section 3.)

As in Honolulu, the flat rate—when you can get it—is generally a better bargain than mileage rates on Kauai. Most people average 50–100
miles a day on a two-day visit to the island. If you do, the flat rate will
almost certainly be cheaper, but it's always better to take a minute with a
pencil to work it all out. Remember that either on mileage or flat, you'll
have to buy your own gas with any agency. Be aware that in busy periods,
however, many companies will cancel their flat rates entirely, and also up
their mileage rates.

Here are some fairly dependable Kauai rental car agencies, and an
observation or two about them. All but Tropical have an office at Lihue
Airport. In all except Watase, you may make advance reservations by
calling their Honolulu offices. (Check the Oahu telephone directory for
those numbers.)

Avis Rent A Car (Tel. 245-3512) strangely has a cheaper mileage rate
and more expensive flat rate than Hertz at this writing. **Budget Rent A
Car** (Tel. 245-4572) once laid the insurance pressure on us hard here.
But we resisted and found the car, at least, satisfactory. **Dollar Rent-A-
Car** (Tel. 245-4708), with an office at Lihue Airport, may have a good
deal on renting camping equipment to go with the car.

Hertz Rent A Car (Tel. 245-3356) is generally the top-dollar car here
as in many other places. **National Car Rental** (Tel. 245-3502) presum-
ably still gives Green Stamps. **Robert's Kauai U-Drive** (Tel. 245-4008)
also has jeeps and VW buses. **Tropical Rent-A-Car Systems** (Tel. 245-
4912) is a long-time personal favorite for low flat rates and usually good
service (there's no airport office; call and they'll come pick you up).
Watase's U-Drive (Tel. 245-3251) is a good local outfit which has mileage

rates (generally low) only. And **Holiday Car Rentals** (Tel. 245-6944), a new firm, has been getting a lot of attention for its low rates. Unfortunately its rather tacky gas-tank policy takes the edge off the bargain.

Until recently, driving on Kauai was a pretty informal thing. But not long ago, the very first stop lights came to the island. There still are only two, and there should be more. Also Kauai drivers tend to be informal in their traffic habits. The Honolulu *Advertiser's* barefoot Kauai correspondent with the untenable name Jan TenBruggencate points out that there are still three more things any *malihini* driver is just going to have to grin at and bear up with—following in the wake of a tour bus, getting stuck behind a giant sugar cane truck loaded with stalks (don't try to pass them in an open convertible), and nosing the exhaust pipe of a little old retired plantation worker who chugs along at 35 miles per hour no matter where he is.

But here's a couple of upbeat notes: There is virtually no parking problem on Kauai. And most Mainlanders feel that traffic is mild compared with back home.

What about the **bus**? Although there is no authentic public-supported transportation on the island, a small private omnibus line was in operation until the recent hurricane blew them right out of business, either temporarily or permanently. Better phone owner/driver Fred Allen at 822-9532 to see if he's managed to crank up his old "Aloha Bus" to run again between the Kauai Surf Hotel and the Coconut Plantation.

Motorcycles. Every now and then, somebody begins revving up some cycle rentals, but one of our old standbys has thrown in the oil rag. You might check with **Yamaha of Kauai** (Tel. 245-6612) on Rice Street. If they can't help you with a rental, they might sell you a used machine! Sorry. That's the best we can do this year.

Motorized bicycles. There are usually two or three outfits renting these. Try **South Shore Activities** (Tel. 742-6873) at the Sheraton. Whatever the rates are, we'd advise comparing them carefully with what you would pay for a rental car. Chances are, if there are at least two of you, you'll be further ahead in something with four wheels.

And **bicycles**—the pedal kind. Some hotels have them, and more are talking about it. We found rental racks at the Kauai Surf, the Poipu Beach, and the Sheraton Kauai. Also, the Smiths (of the riverboat Smiths) are pumping up this business, too. You can pedal away on 10-speed models from **Smith's Boat Service** (Tel. 822-4111) at the marina in Wailua. Also in Wailua, a little past the Sea Shell restaurant, you'll find **Kinipopo Bike Rentals** (Tel. 822-3630), with perhaps a wider choice of models. Over in the Poipu area—actually in Koloa—is **Surf n' Cycle** (Tel. 742-6633). Rates average more than $5 a day, and, incidentally, that's about the price to fly your bike from Honolulu on either jet airline.

4. The Hotel Scene

By torchlight, sunlight, candlelight, and moonlight, we have prowled over the major accommodations on Kauai, and we cheerfully report that with a few dusky exceptions, the value-for-dollar picture is pretty bright.

You'll probably base your choice as much on location—whether you prefer to be the village mouse or the country mouse, or to be a club-jumper or a beachnik—as you will on the particular amenities offered by hotel managements.

And if you're a budget squeezer, remember that even the most modest twelve-dollar Kauai double is planted in lush, spring-like surroundings that money simply can't buy in the most prestigious establishments in Chicago, Cleveland, or Milwaukee.

The hotels we have inspected fall into four major geographical sectors—*Lihue-Nawiliwili*, which is about as close as you can get to "downtown Kauai." Then there's *Wailua-Kapaa*, the east shore action central for many hotels and where more people check in than in any other neighborhood. Third is *Poipu Beach*, a heavenly strand somewhat isolated from the mainstream and other beaches, about 20 minutes' drive southeast of Lihue. Except as noted, all hotels in the area have fully recovered from the effects of Hurricane Iwa. Lastly, we looked into some fairly expensive havens in *Hanalei*, which may be about as far removed from reality as you can get, way up on the north shore. (WARNING: Winter swimming at any north shore beaches can be dangerous.)

Hotels we have listed in the *Expensive* category rent out most of their double rooms from about $70 per day on up. In our *Medium* group, two persons will pay from about $30 to $60 for 24 hours. And *Budget* hotels will happily put up a pair for something between $15 and $30. Prices may change, of course, so those mentioned on these pages should be thought of only as a general guide.

EXPENSIVE HOTELS

The leader is the **Coco Palms Resort** (Tel. 822-4921) in Wailua. It is also a sightseeing attraction, and even if you're not lucky enough to tuck under the covers there, by all means go see it, wander its palm-shaded property, dine on the lagoon-side terrace, and feed the tilapia.

For those who do check in, here's some of what you'll find: high-peaked, church-like lobby with mammoth chandeliers and stained-glass windows; up two steps to a split-level reading alcove; grounds with three outdoor swimming pools; tiny zoo out back; nine tennis courts; thatched "Chapel in the Palms," built for "Sadie Thompson" (weddings easily arranged); three dependable restaurants—the Lagoon Dining Room, the Flame Room, and the Coconut Palace; nightly entertainment; lounge/bridge over the entrance road; miles of pathways wandering through scores of palms; famous torch-lighting ceremony nightly around the lagoon (the honors Elvis Presley performed in "Blue Hawaii"); the public Wailua Beach (no beach services) across the busy road from the resort.

Only a very few of the Coco Palms' 427 rooms are standard doubles at around $65. We like the Superiors for about $78 in the Sea Shell wing: blue-and-white decor; famous genuine giant clam-shell wash basins; refrigerators; several other extras. Try for Sea Shell rooms overlooking the lagoon. Deluxe rooms in the Alii Kai ("Chief of the Sea") section are around $88. We saw Room 444 and loved the custom tiles, wrought iron, and white rattan furnishings.

The Kings' Cottages and Queens' Cottages, running from $115 to $125 this year, however, are perhaps the most dramatic features of the hotel and are unsurprisingly popular with honeymooners. Decor in red and green and stone and wood; cane lamp over the punee; drop curtain to mask the royal purple bedrooms from the lanai; small, hidden yardlet with a unique outdoor lava rock bathtub for private soaping in the sun. (Make sure you don't get the cottage right next to the dining room where some guests have written to us about the kitchen noise late at night and early in the morning.) The new Prince of Hawaii cottage ($155) we have yet to see. (*Reservations from AMFAC Hotels, P.O. Box 8519, Honolulu, HI 96815.*) On Kauai, the Coco Palms wins our lowest bows—and highest recommendation.

A fond second place has to go to the lively **Sheraton-Kauai Hotel** (Tel. 742-1661), which is still recovering from Iwa, the November 1982 hurricane whose 30-foot waves swept away virtually the entire original section of the hotel. Happily, the Sheraton had already opened its new and better wings on the inland side of the road, and these weathered it all very well. Moreover, the gardens are even more attractive now than they were before the storm. In spite of—or because of—the hurricane, the hotel seems to have developed a new *esprit de corps* that matches its improved facilities:

Ideal location on a good section of Kauai's beautiful Poipu Beach; several four-story buildings scattered around lovely grounds, all connected by elevated walkways; some parts forming an architectural impression of a small Japanese village; high-peaked, open lobby with tile floors and baskets of greenery; downstairs still guarded by grouchy old Waha, the parrot (he barks, too, but his bite is worse!); large poly-sided pool and The Trellis, a pool bar; popular Pareo Pub for happy hours; Lanai Terrace restaurant (where the catch of the day sometimes has been caught by fisherman/chef Bert Matsuoka himself); the old Shell Dining Room perhaps reconstructed this year under a new name.

Six Garden Wing buildings with accommodations oriented either to pool or ponds; rooms here ranging from $75, $85, and $90 depending on view; fourth-floor units featuring high "cathedral" ceilings; ground-floor models convenient to pool or gardens via the lanai doors; beds all double-doubles or king-size; good furnishings throughout; TVs and *TV Guides;* paintings by artist Pegge Hopper in every room; 114 rebuilt Ocean Wing units *makai* of the road opening April 1984; deluxe rates over there at $110, $120, and $200; some accommodations in all categories equipped for the handicapped; temporarily no room service available. Say hello for us to helpful assistant manager Ken Harding, who grew up in Washington, D.C. (*Reservations from Sheraton Hotels in Hawaii, P.O. Box 8559, Honolulu, HI 96815.*) Like Phoenix rising from the mud, the Sheraton-Kauai is ready to fly again—perhaps higher and better than ever before.

Some say the title for Garden Isle elegance should go to the **Waiohai Hotel** (Tel. 742-9511), a 460-room Gargantua also on Poipu Beach. Built to withstand a tidal wave, it received no structural damage from Hurricane Iwa. The Waiohai occupies the site of a modest and fondly remembered lodge of the same name that was about one-tenth the size of this baby, and today it rather self-consciously tries to recapture the slower pace of an earlier day with its plantation-theme decorations:

Four-story, W-shaped plant on 11 recently relandscaped acres; marble-floored, open-air lobby with four-story windows; teak and brass accents abounding; the largest, most artistic lobby wind chime you ever did see; two garden areas between arms of the "W"—the Ginger Courtyard with fragrant, white flowers, and the Rainbow Courtyard with multicolored blossoms; each court with a pool, but one surrounding a semisunken bar (neither is deeper than five feet, so no diving); six tennis courts; two (later three) expensive restaurants, including the Waiohai Terrace (on the viewful site of the old hotel's restaurant) and the haute-cuisine Tamarind (which we enjoyed); cellar-sited Wine Room still being shoveled out of the sand on our recent visit; Jackstraws, an atmospheric bar; the Tamarind Lounge probably with versatile Kimo Garner at the keyboard; a large physical-fitness center with all the appropriate accouterments.

Rooms (nearly all with ocean view) have hidden color televisions; prestocked refrigerators; wet minibars; mirrored doors; patterned walls, upholstery, and bedspreads; small couches with tiny coffee tables; some rooms without desks or sit-down tables; very fancy bathrooms; small lanais with uncomfortable outdoor furniture. Due to design deficiencies, many rooms do not admit enough sunlight during the day, especially the one we drew in the armpit of the W at the back of the court. At least one guest has complained that the fluorescent bed lamps are unflattering. Rates for '84 run $83 for Standards, $103 for Superiors (same rate for three persons), and $137 for Deluxes (same rate for up to four). Large suites go from about $275 to $675, and some are good deals for two or three couples sharing.

The Waiohai is controversial among local residents who fought its construction and did succeed (thankfully) in limiting it to four stories. Our own stay was okay. (*Reservations from AMFAC Hotels, P.O. Box 8519, Honolulu, HI 96815*.) Although we, too, miss the old Waiohai, the new model is still recommended for Kauai capers—and most especially to beach lovers.

Also on Poipu Beach, the **Kiahuna Plantation** (Tel. 742-6411) is a resort condominium haven. Many of its buildings were damaged during the hurricane, and at this writing its accommodation operation has not yet reopened. But they should be ready by January 1984: About 300 apartments in some 40 cottage-style cedar and redwood buildings rambling over 20 acres; some units right on the sand; others set back a long way; famous but somewhat yo-yo Plantation Gardens restaurant on the property (see Section 5); ten tennis courts (free to guests); swimming pool a long hike from the beach; new golf course (the only one in the neighborhood); accommodations decorated in bright colors; no TVs except by special arrangement ("This is a place for families to have fun together," said management. "We find our guests never miss it."). One-bedroom models $74 to $189 for two as 1984 begins; two-bedroom units for four persons from $138 to $238. (*Reservations from Village Resorts, Inc., Suite C-211B, 50 S. Beretania St., Honolulu, HI 96813*.) It's not cheap, but for its type of private ambience, and certainly for avid tennis buffs, it could be a winner.

Closer to the county seat of Lihue, the highrise **Kauai Surf Hotel** in Nawiliwili has just finished a half-million dollars' worth of renovations throughout its massive structure. At eleven stories, it's the only "skyscraper" on the island. (Alarmed county officials passed a four-story limit on everything soon after the Surf was built in 1960.) It's the only hotel on Kalapaki Beach, a popular public area:

Spacious, well-manicured grounds with many pathways; golf course up on the hill; eight tennis courts nearby; large swimming pool; separate convention center; large, sunny lobby with polished tiles; Golden Cape restaurant in the penthouse (often good, but check the prices); two lesser dining rooms; Destination Discotheque; comfy Golden Cape Lounge open late-late way-way upstairs; popular Planter's Bar at ground level; a good group of shops; zillions of activities to sign up for.

Our standard double (now $69) left a lot to be desired. The $83 superiors and $95 deluxes are better. We thought that the staff was a little too offhand and room maintenance not all it should be. Nevertheless, it's a good hotel and a prestigious address. (*Reservations from Surf Resorts Hawaii, P.O. Box 8539, Honolulu, HI 96815*.) Okay for the outlay.

At the end of hard-to-find Papaloa Road between Wailua and Kapaa, a Japanese *Torii* gate welcomes you to the **Kapaa Sands Apartments** (Tel. 822-4901), a neat collection of little duplex houselets along a narrow beach. They come with fully equipped kitchens and most are the same rate (about $65 to $75) for up to four persons. (Some small studios for two rent for about $50.) There's a pool, but no dining room, bar, or anything central like that. (*Write Harriet Kaholokula at R.R. 1, Box 3-H, Kapaa, Kauai, HI 96746 for bookings*.) A haven of its type.

The 311-room beachside **Sheraton Coconut Beach** (Tel. 822-3455), not to be confused with the aforementioned Sheraton Kauai, is the former Holiday Inn at the far end of the Coconut Plantation complex: Rambling, four-story structure with a modernistic, 40-foot waterfall in the lobby; koa wood planters and lots of stained glass and tapestry on the ground floor; same old Voyage Room restaurant, partly outdoors, and Cook's Landing, an indoor/outdoor bar near the pool; special *hale* under the palms for the Sheraton *luau*; several sports activities including tennis (3 courts), volleyball, shuffleboard, and a putting green; fairly good beach, except for the tiny pinecones from the ironwood trees that bother your sensitive tootsies.

Rooms with color TVs, 80 percent with ocean views, but nearly all with tiny, triangular lanais. For bigger balconies, choose the oceanfront Deluxes at $110 for two. Other rates go down to $70, but try not to draw the unit we had across from the Coke machine and noisy laundry room. (*Reservations from Sheraton Hotels in Hawaii, P.O. Box 8559, Honolulu, HI 96815*.) Wear your zoris to the beach and you may love it.

We haven't been through the 140-room **Poipu Beach Hotel** (Tel. 742-1681) lately, but it pales considerably in the shadow of the next-door Waiohai, under the same ownership. Rates range from $60 to $80 this year. (At one time there was a plan to make this a *part* of the Waiohai, and we hope that idea doesn't surface again. We were never very fond of the place personally.)

Many may prefer the long drive out to the dramatic and still-developing recreational community **Princeville at Hanalei** (Tel. 826-6561), which boasts one of the best golf courses in the entire state. Spread out on a section of 1,000 acres, there are several rentable condominium clusters administered by the Princeville Management Corp., each considerably separated from the other. More are under construction. None, incidentally, is right on a beach, but the sands are not far away.

Princeville's "front desk" is in a building fronting the shops at Princeville Center, just off Kuhio Highway. We've seen beautiful interior furnishings at these condos in big sky country, but we still get the feeling that we are too far away from things, although they are certainly convenient for drive, slice, and putt addicts. Tennis courts and a swimming pool are also available, and there are four pleasant restaurants in the vicinity.

Princeville will be nicer when it is more grown up—with a genuine hotel down by the beach, more trees, and a mature personality. Meanwhile, daily rates run from about $70 for one-bedroom apartments (sleeping up to 4) to about $160 for three-bedroom apartments (up to six people), all with daily maid service. (*Reservations from Princeville at P.O. Box 121, Hanalei, HI 96714.*) We've never heard a discouraging word about Princeville from its guests, and dedicated golfers surely rate it much better than par.

Another condominium operation, **Hanalei Bay Resort** (Tel. 826-6522), was closed for seven months after sustaining wind damage from Hurricane Iwa, but now appears to be back on its feet. It occupies 20 acres of land, not part of the Princeville organization, but in the same complex. Excellent Bali Ha'i Restaurant in the central building; popular Happy Talk lounge; 11 tennis courts; two swimming pools.

Generally attractive one-, two-, and three-bedroom units in buildings named after fruits—or was it trees? (we checked out the Guava Building); lots of space and good facilities in the units, including washer/dryer, good kitchen equipment with garbage disposals; no air conditioning; overhead fans. Rates begin at about $66 (for two) and go up to about $250 (for up to seven). (*Reservations from Village Resorts, Inc., Suite C-211B, 50 S. Beretania St., Honolulu, HI 96813.*) Expensive, certainly, but certainly nice, too.

Further out, in Haena, is a more rustic apartment operation, the **Hanalei Colony Resort** (Tel. 826-6235), on a rocky beach almost at the end of the northern road. Lots of greenery, including palms, *hala*, papaya, *ti* leaves, and hibiscuses; new pool; about a dozen houses, each with four spacious apartments; full kitchen and fridge; ample storage; king-size beds; no TV; restaurant on the property; daily maid service extra. We prefer the downstairs lodgings where the *lanai* gives private back-door access, too. Rates run about $70 to $100 for two-bedroom apartments. (*Write the hotel at Hanalei 96714.*) The word "resort" is certainly a misnomer, and there's no good ocean swimming in the winter. Otherwise it's not bad for an isolation-comfort combination.

MEDIUM-PRICED HOTELS

Although their snazzier rooms may run higher, here is a group of hotels and condos where you can usually come up with a decent double for $60 or less per night.

Besides those establishments listed below, sometimes private homes can be rented for short terms at comparable rates. If you're already on

Kauai when you read these words, drop in to some local real estate agencies that handle vacation rentals.

Top medium-budget place is occupied by the 243-room **Kauai Beach-Boy** (Tel. 822-3441), two strokes and a kick from the Sheraton Coconut Beach along the same shoreline in the Coconut Plantation complex: Friendly reception in a somewhat cluttered lobby; dining in the high-ceilinged Hale Ani Ani restaurant (where our own luck was good); Hale Kai Boogie Palace Bar (outrigger canoes "fly" from the roof); parquet dance floor; downstairs beauty parlor; several shops; angular pool in well-kept lawn; Menehune Snack Shop beside the kiddie pool; myriad extracurricular activities including tennis, volleyball, ping pong, etc.

Some units directly on the beach; neat bedrooms; all air-conditioned; washbasin separated from sleeping chamber only by a room divider; shower and toilet, however, with a genuine door; some teak-like furnishings; sliding door to the *lanai*; light-patterned wallpaper (unusual in Hawaii); clock radio (a rare blessing); no room service at all. Doubles for $49 or $58—$68 for the best beachside locations; third person $6 extra. (*Reservations from AMFAC Hotels, P.O. Box 8519, Honolulu, HI 96815.*) The Kauai Beach Boy is tanned, healthy, and a handsome choice for the price.

One of these days, we're going to stay at least a day or two at the **Kauai Sands** (Tel. 822-4951) because we find it hard to rank. Adrift on a hard-to-snag road just before you get to Coconut Plantation, its facilities seemed somewhat lusterless. Not so its bubbly staff, however, all of whom couldn't have been more friendly, warm, and helpful during our short visit to the property. These personalities could make up for a lot of ordinary furniture. Calling itself "the only Hawaiian owned and operated hotels in the world," Hukilau Resort Hotels, the owner, also has one hostelry on Maui and three on the Big Island. On Kauai, neat doubles went for about $35 to $50 when we looked in. (*Reservations from Hukilau Resort Hotels, Suite 1201, 2222 Kalakaua Ave., Honolulu, HI 96815.*) Our verdict? A plain Jane, but probably with a beautiful soul.

Another hostelry about which you may disagree is the **Kauai Resort Hotel** (Tel. 245-3931), which we thought lacking in atmosphere on our own short stay. Enviable location alongside winsome Lydgate Park; gigantic high-roofed lobby which can fill up with 200 milling people at the crack of a bus door; somewhat overdone rock garden outdoors; tiny, perfectly round swimming pool, access to park beach; very-decorated restaurant; buffet liked by island residents. Our standard double in the big building seemed sterile, but sells for about $52 now. There are cabanas for $41, and perhaps they are a good deal. (*Reservations from Hawaiian Pacific Resorts, 1150 So. King St., Honolulu, HI 96814.*) We'll try this one again.

We've heard good things about the **Wailua Bayview Apartments** (Tel. 822-3651), overlooking the ocean just a shell's toss from the Sea Shell Restaurant. One-bedroom units rent in the $60 range. We've yet to confirm this for ourselves, however.

BUDGET HOTELS

We found three good low-priced bargains and have stayed in two of them briefly. The best in this price range perhaps is the **Hotel Coral Reef** (Tel. 822-4481) in Kapaa: attractive palm-fringed setting for two buildings; office in the older wooden structure fragrant with many blooms; open-air loungette with Japanese garden; narrow beach outside, okay (not great) for swimming; a short walk to the town pool. Some rooms with refrigerator; nicest nests in the newer building about $30 for two; doubles in the old building maybe $20 now; no discount for singles. There are also two spacious, two-bedroom family rooms, perhaps $30 for a couple and two *keikis*. Some readers have reported difficulties making reservations by mail, but once they check in most seem to love it. (*Write to the hotel at 1516 Kuhio Highway, Kapaa, Kauai, HI 96746.*) We doubt you can beat it at those prices.

A brief, incognito stay in the **Ocean View Motel** (Tel. 245-6345) in Nawiliwili certainly kept dry our enthusiasm for Spike Kanja's place. TV lounge downstairs; no frills like pictures or phones in the rooms; not quite Spartan but usually spotless doubles for $20 to $25; singles begin at $17. And is there an ocean view at the Ocean View? You bet! It's way in the distance across the road, but you can walk there as well as to the terrific Kalapaki Beach where you may play footsies with those paying more than four times your O.V. rate at the luxurious Kauai Surf Hotel. (*Write Spike at R.R. 1, Box 192, Lihue, Kauai, HI 96766.*) It's no Ritz, but it's priced right.

An unusual bargain, if the location is okay and you reserve far enough ahead, is at the state-owned **Kokee Lodge** (Tel. 335-6061). This is not a hotel or condo, but a collection of a dozen cabins about 4,000 feet up in the cool forest at Kokee State Park, on the edge of the Alakai Swamp, a l-o-o-o-n-g way from the action. Surrounded by miles of hiking and hunting trails and several trout-fishing streams, the rustic accommodations are furnished with refrigerators, stoves, showers, dishes, utensils, sheets, towels, pillows, blankets, and a woodburning fireplace. A small restaurant/bar is nearby. Rates are $25 per cabin for either the small units (sleeping three) or the large ones (sleeping seven). Understandably this relatively nontropical, high-altitude haven is often filled with Hawaii residents in the summer. Maximum length of stay is five days. (*Reservations from Kokee Lodge, P.O. Box 819, Waimea, Kauai, HI 96795, and a $25 deposit is required.*) This revitalized operation is now run by Olson and

Johnson, personal friends of ours, along with another couple, all of whom are serious about doing a good job.

If you want to establish yourself in the center of Metropolitan Lihue, try the **Tip Top Motel** (Tel. 245-2333), whose bakery is justly famous for Portuguese sweet bread (*pao dulce*) and macadamia nut cookies. There's a cafe, of sorts, and clean *air-conditioned* bedrooms ran about $20 single and $25 double the last time we looked in. Better recheck those prices later. (*Reservations direct from the Tip Top, 3173 Akahi St., Lihue, Kauai, HI 96766.*) Not really tip-top, but then neither are the prices.

Three other tiny places we didn't get to see include the **Hale Lihue** (Tel. 245-2751), 2931 Kalena St., Lihue, HI 96766, the **Ahana Motel Apartments** (Tel. 245-2206), 3115 Akahi St., Lihue, HI 96766, and the **Motel Lani** (Tel. 245-2965), P.O. Box 535, Lihue, HI 96766. All have some double rooms for $25 or less. Singles run around $20.

Richard Netherwood of Alameda, Calif. likes the **Kahili Mountain Park** (Tel. 742-9921): "Quiet, clean and rustic. Beautiful setting with somewhat worn but adequate facilities. Enjoyable furo. Take bug repellent. Not a place for people who don't like living with lizards and large insects." (Doubles with kitchens run about $15 to $35.)

5. Kauai Restaurants and Dining

Of the four relatively populous islands in the state, Kauai is certainly the least known for culinary excellence. But all things are relative, and happily there are some delicious exceptions to the general fare.

LIHUE-NAWILIWILI DINING

The top restaurant in the neighborhood, in more ways than one, is still the elegant **Golden Cape Dining Room** (Tel. 245-3631), crowning the eleven-story Kauai Surf Hotel in Nawiliwili. Its long carte runs from such winged delicacies as Chicken a la Kiev to a Royal Chateaubriand for two. The food is merely excellent, but the atmosphere is delightful. Complete dinners run about $25. Get there early to enjoy the spectacular view over the harbor. Another restaurant at the Kauai Surf is the **Outrigger Dining Room**, on stilts over the beach. A lot depends on the staff on duty, but we got along all right for breakfast.

There are two or three champion steak-mahimahi-lobster addresses on Kauai, and debates continue to be waged over the charcoal fields. The traditional winner is **J. J.'s Broiler** (Tel. 245-3841), 2971 Haleko St., which some say put the "cow" in "cow-why." It's in the refurbished quarters in the third of four nineteenth-century German plantation foremen's houses. It's always great for lunch. Unfortunately, flying bugs can be an annoyance in the evening, depending on the weather and the season.

Lihue now boasts no less than five—count 'em, five—interesting Chi-

nese restaurants. One of the best bargains is **Ho's Garden Restaurant**
(Tel. 245-5255) at 3016 Umi St., in a tiny building near the Hawaii Visitors Bureau office in the center of town. Certainly the most unusual setting is occupied by the **Genting** (Tel. 245-6520), which is in the back of
the Shell service station in the Garden Island Plaza on Route 56. Sweet-
and-sour pork sells for about $4 for a large serving. A great place to gas
up and change your oil (and you can have your car worked on, too).

The third Chinese establishment is the **Lihue Cafe and Chop Sui** (Tel.
245-6471) at 2978 Umi St., not far from Ho's. We haven't been in, but we
heard from a couple who enjoyed it. Closed Mondays. The **Kauai Chop
Suey** (Tel. 245-8790), in the Menehune Shopping Village across from
the Kauai Surf, is a little more expensive, but some think it's worth every
penny. Pleasant decor and service. Try the Shrimp Canton. Last, and
perhaps least from the strictly culinary point of view, is the revered old
Club Jetty down at Nawiliwili Harbor. The people are friendly, and the
combination "down-home" and nautical atmosphere is fascinating. Nobody really goes for the food, but it's certainly okay if a little pricey. The
place is much more lively late at night (see Section 11).

Moving into the Japanese column, now, the best low-price bargain has
to be **Restaurant Kiibo** (Tel. 245-2650) at 2991 Umi St., across Rice
Street from the County Building. (It's in the phone book under "R.") Try
the shrimp tempura, and wash it down with *sake* or Japanese beer. Much
better known, more expensive, and perhaps a little more tasty overall,
too, is **Kintaro** (Tel. 822-3341). It also boasts the only genuine *sushi* bar
in Kauai. Also with Nipponese specialties is the little **Barbecue Inn** at
2982 Kress St. Sorry, we haven't been in, but we've heard a good word or
two from those who have.

The only Italian address in Lihue now is the **Casa Italiana** (Tel.
245-9586), which is winning friends for its long menu as well as its *northern* Italian goodies. It's at 2989 Haleko Road, near J.J.'s, in a little stucco
casa said to be haunted by the German plantation manager who built
it 100 years ago. He may stamp around upstairs from time to time in
his jackboots. If the spirit is willing, perhaps the Italians and Germans
will remain in peaceful coexistence when you and your doppelganger
float by.

Two Mexican entries compete in Lihue. Closer to things is **La Luna**
(Tel. 245-9173), in the Menehune Shopping Center, although one reader
proceeded to give it the Pancho Villa treatment in a letter to us. We
haven't tried it, but we did recently get to **Rosita's** (Tel. 245-8561) at its
new address in the Kukui Grove Center. It's decorated in almost a Mexican musical-comedy motif, with many high-backed, very *grande* booths.
The food was innovative and generally *muy bien, gracias.* Try the unusual
crab enchiladas or stuffed steak Tapacania.

There's plenty of genuine, penny-pinching local atmosphere at the **Tip Top Cafe**, which is a bit of a misnomer, at 3173 Akahi St. The Lihue businessmen's lunch favorite is probably still **Kenny's**, at the entrance to the rotunda in the Lihue Shopping Center.

Another local choice is **Ma's Family, Inc.** (Tel. 245-3142), formerly Ma's Place, at 4277 Halenani St., just in back of the Kress store, particularly for fresh malasadas. Catch these operating hours: Open Monday to Friday from 4 A.M. to 2 P.M. and on Saturday and Sunday from midnight to 10 A.M. Kauaians disagree with my own Ma, who used to say nothing good ever happened after midnight, and point to their Ma's as the proof. And now Ma's nephew has opened **Dani's** (Tel. 245-4991) at 4201 Rice St., next to the fire station. Another "local kine" coffee shop, Dani's also has some strange hours: Monday to Friday 5 A.M. to 2 P.M., Saturday midnight to 2 P.M., and Sunday midnight to 11 A.M. (Don't ask me, ask Ma's nephew!)

Before we leave the Lihue area, let's assure all timid souls that yes, the county seat does have a **Kentucky Fried Chicken**, where the public waits while the colonel cooks; a **McDonald's**, which is like any one anywhere else, except maybe pricier; and a **Dairy Queen** or two, where we would keep strictly to the one product that made it famous and skip everything else.

Those three draw a late snack crowd, of course. But for something with more fun and local flair, try the **Hamura Saimin Stand** at 2956 Kress St. The saimin and barbecue sticks are cheap and really *ono-ono*. It doesn't close its doors until 2 A.M.—sometimes an hour or two later.

DINING FROM WAILUA TO KAPAA

Despite that awful name, **The Bull Shed** (Tel. 822-3791) continues to round up beef lovers over in the Waipouli/Coconut Plantation area. Try not to get seated in the hallway. Careful, because the popular **Rib 'N' Tail** (Tel. 822-9632) in Kapaa just changed owners. The name refers to a combination dish of prime roast beef rib and prawns. Hope it's just as good, and please let us know, too. If you don't mind cooking your own, try **Create a Steak** (Tel. 822-3390) in the Coconut Plantation.

The **Coconut Palace Dining Room** (Tel. 822-4921) is certainly attractive, but the gourmet menu seemed beyond the abilities of whoever was panning things out in the kitchen during our dinner stop. We have also dived into the **Lagoon Dining Room** in the same hotel for breakfast and lunch. It is very pleasant, including that unforgettable view of 132 palms reflected in the still, blue water. The buffet is still inexpensive. We weren't too taken with the mass feeding operation in the cavernous **Wailua Marina Restaurant** across the river by the boat landing. Prices, however, seemed on a fairly even keel.

There are two Italian *ristorantes* in the neighborhood. One is **Beef 'N' Pasta** (Tel. 245-6832) in the "old plantation" block at the wide place in Route 56 called Hanamaulu. An interesting free museum winds around this pasta *puka* in the wall. (Pull up where you see the 12,365-pound, 9-foot-4-inch-diameter main gear drive from the old Kilauea sugar mill, and walk inside past the post office. On your left you'll find steak, seafood, and various Roman specialties.) The other is **Grandfather's**, an informal, inexpensive *casa* in the Coconut Plantation. Besides veal scallopini and the like, they're featuring freshly caught fish of the day, reportedly at sea-bottom prices.

What used to be just a lunch wagon in Hanalei has now been parked in a more or less permanent address in Kapaa. That is **Tropical Taco** (Tel. 822-3622), in the shopping center. T.T. has been known for several years, now, as the home of Hawaii's 10 best tacos, all containing tons of refried beans, large amounts of ground beef, plenty of lettuce and tomato, lots of shredded cheese, hot sauce, and a whopping lump of sour cream on top. You need a spoon and maybe a half-hour to do justice to it. We have not yet tried **El Cafe** in the Roxy Theater Building nearby, but Paul Lowe wrote us from Anchorage to say he loved it. We also keep hearing great things about the **European Deli & Patisserie** (Tel. 822-7788) at 4-901 Kuhio Highway. Look for the orange awning.

Also in Kapaa, a Lancaster, Calif., reader said he found Hawaii's finest breakfast at the **Kountry Kitchen**. We followed up and basically agree. Try the Polynesian omelette.

KOLOA-POIPU DINING

The finest restaurant on this end of the island today has to be the **Tamarind Room** (Tel. 742-9511), and some would logically rate this classical Continental and Asian establishment the best on Kauai, ahead of the Golden Cape. But while the G.C. enjoys an atmospheric vista, the Tamarind must rely on an elegant brass, pink, and blue decorating scheme within its dark, windowless cavern in the Waiohai Hotel. (We always carry a penlight for places like this just to illuminate the menu.) One anachronistic pretension is handing women a menu without prices listed; Sara immediately demanded—and got—the real thing. We experienced very attentive, professional service. Our party of four enjoyed the Hong Kong Steak, steamed fish, Hot and Spicy Chicken, and the house wine and got away for not much more than $100 (plus tip). Incidentally, out of a hundred or more different restaurants we've patronized in Hawaii, this was the very first to hand us silver chopsticks!

The traditional fine dining restaurant in Poipu is the **Plantation Gardens** (Tel. 742-1695). It's a former sugar plantation manager's nineteenth-century home, carefully restored and planted in the center of seven acres of exquisite tropical foliage which is, in turn, part of the Kiahuna Plantation resort.

While waiting for a table, examine the museum/lounge with its *poi* pounders, tapa beaters, game stones, lamps, sinkers, feather gourds, and calabashes preserved from Old Hawaii. Be careful with your drink if you wait at a "cocktail table" that was once a hollowed-out *poi*-pounding board. (I spilled my Bloody Mary into history.)

After all that, we must say that over the past few years the chefs have rolled in and out of here like waves off Poipu Beach, so the cuisine, at least, has simply been inconsistent. Our advice is to go while it's still light, sit at a table on the lanai by the window, and order something dependable like steak or mahimahi. After dinner, finish off with a cognac or liqueur in the outdoor bar. The Plantation Gardens has it all over anyplace else on Kauai for atmosphere.

In a very different vein, we have become recent fans of one do-the-work-yourself place in Koloa called the **Koloa Broiler** (Tel. 742-9122), at least for lunch. Inside a rickety old green-and-white building right on the main drag, you can still enjoy a burger and salad bar for around $3, a top sirloin for perhaps $8, and several things in between. While you're salting and turning your meat, you can read the nearby sign: "Known worldwide for our famous chefs!" (Sit outdoors on the lanai.)

Sadly, the **Beach House Restaurant** was carried out to sea by Hurricane Iwa. The owner is rebuilding, however—a little farther away from the ocean. The same management, incidentally, has just purchased **Kona's** (Tel. 742-6433), a popular address in the Poipu Kai condo. It's on our list for a try this year.

HANALEI RESTAURANTS

The champion performer in this northern neighborhood is now the **Bali Ha'i** (Tel. 826-6522), in the hard-to-find Hanalei Bay Resort which is inside the gigantic Princeville complex. It's worth the trouble, however, for a glorious site with views through the open walls to sea and mountains. Unfortunately the railing blocks the vista when you sit down. For lunch we had a seafood salad with honey-mustard dressing and Cannellone Crepes (with veal and mushrooms). For dinner, try the baked salmon, rack of lamb, the scampi, or the Monte Cristo sandwich. This place brought in a consulting chef who taught the kitchen staff how to make a lot of tasty dishes. The chef has since bid adieu, but the talent lingers on as long as the same crew keeps on cookin' at the Bali Ha'i. Usually a good choice.

A popular address in Hanalei itself is **The Dolphin** (Tel. 826-6113), in a rustic cabin on the side of the Hanalei Trader general store: lacquered tables in tapa designs; glass-ball and paper lamps; captains' chairs; screens over the windows; Bombay fans; lots of wooden fixtures; lighted aquarium by the bar. We had a pleasant breakfast there, but it is well-loved for dinner, too. Honolulu *Star-Bulletin* columnist Dave Donnelly praised the Ratatouille appetizer. There are several steak, lobster, chicken, and fish entrees, adding up to seven to eleven clams, and a surprisingly complete wine list. The Dolphin knows some good tricks.

There are three dining salons open in the Princeville at Hanalei resort and golfing complex. The **Beamreach** (Tel. 826-9131), a neat, second-story entry overlooking the greens, features hand-carved sandwiches at lunch and steak/seafood at dinner. It's a favorite. Also smacking a lot of happy Kauai lips is **Chuck's Steak House** (Tel. 826-6211) in the new shopping center. Jerry and JoAnn Cole, who get around on Kauai, remember great ribs and the Sunday brunch. Another old reliable in the neighborhood is the **Princeville Lanai Restaurant** (Tel. 826-6228). Dancing and entertainment are often on tap there.

Also in Hanalei, a nightclub that used to serve a few meals on Fridays has now heated up the fires on a daily basis. **Tahiti Nui** (Tel. 826-6277), indeed owned by a woman hailing from Big Tahiti, dishes out breakfast, lunch, and dinner. And the Chinese restaurant in the new Ching Young Village, **Foong Wong** (Tel. 826-6996), has been packin' 'em in lately, too.

THE ROUTE TO KOKEE

Turning now to the southern route, there are four or five stops highly recommended by the Kauai *cognoscenti*. In Hanapepe (or actually between Eleele and Hanapepe), about 17 miles from Lihue, is the **Green Garden Restaurant** (Tel. 335-5422), serving all three meals in an open garden. The food is usually excellent, but the crowds are sometimes discouraging. Try the famous *lilikoi* (Hawaiian passion fruit) chiffon pie. A short way past that, on the same highway, is **Conrad's and Wong's** (Tel. 335-5066). We haven't been in since it was called Mike's Cafe, but the new dual-ethnic operation is run by two former Waikiki hotel chefs who thought they might hit the sunset in Kauai. Reports have been shining.

The traditional stop in Waimea for simple family food at modest prices is **Oa Oa** (Tel. 338-1671). In Kekaha you'll find the **Traveler's Den** (Tel. 337-9922), a local luncheon favorite that also houses a pastry shop. (No dinners.)

Near the end of Route 55, way up in the heavily forested Kokee (that rhymes with "okay") State Park, is the recently refurbished, revitalized, and remanaged **Kokee Lodge Restaurant** (Tel. 335-6061). Now serving all three meals, the Kokee dining room and its connecting bar reportedly have taken one giant step up from "okay" to *ole!*

6. Sightseeing Kauai

With just a little advance attention, semi-circumnavigating the island could hardly be more fun or more easily planned. The good two-lane road runs about three-fourths of the way around, and the starting point must begin more or less in the middle of that highway. So Kauai almost automatically divides itself into two one-day round trips for the casual wanderer.

On the other hand, dedicated explorers determined to exhaust the possibilities could poke around for two weeks, or even two months, for that matter, and still leave some important stones unturned.

Here is our own highly personalized list of sightseeing targets. We've eliminated some (the library, the new state building, etc.) from the standard itinerary whenever we felt they might take some time and attention from others we felt were more worthwhile.

They are listed in the order you'll come across them using the two-route system. In either case, plan on following the road to the very end (46 miles each way from Lihue on the southern branch and 40 miles on the northern one). Each has its pot of gold which must be reached to be enjoyed.

Leave early in the morning to avoid driving behind tour buses, and you may want to tuck a picnic lunch into the car. If you're going to Kokee in the winter, toss a sweater or a jacket for each of you in the back seat. You may need them.

LIHUE TO KOKEE, AND THE KALALAO VALLEY

From the airport, it's 2 miles (via Route 57) to **Lihue** ("Lee-*hooey*"), the county seat. The twin stacks of the **Lihue Sugar Mill** (no visitors) will tell you you're there. Rice Street (Route 51) is the main drag.

Near the Lihue sugar mill are the **Haleko Shops**, four nineteenth-century buildings, two of which are now restaurants (J.J.'s Broiler and Casa Italiana).

Just across the street is the Lihue Shopping Center. Notice the little *two-colored* bougainvillaea "trees" which brighten up the parking lot when they are in bloom. They are made of carefully twisted vines of orange- and blue-blossomed varieties and then mounted on a tree-like metal frame.

A block farther down Rice Street on the left is the double-structured **Kauai Museum** (Tel. 245-6931, admission is $2, children free, 9:30 A.M. to 4:30 P.M., Saturday til 1 P.M., closed Sunday). Permanent "Story of Kauai" exhibit in the Rice building; art shows and changing exhibits including cultural heritage displays in the Wilcox Building; authentic materials and Hawaiiana books for sale in the gift shop. Save the museum for a separate day, however.

Continue on Route 51 to see **Kalapaki Beach** fronting the island's only tall building, the luxurious eleven-story Kauai Surf Hotel. The area is called Nawiliwili, and its harbor is used by ocean-going and interisland vessels, including the interisland cruise ships *Independence* and *Constitution*.

At the point where Route 51 ceases to be Route 51, a spur called Niumalu Road—then Hulemalu Road—continues on to the **Alekoko Fishpond**, a mysterious mullet-raising lagoon said to have been built by Menehunes, the "little people" who may have been the island's first residents. Whoever did it constructed an ingenious wall more than 900 feet long in order to cut off a bend in the Huleia Stream. Legend says the Menehunes engineered the entire project overnight for a princess and her brother but under the stipulation that no one would watch them at work. Unable to restrain their curiosity, the royal *keikis* crept up to have a peek, were seen by the elves, and were turned into twin pillars of stone for their transgression. They still stand on the side of the mountain above the pond.

If you want, you may continue on the gradually worsening road to eventually hit Route 50 at Puhi. However, we recommend retracing your route back to the junction with 580 and turning left on it. On your right are the **Menehune Gardens** (Tel. 245-2660), although they may not be too well marked. Admission is $2.50 for adults, 50 cents for children under 12, and it's open 10 A.M. to 4:00 P.M. daily. You'll probably be guided through the garden by owner Melvin Kailikea, who still wears his WWII air-raid warden's helmet while describing the flowers, plants, and trees you rub noses with along the long, meandering pathway. The garden's glory is the gigantic Chinese Weeping Banyan tree, planted in 1896 and still growing. (Mrs. K. told us she had measured some of the aerial roots lengthening at a rate of five feet in eight months!) Although a piece of the banyan was taken out by Hurricane Iwa in 1982, this may still be Hawaii's largest tree, occupying nearly an acre of land. The enthusiasm of the Kailikeas makes the hike worth the price of admission.

Not far away is the **Grove Farm Museum** (Tel. 245-3202), a private, 80-acre historic site recalling plantation days on Kauai. The buildings comprise the former home of the Wilcox family, who ran the Grove Farm Plantation for more than a century. Things are almost exactly as they were when it was lived in, including furniture and household items dating from several different periods ending in 1978 when the last resident Wilcox died. Admission is $3 for adults, $1 for children, on a 1½-hour guided tour in small groups. Tours begin promptly at 10 A.M. and 1:15 P.M. Monday, Wednesday, and Thursday only, and *advance reservations are required*. (Call the above number, a day or more beforehand if possible. They'll give you exact directions to the homestead.) We thoroughly enjoyed it; tell 'em we sent you!

When you reach Route 50 (Kaumualii Highway), take it to the left. Continue through the village of **Puhi**. In another mile or so you'll come across one of those HVB warrior markers labeled **Queen Victoria's Profile** and pointing with undue assurance to a mountain ridge a few miles away.

We've passed that area dozens of times, strained our eyes, and finally after several trips were able to trace out what must be Queen Victoria's stubby form. The secret is to know not only that her hair is tied in a bun, not only that she is lying on her back in a most unroyal manner, but also that she has an admonishing finger raised toward Nawiliwili Harbor. She is supposed to be saying, "Now, Willy Willy!" in a scolding manner. The legend dates back to somewhere between 70 and 80 years ago, the "Willy Willy" being Victoria's cousin, Kaiser Wilhelm of Germany. Good luck and God save the queen if you want to search for this kind of thing, but just be careful not to drive off the road.

In September and October in this area, we are much more interested in gathering the *lilikoi* (yellow passion fruit) off the road and trees in the immediate neighborhood. Delicious!

We suggest another side loop to the south onto Route 52, or Maluhia ("Serenity") Road. Drive through its wonderful tunnel of towering eucalyptus trees to the diminutive and somnolent town of **Koloa**. A glance at that main street with its weatherbeaten false fronts will take you back a hundred years. We always liked Koloa just the way it was, and we hope the new "restoration" will do it no harm. Kauai's first sugar mill (1835) stands in ruins across the street from the business block.

To reach the most beautiful beach in southern Kauai, take the Poipu Road down to Poipu Beach. A few nice hotels are located here, although there is public access to the same sands at **Poipu Beach Park**. This is a fine location for swimming and snorkeling.

Returning toward Koloa, you can first take the side spur to **Spouting Horn**, which is one of those shoreline lava tubes through which the waves shoot very dramatically, often on a day other than the one you happen to come down to see it. It's very much like the Blow Hole on Oahu, but when this one is working well, it emits a strange, low moan following each eruption. A new park has just been completed there, and some think the whole place has been overbuilt.

Kauaians, incidentally, agree that the Spouting Horn has changed to only a little squirt in recent decades. One story told is that it used to shoot hundreds of feet into the air until the owners of nearby sugar fields determined that the windblown salt-water spray was ruining their crops. Their solution was to dynamite the rock, making the hole larger and the fountain much less tall. Could be, but we'd certainly rather believe the opening has just become eroded over the years!

At Koloa again, take Route 53 (also called 530) west. If you're lucky, and it's a Tuesday or Thursday, you can turn left on hard-to-see Hailima Road for about two miles and then find the 186-acre **Pacific Tropical Botanical Garden** (Tel. 332-8131). Not widely known, this private tropical plant research center gives two-hour tours for $7 on Tuesdays at 9 and 10:15 A.M. and on Thursdays at 9 A.M. Unfortunately we've never managed to stop by on the right day, but Maverick readers who have stumbled across this garden have praised it as the highlight of their trips. (Better phone first for exact directions.)

Rejoining Highway 50 at Kalaheo, you might keep an eye out for the **Olu Pua Gardens** (Tel. 332-8182), a former plantation manager's estate now opened as a botanical attraction. The self-guided tour is attractive and interesting, but it seemed a little overpriced to us at $4 a ticket. (Maybe you can get a two-for-one discount coupon in your rental car *Kauai Drive Guide* magazine, as we did.) Incidentally, former President Richard Nixon was a houseguest here in 1979.

Make a brief stop at the **Hanapepe Valley Lookout**, indicated by an HVB warrior marker. Years ago, the view was capped by a dramatic windswept 326-foot-high waterfall. But in recent decades its headwaters have apparently been tapped for sugar field irrigation, perhaps by the same folks who fiddled with Spouting Horn. Still, the valley forms an impressive vista.

A mile past **Eleele** ("Elly-Elly") is the village of **Hanapepe** ("Hah-nah-*pay*-pay"), which boasts it is the "Biggest Little Town on Kauai." It's a happy place today and bears no mark of its 1924 tragedy when at least 20 people were killed here in an all-out battle between police and striking sugar cane workers. (We once saw a hillside covered with hundreds of multicolored flowers at one of the two entrances to this town.)

If it's lunchtime by now, try the Green Garden Restaurant or Conrad's and Wong's, both on the main highway. (See Section 5—"Restaurants and Dining.")

If you find you've been clipping right along, you might take the one-mile detour on Highway 543 to the ancient **Salt Ponds** (look for Lokokai Road, then Kaalani Road) and the nearby mild beach. Here the Hui Hana Paakai O Hanapepe (Syndicate of Hanapepe Salt Makers) has kept alive the ancient Hawaiian art of salt-making, during the spring and summer months. The salt-drying beds date back at least to the seventeenth century and perhaps to several hundred years before that. Captain James Cook's crew observed and wrote about the Hanapepe salt ponds in a description which is still accurate today. Cook surely replenished the H.M.S. *Resolution*'s own supply of salt during his 1778 discovery trip to Kauai. The salt is still popular with modern Hawaiians for seasoning, and some family recipes call only for Hanapepe salt. Supercautious health regulations now prohibit the sale, and we suspect that it's the "impurities" which provide the special flavor. The salt is highly prized for gifts, however, and you may be able to talk somebody out of a pinch or two.

In and around the nondescript village of **Waimea**, the former Polynesian capital of the island, there are three "musts," at least two of which don't impress us a lot. (If you're running late, we suggest saving them all for the return trip, pushing on instead toward Kekaha and Kokee.)

The first of the three is the old **Russian Fort**, a pile of lava stones on your left, about 5½ miles from the junction of Highway 543. It was built in 1817 in the shape of a six-pointed star by a German doctor named Georg Anton Scheffer, who was also a former Moscow policeman and international adventurer. Although built ostensibly for Kaumualii, the King of Kauai, it flew the Russian flag over its 30-foot-thick walls.

Scheffer also built a Russian fort in Honolulu where the Aloha Tower now stands, leaving the capital only with "Fort Street" today as a reminder. And there were two more Russian forts built by Scheffer near the Waioli River on Kauai's north shore, but those have virtually eroded away.

At any rate the czar never backed up his ambitious Hessian, being more interested in Russia's well-established colonies in Alaska. Scheffer and his soldiers eventually left. For some unknown reason, King Kaumualii continued to fly the Russian flag over the structure for a number of years.

So the tumble-down fort remains symbolic of what might have been.

Just past the bridge over the Waimea River, you may turn left toward Lucy Wright Park to see **Captain Cook's Landing**, a spot on the beach now denoted by an unimpressive marker. Captain James Cook discovered the Sandwich Islands just about here, stepping on the sand just at the river's mouth at about 3:30 in the afternoon, January 20, 1778.

Off the highway, on Menehune Road opposite the suspension bridge, about 1½ miles in is a low, mysterious structure, most of which has long ago been buried in the thoughtless construction of the road. The Peekauai Ditch, now generally known as the **Menehune Ditch**, is said to be the work of this strange, small race, built either prior to the arrival of the Polynesians or, according to one account, at the bidding of the Hawaiians when the Menehunes lived on Kauai as a low-caste people.

That legend says a Hawaiian king named Pe, who sought to improve low-land irrigation, hired the Menehunes to build the aquaduct. As usual, the Menehunes completed the job during one night, and they received a *luau* of shrimp as a reward. With great joy, they returned to the mountains back of Puukapele and their shouts are still recalled in an old Hawaiian chant: "The hum of the voices of the Menehune at Puukapele, Kauai, startled the birds at the pond of Kawainui at Koolaupoku, Oahu."

We happen to live not far from the pond of Kawainui on Oahu and we can state with some assurance that there would have to be lots of Menehunes for their hum to carry more than 130 miles. At any rate, they were marvelous stonemasons, and archeologists agree that the Hawaiians were not capable of building such sophisticated cut and keyed masonry. It is also doubtful the work could have been performed with stone tools, which gives rise to even greater mysteries. Look for the stone wall; many drive up here and miss the whole point of the place.

We'd recommend going on Route 50 as far as **Kekaha** before turning on Route 55 toward Kokee. (Better not take the road *up* from Waimea because of cane truck traffic.) Check your gas gauge; by the time you return to the coast, you'll have traveled about 40 more miles, no mile of which passes a working pump. If you still haven't had lunch, look for the Traveler's Den Restaurant on Kekaha Road, the town's main street. And picnickers should note that this is the last neighborhood with a grocery store, too, before they head up into the mountains.

We don't recommend taking Route 50 to **Barking Sands**, by the way, because you'll be disappointed when the military folks won't let you in. This famous attraction is now part of the Pacific Missile Range, and serves as a reminder that our armed forces have placed much of Hawaii "off limits" to the taxpayers.

The most determined hikers can invade along the beach for some miles, however, since the shore is state of Hawaii land up to the high water mark. You're supposed to slide down a certain sand dune to hear the "woof-woof" of a German Shepherd. And they say that you can also pick up some of the sand, clap it together, and produce something like the "yap-yap" of a Chihuahua. The sand includes ground-up coral and lava, and that's the secret of its "bark." But on top of every other difficulty, it's supposed to sound off only on a very dry day.

On the way up, up, up Route 55, you will eventually catch a good view of isolated **Niihau**, about 17 miles out into the ocean. Called the "Forbidden Island," it is the last example of old—really old—Hawaii. Fewer than 250 people live there, virtually all of whom are pure-blooded Hawaiians. They still speak Hawaiian in day-to-day conversation, although their English has improved since the invention of the transistor radio. There is no electricity—nor telephone, television, guns, doctors, liquor, and jails—on Niihau. All these are forbidden.

Visitors are absolutely *not* welcome, but this time it's not the military which declares the *kapu*. Nor is it the Hawaiian *paniolos* you'll see waving happily if you fly over Niihau by helicopter. Since 1864, the entire 72-

square-mile island has been owned by one *haole* family, and all the Hawaiians work on their ranch. Contrary to legend, the residents of this
twentieth-century semi-serfdom *may* move back and forth, although
some who did leave reportedly had difficulties competing in modern life
and returned to the island permanently to tend the cattle and sheep or
gather wild honey.

Sights there must be on the Forbidden Island. A unique white coral
heiau is rumored to survive in good condition there. And the island
contains Hawaii's only large (841 acres) natural lake. But few non-
Hawaiians have visited Niihau—including us.

Eleven miles up the road from Kekaha at a fork in the road, an HVB
warrior sign indicates the main lookout for **Waimea Canyon**. Park the
car and take the steps to experience a startling sight for such a small
tropical island. Mark Twain called the chasm the "Grand Canyon of the
Pacific." That's an exaggeration, but its size and depth are still amazing.

The opposite side of the canyon is broken into three enormous tribu-
tary canyons, giving some added depth to this panorama. There are
many colors at midday with pinks, greens, and browns predominating.
Later in the day, purples, blues, and lavenders usually take over the
scene.

To your left you may see the distant Waipoo Falls tumbling 800 feet
over a cliff, its narrow flow disappearing behind a hill before it hits bottom. There is seldom any wind, and if there are few people at the lookout you'll be impressed with the overwhelming quiet of it all. You can
sometimes see the ribbon-like Waimea Stream about 3,000 feet below,
but everything is so far away that there is neither sound nor movement.
The only motion you can perceive will be the flight of the long-tailed,
white *koai* birds as they scout out the crevices and pillars.

Waimea Canyon alone is worth the 38-mile trip from Lihue, but we
think the very best is a little farther along the same road.

Push on another 8 miles into **Kokee State Park** (Tel. 335-5871). There
in the forest you will find a restaurant, rental cabins (see Section 4), a
natural history museum and many hiking trails, including some which
traverse the 30-square-mile **Alakai Swamp**. From mid-June until early
August, you may pick up to the limit of ten pounds of the delicious
Kokee plums which grow in the park. Some folks come all the way from
Honolulu to do just that.

But then head for Kokee's crowning glory, the **Kalalau Valley Lookout**, and pray that no cloud will drift along to obscure the view. At an
elevation of 4,000 feet, it is a magnificently impressive panorama over a
vast valley which slopes steeply down to the shore far, very far, in the
distance. To try to describe the hogback cliffs, the lush vegetation, the
distant narrow waterfalls, the feeling of endless space, seems useless.

We had read Jack London's description of the valley and have since looked at many photographs taken from this point, but no writer or photographer has ever managed to capture completely the feeling we received standing right there for the first time.

The Kalalau Valley below you today is completely non-populated, although the natural vegetables, fruits, and other foodstuffs which once supported hundreds of families are still growing there. No highway could ever reach it, and plain old loneliness drew nearly everybody out about a hundred years ago.

Please be warned that despite what you may have heard, there is no trail from here down to the beach. Hikers regularly get into trouble in the area, and in 1978 one man died trying to make it down.

Only experienced mountaineers can enter the valley from Kokee. But almost anyone in good physical condition can make the 18-mile hike to the Kalalau beach from Haena on the north shore, we're told. And from May through September, when the seas are calm, it's fairly easy to land on the beach in a canoe.

Kalalau Valley, by the way, is the setting for the Jack London short story "Koolau, the Leper." In the tale, one man defends his right to live and die with his family alone in Kalalau Valley, killing off one by one the authorities who would ship him away to live alone in the leper colony on Molokai. It's based on a tragic story that took place here around the turn of the century.

On the way back down the mountain, look carefully for the Canyon Rim Road on the left about two-thirds of the way along. (On our last trip it was poorly marked.) It's a twisting and turning route, but a paved road which provides several other views of Waimea Canyon. Drive carefully and you'll end up in the village of Waimea (not Kekaha), so you can see its sights—the Menehune Ditch, Cook's Landing, and the Russian Fort—if you missed them before.

THE NORTH SHORE AND HANALEI—HOME OF BALI HA'I

You definitely will not need your sweater for *this* trip, but you may want to dredge up an ancient Hawaiian curse if you should forget your bathing suit. There's also a rough but famous hiking trail at the end of the road, so you might throw a pair of "sensible" shoes in the car, if not a good set of boots. (Two miles along that trail, incidentally, you may feel more in style streaking into the water *without* any bathing suit.)

The highway runs about 40 miles. Stretches of the route which go along the beaches are in the Wailua and Kapaa areas and on part of the road past Hanalei to Haena. There are beautiful views of oceans and mountains, bays and valleys, and many unmarked beaches which may be reached by well-worn paths. The most intrepid sand-seekers will use this route to find their goal—the beach without a footprint.

Before leaving Lihue on Route 56 (Kuhio Avenue), you might like to turn right into the grounds of **Wilcox Hospital** for a moment. Without leaving your car, you can see there, next to the parking lot, an entire field of photoelectric cells. Today the sun provides virtually all the power needed by this community institution.

About a mile north of town there's a wide spot in the road called **Kapaia**. Turn onto the dusty pavement to your left and wind through the sugar cane fields for a long, dull 4 miles on a narrow road to reach **Wailua Falls**.

Wailua means "twin waters," and if you look over the side of the road, you'll see a double torrent of water throwing itself over an 80-foot cliff. It's particularly dramatic after a heavy rain. The pool at the bottom is ringed with *hala* trees and tropical flowers. There used to be a tricky path down to this basin, but we couldn't find it.

Back on the main highway, the next hamlet is **Hanamaulu**. Stop at the giant gear wheel to see the free museum both outside and inside the battery of old wooden buildings.

Another mile on is the entrance to **Lydgate State Park** on the site of an ancient temple of refuge. The ruin is still there, under the palms next to Wailua River and the sea. It was to this place that a Hawaiian of any rank could run after he had broken a sacred *kapu*. No one could touch him in the temple of refuge, no matter how serious his crime.

Nearby, when the tides remove the sand, there are a group of black rocks bearing mysterious primitive carvings called **petroglyphs**. Some believe they had fairly sophisticated meanings. Other experts say that they are little more than centuries-old doodles.

Back across the main highway, just before the Wailua River bridge, is the **Wailua Marina**, where Smith's Motor Boat Service and the competing Waialeale Boat Tours conduct cruises up the river to the beautiful **Fern Grotto**. (See Section 7 in this chapter.)

Unless you know someone with his own canoe, the only way to reach the grotto is along with scores of other people all in the same boat. Rather cloying music and entertainment are provided along the route and at the site. But the river is lovely, and so is the grotto, where ferns grow upside down and hang from the top of the cave—even if your boat crew does feel compelled to sing the "Hawaiian Wedding Song." Either boat company, incidentally, will arrange a genuine wedding in the Fern Grotto.

The broad Wailua River is known as the only navigable river in the Islands. It was deeper and swifter in times gone by before it was tapped upstream for irrigation. Sailing vessels used to beat their way up the river. During the American Civil War, a northern ship made it over the sandbar to hide on the river while dodging the Confederate ship *Shenandoah*, then thought to be prowling Hawaiian waters.

Almost next door to the Wailua Marina and rapidly becoming one of those "must" commercial parks is **Kauai's Paradise Pacifica** (Tel. 822-4911), a 31-acre botanical collection where you can take a one-hour guided open tram tour or walk around by yourself for as long as you want. There's a couple of strange elements around, like a fake Easter Island statue that looks like former president Nixon and a puce-colored "Filipino Village." The flowers and trees are beautiful and interesting, but we think it's somewhat overpriced at $5 a pop, whether you take the narrated tram or not. If the mosquitoes are not too much in season, the nighttime show is supposed to be pretty good, although we've never seen it personally.

Just across the Wailua River bridge on Route 56 and to the left is the **King's Highway**, so called because his majesty, upon beaching the royal canoe, would be carried to his house while still seated in the craft rather than take the risk that his blue-blooded feet might be soiled by common ground. Today the King's Highway is called Number 580, and it will lead you first to the **Holo-Holo-Ku Heiau**. It's perhaps the oldest *heiau* on Kauai and one of the few such temples in Hawaii where human sacrifices were taken. Look for a huge rock at the southeast corner of the ruins. The blood has washed away, but that was the sacrificial stone.

A few yards away is the **Pohaku-Ho-o Hanau**, a collection of sacred stones where royal women came to give birth to royal babies. The sanded platform in front is thought to be the floor of the shelter built for the expectant *alii wahine*.

Beyond these birthstones at the top of the hill is a famous *heiau* where the Kauai king's house and private temple were situated. Following a trail below the *heiau*, you might come across the famous **Bell Stone**. This one still rings, and the sound you hear is exactly the same as that heard hundreds of years ago bringing news of a noble birth or similar auspicious event. Nevertheless, we've been unsuccessful in rooting this one out. If you find it, please let us know how you did it!

Also on the same road, an HVB warrior marker will tell you where to get a distant view of **Opaekaa Falls**. They might be nicer if you could get closer, but you can't.

Returning to the main road, on your left is the Coco Palms Resort (see "Hotels"), set down in a once-sacred coconut grove formerly owned by the queen of Kauai. Later it served nicely as a copra plantation. The charming little lagoon, around which the resort now holds its evening torch-lighting ceremony, was in ancient times a pond to sweeten and fatten salt-water fish.

A mile north of Wailua and Coco Palms is Waipouli, now the home of the recently constructed **Coconut Plantation** complex. It includes an attractive shopping center called the Plantation Market Place (See "Shopping"). Two hotels are there, the Sheraton Coconut Beach and the Kauai BeachBoy, as well as about three or four restaurants.

Photographers love the village of **Kapaa** farther up the road for its weatherbeaten, false front main streets. Would that it would never change.

Because everybody talks about it, and because there's an HVB marker pointing it out, be aware of a mountain-top configuration visible from Kapaa that's supposed to look like a **Sleeping Giant**. Just like Queen Victoria's Profile on the southern route, this doesn't wake us up, either.

So if you can't make out the Sleeping Giant, have a look later at the somewhat enhanced photograph on the luncheon menu at Coco Palms. There you can see something of what you're supposed to grasp on the mountain. (And the "legend" printed on that menu is as good as any other for justifying the Kauai Gulliver.)

At **Kealia**, about a mile farther along the road, athletic visitors used to search out the **Waipahee Slide**. Unfortunately, this natural rock slide into a pool of water has been closed indefinitely for safety reasons.

Returning to Route 56, the road through the townlet of **Anahola** used to cut through acres and acres of green pineapple fields. But nearly all Kauai pineapples have now *pau*-ed out. More's the pity, because Kauai pineapple has always seemed to us to be about the sweetest grown in the state. It will be some consolation, though, if the land is given over to the raising of the famous Anahola watermelons.

About three-quarters of a mile past Anahola, there's another HVB warrior marker pointing out the **Hole in the Mountain**. This natural feature, which sparked many legends in the old days, was virtually covered by a rock fall in 1981. Unless someone puts forth the effort to dig it out, and it doesn't seem as if they will, the Hole in the Mountain is now a thing of the past.

An unromantic geologist has declared the narrow, serrated crest and the hole through it are the products of "subaerial erosion" which is to say it's been awfully windy up there for a long time.

At **Kilauea**, either on the way out or on the way back, take the two-mile-long road out to the 1913 **Kilauea Lighthouse**, operated by the U.S. Coast Guard, but whose grounds are open to all between noon and 4

P.M. weekdays, and from 8 A.M. to 4 P.M. Sunday. (Closed Saturday.) Perched on a high bluff above a restless and sometimes violent sea, this unusual clamshell lens beacon is the world's largest of its type. Nevertheless, the lighthouse has outlived its usefulness, and it blinked out late in 1976, apparently for good. A smaller beacon nearby now does the job. In spring and summer, the comical red-footed booby birds make their somersault landings near here to nest and raise their young. Other birds are also seen here.

Sadly, the second **Slippery Slide** in this area has also been closed. Farther along is the **Kalihiwai Valley Lookout**, then **Anini Beach**. (Two miles from the highway, this could be your "beach without a footprint" on a weekday.) Swimming is excellent.

The next stopping point is a scenic vista indicated on the left. If you miss it on your way out, don't speed by coming back. The **Hanalei Valley Lookout** is one of the famous views in the Islands. The broad panorama includes taro patches, vegetable crops, sugar cane and a few rice paddies, all bisected by the gleaming Hanalei River, and backdropped by three majestic mountains.

Nearby is **Princeville at Hanalei**, a 1,000-acre recreation community, known especially for its two championship golf courses.

The main road descends a hill, and you'll find yourself crossing the rickety 1912 bridge you probably saw from the Hanalei Valley Lookout. Along the river, you might notice a herd of contented cattle. The far distant mountains sometimes spring forth with dozens of waterfalls, some of which drop a thousand feet or more.

In **Hanalei**, headquarters for members of the counterculture and wealthy escapists, there are two general stores, two restaurants, and one interesting bar (Tahiti Nui). Nick Beck's **Hanalei Museum** (adults $1, children free, irregular hours) has a small and interesting private collection of artifacts gathered from an earlier day.

The **Waioli Mission House**, one of those nineteenth-century New England prefab jobs, was put up here in 1836. It's completely outfitted with period furniture, including a bedwarmer brought around the horn by a missionary wife who just didn't know what to expect of the climate so far from home. Admission is free; visiting hours are approximately 9 to 12 and 1 to 3 Tuesday through Friday. Guided tours are available. Follow the double-track cement driveway through the white picket fence to locate this charming building.

You can swim at the majestic beach on **Hanalei Bay**, but only if you stay near the old pier where waters are calmer. As with any of Hawaii's beaches, it's safer to enter deep water only where you see others doing so. (See Section 8.)

From here on, the road will wind through tiny one-lane bridges and along scores of beautiful beaches. One shoreline you won't want to miss is **Lumahai Beach** on which Mitzi Gaynor vowed to "Wash that Man Right Out of My Hair" in "South Pacific." You'll see it first from on high (sometimes an HVB sign is posted there). There's a steep trail down through the pandanus trees to the sand itself if you want to comb the beach for the little green olivine stones that often wash up there. But swimming is safe on that beach *only in the summer* when the water is calmer and even then *only for the expert.* There is an undertow and the ocean currents are very tricky at this point.

Pass **Haena Beach Park** (*absolutely no swimming*), and you'll see three sets of caves. The first is **Maniniholo Dry Cave** named after the head fisherman of the Menehunes. It's the end of a lava tube running for several hundred yards under the cliff.

About a mile farther are the **Waikapalae and Waikanaloa Wet Caves**. The Hawaiians claim they were dug by Pele, the fire and volcano goddess, when she first sought a home in the Islands. Twice she hit fresh water instead of the fire in the center of the earth, so she moved on. The usual clear water in Waikanaloa mysteriously turns milky from time to time, and no one knows why. We'd skip the one up the steep difficult side road.

The road ends at **Haena Point**, directly in front of Ke'e Beach where there is good, safe swimming and excellent skin diving.

At Haena Point begins the 11-mile trail to Kalalau Valley Beach along the famous and rugged **Na Pali Coast**. Lots of young folks hike along the trail at least 2 miles to the mellow-minded beach called Hanakapiai ("hah-nah-*cop*-pee-eye"), where they often find more people without clothes than with them.

Don't even make the short late trip in the afternoon, however. The trail is treacherous in lengthening shadows and impossible after dark.

For maps and more information on this and other trails on Kauai, write Kauai Forest Reserve Trails, Department of Land and Natural Resources, Division of Forestry, P.O. Box 1671, Lihue, Kauai, Hi. 96766.

7. Guided Tours and Cruises on Kauai

There are five tour bus companies on the island, including three old big-bus standbys with offices at Lihue Airport, and two more laid-back outfits that specialize in small van tours.

Taking the latter two first, **Holo Holo Kauai** (Tel. 245-9134), which made minivan tours popular on Maui, has branched out to the Garden Isle. We've been very happy with their tours on the Valley Island and we imagine they're pretty good over here, too. At this writing, they have an all-day North Coast tour as far as Haena for about $35 per person, a Waimea Canyon and Polihale Beach excursion for about $40, and a few other arrangements. (You can phone 24 hours for information and reservations.)

Next, a husband-wife operation called **Niele Tours** (Tel. 245-8673) is gaining ground on Kauai. Norman and Kathy Valier list several full-day tours at competitive rates. All trips are limited to 12 persons in their air-conditioned minibuses. Call or write the Valiers at P.O. Box 239, Kapaa, Kauai, HI 96746.

The three more traditional companies include **Robert's Hawaii, Inc.** (Tel. 245-3344), now a statewide company for which Kauai was the ancestral stamping ground; **Gray Line Hawaii** (Tel. 245-3344), owned by InterIsland Resorts, but up for sale at last report; and **Kauai Island Tours** (Tel. 245-7777), which may be all right although we don't know much about them.

BOAT CRUISES

Two companies compete on the 3-mile river run to Fern Grotto. **Smith's Motor Boat Service** (Tel. 822-4111) has been in business much longer, and it offers scheduled trips every half-hour daily from 9 A.M. to 4 P.M. Each lasts an hour or a little more and costs $7 for adults and $4 for children under 12. They also cast off on a Hawaiian Night Luau Cruise Tuesday and Thursday at 6:15 P.M. for 2½ hours. Adults are $18 and children $11 for that. For a ticket without a dinner, the price is $12 and $8 respectively. Fares may be up later in the year. The other company is **Waialeale Boat Tours** (Tel. 822-4908). Prices are similar, but many individual travelers prefer this company to avoid the massed battalions that are often booked on the Smith armada during the day.

Several interesting "cruises" are now being offered by Gary and Bob Crane through their **Island Adventures, Inc.** (Tel. 826-9381). We enjoyed Gary's company on their kayak trip up Huleia Stream. The 3-hour tour, one to a boat, includes a box lunch for about $30. (These boats are special models, called "Royaks," and are much less likely to tip than the traditional Eskimo variety.) The brothers also offer trips on the Kalihi Wai River up to a waterfall on the North Shore and a paddle/snorkeling tour at Haena, neither of which we've taken yet.

Unusual excursions are also offered by **Na Pali Zodiac** (Tel. 826-9371), taking passengers in rubber boats to virtually inaccessible beaches and coves along the rugged Na Pali Coast. Four trips include the Morning Excursion for $40; Camper Drop-off at Kalalau Valley for $40 one way, $75 round trip; Day Expedition for $70; and the Sunset Cruise for $40. (Children's prices are about 25 percent less.) We have yet to make the trip ourselves, but reports are favorable. You can write them at P.O. Box 456, Hanalei, HI 96714. Tell 'em we sent you.

Some more conventional trips on the ocean this year may include sailing aboard the 45-foot catamaran **Kalapaki Kai II** (Tel. 245-3631, Ext. 7666). Several cruises run into Kalapaki Bay from the Kauai Surf Hotel. Also the **International Sailing Academy** (Tel. 245-9290) is on the same bay offering lessons, rentals, and rides in hobie cats and other small boats.

BIRD'S-EYE VIEWS

The popularity of Kauai helicopter flights over the past several years has resulted in a proliferation of competing companies offering tours in and out of some of the most spectacular scenery in the Pacific.

The companies buzzing around at this writing all fly four- or six-passenger Bell Jet Rangers, headquartered at different airports and heliports around the island. You can either charter the entire aircraft, for $400 or so per hour, or you can buy tours on a per-seat basis.

Here are some sample tours, and our guesses as to their length and current fares (they will vary depending on the location of pickup points, of course):

Waialeale Crater, 15 minutes, $35. Na Pali Coast, 20 minutes, $45. Waimea Canyon, 30 minutes, $60. Around the entire island, including all the above and other areas, 45 minutes, $90.

Corporate and personnel changes may be made so rapidly in helicopter companies that it's difficult to recommend any one over the others. However, we will say that the granddaddy of the chopper firms is **Jack Harter Helicopters** (Tel. 245-3774). Harter's wife is a professional photographer, and he's used to covering all the good angles. **Kenai Helicopters** (Tel. 245-8591), a statewide firm, is also popular and usually good (although we had one letter from a passenger who severely criticized his flight). **Island Helicopters Kauai** (Tel. 245-8588), a one-man operation, was set up after its owner split with Kenai. **South Sea Helicopters** (Tel. 245-7781) and **Menehune Helicopters** (Tel. 245-7705) are two newer firms we know very little about.

Helicopters can be nice any place in Hawaii, but somehow Kauai retains the reputation as the most fun in a chopper—*if*, of course, you can stand the financial altitude.

At this writing, there is also one fixed-wing sightseeing plane in operation available through **Kauai Adventures** (Tel. 245-6035). Advertising a three-passenger Cessna, the firm lists fares per person varying from $25 through $65. We know absolutely nothing about them—including whether they'll still be in operation after the ink dries on these pages.

8. Water Sports on Kauai

There are at least 23 major beaches and bays on the island, but not all of them are safe beyond the shoreline. Generally, the north shore is best for winter surfing and summer swimming. The south shore is the opposite—fine for a summer surf and for milder winter swimming. Obviously there are several exceptions, and the east side is good off and on for both water activities the year around. There are few, if any, good locations for snorkeling or scuba diving on Kauai. Here are some of the beaches:

Anahola Beach Park. Excellent swimming and wading; good skin diving; good surfing a long way out; fishing and shelling okay; barbecue pits and picnic tables; tent camping only.

Anini Beach. Excellent swimming and wading; well protected; good skin diving; winter surf for experts only; reportedly great torch fishing; shelling; barbecue pit and picnic tables; tent camping only.

Haena Beach Park. Swimming positively unsafe! (But there is good swimming and good skin diving at Ke'e, a little farther at the end of the highway.) Fishing; shelling; picnic tables; barbecue pits; tent and mobile camping permitted.

Hanalei Beach Park. Swimming safe at the old landing only; excellent surfing early morning and late afternoon; tables, barbecue pits, and pavilion; tent camping only.

Hanamaulu Beach Park. Former water pollution problems said to be corrected; poor skin diving; shelling okay; tables, pits, and pavilion; playground; tent and mobile camping permitted.

Kapaa Beach Park. Good swimming; fishing; tables, barbecue pits, and pavilions; tent and mobile camping permitted.

Kekaha Beach Park. Rough surf; strong ocean currents; tables, pits, pavilion, and playground; tent camping only.

Lydgate State Park. Good swimming; picnic tables; barbecue pits; no tent camping due to problems with local bullies.

Lumahai Beach. Not recommended for swimming. Beachcombers look for small, green olivine crystals in the sand here.

Na Pali Coast. Dangerous swimming everywhere, especially in winter.

Nawiliwili Park. Excellent swimming at Kalapaki Bay; good for beginning surfers; fishing; picnic tables and barbecue pits.

Poipu Beach Park. Good swimming and skin diving; excellent body surfing here and at nearby Brennecke's Beach; fishing; shelling.

Polihale State Park. Good swimming in summer; hazardous in winter; fishing; shelling; tables and barbecue pits; tent camping only.

Salt Pond. Good swimming; occasional summer surfing; shelling; fishing; tables, barbecue pits, and pavilions; tent camping only.

Wailua Beach. Good swimming; good beginners' surf when waves are small; dangerous when surf is big due to strong currents.

SCUBA AND SNORKELING INSTRUCTION

Some of the best snorkeling and skin-diving waters in Hawaii are in Kauai, and now there are five diving firms to help you enjoy them.

We were very impressed with the efficient yet fun-loving operation run by Terry O'Halloran and Barbara Brundage at **Fathom Five** (Tel. 742-6991) from modest headquarters next to the Chevron station in Koloa. Snorkeling lessons and tours start at $20, and introductory scuba runs $55 for a half-day trip. Other dependable outfits include **Kauai Divers** (Tel. 742-1580), also in Koloa, and the three headquartered in or near Kapaa, **Sea Sage Diving Center** (Tel. 822-3841) at 4-1378 Kuhio Highway, **Aquatics Kauai** (Tel. 822-8422) at 4-733 Kuhio Highway, and **Ocean Odyssey** (Tel. 822-9680) in the Coconut Plantation Market Place.

9. Other Sports

There are five golf courses on Kauai. The most famous and beautiful is the **Princeville Makai Golf and Country Club** (Tel. 826-6891), site of the 26th World Cup Golf championship tournament in 1978 and 1979. The 27 holes will soon be augmented by 36 more (all designed by Robert Trent Jones). Several packages are available with accommodations. (Call the "800" number in the appendix for details.) The new **Kiahuna Plantation Golf Course** (Tel. 742-9595) has just opened the last 9 of its 18. The county-supported **Wailua Golf Course** (Tel. 245-2163), which you won't book through a travel agent, is a sleeper. Golfing writer Grady Timmons has reported that the back nine may be the best nine holes in the state. The **Kauai Surf Golf & Country Club** (Tel. 245-3631) is high on a windy peninsula at Nawiliwili. For us duffers, there's the 9-hole **Kukuiolono Park Golf Course** (Tel. 332-9151), which charges reasonable green fees; a cart is optional.

Tennis. Several hotels have courts which are available (usually free) only to their guests. Free public courts are open in the villages of Lihue, Kalaheo, Kapaa, Hanapepe, Koloa, and Waimea.

Hotels which have courts available to non-guests, too, include Coco Palms (Tel. 822-4921), the Kauai Surf (Tel. 245-3631), Kiahuna Plantation (Tel. 742-6411), the Princeville Makai Tennis Courts (Tel. 826-6561), and the Hanalei Bay Resort (Tel. 826-6522).

Kauai has two riding stables: the **Highgates Ranch** at Wailua Homestead (Tel. 822-3182), where a reader suggests asking for "Rose," and **Po'oku Stables** (Tel. 826-6777) at Princeville. Both charge about $7 per hour. Either may have special picnic, moonlight, breakfast rides, etc.

Hiking enthusiasts should write the Kauai Forest Reserve Trails, Department of Land and Natural Resources, Division of Forestry, P.O. Box 1671, Lihue, Kauai, Hi. 96766, to ask for lists and maps of trails on Kauai. Permits are not needed for hiking, but you must have them for camping. They're free for state parks, however, and available from the above office in the State Building, corner of Hardy and Elua streets in Lihue. Camping permits for county parks cost $3 per person per night and are issued at the Kauai War Memorial Convention Hall, 4191 Hardy St., Monday–Friday, or by the police department after hours. Kauai Kops, incidentally, are notoriously merciless if you have no permit.

Non-resident hunting licenses are available for $15 from the same State Department and address as the above, except it's the Fish and Game Division you go to see. They'll bring you up to date on the latest regulations, bag limits, and seasons for wild goats, wild boar, blacktail deer, pheasant, quail, doves, and partridge. (There is no commercial hunting guide service on Kauai.)

10. Garden Island Shopping

There is not a lot for sale on Kauai that you won't also find—usually cheaper—in Honolulu. There are now seven main shopping complexes: The **Lihue Shopping Center** in the center of town, the **Rice Shopping Center**, a group of sixteen shops congregated at 4303 Rice St., the new and snazzy **Kukui Grove Center**, just out of Lihue off Route 50, the **Menehune Village** at Nawiliwili just across from the Kauai Surf Hotel, the **Market Place at Coconut Plantation**, now more than 60 shops among the three hotels and several restaurants at Waipouli, the **Princeville Shopping Center**, an 1800s-style, wood-frame architecture center, which is bringing some life to the Princeville resort up near Hanalei, and the new **Ching Young Village** in Hanalei itself near the old Ching Young general store.

Many hotels have shops on the premises, but remember that in Kauai, as elsewhere, hotel shops usually must recover more from their customers in order to pay for higher real estate costs.

ARTS AND HANDICRAFT

Hawaiian art by island artists is sold in the **Makai Art Village** (Tel. 245-4580) in the Kauai Surf Hotel. Oils run from $10 to $400, and water colors from $30 to $175.

The Kauai Museum Gift Shop (Tel. 245-6931), 4220 Rice St., offers imported Polynesian and local handicraft, jewelry, shell leis, and Hawaiiana books and prints. You need not pay the entrance fee to the museum to visit its shop.

On the *makai* side of the highway north of Hanamaulu, the **Hard-wood Factory** (Tel. 245-2061) carves its products only in the workshop to the rear and sells them in the display room out front. If you visit at just the right moment, you can watch them cutting up a giant *koa* log on the ancient outdoor sawmill. Prices run from about $2 for a small, papaya-shaped dish up to $400 or so for a resin-coated monkeypod coffee table. One reader, who thought their products rather ordinary, liked instead the offerings at the **Kong Lung Store** (Tel. 828-1731) in Kilauea.

Rehabilitation Unlimited Kauai (Tel. 822-4975), across Highway 580 from the Coco Palms Hotel, invites visitors into its workshops where the handicapped manufacture coconut, *lauhala*, and shell products. Prices run from about 75 cents to $30. Open Monday through Friday, 8 A.M. to 4:30 P.M. Closed Saturday and Sunday.

HAWAIIAN WEAR

The **Happy Kauaian** now seems to have branches scattered every-where over the island. The traditional old-timer is **Tad & Mary's**, which has moved from Lihue to the Kukui Grove Center. In Kapaa, **Marta's Boat** (Tel. 822-3926) is mainly a mother/child boutique. In the Kukui Grove Center, we thought **Deja Vu** a rather strange name for a clothing store until we realized that indeed we had seen most of their fashions before.

BOOKSTORES

Competing on opposite sides of the mall at Kukui Grove are **Walden-books** (Tel. 245-7162) and **Rainbow Books**, which shares digs with a cof-fee shop and art gallery. They are obviously run by sage business people, since we saw copies of the Maverick series at both of them! (Tell 'em we sent you.)

DEPARTMENT STORES

The island's only homegrown department store, Kauai Stores, has now bit the dust. Opposite ends of the Kukui Grove Center are anchored with **Liberty House**, a branch of the Honolulu firm, of course, and **Sears, Roebuck and Co.**, of Chicago and points north, south, east, and west. A planned opening of Penney's at Kukui Grove was postponed, like many projects, in the economic fallout following Hurricane Iwa.

SOUVENIRS

For the general run of gimcrackery, you'll still find the best prices at **Woolworth's**, now moved over to the Kukui Grove Center.

The barnlike structure at the junction of Highways 50 and 53, formerly called the Tourist Trap, then the Hawaiian Trading Post, has now been sold again and is called the **Paradise Trading Co**. We liked the original title best for its honesty.

11. Nights on the Town on Kauai

Few come to Kauai to "make the scene," and if they do, they must have gotten it mixed up with somewhere else. Most folks say that Kauai after dark is just that—dark. There are a few up-beat and shiny exceptions, however.

The **Golden Cape Lounge**, on the top floor of the Kauai Surf Hotel and across the foyer from the restaurant of the same name, is a popular night spot. Bill Lucidarme and his trio or quartet will no doubt still be there from about 10 P.M. till 2 A.M. No cover charge.

The **Planter's Lounge** in the same hotel has a Polynesian show some nights. The bar is made from four cars of a tiny plantation train. Also in the Kauai Surf, the **Destination**, formerly a top disco, had been turned into a sort of sing-along piano bar the last time we swung through.

In Waipouli, you'll find the disco formerly called the Observatory when it was started by a Kauai optometrist. Perhaps it set its sights too high, for it's now been sold and renamed the **Vanishing Point**. It's still popular enough, probably because it's one of the very few spots on the island open until 4 A.M. It's upstairs over Waipouli Chop Suey.

The **Club Jetty**, right on the pier at Nawiliwili, is a local institution. It's the oldest nightclub on Kauai, it looks it, and it's better for it. There's a Polynesian show about 9:30 P.M., and dancing after that (the owner, Auntie Betty, becomes the deejay). Sometimes it imports modern musical groups from Taiwan, Japan, Hong Kong, the Philippines, etc. Note the sign declaring: "Barefoot Dancing Prohibited." The fact that they have to put up such a sign in the first place tells you a lot about the Jetty in the second place. Open until about 4 A.M. Closed Tuesday. We like it for its special atmosphere.

You may find good Polynesian shows at the **Kahili Room** in the Kauai Resort Hotel, or in the open longhouse at the Sheraton Coconut Beach, but this scene can change quickly. Lately the **Paddle Room** at the S.C.B. has been experimenting with dinner theater on Wednesday and Sunday with the local thespians putting on Neil Simon plays and the like. (Do not confuse this Sheraton with the other one at Poipu Beach.)

The buffet luau at **Kauai's Paradise Pacifica** (Tel. 822-4911) may still be sold only in conjunction with daytime admissions to the gardens or the nighttime Polynesian show in the amphitheater. Better recheck.

The piano bar in the **Jolly Roger** restaurant, at the Coconut Plantation, is popular with the 20s and 30s crowd. Nearby, the **Hale Kai Boogie Palace Bar**, a mouthful in the Kauai BeachBoy Hotel, usually starts throwing out hard rock music into the night after 9:30. Sometimes live shows are brought in, too.

The shining nighttime star in Hanalei is generally the **Tahiti Nui**, which serves up local entertainment on a spontaneous basis. Songs are mainly Hawaiian, but its female owner is an expert in Tahitian melodies, too. This is a favorite bar with a hip, local crowd, and when it's hot, it's hot.

12. The Lihue Address List

Art Supplies—The Art Shop, 3196 Akahi St. Tel. 245-3810.

Barber—Benny's Barber Shop, 3204C Kuhio Hwy. Tel. 245-6062.

Beauty Salon—Towne House Beaute Salon, 103A Lihue Shopping Center. Tel. 245-2293.

Camper Rentals—Beach Boy Campers, Nawiliwili. Tel. 245-3866.

Chamber of Commerce—2970 Kele St. Tel. 245-4920.

Dry Cleaners—Up-To-Date, 3088 Akahi St. Tel. 245-6621.

Fire Department—4223 Rice St. Tel. 245-2222. (Emergency: 911.)

Fishing Supplies—Lihue Fishing Supply, 2985 Kalena. Tel. 245-4930.

Florist—Pua Lani Florist, 4444 Rice St. Tel. 245-4717.

Hawaii Visitors Bureau—3016 Umi St. Tel. 245-3971.

Hospital—Wilcox Hospital, 3420 Kuhio Hwy. Tel. 245-4811.

Laundromat—Lihue Washerette, lower level, Lihue Shopping Center.

Pharmacy—Longs Drug Store, Kukui Grove Center. Tel. 245-7771.

Police Headquarters—3060 Umi St. Tel. 245-9711. (Emergency: 911.)

Post Office—4441 Rice St. Tel. 245-4994.

Public Library—Main Branch, 4344 Hardy St. Tel. 245-3617.

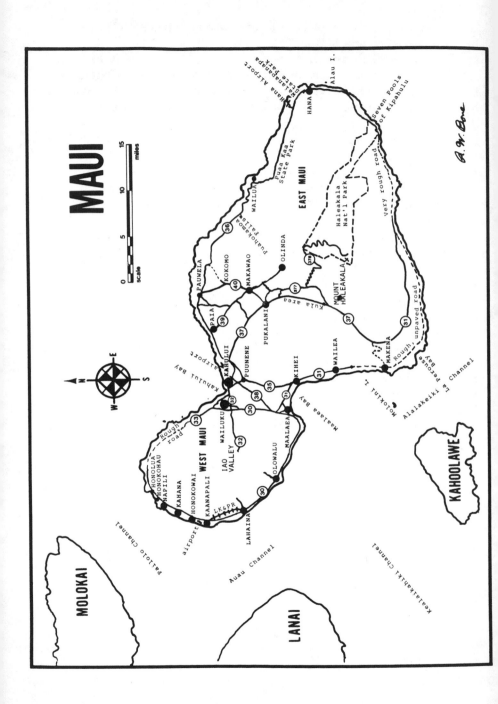

7

Maui,
the Valley Island

1. Around the Island—the Beauty of Success

Local pride flatly sums up Maui in an often-seen declaration: *Maui no ka oi!* In older and more warlike times the phrase was translated as "Maui over all!" Today it simply means "Maui is the best!"

Maui is certainly a three-way favorite. First, it attracts more visitors than any other Neighbor Island. Second, it is the fastest-growing island in the state; its population stands at 70,000, having taken a 60 percent jump over the last decade.

Third, its economic future looks particularly bright. Although the other islands are phasing out their traditional sugar and pineapple plantations in greater or lesser degrees, Maui continues to produce these products in relative abundance. Maui is also particularly suited to raising several other kinds of agricultural products.

Some worry about Maui's rapid growth, predicting mistakes that would create a hodgepodge of uncontrolled development. But blessed with some cool heads, the county and the builders have so far managed to make generally high-quality plans for both vacationers and residents.

Maui is the second largest of the Islands in land area. It measures nearly 729 square miles, 120 square miles more than Oahu, where Honolulu is located. Yet Maui numbers less than one-tenth the population of Oahu. All things considered, Maui is lucky that the king moved the capital from Lahaina, Maui, to Honolulu back in 1843.

As every Island has its sobriquet, Maui is known as the "Valley Island."

In recent years it has been explained that because Maui was created by two massive volcanoes, an isthmus appeared between them and that this is the "valley" of the Valley Island. But this effect occurs on Oahu and the Big Island, too.

Author Stanley Porteus was more likely correct forty years ago when he said the old Mauians nicknamed their island for the Iao Valley, the dramatic green slash that cuts nearly to the heart of the ancient West Maui volcano and that figured so prominently in the island's history. There thousands died when Kamehameha the Great, with the help of his *haole* technical advisers and their cannon, finally decimated the defending army of Maui after trapping it in that exitless gorge.

Topographically, the island displays three great natural characteristics: the incredibly rugged, often impassable, and largely unexplored mountains of West Maui; the low ground in its center on which are planted the towns of Wailuku and Kahului and thousands of acres of sugar cane; and the massive, sleeping volcano of Haleakala (pronounced "holly-ah-kah-*lah*"), whose cool and rarefied summit looks down 10,023 feet to the warm ocean below.

It's been said that residents of Maui may choose their climate. They can live in Lahaina, whose name means "merciless sun." Lahaina is warmer much of the year because steep, brooding mountains block it from the cool trade winds. These refreshing breezes do reach Kaanapali just three miles away, however. And they ventilate Napili, a few miles farther on, even more.

The trades also sweep the central isthmus most of the year. And the farther you drive up Haleakala, the cooler it gets, winter or summer. On the fertile slopes grow Mainland fruits, vegetables, and flowers which would never survive at tropical sea level. Here are the delicious Maui onions, russet potatoes, rows of rosebushes, and fields of African protea blossoms.

Some years, perhaps in February or March, it really does snow atop Haleakala, transforming that already beautiful but desolate landscape into a white, nonobjective sculpture unduplicated anywhere else in nature.

Last, those who seek the lushness of a rain forest, or perhaps a tropical version of a green Irish countryside, may settle at Hana. The village and its surrounding area receive an annual rainfall of more than 70 inches, almost all of which blessedly falls during the night.

The island is named after the demigod Maui, whose exploits are celebrated in the legends of all Polynesian peoples. In Hawaii, his fame was assured after he ascended Haleakala (literally, "House of the Sun") one night, determined to set a lower speed limit for the sun's trip across the sky. As the sun arose from its house, Maui took careful aim and lassoed the hot beast by its genitals, not releasing it until it promised to proceed more slowly in the future. This fantastic feat was accomplished mainly so Maui's mother would have more time to dry her tapa cloth in the sun's rays.

The sun told its captor it would take it easy henceforth, and it may now be safe to say that the whole world benefited from Maui's imposed daylight saving time. Today you may ascend the House of the Sun, wait for the dawn, and watch the sun lift himself from his bed at the end of the sky. It's one of the most beautiful, moving events on earth.

2. The Maui Airports

The Valley Isle has three airports, including the state-run fields at Kahului (for jet traffic) and Hana (prop planes only), and for the moment, at least, the private airstriplet in the luxury hotel area of Kaanapali (pronounced "kah-ah-nah-*pah*-lee"). Like Hana's, it operates only by day. All these handle scheduled interisland flights.

The island's main terminal, which is often hopelessly overcrowded, is at **Kahului Airport** in the flatland between Maui's two mountainous areas. Distances will be important on Maui, so remember that these runways are 2 road miles from the Kahului business district, 5 miles from Wailuku, 9 miles from Kihei, 15 miles from Wailea, 25 miles from Lahaina, 29 miles from Kaanapali, and 35 miles from Napili/Kapalua.

Kahului is the only Maui airport that operates at night. But unless you're going to your hotel by taxi or shuttle, plan your landing in full daylight, leaving enough time to rent a car and find your hotel before dusk. The first time we set foot on Maui, we had one dickens of a time finding Kaanapali after a long drive in the dark and in the rain.

Over 1984 and 1985, the Kahului terminal will be going through a massive expansion program with as-yet-untold effects. As of the day before yesterday, anyway, here was the layout of the terminal:

It is basically one large room, completely open on the side away from the runways, like an outsize Hawaiian *lanai*. The Hawaiian Air baggage carrousel is in the west. Aloha Airlines' and Mid Pacific's baggage claim is under an overhang outside the building on the west wall. The check-in counters for Aloha Airlines (Tel. 244-9071) and Hawaiian Airlines (Tel. 244-9111) are on the east wall. A Hawaii state visitors' information kiosk is in the center of the building, almost under the Chinese banyan tree. Agricultural inspection counters for Mainland-bound passengers are between the tree and Aloha's check-in.

The airport restaurant is up the stairs on the east side, above the Hawaiian departure lounge; the snack counter (maybe a dollar for a small glass of guava juice), the souvenir shop, and the news kiosk are on the west side. The lei stand (which sometimes sells Maui onions and pineapples) is next to the carrousel.

Also near that baggage wheel is a lighted board offering free telephone service to some hotels and to rental car agencies that do not have booths at the airport. Through the nearby door—on the outside of the building—you'll find the booths for about a dozen U-drives that *are* there, as well as other counters serving a taxi company and a tour agency or two. Check-in counters for Mid Pacific Airlines (Tel. 242-4906) and United Airlines (Tel. 244-7602) are on the south, or runway side, wall next to the new Aloha departure lounge wing—Gates 6 to 11. Headquarters for the small commuter airlines such as Royal Hawaiian Air Service (Tel. 244-3977) and Princeville Airways (Tel. 242-9661) are outdoors, a short walk away in a tiny wooden building just past the control tower.

Fifty twisting road miles and more than two hours of hard driving from Kahului Airport is the **Hana Airport** (Tel. 248-8208). By light plane, the two strips are less than 15 minutes apart. There's not much at the Hana terminal but a check-in counter for Royal Hawaiian Air Service (Tel. 248-8328), a drinking fountain, two rest rooms, and benches (choice of outdoor or indoor).

If the Hotel Hana Maui or the Hana Kai Resort is expecting you, there will be a hotel minibus to pick you up from the airport. Or you can order a rental car from either of these two hotels to meet you at the terminal. Otherwise you're on your own, 4 miles from the village. (Special note to backpackers, however. It's only a short hike from Hana Airport to Waianapanapa State Park, where camping is permitted and where cabins are for rent if there's a vacancy.)

Maui's third airstrip, a private beachside runway seemingly created by mowing down a narrow swath of sugar cane, is the **Kaanapali Airport** (Tel. 661-3132), accepting interisland flights only from the Cessna 402s of the Royal Hawaiian Air Service. In contrast to Hana, there's some lively activity surrounding this modest little structure nestled in a grove of palms. You'll find four or five rental car stands, counters for Royal Hawaiian (Tel. 661-0548) and Kenai Helicopters (661-4426), a regular jitney service to the nearby hotels, and the little Windsock cocktail lounge up the carpeted spiral staircase.

Last year Amfac Resorts, which owns the airport property, announced that the facility would be closed so that it could build two hotels and a condo there. However, there has been a temporary reprieve for the strip until a new location is decided on farther *mauka*, and aerial operations are moved there. We can only hope the Kaanapali Airport's atmosphere is carried over there, too.

3. Transportation on Maui

By taxi, it will cost you about $20 for the long run between Kahului Airport and your Lahaina or Kaanapali hotel. If four persons take the cab and share it equally, the rate is better—about the same or less per person as **Grayline** (Tel. 667-9005) will charge you for a seat on the bus.

But for that $20, or a little more, you can rent a car and drive it yourself for 24 hours. Automobile rental turns out to be the best transportation bargain on Maui, since the distance between the airport and the most popular hotels is so great.

Car rental on Maui is such a fiercely competitive and volatile industry that the rates and companies seem to change daily. At last count there were no less than forty-five (honest—45!) different rental car companies on the island. We have never seen fewer than thirty such companies there at a time. This competition serves more to confuse the picture than to clarify it. But if you are searching for the lowest rates, the principle remains the same: Pick a company that has no address in the airport high-rent district. (The heck of it is that even if you do choose a company from among the rental car booths on the property, you will probably have to be vanned to the company's parking lot a mile or two away from the airport, anyway.) And if you're planning to bring your car back late, be sure to find out if the rental agency closes before your flight out.

Here's a piece of advice from Dave Donnelly, the well-driven columnist for the Honolulu *Star-Bulletin*: Don't rent a standard-shift car if you're planning to twist and turn over the 50-mile route to Hana. "So I saved a buck, but 2½ hours later I was a basket case!"

Speaking of Hana, it is virtually impossible to rent a car there unless you are a guest at one of the two main hotel operations.

During peak periods—June through August and December through March—it's pretty risky to arrive on Maui without advance reservations for cars. Following is a list of some of the better-known companies. As we said, there are a lot more, but these have all been around for a few years. All these except Tropical, Kamaaina, Tom's, El Cheap-O, and Rent-A-Wreck have offices at Kahului Airport. All but Tom's, Rent-A-Wreck, and El Cheap-O have Honolulu offices with numbers listed in the Oahu directory, so you can make reservations before leaving the capital. The Maui numbers, however, are given here:

American International Rent-a-Car (Tel. 877-7604); **Avis Rent A Car** (Tel. 871-7575); **Budget Rent A Car** (Tel. 871-8811); **El Cheap-O Rent-A-Car** (Tel. 877-5851); **Hertz Rent A Car** (Tel. 877-5167); **Holiday Rent-a-Car** (Tel. 877-2464), a new one, but perhaps a good bet; **Kamaaina Rent-a-Car** (Tel. 877-5460), a Maui outfit that sometimes has good summer rates; **National Car Rental System** (Tel. 877-5347), which still gives Green Stamps; **Rent-A-Wreck** (Tel. 877-5600), which offers used cars for rent; **Robert's Hawaii Rent-A-Car** (Tel. 877-5038); **South Seas Rent-A-Car** (Tel. 877-6568), now under new and better management; **Tom's Car Rentals** (Tel. 871-7721); and **Tropical Rent-A-Car Systems** (Tel. 877-0002), a personal favorite throughout the state.

MOTORCYCLES AND BICYCLES

The new motorized bicycles (no license required) have invaded Maui. **Go-Go Bikes Hawaii** (Tel. 661-3063) are racked up at each of the four big hotels in Kaanapali. They putt out for perhaps $15 a day. Some of the Go-Go stands also rent conventional pedal bikes for $5 a day. In Lahaina, try the **South Seas Moped Rental** (Tel. 661-8655). It's parked at 1248 Front St., in the "historical Lahaina cannery."

There are some special bike paths on Maui, by the way. One well-used trail has now been paved all the way from Lahaina to the Kaanapali resort area. Nevertheless, Maui motorcyclist Ron Youngblood, an avid hog and chopper addict, points out that in other areas—like the central valley and places such as Olowalu and Pukalani—any kind of two-wheeler will have to fight winds that habitually gust at speeds up to 40 miles per hour.

DRIVING ON MAUI

You'll feel safer with a four-wheel-drive vehicle—a Jeep, a Bronco, or a Land Cruiser (a sort of Japanese Jeep)—if you're planning to drive the rough northern route on West Maui or the rougher portions of the southern route on East Maui, either one a piece of potentially axle-busting terrain. These dirt roads, incidentally, are prohibited to you under normal rental car contracts, so if you break down on them, you'll have to bear all the expenses.

Except for the teeth-rattlers just mentioned, the main roads on Maui are as well maintained or better than those on Oahu. There are usually two lanes only, however, and you'll find no real divided highways on the island. Local drivers are generally considerate; many other drivers seem confused, since there are so many cars driven by visitors to the Valley Isle. And for some reason or other we see more cars on Maui with one headlight out than on other islands.

The road to Hana (Highway 36) is feared by some for its 617 twists and turns, and the possibility that a landslide might block the road in rainy weather. Any one of its miles of splendiferous views also may distract a driver from his steering wheel.

And when going up Haleakala, remember that you will end up at 10,000 feet, which is high enough to make some folks feel a little woozy from the rarefied atmosphere. We never take that trip without another driver in the car.

Driving to Kaanapali, be aware that the resort has three entrances off the Honoapiilani Highway, 3 miles past Lahaina. Take the third entrance for the airport and the Maui Kaanapali condominium. Take the second for the Royal Lahaina Hotel. Take the first for everything else.

OTHER FORMS OF TRANSPORTATION

There is no genuine public transportation on Maui. Between the Airport and Wailea, you can catch the **Grayline Wailea Shuttle** (Tel. 877-5507), which will take you to Wailea (the Inter-Continental and Westin hotels) for $6 a seat. Over in West Maui, the little outfit called **Shoreline Transportation** (Tel. 661-3827) runs from Lahaina about every half-hour through the Kaanapali hotels, shopping areas, and airport, and then sometimes as far out as Napili for fares of around $2 per seat. Then there's the **Kaanapali Jitney** (Tel. 661-0089), a green, double-streetcar-like vehicle that runs on rubber tires instead of rails. This one tours the Kaanapali resort area only, chugging between the airport, the hotels, the Whalers Village, and the Kaanapali station of the LK&PR railroad line. The fare may be $2 for an all-day ticket this year.

And the train? Yes, there really is one, but it's mostly for the thrill of the ride and seems rather costly when considered as straight transportation. See the details in Section 6, "Sightseeing."

4. The Hotel Scene—Luxury in Lilliput

There is one area for a Maui vacation headquarters that outdistances all others on our personal yardstick of desirability. This is the short stretch of shore that runs from **Lahaina to Kaanapali.**

Lahaina, the once-bawdy old capital of the Sandwich Islands, is today a living museum. It hosts no luxury hotels, and has no beach to speak of. However Kaanapali, just three miles farther along the road, was once *only* an area of beautiful beaches. The only thing that extended higher in the air than a grass shack was a 100-foot-tall volcanic promontory called Black Rock. Today the grass shacks are all gone, and Black Rock is the foundation of the Sheraton-Maui Hotel.

And the Sheraton, in turn, is only one of a group of luxurious hostelries that have sprung up along the breakers over the last dozen years. They are all tied together by the bright green strip created by the 36-hole Royal Kaanapali Golf Course.

Farther along the same coastline are the villages of **Honokowai** and **Napili**, which reach just about the limit of remoteness for staking your claim in the sands. The luxury Kapalua resort is virtually at the end of the line.

A more recently developed shoreline runs from **Kihei** ("*key*-hay") through **Wailea** ("why-*lay*-ah"). These lie along some lovely and sparsely populated beaches down the southern neck of the low area separating West and East Maui.

The Wailea neighborhood now rivals Kaanapali in attractiveness, and sun-seekers searching for a more peaceful, somewhat less peripatetic vacation than they might find at Kaanapali are settling in nicely at Wailea. Unlike Wailea, Kihei has been developed by many different owners, and that area is now somewhat helter-skeltered, although both Wailea and Kihei have at least taken the pressure off the West Maui areas.

There are also a few hotels in the twin communities of **Wailuku** and **Kahului**, which serve as the county seat and airport gateway respectively. These are relatively workaday little towns and of not a whole lot of interest to short-term visitors.

Certainly in a class all by itself is the little bay, village, and state of mind called **Hana**. A tropical and sociological wonder, "Heavenly Hana" stays that way mainly because of its extreme isolation from the rest of Maui and from the rest of the world. It was here that Charles Lindbergh came "home" for the last time in 1974. There are only two hostelries in Hana with more than five or six rooms, and one of them is one of the most costly hotels in the Islands.

Maui Condomania. If you drive along the coast from Kaanapali to Napili, you may see some modern apartment buildings, a few of which may hang out signs: "Beautiful double room, $40 nightly." These are not hotels, but the simplest version of an innkeeping concept called "condominium hotels" or "resort condos." Hawaii has the largest number of hotel condo units in the nation, and Maui has more than any other Neighbor Island.

Resort condominiums are not set up by a person or a corporation, but by a limited partnership, a venture that may include as many as 200 people—investors or second-home owners—who have proprietary rights over at least one of the units. Owners share in the maintenance costs, and all common areas are held jointly. The number of units available for rental varies, depending on how many are occupied by owners or long-term lessees.

Smaller places offer rooms or apartments—period. There may be no restaurant, no beach services, infrequent maid service, and no professional management. The amenities in your flat will depend largely on how often the owner of the unit stays there himself. If he visits frequently, there may be a good color TV, fine furniture, and a set of fine china. If he doesn't, there may be nothing in the unit except the basic equipment all the partners have agreed to provide.

The larger condominium operations, however, have been coming into their own, offering more hotel-like facilities. Many of these are now excellent bargains that can compete with hotels offering the same luxury amenities. Beyond the usual hotel arrangements, most include full kitchens for no more money than you might pay for a comparable room without such conveniences in a conventional hotel. And rates are generally based on the size of the unit itself, not on the number of people who will be occupying it.

We have divided up our selection of accommodations (including a few proven condos) into Expensive, Medium, and Budget categories, and we have listed them generally in the order of our personal choice within those groupings. (The exception is the Hana hotels—there are only two, plus a set of cabins—which are listed at the end of each price classification.) Rates we have mentioned should only be taken as a general guide, although we believe they are correct at press time.

And, as always, tell 'em we sent you!

EXPENSIVE HOTELS

The 815-room, triple-towered, $80 million **Hyatt Regency Maui** (Tel. 667-7474), Maui's most dazzling hotel, opened in late 1980 on Kaanapali Beach. Developed by Honolulu millionaire Chris Hemmeter, the hotel set out unabashedly to outshine anything else on the island, if not the entire state, and in many ways it succeeds admirably:

Mammoth entranceway flanked by massive, million-dollar Chinese vases; valuable Oriental artworks scattered over the 20-acre campus; two dozen elegant shops in the ground-level promenades joining the three structures; scads of tropical gardens with scads of tropical birds; dramatic, free-form, one-acre swimming pool (divided into two areas by a swimmable waterfall hiding the Grotto Bar, and also featuring a 130-foot slide).

Long list of guest facilities and activities including saunas, massage room, exercise room, jacuzzi, library, pool table, electronic game room, scuba and snorkeling lessons and excursions, volleyball, shuffleboard, tetherball, boating, etc.; five tennis courts, with a teaching pro; Kaanapali golf links next door; four expensive restaurants, including the mirror-lined Swan Court, the chocoholic-bar-equipped Lahaina Provision Company (above the waterfall), the Italian-flavored Spats II, doubling as a popular basement disco, and the poolside Pavilion Restaurant, the priciest "coffee shop" you ever did see; several bars; entertainment in the Sunset Terrace or the plastic-roofed, tree-full Grand Ballroom; unfortunately inconvenient parking in the back lot behind the hotel.

Guest bedrooms in three wings—the rectangular Napili Tower to the west and Lahaina Tower to the east, and the atrium-hollow Kaanapali Tower in the middle; all units with at least a peek at the ocean; all with luxury facilities, except strangely with narrow *lanais*; decor running to brown and beige; most rooms divided by a credenza into sleeping and sitting areas. Current rates (single or double): Garden View, $125; Mountain View, $145; Ocean Front, $165; Regency Club, $185; and Regency Club/Ocean Front, $195. These are higher tabs than even the Hyatt on Waikiki Beach, and unlike the other Hawaiian Hyatt, this one no longer has any summer reductions. Our guest reports are still mixed on employees and service, but all praise the facilities and dramatic layout. *(Reservations through the Hyatt chain or the Hotel Hyatt Regency Maui, 200 Noheo Kai Dr., Lahaina, HI 96761.)* The Hyatt wins our highest recommendation on Maui.

Also in Kaanapali, the **Sheraton Maui** (Tel. 661-0031) has two "ground" floors, one with the lobby, the other eight stories up on top of Black Rock, the extinct volcano crater from which the ancient Hawaiians said warriors leaped off to join the spirit world. Today leaps are being held nightly. As the climax of the evening torch-lighting ceremony, a *malo*-clad employee dives into the sea from a rocky ledge. We've stayed at the Sheraton from time to time, and here are our impressions from a recent inspection up, down, and around this unique establishment:

Large, moon-shaped swimming pool; wide, wide, wide beach a few steps away; smaller pool by the cottages; three tennis courts; golf privileges on the nearby courses; pathways for explorers winding around Black Rock; elevator making a faster and easier route up the Cliff Tower; viewful Discovery Room restaurant at the top; Barkentine Bar next door (open about 5:30); Black Rock Terrace restaurant by the main pool.

There are 503 bedrooms in three areas, ranging from Standard doubles at $105 in the Garden Tower through Deluxe units around $120 in the just-refurbished Ocean Lanai buildings on the face of the rock, to the handsome Ocean Front Cottages about $155 (and for which reservations may only be confirmed by the Sheraton-Maui directly). There are also suites in the Cliff Tower, about $200 in high season. *(Reservations through the Sheraton chain or from Sheraton Hotels, 2255 Kalakaua Ave., Honolulu, HI 96815.)* After a quarter century, there is evidence of some hard knocks on the premises, and some of the staff seemed a little stiffer recently than in times past. Nevertheless, as a sightseeing attraction, an architectural achievement, and a convenient base for Kaanapaliing, we have to declare this choice as solid as the rock on which it sits.

Way over in Wailea, the 1,450-acre luxury resort community built by *kamaaina* sugar firm Alexander & Baldwin, Inc. is anchored by the 600-room, $26 million **Inter-Continental Maui** (Tel. 879-1922). Its far-out location on the bosom of East Maui affords some spectacular views of Kahoolawe, Molokini, and West Maui: Greens beckoning from the nearby Wailea Golf Course; 14-court Wailea Tennis Club also a short serve away; white stucco and dark wood architecture throughout; towering, eight-story Lahaina Building suitable for tour groups; one Main Building for central services; long, open-air lobby with its Lobby Bar; a dozen tasteful shops; string of eight low-rise structures generally housing non-group travelers; lava-rocky coastline between lovely Wailea Beach and Ulua Beach; three pools (at least one always sheltered from the wind); one of Maui's most attractive outdoor luaus; miles of meandering pathways with benches; full beach services; sports, crafts, and many extra activities for guests; handy "guest relations desk" with concierge-type services; five restaurants, including the Makani Coffee Shop, the Lanai Terrace (pleasant for Sunday brunch), and the fancy seafood dining salon named La Perouse; sculpture and other art scattered here and there.

We saw neatly appointed bedrooms in browns, yellows, and oranges. Several had king-size beds; some had twin doubles. All had good baths, individual *lanais*, and air conditioning. TV/radios are now in all units. Figure $75 to $135 daily for two here, depending on your view. But we saw no bad views—just some that gazed toward Haleakala instead of the waves. Suites run from $140 to $555. Children under 18 free in their parents' room at any price level. Special Family Plan April 1 to December 23 includes complimentary adjoining room for the youngsters. *(Reservations from the hotel at P.O. Box 799, Kihei, HI 96753.)* If the Wailea resort itself were nearer the action, both this hotel and the next one would rank above the Sheraton in our book. Certainly a handsome choice.

Next door, the newer and smaller **Westin Wailea Beach Hotel** (Tel. 879-4900) is a bright alternative that some logically place at the top of the list. It's operated by the United Airlines chain that links Honolulu's Ilikai, the Big Island's Mauna Kea Beach, and several Mainland hotels: Colorful, cheery lobby; same Wailea Resort golf (36 holes) and tennis (14 courts) as the neighboring Inter-Continental; large pool amid innovative landscaping (also fine for wheelchairs); waterfall and meandering lagoon; lovely crescent of beach beyond; Hawaiian language and history classes; special honeymoon packages; summer children's programs; three restaurants, including the award-winning Raffles, the Palm Court, and the Maui Onion down by the pool; drinking on the Sunset Terrace or at Lost Horizon, a Shangri-la for the disco set; large game room.

A total of 350 well-furnished, nicely decorated units with full luxury amenities (including refrigerators); free local phone calls; two rooms especially equipped for the handicapped. Most double rates now about $200 for Beach Front, $150 Ocean View, $130 Garden View, $115 Mountain View; slightly lower after April 21 to December 16; some sumptuous suites from $325 to $650 (all year); four sleeping wings with the Mokapu Wing, the separate one down near the beach, the most desirable; the Makai wing our second favorite; some Ocean View rooms recently downgraded to Garden View (instead of cutting down the greenery). It's expensive, but many love the place, and service standards are second to none on the island. *(Reservations through the Westin organization or the hotel at Wailea, HI 96753.)* Perhaps it's not quite the champion, but it's certainly a challenger.

Far beyond Kaanapali, a double-deluxe resort on West Maui's most beautiful beach is the **Kapalua Bay Hotel and Villas** (Tel. 669-5656), created by Laurence S. Rockefeller but now turned over to Regent International Hotels (which runs the Halekulani on Oahu), and the only hotel operation in the Kapalua resort.

Developed alongside two championship, 18-hole golf courses designed by Arnold Palmer; sloping site made even more gentle by design of the hotel on four levels in six buildings joined in a "Modified C" plan; three-story-tall lobby with views to trees, grass, pool, the ocean, and the islands beyond; Bay Lounge in the lobby with evening entertainment; two-tiered Dining Room (no fancy name), for informal lighter meals one level below, bisected by a moving waterway; separate and well-regarded Bay Club Dining Room a beach length away; the Grill & Bar, a casual local favorite up by the Golf and Tennis Garden; Crown Bar (with evening entertainment) next to the Dining Room; usually excellent Plantation Veranda, an enclosed, U-shaped, Hawaiian-look room serving dinner only (specializing in Nouvelle Cuisine and serving more California wines, fewer European vintages than the Dining Room); nightly movies on the property; 10 all-weather tennis courts; large, 12-corner swimming pool with bar/snack bar; many organized athletic activities.

Rooms are divided into 108 Ocean Views, 83 Garden Views, and 3 suites. Reflecting a major change in philosophy, Modified American Plan (two meals) is no longer required but is available at $43 per person. Rates for 1984 run from $160 for Standard rooms up to $415 for some of the suites. Hotel units are large and near duplicates of each other, with rate classification based on their position relative to the ocean: All decorated in either blue or rust tones; king-size bed or twins; air conditioning, but also Bombay fans; original art in each chamber; hidden fridgelette under the tiled dry bar; color TVs, now (a departure from the original isolation plan); his-and-hers bath with separate double sinks, separate double closet, and separate tub and shower; 130 Condo "Villas" now under the same management, but as yet uninspected by us.

Because of its distance from the action, this hotel has had to drop its original elitist plans, and partly turn to groups to keep the room night count up, a policy which drew heated criticism in one letter we received from a guest last year. *(Reservations through the Regent group or the hotel at One Bay Drive, Kapalua, HI 96761.)* A far-out beauty, to be sure, and perhaps too far away for some.

Back in Kaanapali, a vetéran contender still loved by many is the **Royal Lahaina Hotel** (Tel. 661-3611), a neighbor of the Sheraton, but on a different stretch of beach. The hotel has just been bought by Pleasant Hawaiian Holidays, a large tour wholesaler in California, and this presages the appearance of more group traffic and tighter fiscal policies. Nevertheless, the hotel has finally managed to divest itself of the old Aloha Tower condo operation next door that was once the trouble-plagued Maui Hilton and has now become the Maui Kaanapali (unreviewed by us). The Royal Lahaina management continues to be by Amfac Hotels, certainly a plus. Today it is mainly one 11-story building with rooms overlooking the cobalt blue ocean or the electric green Kaanapali Fairway Number 8, with a few smaller buildings and 31 wonderful little cottages.

Generally friendly welcome in monkeypod-paneled and wallpapered lobby; Franciscan-tiled floor; a bellhop for your bags only if you ask for one; a half-dozen swimming pools besides that most beautiful pool of all called the Pacific; terrific views (Lanai on the left, Molokai on the right); eleven tennis courts; two putting greens; several restaurants, including the Alii Dining Room and its nightly Polynesian show; two cocktail lounges; the Foxy Lady Discotheque.

Bedrooms in cool and comfortable greens and blues; generally excellent appointments with imported rattan, glass-top tables, and pillowed easy chairs; double rates ranging from about $80 to $120, depending on position; magnificent sea view corner suites about $250. (We marveled at the 1131–1132 connection, for example.) But the cottages—*no ka oi!* There are four units per building, but somehow each seems private. Delightful bedrooms open to the breeze on two sides; luxurious shag rugs; dark-stained rattan and teak furnishings; second-floor units with private lanai; bottom units with back door opening right to the beach our personal favorites; all equipped with refrigerator, TV, and several extras; cottage rates about $100 to $125. One reader has complained that the walls are too thin in the cottages too far from the sound of the ocean. *(Reservations from Amfac Hotels, P.O. Box 8519, Honolulu, HI 96815.)* If not quite so royal, it's still a professional operation.

Vastly improved over the past year or so is the 556-room, S-shaped **Maui Surf Hotel** (Tel. 661-4411), also in the Kaanapali complex and next door to the Whalers Village shopping/museum site. Mammoth entrance with lava rock pillars; gracious reception; open-sided lobby with polished tile and a soft rug; an arcade of shops; Eight Bells Coffee Shop with you-guessed-it lined up outside; Quee Queg Restaurant (much better these days); Pequod Bar, decked out like a whaling ship; same beautiful beach as that of the Sheraton; three tennis courts; two swimming pools; new beachside recreational complex; perhaps about one elevator short of what it needs. Many king-size beds and color TV/FM/AM combinations; happily, rates up from last year by smaller amounts than many other hotels; ocean-view Deluxes a knockout at $105; some $90 Superiors also overlooking the waves; Standards at around $80 for viewing mountain greenery.

One of a family of four, this one is much better than its Surf sister on Kauai, though perhaps still not up to its two sophisticated siblings on the Big Island. *(Reservations from InterIsland Resorts, Box 8359, Honolulu, HI 96815.)* We've been getting much improved guest reports on the Maui Surf, and we're happy to move it up a couple of notches for 1984—maybe more later.

A well-maintained resort that offers a lot for your money is the **Napili Kai Beach Club** (Tel. 669-6271), just before Kapalua. If we seem to rank it further along the chapter than we might, that reflects its mileage down the pike—a definite disadvantage for some—rather than its service and facilities, which we cannot fault. It is some way from the action-central areas of Kaanapali and Lahaina (10 miles), and 35 miles from Kahului Airport. But if semi-isolation is no problem, here is a total outdoor activity center in one hotel-condo complex: Large, well-landscaped grounds snuggling up to two beautiful beaches; tremendous selection of *alfresco* sports including tennis courts, croquet, shuffleboard, putting, snorkeling, you-name-it; no extra charge for most sports equipment; some organized activities like Mai Tai parties; new outdoor barbecue now sizzling; dependable Restaurant (formerly "Teahouse") of the Maui Moon; entertainment nightly; five swimming pools; eight buildings including a tiny "Hideaway Cottage."

The rooms we saw were lovely, in neo-Japanese decor, and all overlook the ocean. To be right next to the sand, however, ask for Standard rooms in the Lahaina Wing ($100 double studios or $115 double suites). Studio prices for two run $135 in the luxury units. Suites in the Honolua Wing go for $160, and the price is $225 for four to six persons in that Hideaway Cottage. *Credit cards are not accepted. (Reservations from Napili Kai Beach Club, Napili Bay, HI 96761.)* Despite the distance, a devoted clutch of annual returnees wouldn't consider anyplace else.

Much closer to the center of things, the 364-unit condominium operation called the **Papakea Beach Resort** (Tel. 669-4848), a little north of Kaanapali, is winning friends and influencing visitors. There's a narrow strip of beach at low tide, a couple of inviting pools, tennis courts, well-landscaped gardens, and several guest activities. Well-furnished living units on four floors offer color TVs, washer/dryers, good kitchenettes, and overhead fans, but no air conditioning. Like some other condos, this one has maid service *every other* day.

Rates run from $84 to $94 for studios through perhaps $105 to

$120 for one-bedroom models sleeping four, to $155 to $170 for two-bedroom apartments. Substantial summer discounts beginning April 1. The L. W. Reynolds family of Ontonagon, Mich., has written in praise of the helpful staff and the well-kept units. *(Reservations from the resort at Kaanapali, HI 96761.)* Perhaps a happy find.

Back inside the Kaanapali Resort itself, the twin-winged, 720-room **Maui Marriott Resort** (Tel. 667-1200) is Marriott's 100th link in the chain, and the first to be forged in Hawaii: Windy, 15-acre, oceanfront site near the Hyatt; recently improved landscaping; open-air lobby surrounding pools and fountains; conveniently separate group and independent check-in; pleasant folks on duty there; long, open courtyard acting like a walk-in Venturi tube; many outdoor activities; two grown-up pools and one kiddy pool; five tennis courts; often difficult parking; four restaurants, including the Kaukau Grill, a poolside snack bar, the Moana Terrace (open to the ocean when weather permits), the well-liked Nikko Steak House (featuring Japanese teppanyaki), and the fine-dining Lokelani Room; several bars, including the swinging Banana Moon "entertainment lounge."

Accommodations in two nine-story towers, the Lanai Wing and the Molokai Wing; generally large rooms with king-size or twin-double beds; convertible couches sleeping two more; luxury accouterments including color TVs, lanais, etc.; rates from $100 with a golf-course or mountain view through $130, $150, and $175 for increasingly greater vistas of the ocean.

We thought the hotel not well designed for the site on which it sits. One of its most scenic spots, on the ground floor by the beach, is used for that Japanese steak house, which is air conditioned and only open after dark. And with the repetitious black railings, the courtyard facades of the two towers seemed to have all the charm of a cellblock at San Quentin, although new planter boxes with trailing vines may provide an escape from that impression. *(Reservations through the Marriott chain or from the hotel at 2341-A Kaanapali Parkway, Lahaina, HI 96761.)* Our own stay was okay, and letters from readers have been generally favorable too.

Deluxish accommodations in old Lahaina itself are possible in the seven-story **Lahaina Shores Hotel** (Tel. 661-4835), which really is a condominium-apartment operation, under the biggest American flag you ever saw in your life: On the water at the east end of town; a narrow beach of sorts, a rarity in Lahaina; attractive, old-style façade with colonnades and balustrades; spacious lobby in subdued tones; swimming pool and jacuzzi out on the Astro-Turf; no restaurant or bar, but plenty of those near enough anyway.

All living units with full kitchen, air cooling, and color television; lots of lemon-yellow and lime-green decorations; a panorama outside that just can't miss. Mountain-view studio doubles for $58; similar rooms on the ocean for $64; deluxe separate-bedroom units for $77 facing *mauka* or $90 on the water-and-sunset side of things; some deluxe penthouses in the $100 range; ground-floor units with access from inside or outside. There's no charge for children 6 or under, so this might be a good family alternative. Manager "Butch" Soares is still in charge. *(Reservations from the hotel at 475 Front St., Lahaina, HI 96761.)* Good for its type, if you want that location.

Last on our list of higher-priced choices for West Maui is the **Kaanapali Beach Hotel** (Tel. 661-0011), on the beach for which it is named, and not to be confused with any similarly named establishments. The rooms are, well, okay (try for the ground-floor units for easy access to the beach and the cartoon whale–shaped pool). But we think the general layout is less than inspiring and that too many cost-cutting measures are in effect. It seems heavily used by groups, making some independent visitors feel alone in the crowd, and we continue to receive letters critically inclined toward this hotel. Standard doubles for $70; Superiors for $82; and Deluxes for $92. *(Reservations through Amfac Resorts.)* We would prefer to pay a little more to stay elsewhere—like any other Amfac hotel in Hawaii.

Two more condo possibilities include the popular **Kaanapali Shores** (Tel. 667-2211) near Papakea, in the $100 range, and the **Whaler** (Tel. 661-4861), right on Kaanapali Beach, for around the same fare. We have not yet been on a full inspection of these two.

Now, how about Hana? To a large extent, the attraction of the **Hotel Hana Maui** (Tel. 248-8211) is simply the lush, unspoiled environment of Hana itself. Located smack in the modest little village, it's a collection of several low-roofed buildings, around which wind its own private gardens and 18-hole pitch-and-putt golf course:

Open patio-style lobby with a fountain of flowers; several public areas indoors including sitting room, cardroom, etc., off the restaurant and open-air cocktail lounge; many outdoor facilities and activities including heated swimming pool, two tennis courts, shuffleboard, croquet, table tennis, golf, weekly cookouts, *luaus*, and so on.

Swimming is on Hamoa Beach with private access a few minutes away by hotel shuttle. The staff will handle all arrangements for car rentals, horseback riding, hula and ukulele lessons, bicycling, and nearly anything else you can think of except a Broadway show. There are many different types of accommodations, all single-story, running from about $180 per day for two (including all meals) on up to the Alii Executive Home for $550 per day. There are no TVs or air conditioners needed or available. Better book a year in advance for a Christmas vacation. *(Reser-*

vations from the hotel direct at Hana, HI 96713.) It's expensive, but to many its unique style is worth every blue chip.

MEDIUM-PRICED HOTELS

First, here are some lodgings on which Sara and I do not agree. I happen to like very much carrying my own bags up the creaky wooden stairs of the octogenarian original building of the **Pioneer Inn** (Tel. 661-3636) on the waterfront in Lahaina. There in a lopsided old room with a fan circling overhead and whose shivering timbers are only held together by multitudinous layers of white paint, I can lie down and hear the rinky-tink piano coming from below in the Old Whaler's Grog Shop. That's a genuine antique bar like none other in Hawaii. Then I can wander out on the ancient veranda and scan Lahaina Harbor, the scene of drama, history, and the passing Hawaiian parade for two centuries. There is a pool, of sorts, but no room service. Doubles in the original building are about $30 with bath or perhaps five dollars less with down-the-hall facilities. Creatures of comfort who choose the new wing in the rear (we must admit, it *is* nice) will pay about $40 for two. (But the Spencer Tracy-Katharine Hepburn Suite is up front.)

Now, why do I like it? Listen to some of these house rules posted on opening day in 1901: "Women is not allow in you room. If you wet or burn you bed you going out. You are not allow in the down stears in the seating room or in the dinering room or in the kitchen when you are drunk. You must use a shirt when you come to the seating room." *(Reservations from the hotel at 658 Wharf St., Lahaina, HI 96761.)* Sara says it's like sleeping in an old museum, and I say yup, that's just why I like it!

The 49-unit **Noelani** (Tel. 669-8374), out past Kaanapali at Honokowai, is one of the nicest small condominium-apartment buys we've seen. No lobby or central meeting place; two palm-lined pools, however, both near the ocean; pleasant grounds; postage-stamp beach a short stroll away; nicely furnished units in three buildings; full kitchen facilities, dishes, etc.; all with TV on the cable; some with washer/dryer; all with ocean views; maid service once a week; management-sponsored free Mai Tai parties.

Studio units only in the older two structures and larger studio units in the new building in either blue or orange motif, all for about $50 for two; one-bedroom apartments for about $65 double; $7 per extra person in the high season only; two-bedroom units sleeping four for $85; monthly discounts available. *(For the latest scoop, write the Noelani at 4095 Honoapiilani Highway, Lahaina, HI 96761.)* A happy find.

Good ole **Maui Lu** (Tel. 879-5881), the pioneer in the Kihei area, is owned by—and especially popular with—Canadians. It's across the road from the beach where Captain George Vancouver is thought to have landed in 1792, now marked by a Canadian totem pole. You'll find a swimming pool shaped like a huge map of Maui, two tennis courts, the former Longhouse Restaurant just renamed Jesse's (with Jesse Nakooka still hosting the six-night Polynesian Dinner Review), the Hale Kope coffee shop, popular Thursday Aloha Mele luncheons; and the three-times-weekly Maui Lu-au, now packing them in at about $30 a ticket.

The rambling collection of buildings makes for widely varying rates and types of accommodations, but all have refrigerator, coffee maker, TV, and air conditioner. Some feature cooking facilities. Doubles run from $50 on up to $65 or so. *(Reservations from the hotel, 575 So. Kihei Rd., Kihei, Maui, HI 96753.)* Stay with the lower rates for the best deals.

Back in Lahaina, the **Lahaina Roads** (Tel. 661-3166) is somewhat removed from the main drag at 1403 Front St. The "beach" is better for snorkeling than for wading, but there's also a pool. Parking is underneath the building: Total of 34 condo apartments; private *lanais*; wall-to-wall carpeting; all with TV; washer/dryer; all with kitchen facilities; no maid service; no restaurant. One-bedroom apartments for about $55; two bedrooms for $63 or so; penthouse (sleeping four) for perhaps $120; long-term rates available. *(Write to the above address at Lahaina, HI 96761.)* The Roads is no superhighway, but it's passable.

To us, at least, the least desirable lodge in Lahaina is the **TraveLodge** (Tel. 661-3661) at 888 Wainee St. Formica, polyethylene, and mass-production furniture were everywhere. It's a long way from the shore, and as we walked through after a ho-hum breakfast in its spiritless diner we couldn't escape the feeling that we were poking around a motel along the Ohio Turnpike. All-alike doubles rent for around $45. If you put ketchup on your roast beef, you might like it. We thought it out of place—by about 3,000 miles.

In Kahului, the **Maui Beach Hotel** (Tel. 877-0051) and its Siamese twin, the **Maui Palms Hotel** (Tel. 877-0071), are not recommended by us until further notice. (The Maui Hukilau, see below, is cheaper and better.)

Now, out at Hana again, the "other" place to stay in town is at the **Hana Kai Resort Apartments** (Tel. 248-8435), a 20-unit condominium with daily maid service. Two buildings in a lovely setting right on the water; an "unofficial" swimming pool (it's all right but doesn't have the approved kind of filter or something); no restaurant (bring your own fixin's or eat dinner at the expensive Hotel Hana Maui); free pickup from the Hana airstrip. The hotel will arrange rental cars, horseback rides, and other activities. Studio apartments with all equipment for $53 double; one-bedroom apartments for $69, extra people for $6 each. Naval Commander (retired) Joe and Sina Fornier are your hosts, and they keep everything on an even keel. *(Reservations from P.O. Box 38, Hana, HI 96713.)* A shipshape choice.

BUDGET HOTELS

No doubt about it, the best bargain in low-priced hotels on Maui today is still the little **Lahainaluna Hotel** (Tel. 661-0577), especially if you land one of its better units. Upstairs in one of those reconstructed buildings in the Lahaina historic district; 100 percent air-conditioned; B&W TV in all units; good, glass-door showers; clean floors. Best bargains are the units on the front, with honest-to-whale waterfront views; cells in the back seem more claustrophobic but still neat; at last report even the most expensive units were still holding at $30. Single rates the same as doubles; $6 per extra person after two; no checks, but credit cards okay; absolutely no confirmation without a deposit; maid service three times per week; two days' minimum stay. *(Reservations from the hotel, 127 Lahainaluna Road, Lahaina, HI 96761.)* We've tried it and—for the Bare Bones category—we like it.

Over on the windward side, the best deal is the **Maui Hukilau/Maui Sands Hotels** (Tel. 877-3311), now combined in Kahului. Although physical facilities are excellent for the price, the dullsville location plus the number of groups that pour into Kahului hotels combine to rank them lower on our scale than they might otherwise be. If you arrive on Maui without reservations, you might snag a decent leftover double for $35 or so, plus the price of a phone call. Speaking of phone calls, absolutely no long-distance or interisland calls can be made from the rooms. (Boo!) On the other hand, local phone calls are free. (Yay!)

And now, Hana for the budgeteer? Since we wound up each of the previous two categories with accommodations in Hana, we should mention that the low-cost traveler might be put up there in the rustic cabins at **Waianapanapa** ("why-a-noppa-noppa?") **State Park**. There are furnished units sleeping four to six at rates from $10 to $30 a day. All are completely equipped with kitchen, etc. (For the most up-to-date report, write to the Division of State Parks, P.O. Box 1049, Wailuku, HI 96793. On Maui, telephone the Parks Division at 244-4354.) Why-a-not?

5. Maui Restaurants and Dining—Supper by Sunset

Does Maui have restaurants? Does it ever! They roll in and roll out, sometimes appearing and disappearing with the rapidity of the waves off Kaanapali. Occasionally a famous name will stick around for a while, but even then there may be a swinging door back in the kitchen to accommodate the incoming and outgoing chefs. It is not uncommon at all for a cook to prove his giblets on Maui, only to be shanghaied and hauled off to a juicier kitchen in Waikiki.

LAHAINA AND VICINITY

Longhi's (Tel. 667-2288), hard by the traffic in the quaint, white building at 888 Front St. (corner of Papalaua), has now expanded to the upper story. There are no reservations and no menus, and the first surprise comes when your waiter pushes aside a Boston fern and sits down at your table. Oozing sincerity, he leans forward and in respectful tones recites the "verbal menu." Notwithstanding some of these "hipper than thou" attitudes, the classic Continental food is always good, usually excellent, and sometimes superb. Better get there early (maybe around 6). Looking back, our only grouse was the background of street noises through the open-air, curbside structure. This may be improved if you can snag one of the new tables upstairs.

The aerial-motif **Bluemax** (Tel. 661-8202) takes off at lunchtime and dinnertime in the wide-open cockpit above 730 Front St. The "Max" is, in reality, aviation pioneer John Laurance, who has decorated the place with early Hawaii aircraft photos, propellers, and other Wild Blue Yonder paraphernalia. We landed on a good menu of French Provincial cuisine, our crew of three then flying high on the stuffed pork and the salmon dishes that were specials that night. Most dinner entrees are about $13 to $15. Service was skillful and friendly. (We did have one reader report of a rough flight here last year, however.) Go at noon to efficiently peruse the old pictures as well as the picture-postcard 3-D view of the Lahaina Roadstead. Usually a real joyride!

Just off the sidewalk in the Lahaina Market Place, **Gerard's** (Tel. 661-8939) is this year's genuine Gallic champion in Lahaina. Monsieur Gerard Riversade tends everything himself in the kitchen, leaving the dining room to Alfons, his equally atmospheric maître. We found pleasant but unpretentious surroundings, with two dozen or so white-tableclothed tables set on a brick floor. The menu varies daily, depending on the availability of ingredients, but many classic veal, duck, fish, and chicken specialties—all with a variety of French sauces—are served. Order carefully. Our meals for four (with a modest wine) came to $100. (Closed Sunday.)

The traditional longtime French kitchen on the island is all by itself nearly 6 miles east of Lahaina at **Chez Paul** (Tel. 661-3843). It's ensconced at the end of a wood-frame general store and almost hidden in a clump of trees off the highway at Olowalu. (Don't try to find it at night if you didn't see it during the day.) Only about fifteen tables in one modest room; reservations a must; single diners not taken; candles on white tablecloths; no view; no fancy decor; just excellent *cuisine française* at prices which are *not* cheap.

We had Filet of Sole Meuniere and Veal Valdotin, a casserole dish with veal, two sauces, and ham and cheese. Others swear by the creamed soups. The Gallic owner/chef is Paul Kirk. We've never met him, never heard a discouraging word about his accomplishments, and have none ourselves. Closed Sunday *and* Monday. Recommended. Somehow we missed **La Bretagne** (Tel. 661-8966) again, but Madge Walls, the savor-savvy dining editor of the Maui *News*, says there are many unusual dishes from Brittany there, all of which are worth a try. It's in a private house, officially at 562 Front St., but actually a little off the street at Malu Ulu O Lele Park. It's on our list for future degustation.

Back in town center, the 1901 Pioneer Inn Hotel (Tel. 661-3636) hosts two restaurants. The **Harpooner's Lanai** is open for breakfast and lunch, but we recommend it heartily *only* for breakfast. You'll see and hear a marvelous selection of town characters along with your pancakes. At lunchtime, however, we have been gassed in our chairs by the battalions of tour buses which leave their diesel motors idling nearby.

On the other side of the same historic building is the dinner-only **South Seas Patio**, which features a broil-your-own steak, chicken, or fish dinner for about $6, and includes the all-you-can-eat salad bar and baked beans. One of the best dinner bargains on the island.

Under the same management is the **Lahaina Broiler** (Tel. 661-3111) at about 885 Front St. At night the Broiler is lit up literally like a Christmas tree. Whaling ship decor with kegs, floats, glass balls, and wooden pilings; open-air view from the rail of the islands of Kahoolawe, Lanai, and Molokai; pounding waves seemingly threatening the underpinnings. We've had delightful breakfasts here (bacon, eggs, toast, coffee, juice, and tax for about $4) and enjoyed playing footsies with the little crabs who sometimes search for crumbs along the rail. Watch out for your valuables. One slip, splash, and they belong to King Neptune. Service was unprofessional but friendly. We've had some complaints about evening dinners. Certainly good for the forenoon, anyway.

Sorry, but we did not like the service or lunchtime fare at **Kimo's**, 845 Front St. The setting is delightful, and nearly everyone says that things are fine at dinner. We've yet to come back in the evening. However, we are now skipping **Blackbeards**.

On the *makai* side of the street, but not nearly so far along, is the well-named **Oceanhouse** (Tel. 661-3359) at 831 Front St. It's a double-decked nautical emporium with both the downstairs dining room and the overhead Carthaginian Bar gazing down on floodlit waves. You can take the salad bar alone for about $8. Meals run from sauteed filet of mahimahi for about $10 to lobster tail for about $18. Not a fancy place, but we experienced fast, friendly service.

Down an alley called Wahie Lane behind 834 Front St. is an Italian hole-in-the-wall called **Alex's Hole In The Wall** (Tel. 661-3197). Pasta dishes are in the $8 range, with Veal Scallopini for perhaps $16. Closed

Sundays. Recently expanded but still deservedly popular. Across the street at No. 839, **Greenthums Over The Ocean** almost places you *in* the ocean on heavy sea days. We had some nice salad and a lasagna for lunch, but watch those waves!

Across Front Street from the town park and banyan is the **Banyan Inn** (Tel. 661-0755), an old cement-floor, no-nonsense place which has now been renovated. It's fish and steaks, mostly. Top it off with *lilikoi* (passion fruit) or some other fresh fruit pie. Some good local entertainment is served with the fixin's some nights.

The **Whale's Tale** (Tel. 661-3676), next door to The Wharf, deserves its own long-taled reputation. The high-beamed ceilings, stained-glass lanterns, and open-air balcony are typical of Lahaina reconstruction decor, restaurant division. We enjoyed drinks in its Whale Watchers Saloon, but somehow never got back for dinner. It serves until 11 P.M. (sinfully late for Lahaina), and Hawaii's gourmet-cartoonist Harry Lyons reported he heartily enjoyed his Roast Duck a l'Orange. A la carte choices will run $12 or more here now.

Le Croissant d'Avignon, in the Wharf shopping center next door, specializes in quiches. Another favorite Lahaina bakery is **The Bakery**, strictly a carry-out though, at 991 Limahana Place on the other side of the highway.

We do not suggest setting your course for the **Chart House** at the north end of town. And the **Voyager** restaurant in the Lahaina TraveLodge was less than inspiring. Our own wake-up meal there was unspecial except for the lone, long hair that came with the bacon. The submarines at **Togo's Sandwich & Delicatessen** might blast you out of the water at $7 or so. Nevertheless, they make for a hearty meal in your own cabin. Look for them in the Lahaina Shores Village at 505 Front St. Up on the highway, **Chris' Smokehouse** (Tel. 667-2111) is pretty good for ribs, chicken, and the like. **Fujiyama**, in the Lahaina Square, isn't bad for Japanese food, but it adds up to a lot of yen. The **Golden Palace** is the only Chinese restaurant in Lahaina. Okay, but it's no Ming Yuen (see Kahului).

Want a completely local, down-home, non-tourist, cheap steak-and-beer kind of place in Lahaina? Then search out **Naoke's Steak House**, far down the line at 1307 Front St. It's open 'til about 1 A.M., and still serving big, 16-ounce steaks for perhaps $7.95 or so *with* salad, and *with* rice, too. Hawaiian food (*kalua* pig, etc.) is also available and reportedly good.

KAANAPALI

With two or three exceptions, Kaanapali dining is pretty much hotel dining, and these inns are not always consistent in the quality of their meals, perhaps because some of the chefs are as transient as their customers.

One of the exceptions is the proudly strutting dining room called **The Peacock** (Tel. 667-6847), a Continental/Polynesian entry now firmly installed in the former golf clubhouse at 2650 Kekaa Drive (near the Maui Eldorado condo): Shining ceiling of LED indicators inside plastic tubes; long, low room with wicker tables (the bases can get in the way of long legs); deep red tablecloths; open to island breezes (no air conditioning). Our party enjoyed some excellent dishes including turtle soup (you add the Sherry), Veal Oscar, Tournedos Forestiere, and fresh island opaka-paka (red snapper), all attractively prepared and deftly served. The lamb curry is also reported to be excellent. Wide-ranging prices from $13 to $25 for dinners. The Peacock has been spread out by the same folks who run the famous Quail Lodge on California's Monterey Peninsula. Now it's perhaps the most dependable Kaanapali address for lunch and dinner.

A little less imposing is a seafood room on the shoreline next to the Whalers Village complex called **El Crabcatcher** (Tel. 661-4423). You can choose the full dinners in the $14 range or some "light suppers" (crab custard quiche, or crab Louie salad, etc.) for around $10. Try the shrimp scampi maybe. This one is also drawing discriminating local traffic from Lahaina and points east.

If hotels were to seek a plethora-of-restaurants prize, it would probably be won by the several kitchens on the grounds of the Royal Lahaina (Tel. 661-3611). **Moby Dick's** is one of the better ones for seafare-ing. Try the duck in peanut sauce or other exotica at **Don the Beachcomber**.

Nearby, we haven't yet tried the **Paniolo Steakhouse** in the Maui Kaanapali condo. This place recently changed hands, so its future is in doubt. Meanwhile, what everyone comes over to see is the famous oil painting of "Stella," the nude who startled Chicago when she was unveiled at the World's Columbian Exposition in 1893.

The **Rusty Harpoon** (Tel. 661-3123) in the Whalers Village offers broil-your-own lunches and dinners catering to a young, hip crowd. My lunchtime cheeseburger was around $4, and I did all the work. Dinner looks like a better bargain. Light and dark beer on draft. A possibility. **Ricco's** in the same area is the place for pizza, made from Ricco's mother's own recipe. The **Sea Scoop** is sometimes a good bet for sandwiches and a malt.

Over at the Sheraton-Maui Hotel (Tel. 661-0031), the **Discovery Room** may be found atop Black Rock, providing unequaled views over the nearby land-, sand-, and seascape. It may be worth dropping into when good entertainment is on stage, but there are several bad tables and some readers have complained to us of patronizing service. The formerly good breakfast buffet there just isn't any more, either. Down the elevator, the **Black Rock Terrace** now serves a no-reservations a la carte dinner, sometimes including a delicious sunset.

The teppanyaki at the **Nikko** Japanese steak house in the Maui Marriott is expensive, fun, and usually good, too. The **Lokelani Room** in the same hotel has been doing swimmingly with a different lobster specialty every night.

In the Maui Surf Hotel (Tel. 661-4411) we only hit the **Surf Side Coffee Shop**, which is much improved from a year or two ago. Ditto for the **Eight Bells Dining Room** and especially the nearby **Quee Queg** restaurant, which has become a favorite of one regular reader of this volume.

NAPILI

The dining rooms associated with the Kapalua Bay Hotel (Tel. 669-5656) are expensive, but usually excellent. You dress for dinner in the **Dining Room** and coats and ties are also strongly suggested in **The Bay Club**, which is down the beach a bit and not attached to the hotel. There's no view at the **Plantation Veranda**, an elegant inside room. A local favorite between the tennis garden and the golf club is the informal **Grill & Bar**, especially for lunch.

The French-style restaurant in the Napili Shores Resort has changed its name again. (In the past, it was The Bistro and before that Le Tournedos.) We haven't been in since it went through its latest transformation, although reports are encouraging. Let us know if you go.

The nearby **Restaurant of the Maui Moon** (Tel. 669-6271) is a winner, especially since they stopped calling it a "teahouse." Continental cuisine with island accents; entertainment nightly except Sunday; Friday-night show featuring offspring of the hotel staff. Dependable and enjoyable.

Not far away is the dinner-only **Pineapple Hill**, a former plantation manager's home in a lovely hilltop setting. However, we have received several complaints about this place in the past year, so it's off our list until further notice.

KIHEI

In Kihei, **Jesse's** (Tel. 879-1511), formerly the Longhouse in the Maui Lu Hotel, is still long on reputation. Some delicious prime rib is served here on the one-price buffet. But *the* event on Thursdays at 11 is the Aloha Mele Luncheon, a real Hawaiian hoedown.

A French restaurant called **Robaire's** (Tel. 879-2707)—and it *is* spelled that way—is shepherded by Robert (pronounced "Robaire") Goueytes, who used to be at home on the ranges at New York's Le Pavillon, Le Jockey Club in Madrid, and the Cafe de Paris at Biarritz. The secret to his success may be his personal supervision over each dish. You'll find the place at 61 So. Kihei Road, next to the Suda Store.

Also in Kihei today is **La Familia** (Tel. 879-8824), a branch of the Mexican Familia from Wailuku. Probably as good a bet here at 2511 So. Kihei Road as there. The **Island Fish House** (Tel. 879-7771) is dependable and popular for finny fare. It's tied up to 1945 So. Kihei Road. And some health-conscious diners are happy with the Pritikin diet meals at the condominium **Mana Kai-Maui** (Tel. 879-1561). We haven't been in.

WAILEA

The restaurants at the Hotel Inter-Continental Maui (Tel. 879-1922) are gaining recognition now from both local and traveling folk. The seafood-oriented **La Perouse**, decorated in a wide variety of Oriental silks, African antiques, etc., seems to specialize in anything you won't find elsewhere. How about an appetizer of Prosciutto with Kiwi Fruit, soup of Breadfruit Vichyssoise, a salad of Kula Wilted Spinach, and perhaps a main course of Dover Sole in Macadamia Nut Butter? Now that coats and ties are no longer required, we'll be in for some of that.

Next door, in the Wailea Beach Hotel, the award-winning restaurant called **Raffles** (Tel. 879-4900) has been making a name for itself. The restaurant editor of *Travel/Holiday* magazine, Robert Lawrence Balzer, recently invaded the kitchen, donned an apron, and created some new dishes, which have since been added to the menu. The atmosphere seeks to re-create that of the Singapore Raffles Hotel, with polished teak floors, Oriental rugs, bronze chandeliers, and the like. In the same hotel, the **Palm Court** has been offering a good champagne brunch every day.

Near the golf course, the **Wailea Steak House** was for sale the last time we drove through. Its score will have to remain a question mark for the moment. **The Set Point**, dressed in yellow and white at the Wailea Tennis Club, offers second-floor fans a chance to munch some sandwiches while keeping tabs on the action on the courts below. This may be the only dining room on Maui that keeps your jaw moving from side to side as much as up and down.

WAILUKU-KAHULUI

Mexican food fans must try **La Familia** (Tel. 244-7481), a labor of love carved out of a run-down block at 2119 Vineyard St. *Delicioso!* Maui is not particularly known for Oriental fare, but **Ming Yuen** (Tel. 871-7787) probably still serves the best Chinese food on the island. It's off the main track (Route 380) at 162 Alamaha St. in the Kahului Industrial Area. Then the all-you-can-eat Imperial Buffet Dinner, a six-day Japanese extravaganza in the **Maui Palms Hotel** is *ichi ban* (but not on Sunday). Also on the Japanese file, try **Tokyo Tei** (Tel. 242-9630) at 1063 Lower Main

St. for the shrimp tempura (and other goodies) or **Archie's** (Tel. 244-9401), on the same street at No. 1440 (lots of soups). Both are in Wailuku, and both are often jammed at lunch.

The nicest place for a businessman's lunch these days is the **Island Fish House** (Tel. 871-7555), where Mr. Hugo's used to be at 33 Lono Ave. in the Alexander & Baldwin Building in Kahului. This one was launched recently by the parent Island Fish House in Kihei.

A good local place for breakfast—and maybe a modest lunch—is **Ma-Chan's** (Tel. 877-7818) in the Kaahumanu Shopping Center in Kahului. No fancy surroundings, but a popular place with permanent residents of the neighborhood.

KULA

On the way up—or down—Haleakala are the **Silversword Inn** (Tel. 878-1449) and the **Kula Lodge** (Tel. 878-1535) in Kula. Both serve up breakfast and heaps of mountain atmosphere along Highway 377.

MAKAWAO

The **Makawao Steak House** (Tel. 572-8711) has a good salad bar and offers intimate dining in this Up-country neighborhood. Somewhat more informal is **T-Bar Junction** in the new shopping center in nearby Pukalani. Also in Pukalani, right on Highway 37, the cafe called **Bullock's of Hawaii** has been serving up "moonburgers" and guava milk shakes to satisfied customers for years.

PAIA

In this tiny town, a jumping-off place for the Hana trip, there are two choices for semi-serious dining. **Dillon's** (Tel. 579-9113) is right in town, and a good choice for steaks, chops, and fish. Then there's the more-famous **Mama's Fish House** (Tel. 579-9672), which is actually about a mile out of town at Kuau Cove. It still serves up a good seafood dinner—including Mama's papaya-seed salad—for around $13. (It opens at 5 P.M.)

HANA

In Hana itself, there is literally one single address for dinner, and that's the expensive spread at the **Hotel Hana Maui** (Tel. 248-8211). We've enjoyed the buffet lunch there, too. You can also eat from about 11 A.M. to 4 P.M. for about $5 at the **Hana Ranch Restaurant** (Tel. 248-8255), whose address we've misplaced, but just ask anyone. Down at Hana Beach Park, **Tutu's Snack Bar** keeps turning out saimin, hot dogs, hamburgers, etc., until about 5 o'clock.

6. Sightseeing Maui

Points of interest on the island of Maui divide themselves naturally into four general areas, and many visitors schedule their Valley Isle stay for a total of four days.

This is not to say you can't have a good time on only a two-day trip. And you could easily spend more than a month on Maui, devoting a week to exploring thoroughly each of the different island neighbor-hoods, with an occasional day of rest on some deserted beach. There are also miles and miles of trails, virtually impassable without a four-wheel drive, not to mention even more obscure paths through the wilderness, elusive to all but dedicated hikers.

As described in this chapter, the four areas include the following:

West Maui, beginning at Kaanapali, concentrating on Lahaina, and continuing down the coastline as far as the village of Maalaea.

Central Maui, which takes in Kihei, Wailea, and everything in the "neck" of the island. It includes, too, the airport village of Kahului, the county seat of Wailuku, and Iao Valley—its parks and its "needle."

Haleakala, for which the trip first runs along some 30 miles of moun-tain greenery in "Up-country Maui" and then winds on up to the crater rim itself at 10,023 feet.

Hana, the unique and unspoiled village and its lush countryside. It is reached by a route so long and winding that many visitors save it for a separate trip on another visit—and that's just what keeps Hana the vir-ginal tropical wilderness that it is.

WEST MAUI—KAANAPALI, LAHAINA, OLOWALU, MAALAEA

If you're staying in the neighborhood, one of the first things you'll notice about **Kaanapali Beach** is how really gorgeous four long miles of gently curving, wide, wide sand can be. A dozen years ago, this was about 1,000 wild acres, used largely as a dumping ground for bagasse, the waste product of the Pioneer Sugar Mill. Today, two golf courses provide a neat, green carpet along the strand, studded here and there by a hotel or resort building.

Across the water you will see the outlines of Molokai and Lanai, giving you the feeling as nowhere else in Hawaii that you are indeed living among a community of islands.

The beach is divided in two halves by a large volcanic cone called Kekaa, or **Black Rock**. A sacred cliff in ancient times, the rock today is used as the base for the Sheraton-Maui Hotel. It may sound like a sacri-lege, but even the most severe critics of modern building in conflict with natural wonders must give the Sheraton its due. The effect is magnifi-cent, and a walk over its grounds is certainly recommended.

Nearby, still in Kaanapali, is the answer to a common husband-wife dilemma, the genuinely unique **Whalers Village**. This handsomely designed shopping bazaar occupies us elders easily for an hour or two. There's plenty of room for the kids to run, too, plus a whaleboat to "sail," old bells to ring, and the like.

The 100 exhibits show the effects of whaling on Maui's past. There's an entire skeleton of a 40-foot-long sperm whale hanging around, plus at least a dozen shops, including a couple of restaurants, and a movie theater in the same complex. (See also Section 10, "Shopping.") It's a marvelous browsing place. Don't miss it.

Kaanapali also provides the western terminus for the little **Lahaina, Kaanapali & Pacific Railroad**, a reconstructed 1890 sugar cane train (with passenger cars) operating between Kaanapali and Lahaina. The 6-mile, half-hour run is made about five times daily in each direction. Strictly on a per-mile basis, the fare is a little steep—$4.25 one way and $6.50 round trip for everyone aged 13 and older; $2 one way, $3.25 round trip for preteens. You can walk to the two Kaanapali depots, one just across the highway from the airstrip and the other across from the Maui Eldorado condo, or take the green articulated Kaanapali Jitney to the station ($2 round trip). The railroad provides a free bus on the other end of the line to get its passengers from the Lahaina depot to the center of town. Getting there is all the fun, and you may find the LK&PR worth the tab.

Lahaina, the scene of so much adventure in James Michener's novel *Hawaii*, was the capital of the Islands from the time Kamehameha the Great rested there after conquering Oahu in 1795 until 1843, when his son, Kamehameha III, moved himself and the seat of the kingdom to Honolulu.

Lahaina's turbulent period ran from the early 1820s—when the whaling ships and the missionaries first arrived, bringing all at once the concepts of both sin and salvation—until late in the century when the rise of the petroleum industry reduced the demand for whale oil. The missionaries, whose homes and missions had even been shot at by water-borne cannon, apparently won by default. The whalers stopped coming, and the principal "sights" of Lahaina today are the real beneficiaries of all this—the whales themselves.

If you visit Maui between late November and early May, you might see the whales rolling, jumping, and skylarking offshore. Often they are within the 9-mile span of water between Lahaina and the island of Lanai, cavorting on the very spot where as many as 400 whaling vessels once tied up deck to deck, almost forming a floating bridge across the Auau channel.

You can walk to most of the interesting spots in Lahaina. We'd begin with the East Indian **Banyan Tree**, the oldest and perhaps the largest in all the Islands. It was planted in the center of the square by William O. Smith, the sheriff of Lahaina, on April 24, 1873, to celebrate the fiftieth anniversary of Protestant missionary work. In 1973, more than 500 persons gathered in its 2/3-acre shade to mark its first century.

Fronting the mammoth tree is the **Lahaina Courthouse**, built in 1859 from stones cannibalized that year from Kamehameha III's old decaying palace several blocks away. Today it serves as Lahaina's police station and galleries for the Lahaina Art Society.

The crumbled walls you see nearby represent the corner of the old **Waterfront Fort**, put up in 1831 as a show of force to the whalers. They had been picking fights with the missionaries who disagreed with the sailors over visitation rights for native girls to their ships, and some cannonballs had even whistled into the church compound. The fort was demolished in 1854. In recent times, when Lahaina began honoring its lusty past, there wasn't much that could be done about rebuilding the fort without the unthinkable act of removing the banyan tree. So they rounded up some coral blocks and rebuilt just a corner of the structure —as a "ruin" that never existed in the first place!

In front of the courthouse is the **Lahaina Small Boat Harbor**, filled with a colorful mixture of private and commercial craft. The local cruise boats, fishing charters, and glass-bottom vessels are all tied up there.

The original building of the **Pioneer Inn**, across the street, was put up in 1901, when activity in Lahaina was at a low economic point. It was mainly built as a convenience for passengers on the interisland ferry which used to dock nearby. Incredibly, the landmark has remained virtually untouched. There's a wonderful old bar there on the other side of a pair of batwing doors which appears to be right out of Somerset Maugham. It's a favorite watering hole for yr. obt. svt. at least once in every voyage to the old capital.

Tied up to the wharf out front is the museum ship now dubbed **The Brig Carthaginian**. There once rested here a lovely old square-rigger called the *Carthaginian*, used during the filming of *Hawaii*. But someone ran it up on the reef in 1972, hopelessly foundering it, and everyone was heartbroken. The steel-hulled vessel now parked at the same pier was obtained at great effort from Denmark by the Lahaina Restoration Foundation, sailed 12,000 miles to Lahaina, and determinedly renamed *Carthaginian II*. Although a sorry-looking craft at the beginning, it has gradually been restored authentically as a square-rigged vessel of the 1800s (though the ship actually dates only to 1920). The exhibits below deck are interesting, and there's also a good video show about whales. (Open 9 to 4:30 daily; admission $2.) Although everybody who knew it misses the original, this newer incarnation of the *Carthaginian* is certainly worth a visit.

Just inland from that ship is a set of low ruins partly under plexiglass, the remains of the **Brick Palace**. Almost certainly the first western structure in the Islands, the palace was somewhat amateurishly built around 1801 by two ex-convicts from Australia expressly for the first King Kamehameha.

A short walk along the waterline from the above is the **Hauola Stone**, believed to have been a sacred healing place for the early Hawaiians. You'll have to look over the edge of the seawall to find it. It is shaped like a chair.

Catercorner across Front Street from the back of the Pioneer Inn you'll see the **Baldwin House** (Tel. 661-3262), the proud showpiece of the Lahaina Restoration Foundation. Built in 1834, it housed the medical missionary Dr. Dwight Baldwin and his family from 1838 until 1871. Through crude vaccination techniques, he saved the people of Maui, Molokai, and Lanai from the smallpox epidemic that plagued the Islands in 1853. The admission price includes a tour by one of the gracious Lahaina ladies active in the foundation. (Open daily 9:30 A.M. to 5 P.M., admission $2.25 for adults, free for children.) We also recommend the little booklet "Story of Lahaina," which they sell there for about 50 cents. Next door is the **Master's Reading Room**, a two-story coral building built by missionaries for the use of ships' officers. Today it serves as headquarters for the Restoration Foundation.

A 10-minute walk down Front Street and up Prison Road will take you to the place all the coral stones from the demolished waterfront fort went to. The **Hale Paahao**, translatable as the "stuck-in-irons house," is a prison built by convict labor at a leisurely pace from 1852 to 1854. (The walls are original, but the wooden cellblocks inside have been rebuilt.) It housed drunken sailors and Hawaiians alike.

If you have time, you can walk along Wainee Street to Shaw Street and look behind the recently rebuilt Wainee Church for the **Wainee Churchyard**. Perhaps as many as a third of the stones mark the graves of children—missionary babies who just couldn't make it because of hardship and disease. Many famous citizens of old Lahaina are also buried there.

You'll have to drive or ride toward Lahainaluna to see the **Pioneer Sugar Mill**, which has been in continuous operation since 1860. Farther *mauka* along the Lahainaluna Road is the **Lahainaluna High School**, built by its own first students in 1831 as a mission seminary school. It's not open to the public, but on its grounds is the **Hale Pa'i** ("House of Printing"), which is sometimes open. That 1834 printing house, recently restored, is the site of the first newspaper printed in the Islands—or west of the Rockies, for that matter. The volunteer curator there may print a page from an old school book for you while you wait. (Admission free.)

Six miles east of Lahaina along Route 30 is the easily overlooked village of **Olowalu**, which is the entry point for the equally obscure dirt road to the **Olowalu Petroglyphs**. The way is no longer marked by a Hawaii Visitors Bureau "warrior" sign. There are about three dirt roads leading *mauka*, but the right one runs by a water tower maybe 100 yards west of the Olowalu General store, almost hidden itself in a clump of trees.

About a mile in, you may see the remains of a wooden stairway that used to help everyone up to inspect the 200- to 300-year-old rock carvings. Today, most of that has been removed to discourage vandalism, and you will have to make like a mountain goat to scramble up the side of the cliff. If you're not that agile, and/or if you're going to the Big Island—where the petroglyphs are somewhat more accessible in the Puako area—these just might not be worth the effort to see them.

Continuing on Highway 30, you might look up the hill from time to time to catch a glimpse of the winding old road, especially above the outcropping, which you burrow through in a tunnel. That's the route people like Herman Melville and Mark Twain used to travel on horseback between Lahaina and Wailuku. Maui seemed a much bigger and more adventurous island in the last century, we'll wager.

Stop at **McGregor Point**, which is now only labeled "Scenic Point," to obtain a good view of East Maui (and Haleakala); Kahoolawe, the island the U.S. Navy uses as a great big bomb and shell target range; and Molokini, the little islet which pokes up above the water about halfway between Maui and Kahoolawe. From the air, it's obvious that Molokini is a little volcano crater, breached on one side by the sea, giving it a half-moon shape. A fish sanctuary, it's ideal for snorkeling and scuba diving. (See Sections 7 and 8.)

A few miles farther along the road, on the shores of Maalaea Bay, is **Maalaea**, today sloppily pronounced "mah-*lie*-ya" by local folks. The tiny village has a small market, a gas pump, a Coast Guard station, a small boat harbor, and Buzz's Restaurant.

CENTRAL MAUI—KIHEI, WAILEA, AND IAO VALLEY

Those on a limited schedule could skip this trip, with the possible exception of Iao Valley.

The coastline from Maalaea to Kihei has formed the traditional war-canoe invasion beach for centuries. The U.S. Armed Forces in the 1940s were aware of this; along Route 31 you may still catch sight of one or two structures overgrown by weeds or sugar cane. These were the **World War II Block Houses**, hastily constructed to prevent the Japanese invasion that never came. You may also still see some tank traps—cement boulders with spikes of railroad rails bristling from them.

Several little beaches along the highway may be reached by short access roads. On some you will find no one else in sight, probably because of the steady and often bothersome wind that comes up at noon and continues until dusk. On many of these beaches, U.S. Marines stationed on Maui trained for the assault on Japanese-held islands in the South Pacific during the war.

Opposite the Maui Lu Resort is the **Vancouver Monument**, thought to mark the point where Captain George Vancouver landed in the early 1800s. The marker is a totem pole, recalling Vancouver's association with western Canada. The Maui Lu Resort across the road is run by and caters to western Canadians, and somehow all this ties in together.

The little village, area, or whatnot of **Kihei** ("*key*-hay") is not attractive, and many tasteless condos sprouted up in the area in the 1970s. It may help that the new *mauka* highway now manages to bypass all of this hodgepodge.

If you continue driving on either road you will enter the **Wailea Resort**, the well-planned resort community executed by Alexander & Baldwin, a *kamaaina* company that once devoted its attention entirely to sugar. Instead of cutting the public off from the five beautiful beaches next to its land, A&B built a minipark at each with parking lots, paved access, and some rest rooms for everybody, and then turned these facilities over to the county government.

There are two beautiful 18-hole golf courses, plus an 11-court tennis club. The luxurious Hotel Inter-Continental Maui is between **Ulua Beach** and the larger **Wailea Beach**, and the handsome Westin Wailea Beach Hotel is on nearby **Mokapu Beach**. The Wailea Shopping Village, a smallish complex, is also on the property near the highway.

The paved route (Wailea Alanui) ends a short way past **Polo Beach** and the somewhat intrusive Polo Beach Club building. The dirt road is passable at least to **Makena Beach**, one of the most popular public swimming and surfing shores on the island. *Warning:* Leave nothing valuable in your car, and watch your belongings in general, if you go swimming in the area.

Unless you have a rugged vehicle, you should turn back here. We *do not* recommend the temptingly short but very rough winding road up the mountain between Makena and Ulupalakua, even if someone tells you the route is "okay." (It may be reasonably passable one day, but not for the next 10 days.) Improvements will come here some day, and when this route is finally smoothed out, we will be among the first to try it as an attractive alternate course to "Up-country" Maui and access to Haleakala.

Retracing your route past Kihei, you can turn off onto Highway 35 for a quick march to **Kahului**, Maui's deepwater port and site of the island's well-designed jet airport. **Baldwin Beach Park**, near Paia, is about the only good beach on the windward side of the island. Personally, we don't like the atmosphere there all that much.

The rest of Kahului is composed mainly of shopping centers, gas stations, and housing developments. You can continue along Highway 32 (Kaahumanu Avenue) into its twin city, **Wailuku**, the older county seat. The older section of Wailuku is in the foothills of the West Maui Mountains. Of the things that are generally pointed out to visitors, we like the little 1832 **Kaahumanu Congregational Church**, the oldest extant church on Maui. It's near the county government buildings on Route 30, just off Main Street.

The only "don't miss" in Wailuku with which we strongly agree is on the left and just a little farther along Highway 32, the same road that leads to Iao ("ee-*yow*") Valley. This is the **Hale Hoikeike**, the Maui Historical Society museum (Tel. 244-3326). The first part of the stone structure was put up in 1842, and it became the home of local schoolmaster and artist Edward Bailey. Several of his works are exhibited there. There are also many artifacts from both stone-age Hawaii and post-Cook periods on display, including items brought to the Islands by the missionaries. (Open 9 A.M. to 3:30 P.M., Monday to Saturday, $2.50 adults, $1 children.)

Farther up the road you'll see **Kepaniwai Park**, whose charming, peaceful grounds belie its violent past. Kepaniwai, which takes its name from the stream running through it, means "damming of the waters" and refers to the 1790 slaughter by Kamehameha of the Maui army. The bodies filled the brook, causing *kepaniwai*. (And the water ran red down the valley, too, causing another name change in the village at the bottom: *Wailuku* means, loosely, "Bloody River.") Kamehameha won the battle, incidentally, by introducing cannon into local power politics for the first time. The cannon, named Lopaka ("Robert"), was manned by the king's *haole* advisors John Young and Isaac Davis. Some of the first and still highly revered whites in the Islands were not exactly men of peace and good will.

Kepaniwai Park was built as a cultural tribute to the ethnic groups that settled on Maui. There are separate pavilions for Japanese, Filipino, Chinese, Hawaiian, early American, and Portuguese groups.

A little farther up the valley, and on the right, is a spooky natural formation, the **John F. Kennedy Profile**. At one time it was thought that the natural rock formation closely resembled the late president, although as memories dim it may not be as effective for some. It seems strange, however, that the face was apparently not noticed until after the president died.

The end of the road is in **Iao Valley State Park**, the spot that Mark

Twain in typical hyperbole called the "Yosemite of the Pacific." The park is at the eroded center of the ancient volcano that created West Maui. The valley floor is already 2,250 feet above sea level, but the most startling feature is a spire of gray and moss-green rock called **Iao Needle**. It doesn't look very tall because there's nothing on top of it to provide a comparison, but this natural basaltic form rises another 1,200 feet above your head.

The green-carpeted cliffs in the valley inspired another writer, Robert Louis Stevenson, to coin a word to describe it—viridescent. The moss and small ferns do seem almost to glow when the sun catches them at just the right angle. The cliffs rise about twice as high as the needle, incidentally. When there has been a heavy rain in the neighborhood, a spectacular waterfall is often seen nearby.

There is a 1½-mile-long trail in the valley, but in the winter you may want to remember that the sun goes down quickly, leaving you in a very cool shadow as early as 3:30 P.M. The Hawaiian word *iao* is often translated as "facing the dawn," and the steep valley which bears the name has no sunsets.

They say Iao Valley by moonlight is a beautiful experience, and that one's sense of perspective becomes quite confused and the valley appears much smaller in the lunar illumination. Those who have spent a night in Iao Valley under a full moon say it's far from a frightening experience. They are comforted by the splashing of the little brook and the lights of Wailuku and Kahului, which can be seen in the distance. We hereby resolve to do this before many more moons have gone by.

THE HALEAKALA TRIP—KULA AND POINTS UP, UP, AND UP

Measured from the airport, the trip to the summit of Haleakala, the "House of the Sun," is only 36 miles. It will take you about 2½ hours in each direction, however. With the stops you'll want to make in Kula and at the observatory points, it would be a darn good idea to start very early. The crater will probably be cloudy at midday and clear in midmorning or late afternoon. Dial the National Weather Service recording, 877-5124, for a weather report on viewing conditions. There is also a national park recording, updated less frequently, at 572-7749. If you want to check with the park rangers live, call 572-9306 until 4 P.M.

No matter how warm it is at sea level, take a wrap to put on at the summit. (Going up to see the sunrise, especially, many borrow blankets from their hotel rooms.) It will be downright chilly at 10,023 feet at any time of year. A second caveat: If you suffer from high blood pressure or have any other trouble with rare air at high altitudes, let someone else drive the car. Pull over to the side if you begin to feel light-headed at any point during the trip.

If you've got plenty of gas in the tank, water in the radiator, and perhaps a picnic lunch and a thermos of hot coffee in the back seat, start off along Highway 37 out of Kahului.

Your first sign of civilization over the rolling hills of "Up-country" will be **Pukalani**. There are a couple of gas stations operating there, in case you really *did* forget to fill up down below. Bullock's of Hawaii, a snack and gift shop, is not bad for a "moonburger." (See Section 5.)

At the junction with Route 377, take that road. It's also known as the Upper Kula Road, and it will lead you over some particularly pleasant pastureland and along stands of eucalyptus and pine trees to **Kula**, the center of the vegetable and flower-growing industries on Maui. The air is nearly always more bracing up here, giving rise to the local slogan "It's cooler in Kula."

You'll soon come across the two little chalet-hotels near each other at the 3,300-foot level. Both the Kula Lodge (Tel. 878-1535) and the Silversword Inn (Tel. 878-1232) have dining rooms, cozy lounges, and fireplaces. Persons who plan to spend hours hiking or riding in Haleakala might want to consider their rooms. Doubles run around $35.

A little farther along is the junction with Highway 378, the route that will eventually take you to the top. Almost immediately, it begins its twists and turns, and along about here you'll be glad you brought your sweater or jacket.

If it's still morning, you may be able to see all the way down to the ocean while you continue to climb. If it's later in the day, you may be driving through mist and rain. If it seems foggy, don't give up. It could still be a beautiful day where you're going, in the land beyond the clouds.

At about 7,000 feet above the ocean there's a side road off to the left to **Hosmer Grove Campground** about one quarter mile in. If you brought a picnic and you're hungry now, this glen full of exotic shrubs and trees is the traditional place to eat it. There are rest rooms, a couple of picnic tables, a barbecue pit, and probably no one else to talk to.

Just ahead is the entrance to **Haleakala National Park** and the park headquarters. Incidentally, this was the first building we ever saw in Hawaii that was centrally heated, radiators being about as common as snowmen in the state. Load up here on information, literature, etc.; this is also the place you secure your camping and hiking permits, if needed.

In the front yard of the building are planted several examples of silversword, that strange, delicate plant that grows only on Haleakala and high up on the Big Island, and nowhere else in the world. It blooms just once, and dies shortly afterwards.

And in case you don't see them in the wild, there are a couple of specimens of *nene*, the Hawaiian native goose, penned up in the back yard.

The *nene* has a black patch over his eye, but more significant is the lack of webbing between the toes. Over the centuries, this feature has evolved for living among the rough lava flows, whereas webbing, of course, is more suited for paddling around in a lake.

From headquarters it's 11 more miles to the summit. There are two overlooks to the crater on the way, Leleiwi and Kalahaku, but save them for the trip back. Push on to the Visitor Center at 9,745 feet, where the park rangers give occasional talks. (It used to open at dawn to welcome the sunrise crowd, but because of current federal economy moves, the hours have been unfortunately restricted to 8 A.M. to 3 P.M.) A little further, the unattended observatory at the summit (open 24 hours) is the traditional place to watch the sunrise.

The beautiful scene of desolation spread out in front of you has been compared to the mountains of the moon. It's an awesome crater—seven miles long, two miles wide, 8,000 feet deep—supposedly enough to hold the entire island of Manhattan, Bronx to Battery, East Side to West Side, subways to skyscrapers. Throughout this huge crater are smaller craters, a miniature mountain range of cinder cones. Everywhere there are muted colors—rust, gray, purple, brown, black, yellow, and an occasional pink.

The way to really experience the Haleakala Crater is to hike or take horseback trips into it. There are 30 miles of well-marked trails, and excursions are occasionally conducted by park rangers. Three cabins are within the crater, none closer than 7-1/2 miles from the rim observatory. Fees are cheap, but the cabins are booked months in advance, and the bookings are made by National Park Service lottery since requests far outnumber the bunks available.

Full information on hiking, riding, and camping may be obtained in advance by writing the Superintendent, Haleakala National Park, Box 537, Makawao, Maui, HI 96768. On Maui itself, you may telephone the park headquarters at 572-9306.

If you didn't enter the crater and missed seeing examples of the silversword there or at park headquarters, you will have another chance near the **Kalahaku Overlook** on the way back down.

At the bottom of the crater road—Route 378—you may want to turn left (south) on 377, Kekaulike Avenue, and search out a commercial protea flower farm. One we like very much is the **Maui Sunburst** (Tel. 878-1218), on the somewhat hard-to-find Copp Road, which is about a mile and a half from the end of 378. Say "Hi" for us to Carver or Skelly, the bachelors who run the operation—and to their girlfriends who help out during busy periods. (Closed Saturday.) Unfortunately, Copp Road is marked better at its junction with the lower road, Route 37.

Even farther south, another 10 miles or so along the narrow and twisting portion of Route 37, you will eventually arrive at Ulupalakua Ranch and the tasting room of the **Tedeschi Winery** (Tel. 878-6058), in a century-old jailhouse (open 10 A.M. to 4 P.M.). For a few years, now, the winery has had only pineapple wine to offer—Maui Blanc and the sparkling Maui Brut. (Not bad, considering what it is!) But sometime in 1984 Emil Tedeschi is scheduled to unveil the real stuff—a champagne and a red table wine made from the Carnelian grape.

HANA—THE SPIRIT OF OLD HAWAII

"Heavenly Hana," they call it. And maybe it is that way because it's almost as hard to get to. Officially it's just under 53 miles from Kahului Airport on Route 36, but that's a trip that will take nearly three hours each way when the weather is good. When it's not, well, you just don't go. If there's a washout on the road, you could be trapped for hours.

We've been to Hana both by land and by air, and you might want to consider taking the plane, too. Royal Hawaiian Air Service flies there, as well as some charter or tour trips out of Kahului like Paragon Air. When we flew in once, we rented a car to explore the immediate area. But you can't "deadhead" a rented car into or out of Hana. You either have to fly both ways or drive both ways.

Check your gas and your tummy in the village of **Paia**, a last-chance stop on the way. Ten miles later the road gets rough and your safari has begun.

Now right about here is where we should say that travelers vary widely in their reaction to the Hana road. We get letters annually from some readers who ask how we could have the nerve to put them on such a terrible, difficult, narrow, and winding road. Others write to tell us that they don't know what we were making such a fuss about. The route was fine, they say, and well worth the rewards. So there you are; you'll have to make up your own mind.

You'll find plenty of tempting places to stop, but don't lose track of your time. There are some occasional freshwater swimming holes. A favorite of ours is at **Puohokamoa Falls** almost halfway to Hana. Other wonderful picnic spots include **Puaa Kaa State Park**, where two waterfalls and a pair of natural pools occur right beside the highway, and **Kaumahina State Wayside Park**, where trees and flowers are labeled along a short nature trail.

You'll see fascinating vegetation along the road, like the giant *ape-ape* ("*ah*-pay, *ah*-pay") leaves, African tulip trees, and breadfruit trees. If you like guavas, sometimes you can pick up hundreds along the road to **Hana Airport**.

About a half mile farther from the airport road is **Waianapanapa State Park** ("why a *nah*-pah *nah*-pah"), which offers camping or rustic accommodations in a dozen cabins (if you've made advance reservations). Also in the park are trails through the *hala* or pandanus trees to hard-to-find **Waianapanapa Caves**, where you can swim underground in some water-filled lava tubes.

Here's another trick we haven't tried, but some readers have managed to make it under these instructions: At low tide, there's a second chamber in the cave which you can locate only by floating something ahead of you like a surfboard with a light on it. If you do, you will find a natural rock throne where a Hawaiian princess once tried to hide from her jealous husband. But he saw in the water the reflection of her feather *kahili* (the symbol of royalty), entered the secret chamber, and killed her there along with her servant. Today the water is supposed to turn red every spring in supernatural testimony to that tragedy.

As you enter Hana, there's a fork in the road. Either route will take you into the village, but the rougher road on the right follows the high ground and provides the first distant view of the lovely **Hana Bay**. The beach park down below is a beautiful picnic site, but the swimming is not all that great. In ancient times, this gentle and peaceful inlet witnessed countless invasions from the Big Island, only 30 miles away. The **Hotel Hana Maui**, the town's principal means of support, is the only place in town open for dinner. (See Sections 4 and 5.)

Across the street from the hotel is the charming little **Wananalua Church**, built in 1838, appropriately enough on the site of a *heiau*, thus physically supplanting the old religion with the new. As much of a sight as any in Hana is the funky commercial establishment made famous in the now seldom-sung song, the **Hasegawa General Store**. Here's where you get the bumper stickers with Hana's solution to gasoline and pollution problems—"Get a Horse," it advises. (And it looks like Hasegawa's just might sell you one, too, right off the counter.)

The paved but very rutty road (Route 36) continues through the lush and unhurried countryside for 10 miles or so beyond the village of Hana. On quiet weekdays, you may have trouble skirting the sleeping dogs in the road so you can drive through. But dogs aren't the only hazards.

On one trip, we saw a sign which declared in no uncertain terms: "Beware of Goat!" Suddenly we saw the Big Gruff Billy himself, trying to stare us down from the shoulder of the road. And another notice farther on slowed us even more. "Caution for Little Pigs Crossing Road," it said, alongside a silhouette of three little porkers. These we didn't see in the flesh, but it wasn't for lack of looking!

A few miles out of town a sign indicates **Hamoa Beach**, on a separate loop off the main road. Not as beautiful as it's sometimes cracked up to be, the sand is reached over land owned up by the Hotel Hana Maui, which maintains the beach as part of its private facilities. (Some Mavericks have reported that they have successfully invaded this beach despite all the intimidating signs.)

Continuing along the main road, you may be able to catch sight of the Big Island across the Alenuihaha Channel. In the winter, look for the snowcapped peaks of Mauna Kea and more-distant Mauna Loa.

The large cross you will soon see at the side of the road is dedicated to Helio Kawaloa, an early Catholic Hawaiian who converted 4,000 more to his faith. He is buried down the hill in the ruins of the deserted Wailua village. A little ways farther is **Wailua Falls**, a dramatic cascade that thunders down beside the road. You may get a better look at it on the way back if you have time then.

Just when you think there is no such thing, you round your last curve to find the **Seven Pools of Kipahulu**, sometimes (incorrectly) referred to as the Seven Sacred Pools, 10 miles from Hana. Since the Kipahulu Valley down to the ocean is now part of Haleakala National Park, you will probably find a park ranger there to answer your questions about the area. (Sometimes he conducts special field trips. Telephone 248-8260 for information.)

The road crosses the stream between pool number four and pool number five. Park your car in the parking area beyond the bridge and walk back to it and then down along the lower pools to the ocean. Swimming, picnicking, and camping (with permit for the latter) are most certainly allowed.

If you want, you may continue for a little over two miles farther along the road to visit **Charles Lindbergh's Grave**. The great aviator picked out and cleared the site himself more than a year before his death. He chose the churchyard of the 1850 Kipahulu Hawaiian Church, a couple hundred yards off the road. (Not to be confused with St. Paul's Church nearby.) The grave, now marked with a simple marble stone, is *makai* of the church. Lindbergh died August 26, 1974, and was buried the same day, in accordance with his instructions.

7. Guided Tours and Cruises on Maui

Robert's Hawaii, Inc. (Tel. 877-5038), an all-Island firm, and **Maui Island Tours** (Tel. 877-5581), a Maui agency, begin their tours in Kahului. Two other companies—**Grayline Maui** (Tel. 877-5507) and **Holo Holo Maui** (Tel. 661-4858)—offer theirs originating at Kaanapali. Arrangements can be made with any of these for pickup in the Wailea area. All but Holo Holo Maui use big buses, limousines, and vans. Holo Holo prides itself on offering tours in minibuses only.

Some typical bus tours include the following:

Iao Valley-Haleakala Crater. 10 hours. From your Kaanapali Hotel, via Wailuku, to see the Iao Needle and then way up to the crater. This is a long trip, and in winter it will be dark before you get back to your hotel.

Kaanapali-Iao Valley-Kula Drive. 8 hours. Similar to the above, but instead of continuing up to see Haleakala crater, you turn around in Kula, the village on the slopes.

Lahaina. 3 hours. From your Kaanapali hotel, the tour takes you to old Lahaina town, stops at the old prison and the fort, and brings you back again.

Small van or minibus tours are much more numerous, flexible, and changeable. As of this writing, Holo Holo Maui, for example, has the following set of tours in 12-passenger vehicles (don't hold us to these estimated prices): Heavenly Hana, $50; Haleakala Sunrise, $40; Haleakala and Central Maui, $40; Iao Valley and Lahaina, $55; Haleakala Sunset, $50; and the Circle Island Tour, $50. (Reservations at P.O. Box 1591, Lahaina, HI 96761.) We've taken one tour with the laid-back Holo Holo operation, and we like them very much.

Another small van tour for anyone who makes it into Hana, whether by air or by any other means, is the unique and personalized **Tiny's Hana Tours** (Tel. 248-8685). Tiny's is one van and one man, named Viewed "Tiny" Malaikini, a 300-pound-plus musical Hawaiian born in Hana who's been around the world and come back home again. A large part of the attraction is Tiny's jovial but respectful personality, and he'll tailor his tour to the wants of his passengers. At the moment, Tiny's tours are selling for $25 per person for three hours and $50 for six hours. (You can reserve in advance by phone or by writing him at P.O. Box 41, Hana, HI 96713. Bookings are also made through Royal Hawaiian Air Service or Paragon Air —see "Air Tours" later.) Tiny's is the only game in town—and it's a good one, too. We enjoyed Tiny's tour last year, so say hello to him from us!

BOAT CRUISES FROM MAUI

Heading into the waves directly from Kaanapali Beach is **Sea Sales** (Tel. 661-0927), headquartered at the Sheraton Hotel. Their catamaran *Seahorse* offers a three-hour luncheon cruise with a snorkeling expedition for perhaps $40, and a sunset cocktail sail with open bar for about $30.

There are several vessels to choose from at the boat harbor in front of the old courthouse in Lahaina. Those designed primarily for fishing or scuba charters will be found under our Section 8, "Water Sports." Here are those offering regular cruises:

Lahaina's large (65-foot) glass-bottom boat, named (with no apologies for the spelling) the **Coral See** (Tel. 661-8699), cruises clearer waters than do the glass-bottom craft on Oahu. Half-day picnic/snorkel tours, with equipment, instruction, and lunch, now run about $40 (children half price). From December through May, two-hour whale-watching cruises are scheduled on the *Coral See* for about half those rates.

With five departures a day, the souped-up, 52-foot Chinese junk called the **Lin Wa** (Tel. 667-9266) offers 1½-hour glass bottoming for around $10, or kids for $5. If you bring a bathing suit, you can help feed the fish. (Both the *Coral See* and the *Lin Wa* have just been put under the joint management of Captain Jon S. Dilloway, P.O. Box 596, Lahaina, HI 96761.)

Scotch Mist Charters (Tel. 661-0386) launches several sails aboard the 36-foot sloop *Scotch Mist* or the 50-foot yacht *Scotch Mist II*. Two-hour sails begin at about $35. There is also a full-day sail around the Island of Lanai for about $90 and several other trips. Call Skipper Dan O'Brien, or write him at 98 Haleleo St., Lahaina, HI 96761 to make advance reservations.

Cruises to Lanai are also launched by three other outfits. The Frederick Lewises from Bakersfield, Calif., wrote to us to highly recommend **Seabird Cruises** (Tel. 661-3643). In the two-masted ketch *Viajero*, they set sail for an all-day Lanai cruise. With breakfast, lunch, snorkeling, and Lanai bus tour, the whole excursion may run around $60 this year (half-price for junior sea scouts). There may also be a five-hour Picnic Snorkel Sail for around $35, a Sunset Mai Tai Sail (two hours) for around $25, and a Cocktail Dinner Cruise (roast beef, open bar, entertainment) for around $40. Seabird now also operates the catamaran *Ono Mana* (formerly the *Aikane II*), on an all-day round trip to Molokai for about $65, including breakfast, lunch, and cocktails.

Another buoyant boat operation with Lanai trips is **Windjammer Cruises** (Tel. 667-6834), a branch of a Honolulu operation. Windjammer launches its 65-foot schooner *Spirit of Windjammer* for that trip (about $60 for an all-day sail) or for their evening dinner cruise (about $35). We've happily sailed with these people in Honolulu, but have not yet climbed aboard on Maui.

The 50-foot trimaran *Trilogy*, built by the late E. J. Coon, is still operated by his family as **Trilogy Excursions** (Tel. 661-4743). The daylong sails to Lanai go Monday through Friday for about $90, including breakfast, a car tour of Lanai, snorkeling, and lunch. This is also a popular trip, and parties are kept small. (If necessary a second, 40-foot trimaran, the *Kailana*, is also put in service.) We've had several letters about the Coons, universally in praise of the operation despite the fact that it's a little more expensive, and we intend to make the trip ourselves one day soon. Phone or write Jim Coon or his family at P.O. Box 1121, Lahaina, HI 96761.

A sleek, fast 47-foot luxury powerboat called the *Unicorn I* is run by **Unicorn Tours** (Tel. 879-6333) almost daily between Maui and Lanai or Molokai. Morning or afternoon round tips, including a bus tour, will run about $55 this year. A full-day trip, with lunch, runs about $80. (Backpackers report they have managed to arrange a one-way interisland trip via the Unicorn connection.) A Maverick reader has written very critically of her trip on the **Alihilani**, out of Lahaina.

A new and well-run snorkel cruise sails out of the Maalaea Harbor every morning at 7:30 A.M. aboard the *Wailea Kai*, run by the **Ocean Activities Center** (Tel. 879-4485). The 65-foot catamaran heads for the tiny, half-moon-shaped islet of Molokini, which cradles a marine conservation area. On the way the crew instructs you in safe and fun snorkeling activities, then turns you loose under their watchful eyes to observe the hundreds of kinds of multicolored fish under the surface. With a light breakfast and lunch, the price will be around $50 in 1984. We went along as observers and were impressed with the entire operation. In season, the *Wailea Kai* also launches two-hour whale-watching cruises in Maalaea Harbor, an excellent observation area, for around $25. And there's a Sunset Champagne Sail, with dinner and drinks, for around $35. (Reservations from the phone number above, at either of the Wailea hotels, or from the Ocean Activities Center at P.O. Box 1082, Kihei, HI 96753.) Tell 'em we sent you!

Besides the above cruises, there will surely be others riding the waves this year. Three booking services try to stay afloat on a changing sea of information. Besides the Ocean Activities Center (above), you might check with the **Aloha Activity Center** (Tel. 667-9564) in the Whalers Village and at The Wharf in Lahaina, or the **Maui Visitor Information & Activity Center** (Tel. 661-8340) on Halawai Drive in Lahaina. These agencies draw a commission from the boats themselves, so it should not cost you any more to make your bookings through them.

AIR TOURS ON MAUI

The flight patterns change rapidly, but this year's big whirlybird for sightseeing seems to be **Maui Helicopters** (Tel. 879-1601), a four-passenger Hughes 500C jet helicopter stationed at the Hotel Inter-Continental Maui. Three tours include Remote Excursion, Keanae's Coastline, and Hana, about $100 per person; Panoramic Journey, Hana, Seven Pools, and Haleakala Crater, about $130; and Maui Unlimited, the entire island, $175.

Three other chopper firms are on Maui. **Kenai Air Hawaii** (Tel. 661-4426), an extension of the Honolulu company, has three Maui tours with departures from Kaanapali and Kapalua. They are the Maui Deluxe, including Haleakala crater and Hana, with a touchdown in an inaccessible area for about $165 per person; West Maui and North Shore of Molokai, including Kalaupapa and a stop at an otherwise inaccessible beach, $120; and Maui's West Coast and Mountains and Iao Valley, about $90.

Papillon Helicopters (Tel. 669-4884), a branch of the Kauai company of the same name, is headquartered at Kapalua. Their four main tours are the West Maui Fantasia, including the West Maui Mountains, Iao Valley, and Lahaina for about $100; Molokai Voyager, an air tour of the southern and northern coast of Molokai and the Kalaupapa Peninsula for about $140; Sunset Fantasy, including Molokai and Shipwreck Beach on Lanai, about $165; and Maui Odyssey, the West Maui Mountains, Hana, Kipahulu Valley, inside Haleakala Crater, including a wilderness champagne picnic snack, about $225.

South Sea Helicopters (Tel. 667-7765), a newer company, also offers several tours, including a 1-1/2-hour flight called "Pacific Fantasy" covering the entire island. With a beach stop and a meal, it runs about $135.

Touring helicopters get most of the publicity, but good bargains can sometimes be found on fixed-wing aerial tours in Hawaii. In Maui, the best of these is probably **Paragon Air** (Tel. 244-3356). Pilot Peter Wolford and his wife have organized two aerial programs, a one-hour tour of East Maui for $75, and an hour and 45-minute tour that adds to that Lanai and Molokai for $110. Combination air/ground tours have been set up, too, including one that connects with the above-mentioned Tiny's Tours of Hana for a total cost of about $100 per person. We've flown with Peter in his sleek, high-winged Italian Partenavia, and enjoyed every thrilling second of it. If you go, give him our warmest happy landings!

Horseback riding? For this turn around the track, anyway, we cover that in Section 9, straight ahead a couple of furlongs.

8. Water Sports on Maui

Of Maui's 150 miles of coastline, some 32-1/2 miles are lined with beaches. Many are not even named, which does not dim their popularity with beachcombers, surfers, swimmers, snorkelers, or fishermen.

We stick stubbornly to the southerly shores. Despite local pride, there is virtually no good swimming along the entire windward coast of Maui—or if there is, please tell *us* about it. We couldn't find a decent beach over there except for **Baldwin Park**, near Paia on the road to Hana. It's often populated by youthful beer drinkers, and some say that the sharks are all on the shore at Baldwin. The offshore current is also strong.

Kahului Beach behind the Kahului hotels is almost a joke. Sup-

posedly, however, it's good for hunting "Maui diamonds," which are actually little white quartz stones. We never saw any, but then we didn't
look very hard.

All the most desirable beaches are leeward, or on the southern shores.
Here are some selected targets for beachniks there, progressing generally from west to east:

Honokohau Beach, near the end of the paved portion of Highway 30.
Good swimming, surfing, fishing, and shelling. **Pokakupele Beach**,
sometimes called Windmill Beach, is better for fishing and shelling than
for swimming.

Honolua Beach has good swimming, surfing, skin diving, and scuba
diving. One of the finest habitats for live coral and reef fish in the state, it
has now been named a State Marine Life Conservation District.

Makuleia Beach has good swimming and fishing. **Honokahua Beach**
has good swimming, snorkeling, and skin diving.

Kapalua Beach, also known as Fleming Beach, is one of the finest
beaches on Maui for swimming, snorkeling, skin diving, and scuba. The
Kapalua Bay Hotel opened right on this beach, but there is public access
from an obscure road.

Napili Beach fronts the Napili Kai and other hotels on Napili Bay.
There's good swimming, snorkeling, surfing, skin diving, and scuba diving there. **Honokowai Beach Park**, at Honokowai, offers fair swimming
and snorkeling off narrow sands.

Kaanapali Beach. Three miles of beautiful sandy beach fronting
more than a half-dozen luxury hotels and condos. Good swimming except when the surf is high (look for the red flags put out by the hotels).
Good body surfing fronting the Sheraton.

Lahaina shoreline. Little beach—except a bit of sand at the Lahaina
Shores Hotel—but there are excellent spots dotted along the entire
Lahaina coastline for swimming, surfing, shelling, fishing, snorkeling,
and skin diving in shallow water.

Launiupoko State Park, a wayside picnic park you'll notice between
Lahaina and Olowalu. Nobody likes to talk about it much, but the surfers
call this area "Shark Pit." It is indeed a breeding ground for small sharks
during May, June, and July. It's not a good swimming area, anyway, although it's okay for fishing and hunting shells.

Olowalu Shore, near Hekili Point. Not only are there good swimming, surfing, fishing, skin diving, and scuba diving, but this is the best
place for hunting those "Maui diamonds," described above at Kahului
Beach.

Kihei Memorial Park. No swimming. Picnic only. **Kalama Beach
Park**. Heavy coral here makes for poor swimming. **Kamaole Beach**

Parks I, II, and III all have excellent swimming and good snorkeling and fishing.

Keawakapu, Mokapu, Ulua, Wailea, and Polo beaches. These five beaches, which were developed by the Wailea Resort, are excellent for swimming. There's also good fishing and snorkeling around the rocks. When the waves come in during the summer months, they are excellent for body surfing.

Makena Beach. Popular until recently with an exclusive surfing coterie, but now gaining in general use. The winter surf is big, but when waters are tame it's also a good swimming, fishing, and shelling area. (*Caution:* There are often thefts from cars in this area.) **Little Makena Beach**, just the other side of the rock promontory at Makena's north end, is Maui's most famous nude beach.

The Nuu Shore. Running from the Makena beaches to La Perouse Bay, this rugged area of dirt trails and steep cliffs does offer good shelling and fishing. Surfing is for experts only at La Perouse Bay due to the steep cliffs and razor-sharp lava fingers in the area.

Hana Beach Park. This picturesque beach at the village of Hana does offer good swimming and fishing. **Hamoa Beach.** Near Hana, all land access to this beach is controlled by the Hotel Hana Maui, making it almost a private beach for the hotel's guests only. Swimming and snorkeling are excellent, but the gray sand is certainly not as lovely as many others found in West Maui.

FRESHWATER SWIMMING

There are several natural pools along Highway 36 to Hana and beyond, nearly all at the bottom of waterfalls. Some of these include Waikamoi Stream, Puohokamoa Falls, Haipuaena Falls, Koolau Park, Puaa Kaa State Park, Hanawi Falls, Waianapanapa Cave, and the famous Seven Pools of Kipahulu.

SCUBA DIVING AND SNORKELING

Some of the best diving grounds in Hawaii are found in the channel running from Olowalu to Kaanapali. The coastline from Kihei to Makena is also good, as well as at Napili Bay and Fleming Beach. But divers should check with local experts to be fully aware of hazards in these waters. Snorkelers will also find beautiful viewing in the same areas, but generally close in to shore. (An exception is at Molokini Island; see below.)

Instructions and equipment rental are available at four dive shops in Lahaina. These include **Central Pacific Divers** (Tel. 661-8718), the granddaddy of most of them, at 780 Front St.; **Lahaina Divers** (Tel.

667-7496) at 710 Front St.; **American Dive Shop** (Tel. 661-4885) at 628 Front St.; and **Hawaiian Reef Divers** (Tel. 667-7647) at 129 Lahainaluna Road.

Two dive shops now have Kihei addresses. They are **Kihei Sea Sports** (Tel. 879-1919) at the Kihei Town Center, and **Maui Dive Shop** (Tel. 879-3388) in the Azeka Place Shopping Center. At any of these, figure about $50 for a half-day of scuba instruction, if the shop arranges everything.

Accomplished divers may experience some fascinating underwater adventures. Central Pacific likes to take its people to the huge underwater caves called the Lanai Cathedrals, 60 feet down, or to a sunken navy submarine, the former U.S.S. *Bluegill*, scuttled in 1972. But caution: The *Bluegill* rests on the bottom in more than 140 feet of water —much too deep for the novice diver. Several beginners have gotten in trouble diving to see the submarine in the past few years.

SPORT FISHING

No license is required for deep-sea fishing. Catches include marlin, mahimahi, aku (skipjack), barracuda, kawakawa (bonito), ulua (jack crevalle), ahi (yellowfin tuna), wahoo, and bonefish.

There are several well-known charter outfits, many of which sail from the small boat harbor at Lahaina and some from the marina at Maalaea. All officially charge about $275 for a half day (four hours) and $400 or so for a full, eight-hour day for the entire boat (up to six persons). Some will stick to these official rates, but you might try to make your contacts in person to see how good a deal you can snag when the captain doesn't have to pay an agent's commission. Many will also set up trips on a "share-boat" basis.

The numbers of skippers who have skipped on and off the Maui charter scene over the past few years has been too much for us to keep up with, so we can no longer list individual boats and crews. If you're interested in deep-sea fishing, either (a) go down to the docks in Lahaina or Maalaea and strike up a conversation with a captain or his mate; (b) seek advice from your hotel activities desk; or (c) call any of the three Maui activities centers, who are up on the latest boats and rates available. The Aloha Activity Center (Tel. 667-9564), the Ocean Activities Center (Tel. 879-4485), and the Maui Visitor Information & Activity Center (Tel. 661-8340) should have all the dope on charter fishing, and, of course, lots of other activities.

9. Other Sports on Maui

On Maui, hunting is becoming almost as popular a sport as fishing. Year-round game mammals include the wild boar in the West Maui mountains and goats on the northern and western slopes of Haleakala. Bag limit is two each per day. Game birds include pheasants, doves, quail, wild turkey, francolin, and chukar partridge in the Kula-Kahikinui Game Management Area.

Licenses for non-residents are $15. All hunting is under State of Hawaii jurisdiction, so up-to-date information on Maui hunting should be obtained from the Division of Fish and Game, Hawaii Department of Land and Natural Resources, State Building, Wailuku, HI 96793. The telephone number is 244-4352.

MAUI GOLFING

There are at least eight golf courses open to the public on the island, and naturally they are used all year round. The most famous is the site of the annual Women's Kemper Open, the **Royal Kaanapali** (Tel. 661-3991), North and South Courses, which wind regally through the Kaanapali resort area.

The **Wailea Golf Club** (Tel. 879-2966) is split into a Blue Course and a Red Course. The newer **Kapalua Golf Course** (Tel. 669-8044), designed by Arnold Palmer, is the nucleus of the Kapalua Bay Resort. Each of these resorts has 36 holes.

Other courses include the **Maui Country Club** (Tel. 877-0616) at Sprecklesville, the **Waiehu Municipal Golf Course** (Tel. 244-5433) at Waiehu, the **Makena Golf Course** (Tel. 879-3344) at Kihei, and the **Pukalani Country Club** (Tel. 572-1314) at Pukalani.

THE TENNIS SCENE

There are two obvious tennis centers serving Maui. First is the 14-court **Wailea Tennis Club** (Tel. 879-1958) in the Wailea Resort near the Maui Inter-Continental Hotel. This is the site of the annual Seiko Super Tennis International Tournament in late September or early October. Three courts are lighted; another three are grass. Play in the morning or early afternoon to avoid the wind.

The **Royal Lahaina Tennis Ranch** (Tel. 661-3611) has 11 courts, at least 6 of which are lighted. Spectator tennis is often centered at the hotel in the stadium court. The **Kapalua Tennis Garden** (Tel. 669-5677) is now open at the Kapalua Resort.

Community courts are set up at Wailuku, Lahaina, Kihei, and Hana, all administered by the Maui County Department of Parks and Recreation (no charges). In addition, a few courts are set up at some other hotels (one or two courts each), which are primarily available to guests in those hotels.

MAUI BY HORSEBACK

We're not sure these should really be filed under "Sports," since the horses get all the workout. But anyway, there are a few good riding tours on the island. (We'd particularly like to have your reaction to any of the outfits listed below.)

One of the best is run by Jerry and Margaret Thompson at **Thompson's Ranch and Riding Stables** (Tel. 878-1910) up in Kula. The Thompsons offer one- and two-hour escorted trail rides around their Upcountry ranch, which is certainly scenic enough, for about $12 per person per hour. But the best deal is probably the $100 all-day trip into Haleakala Crater. To get to the ranch take Route 37 past the main part of Kula, turn left at the sign to the Kula Sanatorium and Hospital, then an almost immediate right onto Thompson Road, which, after a mile and a half, leads to the ranch. Jerry says many of his riders have never been on a horse before, so he has some gentle mounts available. (Say "howdy" for us.)

In West Maui, you might try **Kaanapali Kau Lio** (Tel. 667-7896), which offers two-hour guided rides on their sloping meadows above Kaanapali for about $30 per person. You can't drive there, though. Call the phone number and they'll pick you up.

Meanwhile, back in Hana, *the* place for horseback riding this year is supposed to be the **'Ohe'o Riding Stables** (Tel. 248-7722). Again, our personal knowledge is limited, so if you go, let us know.

Horse racing? Sometimes. Usually every other Sunday during the summer at the County Fairgrounds in Kahului, at the annual fete itself in October, and on other varying occasions throughout the year. But caution: *Betting on any horse race is strictly forbidden by state law!*

HIKING AND CAMPING

Write or visit the Division of State Parks, Hawaii Department of Land and Natural Resources, State Building, Wailuku, Maui, HI 96793 (or Tel. 244-4354) for the most up-to-date regulations on hiking and camping in state parks. Camping permits are required, but the state ones are free.

The three state parks with camping permitted are **Kaumahina** (tent only) on the road to Hana, **Waianapanapa** near Hana Airport, and **Polipoli** on Route 37 near Kula.

County camping information is available from the Maui Department of Parks and Recreation, War Memorial Gymnasium, Kaahumanu Avenue, Wailuku, Maui, HI 96793 (Tel. 244-5514). Permits are $1 per day. County campsites include **Baldwin Park** in Paia, **Hookipa Beach** off the Hana Highway, and **Rainbow Park**, also near Paia.

There are 30 miles of hiking trails meandering inside Haleakala Crater, and the National Park Service offers conducted tours in the summer. There are also several campgrounds within park boundaries. For detailed, up-to-date information, write the Superintendent, Haleakala National Park, P.O. Box 456, Kahului, Maui, HI 96732 (or Tel. 572-7749).

Dedicated hikers may also want to touch base with the **Mauna Ala Hiking Club** (Tel. 572-8338), P.O. Box 497, Makawao, Maui, HI 96768. The club conducts Saturday and Sunday hikes, and visitors are welcome to join in.

10. Valley Isle Shopping

Visiting browsers will generally enjoy poking around more in Lahaina and Kaanapali than in the more bread-and-butter emporia in Wailuku and Kahului.

You will find a surprising number of unusual gift items—Polynesian fabrics, clothes, wood, lauhala, and shell products; jewelry made from such locally harvested material as pink, black, and gold coral; and "Maui Diamonds." Local handicrafts in wood, clothing, leather, shell, etc., are sold as well as modern scrimshaw—delicate carving on whale teeth, walrus ivory, or similar material. Outside the more expensive hotel shops, prices often rival those in Honolulu. And there are genuine bargains to be found in some Maui establishments by dedicated shoppers.

In **KAANAPALI** you'll find the local equivalent to *chic*, clever bazaars like Honolulu's International Market Place or King's Village. This is the **Whalers Village**, a combination shopping center and museum containing about 25 stores and rambling over 8 acres adjacent to the ocean between the Kaanapali Beach and Maui Surf hotels. The village is open seven days a week, 9:30 A.M. to at least 5:30 P.M., but until 9 P.M. on Thursday and Friday. Pick up a free map (sometimes) at the main entrance just off the Kaanapali Parkway. Here are a few shops that interest us there:

Ka Honu (or the Wood Shop, Tel. 661-0173) is owned by local name sculptor Sam Kaai, but he no longer sits down there to carve. He imports crafts from the South Pacific, many of them of museum quality. Authentic Maui crafts include beautiful feathered headbands from Kula, starting at around $40. **The Book Cache** (Tel. 661-3259), nearby, is a pretty well-stocked bookstore. Besides contemporary and standard literature, it has a large line of Hawaii books and local publications. If you're lucky, you'll meet helpful Lynn Rogers there.

We understand they still design and fashion jewelry on the premises of **De Anko's** (Tel. 661-0139). Ask here about "Maui Diamonds," which should only be considered at well-established stores. **Narwhal Shoppe** (Tel. 661-3517). Gift shop with very attractive displays in a nautical theme. It features some unusual tiles, glassware, ceramics, and sculptures.

Pier 49 (Tel. 661-4034), with the works of about 30 scrimshanders, will be glad to talk to you about scrimshaw. **Liberty House** (Tel. 661-4451). The West Maui branch of the famous Honolulu department store. Look here for good-quality resort wear, Polynesian clothing, lingerie, gourmet foods, and many other items.

In **LAHAINA**, the most interesting establishments are still generally along Front Street, the town's main thoroughfare which fronts the ocean. This is not some centrally engineered set of shops, but a wonderful collection of ramshackle buildings, many of them left over from Lahaina's days of gore and glory. There are a few newer structures, but they are strictly converted according to a conscientious code so they will retain the nineteenth-century motif of the town.

We recommend you start your ramble in the Hotel Street arcade of the Pioneer Inn and then move into Front Street for a five-block shopping serendipity, perhaps ending with a snack at any of the little restaurants or sandwich stands there:

Jack Ackerman's Maui Divers, the first place you come across, disappoints us terribly. The black coral is okay, if you like it. But the "Maui Diamonds" we saw there are actually quartz cut, shaped, and polished so they look like real diamonds. They are *not* real diamonds, of course, and they are not even from Maui. **Super Whale**, also in the Pioneer Inn Arcade, specializes in children's wear.

Across Front Street from the square is the fairly new complex called The Wharf, a high-density, thick-wood, heavy-handed shopping center that is out of key with Lahaina's more delicate architectural pattern. The shops there are nicely air conditioned, however, a plus in this sunny neighborhood. One we especially liked is **Upstart Crow and Company** (Tel. 667-9544), which manages to marry a delicious coffeehouse with a well-stocked bookstore. The **Maui Mad Hatter** (Tel. 661-8125), which we always thought was fun in Wailea, has now moved in here.

Moving along Front Street, now, **Dorolen of Lahaina** (Tel. 661-3565) calls itself the house of the Lahaina *muumuu*. It also has hand-embroidered dresses, accessories, and costume jewelry. We don't know much about **Apparels of Pauline** next door, but remembering the movie "Perils," we've always enjoyed the name.

The Kite Shop (Tel. 661-3159), at No. 709 Front, is certainly unusual. They've gathered up every kind of kite known to man or bird, selling from about $2.50 to $75. The most popular item is a 45-foot-long Dragon Kite, weighing 2.8 ounces and made from Mylar for about $12. (Very practical for mailing.) A couple of doors away, the **Vagabond** (Tel. 661-8616) should be called the "Bagabond." Just about every kind of Gladstone and duffle is sold there.

The Gallery (Tel. 661-0696), at 716 Front across the way, features a veritable museum of art and antiques from the Orient. Exquisite pieces of jade, porcelain, etc., are for sale to collectors.

The former Whaling Port Curio and Shell Shop, at 724 Front St., has been sold by malacologist Charlie King to his son-in-law and renamed the **Native Chimes and Shell Shop** (Tel. 667-7084). We think it suffered in the modernization, but you'll still find some of Charlie's unusual specimens for sale there. Incidentally, the **Hop Wo Store** at 728 Front will give you some idea what all the businesses used to look like along here.

At No. 762 Front St., **Far Out Fits** is founded on a belief in flying saucers. Perhaps more interesting for its far-out philosophy than its tie-dyed and silk-screened outfits.

The Lahaina Market Place, which contains several shops at the corner of Front and Lahainaluna, is worth entering for a short stroll. A few steps down Lahainaluna Road is the **Nagamine Poster and Photo Gallery.** It has some nice things, although they weren't all that friendly to us when it looked like we weren't going to buy.

David's of Hawaii (Tel. 661-4009), now moved to No. 815, carries some unusual vintage "silkie" aloha shirts from $75 to $250, besides the modern variety.

Set back from the street, behind a yard full of greenery in a 75-year-old green house, is the **Old Poi Factory** (Tel. 661-4610) where we saw some good, modern designs in women's wear by a couple of modern *wahines* who are really into clothes. We also like the attractive display at the **Lahaina Scrimshaw Factory**, at 845 Front St., next to Kimo's. Up the street at No. 851, the **South Seas Trading Post** (Tel. 661-3611) offers generally expensive—but good—handicraft from several South Seas islands. These folks seem to know their stuff.

Sea Breeze (Tel. 661-0863), 855 Front St., is a pretty well-equipped souvenir shop where you can lean right in the window over the display cases. We almost bought one of those cheerful wind chimes for $12, but settled for a $2.50 poster. **Crazy Shirts** (Tel. 661-4775), up the street, has Hawaii design T-shirts from $7 to $12. Go in to see the figurehead from the old *Carthaginian*, the photographs of her 1972 sinking, etc.

On the opposite side of the street, M. J. Marcial designs and makes custom emerald jewelry on the premises of **Emeralds International** (Tel. 661-8705).

An attractive address for scrimshaw and other nautical items is **The Whaler** (Tel. 661-4592) at 866 Front St. The owner is Chuck Sutherland, one of Maui's senior scrimshanders, and he and his staff tell some interesting—and authentic—stories.

Finally, off Papalaua Street, just *mauka* of Front Street, is the **Lahaina Shopping Center**, with groceries, drugstores, hardware shops, and other places suited to more prosaic needs. Two establishments worth noting,

however, are the **Nagasako Variety Market** (Tel. 661-4108), which carries small sizes in soap powders and other handy condo miniatures, and
its sister organization, **Nagasako Super Market** (Tel. 661-0985), which
we like better than Foodland across the street in the Lahaina Square. In
fact, Nagasako's market is probably the best place to stock up on staples,
unless you're going into Kahului.

Out at **WAILEA** is a small complex called the **Wailea Shopping Vil-
lage**, not far from the Hotel Inter-Continental. You'll find branches of
Carol & Mary, an exclusive Honolulu women's specialty shop, and of
Chapman's Men's Wear, also expensive, for male resort wear. We liked
one unusual stitchery shop called **The Crewel World** (Tel. 879-1880).
You may find something to keep the kids busy there, too.

In the old town of **WAILUKU** you might like to peek into the **Maui
Rehabilitation Center** (Tel. 244-5502) at Cameron Center, 95 Mahalani
St., which has authentic Hawaiian handicrafts made by the handicapped
on the premises. Also in Wailuku, many search out the famous Japanese
cookies with the sweet bean filling called *manju*. They're made only at the
Home Maid Bakery (Tel. 244-7015), but you can buy them at 1005 East
Lower Main St., too. About $3 a dozen, they're a delicious Maui specialty.

In **KAHULUI**, if you're at the Maui Mall Shopping Center, drop in to
Pieces of Dreams to see some unusual imports. For groceries, by the
way, **Star Super Market** nearby is about the cheapest on the island, although some prefer **Ooka's Super Market** (Tel. 244-3931) at 1870 Main
St. Also in the Maui Mall, now, is an excellent branch of **Waldenbooks**
(Tel. 877-0181), and a smellorific store called **Sir Wilfred's Coffee, Tea
and Tobacco Shop** (Tel. 877-3194). Look for the antique Indian outside.
Almost next door is the famous **Tasaka Guri Guri Shop**, which makes
the best *guri guri* ("goody goody") Japanese ice cream in Hawaii. Actually, it's a kind of sherbet, and locals like it on top of sweet *azuki* beans.

The prestige shopping complex in Kahului is Kaahumanu Center.
In some ways it's an architectural echo of Honolulu's Ala Moana, studded by **Sears** on one end and by **Liberty House** on the other, with lots
of Honolulu-headquartered emporia in between. We like to browse
through the **Book Cache**. You'll find island fashions at **Otaheite**, a boutique. **Camellia Imports Seed Shop** has those dried Chinese seeds island
youngsters like to chew on. At **Karen's Fruit and Floral Boutique** you
may see samples of protea blossoms, if you missed them up at Kula.

Foremost among miscellaneous Maui specialties is pineapple, of
course. All the pineapple grown on Maui is, in theory, reserved for can-
ning. Actually you can buy some Maui pine fresh if you find the **King
of Hawaii** brand. The sweetest, tastiest Maui onions are those from
M. Uradomo Farms. And the best pastries (aside from the previously
named *manju*) are those turned out by the **Komoda Bakery** in Makawao.

Finally, a word about potato chips. Ever since articles on Maui's potato chips appeared in the *Wall Street Journal* and some other Mainland publications, there has been a run on virtually all potato chips on the island. It may surprise you—as it did us—to learn that there is more than one potato chip factory on Maui, at least two of them apparently having been set up more recently. It is distinctly possible, therefore, that you may pick up and crunch into Brands X, Y, or Z.

If you want to be sure to buy the right product—the one that often looks like the rejects of a real potato chip factory—search out the "Kitch'n Cook'd" label. These are the real Dewey Kobayashi, and if you can't find them in the stores, you might like to line up at the **Maui Potato Chip Factory** (Tel. 877-3652), at 295 Lalo Place in Kahului.

11. Maui Nights on the Town

The Valley Island swings like a tree-full of mynahs in a high wind. In fact, Maui's *hele on* stance after dark is precisely what makes it difficult to publish an up-to-date report. It is not like Kauai, for instance, with its base of well-established watering holes where year in and year out you find the same crowd soaking up rhythm, alcohol, and *hoomalimali*. Instead, you'll find a night-life scene with a volatile collection of bars and clubs opening and closing as frenetically as a family of octopuses swimming through a revolving door.

If there is any consistency on the night scene, it will be found in the cocktail lounges and club rooms of the major Kaanapali hotels:

THE disco on the Kaanapali Kampus this season is **Spats** in the Hyatt Regency Maui. It's recorded rock, but the beat goes on almost 'til dawn. Rocker-readers have reported that it's hopelessly crowded on Friday and Saturday, though.

A similar attraction, but for a younger set, is the **Banana Moon** lounge in the nearby Marriott. It's also often mobbed on weekends. Two other dens for disco and rock fans include the **Foxy Lady** and the **Wet Noodle** in the Royal Lahaina Hotel.

Polynesian shows are offered at several hotels, but the best luau/entertainment combinations now are probably the **Aloha Luau** at the Sheraton-Maui in Kaanapali and the **Inter-Continental Luau** over in Wailea. The **Maui Lu-au**, in the Maui Lu Hotel in Kihei, also has its loyal fans. The similar **"Drums of the Pacific"** show at the Hyatt Regency may be okay, but there's no way you're going to get us to the buffet/show at the Kaanapali Beach Hotel.

The best long-running and consistent stage show on Maui has to be **"Here is Hawaii"** in the Kapa Room at the Maui Surf Hotel (Tel. 661-4411) in Kaanapali. Unlike many poly-Polynesian shows, this one is *all* Hawaiian (no Tahitian or Samoan hulas, etc.). You'll find a lot of good history and good fun here, as the show enters its third year on the boards. (Jim Luckey, director of the Lahaina Restoration Foundation, told us he's seen the show six times!) The dinner/show package may come to $30 or so this year, but you may be able to book the show only. Recheck on the scene. Also in the Surf, the **Pequod Bar**, apparently made from the deck of an old sailing ship, attracts nautical buffs by the boatload.

Outside the Kaanapali hotels, but still in the resort area in the Whalers Village, the **Rusty Harpoon** (Tel. 661-3123) sometimes hooks some up-and-coming groups for its lounge acts. It's a smooth place for a sunset, but also mellow for midnighting. Its resident mixologists, by the way, specialize in about a dozen different daiquiris. (Cash only. No credit cards or traveler's checks.)

In **LAHAINA**, our all-time favorite Maui bar is the **Old Whaler's Grog Shop**, the lopsided landmark tavern in the corner of the old Pioneer Inn. Good drinking and a spirit of camaraderie are generally available at any hour, but the seasoned old floorboards really jump when someone sits down at the rinky-tink piano late in the evening. It's very popular with the young singles crowd, but some of us in our Fabulous Fifties like the place, too.

The top-deck Carthaginian Bar above the downstairs dining room in the **Oceanhouse**, at 831 Front St., is inviting. Sit next to the windows for a floodlit view of the breakers below. Perhaps ideal for a quiet *tête-à-tête*, not for a foot-stomping hoedown. Open until 1 or 2 A.M.

Another top-floor entry, particularly pleasant for early evening tippling, is the bar at the **Whale's Tale Inn** at 666 Front St., behind the Pioneer Inn. Sit on the *lanai*, near the corner, to overlook the famous Banyan Tree, the courthouse, the ocean, and, perchance, the whales in the channel.

Not far away, on Friday and Saturday nights, you'll find an appreciative local crowd taking in the Hawaiian music at the **Banyan Inn**, the open-sided restaurant at 640 Front St., opposite the big banyan tree.

The "now generation" crowd seems to go for the **Bluemax** (Tel. 661-8202) at 730 Front St. It's an aviation-theme restaurant in the early evening, but then it takes off as a live-band lounge from about 9 P.M. to 1:30 A.M. nightly. A loft-full of comfortable couches and a wild-blue-yonder decor of old aircraft memorabilia keep this one on course.

Way out in **NAPILI**, the Napili Kai Resort is proud of its **Restaurant of the Maui Moon**, which offers the usual Polynesian show on most nights. But on Fridays there's a welcome change: all the acts are performed by about 40 children—offspring of the hotel staff. Telephone 669-6271 for show time. It's a real refresher.

In **KIHEI**, "Maui's largest dance floor" is supposed to be at the **Maui**

Lu Resort (Tel. 879-5881), which offers live music nightly in the room recently named "Jesse's." The entertainer of long standing there is Jesse Nakooka. And out of the night scene there is the Aloha Mele Luncheon at noon Thursdays, when Jesse teams up with "Auntie" Emma Sharpe to host a popular midday showplace for lots of island talent.

A good living room bar in **KAHULUI** may still be **Apple Annie's** (Tel. 877-3107) in Kaahumanu Center, next to Liberty House. (But better recheck that by phone; we haven't been there in a while.) In the neighboring township of **WAILUKU**, an often-colorful tavern at 2080 Vineyard St. is the **Hale Kukui Lounge** (Tel. 242-9208). There's often a live band, at least on weekends. This one can get rough, though, so give the crowd the once-over before sitting down. If you see any Kukui nuts, pick another Hale.

Not exactly night life, but certainly grand entertainment, is the annual Na Mele O Maui, "the Songs of Maui," a three-day festival held in Lahaina and Kaanapali on one weekend every November.

12. The Maui Address List

Bakery—Nashiwa Bakery, Lahaina Shopping Center. Tel. 661-3188.
Barber—Agena Barber Shop, 782-B Panaewa St. Tel. 661-3187.
Beauty Salon—Hair Horizon, Lahaina Shopping Center. Tel. 661-3466.
Chamber of Commerce—26 N. Puunene Ave., Kahului. Tel. 877-0452.
Doctors—Maui Medical Group, 130 Prison St., Lahaina. Tel. 661-0051.
Dry Cleaners—Maui Dry Cleaners, Lahaina Shopping Center. Tel. 667-2659.
Fire Department—Emergency Tel. 661-0555.
Florist—Lahaina Florist, Lahaina Shopping Center. Tel. 661-0509.
Hospital—Maui Memorial, 221 Mahalani St., Kahului. Tel. 244-9056.
Laundromat—There's one at the Lahaina Shopping Center.
Liquor—Party Pantry, 1217 Front St., Lahaina. Tel. 661-3577.
Pharmacy—Craft's Drugs, Lahaina Shopping Center. Tel. 661-3119.
Police Headquarters—Old Lahaina Courthouse, Town Square. Tel. 661-4441 (but dial 911 for emergency).
Post Office—In Lahaina Shopping Center. Tel. 667-6611.
Public Library—Lahaina branch next to Pioneer Inn. Tel. 661-0566.
Supermarket—Nagasako's, Lahaina Shopping Center. Tel. 661-0985.
Tourist information—Hawaii Visitors Bureau/Maui County Visitors Association, 26 N. Puunene Ave., Kahului. Tel. 877-7822.

MOLOKAI

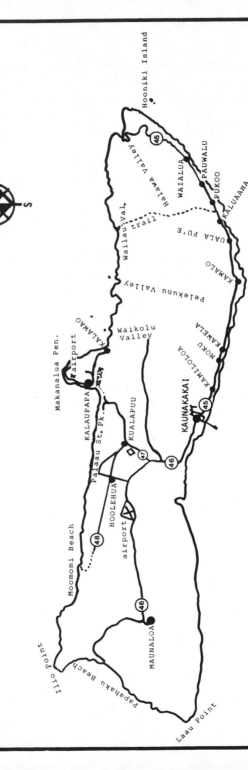

scale

0   5   10
miles

N
W S E

Iilo Point

Moomomi Beach

Papahaku Beach

Laau Point

MAUNALOA
46

HOOLEHUA
airport
48

Palaau St. Pk.
KUALAPUU
47
46

Makanalua Pen.
KALAUPAPA
airport
KALAWAO

Waikolu
Valley

Pelekunu Valley

Wailau Val.
trail

Halawa Valley

Hoonuki Island
45
WAIALUA
PAUWALU
PUKOO
KALUAAHA

UALA PU'E

KAMALO

KAWELA
MOKU

KAMILOLOA

KAUNAKAKAI
45

R.H.Bone

8

Molokai,
the Friendly Island

1. Around the Island—A Land in Limbo

Like the populace of a small town in Indiana, Molokaians seem to be traditionally interested mostly in people—talking because it's fun to talk, and being helpful just because it feels good to be helpful. For this reason, Molokai over the past fifty years or so has earned the subtitle "The Friendly Island."

In old Hawaii, Molokai supported a native population of at least 10,000. During the 1800s, however, new opportunity beckoned elsewhere and the number dropped severely. The population reached a low of 1,006 in 1910. During this black period, Molokai was known as "The Lonely Island" or "The Forgotten Island."

The establishment of pineapple was the island's eventual salvation. In the 1920s and 1930s, there was a rush to return home to unspoiled Molokai and work in the booming industry. Everyone's mood improved, and eventually 7,000 happy people were being supported directly or indirectly by pineapple paychecks.

Then again, fortune turned for Molokai. In the 1960s and 1970s, the island was the only one in the state that was *losing* population, dropping down to around 5,000. With cheaper pineapple production available in foreign lands like Taiwan and the Philippines, Dole closed its Molokai plantation. Last year Del Monte announced that it would also follow suit.

Today, however, a new spirit has sprung back on the island, sparked largely by the construction of the Sheraton Molokai Hotel and other projects. Population is again on the rise, now standing at well over 6,000. A few condominiums are being built and roads have been improved. It looks like the island will never be lonely again.

Molokai is being dragged somewhat against its will into the 1980s, and visitors should realize that there is still some controversy on the island about the ultimate social value of tourism. If this skepticism results in slow, intelligent growth, then it will prove a healthy influence in the coming years.

Meanwhile, tread softly on Molokai. If you do, you'll come across some of the most genuine and ingenuous Hawaiian charm to be found anywhere.

2. The Airports—Hoolehua and Kalaupapa

The terminal buildings at either airport are uncomplicated. The one at Kalaupapa is not much more than a one-room shack. The airport at Hoolehua is eight miles out from Kaunakakai, and it is this one that is usually referred to simply as "Molokai Airport." Hawaiian Airlines has counter space inside the building. Commuter airlines occupy modest kiosks outdoors on the opposite side of the structure from the runway, along with the booths for the island's few rental car outfits. There is also a tiny bar and snack shop in the building.

Molokai's two airports form the gateways to two very distinct places. *There is no ground transportation between them* (except by pack mules—see later). The simple landing strip at Kalaupapa serves the leprosy settlement there near sea level on the little Makanalua Peninsula. Molokai Airport, on the other hand, is "topside"—meaning more than 1,000 feet up the cliff—and it accepts passengers destined for all other parts of Molokai.

If you are going to Kalaupapa, therefore, the most practical way is to *fly down* to it from topside—Polynesian Airways (Tel. 567-6647) goes once or twice a day. Or, if you wish, you may wing directly to Kalaupapa from Honolulu in 25 or 30 minutes via Air Hawaii's or Royal Hawaiian Air Service's propeller-driven Cessnas for about $75 round trip.

Hawaiian Air jets serve Molokai Airport, about an 18-minute flight from Honolulu. Royal Hawaiian Air Service (RHAS) and Air Molokai maintain scheduled flights there as well as to Kalaupapa. Aloha and Hawaiian Air do not fly to Kalaupapa.

3. Transportation on Molokai

There are no buses or other means of public transportation on Molokai. The major hotels will provide complimentary service for their guests to and from the airport or the pier. There are two or three taxis.

Rental cars tend to run higher on Molokai than on other Neighbor Islands. Rates for the traditional competitors have generally been consistent between them, and consistently about 20 percent higher than the minimums on other islands. The rental service most well-known for years is the **Molokai Island U-Drive** (Tel. 567-6156), Box 218, Hoole-hua, Molokai, Hi. 96729.

Molokai now has links in a few local and national chains. **Tropical Rent-A-Car** (Tel. 567-6118) has long been a favorite for relatively low rates. **Avis Rent A Car** (Tel. 553-3866) may cost you more.

If you want to prowl the trails and deserted beaches of West Molokai, you'll need a Jeep. **Royal Rainbow Rent-A-Car** (Tel. 567-6797) is now the only outfit we know that rents Jeeps—at a whopping $50 a day. (And there's no hourly rate, either.) Be aware that many of Molokai's jeep roads are on private land, and there's no telling where you may be con-fronted with a locked gate and the need for prior permission to pass.

The main roads are well-paved, and there are several sightseeing tar-gets to which a passenger car will take you easily. Local residents think traffic gets heavy. Most of the time, however, you might judge it only slightly heavier than in the Mohave desert on a Sunday afternoon.

4. The Hotel Scene

You don't have to stay overnight to have fun on Molokai, but if you do, there are now three full-fledged hotels to put you up, plus a couple of other possibilities. Only one qualifies as a luxury house, but comfort-able rooms may be found in all. The hotels also offer pretty good Polyne-sian entertainment on busy evenings.

The **Hotel Sheraton-Molokai** (Tel. 552-2555) has rooms strung out in several *ohia* wood and redwood two-story buildings, many of them a fair hike from the dining room and lobby. Absolutely the sole Molokai hos-telry to be on a really attractive beach, the Sheraton boasts no air condi-tioning. Indeed, none is needed with the dependable breezes (and some-times gales!) that sweep across the miles of adjoining deserted ranchland to this isolated resort at the island's west end.

By day, the faint outlines of Oahu may be seen, making the Sheraton the only Neighbor Island hotel with the coveted view of Diamond Head. At night, Honolulu glows against the distant sky for late strollers.

Four lighted tennis courts, all surrounded by a high windbreak; an 18-hole championship golf course; two resort shops; an electronic game room; one nice pool next to an attractive bar and dining room; willing, hard-working, friendly though sometimes amateurish service. Doubles under the twirling fans running $85 to $90 (ask for a room near the cen-ter of things); regular suites for about $115; the best facilities by far in the beachside Ocean Cottage Suites at $135 for two.

The success of Sheraton's Molokai venture is still not assured. We wouldn't swim in the tricky surf in any case. (Reservations from Shera-ton Hotels in Hawaii, P.O. Box 8559, Honolulu, Hi. 96815.) All in all, an admirable attempt at carving an oasis from a Hawaiian desert.

Not far from the Sheraton is a rental condo operation, **Paniolo Hale** (Tel. 552-2731), we haven't managed to see yet. Daily apartment rentals begin at about $60 for studios and continue on up to over $100 for some two-bedroom combinations. We'll try to inspect this one soon.

The Hotel Molokai (Tel. 553-5347) is a collection of low, swaybacked buildings in a palm grove about two miles east of Kaunakakai: Very rustic, open-air lobby; nearby Polynesian-wear shop and florist; well-kept lawns; ocean- and poolside dining room with carved totem posts; usually good meals; bar to one side; blimp-shaped but not blimp-sized swimming pool; 56 heavy-timbered accommodations; no room telephone service. Prices have come *down* here recently. The most expensive upper-floor units should cost $51 for two this year. There are better bargains in the ground-floor Long House bordering the parking lot at $41, while mid-range and cooler rooms next to the garden can be had for $46 to $51. (Reservations from the hotel at P.O. Box 546, Kaunakakai, Molokai, Hi. 96748, or telephone the hotel toll-free from Honolulu at 531-4004.) Enthusiastic manager Peter Wheeler seems determined to make you happy. Tell him we sent you.

The traditional runner-up in Molokai is the **Pau Hana Inn** (Tel. 536-7545), known before its remodeling as the Seaside Inn. Conveniently located for foot wanderers on the fringe of Kaunakakai; modest entrance with palm growing through the roof; attractive indoor dining room with lava-rock walls, fireplace, and overhead fans; good, substantial fare; outdoor bar near dramatic, century-old, Bengalese banyan tree; terrace often a popular gathering place for a fun-loving crowd; a chewing-gum-and-bailing-wire piano bar fashioned out of an *upright* piano into a sort of linoleum baby grand; good, large swimming pool. The doubles near the pool (about $50) are newer and pleasanter, and some have air conditioning. The cheaper units are the old Seaside sleeping quarters with some plastic lamination. The lowest priced accommodations (about $20 for twin pillows) are quite basic but adequate for the most dedicated pinchpennies. (Reservations by mail to P.O. Box 860, Kaunakakai, Hi. 96748, or in Honolulu, telephone direct at 536-7545.)

Two more condominium-apartment operations (not hotels) have opened on Molokai. One, **Wavecrest** (Tel. 558-8101) is 25 miles from the airport on Molokai's windy eastern shore. There's a swimming pool, two lighted tennis courts, and a grocery store (the only one for miles around). We thought the units seemed uninspired, but at about $65 for two bedrooms, they could certainly be bargains for groups of four. (One-bedroom units for 2 vary between $30 and $40 this year.) There are full kitchen facilities, color TV, daily maid service. And the whole thing is on the water's edge, but we didn't think much of the beach.

The other is **Molokai Shores** (Tel. 553-5954), closer to Kaunakakai.

One-bedroom apartments (holding four) were renting for $50, and the two-bedroom jobs (sleeping six) were running at $74, the last information we had. We'll check in or check out this address sometime soon.

5. Restaurants and Dining, Molokai Style

The salons to load up on serious viands are at the trio of hotels. The Ohia Lodge in the new **Sheraton-Molokai** (Tel. 552-2555) has captured more attention, now, especially with its Saturday night buffet. Also the hotel has its Paniolo Broiler, featuring steaks and chops over *kiawe* charcoal.

At the **Hotel Molokai** (Tel. 553-5347), we enjoyed a buffet lunch in the hotel's attractive oceanside restaurant. Sunday evenings there is sometimes a "Broil Your Own Steak Family Cookout." Actually, our resident Molokai spy says the hotel has quietly become the island's finest dinner restaurant. The dining room in the **Pau Hana Inn** (Tel. 553-5342), a former favorite, is now off our list. Sorry.

Outside of those, there's a tiny Chinese restaurant called the **Hop Inn** (Tel. 553-5465) and a modest snack shop with a few booths and tables called the **Mid-Nite Inn** (Tel. 553-5302) on Ala Malama Street, the main drag of Kaunakakai. The Mid-Nite Inn, incidentally, closes at 9 P.M. Also **Gladys' Saimin Parlor** has been packin' 'em in until all hours.

Breakfast? Try those wonderful fresh doughnuts, sweet rolls and special Molokai bread at the **Kanemitsu Bakery**. They have a counter and booths behind the shop.

6. Sightseeing Molokai—Delightfully Lonely Exercise

With a rented car, most people find they can see what they want in a day or two. With a jeep, you'll need at least two days to cover it all, since more sights which are relatively inaccessible by low-slung sedans will be open to you.

Using any of the hotels as a starting point, we'll divide our "topside" trips into west and east of them. Following this is a separate discussion on visiting the leprosy colony at Kalaupapa.

THE ROAD WEST

The principal village, **Kaunakakai** is pronounced "cow-na-cock-*eye*," and is the reason a Hollywood songwriter composed "The Cockeyed Mayor of Kaunakakai" during the 1930s. Incidentally, there is no official mayor of Kaunakakai because all of Molokai is merely a part of Maui County—which does have a mayor in the county seat of Wailuku on the Island of Maui.

Kaunakakai, population 500 or so, is known principally for its main thoroughfare, Ala Malama Street, with its wide, empty pavement flanked by a collection of wooden, false-front commercial buildings. It is reminiscent of Tombstone, Arizona, in the 1860s. With new prosperity, however, the paintbrushes have come out. Some say the former weather-beaten charm of the street is now being glossed over.

Kaunakakaians are proud of their **wharf** on which you may drive nearly a half-mile out over the ocean. Until recently, huge barges were berthed here to load the tons upon tons of pineapple produced on Molokai and destined for the cannery in Honolulu. Pineapple production has been virtually phased out, however, and unless that pier can be kept busy loading such goods as potatoes and onions, some say Kaunakakai may yet turn into the ghost town it already resembles.

Near the canoe shack just west of the approach to the landing is the foundation of **Kamehameha V's Summer Home**. That monarch, who reigned from 1863 to 1872, is a sort of unofficial patron of the past to Molokai. Several things are named for him, including Route 46.

A couple miles west along the Kamehameha V Highway is the **Kapuaiwa Grove**, which still contains hundreds of coconut palms, the remnants of the 1,000 planted by the king in the 1860s. The spring which still bubbles there marked the center of a town square. You may explore what's left of the grove, but be warned that there is always a danger of falling coconuts.

Directly across the road from the coconut grove is **church row**. There are about ten houses of worship there now. Any church with at least a few Hawaiians in its congregation may build there on lands granted by the Hawaiian Homes Commission. Molokai's only rush hour occurs here—at noon on Sundays when they all let out at once.

If you're not pressed for time, continue on Route 46 to the left after the junction with Route 47. (If you are in a hurry, skip the next six paragraphs.)

Past the airport, the land becomes dry and brown. Until a couple of years ago this area was a deep green, paved with thousands of neat rows of pineapple plants. What to do with the land today is the subject of a special government task force, and along here you may see some experiments—an onion farm here, a tree nursery there.

At **Puu Nana** ("Viewing Hill"), elevation 1,381 feet, you may be able to see 30 miles over the ocean to the Island of Oahu on a clear day.

At the end of the paved road is the former Dole plantation village of **Maunaloa**. (Dole has already closed down its Molokai pineapple operations.) Look for a post office (Zip 96720), and a branch of Kaunakakai's Friendly Market. They've closed down the movie theater showing Filipino films. The fancier residences up on the hill were the managers' houses. Maunaloa is (or was) about as typical an example of a Hawaii plantation town as you can find.

Through the scrub growth in this area are many dirt roads. One paved one, however, will take you to the new Sheraton-Molokai Hotel at **Kepuhi Beach**. Some other strands along the same coastline are still deserted. Now open, too, is a wildlife park which has been stocked with such exotica as giraffes and antelope. (See Section 7.)

Returning along this spur of Highway 46, you may want to take the little road that circles behind Molokai Airport. If we had not been traveling with the Imamura family of Kaunakakai, we never would have known it, but those little hills or mounds along the road are actually overgrown hangars and bunkers left behind by the Army Air Corps after World War II. Carolyn Imamura told us she explored the ruins as a child, but now they are largely caved in and dangerous.

At the junction, take Highway 47 north. You will pass the **Kualapuu Reservoir**, a water source of some local pride. Holding 1.4 billion gallons, it is the world's largest rubber-lined body of water and the home for a few families of mallards. Is it worth a stop? Well, we were more impressed when we looked it over from the airplane.

Above **Kualapuu**, a Del Monte company town, the countryside becomes greener and more hilly. The yellow fruit you may see in the bushes lining the road are guavas, and they're delicious raw or made into jams and jellies.

Continue on the new road into **Palaau State Park** and to the parking lot at the end of the highway. Two short trails lead from there. The footpath to the north will lead you in about three minutes to the **Kalaupapa Overlook**. From a 1,600-foot cliff you look through space down to the Makanalua Peninsula holding the last few remaining residents of the leper colony. The colony was established in 1866 originally as a place of quarantine. Today, of course, leprosy has been contained by sulfone drugs, but about 200 residents remain—perhaps because the location is beautiful, but mainly because it is home. The view from this point, from which you also catch a glimpse of the inaccessible north shore and its 3,000-foot cliffs, is one of the most famous and dramatic in the world. Don't miss it.

The other trail runs through about 150 yards of forest, a 10-minute walk accompanied by the whistling wind in the eucalyptus trees, to the famous **Phallic Rock**, also called Kauleonanahoa. A Brobdingnagian natural feature, the stone organ has naturally given rise to certain legends, and one is explained on a nearby plaque. In ancient times, barren women made a pilgrimage to this sacred rock so that they might be able to conceive.

Along the trail on the way back out of the woods, look for a large stone suspended so that there is a tiny tunnel underneath it. There are the only **petroglyphs** we have seen on Molokai. You'll have to lie on your back and wriggle under to have a look. However, well-known travel writer Joan Storey, who was there more recently, says the figures seem to have disappeared.

As you begin the drive toward the park exit, there is a pavilion on your right where forty different species of trees are identified and clearly labeled. Here are also some public picnic grounds, popular with Molokai residents.

Just outside the park, at the sign marking its entrance, is a route to the **original Kalaupapa Overlook**. This road is muddy in wet weather, but some believe this angle provides a more dramatic view of the peninsula than the one we previously described. You cannot see the north shore cliffs from here, but in the foreground you will catch sight of the beginning of the **Jack London Trail**, a 1,600-foot switchback route down to the leprosy settlement below.

Jack London was not the only famous person to make the trek into and out of the colony. But he did write about it, and if the trail is known by any name, it is his. You may follow in his footsteps for a short way or, with proper permission, you may hike or take a mule to the bottom. The trail is still the only land route to and from the isolated peninsula.

On the return trip along Route 47, you may turn right onto Route 48 going first to the village of **Hoolehua**. Some, with tongues in their craw, call it "the home of Molokai's feathered gladiators." Cockfights, however, are highly illegal, so don't count on running across one by accident.

At the end of Route 48, a dirt road continues through private property to the beaches of **Moomomi** and **Keonelele**. If you want to go, you'll probably have to open a gate or two on the way. Just remember to close them behind you. At Keonelele you'll find a good beach and a pavilion. Moomomi boasts the state's sole collection of sand dunes.

Back on Highway 46, just about a half-mile south of the junction with 47, a dirt and gravel road leads toward the east. *If* the weather is neither too wet nor too dry, this can be a dramatic and lovely excursion. (In dry weather, a gate is sometimes closed at the road's beginning because of the danger of forest fire. The key to enter, however, may be obtained from the Division of Forestry in the State Building at Kaunakai. The man to see there is Jim Lindsey.)

About 9 miles in is the famous **Sandalwood Measuring Pit**, a depression in the ground the size and shape of a sailing ship's hull. In the early 1800s, the Hawaiian chiefs had their workers measure the cut sandalwood here before it was sent to the white traders. Use of the measuring pit was discontinued about a century ago when all the sandalwood trees were finally stripped from the island.

Another mile or two brings you to the **Waikolu Valley Lookout**, a dramatic viewpoint over a 3,000-foot-deep gorge. About 3 miles away in the sea you may catch sight of Okala Islet, the same feature you may see from quite a different angle if you journey to Kalawao Park, across the Makanalua Peninsula from Kalaupapa. The view of the valley is usually clear in the morning—but don't count on it.

THE LONG ROAD EAST

To Halawa Valley and back (60 miles) is absolutely a half-day trip, and we prefer to make it in the morning so that we are less likely to be worried about rain clouds along the steep dirt road into and out of the valley. Since Mr. Ah Ping retired and closed his country store near Ualapue, there is no place to get gas en route. Don't forget to check your fuel gauge.

Another step in preparation: If you are planning to visit the Iliiliopae Heiau, you'll need permission and perhaps a gate key from Mrs. Pearl Petro (Tel. 558-8113), but be sure you want to make the hike.

Some travelers prefer to drive directly to Halawa Valley and then hit the other sites on the return trip. To avoid confusion, however, we will describe each point in its order along the route. Don't count on being directed solely by those Hawaii Visitors Bureau warrior signs, incidentally. Many of them had disappeared the last time we made the Route 45 trip.

Route 45 is the portion of Kamehameha V Highway that goes east (as opposed to Route 46 which is also Kamehameha V Highway, but westbound).

Almost immediately you will see the first of fifty-four original **Hawaiian fishponds** built along this coast from the fifteenth to the eighteenth centuries. Some have been wrecked by tides or silt, but many others remain and a few are even operated commercially. The walls, constructed of coral and basalt, formed enclosures used to raise and fatten salt-water fish.

Next, you will come across a village with ancient roots called **Kawela**, 6 miles from Kaunakakai. Kawela was named by a Maui chief, according to research gathered by Cadette Girl Scout Troop No. 311 of Molokai. The chief landed at the nearby **Pakuhiwa Battleground** and saw that the first wave of soldiers were already engaged in a bloody slingshot war. "Kawela!" he shouted, meaning "The heat of the battle!" The area has been called Kawela ever since. The battle itself, incidentally, was one of the decisive ones by which Kamehameha the Great conquered the Islands. They say his war canoes lined the now peaceful beach for 4 miles and that sling stones are occasionally found there today.

St. Joseph Church, about 11 miles from Kaunakakai, was built by Father Damien de Veuster in 1876. Father Damien, famous for his work with leprosy victims in Kalawao and Kalaupapa, also would hike to East

Molokai to tend to this and other parishes. An old wooden statue of the Belgian priest has now been moved here.

A little farther along, a small monument marks the **Smith and Bronte Landing**. In 1927, aviators Ernest Smith and Emory Bronte came down here somewhat inelegantly in a clump of *kiawe* trees, thus completing the first civilian transpacific flight.

We missed it, but a short distance from the fishpond is the **Loipunawai Spring**. Perhaps we were lucky, for among the legends are stories of persons who died of thirst trying to find the spring and others who drank so much when they finally did locate it that they killed themselves. Supposedly this one bubbles up from the ground practically beside the salty sea.

Near Mapulehu, 15 miles from Kaunakakai, is the start of the **Wailau Trail**, a difficult all-day trek to Wailau Valley on the north shore. The valley once held a large community, but it is now virtually deserted except for a few fishermen and *pakalolo* growers who hike to the lonely chasm.

Past Pukoo, and less than a mile off the road, is the thirteenth-century **Iliiliopae Heiau**. This temple, 268 feet long, is said by many to be the most magnificent in all Hawaii. If you have the previously mentioned gate key, you may follow the trail and cross the two streams to see this structure, some say the scene of ancient human sacrifices.

Along here, you will begin seeing the island of Maui across the Pailolo Channel. In the area are several coves with deserted sandy beaches and good swimming. When the water is calm, it is also clear and ideal for skin diving.

As the road begins winding up to a higher altitude, you'll catch sight of the **Isle of Mokuhooniki**, a turtle-shaped offshore rock used as a bombing target during World War II. Today's pilots say it resembles a different animal from the air. They call it "Elephant Rock."

At the top of the bluff is the **Puu-O-Hoku Lodge and Ranch**, which once raised the largest herd of Charolais cattle in the world. Puu-O-Hoku means "Hill of Stars," and there must be a zillion visible on a moonless night from this isolated place.

Just past the ranch entrance is **Kalanikaula Kukui Grove**, one of the most hallowed spots in the Islands. This clump of candlenut trees, with their characteristic gray bark and light green leaves, used to surround the home of a famous and powerful *kahuna* named Lanikaula. Once, when the California Packing Corporation (Del Monte) wanted to clear this land, the company could find no Hawaiian worker who would take an axe to the sacred *kukui* trees.

A few more turns and you will catch your first breathtaking view of the magnificent **Halawa Valley**. Far, far below you'll see a curving beach, then a broad, grassy plain headed by a thick jungle 3 or 4 miles inland. There, two large waterfalls plunge down the side of the cliff. To know that hundreds once lived in that deep gorge adds to its overwhelming beauty and loneliness.

The very rugged 3-mile descent into the valley has recently been paved, but that doesn't help a whole heck of a lot. The road is still narrow and dangerous, and frequent honking at blind curves is certainly advisable. You may still have to back up now and then to let another car pass in the opposite direction.

Halawa Valley is popular with campers, picnickers, and beachcombers. Only two or three families live there permanently today, and they must make do without electricity or telephones. Several houses and a church are just plain deserted.

We didn't hike back to the 250-foot-high **Moaula Falls** on our only trip so far into Halawa Valley. It was late in the day and it looked like rain. (And if that road gets too wet and slippery, well, you could be trapped in the valley for hours—or even days.) Those who have made the trek to the falls say you should follow the road past the old houses, then the trail through the banana trees, generally keeping in sight a water pipe which also runs back to the falls. There is also a stream or two to ford. Allow at least an hour in each direction.

According to legend, you may swim in the pool under the falls if the lizard who lives below the surface is happy. To test his mood, throw a ti leaf on the water. If it floats, he won't bother you. If it sinks, the creature is testy, and you'd better save your swim for another day.

THE TRIP TO KALAUPAPA

The Makanalua Peninsula, often miscalled the Kalaupapa Peninsula, was the scene of unthinkable tragedy and heartbreak in the latter half of the nineteenth century. Today it may be visited easily and absolutely safely. About 200 leprosy patients still live there because of their sentimental attachment to the place. For years, there has no longer been any medical need for the natural barrier cliffs to keep these victims of Hansen's Disease isolated from the rest of Molokai and all the world. And there is also no longer any need to use a euphemism for leprosy, since it is not, after all, a crime or an immoral act. But for the same reason it is terribly cruel to label a person as "a leper."

There are only two ways to reach the settlement on the spit of land so far below the northern *pali*. You can fly from Molokai Airport to the airport at Kalaupapa. Or you may hike or ride a mule down the 3.2-mile switchback trail which descends the 1,600-foot precipice. (Figure from an hour to 1½ hours each way.)

It is not very practical to tour the peninsula entirely on your own hook. The closest thing to that at the moment is to fly down—or hike down (yes, some people do it!)—and arrange to be met at the airport or the bottom of the trail by Father Damien Tours, run by Mr. and Mrs. Richard Marks, who live in Kalaupapa and are themselves patients. (See Section 7—Guided Tours and Cruises.)

Three airlines serve Kalaupapa. Try to fly there via Royal Hawaiian Air Service (Tel. 553-5317), although they won't go from "topside" unless there's a minimum of four people. Also check with Polynesian Airways (Tel. 567-6647) or Air Molokai (Tel. 553-3663). The fare may be about $25 round trip.

On the tour, you will see **Kalaupapa**, the sleepy town which is the site of today's hospital and settlement on the western side of the peninsula. The town is noted for its large number of pet dogs, which are loved by the patients in lieu of the children they are not allowed to have. Young children, who are still considered susceptible to leprosy, remain strictly forbidden. Newborns must be sent away to live somewhere else.

More beautiful than Kalaupapa is the original village of **Kalawao**, now in ruins, on the other side of the peninsula. There still is the little St. Philomena's Roman Catholic Church, built by Father Damien de Veuster. Known today as the Martyr of Molokai, the Belgian priest came ashore in 1873 to help the leprosy victims who were banished there without shelter or provisions. Father Damien himself caught the disease and died in 1889, soon after the church was finished. He has been nominated for sainthood.

Notwithstanding the magnificent scenery at Kalawao, the colony eventually moved across the peninsula to Kalaupapa where it was warmer and less windy. But Kalawao is the place to have your picnic. Sara and I sat down there with Mrs. Marks one sunfilled day and thoroughly enjoyed the incomparable view of the rugged north coast. We watched turtles play in the surf and gave silent thanks that this place of beauty will never again be marred by the tragedies of long ago.

7. Guided Tours on Molokai

The just-mentioned **Father Damien Tours** (Tel. 567-6171), Box No. 1, Kalaupapa, Hi. 96742, offers a standard 3½- to 4-hour tour of the Makanalua Peninsula for about $12 per person daily except Sunday.

But the most interesting, nay, exciting, nay, thrilling way down to Kalaupapa is to sign up with the **Molokai Mule Ride** (Tel. 567-6088). For about $50 per person, you will descend the Jack London trail on a sure-footed mule and sway along the 26-switchback route, down, down, down to the point where you are met by residents and given a guided minibus tour of the peninsula. The rate includes the trail guide, the mule, a box lunch, and the tour, plus transportation between your hotel and the corral. The experience may prove frightening to some (children under 16 are not permitted by Hawaii Health Department rules anyway). The entire excursion takes about six hours. Highly (about 1600 feet high) recommended.

Another strange excursion is the **Molokai Ranch Wildlife Safari** (Tel. 553-5115), an unusual photographic hunting trip through the Molokai Ranch Wildlife Park, for about $10.

They afford passengers in open-windowed vans a chance to view and photograph several types of African animals, many of which are rare or endangered, being raised to supply zoos and other animal parks in the world. These include giraffe, aoudad (Barbary sheep), Indian black buck, eland, sable antelope, oryx, impala, ibex, and the greater kudu.

Also, **Grayline Tours** (Tel. 567-6177) takes standard trips which may be arranged at your hotel. The tab for the five-hour "Grand Tour" is about $25 for adults, half-price for children under 12. It will take you over a route from the Kalaupapa Overlook to Halawa Valley. There is also an East End tour for around $20, and a Kalaupapa Lookout tour for around $15.

Molokai also has some cruises this year, most on a 42-foot sloop called *Satan's Doll* from **Molokai Charters** (Tel. 553-5045). There's a sunset cruise at $20 and a round trip to Lanai for $50. Several kinds of charters are available. Talk to Captain Richard Reed about it all.

8. Water Sports—Privacy on the Sands

There are no good beaches at Kaunakakai. The very best sandy shoreline is on the extreme west coast of Molokai, at **Papohaku Beach** and Kepuhi Bay next to the Hotel Sheraton Molokai, although the currents are often treacherous there.

Local folk like to swim on the north shore at **Moomomi Beach** and **Keoneiele Beach**. To reach these, follow Highway 48 to the end—and then keep going on dirt roads and hope.

The easiest beaches to drive to are those on Highway 45 to the east. They begin about 10 miles from Kaunakakai, but our favorite is **Waialua**, about 20 miles down the road. Swimming and skin diving are excellent at this ummarked strand. Along there the shore fishing becomes good, too, particularly at **Morris Point**. (Your luck may also be running at the end of that half-mile-long pier back at Kaunakakai.)

The beach in picturesque **Halawa Valley** is popular for skin diving. Nearby is one of the few good surfing spots on Molokai, and fishing is fine in the bay from August to November. You can swim in the bay and, of course, at the foot of **Moaula Falls**, about an hour's hike inland from the beach.

Some of the best deep-sea fishing in the Islands is found at Penguin

Bank, a submerged peninsula off the southwest coast of Molokai. Although this wide, shallow area is mostly plied by charter outfits out of Honolulu or Lahaina, there are two or three Molokai operations who also know the waters. The aforementioned *Satan's Doll* also takes fishing charters. Also, check with **Sportfishing Molokai** (Tel. 567-6571) about the 27-foot fishing boat *Maikai*, probably available for $200 a day, or the **Molokai Fish & Dive Corp.** (Tel. 553-5926), a newer firm which may be running various snorkel and scuba trips, too.

9. Other Sports on Molokai

The Kalua Koi championship golf course (6,705 yards) is now open at the Sheraton. Also, the Del Monte people have a 9-holer at Maunaloa, and there's a hilly set of links at Kualapuu.

For hunters, there are several thousand acres of public game. As on Lanai, you may hunt axis deer and wild goats in season, as well as several kinds of game birds. Full information on the latest season dates, bag limits, etc., is available from the Department of Land and Natural Resources, Division of Fish and Game, 465 South King St., Honolulu, Hi. 96813.

The Sheraton offers tennis, horseshoes, volleyball, and other activities to its guests. Similar facilities are available at Hotel Molokai and at the Wavecrest condominium at Uala Pue.

10. Shopping—Just Looking?

Kaunakakai has all the shops and stores needed to provide most day-to-day needs for a community of 6,000. Most of these are located on Ala Malama, the main street of the village.

Fay's One Gift Shop, way out in Maunaloa, is now the best arts and crafts shop on the island. In a tiny building, she has jammed many original items, including carvings, shells, Hawaiian quilts, and other locally made goodies. We can only hope it will remain the same. Another place we haven't seen in awhile is **Mololani Crafts**, a project for the handicapped, headquartered in a building more or less behind the town baseball diamond. Best buys are the *lauhala* hats and mats.

There's a branch of Honolulu's **Liberty House** at the Sheraton. And at the Hotel Molokai, drop in at the **Jo's of Molokai Gift Shop** (Tel. 553-3444), operated by Jo and Bob Johnson, retired TV folk. (Bob is the recorded voice on "Mission Impossible" who promises to self-destruct in five seconds!) You might ask there to see a nice souvenir book called *Molokai, the Friendly Isle*, by Molokai resident Marlene Freedman.

Browsers might also enjoy reading the three bulletin boards set up in different parts of town. There's a wealth of fascinating information about bazaars, garage sales, festivals, and anything else that is *au courant* in Kaunakakai.

11. Nights on the Town

The last time we looked, there were four places to make the night scene. Three of them are the **Sheraton Hotel**, the **Hotel Molokai**, and the **Pau Hana Inn**. At the latter you'll probably find a more local crowd gathered out back underneath the beautiful old banyan. Live music and dancing are available at the hotels.

12. Address List

Molokai folk don't hold much with the names of streets and numbers. Just ask anyone for what you want. They'll tell you or go out of their way to take you there.

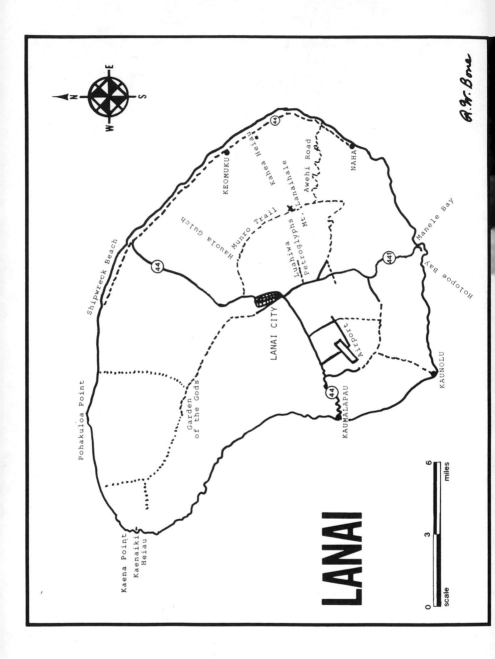

LANAI

scale
0   3   6
miles

9

Lanai,
the Pineapple Island

1. Around the Island—A Green and Rugged Experience

Somehow a myth is perpetuated in Honolulu to the effect that the island of Lanai consists of virtually nothing but pineapples. It's true that there is an abundance of the big, fat, golden and delicious fruit there. The 16,000 acres planted on Lanai make up the largest single pineapple plantation in the world, and it is the island's only industry.

But Lanai doesn't consist of a mere 16,000 acres. It totals about 90,400 acres—nearly 140 square miles—so less than one-fifth of that island is planted in pineapple. The rest? Well, much of it is ripe for your exploration.

"But it has only 20 miles of roads!" the myth-makers exclaim. Wrong again. Lanai has only 20 miles of *paved* roads. We put well over 100 miles on a jeep on Lanai recently and had a darn good time doing it, too.

True, Lanai is not for everyone. If you aren't prepared to bounce around in a jeep over dusty and rocky routes, don't go. But if you're young or in good health, want to blaze some trails and find historic sights with few signs to guide you, and maybe meet only two or three fellow visitors, then you'll enjoy Lanai as much as we did.

The Dole Company bought the entire island in 1922 for $1.1 million. That firm is now owned by Castle & Cooke, Inc., which eventually bowed to union pressure and sold nearly 2,000 acres of company housing to employees at very cheap rates. Today about 65 percent of the families who live there proudly take care of their own tiny houses and gardens. Nevertheless, the company still owns nearly 98 percent of the island.

If you stay overnight at the Lanai Lodge, you might awake to hear the whistle blow at 4:30 A.M., in the middle of the dark, cool night. That means the weather's dry and there's work today.

If you were one of the 2,000 Filipino workers who live in Lanai City, you would eat your breakfast swiftly and then get dressed as quickly as you could in an incredibly thick outfit to protect you from the hot sun and the sharp crowns of the pineapple. If you got to the trucks in an hour and a half, you'd be in the fields in time to earn a full day's pay.

2. Lanai's Airport and Flights

As you descend closer and closer to the prickly pineapple fields, it's hard to believe that there's really a smooth runway down there—one which stretches enough to accommodate the DC-9 Fanjets of **Hawaiian Airlines** (HAL) as well as their funny-looking DASH-7 jet props.

Aloha Airlines doesn't fly to Lanai, so your best choice of craft is either Hawaiian Air or the twin-engine, nine-seat Cessnas flown by **Royal Hawaiian Air Service** (RHAS) or **Air Molokai**.

We flew Royal Hawaiian to Lanai recently since we like the personal contact with the pilot who points out things to ooh and ah at from the low-altitude propeller flight.

About the only point to remember about the Lanai terminal building itself is that it is only open when flights are due. Otherwise its doors—including the lavatories—are securely locked. This becomes important after a day of jeep riding on dusty, red-dirt roads when you thought you could clean up quickly in the restroom just before catching the plane out. For other types of emergencies, ask the airport firemen in the corrugated metal shack next door.

The airport is five minutes' drive from Lanai City.

3. Transportation on Lanai

The scheduled planes into Lanai are usually met by the island's only taxi, driven by either **"Molokai" Oshiro** or Mrs. Oshiro. If they are not there, you can telephone them at 565-6952 from the pay phone on the outside of the terminal building. If you are going to arrive on Sunday, be sure to make advance arrangements.

The Oshiros also own one of Lanai City's two gas stations, and now the only rental car agency. We signed out a jeep from them once, and with the use of the compound low gear (four-wheel drive) on occasion, we were able to reach any point on the island where any other vehicle had ever preceded us.

The other gas station, now called **Lanai City Services** (Tel. 565-6780), is also in the U-drive business, and reportedly manager Don Cotten runs a much more laid-back operation. Expect to pay $55 or $60 a day for a Jeep or some similar four-wheel-drive vehicle. Oshiro or Cotten will be glad to provide a passenger car for about half those rates, but there is little reason for renting one unless you are in Lanai on business and have no reason to sightsee. Nearly anything of interest can only be reached with a rugged vehicle. Not every road will require switching into four-wheel drive, but the high undercarriage will serve to carry you safely over rocks and other objects hazardous to low-slung passenger automobiles.

The unpaved roads, particularly those through pineapple fields, are very, very dusty (and, on occasion, very, very muddy). Although it may be fun to take the top off and put the windshield down on either the high-up ridgeline Munro Trail or the beach roads, we'd advise against it in the red-dirt plantation area.

Traffic is no problem on the few miles of asphalt. On the one-lane dirt jeep trails, get in the habit of honking your horn on blind curves. However unlikely, another vehicle could come along. There are no traffic lights, but there are stop signs in the city limits plus about six policemen who do, they tell us, hand out tickets to tourists. Parking is free everywhere, and we never saw a "No Parking" sign on Lanai.

There is no public transportation on the island. Young folks generally have good luck with hitchhiking, except that local residents are seldom heading as far as such sites as petroglyphs, ancient *heiaus*, ghost towns, or the Garden of the Gods. If you have a pack on your back for serious exploring, however, and just need a lift to where the trail begins, chances are somebody will take you closer to it.

There are no bicycles, motorcycles, or horses for rent on Lanai. Hawaiian Airlines will fly your bicycle to the island for $5, however.

4. The Hotel Scene—Your Choice of One

Set atop a grassy knoll in a cool forest of stately Norfolk pine trees 1,600 feet above sea level is the tiny **Hotel Lanai**, the only hostelry on the island. Built in about 1927 by the Dole Corporation for its official visitors, it still serves that function, but it is also open to all comers.

There's a charming, knotty-pine dining room with a fireplace, guns, and heads of deer and sheep at one end of the room. The hotel's spacious, creaky verandah now serves as the town's only bar. (Order your Scotch and soda through the same window where you registered for a room.)

The white-frame structure has 10 very nice rooms, some doubles and some singles, all with toilet and shower. A few have private entrances so you won't have to track all that red dirt through the house after a day of sightseeing.

The entire hotel has been renewed from the roof on down by the new owner, the widow of the man who shepherded the Hotel Hana Maui for many years. The newly enlivened deluxe rooms with designer bed-spreads and original art now rent for $58. Some standard twins go for $45. In the best deal of all for groups or large families, the hotel also now rents out two nearby fully equipped *houses* (three-day minimum stay), in-cluding a three-bedroom model, sleeping six, for $65 per day and a four-bedroom house, sleeping ten, for $110 per day. (Reserve at the Hotel Lanai, Lanai, Hi. 96763 and include one night's deposit.) Say hello for us to Alberta de Jetley, who has turned this hotel into the plushest thing Lanai has seen since the beginning of time.

5. Dining and Restaurants—Your Choice of Three and One-Half

By far the best restaurant in Lanai City is the dining room in the **Hotel Lanai** just mentioned. Complete dinners run about $15. At break-fast or dinner, you'll probably find yourself exchanging sightseeing in-formation with other guests.

For lunch, there's a sort of all-around goody shop called **S. T. Proper-ties** on Seventh Street. It has a soda fountain inside, and it used to be named the Lanai Fountain. Lots of folks hereabouts still refer to it as "The Fountain." Anyway, it serves pretty good hamburgers. Next door, **Dahang's Pastry Shop** is now serving a local-style breakfast and lunch. The morning meal runs about $3 with all the trimmings. You can get a noontime sandwich for under $2.

Or you can buy food fixings at Richard's Shopping Center, 434 Eighth St., or the Pine Isle Market, just up the street at No. 356. Both are gen-eral stores.

For our own lunch, we had the hotel make up some sandwiches and other accessories which we consumed on the road, high, high up at Lanai-hale, and far, far from the maddening mob. You never knew a crunch into ham and cheese could taste so good—and sound so loud!

6. Sightseeing Lanai—Fun, but Rugged

Lanai has its fair share of sightseeing points, but they're about the hardest targets to hit of any in the Islands. Frankly, there's some serious local sentiment for maintaining the obscurity of many of the historical locations, under the theory that those who really want to find them badly enough will manage it somehow, and that casual wanderers can be dan-gerous. And it is true that such valuable relics as petroglyphs, ghost towns, and archeological sites have been defaced and damaged. Unfor-tunately, there are no facilities for guarding these important sites.

Once upon a time there were as many as twenty Hawaii Visitors Bu-reau warrior markers on Lanai, but all except two or three of these seem to have disappeared. Even some road signs in the hinterlands have been uprooted or at least not replaced when knocked asunder by wind, rain, or the wrath of the *akuas*.

Another problem in traversing Lanai is simply that there are *too many roads*. Every time a pineapple field is replanted or redesigned, the bull-dozers are brought in to cut some new roads along the rows of fruit. Even some old routes indicated on maps are impossible to tell from just another pineapple road as it makes its way through the plantation.

One of the helpful techniques we have found for locating old roads is simply to drive along the periphery of the pineapple plantings, keeping the fruit on one side of the jeep and the undeveloped scrub growth on the other. Then, when you see one of the "pineapple roads" cross your path and head off into the bushes, it could be the track you're look-ing for.

Use our directions here as general guides, but the way to improve your chances of finding the right road is to ask first at the Hotel Lanai. There's a map on the wall that marks several sites you may not find listed elsewhere. (If you're reading these words before leaving for Lanai, hie yourself down to Honolulu Bookshops or another place which sells the University Press of Hawaii's map of Molokai and Lanai. It's about $3 well invested, even if it, too, isn't entirely accurate.)

The courses to follow generally divide themselves into five. Each one of four routes heads off more or less in a different direction. And a fifth road makes its way up along the ridgeline to the top of the mountain and down again. All radiate more or less from Lanai City, a patchwork of little houses in the pines positioned in the approximate center of the island.

THE NORTHWEST ROUTE

A well-traveled dirt road entitled the Kanepuu Highway begins its trek to the far corner of the island by running through pineapple fields, but eventually emerges into the open, dry country which has probably not changed much for hundreds of years.

After about 7 miles, the road comes to the **Garden of the Gods**. Most dramatic at sunrise or sunset, the bizarre landscape is dominated by a canyon of buttes, pinnacles, and weird lava formations, all cut into the red dirt and bordered by green grass.

Farther along, the road gets rougher, but you can follow it when the weather's good to **Kaenaiki**, the site of the largest *heiau* on Lanai. There used to be a spur from there to **Kaena Point**, which served as an exile colony for adulterous Hawaiian women for a brief period in 1837. Lately the road has been closed, however.

THE NORTHEAST ROUTE

Here's one that's paved, or at least it is for the first 8 miles down the slope as far as the windward shore. That's where it begins to be interesting, and it divides into two sections.

Just before the end of the macadamized section, take the Poaiwa Road to the left. This winding, dirt-and-sand track dives through tunnels of *kiawe* trees (plenty of ducking necessary if you're in an open jeep) and eventually leads to **Shipwreck Beach**. You'll pass several squatters' shacks built out of the timbers of foundered vessels. At the very end of the road, you'll probably see at least one modern ship aground, deserted and just waiting for the waves to pound her into submission against the offshore reef. The craft is an old "liberty ship," still holding out since its beaching during World War II.

With the trade winds funneling through the Pailolo Channel between Molokai and Maui (both islands visible in the distance), hundreds of large and small craft have been scuttled on this shore, either by accident or design, for more than 150 years. There have been fewer shipwrecked in recent decades since whaling vessels no longer congregate in the Lahaina Roadstead across the 9-mile channel between Lanai and Maui.

Leave your jeep at the end of the road and head on foot for a cement structure that looks like it might have been a World War II gun platform. Near there, the rocks on the ground have been marked with white paint and an occasional arrow by Lanai Boy Scouts. Follow these for a few hundred yards to see a good collection of **Hawaiian petroglyphs**. The gateway boulder to this ancient grotto of pictorial graffiti is marked in commanding strokes, "Do Not Deface!"

If you return to the end of the paved portion of Highway 44, you can continue south on the dirt along the waterline to the ghost town of **Keomuku**. The village was abandoned in 1901 when the nearby Maunalei Sugar Co. failed. Nestled in a lovely coconut grove, most of the old houses were, for some reason, just razed in 1973. The rickety wooden church remains, however.

Just down the road, you'll see why the Hawaiians say the plantation closed down. There is the **Kahea Heiau**, some of whose sacred stones were taken by the *haoles* to build the sugar railroad. Not long after the shrine was disturbed, the mill's sweet water turned salty for no earthly reason. (We also saw some interesting petroglyphs on the large stones near the *heiau*.)

If you follow this windward dirt road for the full 15 miles, you'll eventually come to the site of the old Hawaiian village called **Naha**. There is some "paved" road here—paved in stones by the old Hawaiians centuries ago. But cobbled or not, here your jeep road ends. Unless there's been a new cut made by the bulldozers since we were there, you'll have to turn around.

THE SOUTHWEST ROUTE

A really good stretch of two-lane highway, this end of Route 44 goes past the airport road and winds down the bluff to **Kaumalapau Harbor**, and it is a busy thoroughfare during the picking season. The harbor was built to transfer millions of tons of pineapples from the enormous trucks to the enormous barges which then speed them off to the enormous Dole cannery in Honolulu. In the summer, you may watch this operation in progress.

Just past the airport road, long before you get to that harbor, however, there is another paved road which turns off the Kaumalapau Highway to the left. If you have a jeep, a rugged constitution, a determined nature, plenty of time, and a deep interest in seeing the vast remains of a once-populous village frequented by Kamehameha the Great, you can turn here to begin the trek to **Kaunolu Village**. A rough shoreline community, now completely deserted, it was Kamehameha's favorite fishing ground.

The pavement peters out into a dusty red pineapple road at a point nearly opposite the end of the airport runway (the elevated area to your left). Now scan the horizon to your right on a search for the only man-made structure in view, a tubular-like building which is the covered antenna for an aircraft electronic navigations station. From this distance, it looks something like a rocket ship or a lighthouse. Head out across any pineapple road over the rolling plantation until you reach that building, located right on the border between the pineapples and the uncultivated countryside.

Next, continue to drive generally south along the edge of the plantation, always keeping the pineapple (or plowed pineapple fields) to your left and the rugged grassland to your right, for about 1.8 miles. There, the Kaunolu Road heads into the bush to your right. If you're lucky, there *may* be a wooden sign to reassure you.

The incredibly rough road bumps down, down, down for 2 miles (it may seem more like 10) before you reach the rocky ruins of the village. But then, wow!

Park your jeep, and climb around the "city," being very careful not to stumble and fall into any ravines or over any *palis*. There are the ruins of **Halulu Heiau**, and you can soon begin to imagine the place full of activity as it must have looked with a hundred or more grass houses scattered over the terraces, where only piles of rocks and remnants of hillside trails now remain. (The rocks, incidentally, are believed by some to contain the spirits of the former residents. Those who want to stay on good terms with these Hawaiian ghosts will demonstrate it—as we did—by piling at least one rock on top of another, larger rock, thus restoring a fallen warrior to his former dignity.)

You may find yourself standing on the brink of the eastern bluff, just above the gulch. This, they say, was the site of the king's house. From here, you can see **Kahekili's Jump**, a 62-foot-high cliff from which Kamehameha's bravest soldiers would, on his command, leap into the sea. Those who were strong and pure of heart would have no trouble clearing the 15-foot ledge which protrudes below. Others, who could not, would instead enter the spirit world, leaving their broken bodies with the rocks at the water's edge.

THE SOUTHEAST ROUTE

This, too, is a main paved road to the shore with almost a Mission Impossible side trip of nevertheless unusual value. The conventional route is to follow Manele Road (State Highway 441) to the twin inlets of **Hulopoe Bay**—a lovely beach park with picnic tables, barbecue pits, and excellent swimming—and the nearby fork in the road to **Manele Bay**, the site of a rather plain, small boat harbor where you'll land if you're one of the few visitors to Lanai to arrive by sea. (Several cruise boats from Lahaina, Maui, offer excursions to Lanai, and this could be an unusual way to effect an interisland trip. See the Maui chapter, Section 7, "Guided Tours and Cruises.")

But the side trip off Highway 441 to see the **Luahiwa petroglyphs** is the most tantalizing—and the most frustrating—project for many visitors. Among the best preserved in all the Islands, this large collection of boulders engraved with hundreds of Hawaiian figures would be easy to reach if the roads were marked, but they are not.

About a mile south of Lanai City on Route 441, look east toward the foothills until you see a silvery water tower, an easy landmark to find. Below this tank, almost down to the level of the pineapple fields, is a more obscure little yellow building (or at least it was yellow the last time we were there) which houses a humming electric transformer. The petroglyphs are approximately 50 feet up the hill above this high-voltage shack, and a little south of it.

After parking our jeep at the little building and making an agonizing climb up a near-vertical cliff through the underbrush, we finally came to—another road! (Later we found the same road on wheels, but it is hopeless to describe the maze of rust-colored trails we blundered through in order to do so.)

The scatter of inscribed boulders in the grove of trees and sisal plants on the nearby hillside was magnificent. There were petroglyphs we hadn't seen represented in any books, and we marveled at such images as the magnificent large war canoes, complete with sails and outriggers. Also there were men on horseback, so these were apparently drawn after the *haoles* came to Lanai with their strange snorting beasts. We thought then that it was a historical pity that the Hawaiians did not bring the newcomers to such stones to describe what significance was attached to their scratches, if not to read aloud the stories inscribed there.

The boulders appeared to march up and up the hill, one by one, in a zig-zag pattern. Each rock seemed to call us to climb again and see just one more group of pictures, farther and farther up the bluff in a continuing quest to pry some meaning from it all. It seemed each rock had some different story to tell—about families, dogs, pigs, birds, and little concentric circles which could mean trips around the island, or, perhaps, rainbows. There were petroglyphs on top of petroglyphs, so surely they had not yet all been studied exhaustively. Who would perceive the solution to their mystery?

THE MUNRO TRAIL

Sometime after the turn of the century, a New Zealand naturalist named George C. Munro came to Lanai with seeds, plants, and flowers from his native land which he decided would flourish up along the ridgeline of Lanaihale, the 3,370-foot-high mountain which today watches over Lanai City and the pineapple plants below.

So Munro proceeded to sow a little New Zealand way up high, and not the least of these botanical wonders were hundreds of Norfolk Island pine trees. These proved to be so efficient at gathering moisture from the air that they were also successfully seeded in and around Lanai City to alleviate the desert atmosphere.

Our jeep trip through the upland rain forest along the Munro Trail was a particular delight for Sara, herself a displaced New Zealander. She recognized such familiar home-grown specialties as *manuka* and other wildflowers and tree ferns which descended from her countryman's munificence long ago.

The Munro Trail is often—and rightly—the first excursion taken by a visitor to Lanai. Pack some sandwiches and take Route 44 past the golf course about a half-mile; then turn right onto the dirt road at Koele. Always follow the more well-traveled track, even when it appears to go down instead of up, not far from the beginning of the route. Or, better yet, get some up-to-date advice from the Hotel Lanai. Alberta de Jetley tells us that the cemetery road is now a better beginning to the trail. Keep a sharp eye out, and you may see an axis deer, as we did on our own gambol over the trail.

You'll pass the **Hookio Ridge**, the fortified notches in the landscape where Lanai warriors unsuccessfully defended their home from an invasion launched from the island of Hawaii in 1778.

Nearby is the 2,000-foot-deep **Hauola Gulch**, seen best from a foot trail that leads to an overlook. But where we shut off the motor, were deafened by the silence, and settled down to picnic was at the **Lanaihale Overlook**. There you can see the islands of Maui, Molokini, Kahoolawe, and, on a clear day, Oahu, Molokai, and Hawaii.

From Lanaihale you must continue around the remainder of the 7-mile circular route until it joins Highway 441 via Hoike Road.

The Munro Trail is Lanai's zenith—a "must," we think, for all comers.

7. Guided Tours and Cruises

Jimmie Nishimura, now in his seventies, has sold the gas station and tour operation he ran for most of his life. However, Jimmie is still there at **Lanai City Services** (Tel. 565-6780), although semiretired. If you could talk him into giving you a tour, it would probably be first rate and cost around $25. Jimmie's replacement as tour guide has not been named at this writing.

On the cruise file, a new operation, **South Sea Island Charters** (Tel. 565-6650), was launched last year. The 55-foot yacht *Loco Viente II*, piloted by Gail Chapin, will take two to six people on a three-hour sail out of Manele Harbor for a charter price of $150. She also has several longer cruises through all the islands from a Lanai base. You can make bookings through the Hotel Lanai.

Lanai Sea Charters (Tel. 565-6958) will tailor its trips to suit you, the sailor. Several different arrangements are available. Bob Moon, captain and instructor, will meet you at Lanai Airport or even send out his boat to bring you over to Lanai from Maui, if you prefer. Better write him in advance at P.O. Box 401, Lanai City, Hi. 96763 to find out the latest information.

Several other sailing trips may be organized from Lanai in 1984. Chances are all the latest nautical scuttlebutt will be available from the Hotel Lanai.

8. Water Sports on Lanai

There is good swimming, some snorkeling, so-so surfing, and several excellent spots for shore fishing.

Hulopoe Beach is one of the best beaches in the state, usually safe for swimming except during rough seas. Sometimes there is good body surfing. Camping is possible with a permit from the Koele Company.

Manele Beach, next door, is more suited for docking of small boats than swimming, although there is some sand leading up to the calm waters. Most people swim at Hulopoe, however. There are picnic tables and grills at both, but *no drinkable water*.

Shipwreck Beach is fine for wading, shore fishing, and certainly beachcombing.

Kaunolu, which was Kamehameha's favorite fishing grounds, still is good fertile territory for shore casting, they say. We wouldn't swim in these crashing waves and near those rocks, however, on a *kahuna*'s double-dare!

Kaumalapau Harbor is also popular for shore fishing, once the pineapple truck and barge activity has ended for the day.

SPORT FISHING

There are no charter boats stationed at Lanai, but some will come over from Maui on request. Approximate rates for half-day charters are $250, for full days $350. Waters around Lanai are known for catches of ahi, aku, kawakawa, mahimahi, and ulua.

9. Other Sports on Lanai

There is the 9-hole **Cavendish Golf Course** ($5 a day for out-of-towners; no carts and bring your own clubs) and four free tennis courts at the school (bring your own rackets and balls). You can also use the archery club's range free (again, only if you've tucked your bow and arrows into your bags).

HUNTING

If a Honoluluan knows anything more about Lanai other than "it's paved with pineapple," he knows it's an island of good hunting. In the latter fact, he is correct. The island has been stocked with several kinds of game particularly for hunters.

Axis deer, Mouflon sheep, and pronghorn antelope are the larger animals in season, although the recently imported antelope have not been surviving very well on the island.

Many game birds are hunted, some of which will make a quick bag limit. These include the ubiquitous Chukar partridge, bamboo partridge, ring-necked pheasant, barred dove, black francolin, grey francolin, lace-necked dove, Gambel's quail, and the Rio Grande turkey.

Seasons, limits, and hunting licenses are set up, both by the Koele Company (which controls hunting on and near pineapple land) and the state (which sets the rules everywhere else). For information write to the Chief Ranger, Koele Company, Lanai City, Hi. 96763, or call 565-6661 on Lanai or 531-4454, a direct line from Honolulu.

Basic charge for hunting on Koele (Castle & Cooke) land is $180 per hunter per day. If you've never hunted there before, a guide is required, and they cost $150 to $200. The guide will take care of just about everything except firing the shot, including pickup from the airport, providing a light breakfast, finding the deer, gutting it later, packing the meat and the trophy, etc. If you don't stay at the Hotel Lanai, the Koele Company can sometimes provide basic one-bedroom hunter's cottages, sleeping two, for $50 a night. If you forget your gun, the Koele Company will rent you that, too.

If you're interested in hunting on state land, on Lanai or elsewhere in Hawaii, write to the Department of Land and Natural Resources, Division of Fish and Game, 465 South King St., Honolulu, Hi. 96813.

One other sport which is not regulated—except that it is completely illegal—is **cock fighting**, which is very much part of the tradition and culture of the Filipino plantation workers. By asking around, they say, you can attend a cock fight any Sunday. (We haven't.)

10. & 11. Shopping and Nights on the Town

The first isn't recommended for the visitor. And the second just isn't. Have a short one on the *lanai* of the Hotel Lanai and then go to bed early like everyone else. (The bar closes at 9:30 P.M. anyway.)

10

The Island of Hawaii —the "Big Island"

1. Around the Island—A Sizable Hunk of History

The Big Island is what Hawaii is all about.

Just under its surface, the liquid fire of creation still lives, its vaporous breath always visible and smellable, even in the most quiescent periods. Sometimes it emerges in a spectacular display to remind us that human life is only a very recent and relatively insignificant feature on this or any other island.

New lava may pour forth, either from one of the great calderas in the Volcanoes National Park, or squeezed through massive fissures that open far away in the earth, perhaps near villages and farms and nowhere in the vicinity we think of as the volcano area.

The hot material, at once destructive and constructive, then moves over the land decimating the works of man until it reaches the sea, there building up a new shoreline and still more real estate on the island of Hawaii. It is the only such island in the chain that is physically still growing in size.

According to Hawaiian legend, the island is the dwelling place of Pele, the goddess of the volcano. Her house is said to be in whichever crater is currently the hottest and most frequently active. The ancient Hawaiians were justly afraid of Pele, for her wrath claimed a number of their souls. It is interesting, though perhaps not significant, that lives virtually ceased to be lost to Pele in modern times, and her antics have become relatively predictable. During a volcano eruption, the National Park Ser-

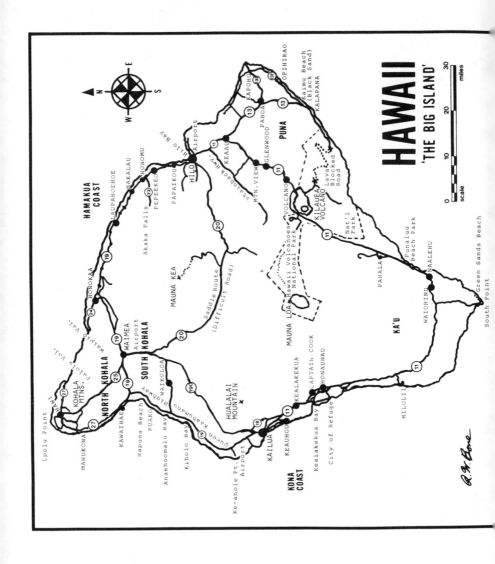

vice does its best to find safe places for everyone to watch the show and to direct the public to these areas.

Three mountains dominate the Big Island landscape. Hualalai, the shortest, and Mauna Kea, the tallest, are considered dormant (but not extinct) volcanos. Mauna Loa, nearly as lofty as the 13,800-foot Mauna Kea, is officially an active volcano, although its eruptions are infrequent. Mauna Loa was relatively quiet for twenty-five years, in fact, until it let loose a spectacular, one-day outburst in July, 1975. It will, however, erupt again.

Hawaii's most active volcano, Kilauea, does not seem to be a mountain at all. Its major crater is a gigantic, ever-steaming circular pit on a plain at about the 4,000-foot level on the gentle slope of Mauna Loa. Between 1959 and 1975, Kilauea erupted two or three times a year, either from the crater area or farther down the "rift zone" in the Puna District. Then the action slowed for a time, with an eruption about every other year. In 1982, however, there were two short outbreaks of lava directly inside Kilauea crater, and these drew thousands of spectators to the rim day and night to watch the sound and light show below. Then, in 1983, Kilauea erupted spectacularly off and on throughout most of the year, although almost always away from the crater in out-of-the-way forests that were only accessible to scientists. On two occasions, however, lava flowed slowly down the mountain into an isolated residential area, and eventually it claimed several houses. As always, no one was hurt.

The island has hosted many key events in human history, not the least of which was the visit of the great British navigator Captain James Cook, at first worshipped and then killed by the Hawaiians at Kealakekua Bay in 1779. It was on Hawaii, too, that Kamehameha the Great first plotted and fought his way to power and then went on to extend his empire over the entire string of islands. Christianity gained an important step here in 1824, when the converted Chieftess Kapiolani publicly and successfully defied Pele in a ceremony at Kilauea Crater in front of scores of trembling witnesses.

Today, of course, the Big Island is not all volcano. Its county seat is Hilo, a mixture of modern and rustic structures at the mouth of the Wailuku River, and a center for the colorful orchid and anthurium growing industry. North of Hilo is the dramatically rugged Hamakua Coast, ending in the deep green slash of Waipio Valley. And near that is the vast, rolling cattle and cowboy country of Waimea.

Still farther north is the former sugar land and economically depressed peninsula of Kohala. The western coast is called Kona, a sunny and dry neighborhood which includes the former stamping ground of Captain Cook, King Kamehameha, Captain George Vancouver, and the first missionaries to the Islands. Today the Kona coast boasts the only commercial coffee crops in the U.S. and perhaps the best deep-sea fishing area in the world.

The southern land mass is Ka'u, which received the first Polynesian settlers to the Islands and is now sparsely populated. It is the home of the "southernmost" everything in the United States.

Then there is prosperous Puna, which has, at the same time, some of the most desolate parts of the island in its volcanic areas and some of the most tropical and lush acreage where the soil has escaped the flows of lava.

Strangely, the Big Island has few tourists for its size, due at least partly to the confusion caused by its own name. (Local boosters complain that even travel agents have been known to get off the plane in Hilo and ask the way to Waikiki Beach—and worse, to ask in Honolulu to be taken up to the volcano!) This is a shame, for in many ways this island offers unique sights and experiences that cannot be duplicated in the state—or in any other state, for that matter. For its special features, it just might be the best bargain for visitors who want to choose a single destination with lots to see and do but still without the hustle-bustle of Honolulu or Maui.

So islanders virtually never call the island Hawaii, unless they can use the term "*on* Hawaii" to contrast with the phrase "*in* Hawaii." There have been attempts to nickname the island of Hawaii as "the Orchid Island" or "the Volcano Island," but those terms usually fall on inattentive ears at home. The island's dominant characteristic will always be its size—more than twice the land area of all the other islands combined—and its name will always remain simply "The Big Island."

2. The Airports on Hawaii

Five civilian airports are scattered over the Big Island, but up to three may be about to fade from the scene. The **Kona Village Airport**, serving an exclusive resort community, has already lost its only scheduled service, and now serves primarily as an emergency strip.

The tiny **Upolu Airport** (Tel. 889-9958), on the windswept land's end at the northernmost tip of the island, still receives occasional flights from the prop planes of the Royal Hawaiian Air Service.

The attractive, well-maintained **Waimea-Kohala Airport** (Tel. 885-4520) at Waimea, like the Upolu and Kona Village strips, may be doomed by a new fast highway in the vicinity. Kamuela/Waimea, the center of the ranch and cattle country, is still served at this writing by Royal Hawaiian and very infrequently by Hawaiian Airlines. (No taxi or bus service is available, but you can probably get someone to drop you off in town.)

Kona's outdoorsy **Ke-ahole Airport**, about 15 minutes' drive north of Kailua-Kona, is one of two full-size gateways to the Big Island. It has several flights a day from all other islands via the jets of Aloha Airlines and Hawaiian Airlines, the jet props of Mid Pacific Airlines, and the propeller-driven Cessnas of Royal Hawaiian Air Service. It has also just begun receiving jumbo-jet flights from Chicago and Los Angeles via United Airlines.

Set up in a string of eight or ten little Polynesian style, open-sided buildings, the terminal is divided into two general areas. Hawaiian Airlines occupies the southern or Kailua extremity, while Aloha Airlines has the opposite end, with facilities arranged in a near-mirror image to Hawaiian's. Consequently, there are two of nearly everything at the airport—two snack bars, two sets of restrooms, two state information counters, et cetera.

Royal Hawaiian Air Service has a completely separate hut a few steps north of Aloha's arrivals area, across from a tour bus parking area.

Over a footbridge in the very center is a small building devoted to a line of automobile rental counters, with their vehicles parked in the lot behind them. Firms represented at the airport when we last checked included Hertz, Avis, National, Budget, Dollar, Robert's, American International, Marquez, Liberato's, and Phillips. (Two or three other companies are in Kailua and will arrange an airport pickup for customers. See next section.)

There is no public transportation available at the airport. It will cost you about $7 for a seat on the Gray Line limousine for the nine miles to Kailua or perhaps $10 via one of the three or four taxi companies available—up to $15 to hotels in Keauhou.

Over on the windward side of the island, the half-mile-long terminal at Hilo's **General Lyman Field** serves all interisland flights as well as those from Kona on United Airlines, which gas up in Hilo before leaving for the Mainland.

Passengers from all jets enter the terminal on the second floor through one of seven loading bridges attached directly to aircraft doors. Baggage claim carrousels are down the escalator on the ground floor. In one end of the building there is a state VIP (Visitor Information Program) booth and three lei stands. The Island King of Hawaii gift shop is next door.

The cafeteria-style restaurant, just across the hall, is another in the Host International chain, also represented at Honolulu Airport. A package food store (macadamia nuts and all that) is nearby.

Rental car agencies are outside opposite the center of the new complex. They will probably still include Hertz, Avis, National, Budget, Robert's, American International, Dollar, Liberato's, Marquez, Holiday, and Phillips.

As in Kona, there is no public transportation from the airport—not even in a "stretch-out" limousine. But since the airport is practically inside the city and near many hotels, taxis are not so bad—about $4 or so. (Backpackers may prefer to hoof the 3 miles into town.)

The terminal is attractively landscaped and even features some small waterfalls using water collected from the building's roof. (And in Hilo, that should certainly be a dependable source!)

3. Big Island Transportation

The most practical transportation for visitors on the Big Island is a rental car—or even a jeep, if you are heading to more rugged and wilder areas.

At any given time, there are at least a dozen very competitive car rental firms on the island. Those with offices at the two major airports are more convenient, of course, and usually more expensive, too.

Since distances are so great compared with other islands in the state, many will prefer to rent a car on flat rates—with no mileage charges. Be aware, however, that this is difficult to do during the busiest seasons of the year when there are many customers and fewer cars.

Flat rates for most companies go into hiding in February and don't come out again until about April. They might disappear again in July and August. (If you are in Honolulu planning a Big Island trip, you can look up and call the Honolulu phone numbers for some of these outfits, questioning them on their rates and then making reservations for cars.)

Here is a list of some Big Island car rental companies as they exist at the moment, although more mergers and closures are being rumored. Unless otherwise indicated, all have offices at General Lyman Field in Hilo and the Ke-ahole Airport in Kona, and the Hilo and Kona phone numbers listed here are for those terminal locations.

Be aware that if you rent a car in Hilo and turn it in in Kona—or vice versa—you'll probably pay a drop-off charge of as much as $8. So compare this with your air fares. To drive from Hilo all the way around to Hilo again and then fly back to Honolulu may only cost you about $3 or so more than turning in your car in Kona and flying to Honolulu from there. For one person making the complete circle, it's a net saving of $5. For a couple, it works out at about the same price (with gas, anyway), and you'll see a lot more countryside (on the ground and in the air) in any case.

National chains:

Hertz Rent a Car (Hilo 935-2896, Kona 329-3566, Kamuela 883-9400), which specializes in Ford products; **Avis Rent a Car** (Hilo 935-1290, Kona 329-1745), which generally has Chrysler cars; **National Car Rental System** (Hilo 935-0891, Kona 329-1674), which usually features GM products; **Budget Rent-A-Car** (Hilo 935-6878, Kona 329-3581), which is connected with the Slim Holt Tour operation; **Dollar Rent-A-Car Systems** (Hilo 961-6059, Kona 329-2744), which will also rent you camping equipment for pretty good rates; and **American International Rent-A-Car** (Hilo 935-1108, Kona 329-2926), which has a good fly/drive deal with Air Hawaii.

Statewide chains:

Robert's Hawaii U-Drive (Hilo 935-2858, Kona 329-1688), which is well established and well known in the Islands; **Holiday Rent-a-Car** (Hilo 935-5201, Kona 329-1752), a new go-getter; and **Tropical Rent-A-Car Systems** (Hilo, 688 Kanoelehua Ave., Tel. 935-3385, Kona, in Kailua, Tel. 329-2347), a longtime favorite of ours.

Local Big Island companies:

Phillips U-Drive (Hilo 935-1936, Kona 329-1730), which had low weekly flat rates recently, too; **Hilo Motors** (Hilo only, 1177 Kilauea Ave., Tel. 961-5225), which also rents jeeps; **Liberato's Rent A Car** (Hilo 935-8089, Kona 329-3035); and **Marquez U-Drive** (Hilo 935-2115, Kona 329-3411).

Keep in mind that the rental situation sometimes changes daily in regard to rates, ownership, types of deals, etc. Before renting a car anywhere in the Islands, please see our discussion on the subject in Chapter 5, Section 3.

Camper Rentals. For those intrepids who want to guide their own hotel rooms over Big Island byways, there are now two firms to consider. The long-established recreational vehicle renter is **Travel/Camp** (formerly Holo-Holo Campers, Tel. 935-7406) where Gordon Morse can provide any of nine sizes, from a toiletless compact cabover sleeping two for about $50 a day on up to a 21-foot motorhome, sleeping five, with full bathroom and generator for $75 a day. He has lots of rules, so you'd better write for details to P.O. Box 11, Hilo, Hi. 96720.

Beach Boy Campers (Tel. 961-2022) has a Datsun "mini-cabover," sleeping four, from $40 to $50 at this writing. (We've tried neither of these outfits personally, and we'd like to hear from readers who have.)

Driving on the Big Island. In general, the roads are good and well marked, although some maps you may pick up list the old route numbers in the Waimea-to-Kona neighborhood, which has changed around somewhat. (Part of Route 19 has become 190, Route 26 has become part of 19, etc.)

• In Hilo, watch your stop signs carefully. There are a few streets which look like they ought to be through ones for you, but they're not. Also, considerable street-widening and other surface repairs are expected in Hilo over the next year or so. And by all means, be sure your windshield wipers are working all right.

• We do not recommend taking the Saddle Route (54 miles on Route

20 between Hilo and Waimea). In addition to its being narrow with several rough spots and some very tight turns, the road is often wet and foggy and regularly used in massive military maneuvers. There are no gas stations or emergency services of any kind along most of its length, and in case of any mishap, help could be a long time coming and eventually very expensive. If you insist on trying it, do so in the morning only, and then only when the weather is clear. The Saddle Road may look on the map like a faster way to Kona than the northern route, but it decidedly is not.

● Make a practice of keeping your gas tank full all over the Big Island. Stations have a way of closing early when you don't expect it, and there are such frightening stretches as that 50 miles between the villages of Captain Cook and Naalehu with not a gas pump to be seen! (It's even worse than that when Naalehu and Captain Cook roll up their respective sidewalks!)

County buses. In 1974, Hawaii County finally christened a new countywide transit system, and it has proven to be a success. Taking a cue apparently from Honolulu, they made the new vehicles colorful, painting most of them lavender and white, and labeled them with the pidgin slogan *Hele-on*. (That may be loosely translated as "go-go.")

The Hilo bus terminal is between Kamehameha Avenue and the Bayfront Highway, about opposite the foot of Mamo Street. You pay on the basis of how far you *hele* (25 cents for some short trips, but $2 from Hilo to Kailua-Kona), and schedules are usually designed to be of more service to workers than to island visitors. An exception is the Banyan Drive Shuttle, which operates between the hotels and the downtown precincts, between 10 A.M. and 3 P.M. Monday through Saturday. The maximum fare is 25 cents. The latest bus information is available from the Mass Transportation Agency (Tel. 935-8241).

4. The Hotel Scene—Hilo, Kona, and Inns Between

Most lodgings on the Big Island fall into two general areas. First, there are those in the county seat and overseas gateway to the island, the citilet of *Hilo* (either in the shoreline Banyan Drive area or downtown). Second, and 100 road miles across the island, most other hotels are located in the popular resort area of *Kona*, mostly in the neighboring villages of Kailua (sometimes called Kailua-Kona) and Keauhou ("kay-ow-*ho*"), which are 7 miles away from each other.

In addition to these, there are a half-dozen or so country hotels scattered about the island. Generally speaking, all except one—the Volcano House—are very modest choices.

Last, but certainly farthest from least, there are two exclusive hostelries which qualify not just as hotels but as entire centralized vacations in

hemselves—the Mauna Kea Hotel and the Kona Village. These resorts
vere designed for the most affluent travelers to Hawaii, and have very
pecial features which place them in a category of their own. They bring
1p the end of this section.

IOTELS IN THE CITY OF HILO

Hotels in Hilo usually are located in a cluster along Banyan Drive, an
attractive waterfront avenue not far from the airport, or else they are
nearer the center of Hilo itself, where they are somewhat separated
from each other. With exceptions, we lean toward the location on Banyan Drive for views, general atmosphere, and the opportunities for casual strolling in pleasant, not-too-commercial surroundings. (Remember
that there are no—none—absolutely zero—Hilo hotels located on a
sandy beach.)

The hotels we have considered in Hilo fall into two price ranges,
which we have labeled "expensive" and "moderate."

EXPENSIVE HILO HOTELS

There is only one outstanding choice. That is the tightly run **Naniloa
Surf Hotel** (Tel. 935-0831), an InterIslands Resorts entry that sparkles
with professionalism in every corner from garden to gable. Set just a
little back from Banyan Drive, it features: a rambling internal structure
based around two 10-story wings; airy lobby opening onto a viewsome
lanai; separate group tour check-in area relieving the crush; wonderful
vistas of Hilo Bay and—when you're lucky—faraway Mauna Kea; two
main floors, the lower on the sea side; spacious and green grounds featuring an unusual barringtonia ("fish poison") tree; new tennis courts;
meandering walkways along the lava-studded shore; kidney pool with
more sun space than water content; poolside Samurai Bar (11 A.M. to 8
P.M.); adjoining Hutu Terrace coffee shop (where we had an enjoyable
breakfast); cozy Hoomalimali Bar for later dancing and tippling; Polynesian Room Discotheque; good, dependable dining in the Sandalwood
Room; top Honolulu and Mainland acts in the new half-million-dollar
Crown Room, the city's premier night club; several attractive shops on
two levels.

There are 386 well-appointed bedrooms, and the ones we saw sported
TV, radio, air conditioning, and several thoughtful extras. Unfortunately, windows don't open in 503, 504, and some other cheap rooms. Excellent housekeeping and maintenance everywhere we poked; reportedly good room service; twin bedrooms about $50 to $72; suites from
$135 to over $300. (Reservations from InterIsland Resorts, Box 8539,
Honolulu, Hi. 96815.) Despite some newer entries on the scene, the
Naniloa remains the Queen of Banyan Drive and probably of all Hilo.

Also on Banyan Drive, the **Hilo Hawaiian Hotel** (Tel. 935-9361) captures a solid second, and almost anyone would be happy there. The hotel's architecture is a somewhat uninspiring green-and-white reflection of its sister Hilo Lagoon (see below): massive porte-cochere offering plenty precipitation protection; best location on the drive, next to Liliuokalani Gardens; large lobby/lanai featuring Coconut Island in the back yard, Mauna Kea in the background; less outdoor real estate of its own than nearby Naniloa, but a larger swimming pool; four resort shops in four pagodas out front; Menehune Land cocktail lounge with leprechaunish murals; cool blue Queen's Court dining room with a pleasant view.

Total of 290 rooms; individually controlled cooling; color TVs; red-white-blue-striped bedspreads; some units needing more pictures; modest twin standards facing town for $45, oceanfront superiors a little more; deluxe and roomier accommodations for $50 and $60. (Reservations from Hawaiian Pacific Resorts, 1150 South King St., Honolulu, Hi. 96814.) We call it a little cool, but comfortable and reasonably priced.

In a figurative jump into town, the **Hilo Lagoon** (Tel. 935-9311), recently sold to Quality Inns, is next to the Kaiko'o Mall, Hilo's principal shopping center. It is also convenient for government types over from Honolulu because of the neighboring state and county buildings. Spread-out lobby in coral greens and blues, often milling with spread-out tour groups and acres of luggage; reception area somewhat cluttered with signs, advertising, show windows, souvenir counters, etc.; plenty of seats and often plenty of people sitting; curving stairway connecting to lagoon and lower-level restaurants; basement Tiki Garden dining room where our buffet breakfast was far from charming; Windjammer Cabin bar in nautical notes; Paniolo Steak House with big-sky panorama from the tenth story (open 6 P.M.). Generally undistinguished bedchambers with some good views from the high floors in the $35 to $45 range. The Lagoon has also held the line on prices. Quite group-happy, and for the FIT (free and independent traveler) we think it's good enough—but far from great.

MODERATELY PRICED HILO HOTELS

Top choice in this lower category has to be the charmingly rustic **Uncle Billy Kimi's Hilo Bay Hotel** (Tel. 935-0861). Surprisingly homey lobby with lots of light rattan and thatching, even including the chandeliers; tapa cloth everywhere the grass won't go; smells a bit like a hay-mow—not objectionable at all; attractive, bucolic bar; Kimo's Restaurant attached; shopping arcade; Hawaiian garden out back between two residential wings; pond full of colorful carp; lots of bamboo and *hala* trees; attractive bay views at the end by the ample pool.

Very neat, spacious rooms, with some ground-floor models opening right onto the garden (as well as the hall); TVs and air conditioners in all rooms; several with fridge and kitchen sink (costing $5 extra); room prices perhaps holding between $32 and $47 for doubles, $29 to $44 for singles, depending on location. This is a Hawaiian family operation under the avuncular wing of Uncle Billy Kimi, who also owns the adjoining Uncle Billy's Restaurant. (Write him at the hotel, 87 Banyan Drive, Hilo, Hi. 96720.) On our APC Scale—atmosphere, personality, and character—at this lower price range, it wins highest marks.

We also like—most of the time—the 139-room **Hilo Hukilau** (Tel. 935-0821) which sits almost at the end of the airport runway, a little bit off Banyan Drive, and not next to the ocean. Open, lauhala-and-tapa-cloth lobby overlooking pleasant pond and greenery; two internal patios, one with lava rock garden, the other with tables and pool; locally popular restaurant and bar off the lobby; small gift shop; some slippery corridors. Widely varying rooms (one we stayed in had a TV but was short on windows); the nicest units with lanai overlooking the lagoon; double prices $28 to $34; singles $25 to $31. (Reservations from Hukilau Resorts, 2222 Kalakaua Ave., Honolulu, Hi. 96815.) A friendly place, and peaceful, too, between landings and takeoffs.

We once got to stay at the engaging little **Dolphin Bay Hotel** (Tel. 935-1466), which has only 18 units far away from the ocean in a Hilo-green residential area called Pueo. We're tempted to keep this gem a secret, since it can't handle large crowds anyway. There are no TVs to drown out the rustling palms, no pool, and no air conditioners, but plenty of space cooled by oscillating desk fans. All units have kitchenettes, and their managers manage to keep it all as deliciously clean as the inside of a fresh coconut. (They might even give you a coconut to compare!) Doubles will run from $26 to $48 this year, with $7 per extra person. Singles start at $19. A car is a must, and you should reserve far in advance for peak periods. (Write to John Alexander, the manager, at 333 Iliahi St., Hilo, Hi. 96720.) A tropical charmer.

Somebody at the **Hilo Pacific Isle TraveLodge** (Tel. 935-7171) finally wised up and cut the prices in half. Therefore this lackluster entry at the bottom of the previous category in '83 becomes a valid budget possibility for '84. You can't fault its Banyan Drive location, but many TraveLodges, including this one, have that discouraging sameness about them: Strictly a vestigial lobby, more like a front desk on a front porch; heavily used and abused by groups; corridor with vending machines, etc.; oceanside pool; dark cocktail lounge/piano bar; Voyager Restaurant, also sealed against a ray of daylight; a few rooms on the very end with nice views; some units with refrigerators and TVs but virtually no closet space; most doubles now in the $30 range; a few perhaps under $25. (Reservations from the hotel at 121 Banyan Drive, Hilo, Hi. 96720.) A possibility in a pinch.

The **Hilo Hotel** (Tel. 961-3733) is cheaper, and that's as it should be. Midtown location way behind a gigantic kapok tree near the corner of Kinoole and Kalakaua; rocking chairs on the front porch; tiny lobby in beige and black; well-regarded Restaurant Fuji with Japanese menu; swimming pool out back; TV for all in the rec room. Total of 57 well-used billets; some singles a bargain at $15; doubles running $20 to $25. (Don't write; drop in and have a look first.) Affectionately regarded locally—just like the Old Gray Mare.

Some would consider the Hilo Hotel a toss-up with the **Polynesian Pacific Hotel** (Tel. 961-0426), taking into account the latter's better location on Banyan Drive. That's not enough for us, however, and didn't make up for the poor maintenance and housekeeping we found on our own stopover. Doubles are about $20. We judged it okay *only* for the most ascetic travelers who can't find anything else in the price range.

HOTELS IN KONA

Many consider the resort area of Kona to be bounded by the village of Kailua on the north and Keauhou Bay 7 miles south, so the principal hotels appear in those two areas. (Kona Coast hotels outside those boundaries will be discussed later.) As it happened, from our latest research rounds, the Kona hotels fell naturally into three price categories which we have labeled "expensive," "medium," and "budget." Expensive hotels will be found in both Keauhou and Kailua, but all the medium and budget entries are in Kailua only.

EXPENSIVE KEAUHOU/KAILUA-KONA HOTELS

The revolutionary architecture and landscaping in the massive, 537-room **Kona Surf Hotel** (Tel. 322-3411) in Keauhou makes it the strong favorite; huge, rambling structure in five irregularly shaped wings (be sure to get a hotel map) within walking distance to Keauhou Bay, with a little beach and cruises available; dramatic open lobby with intaglio mural; several lush gardens; lots of sports activities including golf, tennis (with pro and pro shop), volleyball, driving range, putting green, two swimming pools (one huge salt-water pool with a slide); sauna bath; massage salon; many shops; Pacific and Asian art and sculpture collection spread throughout the structure; occasionally visiting manta rays in the floodlights after dark.

The hotel boasts several attractive restaurants and bars, including cave-like Puka Bar (7:30 to 12); Poi Pounder show bar and discotheque; Pele's Court coffee shop (where we had a pleasant breakfast); open-air

Nalu Terrace sometimes serving buffet breakfast; Nalu Bar, next to the salty pool; the S.S. James Makee Dining Room, named for an early inter-island· steamship, and now one of the two or three top restaurants in Kona.

The bedrooms are found in five wings named after five islands; the Maui Wing our preference; some rooms with king-size beds; others with double-doubles (not twins); eye-soothing views over rocks and seas; large lanais; tapestries in Hawaiian quilt designs; carpeted baths; generally colorful decor throughout; a few lower-floor standards at about $70 a day; superiors and deluxes $85 to $95. (Reservations from InterIsland Resorts, P.O. Box 8539, Honolulu, Hi. 96815.) A relatively high-priced gem for Hawaii, but for those who seek this kind of luxury, worth every carat.

A couple of miles closer to Kailua, the **Keauhou Beach Hotel** (Tel. 322-3441) is still considered by many to be the best inn in the vicinity, bar none; beachette which looks larger in pictures than in life and fascinat-ing tide pools for shoreline life explorations; several ancient Hawaiian historical sites nearby; undistinguished building façade; small foyer; sev-eral good shops, including Liberty House branch; small pool with falls; shuffleboard and badminton; three lighted tennis courts (and pro); one putting green; Kona Koffee Mill coffee shop with view of hotel entrance-way; Sunset Rib Lanai dining room and Sunday Brunch locally favored; new branch of Don the Beachcomber restaurant.

Total of 317 nicely furnished rooms; color TVs; Hawaiian tapa-cloth-design bedspreads; historical engravings on the walls; attractive wood-and-leather chairs; some refrigerators with cold water awaiting; rates from $46 to $75 daily for two. Management by the veteran Amfac orga-nization is paying off in quality. (Reserve at Amfac Hotels, P.O. Box 8519, Honolulu, Hi. 96815.) We've never checked in here ourselves, but we know several who have and liked it a lot.

In the village of Kailua, the leader is still the **Kona Hilton** (Tel. 329-3111), which dominates the southern skyline. Walking distance to village signs along the shoreline; dramatic exterior with lots of hanging plants, bougainvillaea, and other flowers; three large main structures; massive Grecian pillars in the public areas; airy, breezy lobby reached via a bridge over a lagoon (drop a piece of bread and watch the carp crowd around); small beach nearby; large pool; four new tennis courts; several shops; Mele Mele bar open to the sea; Windjammer Lounge being trans-formed into a nightclub at this writing; elegant Hele Mai Restaurant (high prices); Kona Rib Hale (where locals praise the prime rib); Sing-A-Long piano bar.

Total of 452 well-decorated rooms with views over ocean, mountains, or village; several with original paintings on the walls; widely varying prices running from $57 to $110 for twins all year. (Reservations from Hilton Hotels, 2005 Kalia Rd., Honolulu, Hi. 96815.) We think it's no longer tops, but it's still convenient and recommended.

The **Hotel King Kamehameha** (Tel. 329-2911) has ruled the north end of Kailua town since 1976 after the venerated old King Kam was dynamited off the beach. Certainly the grounds, with their historical displays, are beautiful and interesting; the nighttime torch-lit atmosphere around the pool and the ocean is delightful; and the location is convenient, with a regal shopping center built right into the twin-hulled complex. There are four tennis courts off to the side and a tiny bathing strand along a calm cove. So far we have remained generally disappointed with cuisine and food service.

Upstairs, the suites are fit for a king, but many other rooms are too pawn-sized and uninspired for a luxury-class Hawaii hotel. Five classes of accommodations run from $55 to $90 this year. The helpful staff makes up for a lot. (Reservations from Amfac Hotels, P.O. Box 8519, Honolulu, Hi. 96815.) The Kam is not a bad King, to be sure. But he's far from the top of the heap in his category.

Last on our luxury scale is back in Keauhou again at the 454-room **Kona Lagoon Hotel** (Tel. 322-2727), an architectural achievement next door to the Keauhou Beach Hotel: Three bodies of water—the ocean, a kidney-shaped pool, and the artificial lagoon, to justify the name; large lobby decorated with pictures of last night's luau; color TV in one corner; electronic games for lobby loungers; two tennis courts; Tonga bar and dining room with tapa designs; Wharf Restaurant in blues and greens, serving steaks and seafood; high-peaked Polynesian Long House dinner/show room with glass ball chandeliers across from the huge porte cochere; popular Japanese restaurant surrounded by flowers and water. Upstairs, all the twin double-bed rooms face the mountains, and the twin-bed rooms face the sea. Rooms are rather small, and nearly all except suites are priced about $42 to $54 for 1984. (Reservations from Hawaiian Pacific Resorts, 1150 South King St., Honolulu, Hi. 96814.) We don't really object to this hotel, but all things considered—little beach, group-heavy, distance from the action, room size, etc.—we do prefer all the previously listed Kona addresses this year.

MEDIUM-PRICED KAILUA HOTELS

This year's moderately priced Kona sleeper is the **Kona Bay Hotel** (Tel. 329-1393). Actually, the hotel is the 123-room annex—once known as the Maunaloa Wing—to the venerable Kona Inn, which closed in 1978 and was to be partly razed, partly converted into a shopping center. Now to everyone's surprise, a section of the old inn has been brought back to life again as a hotel through a little magic and a lot of hard work by veteran hotelworkers, members of the younger generation in the family of Uncle Billy Kimi, proprietor of the Hilo Bay Hotel.

The air-conditioned units, virtually all alike, come in standards (B&W TV) perhaps $37 double, superiors (color TV) for $42, and deluxes (color TV and small refrigerator) for $46. (Add $7 for an extra person.) We were happy with our own short stay. (Write the hotel at 75-5739 Alii Drive, or phone Uncle Billy's toll-free number in the appendix.) Probably a good bet at those rates.

A more whoop-it-up favorite with many is the **Kona Seaside** (Tel. 329-2455), which seems to cater to a lively young single crowd. Midtown location at the corner of Kuakini and Palani, a *maika* stone's throw from the King Kam; set back behind the bougainvillaea and the old outriggers; darkish, low-ceiling lobby with large tiles; wood paneling; windows on high; no bar or restaurant; ample swimming pool; deluxe doubles on the fourth floor for $45 with ocean view; superiors on the street corner maybe $40 (where some staff members say you can watch the cars crack up!); some first floor standards in the $35 range for two; singles about $3 less in each category. (Reservations from Hukilau Resorts, 2222 Kalakaua Ave., Honolulu, Hi. 96815.) Plainer than some Hukilaus, but perhaps a good place for a crash.

The general manager of the **Kona White Sands** (Tel. 329-3210) has just written us, asking to be mentioned in this book. While we can't specifically recommend a place until we've had a chance to inspect it, we rather like the sound of it. There are just ten apartments in an office building across the road from White Sands Beach, 3½ miles south of Kailua. With full kitchens and an ocean view, rents run from about $35 to $40 a day for two. (More details from the hotel at P.O. Box 594, Kailua-Kona, Hi. 96740.) We'll sift through the White Sands in more detail soon.

BUDGET KAILUA HOTELS

There are still a couple of addresses where you might get double accommodations for under $35. One standby is the **Kona Hukilau** (Tel. 329-1655), which is connected with (and almost connected *to*) the above-mentioned Seaside. Convenient address, right in the center of everything; rustic lobby right on the street; popular, low-priced tapa-walled restaurant and aquarium-studded bar; unusual hillside design placing the pool and "ground" floor upstairs. A common *lanai* in front of several rooms at once means you'll run into your neighbors—or at least their feet! There are 104 simple, neat, clean rooms starting at $25 single, $28 double. Walk-in room rates may be cheaper than the published sheet, which includes breakfast. (Reservations from Hukilau Resorts, 2222 Kalakaua Ave., Honolulu, Hi. 96815.) You won't find a lot of frills, but we prefer this one to its Seaside sister.

We finally had a chance to inspect the **Kona Tiki** (Tel. 329-1425), a small, three-story structure about a mile south of Kailua. Just 15 modest but clean units, all with lanai; everything directly on the ocean; no beach, but a nice pool next to the salt spray; free Kona coffee and donuts every morning on the terrace; outdoor barbecue for guest use; new ceiling fans in all the rooms. Twins at $33 have cooking facilities; those at $28 do not. There's a three-day minimum stay. (Write the hotel at Box 1567, Kailua-Kona, Hi. 96740.) A little way from the action, but pretty good for the price.

HOTELS IN THE COUNTRY

There are lodgings of differing quality in Hawaii Volcanoes National Park, Honokaa, Waimea/Kamuela, Hawi, Puako, Waikoloa, Holualoa, Captain Cook, and Naalehu.

THE NATIONAL PARK

You won't find anything anywhere that compares with **The Volcano House** (Tel. 967-7321), now run by Sheraton, and parked smack-dab on the edge of the live Kilauea Crater. Wonderful, commodious sitting alcove off the lobby; large, cheery ohia fire on chilly evenings; leather chairs and nine-foot suede sofa; glassed terrace for volcano-watching or reading; same view from Uncle George's Cocktail Lounge and recently remodeled restaurant; sometimes overcrowded lunch buffets (see Section 5); natural volcanic steam sauna (tip: ask them to heat it up considerably before you go in); golf course across the road.

Just 38 well-furnished, well-maintained, and heated (when it works) sleeping quarters; most strung out in a line and overlooking the crater; a few facing the opposite direction. (Unless you're an early riser, try not to get rooms next to the maids' service closet, where you won't avoid the 8 A.M. clatter and chatter.) A few standard rooms now set at $37 for two; more superiors and deluxes for $44 and $48 (no extra charge for youngsters in the same room); roughing-it camper cabins three miles away for about $10 a day without baths, etc. (Write Sheraton, P.O. Box 8559, Honolulu, Hi. 96815 for reservations.) The Volcano House has a long and fascinating history dating back to at least 1864. Sadly, long-time manager Al Pelayo, who used to tell all the stories, has parted company with Sheraton. Nevertheless, even if it's only for a single overnight, the volcano—and its House—should not be missed.

HONOKAA

Just off Route 19, some 40 miles north of Hilo in the hamlet of Hono-kaa, is the old and well-weathered **Hotel Honokaa Club** (Tel. 775-0678). There is a sort of restaurant and bar, and in an emergency, try for Room #16, an $18 double which has a view of a couple of back yards and the ocean farther away. All the second-floor units are worth the asking price, as a matter of fact. The first-floor units are cheaper, but offer much less, too. Many accommodations have been taken by more-or-less permanent residents, who may know something more about the place than we.

WAIMEA (KAMUELA)

Shed a tear for the wonderful Waimea Inn, which has been sold to the Hawaii Preparatory Academy. One inn that hasn't moved out is the venerable **Kamuela Inn** (Tel. 885-4516), whose painted cinderblocks reminded us of an old motel in northern Georgia. On our own overnight, we found the sheets clean, the water hot, and an electric heater a pleasant accessory. Doubles run perhaps $30 to $40. Possibly nicer is the new **The Lodge** (Tel. 885-4100), run by the Parker Ranch. Incredibly, we ran up against an un-*akamai* desk person who wouldn't let us peek at a room. According to lodge literature each unit has a kitchenette and a gas heater. We saw a color TV in the common card room. Rates at this writing are about $45 for two. Sorry, but we can't recommend what we can't see. Many folks now push on to Kailua-Kona (under an hour) on the new highway, which is the reason the only really good hotel in Waimea is gone forever.

HAWI

The 23-unit **Luke's Hotel** (Tel. 889-6835) in Hawi is an old, old institution in an old, old town. With the only bar and restaurant around, it is the social activities center at *pau hana* time. Some dwelling units are grouped around a scraggly garden courtyard featuring a thoroughly undisciplined flowering cactus. Doubles run around $20.

Strangely, it closes on weekends—which is all right if you've already checked in. But the restaurant closes at 6 P.M!

PUAKO

A modern condominium rental establishment, the **Puako Beach Resort Apartments** (Tel. 882-7711) has opened for visitors. All 38 units are well-appointed apartments with full kitchen and/or wet bar and laundry facilities, as well as a lanai overlooking the small beach. One-, two-, and three-bedroom apartments will probably rent for $40 to $85 this year. If you like Puako, a sleepy place we think of only for its large collection of petroglyphs, it might be an attractive alternative.

WAIKOLOA

The 543-room **Sheraton Royal Waikoloa** (Tel. 885-6789), next to the magnificent, half-mile-long palm-studded beach at Anaehoomalu Bay, 20 miles north of Keahole Airport, opened in late 1981. Also beside an ancient Hawaiian fishpond, the twin-wing building rises six stories above the palms, sands, and old lava flows in North Kona on what they now call the Kohala Coast.

Public areas garnished with *koa*, the strong wood once favored by the Hawaiians for their spears and war canoes; green-and-white raffia furnishings in the breezy, open reception area; free-form pool next to the *luau* garden; field of petroglyphs a short stroll away over the black lava desert; nearby 18-hole golf course; six tennis courts; unusual brassaia tree gracing the sunken Garden Room restaurant; two other dining areas, including the Royal Terrace, a dinner showroom, and the Tiare, a crystal-and-china room open in the evenings.

Bedrooms, all with *lanais*, run from $85 for Garden View through $105 for Mountain View, and from $120 to $140 for lesser or greater views of the ocean. There are also Lagoon Cabanas for $180.

As time goes on, and this resort area develops more, the establishment may overcome the feeling of semiisolation that some guests experience there. The hotel itself is fine and the site is, again, simply terrific.

About five miles north of the Sheraton on the same coastline, and a few miles south of the Mauna Kea Beach Hotel, the dramatic new **Mauna Lani Bay Hotel** (Tel. 885-6622) was opened by Tokyo-based Emerald Hotels last year with its sights set on capturing clientele from its more prestigious neighbor to the north. It still has a ways to go:

A beautiful site bordering one of the best golf courses in the nation, part of the same 3,200-acre resort; 10-court tennis garden; architecturally fascinating six-story, arrow-shaped structure aimed toward the sea; several resort shops; pristine-white beach on a protected cove just a coconut's toss away (love those canopied cabanas!); several ocean activities available; two open atria with gardens, streams, and waterfall; glass-walled elevators for viewing the greenery; spacious, breezy, blue-tiled public areas with oriental accents; ample, free-form swimming pool; separate cloverleaf jacuzzi; historic fishponds with leaping mullet; two decorative restaurants, including the Third Floor (a weak imitation of Honolulu's famous restaurant of that name); and the partly open-air Bay Terrace (where we enjoyed our breakfasts); *both* dining rooms requiring jackets for men in the evening (not the kind of Kona we remember!); a free bus ride to the informal golf-course restaurant for coatless males; several lounges and bars; not outstanding room service.

A total of 351 rooms, more than 90 percent with ocean views; a few gazing toward Mauna Kea (the mountain, not the competition); some of the most commodious accommodations in the 50th state; all in maroon, beige, teak, cane, and marble; some with king-size beds, some with double-doubles; all with fridges, bars, tiny coffee tables, and discreetly hidden color televisions; no radios; good lighting; air conditioning and ceiling fans; large, well-designed triangular *lanais;* luxurious bathrooms. Our room, at least, did not have a table large enough to eat dinner on the evening of our arrival, and the one on the *lanai* was in the dark. Rates for '84 have not changed since '83: $165 for Mountain or Garden View, $180 for Ocean View, $195 for Ocean Front, and $250 for a suite, all European Plan. Modified American Plan (two meals daily) is available at $55 per couple per day extra. For all its flamboyance, the best things the Mauna Lani has going for it are its gorgeous site and its friendly, energetic, unpretentious staff. (Reservations from the hotel at P.O. Box 4000, Kawaihae, Hi. 96743.) In time, it could become the dominant resort on the Kohala or the Kona Coast.

HOLUALOA

An old country inn in somnolent Holualoa, a little rain-forest town about 5 miles *mauka* of Kailua, is called the **Kona Hotel** (Tel. 324-7244), and it should not be confused with any other hotel of a similar name. This wooden structure was put up by owner Goro Inaba's parents in 1926, and it has hardly changed a whisker since. There are even views over Kailua, when the weather is clear. None of the 11 units have private plumbing, and at last report rates were still holding at a straight $9 per person per night. At those tabs—perhaps the cheapest in the entire state—some folks find themselves in a state of euphoria. Others might pick a different state.

CAPTAIN COOK

Another antique hostelry, but one which has kept up a little better with the times, is the 1917-model storefront **Manago Hotel** (Tel. 323-2642) in the village of Captain Cook near Kealakekua Bay. When we stayed there, our son, six at the time, called it "very creepy." Actually, Mr. and Mrs. Harold Manago have done a pretty good job, especially with their new addition out back. The 22 "community bath" rooms in the old ("creepy") section run around $13 single, $16 double. The 42 rooms with ocean view and their very own baths were from $18 to $21 single and $21 to $24 double, the last we checked. Ask to see the very special "Japanese Room," dedicated by Harold and Nancy to his parents. There guests sleep Oriental style on *tatami* mats, etc., for around $35 for two. Again, recommended only to genuine seekers of authentic atmosphere.

NAALEHU

The southernmost place to stay in the southernmost town in the U.S.A. is the **Shirakawa Motel** (Tel. 949-7462). Well, actually it's in Waiohinu, about halfway between Kona and Hilo on the southern road (Route 11), about one minute from the monkeypod tree planted by Mark Twain. Lee and Takumi Shirakawa, coffee and banana farmers, run these modest units on the side in the midst of lush, flower-filled surroundings. Rates run from $20 to $22 for two, and if you're stuck in Naalehu, this is it. Mark Twain might have loved it, but he came by just a little too soon.

LUXURY VACATION RESORTS

There are two more-or-less self-contained destination resorts on the Big Island, and they are so different in conception that they cannot be compared with each other. The larger is the 310-room masterpiece, the **Mauna Kea Beach Hotel** (Tel. 882-7222).

A world apart from Hawaii, the Mauna Kea and its own surrounding 18-hole championship golf course sit alone on a desert, completely encompassing one of the few beautiful beaches on the island. It almost never rains at Mauna Kea, and its 500 acres of greenery are kept alive through a network of midnight-activated underground water pipes and hidden sprinklers.

The Mauna Kea is an excellent hotel, and if it has no one distinctive characteristic, it must take justifiable pride in the fact that whatever one liked somewhere else, one might like it better at the Mauna Kea. It is a formula which has worked on presidents, kings, emperors, and rulers of the silver screen.

Here is the way we saw it: semi-isolated location 68 miles from Hilo, 32 miles from Kailua, 12 miles from Waimea, and 3 miles from Kawaihae; driveway to the hotel winding through the beautiful links designed by Robert Trent Jones; two wings, 208 rooms in the original structure and 102 in the newer Beach Garden building; long, low, terraced façades not obtrusive despite size; everything nestled into the side of a hill; trees, plants, waterfalls, and rock walls extending from outdoors to inside the hotel edifice; two large gardens, one north and one south; spacious lobby overlooking a flower-filled interior court; one flight down to "Promenade Level" and tasteful collection of shops (any vase we picked up in The Gallery was priced at at least $100); Cafe Terrace (seating up to 300 for the famous luncheon buffet); Batik Room and bar in Ceylonese motif served by one kitchen; freestanding, three-tiered Dining Pavilion and newer Garden Pavilion handled by a separate kitchen: Hau Tree Terrace snack shop in the beach area; sauna and massage nearby; very large, circular, palm-shaded, blue-bottomed pool back from the beach;

nine-court tennis park; lots of other lawn and sea games; hotel cata-maran *Mauna Kea Kai* for cruising, scuba diving, snorkeling, etc.; hunting and horses available.

A museumful of Oriental art (more than 1,000 *objets*) scattered throughout the buildings' walkways; mirror-bright, brass-walled elevators with parquet floors to lift you to your room level; elegant bedchambers with separate entrance foyers and dressing rooms; plain, white walls; floral art work; framed seashell collections; bright, solid colors; throw rugs on smooth tile floors; imported Eastern fabrics; wicker and cane furnishings; sliding louvered doors to the ample lanais; bathrooms with mirrored wall; Italian marble basins; refrigerators in all units.

Most expensive ocean-view doubles ($325) and the least costly mountain-view rooms ($250) in the original structure; beachfront units in the newer wing (running $295) closer to beach, pool, and golf shop; suites perhaps twice these rates; all fares with breakfast and dinner (Modified American Plan). (Reservations through the Westin Hotels organization or the hotel at P.O. Box 218, Kamuela, Hi. 96743.) The Mauna Kea means a self-contained vacation in almost a Mediterranean style (you dress for dinner, etc.), as opposed to Hawaiian style. Within this framework, the hotel and its *modus operandi* are superb accomplishments.

The other destination resort is the very private, very plush, and still very Polynesian **Kona Village Resort** (Tel. 325-5555). It is designed for those who want a vacation that is a full escape from reality, free from care about almost anything, and perhaps even some sort of transferal to a separate, very personal world.

There is a perfect, sand-lined cove, rimmed with palm trees and no large buildings. It has little guest cottages scattered here and there along the shoreline and a neighboring pond. These amazing thatched-roof huts, called *hales* ("*hah*-lays"), are constructed in the architecture of several South Seas islands—Hawaiian, Samoan, Fijian, Tahitian, and others. They are interesting as much for what they do not contain as for what they do.

There are no televisions, no radios, no air conditioners, and no keys for the doors. There are excellent decorations, lovely baths, and impeccable maintenance standards. All this is carefully installed on the site of an ancient Hawaiian fishing village.

Entrance to Kona Village is through a private gatehouse on Route 19, where the guard lets absolutely no one in who is not known or expected. After this, a narrow roadway for about 2 miles over the lava fields to the verdant *kipuka* (an "island" untouched by the molten flow); small private airstrip for guests arriving by air taxi (until recently, the only way); lobby/office a separate building at the end of the road/runway; the only phone's in there; special rum punch served to all arriving guests; famous

Hale Samoa, the former main restaurant; Hale Moana dining room in New Hebrides motif; large, circular, lava-lined swimming pool; nearby Shipwreck Bar made from an honest-to-schooner, genuine shipwreck; Island Copra general store. Beach with every facility imaginable; three tennis courts; petroglyphs and other archeological tours; all at no extra charge.

All together, 95 thatched *hales* built with "plush primitive" amenities and representing seven different Pacific Island groups; ventilated by trade winds and overhead fans; no room service (but no one seems to miss it); most units with king-size beds; 24 family units; everything closed for redecoration two weeks at the beginning of December. Current prices are Full American Plan daily double rates of $360 for the oceanfront alii, $320 for the ocean-front deluxe, $290 for the superior ocean view or superior garden suite, $265 for the moderate garden *hale*, and $225 for standard garden *hales*. (A third person is $83, under 12 $53.) All rates include all meals, and there are no extra charges for games, equipment, etc. Special wedding and honeymoon package can be arranged. Write the Kona Village at P.O. Box 1299, Kailua-Kona, Hi. 96740. For the special kind of rustic/elegant isolation it offers, it can't be beat. We've been twice, and we hope to return again and again.

5. Big Island Restaurants and Dining

Since there are two main headquarters on Hawaii, we divide our dining section into, first, choices in Hilo, and then, second, restaurants in Kona (generally, Kailua to Keauhou). After that, there is a brief wrap-up of several country tables, too.

DINING IN HILO

Hilo is not exactly headquarters for the gourmet army of Hawaii, and we have found it difficult to keep up with the openings and closings and other maneuvers of dining rooms in the county seat. Just when we think we've got a dependable winner, something changes—the chef, the manager, or even the owner of the place.

Dining in the hotels is considered dependable, though seldom spectacular. When Hiloans go out on the town, they often head for a steak house, and there is always one currently in vogue. Of course it may or may not continue to sizzle the imagination next year.

One long-standing beef emporium with an excellent local reputation is **Rosey's Boat House** (Tel. 935-2112), slightly out of the way near the baseball field at the corner of Piilani and Laukapu streets in a lava rock and shingle building. We stuck with steak here and were happy enough. Other Maverick readers have liked the fish and the crab, too.

In the Naniloa Surf Hotel, the **Sandalwood Room** (Tel. 935-0831) has always been tasty, at least for seafood. Perhaps the Mahimahi Mauna Loa. Then there's the little **Hutu Terrace** in the same hotel for breakfast. It was pleasant, and service was quick and correct. But try not to get our seat near the pantry.

Outside the hotel complex proper is the **Banyan Broiler** (Tel. 935-5802), which has been building both a lunch and dinner reputation. Fellow Mavericks report some of the best steak, prime rib, and especially oysters and opakapaka (snapper) now hang out here. Prices are reasonable, and there's a live band after 9 P.M.

The **Voyager Restaurant** (Tel. 935-7171) in the Hilo Pacific Isle looks like an extension of their midnight moody cocktail lounge. At our table, we felt adrift in time and space. Dark, dark, heavy, heavy paneling; wine-red carpets; some red-orange lights in the wagon-wheel chandelier. Food was okay, but in Hawaiian seas, it seems a crime to be so cut off from the climate—like taking a voyage below the waterline.

If it's raining, but you still want to feel outdoorsy for breakfast or lunch, head for the **Queen's Court** (Tel. 935-9361), a pleasant coffee shop behind huge plate glass windows in the Hilo Hawaiian Hotel. When the weather's nice, the views over the bay are delightful, from either the window seats or the cleverly conceived raised booths farther inside. Our Geisha Sandwich was hokey in concept, but tasted quite nice. (It was a cheese, egg, and bacon concoction where the only thing "geisha" was a paper parasol.) The Sunday brunch is probably a better deal these days.

Much more fun for dinner, though, is **Uncle Billy's** (Tel. 935-0861), stuck on the side of the Hilo Bay Hotel: lots of tables crowded together; Hawaiian entertainment; Polynesian decor; a friendly, super-casual atmosphere. The food was in the $13 range for dinner, and not really fancy, but the whole family scooted in here one night awhile back and enjoyed almost every minute of it. Go early. One diner complained to us that they were out of salad by 8 o'clock! Strictly a shoes-off place, remember.

Pricewise, the breakfast buffet at the **Tiki-Garden** restaurant in the Hilo Lagoon Hotel at first seemed a bargain at one price for all you can eat. However, it was a clumsy operation when we were there. They just couldn't seem to keep up with it all. However, the **Paniolo Room** (Tel. 935-9311), up top in the penthouse of the same hotel, has become a moderate-priced favorite of many localites, including Steve and Frances Reed, reading and writing partners, who keep up with Hilo restaurant 'rithmetic. The Paniolo pans out good prime rib and bellies up to a solid salad bar.

We eat a better breakfast each time we try **Ken's Pancake House** (Tel. 935-8711), Kamehameha Avenue and Route 11, perhaps still the *only*

24-hour restaurant in Hilo. Strictly a coffee shop in mood and manner, but they're quick, friendly, and the pancakes and waffles are delicious. Their omelets are also excellent. Right alongside Ken's, now, is the new Waiakea-Kai Shopping Center with several fast-food stands.

We did check out **Roy's Gourmet**, which seems to get a lot of attention from the barrel-bottom-budget visitors. The name is a gross miscarriage of definition, in our opinion. We didn't like our meal or the half-dozen others we smelled simultaneously. For substantial fare at reasonable tabs, check into **Dick's Coffee House** (Tel. 935-2769) in the Hilo Shopping Center. It's also an excellent place for bargain breakfasting.

Another good economy choice is the little **Hukilau Restaurant** (Tel. 935-4222), in the hotel of the same name, and within walking distance of Banyan Drive hotels. Sort of a green, white, and yellow decor; Polynesian overtones with overhanging canoe; lots of growing greenery; best positions in the window booths; lines on the glass marking height limits of the 1957 and 1960 tsunamis; substantial meals (steak, fish, chicken) in the $10 range. This place was understaffed on our Sunday night visit, but is popular with an understanding, local crowd. The food was certainly okay for the price.

Chinese restaurants. There are several in Hilo, of consistently varying quality. Often praised for its Cantonese cuisine has been the **Dragon Inn** (Tel. 935-5226), but we think it's been draggin' its tail too much lately. A better bet this year is a good family operation, the **Sun Sun Lau Chop Sui House** (Tel. 935-2808), not far away in barn-like surroundings at 1055 Kinoole St. (Closed Wednesdays.) **Leung's Chop Suey House** (Tel. 935-4066), at 530 East Lanikaula St., receives high praise from Shirley and Sig Rich of Los Altos, Calif. And Ferd Borsch, Honolulu's top baseball writer, who also scores hits in his dining-room contests, recommends **Mun Cheong Lau** (Tel. 935-3040), at the corner of Keawe and Kalakaua streets. Ferd managed to gulp down a gallon of bird's nest soup and then made a steamed pork of himself.

Japanese dining. There are three or four we should mention in Hilo. The traditional and well-deserved favorite is the **K. K. Tei Yakiniku House** (Tel. 961-3791), for which we lost our notes, dammit! We remember it as a long, low building with diners seated in two areas, one very informal, one a little spiffier, next to a well-designed rock garden. Some call its menu a little *haole*fied, but there were gentlemen gourmets from Japan in there with us, too.

In the venerable old Hilo Hotel downtown is the **Restaurant Fuji** (Tel. 961-3733), at 142 Kinoole St. Here the dishes run a little more toward the traditional—less teriyaki and more sushi than you might find elsewhere. The shabu-shabu still might be the best in town. (Some report that the service shuffle-shuffle is the slowest in town, too.)

Food chains. Yes, the two old reliables are now in Hilo. **Kentucky Fried Chicken** whomps it up downtown at 348 Kinoole St. until 8 or 9 P.M. daily, and **McDonald's** is a block *mauka* at 177 Ululani St. We haven't tried these two links, but sources tell us they're right on par.

DINING FROM KAILUA- TO KEAUHOU-KONA

Unfortunately, we are not sure there is any absolutely dependable *haute cuisine* restaurant in the Kona mainstream at the moment, although we wish someone would prove us wrong. There *were* two. They're still open, and maybe, just maybe, you'll be lucky. A strong former favorite was **Dorian's** (Tel. 329-3195) in the small Magic Sands apartment building next to White Sands ("Disappearing") Beach. But disappearing, too, seems to be the consistency of Dorian's, which once served us the best Veal Cordon Bleu we had in Hawaii. Several reports combine now to give this salon a yo-yo rating in our book. It's still a lovely location, especially since a new terrace was tacked on to take advantage of the delicious sunsets. Other than that, we are reminded of the "little girl who had a little curl . . ."

Some still assert the finest galley in the neighborhood is installed in the **S.S. James Makee Room** (Tel. 322-3411), in the elegant Kona Surf Hotel at Keauhou. Also famous for Continental cooking, the room was named after a famous old interisland steamship of long ago. Naturally nautical decor; orange lanterns everywhere; locally caught fish on the *table d'hote*; about $20 for everything. Sadly, service standards sometimes seem to slip astern. To sum up, the SSJMR may not always be a ship-shape choice; but depending on your crew, she may get you where you're going.

For lighter dining, also at the Kona Surf, there is **Pele's Court** (Tel. 322-3411), an open-sided terrace on the ground floor with waterfalls and greenery abounding. There's only a patch of sky, but plenty of sunlight is reflected from the hotel superstructure. We enjoyed our breakfast, although a real damper was the fact that our coffee was spilled a little every time it was repoured.

Reports are very mixed on the new **La Bourgogne** (Tel. 329-6711), a French entry at Kuakini Plaza South, about five minutes' drive on Highway 11 from Kailua. One Kona wag told us he dented his fork on his "radial tire rack of lamb," but then exchanged it for some lamb chops which were just fine. The onion soup and cherries jubilee may also be excellent.

A consistently good choice for prime rib of beef fans is back in Kailua at the Kona Hilton. The **Hele Mai** (Tel. 329-3111) at the hotel also features seafood. Prime rib and mahimahi are now also the stars at the **Sunset Rib Lanai** (Tel. 322-3441) at the Keauhou Beach Hotel.

The **Keauhou-Kona Golf Club Restaurant** (Tel. 332-3700) offers a wonderful view over the greens and the bay. But beyond that, look for an excellent prime rib on Saturday and Sunday nights, good seafood on Friday, and a *delicioso* Mexican dinner on Monday. Try Poki's fudge pie for dessert on any night. Good Hawaiian music, too, and prices designed to keep you humming along with it.

The **Kona Ranch House** (Tel. 329-7061), an attractive building near the Shell station at the corner of Kuakini Highway and Palani Road, is another very professional operation, especially for brunch.

Long-time Kona returnees will be happy to learn that the **Kona Inn** (Tel. 329-4425) is alive and well—as a restaurant, not a hotel. The old inn that ruled Alii Drive from 1928 to 1978 mostly has been converted to a shopping center. But one part that wasn't was the 8,000-square-foot dining room and bar, and, in fact, new life has been breathed into the seaside site by a California firm called Wind and Sea of Dana Point Harbor and San Diego. Choose from an assortment of steaks and chops in the $15 range, or for less price and equal flavor the Chicken Cordon Bleu (with ham and swiss cheese), the Hawaiian Chicken or Vegetable Casserole. Fish of the Day, no doubt unloaded that afternoon onto Kailua Wharf, will also run around $13. Today the Kona Inn is looking better than ever!

We remain completely unimpressed with the restaurant operations in the King Kamehameha Hotel in Kailua, by the way. We experienced expensive, clumsily served, poorly prepared comestibles ourselves, and interviewed others with similar misadventures. The **Marlin Room** and especially the **Veranda Room** are off our list. Across the street, **Quinn's** (Tel. 329-3822) is a moderate-price entry catering more to residents, perhaps. There's a very "laid-back" garden patio in the rear where they serve some good sandwiches and salads.

Just across Palani Street from the King Kam, on an upper deck, is the justly popular **Kona Galley** (Tel. 329-3777). Overlooking Kailua Pier, an ideal setting at sunset; Kona Galley is tastefully decorated in a seafaring motif; lantern-lit; awnings rolled down when trade and the trades are both brisk; quiet music; steak and "today's catch" fish dishes in the $10 range; chicken somewhat of a "?"; popular with a knowledgeable local crowd; open 11 A.M. to 10 P.M. Usually a winner.

Huggo's (Tel. 329-1493), next to the water near the Hilton, has been a favorite hangout for years. Always a beautiful view and a friendly atmosphere, it's a dependable choice for sizable sandwiches and uncomplicated dinners. They're still packing them in for the rib special Thursdays.

Probably a little more expensive, but also with a terrific view, is the **Spindrifter** (Tel. 329-1344), but some say the best staff have been spindrifting away more recently. Its name may change to Jolly Roger in 1984.

The newer **Eclipse** (Tel. 329-4686) has the longest bar on the island—about 18 stools. The menu is Continental, and although initial observations are favorable, we'll still have to wait and see how the Eclipse comes out.

Strict nickel-knucklers, however, might like to sit in at the **Ocean View Inn** (Tel. 329-9998) on Alii Drive near the center of things. The ocean view is there, all right, seen through a fine-mesh screen. Decor is, well, somewhere between unfancy and none at all. There's a large menu, and a faithful neighborhood crowd choosing and chewing some of about 75–100 different dishes. It's okay for the budget conscious. Some meals may still be under $5. (Closed Mondays—and maybe Septembers.)

STEAK HOUSES. The leader in the group has been **The Pottery** (Tel. 329-2277, and do reserve), one of Honolulu's best and which here, too, combines a genuine working pottery with a genuine working restaurant. Recent reports indicate something may be slipping here, however. Dancing Fridays and Saturdays. **Buzz's Original Steak House** (Tel. 329-1571), occupying an attractive, second-story, torch-lit Alii Drive location, has both good steaks and fish. (Better selection for an early dinner.) And the **Kona Bay**, in the hotel by the same name, also combines excellent beef with some chicken and fish dishes the locals call *shaka!*

MEXICAN/ITALIAN FOOD. On the Latin spice file, there is a south-of-the-border spot called **Jose's** (Tel. 329-6391), about 15 minutes' drive south of Kailua along Route 11. Full meals about $7, and *muy popular*, too. But Italian food is a rarity in Kona. The new **Caffe Sport** (Tel. 329-6177) has opened in the Kona Inn Shopping Center and is trying mightily to produce good Italian specialties. Prices are not cheap, however, and the jury is still out on this one, too.

KITCHENS IN THE COUNTRY

After a dining discussion of the volcano area, we begin a culinary swoop around the island, starting north of Hilo and heading counterclockwise using Routes 19 and 11. Restaurants worth mentioning are at Honokaa, Waimea, Kawaihae, Captain Cook, Naalehu, and Kalapana.

NATIONAL PARK AND VOLCANO AREAS

Nothing in the neighborhood compares with the **Volcano House Restaurant** (Tel. 967-7321). Located in the famous old hotel, right on the rim of the crater; day views always good; night views superb only when there's some fiery action down in the hole; Early American decor; patterned wallpaper; glass-ball chandeliers. Many changes are taking place, and at the moment things are as unsettled at the Volcano House as they often are at the volcano.

At noontime, however, the hordes of tour groups that are sometimes bused in by the gross for the buffet lunch make the Volcano House impractical and unpleasant for a midday meal. There is also an expensive snack bar nearby. If you're stuck up there without a car, you'll have to put up with it or gnaw on your boots.

With a car, your choices open up slightly. There's a little-known alternate place to grab a bite about a mile and a half away from Volcano House at the **Volcano Golf Course Clubhouse** (Tel. 967-7331). It can be quite nice, and they sometimes bake their own sourdough bread. (Take a right immediately after the military camp, then cross Route 11.)

But if you find you are on your way along that 30-mile road from Hilo to the national park, you could make a last-chance stop at the *village* of Volcano (look for the sign), just off the bypass, about a mile outside the park border. There are two small places of business there, both selling flowers, groceries, and gas. **The Okamura Store** (Tel. 967-7210) also has a snack bar and even some table service for a short time at around midday. The **Hongo Store** (Tel. 967-9949) is also good for fresh-this-morning Saran-wrapped sandwiches. If it's raining, Mr. Hongo may put out some stools so you can munch in the aisles.

Another food variation you might want to try anyway is to stop on the road at Mountain View, look up the **Mountain View Bakery** (Tel. 968-6353), and pick up a package of their famous rock cookies for nibbling throughout your park visit.

HONOKAA

The traditional watering hole 40 miles north of Hilo is the **Hotel Honokaa Club** (Tel. 775-0678), in a tiny old hotel. It is certainly one of the most unexciting looking restaurants we've seen in many a day. Some may now prefer **Andrades** (Tel. 775-7448) or **The Restaurant** (Tel. 775-7112). However, you might like to search out the **Tex Drive Inn** (Tel. 775-0598), on Highway 19 at the Honokaa School Intersection. They serve all three meals and feature some good Portuguese bean soup and mahimahi sandwiches. But Tex's *pieces de resistance* are his excellent, baked-fresh daily *malasadas* (Portuguese doughnuts). These are all dough, too—none of your frothier air-filled type. Go early. They're sometimes gone by noon!

WAIMEA (KAMUELA)

There is one outstanding chuckwagon up here in cowboy country, the **Parker Ranch Broiler** (Tel. 885-7366) in the Parker Ranch Shopping Center: rich, Victorian decor with booths and tables; French and Italian cuisine, along with plenty of prime beef from the surrounding range and fresh seafood from the surrounding ocean; full meals around $15; cozy Colonel Sam's Cocktail Lounge adjoining. We'd skip the buffet, though, and order off the menu instead. Some readers have complained to us of slow service. The Paniolo Stew has always been very good.

The Broiler doesn't serve breakfast, however. If you spent the night in Waimea, you may want to head for the very modest but friendly and able **Kamuela Deli** (Tel. 885-4147), a drive-in on the highway next door to the Parker Ranch Center. Order through the window, take your plate and sit down, and listen to pidgin-speaking cowpokes at the next table talking over ranch problems. *Ono-ono!* (And in this case, that means yes-yes!)

For lunch in this outback neighborhood, try the new **Redwater Cafe** (Tel. 885-4277), which swings mainly with a vegetarian beat. (There's a hip avocado and cheese sandwich that just won't quit.) If your wallet is much more empty than your stomach, seek out the modest, rustic lunchroom called **Homer's U.S. Meal Service** (Tel. 885-7411) behind the Fukushima store just before entering Waimea from the east. It's simple, clean and cheap—and its Portuguese bean soup is the beaniest! (Open 10 A.M. to 4 P.M.; closed Sundays.)

KAWAIHAE

Kawaihae (pron. "Kah-why-*high*") reminds us of the letter written by a nineteenth-century Scotsman who landed at Kawaihae (then an important seaport) to travel to Hilo: "I went from Sky-High to High-Low with nothin' to eat but a bit o' paste on the end of me finger!"

Today you'll be hard put to find any *poi* on such a route, but you will find near Kawaihae some of Hawaii's most elegant tables at the **Mauna Kea Beach Hotel** (Tel. 882-7222). Most readers will be interested in the famous buffet lunch with its gigantic assortment of gastronomic pleasures on the Cafe Terrace from 11:30 A.M. until 2:30 P.M. Its flat price may now be over $17. Kona columnist and trencherman Harry Lyons advises you to go early, eat plenty, and sit on the ocean side. Dress neatly or they won't let you in—at least cover-ups for women, no tank tops for men. Reservations advised. The $10 parking fee is waived if you eat. Continental, Cantonese, "Ceylonese," and American cuisine are also offered at night at the open-air Dining Pavilion and Garden Pavilion or the Asian-decorated Batik Room. Dinners are dress-up and will likely cost a minimum of $20 per person. It seems somewhat high-priced and stuffed-shirt for Hawaii, but many believe it's worth it. (No credit cards accepted.) In Kawaihae itself, there's good food in a garden setting at the **Harbor Hut**. (Open 6 A.M. to 9 P.M.)

CAPTAIN COOK

Yes, there *is* a restaurant in Captain Cook, at the **Manago Hotel** (Tel. 323-2642), a super-simple, old-fashioned frame false-front on the main drag. Meals are cheap enough—in the four to five dollar range, lunch or dinner, according to our notes. Honolulu *Advertiser* food writer Maile Yardley says Mrs. Manago's macaroni salad is fabulous.

NAALEHU

Halfway between Kailua and Hilo on the southern route, the **Naalehu Coffee Shop** (Tel. 929-7238) is fine, especially for local color.

If you can't wait that long going south, or have somehow already passed Naalehu on your way north, you *might* be able to discover the well-named **Hide-A-Way Restaurant** (Tel. 929-7455). Just off Route 11, they say, on Tiki Lane in the Hawaiian Ocean View Estates. "You can't miss it," but as a matter of fact, we haven't found it yet. (Open 9 A.M. to 9 P.M.; closed Tuesdays.)

KALAPANA

Maybe a mile past the Kaimu Black Sands Beach on Highway 130 is the **Kalapana Store and Drive In** (Tel. 965-9242), a neat and simple operation by go-getter Walter Yamaguchi, proprietor. The last time we were there, Mr. Y. was bubbling over the new government tidal gauge installed in his antique Hawaiian well. You can either snack at his tables or pick up some goodies at the store and munch away at a picnic bench in the southern branch of the Volcanoes National Park a few miles farther along the road. Depending on the circumstances, you might find such a picnic your most memorable meal of all.

6. Sightseeing Hawaii—A Big Project on the Big Island

The first part of this section is devoted to a few sights in Hilo, discussed more or less in the order that seems natural to us.

Some folks want to run up for a quick look at the volcano directly from Hilo, a drive of about 30 miles each way. Personally, we like to build up our sightseeing gradually to that climax, and that's why we choose the long, slow route. If you take the short way, however, you may leap over all our prose and turn directly to the portion on Volcanoes National Park. (The same principle applies if you're going to make a direct push into Puna, a spectacular spur we cover after the volcano. And if you're going to use the Kona airport for your entrance to the Big Island, you would probably want to check out our Kona Coast and Ka'u portion first.)

Now, how to allot time for seeing the Big Island? Although there is no satisfactory way of answering the question as thoroughly as we would like, we believe it will take a minimum of six days and five nights in order to get a good islandwide survey: one full day in Hilo (then your first overnight there); one full day driving the northern road to Kailua- or

Keauhou-Kona (your second overnight in Kona); one full day sightseeing the Kona area (your third overnight also in Kona); one full day driving the southern route to Hawaii Volcanoes National Park (your fourth overnight there); one full day seeing Hawaii Volcanoes National Park (your fifth overnight there again); and one full day exploring the Puna District and the exciting "new" Chain of Craters Road.

We have divided our sightseeing section below into six parts: Hilo; the Hamakua Coast to Waimea; the North Kohala Circle, the Kona Coast and Ka'u; the Volcano Area; and the Puna Spur.

HILO—THE CITY OF RAIN

Rain is a naughty word in the Hawaii tourist industry, but the fact remains that Hilo is often soaking wet. Its average annual rainfall is more than 136 inches, about five times as much as Kailua-Kona on Hawaii or Waikiki on Oahu. There is some recent public relations effort to call Hilo the "City of Rainbows," and maybe it's true. (No one's counting, but there could be more rainbows seen in Honolulu, where it doesn't rain nearly as much.)

If you wake up to the patter of little water drops, don't become discouraged. Have a nice breakfast and then get ready to go out anyway. By late morning, things are often drying out. If so, life in the afternoon can be beautiful. Local boosters, too, are quite correct when they claim that the rain—Hilo's "blessing"—is responsible for much of the green and flowerful beauty that thrives in and around the city.

That gracefully curving avenue outside so many Hilo hotels near the airport is **Banyan Drive**, with most of the banyan trees along it planted by visiting celebrities during the 1930s. There is a plaque by each tree, but some of the then notables are today rather obscure.

The east end of the drive skirts **Liliuokalani Gardens**, done in Japanese style with lots of rocks and pagodas. A nearby footbridge leads to **Coconut Island** in Hilo Bay. When skies are clear, the bay is backgrounded by **Mauna Kea** (13,796 feet), the state's tallest peak, 25 miles away. Mauna Kea means "white mountain," and it is capped with snow in the winter months. It also wears six telescopes on its crown—some of the world's most sophisticated astronomical observatories, but generally not visible from Hilo.

Banyan Drive heads into Lihiwai Street next to the **Suisan Fish Market** at the mouth of the Wailoa River. The market comes alive at 7:30 A.M. Monday through Saturday when the auction is held, with most of the bidding in pidgin. Worth seeing, hearing, and smelling (a clean, fresh fish fragrance), if you can get up that early.

Heading along Kamehameha Avenue toward downtown, the **Wailoa State Park** is on your left. This and lots of other open green space in the area formed part of the business district destroyed during the last tidal wave, or tsunami, which roared into Hilo Bay on Sunday afternoon, May 23, 1960. If possible, enter the park to see the **Wailoa Visitor Center** (Tel. 961-7360), the handsome octagonal structure with an information booth and changing cultural exhibits. (Closed Sundays.)

You can hardly go to Hilo without seeing one of its flower nurseries. One that charges $2 to go through is **Orchids of Hawaii** (Tel. 935-6617) at 575 Hinano St. It's in a low, brown-shingle building behind the Oda family homestead, where it all started as a hobby fifty years ago. Here's one place to find out everything you always wanted to know about orchids, anthuriums, etc., but were too shy to ask. (Of course, everything's for sale there, too—See Section 10.) Open 8 A.M. to 4:30 P.M.

Now under new ownership, **Kong's Floraleigh Gardens** (Tel. 935-4957) at 1477 Kalanianaole Ave., is well worth the charge—it's free. Mr. and Mrs. Akana love to talk about orchids. We also like the well-planned and well-displayed **Nani Mau Gardens** (Tel. 959-9442). There are scores of flowers, trees, and plants we didn't know even existed—things like the beef steak plant, that really does look like lean red meat! It's a little hard to find—3.7 miles from Kamehameha Avenue on Route 11, then a left on Makalika Street for another half-mile or so. Well worth going out of your way, but we only wish the admission were not $2.50. (Open daily, 9 to 5.) It's nice, anyway. Travel writers John and Linda Anderson enjoyed talking with the owners of **Anthuriums of Hawaii** (Tel. 969-6448) in Mountain View. It was interesting, and it was free.

Now this is not exactly an official "sight," but some newcomers who have wandered into **Hilo Dry Goods** at 188 Kamehameha Ave. say the old store with the hand-cranked cash register takes them back to an earlier day. The store has been at the same location—and in about the same condition—since 1920. Actually it's several years older than that.

No history buff should miss the **Lyman Mission House and Museum** (Tel. 935-5021) at 276 Haili St., just off Kapiolani St. The original building, constructed in 1839, belonged to the Rev. David Lyman. It has been carefully restored and is now operated together with the new building next door, which displays ethnic memorabilia from the different cultural groups in Hawaii's population. (Here we learned that the ancient Hawaiians used to carve out wooden cuspidors!) There is also a large collection of natural curiosities and other artifacts. (Open 10 A.M. to 4 P.M. daily except Sunday.) Admission is now up to $2.75.

Nearby, just a little *makai* of the end of Kapiolani Street at 300 Waianuenue Ave., is the public library and its front-yard prize, the **Naha Stone**. A legend decreed that whoever could turn this stone would become king of all the islands. Despite the fact that the stone weighs about 5,000 pounds, young Kamehameha I is said to have performed the feat.

(A strong man from Missouri came to Hawaii in 1973 and showed how he did it. They wouldn't let him mess with the Naha Stone, but he raised a similar banana-shaped rock to its pivotal point and then swung it around. It was more a brain problem than one of brawn, he said.)

A little over a mile up the street in Wailuku River Park are **Rainbow Falls**, which make a thundering torrent into the gorge below. The best time to see the falls is in the early morning, when the sunshine may produce a rainbow in the mist at the bottom. The park is particularly nice now that the state has restored a lot of vegetation in the area and cleaned up the trails.

Farther up the stream about two miles is a point of interest called the **Boiling Pots**. It's not much if you insist on looking at the stream only from the parking lot area. If you want to hike down to the water, however, it's more exciting. In some ways, it's like the Seven Pools on Maui, but with more vigor as the series of falls spills from one pool into another. Some of the water flows beneath a level of old lava and then suddenly bubbles up, as if it were boiling.

Some brochures list a lot more Hilo "sights," but unless you have considerable time on your hands, we suggest moving on up the coast.

THE HAMAKUA COAST TO WAIMEA

Start early in the day, heading north from Hilo on Route 19—the Hawaii Belt Road. After about 5 miles, you'll see a sign announcing a "scenic route." It's a short detour along a narrow road of flowers, birds, one-lane bridges, edible wild guavas, weatherbeaten old churches, and crowing roosters. Take the road. It will rejoin the main highway in 4 miles anyway.

At a settlement called Honomu, turn left on a 5-mile road (No. 22) to **Akaka Falls State Park**. From the parking lot, an easy walk along a paved path fragrant with ginger, orchids, and other flowers, will bring you first to **Hapuna Falls**, which plunge a mere 100 feet, and then to **Akaka Falls**, which feature a 420-foot vertical drop. It's lovely—well worth the drive and the hike. (On the way out, you might like to stop at the restored century-old Honomu Plantation Store.)

About 10 miles farther up the belt road is **Laupahoehoe Point**. View it from the side of the road, or, if you have a picnic packed, drive the 1-mile curving road down to the park and dig in beside the crashing waves. There is a monument in this now-vacant settlement to twenty-four pupils and teachers who were lost here in the 1946 tidal wave.

Way up the coast about 25 miles is the cutoff on Route 24 through the creaky and antiquey village of **Honokaa** (Pop. 1600), which is formally or informally preserved in the Hawaii of the 1920s. It may also be a wetter town than Hilo. In January, 1979, it registered *five feet* of rain in *five* *days!* You can take the side road *makai* (seaward) from Honokaa to the **Hawaiian Holiday Macadamia Nut Company** (Tel. 775-7255, open 8:30 A.M. to about 2:30 P.M.). This smaller operation is more commercial and hokey than the Keeau factory, but some like it better since it encourages a lot of different kinds of orders and offers more kinds of products. (We prefer the Mauna Loa—formerly Royal Hawaiian—brand of nut, but they're both good.) Anyway, if you've seen one macadamia nut factory—whichever one—you've probably seen enough.

Continue on Highway 24 for another 8 miles to the end of the road and the viewpoint for **Waipio Valley**, a dramatic green gouge out of the earth. The 2,000-foot gorge is one of the grandiose panoramas of the Islands, nearly comparable to that at the Nuuanu Pali on Oahu.

The road for conventional cars ends here. If you want to go down into the nearly deserted valley, you'll have to hike or have a jeep and know darn well how to drive it. You can also patronize the Waipio Valley Shuttle (Tel. 775-7121), a jeep service which charges $10 per person round trip for a guided tour. (*Psst.* Not many know there's even a "hotel" of sorts down in the valley. It has no electricity, but it does have a phone—775-0368. We've never seen it.)

After returning through Honokaa, take either fork back to 19, the Belt Highway. The Tex Drive Inn is near the school, but for serious lunching continue for 15 minutes through the cattle country to the Parker Broiler (See Section 5 for both) in the ranch community of **Waimea**. There's always some confusion about the name of this village, since the U.S. Postal Service has decreed that one official Waimea in the state (on Kauai) is enough. Mail for the town is therefore addressed to **Kamuela**. (Actually, the post office for Kamuela is in a separate settlement a mile or two up the road.)

Kamuela is the Hawaiian name for Samuel, and it stands for Samuel Parker, grandson of John Parker, the founder of the **Parker Ranch**. Today it's the second largest single ranch in the U.S.A., consisting of 318,000 acres. (Texas' King Ranch is 860,000 acres.) The Parker spread is headquartered right here in Waimea/Kamuela. Many of the white-faced Hereford cattle you see along the road belong to Parker's herd of some 70,000 head.

In Waimea, the traditional "point of interest" is the **Parker Ranch Museum** (Tel. 885-7655) in the shopping center. The admission price is $2.50, and frankly, we don't think it's worth it. One or two of the few exhibits are perky, and it's a highly polished presentation to be sure. But like many a large company history, it suffers from attacks of sycophancy, lack of objectivity, and confusing genealogical detail. It relies an awful lot on photographs, and the largest portrait in the museum is a three-times-life-size head shot of the current owner of the Parker Ranch,

Richard Smart (whose mother was a Parker). The accompanying 15-minute slide-and-sound show was having considerable technical problems on our visit, but nobody in charge seemed to mind. All-in-all, we call it mildly interesting but wildly overpriced. (Closed Sundays.)

We prefer the much more amateurish museum in the neighborhood, a few miles down the road virtually at the junction of Routes 19 and 25. The **Kamuela Museum** (Tel. 885-4724), winds throughout the home of Albert K. and Harriet K. M. Solomon (she's also a Parker descendant). The Solomons, interesting characters themselves, have the most incredible collection of hodge-podge from all periods of Hawaii—and from everywhere else, for that matter. It's not unlike traveling through your grandmother's old attic, only much more so, and with nearly everything neatly labeled. Its very unprofessionalism has a certain naïve charm, and it was only two dollars when we went through recently. We certainly recommend it at that price. (Open 8 A.M. to 5 P.M.)

If you're running short of time, take Highway 19 about 10 miles down the road directly to Kawaihae and skip this next small, seven-paragraph section. If it's still at least early afternoon, however, consider taking the 50- to 60-mile drive through the North Kohala District, described below.

THE NORTH KOHALA CIRCLE

Route 25 is the high road that heads directly through the Kohala mountains, reaching as high as 3,564 feet, and giving vast views of the coastline below. After about 20 miles, the pavement enters the village of **Hawi**, once an important sugar mill town, and now largely fallen into a state of more-or-less picturesque dilapidation.

Take Highway 27 to the right (east) for a couple of miles to the Kapaau Courthouse to see the **Original Kamehameha Statue**. Cast in Florence in 1880, it was lost at sea on its way to Honolulu. A replica was commissioned, and it is the one installed in front of the Judiciary Building in the capital. Then this original was recovered from the ocean and installed here near Kamehameha's birthplace. Surprisingly, it looks very different from the one at the Judiciary Building. The original is on a lower pedestal, for one thing, painted in bright colors, and has such wild-looking eyes!

You'll pass several semi-ghost towns along the route. The Kohala Sugar Company has shut down, and the state government is trying to pull this area back into solvency again, with only marginal success.

Another 6 miles will bring you to the end of the road and a viewpoint for **Pololu Valley**. It's nice, but a definite second or third to Waipio. Here you'll have to turn around and retrace your route the 8 miles to Hawi.

From Hawi, continue on Highway 270 (some maps may say 27). We once tried—and failed—to find **Mookini Heiau** near the Upolu Airport, and nearly got stuck in the mud. There's an HVB warrior marker pointing out the place, now, and the reconstructed site may be worth seeking out—at least on a dry day.

About seven miles farther is **Mahukona Beach Park**, an important and busy harbor in the days of the Hawaiian monarchy, and the adjoining **Lapakahi State Historical Park**, a project providing employment in this economically depressed area. Restoration of the ancient village is nearing completion, and a brochure describes points along a marked path.

In contrast to the lush mountains above, the return route cuts through desert-like rangelands and lava fields. But you haven't *really* seen lava fields. Not yet. Continue on 27 to Kawaihae, and rejoin Route 19 South.

THE KONA COAST AND KA'U

The harbor of **Kawaihae**, once an important village, still is a significant commercial port, but the village part has all but withered away. Nearby (look for the sign) is the **Puukohola Heiau** (Tel. 882-7218), now a National Historic Site. Originally built around 1550, it was rebuilt by Kamehameha I and dedicated to his war god in 1791. It was to this ceremony that he invited the last remaining rival Big Island chief and then suddenly killed him there in cold blood. With this act, he consecrated his temple and began his island conquests at the same moment.

Almost next door to the *heiau* is **Spencer Beach Park**, one of the most popular beaches on the island. The sands are white, and fishing, swimming, snorkeling, body surfing, etc., are excellent. Tent carriers, this is a good place to put down stakes.

Another mile along the road is the turnoff for one of the country's most prestigious resorts, the **Mauna Kea Beach Hotel**. (See sections 4 and 5.) This may be the loveliest beach on the island, and in 1979, the United Airlines hotel bowed to political pressure and provided public access to it. If you want to use its parking lot, however, it will cost you $10—deductible from any money you spend at the hotel.

One more mile along the main highway is the entrance to **Hapuna Beach Park**, and this one features A-frame cabins which can be reserved from the state, hopefully still under $10 a night.

Also in the neighborhood, just down the road a couple of miles, is the village of Puako and the excellent **Puako Petroglyphs**. To find those Stone Age pictures, drive through the long, narrow village past the church and look for the inconspicuous sign that indicates a narrow lane on your left. (If you miss it, come back from the end of the road about 200 yards.) Park on the road, walk through the gate, and follow the rocky path for 20 difficult minutes. There are acres and acres of the mysterious carvings in three groups. These particular ones are thought to be some of the oldest petroglyphs in Hawaii, and anthropologists are still trying to draw meaning from them all.

You may observe that scant attention is called to petroglyph sites at any location in Hawaii. The sites are, of course, subject to defacing and vandalism, and there are some residents who understandably enough would like to delete all directions to any petroglyph fields. Don't take a chance on running into some petroglyphs somewhere else later. If you're near Puako, this may be your only opportunity to ponder the undeciphered records of an ancient people.

If you have an urge to be a graffitist yourself, stifle it until you return to Route 19 south. Then, for about 5 miles, you may join the hundreds who have recently spelled out messages by placing lines of white coral stones against black lava fields along the highway. Some have reversed the technique, writing with black lava on the white fields of coral which were dredged from the sea nearby to use in the road construction.

This straight black road across 34 miles of sunbaked lava desert is the **Queen Kaahumanu Highway**, on which the ribbon was cut in 1975. Designed to open up the area as a new "Gold Coast," the highway is of equal excitement to land developers and fun-seekers, for several previously hard-to-reach beaches and historic sites are now accessible along the shoreline. (The area is also being called the Kohala Coast, these days.)

A beautiful example is about 5 miles beyond Puako on 19. There a turnoff to the right leads to the white-sand beach at **Anaehoomalu Bay**. No longer deserted, it fronts the new Sheraton Royal Waikoloa Hotel.

The beach itself, which also encloses an ancient fishpond, features hundreds of palm trees poking directly up through the sand. Almost unequaled in its type of splendor, Anaehoomalu Beach is reminiscent of Luquillo Beach in Puerto Rico. Several petroglyph fields and other historical sites are hidden nearby and are slated for special exhibition later. About the only defect of this green Eden on the edge of a desert is that it can be uncomfortably windy sometimes when the Waimeas are brisk.

If you cross Highway 19 and drive for about 5 miles on a private pavement, you'll reach what Boise Cascade already has installed in the neighborhood, the **Waikoloa Village**, an uninspiring (to us) California-style planned community with a few townhouses, a very nice 18-hole golf course, tennis courts, and some riding stables. The road continues to connect with Route 190, the *old* Waimea-Kailua highway.

But unless we have a reason for heading Waikoloa way (like to attend the big April rodeo), we'd skip the drive, turn south again, and "hammer down" across the lava desert toward Kailua-Kona, about 20 more arrow-straight miles. (If you have to go to the bathroom, you can turn in at the **Ke-ahole Airport** in about half that distance.)

The Big Island's real resort town is **Kailua-Kona**. (Actually, its name is just Kailua, but "Kona" is often stuck on its end to avoid confusion with another prominent Kailua on the island of Oahu. And many here say "Kona"—which means the leeward, or west, side of the island—when they are talking specifically about the Kailua-to-Keauhou area.)

Despite some uncontrolled development here, Kailua remains a fairly attractive—if no longer rustic—coastline settlement, a haven for fisher-men anxious to try out some of the world's finest marlin grounds, or for the young, single holidaymaker fishing for any kind of action. Inter-island jets from Honolulu fly into its airport (See Section 2), and it is be-coming increasingly popular both as a primary destination itself or as a gateway to the Big Island.

Many think of Kailua as a 2-mile stretch of street called Alii Drive, studded on one end with the "King Kam" hotel and bounded on the other by the Kona Hilton. Like Hilo, the Kailua-to-Keauhou area, about 7 miles long, has several good hotels, restaurants, and bars. Unlike Hilo, it has much more dependable dry weather and convenient water activities.

The most prominent historical site in the village may be the **Hulihee Palace** (Tel. 329-1877), next to the seawall on Alii Drive, sometimes known as King Kalakaua's Summer Palace. Built in 1838 of coral and lava, it was a royal retreat until 1916. Now furnished in Hawaiian mon-archy (Victorian) period interiors, it is operated as a museum by the Daughters of Hawaii. (Open 9 A.M. to 4 P.M. Monday to Friday, 9:00 to noon Saturday, and closed Sunday. Admission $3 for adults, 50¢ for children.)

Across the drive from the palace is the mission-built **Mokuaikaua Church**, which has remained almost unchanged since 1837. We enjoyed seeing (not eating!) the sausage fruit growing on a tree on the church grounds.

Be sure to walk out on the long **Kailua Wharf**, preferably at weigh-in time, between 4 and 5 P.M. daily when the big fish are hoisted ashore from the charter boats. Nearby on the grounds of the King Kameha-meha Hotel, Amfac Resorts (under the direction of Honolulu's Bishop Museum) has restored the **Ahuena Heiau** and **Kamakahonu**, the last resi-dence of Kamehameha the Great, where he died in 1819.

Alii Drive becomes a narrow country road past the Hilton and winds its way along the shoreline. About halfway to Keauhou is **White Sands Beach**, also known as Magic Sands, and also as Disappearing Sands Beach, since it washes away from time to time, leaving only a lava shore-line. *Caution: Currents are dangerous here. Don't swim!*

Swimming is safer and more fun a little farther on at **Kahaluu Beach Park**, near the Keauhou Beach Hotel. Be sure to see St. Peter's, known as the **Little Blue Church**, a tiny chapel with a blue tin roof built in 1880. Nearby is **Kona Gardens** (Tel. 322-2751), a recently opened historical and botanical park. It was cleared by hand in order to preserve the heiaus, homesites, petroglyphs, and the Great Wall of Kuakini. The only trouble with it is the $5.50 or so it will cost you to get in.

At Keauhou ("kay-ow-hoe") Bay, there is an HVB marker pointing out the **Birthplace of Kamehameha III**. The site doesn't look like much, but the small boat harbor and the little beach adjoining are attractive.

The large structure over by the shoreline is the **Kona Surf Hotel**, a minor architectural masterpiece, worth seeing for itself as well as its ambiance and its art collection. Next door is the Holua Tennis Stadium, site of the 1976 Avis Challenge Cup matches, which were telecast live to the Mainland, but not to Hawaii.

From Keauhou Bay, you can take the side road up the hill, past the Keauhou-Kona Golf Course and continue south, now on Route 11.

Turn right just past Kealakekua on Route 16. On the way down the hill, you might stop at the **Sunset Coffee Mill** (Tel. 328-2411) to see how Kona coffee is milled. Open 8 A.M. to 4:30 P.M. daily. At the bottom of the hill is the formerly active Hawaiian fishing village of Napoopoo (that has five syllables in it) and the historic **Kealakekua Bay** ("Kay-Allah-cake-*coo*-wah"), site of the visit and the tragic death of Captain Cook in 1779. The spot where Cook fell is indicated by a white monument on the distant shoreline. (Virtually impossible to visit, except by boat.) The bay has now been made a marine preserve, and its clear waters are a popular snorkeling and scuba-diving spot. You can also see and walk upon the **Hikiau Heiau**, where Cook conducted a Christian burial service.

Instead of returning directly to the main road, try to stand the rough and bumpy 4-mile road along the coast to Honaunau Bay and the **City of Refuge National Historical Park** (Tel. 328-2288). We still call it that, although it was recently renamed Pu'uhonua o Honaunau, an unfortunate decision on somebody's part; but take note because it is that tongue twister that is used on all the highway directional signs. One of the most fascinating legacies from ancient Hawaii, this area was a religious sanctuary for criminals or prisoners of war. If they reached the sacred grounds ahead of their pursuers, they could escape death or other punishment no matter what they had done or were accused of doing.

Today the well-preserved site has been completely restored, and is run by the federal government as a national historical park. Pick up a map/brochure from the Visitors Center (open 8 A.M. to about 5:30 P.M.) and stroll through the shady coconut and pandanus groves by following numbered markers to the various structures and artifacts. Our youngsters enjoyed the free outrigger canoe ride here; it was the highlight of their trip, in fact. In any case, the City of Refuge is a must for any visitor to the island of Hawaii.

About 2½ miles farther along Route 16 (½ mile before Route 11), there is a side road on the left which leads, after about another mile, to St. Benedict's, the **Painted Church**. This old wooden structure was painted around the turn of the century by its priest in order to bring to his hinterland congregation some ideas of the glories of a European cathedral. It's a little hard to find, but charming when you do.

After you're back on Highway 11 southbound, check your gas gauge. It is at least 40 miles to the next station, or maybe 90 miles if it's Sunday. If you're nervous and if the station at the corner of Highways 16 and 11 is closed, better drive the 10-mile route back north to Captain Cook.

On Route 11 southbound, you may be glad or may wish you had rented a compact car. There are often sharp drop-offs on the *makai* side of the narrow road, so watch carefully in any case.

As you cross the fingers of the **1950 lava flow**, notice that the surface now supports life again, even if it is only represented by copious weeds and flowers. Earlier lava flows have been carved into house lots, and you'll see lots of fancy street names which represent real estate projects based on more fast talking than fast action over the past decade or so.

About 9 miles down the road is the turnoff to a 5-mile bumpy road to the Hawaiian fishing village of **Milolii**. Allow an hour for a visit. It's one of the few examples left of a slower pace of island life. In a few years it may not exist at all.

If you're carrying the fixings for a picnic with you, you may want to turn in at the beautiful botanical grounds called **Manuka State Park**, about 8 miles past the Milolii turnoff.

It's another 12 miles to the turnoff for **South Point**, and that's a rough, 11-mile road to the southernmost point in the United States (all that hoop-la back in Key West, Fla., notwithstanding). If you have a four-wheel-drive vehicle or hiking gear, you can work your way another 2 or 3 miles along the waterline to **Green Sands Beach**, where the shoreline is colored by bits of volcanic olivine. ("Sand size" is as big as Hawaiian olivine gets, by the way. Those stones you see in jewelry stores come in from Arizona and Mexico!)

From that turnoff, Route 11 continues quickly into more verdant country. Suddenly you're in the settlement of Waiohinu, which boasts the Shirakawa family hotel, the only place to stay in the Ka'u district, and, a few yards farther, **Mark Twain's Monkeypod Tree**, which he planted in 1866. (Just between us, the tree was blown over in 1957, and the one you now see sprang from the roots of the original Twain tree.)

The attractive hamlet of **Naalehu** ("nah-ah-*lay*-who") is the country's southernmost community, of course. For all its rusticity, there is a cosmopolitan flavor here. Proof that the Italians and the Filipinos get along well, for instance, are the side-by-side Little Sicily Service Station and the Luzon Liquor Store. (There are a couple of coffee shops here, too; see Section 5.)

Continuing along the route, you may visit **Punaluu Black Sand Beach**, one of two well-known black beaches on the island. (The other is at Kaimu in Puna.) The beach area and the attractive Punaluu Village Restaurant and Museum which adjoins it were heavily damaged by waves in the 1975 earthquake but are today back to normal. The restaurant/ museum and the Seamountain Golf Course nearby are operated by C. Brewer & Co., one of the giant sugar firms of Hawaii. They've now opened a resort condo operation, and a hotel is planned eventually. On the same property is the Ka'u branch of the Aspen Institute for Humanistic Studies, an intellectual "think tank."

The last stop, if you stop, before the national park is the sugar mill town of **Pahala**. Take a left and drive down the main street to see as typical an example of a Hawaiian plantation town as exists any more. The weatherbeaten, tin-roofed structures, some of them on stilts, do seem to live well with all the fresh flowers and shrubbery planted around them.

THE VOLCANO AREA

Entering the Hawaii Volcanoes National Park from the southern road, you'll run across three principal points before you get to the Visitor Center. You can backtrack to them later, if you want, but we'll take them in order here. Readers of this book who have come directly up from Hilo will just have to bear with us as we continue our counterclockwise route for the faithful who have tagged along on our long sightseeing circumnavigation. We're not going into exhaustive detail anyway, since the literature and maps you'll pick up from the National Park Service will keep you saturated with scientific information.

Just a mile or so inside the park boundary is the beginning of the **Footprints Trail**, which leads to the tracks made by a Hawaiian army in 1790 when they unsuccessfully tried to escape a volcanic eruption. Read the exhibit at the beginning of the trail. The hike to the footprints is about 2 miles long in each direction.

Just past the **Namakani Paio Campground** (cabins) cutoff is the Mauna Loa Strip Road which leads first to the **Tree Molds**. These molds or holes were created when the ground beneath your feet was molten lava. The lava encircled the trunks of the ohia trees then growing here, creating a lasting impression. (Watch your step and hold onto your kiddies. Some of these are pretty deep!) A little farther along the same road is Kipuka Puaulu, better known as **Bird Park**. A *kipuka* is a piece of ground left alone by a lava flow. This particular fertile "island" has twenty species of trees in 100 acres. You may see these trees and perhaps several unusual birds while walking the circular 1-mile, self-guided nature trail.

Back on Highway 11 for another 2 miles is the cutoff to the **Visitor Center** (Tel. 967-7311), run by the rangers. Here you will get all your maps as well as up-to-date changes in park facilities. (Remember that the volcano and surroundings form a flexible environment, and roads have a way of being cut off by lava or earth cracks. These may force alterations in routes or even in the availability of certain areas.) Also in the center is a museum and theater which shows movies of volcanic action. (Open until 5 P.M. daily.)

Just across the road from the Visitor Center is the **Volcano House** (Tel. 967-7318), a charming old inn. (See Section 4.)

The hotel is perched right on the edge of **Kilauea Crater**, the vast, ever-steaming, and immense pit which is the awesome center of all activity in this area. (Pronounced "kill-ow-*way*-ah.")

You may drive all the way around Kilauea. The Crater Rim Drive is about 11 miles around. Many adjectives have been expended over the years trying to portray the vents, the steam, the smell of sulfur, the panoramas of black lava and deep rifts in the ground, but it can't be described. It may sound corny, but the volcano, whether erupting or not, just must be experienced to be imagined.

If the weather's good, you may be able to see far in the distance the smooth summit of the other volcano in the park, the 13,677-foot **Mauna Loa**. Kilauea fires itself up fairly frequently, but Mauna Loa seems like a reluctant dragon. It did erupt spectacularly for a brief period in July, 1975, but that was after napping for twenty-five years. If you have a jeep and hiking gear, you may ascend to its huge caldera. See the rangers at the Visitor Center for advice on this and any other hiking trails, including those on the floor of Kilauea Crater.

Meanwhile, there are several other craters to be seen in the immediate neighborhood of Kilauea. Foremost is the **Halemaumau Firepit** ("Hahlay-*Mao*-Mao"), a crater *within* Kilauea, and said to be the current home of Pele, the Hawaiian goddess of the volcano. Nearby also is **Kilauea Iki Crater** (*iki*—"eekey" means little or junior, if you will) and **Keanakakoi Crater** ("kay-ahna-cock-*coy*"), both of which have been active in recent years.

Don't miss the **Thurston Lava Tube**, now that it has been opened again. It was closed during the November, 1975 earthquake by a giant boulder which landed right at the cave's entrance.

One of our favorite walks is **Devastation Trail**, a mile hike through a former ohia tree forest which was killed by the 1959 eruption of Kilauea Iki. It seems almost like a walk on the moon.

It surprised us to learn that volcanic eruptions do not always come from the same crater. In fact, even with a dozen or so craters to choose from, an eruption may pick an entirely new and pristine area of real estate to open up and spew forth lava. (The on-again, off-again eruption of Kilauea during 1983 occurred at an inaccessible spot deep within a forest several miles from the main crater.) And when you leave the Hawaii Volcanoes National Park, well, as we shall see, you haven't really left the volcanoes at all!

The dramatic **Chain of Craters Road**, first opened in 1965, then closed four years later by a series of lava flows that continued through 1974, finally reopened in 1979 along a slightly different alignment. This new section of roadway again allows access to many of the park's long-hidden assets and again provides a route from the center of the national park direct to Kalapana and the Puna District—a longer but more stimulating ramble back to Hilo. (If you take this route from the volcano, the sights described in our next subsection on Puna will be encountered in reverse order.)

Along the road, keep an eye out for a sign pointing out **Mauna Ulu Crater**, whose eruption caused all the trouble hereabouts for more than five years. There still remain traces of the old road, so you can see how it was permanently blocked by the lava. You might be able to discern how the hot, molten material streaked in fiery falls over the various *palis* (cliffs) and then wove its way to the shoreline and exploded into the ocean. The hardened lava to the left and right of the road is supposed to be completely undisturbed, since the road was built without allowing any equipment in any area outside the narrow right-of-way.

If you leave the park on Route 11, it's only 30 miles to Hilo again. You might want to turn right about 20 miles down the road for a 3-mile drive through the nut orchard to the **Mauna Loa Macadamia Nut Factory**, a fairly large operation by C. Brewer & Co. Recorded messages will tell you what they're doing down there on the cracking floor, etc. You'll get a handful of free samples, too, and are they ever delicious!

THE PUNA SPUR

The trip through the Puna District is too often spurned by visitors to the island of Hawaii, but we find it just as interesting and almost as attractive as any other. We take Highway 130 off 11 at Keaau, barrel the 11 miles to Pahoa, and then turn on Highway 132 for a couple of miles to find the **Lava Tree State Park**. It is populated by dozens of standing tree molds created during a volcanic eruption in 1790. The looser lava has eroded away, leaving only the hollow columns where the trees were. *Don't venture off the paths, for there are several dangerous earth cracks in this area.*

Continue on Route 132 to find the site of the village of **Kapoho**, which was slowly buried by a lava flow one day just in 1960. (Everybody got out all right.) You're in the center of town at the crossroads, where there is nothing around you today but black lava.

For a dramatic demonstration of what it means to be overrun by lava, however, continue along the dirt road toward the sea. First, take a left on the side road that runs up a little hill and see the **Kapoho Cemetery**, where just a few of the old headstones poke up from the lava flow. Then get back on the other dirt road again and take it oceanward to the very end and the **Kumukahi Lighthouse**. There the 6-foot-deep flow inexplicably stopped after bowling over part of the fence and blistering some of the paint on the little building under the tower. It's an overwhelming exhibit of potential power.

Back at the Kapoho crossroads again, you can take the narrow and sometimes rough road (137) along the shoreline for 15 miles, past a couple of attractive beach parks. Some of the land along here is slated for property development despite the fact that vulcanologists say this part of the coast is almost sure to be overrun by future lava flows sooner or later. (Big Islanders get very blasé about volcanos and such!) The road rejoins Route 13 at the famous **Kaimu Black Sand Beach**.

Black sand beaches are formed when superheated lava flows into the ocean, causing violent explosions which throw off little drops of black glass. The waves then grind the lava glass down to sand.

This particular beach has been steadily shrinking in size, probably because the entire Puna coast has been sinking into the sea ever since the 1975 earthquake—at least one inch per year. So have a good look at the beach while you can. But it is now illegal to carry away the sand. (*Caution*: Don't swim here, either. The current is tricky and dangerous.)

At **Kalapana**, ask the way to the head of the 1977 lava flow. (Look for Keone Drive, which snuggles right up to the rough stuff. If you have any trouble, Mr. Yamaguchi at Kalapana Store will probably give you directions.) The village was thought to be a goner until the magma stopped and cooled just 400 yards short of the settlement. Also saved was the little **Star of the Sea Painted Church**, which was directly in the path. As with most of the houses in Kalapana, the church's furniture was carted out as the lava approached, but the religious frescos along the walls and ceiling, painted just after the church was built in 1931, could not be removed. Later the pews were returned, and the artwork remains intact.

A little farther along the road there is a dirt road on the left to **Queen's Bath**, a natural fresh-water pool in the rocks once ostensibly exclusive to Hawaiian royalty. It is now a favorite swimming hole for neighborhood youngsters—and visitors, too.

THE ISLAND OF HAWAII, THE "BIG ISLAND"

At the southern entrance to Hawaii Volcanoes National Park is the **Wahaula Visitor Center**, which includes a museum and sometimes crafts demonstrations, and the nearby **Wahaula Heiau**, one of the bloodiest sacrificial *heiaus* in Hawaiian history.

A mile or so inland and up the slope from this point is the crosshatch of streets making up the unlucky **Royal Gardens Subdivision**. The sparsely populated residential area was invaded by slow-moving lava flows several times during 1983, destroying some homes and cutting off streets at odd angles and in strange places. (No one was hurt.) If you decide to go up to have a look, be aware that the independent residents who live there without any public utilities tend to be a little sensitive about their misfortune, and probably don't conceive of their community as a tourist sight yet. Some who have gone in recently report they were asked to donate to a relief fund for those whose homes and property were destroyed.

Drive into the park, and you'll come to the **Chain of Craters Road**. (See the previous subsection on "The Volcano Area.")

If you return to Hilo on Route 13, somewhere on the *makai* side of this 8-mile Kaimu-to-Pahoa section of highway there may be a sign marked "scenic point." Pull over to have a look, although you may not see anything at first. But then a little whiff of steam suddenly appears above a rise, and then the smell of sulfur hits your nostrils for a moment. There, right in the middle of a vegetable patch, is a cinder cone—a little volcano—quietly waiting, the advance guard of a potential beast you may have thought resided miles away up the mountain. It is enough to remind us that the Big Island breathes. It is an island which is still very much alive!

7. Guided Tours and Cruises on Hawaii

There are several major tour bus companies on the Big Island. One good hometown company which offers Big Island tours only is **Jack's Tours, Inc.** (Tel. 961-6666), with offices at the Hilo airport only. A branch of a minibus tour outfit in Honolulu is **Akamai Tours** (Tel. 329-7324).

Rates for most companies are standardized. The firms will vary only in the quality of the tour they give, and, of course, this will depend a lot on the individual drivers.

Group tour escorts say the bus driver (who generally does all the talking) expects a tip of $1 per person at the end of the trip. However we tip strictly on the basis of how much we enjoyed the tour and suggest you do the same. (If you don't feel like tipping, don't tip.)

Following each description below is our guess of what it might cost for a seat on the bus. (The eleven-passenger limousines will be more—sometimes over 40 percent higher.) These are just some of the tours listed, and remember, too, that not all companies offer all tours.

TOURS FROM HILO AIRPORT OR THE HOTELS

Akaka Falls. 2 hours. To the falls and return. Perhaps $10.

Hilo City Tour. 2 hours. Liliuokalani Park, Rainbow Falls, Orchid Nursery. Perhaps $10.

Hilo City Tour, Akaka Falls. 3 hours. A combination of the above two itineraries. Perhaps $15.

Hilo-Hamakua-Kona. 7 hours. The Hamakua Coast to Waimea, Kawaihae, Mauna Kea Beach Hotel to the Kona hotels. *One-way*. Perhaps $30.

Kona via Saddle Route. 4 hours. To hotels in Kailua and Keauhou. *One-way*. Perhaps $20.

Puna—Half Day. 4 hours. Through the Puna District to Kalapana, Black Sand Beach. Perhaps $15.

Puna—Full Day. 8 hours. Through Puna to Kalapana, Black Sand Beach, and back via Mackenzie State Park. Perhaps $25.

Volcano. 8 hours. Hilo City Tour plus the Hawaii Volcanoes National Park. Perhaps $25.

Volcano-Kona. 9 hours. Like the Volcano Tour but continues on to the Kailua or Keauhou Hotels. *One-way*. Perhaps $35.

Kawaihae. 8 hours. Akaka Falls, Hamakua Coast, Waimea, Kawaihae and return via same route. Perhaps $30.

TOURS FROM KAILUA- OR KEAUHOU-KONA HOTELS

(Note: Some of the one-way trips to Kona from Hilo just described may be operated in reverse.)

Kona Historical. 4 hours. To Kealakekua Bay and the City of Refuge and return. Perhaps $15.

Parker Ranch. 8 hours. Waimea and Parker Ranch and return. Perhaps $20.

Volcano Round Trip. 8 hours. To Hawaii Volcanoes National Park via southern route (Ka'u) and return. Perhaps $35.

AERIAL TOURS

As on other islands, this tends to be a volatile business on Hawaii. The companies flitting around the scenery this week just may have flown into financial oblivion by next.

There are at least five in the air at this writing, including three chopper outfits that delight in hovering over steaming volcano craters and two fixed-wing Cessna firms that also buzz the lava land and make some other standard circuits. We haven't buckled into any of this latest crop of dusters.

Kenai Air Hawaii (Tel. 322-9231), a branch of the Honolulu firm, but based at the Kona Surf Hotel, lifts off on two regular helicopter tours. The Moana Loa Crater Deluxe, including a ride through the crater, now costs at least $110. The Kona Coast trip runs around $100. One reader wrote us that he loved the big Moana Loa trip, but it was cheaper then. We haven't taken it. **Kona Helicopters** (Tel. 329-2550) offers tours from a base at the Kona airport, as well as charter flights. Another charter outfit is **Lacy Helicopters** (Tel. 885-7272).

At Ke-ahole Airport, the **Kona Flight Service** (Tel. 329-1474), a fixed-wing operation, sweeps the Kona Coast for about $25 a seat and swoops over the volcano for around $60. Another good conventional charter service is run by **Anuenue Aviation** (Tel. 961-5591), particularly during volcano eruptions.

ROUGHING IT

There are at least two tour companies which offer special, off-the-beaten-path trips by jeeps, Land Rovers, etc., through forests, lava flows, and other sites not normally available in buses or passenger cars:

The Waipio Valley Shuttle (Tel. 935-2983). This is a $10 one-hour guided tour by jeep into Waipio Valley beginning at the valley rim, 8 miles north of Honokaa. It goes to a black sand beach, two large waterfalls, the Bishop Museum Waipio Research Station, the former Peace Corps Training Village, etc. It will drop off passengers who want to stay on to swim or explore and pick them up later.

Holo-Holo Island Safaris (Tel. 935-7406) offers several different kinds of historical and scientific excursions, including winter skiing in the snow field atop Mauna Kea. (See Section 9.) Rates of perhaps $50 per person per day include a jeep, a driver/guide, gasoline, meals, and housing when overnights are arranged. Call owner Gordon Morse personally to arrange everything.

BOAT CRUISES

Virtually all boat rides are offered and taken on the Kona coast, most of them from that long pier in Kailua.

The most popular cruises are operated by **Captain Bean's Royal Canoe** (Tel. 329-2955), a large, glass-bottom boat decked out in the hokiest, gaudiest trappings imaginable. During the day, Captain Bean takes out that 85-foot vessel on about five glass-bottom trips of one hour each, charging $8 per adult, and $4 for children under 12. But his best and most popular trips are the Sunset Dinner Sail at 5 P.M. and the Moonlight Dinner Sail at 8 P.M. For a tab of about $30, Bean serves up a full-course dinner, live entertainment, and a wide-open bar (no minors allowed). Of course a lot depends on your crowd, but folks in Kailua are consistently amused and amazed at the happy sounds that drift over the water from that craft every night.

For a more complete *daytime* cruise, however, we'd prefer the glass-bottom cruiser **Captain Cook VII** (Tel. 923-2061), which makes a three-hour cruise down the coast to the underwater marine preserve at Kealakekua Bay. The boat anchors near the Cook Monument so passengers can swim and snorkel in the clear water before the return trip. Price is now $15 (half fare for children). Snorkeling equipment is provided free. There's no meal, but there is a bar and snack bar on board. Voyages leave at 9 A.M. and 1 P.M. This trip is usually dependable and good.

(Boat trips designed principally for fishing or scuba diving will be described in the next section, "Water Sports.")

Berthed down in Keauhou Bay, 7 miles south, is the 50-foot trimaran sailing yacht **Fair Wind** (Tel. 322-2788), a convenient cruise choice for guests at the three Keauhou hotels. Several kinds of trips are available, and we have received several letters from Maverick readers praising all of them.

8. Water Sports on the Big Island

"What this island needs is a good beach!" is the cry so often raised. Actually, the Big Island has several good beaches, although certainly not as many per mile of coastline as most others. Many are difficult to get to without an overland hike. Of the others, we have divided our picks into areas below.

BEACHES IN HILO

Just one, we think, and that's **Reed's Bay Beach Park**, a banyan-shaded cove of Hilo Bay near the defunct Hotel Royal Kalani. Facilities include restrooms, showers, and drinking water. Calm-water fishing and swimming are okay.

HAMAKUA COAST

Not much of a beach at **Kolekole Beach Park**, although the popular Wailea shoreline is used for fishing and camping.

KOHALA

About 4 miles past Hawi just on the other side of Niulii is **Keokea Beach Park**, which offers swimming on calm-water days. **Kapaa Beach Park** at Kapaa also has camping and other standard facilities (but no drinking water). Hiking, swimming, and fishing are popular, but skin diving is dangerous. And **Mahukona Beach Park** at Mahukona is located next to an abandoned village. There's good swimming, fishing, skin diving, boating, hiking, and camping.

KAWAIHAE AREA

Just off Highway 250 a mile before Kawaihae Harbor is **Samuel M. Spencer Beach Park**. Swimming, skin diving, and fishing are all excellent at this popular white-sand beach. Very crowded on the weekends, however. **Hapuna Beach Park** is also not far, about a mile past the Mauna Kea Beach Hotel going south. Besides a good swimming area, this excellent beach is a popular body surfing spot. Lots of facilities including cabins which may be rented from the State Parks Division at about $10 nightly. You can also swim at the hotel beach, now that public access has been opened. And **Anaehoomalu Bay**, about 5 miles down the road, now fronts the Sheraton Waikoloa Hotel. The palm-fringed beach is one of the loveliest on the island, and popular for swimming and skin diving.

THE KONA AREA

Here the beaches are singularly unimpressive. There is a tiny one in Kailua directly in front of the King Kamehameha Hotel. After that, about 3 miles down the coast, is **Disappearing Sands Beach**, also called White Sands and Magic Sands. Some local folks like to body surf here, but we say that whether the sand is in or out, the current is tricky and dangerous. **Kahaluu Beach Park**, near Keauhou Bay on Alii Drive, is the most decent beach in the immediate vicinity. Swimming and skin diving are fine.

Napoopoo Beach Park, and its black sand beach, is better known as Kealakekua Bay. Skin diving is particularly superb in this calm underwater park off Route 11, *makai* of Captain Cook. And **Hookena Beach Park** is located in an interesting beachside village about 23 miles south of Kailua. There is no drinking water or electricity, but plenty of good swimming, body surfing, fishing, and hiking. Tent and trailer camping, too.

KA'U AREA

Another beautiful camping, swimming, body surfing, and fishing site is on the famous black sand at **Punaluu Beach Park**. Some of the facilities may still be damaged from an earthquake not long ago, however.

PUNA DISTRICT

Not far from Kaimu Black Sand Beach (where you shouldn't swim) is the lovely **Harry K. Brown Beach Park** at Kalapana. Lots of park facilities are here, and swimming and fishing are popular and good.

SCUBA DIVING AND SNORKELING

Most of the Kona Coast is considered ideal for diving and viewing life beneath the sea. Visibility often extends to as far as 200 feet underwater, and there are many colorful fish and beautiful corals to be enjoyed. The best areas are at Kahaluu Beach Park, Keauhou Bay, Kealakekua Bay, and the City of Refuge.

Professional instruction, equipment rental, and expeditions are available and abundant in Kona. One reliable Kailua outfit is **Pacific Sail and Snorkel** (Tel. 329-2021) which leaves twice daily for snorkeling lessons on a nearby clear lagoon. Matriculation fee was still about $20 per pupil when last we checked.

For full-scale scuba diving lessons, however, you might try **Dive Makai Charters** (Tel. 329-2025), which has several program options. Lessons and all equipment run around $80. **ALAS-Kona Divers** (Tel. 325-7640) and **Sea Paradise** (Tel. 329-1415) are still too new to call.

Headquartered down in Keauhou Bay, the attractive sailboat, the **Fair Wind** (Tel. 322-2788), mentioned in our cruises discussion, also offers scuba diving trips and instruction at comparable rates.

SPORT FISHING

Deep-sea fishing on the Kona Coast is world famous, and records are made and broken here annually. Thirsting for marlin and similar deep-water denizens, anglers from everywhere converge on Kailua-Kona every summer for the Hawaiian International Billfish Tournament.

Kona charter boats have half-day, full-day, and now even two-day trips when they sail down the coast to South Point, the commercial fishing grounds.

For convenience, turn your fishing request over to either the **Kona Activities Center** (Tel. 329-3171), P.O. Box 1035, or the **Kona Charter Skippers Association** (Tel. 329-3600), P.O. Box 806, both at Kailua-Kona, Hi. 96740.

You can charter the captain, mate, and the entire boat with all necessary equipment for all day (eight hours) for about $400. Half-day trips run about $300. (If you come back with fish, the skipper and mate will expect a tip.) The bigger boats accommodate up to six passengers, so you can split the expense accordingly. There are also some trips sold by the seat—perhaps $100 for all day.

9. Other Sports—at High and Low Altitudes

The Keauhou-Kona area seems determined to become the **tennis** capital of the North Pacific, and it smashed a solid serve toward that goal in

1976 when the Avis Challenge Cup series opened in the new 2,500-seat Holua Stadium.

In the hotel next door is the **Kona Surf Racquet Club** (Tel. 322-3411): eight courts, three lighted; racket rentals, tennis balls, ball-throwing machine, and private lessons available.

On the other side of the bay, the **Kona Lagoon Hotel** (Tel. 322-2727) has two lighted courts. And a lob away from that, the **Keauhou Beach Hotel** (Tel. 322-3441) has two lighted courts and one unlighted.

In Kailua, the **King Kamehameha Hotel** (Tel. 329-2911) has four courts, two lighted. Also there is one free lighted court at the **Kailua Playground** (which might become available at around midnight), and two unlighted courts in the **Kona Village Resort** which are only for folks on the register there.

In Hilo, there are four free lighted tennis courts at **Lincoln Park** (Kinoole and Ponahawai streets) and free unlighted ones and $5-per-hour lighted indoor ones at **Hoolulu Park** on Kalanikoa Street, and at the **University of Hawaii-Hilo** campus at 333 W. Lanikaula St. Also there are two unlighted courts at the **Waiakea Village Resort** (Tel. 961-3041) for perhaps $2 per person per hour.

In the hinterlands, there are nine—count 'em—nine courts in a spectacular 12-acre tennis park at the **Mauna Kea Beach Hotel**, but they are presently for guests only. Two lighted courts are available at **Waikoloa Village** for $2 per person per hour. In Waimea at the **Waimea Park**, there are two free lighted courts. And four courts are open now at the **Seamountain-Hawaii Resorts** (Tel. 928-8010), next to the golf course in Ka'u. Guests at Colony One are free. Nonguests pay a modest charge.

GOLF LINKS ON THE LAVA

Now that horticulturists and architects have discovered the secret of growing golf courses on lava flows, some spectacular greens and fairways have begun to carpet the Big Island. At last count there were eight, some of them ranking with the best in the world. On all these, we recommend you call ahead for starting times, any day of the week.

The **Mauna Kea Beach Golf Course** (Tel. 882-7222) is still the unofficial leader, designed by Robert Trent Jones, the prolific archon of golf architects. About 3½ miles south, the new **Mauna Lani Resort** (Tel. 882-7244) has been getting rave reviews from everywhere, it seems. Two miles farther than that, the new course at the **Sheraton Royal Waikoloa** (Tel. 885-6789) is also available.

An unusual set of links at the edge of a live volcano form the **Volcano Golf and Country Club** (Tel. 967-7550) in the national park.

An attractive coastal course is the new **Keauhou-Kona Golf Course**

(Tel. 322-2595). The **Waikoloa Village Golf Course** (Tel. 883-9621) is located somewhat up-in-the-air in South Kohola. The **Seamountain Ninole Golf Course** (Tel. 928-8000) is the nucleus of a planned resort down at Punaluu in Ka'u.

The county-operated **Hilo Municipal Course** (Tel. 959-7711) is also 18 holes and much less expensive. There are two 9-hole courses, the **Banyan Golf Center** (Tel. 935-7388) next to the hotels in Hilo, and the **Hamakua Country Club** (Tel. 775-7244) way up the coast at Honokaa.

RIDING IN COWBOY COUNTRY

You can rent horses through the **Mauna Kea Beach Hotel** (Tel. 882-7222) at the Kamuela headquarters of Parker Ranch. The hourly rate, complete with a genuine *paniolo* guide, is about $12 per person.

Also, the **Waikoloa Countryside Stables** (Tel. 883-9335) offers opportunities to ride over many wilderness trails for about $10 an hour. Write either outfit at Kamuela, Hi. 96743.

HUNTING ON HAWAII

Wild goats, feral sheep, bristling boar, and wild Vancouver bull, plus several game birds may be stalked on the Big Island. Some kind of hunting is available the year around. The scenery in the hunting areas is terrific, and even if you don't bag something, you'll have had an invigorating outing.

Game hunting on private lands is not state regulated, but you'll need a license in any case. That's $15 to the Division of Fish and Game, Hawaii Department of Land and Natural Resources. In Hilo, they're at 75 Aupuni St. (Tel. 961-7291), but there are also more than a dozen agents authorized to sell you a license.

The only hunting guide service we know of this year is **Hawaii Hunting Tours** (Tel. 775-0128), headquartered in Paauilo. Check with professional hunter Eugene Ramos about rates and supplies. Write P.O. Box 58, Paauilo, Hi. 96776.

SNOW SKIING? YES!

It seems that more is written about skiing on Hawaii every year, as more and more people become intrigued with the idea of skiing in the tropics. But if you come expecting to find anything like another Aspen, you'll be bitterly disappointed.

Skiing on Hawaii (vaguely from December through April) must be taken as a lark—not as a serious sport. There are no lifts or tows, and all skiing must be accomplished at a dizzying elevation of more than 11,000 feet, where altitude sickness and sunburns are common. On the plus side, the runs are 3 miles long, with no trees or rocks to worry about.

Special vehicles take you to the top of each run. And the ski patrol is on duty in case of accidents.

You'll need a four-wheel-drive vehicle and a free state permit, but if you're determined to try it, the best thing to do is to turn over the whole project to Dick Tillson at Ski Shop Hawaii (Tel. 885-4188), whom you may write at Kamuela, Hi. 96743. All-inclusive rates will probably be around $100 a day, with all equipment provided.

10. Big Island Shopping—from Bamboo to Nuts

In Hilo's Banyan Drive area, we generally weren't impressed with the Waiakea Camp Stores or most of those shops along the side of the Orchid Island Hotel. However, we were intrigued by the joyful jumble of good and bad in the **Polynesian Market Place** in the Hilo Bay Hotel. It sells just about every kind of curio ever made in Hawaii—or anyplace else. Some things were very inexpensive.

You'll find more quality items, however, at the shops next door in the Naniloa Surf Hotel. There seems to be a particularly complete selection of local jewelry in **Hawaiian Island Gems** (Tel. 935-6157), including some good coral and shell work.

Mid-town Hilo, also called Kaiko'o, is generally not so interesting for visitors, although the Hilo Mall Shopping Center is there, equipped with such standard places as Penney's, Kress, and branches of Honolulu establishments. More isolated stores in Hilo include the **Hawaiian Handicraft Shop** (Tel. 935-5587) at 760 Kilauea St., across from the mall, where you may sometimes watch the woodcarver at work. And in the old part of downtown, you might peek into the very local business called the **S. Miyao Gift and Hardware Shop**, at 182 Kilauea St., next to the Dragon Inn restaurant. There are lots of little Oriental items there at lower prices than you'll pay elsewhere.

A late-late everything store? Like on a Sunday night when everything's closed, and you want a newspaper or maybe a box of school clay, or perhaps an old Willkie button? Try the **Hawaii Bargain Store**, at 278 Kilauea Avenue.

For orchids, we'd head directly to the home office, garden, and factory of **Orchids of Hawaii** (Tel. 935-6617) at 575 Hinano St. You'll find several different varieties, along with anthuriums and other flowers. They'll air mail, of course. Several other flower farms are also dependable, including the **Hirose Nursery** (Tel. 959-4561) on Highway 11, just out of town. We recently bought some anthuriums here, and were very impressed with the friendliness and efficiency.

For books, you will enjoy browsing the complete stock in the **Book Gallery** (Tel. 935-2447) in the Kaiko'o Mall, run by Steve and Frances Reed. For a good selection of maps, however, try the **Old Town Printers**

& Stationers (Tel. 935-8927), where the Book Gallery used to be, at 201 Kinoole St. They also have books and gifts.

Macadamia nuts? You can buy them anywhere, so there's really no need to make a special trip to either of the two competing factories. Our personal preference for consistently good-quality nuts is the **Mauna Loa** brand, the large C. Brewer operation. You can visit the factory in Keaau (Tel. 966-9301), but they sell the nuts there at the suggested retail price, and there's not much selection of kinds of products. The mechanical operation is well explained, but it's all relatively prosaic.

The other brand, **Hawaiian Holiday**, is produced with more pizzazz by a family factory up in Honokaa (Tel. 775-7255). Instead of just the nuts and nut brittle, they've combined their macadamias with coconut chips, Maui onions, hickory-smoked this and that, and all kinds of candies in every form possible to make scores of things to choose from.

The factory itself is smaller, more human size, and the country store they've tacked on and gussied up to sell the nuts from is, well, nutty but fun. Both will arrange mail orders to the Mainland (air or surface).

Over in *Kailua-Kona*, the *alii* of shopping centers is the 30,000-square-foot, self-contained mall at the King Kamehameha Hotel. There in the **Crossfire Gallery** you can watch a young artist do wonders with metal sculpture. There's also a link in Honolulu's classy **Liberty House** chain, and a branch of **Andrade's**, this one specializing in women's and children's apparel. You'll see a good supply of locally made jewelry in the **Jewel Palace** and next door in the **Shellery**, and a nice selection of canvas totebags next door at **Traveler's Choice**. The imported arts and crafts at the **Tribal Arts Gallery** are interesting. And some beautiful Chinese china and decorative tiles are featured at the **Orient Gift Shop**.

Most of Kailua's shops are tucked into greater or lesser arcades or plazas that have narrow openings onto the main drag. Some are attractive. Most are a hodge-podge. It's easy to get lost and darned hard to tell someone how to find something. Street addresses mean very little in this higgledy-piggledy set-up. There could be a dozen or two stores at "75–5699 Alii Drive," for example.

We saw some unusual clothes for both sexes at the **Butterfly Boutique** in the Seaside Mall, across from the hotel. Some are locally made.

Old-timers shed a tear today for the more authentic ancient ambience gone with the demise of Emma's General Store in the commercial center of Kailua. On that site, now, is the **Kona Black Coral Shop**, which seems to have some good coral prices. (However, it pays to price them in several places and compare first.)

Just across from Emma's Market Place (yes, they named that after the old store) is a shop called the **Sandal Basket**, which seems to sell more hats than either sandals or baskets.

Past the church in front of the Kona Plaza Shopping Arcade is the **Coral Factory**. Prices may run a little higher here, but the atmosphere is attractive, the products are well displayed, and the clerks are helpful. In the arcade itself, **Neptune's Garden** for years has displayed a good collection of shell craft and the like. The **Middle Earth Bookshoppe** has moved its well-stocked shelves to a site nearby.

Next door, the World Square Arcade presents an interesting semicircular browse. (It's to this site that the free London bus carts you from the hotels in Keauhou.) There **Computer Portraits** will stamp your mug on a T-shirt while you wait for about $10. Technically fascinating.

Often overlooked is the less-showy Kona Coast Shopping Center, just up Route 190, where the supermarkets and many better prices are. **Bell, Book and Candle** (Tel. 329-1441) is up there, now, still offering a good selection of Hawaiian books and recordings plus lots of greeting cards and gifts in some recently expanded quarters.

All in all, remember that Kailua's shops have a way of changing before our perishable research can find its way into print. As in Lahaina, many of Kona's most intriguing stores will be temporary—ambitious boutiques and art huts selling something new, clever, and cute, springing up now here, then there, and later perhaps even moving on to another island when the owners seek new inspiration—"Here today, gone to Maui!" is a favorite expression around here.

11. Big Island Big Nights on the Town

The Island of Hawaii has one excellent, dependable showroom, and surprisingly, it's not in Kailua-Kona but in Hilo, at the Naniloa Surf Hotel (Tel. 935-0831). The well-designed, ground-floor **Crown Room** seats a multitude of 400, giving virtually all an excellent view of the stage, and usually serves a full sit-down dinner (no buffet) for about $25. It brings in top acts from the Mainland as well as the best shows from Waikiki.

Also in the Naniloa Surf is the **Polynesian Room**, sometimes featuring a local hula show in the early evening but turning into a discotheque after about 9 P.M. Keep an eye on the crowd; it's been known to attract some chest-beating disco-rillas on occasion. We'd prefer to meet downstairs in the **Hoomalimali Bar**, where there is usually a lounge act like Boyson, Stan, and Mary Lou Brown, a talented Hilo trio.

You might look for the versatile falsetto artist Bunny Brown and his group, who could still be playing in the **Menehune Land Lounge** in the Hilo Hawaiian Hotel (Tel. 935-9361). A popular and not-too-noisy piano bar is the **Voyager Lounge** at an inside location in the Hilo Pacific Isle, also on Banyan Drive. And a locally favored establishment outside the hotels is the **Green Door** (Tel. 935-6388), usually featuring some kind of entertainment. Stay alert; you may discover the drinks are more reasonable than some fellow customers. It's on the Kilauea Street side of the Kaiko'o Mall, and you'll know the place . . . well . . . by its green door.

On the Kona Coast, one big luau/Polynesian extravaganza for folks who've not yet seen a big luau/Polynesian extravaganza is in Keauhou at the Kona Surf Hotel's "Night in Hawaii." Held Monday through Friday in the **Luau Gardens**, it's good and convenient. However, the most delicious and authentic luau on the island this year is probably the Friday-night-only **Kona Village Luau** (Tel. 325-5555). You must reserve ahead or you can't get in the gate, and you'll need a car to make the 15-mile trip up the coast from Kailua.

The premier Kona discotheque now is the **Poi Pounder** in the Kona Surf which pounds until 2 A.M. On the same property, the **Puka Bar** has been tamed into a lovely lava-rock drinking den with more modest entertainment.

The Kona Lagoon Hotel occasionally installs name entertainment in its **Polynesian Long House** (Tel. 322-2727), which some consider to be the island's best-designed showroom. The bar at **Huggo's Restaurant** is always a pleasant place to watch the progress of a Kona evening.

12. Big Island Address List

Bakery—Mountain View Bakery (famous cookies), Mountain View, Tel. 968-6353.

Barber—Sel's Barber Shop, 145 Mamo St., Hilo. Tel. 935-1771.

Beauty Salon—Gail's, Naniloa Surf Hotel, Tel. 935-9171.

Camping Equipment Rental—United Rent-All, 1080 Kilauea Ave., Hilo, Tel. 935-2974. Kona Rent All, 74–5602 Alapa St., Kailua, Tel. 329-1644.

Chamber of Commerce—Hawaii Island Chamber of Commerce, 180 Kinoole St., Hilo. Tel. 935-7178.

Dry Cleaners—Hilo Quality Cleaners, 865 Kinoole St., Tel. 935-1620.

Fire Department—Emergency Tel. 961-6022.

Hawaii Visitors Bureau—180 Kinoole St., Hilo. Tel. 935-5271. And Marlin Plaza, Kailua. Tel. 329-1782.

Health Food Stores—Hilo Natural Foods, 306 Kilauea Ave., Tel. 935-7022. Aloha Village Store, Kainaliu, Kona. Tel. 322-9941.

Hospital—Hilo Hospital, 1190 Waianuenue Ave., Tel. 961-4211. Kona Hospital, Kealakekua. Tel. 322-9311.

Laundromat—Kaiko'o Coin Laundry, 401 Kilauea Ave., Hilo. Tel. 961-6490. Hele Mai Laundromat, Kailua, Tel. 329-3494.

Pharmacy—Long's Drug Stores, 555 Kilauea Ave., Hilo. Tel. 935-3357.
   Pay'n Save Drug Store, Kailua. Tel. 329-3577.
Police—Emergency Tel. 935-3311.
Supermarket—Safeway, 333 Kilauea Ave., Hilo.
Volcanic Activity—24-hour recorded information, Tel. 967-7977.

Appendix

Since the introduction of limited Wide Area Telephone Service (WATS) to Hawaii, you can dial several numbers in the Island State toll-free from other parts of the United States and Canada. To use these numbers, you must dial the code "800" first. *This should not be confused with "808,"* the standard area code for all regular Hawaii telephone numbers. Through an unfortunate coincidence, it is very similar.

Keep in mind that many of these numbers will not work from certain areas, and that several Hawaii hotels and other facilities do not have toll-free 800 numbers. Also, certain chains encourage reservations by calling other branches of their operations in your local area, and even some 800 numbers do not connect you direct to Hawaii, but to some other central reservations facility on the Mainland. (Here's a tip: The genuine Hawaiian WATS numbers all begin with "367.")

The hotels, rental car firms, and others who answer these toll-free numbers are expecting calls mainly from travel agents. However, if you are an individual traveler making your own arrangements, here is a chance to nail down exactly the kind of accommodation or vehicle you want, without the confusion of going through anybody else. Most of these places will be glad to deal with you directly.

Travel agents, too, will find these 800 numbers useful. By calling them, they can get instant free feedback on their requests. Obviously, of course, all such bookings are tentative, and neither individual traveler nor agent will have confirmed reservations until any required advance deposits have been made.

In all cases, please tell 'em we sent you.

TOLL-FREE NUMBERS FOR SOME HAWAII HOTELS

(Remember to dial 800 first. Note that some hotels associated with each other share the same number, so be sure you know which hotel you're booking into.)

Honolulu and Oahu

Ala Moana Americana. 228-3278
Cinerama Hotels—Edgewater, Reef, Reef Towers, Waikiki Tower. 367-5610
Colony Surf (East and West). 421-0652
Coral Reef. 367-5124 (Canada 663-3602)
Coral Seas. 367-5170 (U.S. only)
Diamond Head Beach. 367-5124 (Canada 663-3602)
Halekulani. 525-4000
Hawaiian King Hotel. 367-7042
Hawaiian Regent. 367-5370
Hyatt Regency, Hyatt Kuilima. 228-9000

Ilikai. 228-3000 (Canada 261-8383)
Kuhiolani. 367-5124
Miramar. 227-4320 (California 622-0847)
Moana and the Surfrider. 334-8484 (Eastern Canada 268-9393, Western Canada 268-9330)
Napualani. 367-5004 (U.S. only)
Outrigger, Outrigger East, Outrigger Surf, Outrigger West, Waikiki Village, Waikiki Surf, Coral Seas, and Reef Lanais. 367-5170 (U.S. only)
Pacific Beach and Pagoda Hotels. 367-6060

Princess Kaiulani. See Sheraton.
Queen Kapiolani. 367-5004
Royal Hawaiian. See Sheraton.
Sheraton Waikiki. 334-8484 (Eastern Canada 268-9393, Western Canada 268-9330)
Surfrider. See Sheraton.
Waikiki Beachcomber. 227-0848 (California 622-0644)
Waikiki Grand. 367-5094
Waikiki Resort. 421-0680 (U.S. only)
Waikiki Sand Villa. 367-5072 (Canada 663-3602)
Waikiki Surf. See Outrigger.
Waikiki Surfside. 367-5124
Waikiki Village. See Outrigger.
Waikikian. 367-5124

Kauai Hotels

Coco Palms. 227-0848 (California 622-0644)
Islander Inn and the Kauai Surf. 367-5360
Kauai Resort. 367-5004 (U.S. only)
Kauai Sands. 367-7000
Kiahuna Beach and Tennis Resort. 367-5020
Princeville—Makai Club Cottages, etc. 367-7090
Sheraton Kauai. 334-8484 (Eastern Canada 268-9393, Western Canada 268-9330)

Maui Hotels

Hyatt Regency Maui. 228-9000
Inter-Continental Maui. 367-2960
Kapalua Bay Resort. 367-5035

Lahaina Shores. 367-2972
Maui Beach. 367-5004 (U.S. only)
Maui Lu Resort. 367-5244
Maui Sands and Hokilau. 367-7000
Maui Surf. 367-5360
Napili Kai Beach Club. 367-5030
Papakea Beach Resort. 367-5637
Sheraton Maui. 325-3535 (Eastern Canada 268-9393, Western Canada 268-9330)
TraveLodge at Lahaina. 255-3050 (Canada 268-3330)
Wailea Beach. 228-3000 (Canada 268-8383)

Molokai Hotels

Hotel Molokai. 227-8338 (Alberta 663-3481, British Columbia 663-3141)
Sheraton Molokai. 334-8484 (Eastern Canada 268-9393, Western Canada 268-9330)

Big Island Hotels

Hilo Bay (Uncle Billy Kimi's). 367-5102
Hilo Hawaiian. 367-5004
Hilo Pacific Isle (TraveLodge). 255-3050 (Kansas 332-4350, Canada 268-3330)
Islander Inn-Kona, Kona Surf, and Naniloa Surf. 367-5360
Kona Village Resort. 367-5290
Mauna Kea Beach. 228-3000 (Canada 268-8383)
Seaside and Sands. 367-7000
Sheraton Waiakea Village, Royal Waikoloa and the Volcano House. 334-8484 (Eastern Canada 268-9393, Western Canada 268-9330)

TOLL-FREE NUMBERS FOR SOME CAR RENTAL FIRMS

(Dial 800 first. Note that some companies operate on all islands, some on only one island.)

American International. 527-0160
Avis. 331-1212 (Oklahoma 482-4554, Canada 261-2100)
Budget. 527-0707
Dollar Rent-A-Car. 367-7006
Gray Line. 367-2420
Hertz. 654-8200

Holiday Rent-A-Car. 367-2631
National Car Rental. 328-4567
Robert's Hawaii. 367-5050
Sears Rent-A-Car. See Budget above.
Thrifty Rent-A-Car. 331-9191
Tropical Rent-A-Car. 367-5140

MISCELLANEOUS FIRMS WITH TOLL-FREE 800 NUMBERS

Aikane Catamarans. 524-6800
Air Hawaii. 367-5198
Aloha Airlines. 367-5250

Aloha Lei Greeters. 367-5255
American Express Travel Service, Hawaii. 367-2333

American Hawaii Cruises. 227-3666
  (California 622-0666)
Charley's Hawaii Tours. 367-5200
Chuck Machado's Luau. 367-5255
Germaine's Luau. 367-5655
Gray Line Hawaii. 367-2420
Greeters of Hawaii. 367-5255
Harrington, Al, Show. 367-5610
Hawaiian Airlines. 367-5320
Hawaiian Holiday Macadamia Nuts.
  367-5150

Hawaiian Holiday Tours. 367-5040
Hokunani Cruises. 367-5270
Kona Activities Center. 367-5183
Mid Pacific Airlines. 367-7010
Papillon Helicopters. 367-7095
Polynesian Cultural Center. 367-7060
Princeville Airways. 367-7090
Trade Wind Tours. 367-5333
Windjammer Cruises. 367-5000

Index

Waikiki hotels, 115-30
Waikiki Shell, 167
Waikiki Shopping Plaza, 225-26
Waikoloa, 384, 403
Waikolu Valley Lookout (Molokai), 346-47
Wailau Trail (Molokai), 348
Wailea Beach (Maui), 314
Wailea Shopping Village (Maui), 334
Wailoa (park, river, Visitor Center on Big Island), 397-98
Wailua (Kauai), 269, 277
Wailua Falls (Kauai), 269
Wailua Falls (Maui), 321
Wailuku (Maui), 29, 284, 290, 315, 334
Wailupe Beach Park (Oahu), 206
Waimanalo Beach Park (Oahu), 182, 207
Waimea (Big Island), 369, 383, 394-95, 400
Waimea (Kauai), 265
Waimea Beach Park (Oahu), 189, 208
Waimea Canyon (Kauai), 243, 267
Waimea Falls Park (Oahu), 164, 188-89
Waimea Valley (Oahu), 189
Waioli Mission (Kauai), 272
Waioli Tea Room (Honolulu), 178
Waipahee Slide (Kauai), 271

Waipio Valley (Big Island), 369, 400
Waipoo Falls (Kauai), 267
Wallabies, 39
Ward Warehouse (Oahu), 176, 228
Washington Place (Oahu), 172
Waterfalls, 32
Water safety, 206
Water sports: Big Island, 414-16; Kauai, 276-77; Lanai, 364-65; Maui, 325-28; Molokai, 351-52; Oahu, 203-11
Weather and climate, 24, 34-37
Weeping Banyan tree, 262
Wet caves (Kauai), 273
Whaler's Village (Maui), 310, 331
Whales, 46, 182, 310, 311, 324
Whaling, 56, 310
When to come to Hawaii, 24
White Sands Beach (Big Island), 404, 415
Wind-powered generators, 79
Wine, 316-17
Wiki-Wiki buses, 3, 99
Wood products, 222

Zoo, Honolulu, 83, 90, 167
Zoris, 22, 23, 110, 222

Please tell us about your trip to Hawaii.
(This page can be folded to make an envelope.)

Place
first class
postage
here

Bob and Sara Bone
The Maverick Guides
Pelican Publishing Company
P.O. Box 189
Gretna, Louisiana 70054

Re: 1984 edition